C0-ARD-427

TABLE OF CONTENTS

ACKNOWLEDGMENTS

For their assistance, the House of Collectibles extends sincere gratitude to the following:

Bill Edgerton of Darien, CT, for his help on music boxes; Fran Mayer of The Mechanical Music Center, also in Darien, CT 06820; Arthur Sanders of The Musical Museum, Deansboro, NY 13328.

For their help on our sheet music section—Pat Cleveland of the Sheet Music Exchange, PO Box 2136, Winchester VA 22601; Sheldon Halper of Westfield, NJ 07090, for his help with automobile sheets; Wayland Bunnell for his help with E. T. Paull; Nancy Israel of Paper Memories, Bethesda, MD 20816; Beverly Hamer of E. Derry, NH 03041.

For their help on our musical instruments section—Richard Smith of Columbus, OH; John Morningstar of The Reed Organ Society, c/o The Musical Museum, Deansboro, NY 13328, for a great job on our new reed organ section; Fred Oster, head of the musical instruments department at Christie's East.

For her help in the general field of music collecting, we thank Dana Hawkes of Sotheby's New York. She is the head of the collectibles department there and is very knowledgeable and cooperative.

PHOTOGRAPHIC RECOGNITION

Ainslee's Advertiser, 1907; Alan C. Lungstrum, West Covina, CA; Bellm Cars and Music of Yesterday, Sarasota, FL; *Circle Magazine,* 1907; *Delineator,* 1907; Kalman Detrich; Edison Laboratories, East Orange, NJ; Edison Winter Home, Ft. Myers, FL; Gould and Hundermark; *Harper's Weekly,* 1905; Manor House Galleries; Metropolitan Museum of Art; *Munsey's Magazine,* 1905; Musical Museum, Deansboro, NY; Paul Spigel Collection; Price Collection; Smithsonian Institution; Steve Freeman Collection; Vestal Press.

NOTE TO READERS

All advertisements appearing in this book have been accepted in good faith, but the publisher assumes no responsibility in any transactions that occur between readers and advertisers.

MARKET REVIEW

Perhaps more than any other collecting field, music collectibles encompass a very wide variety of items. Of course, collectors will specialize in one field or another, but music-related items can run the gamut from 17th- and 18th-century musical instruments through 19th-century mechanical music machines all the way to present day stereo recordings.

Make no mistake; this field is as diverse as any other, and more so than most. To get a feeling for the music-collecting market as a whole is almost impossible; one must review each specialty by itself. It is safe to say, however, that music collecting as a whole is growing every day. Values may fluctuate, but collector interest remains high. Many interesting trends are developing in the marketplace.

Musical instruments are continuing to bring strong values. Of course, a Stradivarius will always bring a phenomenal response, but reasonably priced, fine-quality instruments surface regularly at auctions, through dealers, and in private sales. A fine American banjo from the turn of the century can usually be found for $200 to $400. At a music auction at Doyle Auctioneers recently, an S. S. Stewart 5-string banjo (c. 1899) in original mint condition went for $400, while a Hutchins 5-string banjo (c. 1895) with a fine maple neck and abalone pattern went for only $350. At another Doyle auction, this one held in December 1985, a Firth, Hall, & Pond boxwood-and-ivory clarinet (early 19th century) was played all the way home for $427. Novelty instruments can be a lot of fun. Ocarinas are usually under $100, and kazoos are typically much less than that, about $25 or less. They are fun to play and are highly decorative.

As the collector rises in price, higher-quality instruments can be considered. Still, many collectors would be surprised to know what can be purchased at relatively low prices. For example, at a Christie's musical instruments sale in March 1986, a viola by Wolff Bros. of Germany (c. 1889) sold for $850. At the same sale, a violin by Acoulon & Blondelet of France was taken away for only $400. Bows can also make a delightful and not necessarily expensive collectible. Among the most outstanding sales of the recent past, a silver-mounted violin bow stamped *C. Bazin* of Mirecourt brought $700 at Sotheby's. But bows can also be much more expensive. For example, at the same sale, a silver-mounted violin bow, ascribed to Francois Tourte and sold with documents from Wurlitzer & Co. and Kagan & Gaines certifying its authenticity, brought in $5,000.

Although out of reach for most people, the high end of the musical instrument market must always be mentioned. A fine Italian violin by Camillo Camilli (first half of 18th century) was auctioned at Sotheby's recently for $32,000. A rare and very beautiful ivory recorder offered by Christie's London in late 1985 was had for £27,000 or about $38,000. A very unusual pianoforte in the form of a semieliptical side table by William Southwell of Dublin was also put on the block by Christie's London and did quite well, bringing £25,920 or about $33,900 at the exchange rate at the time. Two auction purchases that attracted a lot of attention were of important violins by Joseph Guarneri of Cremona and Peter Guarneri of Mantua (both early 18th century). They were offered for sale at Christie's London in mid-1985. Peter's work brought in a not insignificant £108,000, or $139,000; but Joseph's was the topper at £135,000, or just under $175,000 at the exchange rate at the time. It is safe to say that instruments such as these will never lose their value, but musical instruments of all prices are doing quite well.

Records and memorabilia is another exciting field. Although this area has typically lower prices than do musical instruments, good investment opportunities are plentiful.

A lot of people are rediscovering the old standards. Linda Ronstadt, Willie Nelson, and Kiri Te Kanawa have all sparked interest in this area by recording LP's of great tunes of the 1940's. Re-releases of albums by Frank Sinatra, Duke Ellington, and Ella Fitzgerald are doing very well. Look for continued growth.

The high end of the record market is also doing nicely. Rare albums such as the Beatles' "Yesterday and Today" with the Butcher cover can bring $500 or more. A private sale reported to The House of Collectibles recently was of Buddy Holly's "That'll Be the Day" LP for $295. One must remember, however, that middle-priced records ($20–$50) can be an equally good investment.

Memorabilia is following records' lead. Lots of new items are on the market, and collectors are responding well. Rock memorabilia is especially plentiful, so values are a bit depressed, but collector interest is higher than ever before. Memorabilia of earlier entertainers, those of the 1940's and 1950's, is doing exceptionally well. A private collector of Ethel Merman memorabilia recently reported a private sale to The House of Collectibles of an 8 × 10 studio photo for $60. Values will continue to rise on these items as interest in this period grows.

Sheet music is probably the fastest-growing hobby in music collecting. People like Pat Cleveland of The Sheet Music Exchange are doing all they can to spread the word about this historical and decorative hobby.

As is common in so many collecting fields, the low end of the sheet music market ($1–$10) is staying fairly stable. Most of the items one will find at flea markets are in this price range, and they can be highly enjoyable. The middle and higher price ranges, however, are where the real price increases are happening. Covers by Fred Manning, Starmer,

Stasny, and Vargas are all doing very well. Coca-Cola, baseball, scarce movie and musical tunes, and personality covers are also very desirable. Dealers have reported a softening in aviation, transportation, and ragtime prices. These areas were very popular only a short time ago, but buyers should now exercise more caution.

The big news in sheet music these days is E. T. Paull. Collectors are grabbing everything they can get. Values are really beginning to rise considerably, though, so get on the wagon; E. T. Paull is a sound investment.

Perhaps the highest value ever paid for a piece of sheet music was in 1985 for "Marie from Sunny Italy," lyrics by Irving Berlin, music by M. Nicholson (c. 1909). A private dealer brought in $1,500 for it. It's plain to see that sheet music is rapidly growing out of the small hobby it once was into a full-grown collectible.

Last, but certainly not least, what can one say about mechanical music machines? They are especially exciting to collectors since they combine all the enjoyable aspects of collecting: they are useful, beautiful, and have historic value as well. This area continues to show expansion in collector numbers and interest, but certain financial factors are beginning to become apparent.

Many dealers and collectors are reporting a growing tendency away from unrestored machines, especially music boxes, due to increasing restoration and refinishing costs. Dana Hawkes, head of the collectibles department at Sotheby's New York, summed it up best when she told The House of Collectibles, "The price of restoration has superseded the price of the music box." An expert restorer's work does not come cheaply. Of course, there is no substitute for quality. An inferior job at half the price is not a good deal. To protect your investment, always use the best. But many people are now wary of unrestored machines, fearing hidden costs. More and more, buyers are sticking to completely restored items. They're more expensive, but there are no hidden costs. Despite some doubts, the market is generally strong.

Early phonographs are doing quite well, showing steady price increases, as are restored disc music boxes. At a collectibles auction at Christie's East in December 1985, a Victor VI phonograph (c. 1905) did nicely at $500, while a Symphonium coin-operated disc music box (c. 1900) brought in $1,400. Reproducing and player pianos are also increasing in value. A restored Steinway reproducing piano will bring in $16,000 to $22,000 depending on the model, finish, and amount of original equipment.

Nickelodeons seem to be softening somewhat in value, as are cylinder music boxes. There are still many devoted collectors out there, but these areas are not growing as rapidly as others. Outstanding cylinder boxes always do very well at auctions however; a G. Baker-Troll & Co.

19¼″ interchangeable cylinder box chimed away at $3,200 at the December 1985 Christie's auction.

Large orchestrions are always the stars of the mechanical music field, and many good examples have been offered recently. A superb Seeburg style "H" orchestrion, 7′3″ high, 6′4″ wide, with a mandolin, bass and snare drums, cymbal, triangle, tympani, castanets, and xylophone with ornate art glass panels was auctioned off for $65,000 at Doyle auctioneers in mid-1985. A somewhat less massive but very desirable Seeburg style "G" brought in a smaller but still healthy $24,-500 at the same sale. Look for steady, continued growth in this area. These items are antiques as well as collectibles.

All in all, music collectors have much to be thankful for. Newsletters, clubs, and societies are around in unprecedented numbers. It's now easier to get started in this hobby than ever before. The best advice anyone can follow is to use all the sources and information possible. Visit flea markets and antique shows, check out showrooms in your area, get in touch with the main club or society in your specialty and see if there's a club near you. It's the people involved that make collecting special. You don't have to own a Guarneri violin to enjoy talking about one. Get out there, study, investigate, meet people, and most of all, enjoy!

STANDARDS USED IN THIS BOOK

All collectors' items are not created equal, and even those that may have started out equal in life are not always found in that condition today. It is impossible in a book of this nature to give valuations on every class of item in a wide range of conditions. Therefore, we have tried to arrive at certain standards, and the user of this guide can, by applying our standards and prices to any items he may encounter, form a fairly accurate idea of the value.

Musical Instruments. It is not expected that antique instruments, especially those dating before about 1890, be in the same condition as when they left the factory. The use to which instruments—especially hand-held instruments—were placed resulted in some surface wear, which is inevitable on nearly every specimen and is not considered to detract from the desirability. Instruments should, however, be **complete** and in good operating condition.

Recordings. Usually, the older a record, the less that can be expected of it condition-wise. "Very fine" for a recording of 1905 would mean still listenable but with surface noise, scratches, etc. Early wax records can be found in mint condition, but this is rare. On the other hand, condition standards are strict on records of the 1950's; these should be in virtually new condition.

Books and Other Paper Items. Depends on the nature of the item and its age. More information will be found in the appropriate sections.

The values given for 8 × 10 signed photographs are for specimens with signature only, or signature plus a very brief message, such as "best wishes." Photographs carrying lengthy inscriptions are worth higher prices than those stated, sometimes double the amount or even more. This varies with the celebrity, so it is impossible to give overall guidelines.

THE PHONOGRAPH RECORD: ITS DEVELOPMENT

The phonograph, one of mankind's most enjoyable inventions, has been with us for slightly more than 100 years. Disc records, however, are just approaching their 100th birthday, which will occur in 1987. But phonographs and records as we know them now—with stereo, vinyl, 45's, and LP's—are of much more recent origin. None of these concepts existed as recently as 40 years ago. The many changes undergone by phono records add, of course, to their collecting appeal. And the fact that their beginnings are not *too* ancient is a plus for the hobbyist; the very oldest discs turn up in the marketplace and are available for collecting. One can zero in on any phase of recorded music that appeals to him, from Edison's scratchy cylinders to vinyl rock, and find it on the market. There's another plus, too: nearly every modern phonograph will play the old 78's. If you collect cylinder records, you'll need to buy a cylinder player if you want to listen to them. This, though, is no real problem. The auction sales and antiques shops frequently offer cylinder players in operating condition. If you can do your own restoration work, or know someone who can, you could save hundreds of dollars by buying a nonoperating cylinder player and repairing it.

Even today, heading toward the close of the 20th century, the phonograph is too recent an invention to be properly appraised. Centuries from now it will probably be considered just as monumental an invention as the printing press, which has been around since the 1400's. There are even some who believe that recorded words will eventually take the place of the printed word! Almost right up until the phonograph's invention, the world at large considered such a machine an impossibility. It was just as much a dream as going to the moon. Writing in the late 1700's, biographer James Boswell lamented that there was no way to preserve the voice of his idol, Samuel Johnson, for posterity. He put forward the suggestion that some method of special notations should be developed, which would indicate tones of voice and characteristics of speaking. Never did he envision a *machine* to capture the human voice—it was too improbable! Yet in less than 100 years thereafter, just such a machine was in existence and was capturing the human voice.

During the 19th century—the "Age of Invention" as historians call it—developments occurred which led gradually up to the phonograph. Mankind acquired more knowledge of science and machinery, and each new invention pointed the way toward fresh worlds to conquer. Again and again, clever inventors accomplished the seemingly impossible—with the steam engine, the photo-camera, and so many other things. Stampedes were made on the U.S. Patent Office, and many a patent holder went literally from rags to riches. This encouraged some people to set themselves up as full-time inventors, and secure as many patents as possible on a wide range of products. By far the most successful was Thomas A. Edison of Orange, New Jersey, to whom credit belongs for bringing the phonograph into being. While the idea for such a device may not originally have been his, he was, nonetheless, the first to build a workable phonograph and then to patent it. This was U.S. Patent No. 200,251, issued on February 10, 1878. Actually, Edison's machine had been perfected the previous year. Thanks to the voluminous, careful accounts kept by the Edison staff, we even know the exact date on which his phonograph played for the first time: December 7, 1877.

Of course, the early phonographs had many faults, especially when compared to present-day models. You couldn't get much volume; tone was nonexistent; music warbled; and the surface noise was, by today's standards, intolerable. But, looking at things in perspective, you have to realize that our ancestors were amazed simply by the fact that the phonograph *worked.* It was very remarkable indeed to have a wooden box that talked or played music. What we see as serious defects in antique phonographs and records were largely overlooked by listeners of that time. Edison himself (and other phonograph makers) did not overlook them; he kept on improving his product until the day of his death, many years later. Each improvement brought a new flurry of sales. The phonograph industry quickly established itself as one of America's biggest money-makers, simply because (as with autos, which came a little later) everybody wanted the latest and the best. People were willing—even anxious—to discard a phonograph they had bought just two or three years earlier, to get the latest model. This brought millions of dollars annually into the industry and touched off many battles for supremacy in the phono-world.

Although cylinder phonographs were very compact, the recordings themselves posed a storage problem. Large collections took up a great deal of space. They were also easily damaged, as it was difficult to handle them without touching the grooves. The obvious solution was a flat record disc, which could be easily stacked. A prototype already existed in the metal discs used in coin-operated "music machines" or jukeboxes of that time. In 1887, a patent was taken out for a phonograph using zinc discs—but not by Edison. Developer of the disc record was Emile Berliner. However, the Edison Company very soon was producing disc phonographs and records and garnered the lion's share of sales for them throughout the 1890's and early 1900's. Thereafter, one development followed hot on the heels of another. In 1894 Columbia Records was established and became one of Edison's main competitors. About that same time, Berliner was bringing out 7-inch records and selling them for half a dollar each. His records were blank on the reverse side and played at 70 revolutions per minute, to conform with the turntable speed of his phonographs.

Each record manufacturer cut his records at a different speed from the competition, so they could be played to their fullest advantage only on *his* phonographs. There was a possible drawback to this: if you already owned an Edison phonograph, you might not want to buy Berliner records and hear them slightly cockeyed. But the philosophy of manufacturers was: sell the phonograph *first,* then sell the records. Companies that made only records (not phonographs to go with them) were very few at first. They tried to take a neutral position and cut their discs at middle-of-the-road speeds, so they wouldn't sound *too* bad no matter whose machine you played them on. Luckily, the listeners did not have overly critical ears. In this kind of situation, the music fan of today would be banging his head against the wall.

As expected, the novelty of the phonograph wore off quickly. Those who bought phonographs in the 1880's were fascinated by whatever issued forth from them—even if they had to strain to catch the words or guess about what the melody was supposed to be. As the public became more discriminating—egged on by press critics, who habitually poked fun at the phonograph—it was obvious that better records had to be put out, not only better-sounding but records of a more diverse, interesting character. Many early records were recitations or readings, such as someone reciting The Gettysburg Address. When music was used, it was often played by rank amateurs and wouldn't have sounded too good even on the best equipment. There were singers who couldn't sing, too, and all sorts of theatrical sins committed on early records. So another battle started up, to produce good records that would have wide-ranging popular appeal. And in time the sale of records far overshadowed the sale of phonographs. The best entertainers were hired. By 1905, nearly every major theatrical celebrity was making phonograph records.

The biggest step in this direction was taken by a man named Eldridge Johnson—not very well known compared to Edison, but whose legacy in the industry is awesome. Johnson had worked for Emile Berliner, then went off to found his own company. In 1901 he started up the Victor Record Company, the ancestor of RCA-Victor. In the 1920's he was bought out by Radio Corporation of America and retired with a huge fortune to pursue his hobby of collecting rare books and prints. Johnson's Victor company made phonographs as well as records, but its records made its reputation. Johnson used different color labels on his records to indicate the type of record, and introduced "Red Seal" records for celebrity recordings. The Victor Red Seal records were the most prestigious of their time. In sound quality they were really no better than anyone else's, but the stable of artists that Johnson succeeded in signing up reads like a show business Who's Who. His top selling (and by far most glamorous) artist was Enrico Caruso. In 1903, Caruso's Red Seal recording of "Vesti la giubba" became the first million-selling record in history. This was no small feat. It is very doubtful that, in 1903, as many as a million households had phonographs. Literally everybody who owned a phonograph bought "Vesti la giubba," and some must have bought more than one copy. This is the equivalent of a modern-day record selling 40 or 50 million copies, which no record has ever sold in a single run on the charts (Bing Crosby's "White Christmas" is over 100 million in sales, but this represents numerous repressings over a nearly 40-year span). Caruso cut many dozens of records for Victor, and their sales alone would have made the company very, very successful. But Johnson had many other top artists in his camp, from opera, vaudeville, the minstrel halls, and you-name-it. In less than five years he built a recording empire that even Edison must have envied.

In 1906 Eldridge Johnson added another feather to his cap. Victor brought out the first phonograph (a console model) with an enclosed horn.

Of course there were still advances left to be made, even though the industry had, in three and a half decades, come a remarkably long way. Two years later (1908) another giant stride was taken by Columbia Records with introduction of the double-sided disc. This type of record —made of pressed wax and double-sided—remained standard until after World War II. It played at approximately 78 rpm and differed not too much from, say, a 78 by Frank Sinatra or Perry Como. It was somewhat thicker and heavier, and of course the sound quality was not quite equal to that of later records. But in physical appearance it was much closer to modern records than it was to its ancestors, the cylinder and the zinc disc.

Victor and Columbia were again at the forefront of progress, when the slower-playing vinyl record came along. In 1948 Columbia introduced the 33 "long play" record. It had an option on the 45 rpm disc but did not follow through, believing that the 45 had limited sales potential. So in 1949 Victor picked up the 45 and began experimenting with it. Very few 45 singles were released until the early fifties, when a number of companies were putting them out. The usual practice was to issue records in both 78 and 45. Companies wanted to phase out 78's as quickly as possible but could not rush things, since many record buyers had phonographs that played only 78's.

Thus, the way was clear for the record boom of the sixties, seventies, and eighties, which now accounts for billions of dollars in annual sales.

AUCTION SALES

Almost all varieties of musical collectibles can be purchased through auction sales. Sales devoted entirely to recordings are held by specialist auctioneers in various parts of the country and, in addition, there are opportunities to buy musical instruments, recordings, and memorabilia at many estate sales that are not billed as music sales. Any serious musicana enthusiast must follow the estate sales in his area closely and attend as many as possible to avoid missing good opportunities. Remember that the items you fail to purchase will be bought by dealers, and you will pay them a 50 percent or higher profit. Don't be afraid of auctions. On the other hand, don't go blindly into an auction sale. Attend the presale exhibition, carefully examine any items on which you intend to bid, then decide on the top price you care to pay. At the sale, stay within these limits. Be especially thorough in inspecting mixed or bulk lots of records, music sheets, etc. It is quite likely that a batch of 100 music sheets will contain just one rarity that makes the whole lot worthwhile and that other bidders have not noticed. A collection of old 78 recordings may appear at the surface very uninteresting but could contain a few first-rate gems. Once the sale is over, it's too late.

PITFALLS

The chief dangers are buying mechanical instruments that fail to operate and personality autographs or other memorabilia that are not authentic.

The buyer of mechanical instruments should always insist on a demonstration before making a purchase or putting down a deposit. When purchasing by mail, have some arrangement with the seller whereby a refund will be made if the item does not prove to be operable. A reputable dealer in mechanical instruments will provide a written guarantee, but this is seldom obtainable from a general antiques dealer who sells instruments only occasionally.

Personality autographs are, unfortunately, often faked. This is something of which the public is not fully aware, believing that a forger would not bother with items that retail for small amounts of money. True enough, a counterfeit Washington or Lincoln letter could be sold for thousands of dollars, while a faked Fabian autograph is worth perhaps a dollar or two, but the latter is much simpler to sell. It is almost impossible to successfully pass off Washington or Lincoln material, but a faker can, very easily, take an 8 × 10 publicity shot of any pop singer, which he purchases for $1, add a signature, and sell it for a profit. There is no defense against this sort of thing except to gain a good knowledge of celebrity autographs, study genuine specimens, and acquire, when possible, either from respected dealers or from collectors who have obtained the autographs directly from the stars. There are many collectors who have duplicate autographs that they are willing and anxious to trade.

"Why buy?" is the motto of some hobbyists, who prefer to get their star signatures from the source—the stars themselves. This insures authenticity and provides a spark of excitement, too. Sometimes you can have the item personally autographed to you, which is a thrill that a purchased autograph will never have. There are various ways to go about this. The best, of course, is to approach the celebrity in person. When that cannot be done, a good alternative is to send a personal letter requesting his or her autograph, along with a stamped return envelope. Stars can be addressed in care of the recording studio for which they work, a TV network, motion picture studio, or even sometimes through a magazine. The best way to get a letter to a star is to find out the name of his agent and send it in care of the agent.

SOME TIPS ON USING THIS BOOK

There's an almost encyclopedic amount of information in *The Official Price Guide to Music Collectibles*. It's been arranged for maximum convenience, and especially convenience-under-fire (when you're at a flea market, for example, and need to find a listing *fast*). All items are grouped into categories and the categories are alphabetized throughout the book. Within each section, the items are listed by artist or manufacturer or by "type," whichever is applicable. As there are numerous different types of collectibles listed, no single system could be workable for every category. Flip through the book and in a couple of minutes you'll get the hang of it!

A few general comments:

With all of the items listed, condition counts. The prices shown are (in cases where no reference is made to the contrary) for specimens in well-preserved condition. Any object that is broken, has parts missing, is badly stained, etc., can normally be expected to sell for less than the price range indicated—usually much less. On the other hand, a perfect mint specimen with no signs of use will often sell for a higher price than shown in our ranges.

In the case of the 45 r.p.m. records, when reference is made to *picture sleeve,* the price indicated is for the record *plus the sleeve.* In most instances we also give the value for the record alone. You can easily compute the value of the sleeve alone (with no record) by deducting the price of the record from the price of the record-with-sleeve. The sleeves themselves are definitely collectors' items.

Values for LP albums are for specimens *with the jackets or sleeves.* The records by themselves are worth considerably less, in most cases only about half as much.

ABOUT THE PRICES

Who agrees about the values of collectors' items? Nobody—and that's the reason for the *Official Guide* series of collectors' handbooks: to serve as an independent monitor of the market. Thousands upon thousands of actual sales and dealers' offerings were reviewed, to arrive at fair market values for the listings in this book. Each price is a *retail* value—the sum charged by dealers when selling to the public. When selling *to* a dealer, you would naturally receive less than these amounts, owing to the dealer's operating costs and profit margin. Instead of a single or "flat" price, a range is shown for every item in this book. This approach is (we feel) fairer to both buyer and seller, since the prices of collectors' items *do* vary from sale to sale. It is entirely possible that some, or many, of these items can be found selling for higher or lower than the indicated range. If you're lucky enough to find a $30–45 record at a garage sale, it might be going for $1 or $2. Sales of this type are not considered when computing market values, since they occur outside the normal collector market. By the same token, in an auction sale, a $30–45 item could reach $50, $75, or even more if bidding is intense. Nothing is certain in the world of collecting. That's why this book is presently only a guide—a map to a road that *you* will need to travel yourself, to see what the terrain is really like.

MECHANICAL MUSIC MACHINES

Music has always been very important to mankind. Not until the many and varied inventions of modern man in the industrial age was one able to enjoy music without actually attending a performance. That is what is meant by "mechanical" music. The player piano, Encore banjo, even orchestrions are basically actual musical instruments with the addition of self-playing mechanisms.

Other machines were invented specifically to make music mechanically; for example, music boxes and roller organs.

The phonograph, though it does not actually fall into either of these categories, was a singularly monumental breakthrough in bringing a wide range of entertainment into the homes of a large segment of the population. This is the primary reason for its survival even today.

The common element in all these machines is that they produce musical entertainment without the live presence of a human musician.

DETERMINING VALUE

The most important factors in determining the value of a machine are rarity, popularity, and condition. Condition is a crucial determining factor in the mechanical musical field. "Fine original working condition" (as it left the maker's hands) is the most desirable state for a machine. It is quite rare that a machine has survived many decades without some needed repair or restoration, as in the case of most pneumatically operated machines. A player piano in original unrestored condition is not worth as much as expertly restored examples.

Unless otherwise described, the value range given in each entry is for a machine in "fine working condition," as close to the original as possible.

Our prices come from many sources, such as auctions, dealer catalogues, publications in the field, and our own experience. There can be great differences between the auction and dealer price for a specific machine. Many rare items just don't seem to come up for sale anywhere else than these sources. One can reasonably allow a 10 percent leeway either way on the prices given to account for geography, inflation, and other variables.

It is difficult to determine the value of a machine that is not in working condition. If the "problem" is just a minor adjustment or missing winding tool (e.g., crank, key, etc.), a fair value should be considerably higher than a machine that needs total restoration. It is up to the buyer and seller to educate themselves so they can exercise discretion as well as recognize a bargain when they see it. (See "Repair and Restoration Guidelines" and "Future Trends.") One noteworthy exception where we have included both "Unrestored" and "Restored" prices is the section on "Pianos—Self-Playing." The reason for this is that so many examples are found in unrestored condition, and the difference in the value of a player piano between unrestored and restored condition is considerable.

A willing buyer and seller can set their own values. In the case of rare desirable items of "museum quality," it is a seller's market and very difficult to evaluate. We have given it our best shot. A landmark auction tomorrow could change everything.

One must not let greed or the imagined prospect of a windfall profit cloud his reason. The reality of the marketplace is that it is rare that one can actually get the listed value of an item. Why? In any particular instance so many variables come into account, not the least being the personality of the parties involved.

The antique field has always been a place where haggling over the price is part of the pleasure in making the deal. A guide is useful as a point of reference and in determining relative values of machines within a specific area.

DATING

As this book is meant only as a guide to the field of musical collectibles, very brief historical information is given. When dates are given at the beginning of each section and in some of the entries, they are meant as a point of reference. The "Further Reading" section contains some excellent reference tools for in-depth historical information.

BUYING AND SELLING GUIDELINES

Both the buyer and seller of mechanical musical machines use the same outlets to further their interests.

The private buyer has the same opportunity to purchase machines at an auction as a dealer and at the same price. Sometimes one can come away with a real bargain, and other times the excitement of the moment can cause the bidders to bring the price higher than realistic market values. It can depend on the basic character of the bidding audience and the overall quality of the merchandise being auctioned off. An audience of mostly dealers can be good for a private buyer, as you are not concerned with profit margins and may be prepared to bid higher. For the seller consigning machines to an auction house, an audience of private buyers and collectors can bring higher prices. You should attend specialized auctions before you decide to consign your machines to them. (See "Auctions.")

The best way to gauge your chances for success at an auction is to keep the following points in mind:

Where and how much advertising for the auction did you see?

Is the audience enthusiastic about the merchandise?

Is the buying lively or is the auctioneer working hard to sell the items?

What is the percentage the auctioneer receives in commission?

Is there a buyer's commission on the winning bid?

Buying and selling through special-interest publications, society bulletins, collectors' newsletters, and similar classified advertising is an excellent way to reach an interested readership and a receptive market. Through correspondence and business dealings one gets to meet and know fellow enthusiasts. One does not have to join the various mechanical musical societies to advertise in their publications. One does have to join the society to receive the publication on a regular basis. (See "Mechanical Musical Societies and Their Publications" and "Publications and Sources for Facsimile Reprints.")

Specialized antique shows are a good way to meet some of the people one has corresponded with through the special interest publications. They are also an excellent place to see a wide variety of mechanical musical items from all over. (See "Antique Shows.")

Dealers and restorers are of course an excellent source for buying and selling machines and parts. For some very specialized and rare items, dealers are the primary and maybe the only way to locate them. They have cultivated sources and contacts the ordinary buyer doesn't know about. Dealers can help you locate restorers with the special expertise you may require. Restorers are also a good source for contacts with other interested buyers and sellers. (See "Dealers and Restorers.")

DEALERS AND RESTORERS

Most of the machines in this book require and deserve expert repair and restoration, to insure and enhance their value. The following are guidelines for finding and choosing a restorer:

1. Mechanical Musical Societies can direct you to fellow members and restorers whom members have used and are satisfied with.

2. Local museums or state museums may be familiar with restorers who have done work for them.

3. Yellow pages and other directories may provide you with a starting point; for example, a local dealer who sells the type of thing you need restored.

4. Dealers and restorers listed in the accompanying section (though this is a very incomplete listing).

A word of caution: When you have chosen a restorer, ask to hear and see work in progress and completed work to be sure you have chosen wisely. The list of dealers and restorers was compiled from many sources. The inclusion or exclusion from this listing of any particular company or person does not constitute a judgment on the quality of their work.

ARIZONA
WENDELL MOORE, 3085 W. Highway 89A, Sedona, AZ 86336. Phonographs for sale.

ARKANSAS
K. R. Powers, 28 Alton Circle, Rogers, AR 72756. Disc and cylinder music box restoration sales and supplies.

CALIFORNIA
ANTIQUE JUKEBOX CO., 2363 East Olympic Boulevard, Los Angeles, CA.

ANTIQUE MUSIC BOX RESTORATION, 1825 Placentia Avenue, Costa Mesa, CA 92627. Varied mechanical musical machines.

BROADMOORE AUTOMATIC INSTRUMENT RESTORATIONS, 1709C 1st Street, San Francisco, CA 91340. Orchestrions and reproducing pianos.

CARL FRICK, 940 Canon Road, Santa Barbara, CA 93110. Catalog of parts and literature.

MUSIC BOX DOCTOR: ANTHONY J. CIUFFINI, 28810 Crestridge Road, Rancho Palos Verdes, CA 90274. Musical box repairs.

MUSICAL AMERICANA TALKING MACHINE CO., 354 East Campbell Avenue, Campbell, CA 95008. Large list of phonograph parts and repair services.

STEPHEN OLIPHANT, 5255 Allott Avenue, Van Nuys, CA 91401. Phonographs for sale.

URBAN ANTIQUES, 1861 Union Street, San Francisco, CA 94123. Variety of mechanical musical machines for sale.

VINTAGE TALKING MACHINES (STEVE AND JUDY FARMER), P.O. Box 558, San Luis Rey, CA 92068. Phonographs for sale, complete restoration including coin-ops.

COLORADO

ART REBLITZ PIANOS, 3916 N. Azalea, Colorado Springs, CO 80907. Restoration services for automatic pianos and organs.

FRERES D'METATRON, 610 Downing Street, Denver, CO 80218. Music Box restoration.

CONNECTICUT

MECHANICAL MUSIC CENTER, INC., 25 King Highway North, Box 88, Darien, CT 06820. One of the largest dealers in mechanical musical machines. Showroom and periodic illustrated catalogs.

MECHANTIQUES, 26 Barton Hill, East Hampton, CT 06424. Buy, sell, trade mechanical musical machines.

YANKEE PHONOGRAPH CO. (SCOTT ZAHNER), 39 Florence Street, Rockville, CT 06066. Phonographs for sale, restoration service.

FLORIDA

RINKY-TINK AMUSEMENTS, 14086 S.W. 142 Avenue, Miami, FL 33186. Player piano and jukebox repair and sales.

GEORGIA

D. B. MUSICAL RESTORATIONS, 230 Lakeview Avenue N.E., Atlanta, GA 30305. Music boxes (restoration services).

ILLINOIS

JUKEBOX SATURDAY NIGHT, 1552 N. Wells, Chicago, IL 60610. Jukebox sales and restoration.

PHOENIX OLDE TIME MUSIC-SALES AND SERVICE, 60 Martin Lane, Elk Grove Village, IL 60007. Specializes in organettes and barrel organs.

REGINA MUSIC BOX CO., INC. (J. HARRY AND NANCY CARMEL), 7013 W. Crandall Avenue, Worth, IL 60482. Disc music boxes, parts, new discs.

INDIANA

CLARENCE W. FABEL, Box 202, Route 3, Morgantown, IN 46160. Cylinder music box restoration.

IOWA

TOM FRETTY, Highway 9 and 65, Manly, IA 50456. Musical antiques.

JUKEBOX JUNCTION, Box 1081, Des Moines, IA 50311. Parts, reprints, etc.

STEVE LOOTS, P. O. Box 119, Des Moines, Iowa 50301. Jukebox sales, parts, reprints.

KANSAS

HILL'S PLAYER AND GRAMOPHONE SERVICE, 1535 Campus Road, Manhattan, KA 66502. Restoration of player and reproducing pianos, also phonograph repairs.

PLAYER PIANO COMPANY, INC., 620 East Douglas, Wichita, KA 67202. Large illustrated catalog of piano and player piano parts.

FLOYD'S BAND ORGAN REPAIR AND COMPANY, 2736 N. 66 Terrace, KA City, Kansas 66104. Band organ rebuilder.

KENTUCKY

AUTOMATED MUSIC SPECIALISTS, 204 N. Madison, Middletown, KY 40243. Repair and restoration of automatic pianos and organs.

LOUISIANA

SHREVEPORT MUSIC CO., 109 Kings Highway, Shreveport, LA 71104. Piano repair.

MARYLAND

DAHLBERG'S KEYBOARD SPECIALISTS AND SERVICE, 12613 Chanler Lane, Bowie, MD 20715. Restoration of organs and player pianos.

ART AND HELEN MUELLER, P.O. Box 9450, Cantonville, MD 21228. Sales of Music Boxes and related items.

THE NOOK FOR MUSIC BOXES (CAROLE W. FETTIG), 4849 Cordell Avenue, Bethesda, MD 20814. Music boxes, buy, sell, repair.

MASSACHUSETTS

ALAN PIER PLAYER PIANO SERVICE, 8 Skyline Drive, Billerica, MA 01821. Restoration service, specializing in pneumatic instruments.

OLD SOUND, Route 134 near 6A, East Dennis, MA 02641. Phonograph display, sales and service.

THE PIANO SHOP (JOHN SPRINGER), P.O. Box 411, 438 Spring Street, Athol, MA 01331. Pianos and players: restoration, buy and sell.

ROLAND A. TRIFF, 11 Warwick Road, W. Newton, MA 02165. Music box sales and restoration service.

MICHIGAN

PIANO PLUS (RICHARD F. LUTIN), 916 North Third, Niles, MI 49120. Player piano, reed organ and music box sales and service.

MINNESOTA

JERRY MADSEN, 4624 West Woodland Road, Edina, MN 55424. Phonographs and related items for sale.

MECHANICAL MAESTRO (ANGELO P. RULLI), 1300 East Third Street, St. Paul, MN 55106. Music box repair.

MISSOURI

CRAIG BROUGHER, 3500 Claremont, Independence, MO 60532. Complete piano and player restoration.

WILLIAM T. SINGLETON, PIANOS, 1101 South Kingshighway, St. Louis, MO 63110. Pianos, nickelodeons, music boxes: restoration.

NEW JERSEY

AUTA MUSIQUE LTD. (JERE AND STEVE RYDER), P.O. Box 65, Cranford, NJ 07016. Music box sales and restoration.

GOULD PIANO CRAFTSMEN, 391 Tremont Place, Orange, NJ 07050. Complete piano service and sales. Specializing in player and reproducing pianos as well as other pneumatic instruments. Pianocorders installations, sales and service.

CHARLEY HUMMEL, 61 Laurel Drive, Wayne, NJ 07470. Buy, sell, trade, repair phonographs and related items.

MEEKINS MUSIC BOX COMPANY, P.O. Box 161, Collingswood, NJ 08108. Music boxes, especially "Regina," restoration services.

OLDE TYME MUSIC SCENE, 915 Main Street, Boonton, NJ 07005. Variety of phonographs and records for sale.

FLOYD SILVER, P.O. Box 274, Vincentown, NJ 08088. Buy, sell, trade, repair phonographs and related items. Also mail order auction sales with emphasis on cylinder and disc records.

NEW MEXICO

ELEMENTS OF TIME (A. PARK SHAW III), 109 Romero N.W., Albuquerque, NM 87104. Music box sales and repair (also clocks and watches).

NEW YORK

ANTIQUES MECHANICAL (RESURRECTED) LTD., "Mainspring House" on the corner of Spring and Main Streets, South Salem, NY 10590. Music boxes bought, sold, and repaired.

ANTIQUE PHONOGRAPH SHOP, 320 Jericho Turnpike, Floral Park, NY 11001. Buy, sell, repair spring operated phonographs.

BORNAND MUSIC BOX CO., 139 Fourth Avenue, Pelham, NY 10803. Swiss and disc music boxes for sale (restoration services).

F. & L. ANTIQUES (FRANK AND LORE METZGER), Box 47, Harrison, NY 10528. Music boxes and automata. Buy, sell, and restoration services.

RITA FORD, 19 East 65 Street, New York, NY 10021. Music box sales.

LEONARD ANTIQUES, Box 127, Albertson, Long Island, NY 11507. Variety of mechanical music items.

MUSICAL MUSEUM (THE SANDERS FAMILY), State Route 12B, Deansboro, NY 13328. Museum Shop repair service for mechanical musical machines. Sale of music rolls for grind organs.

PANCHRONIA ANTIQUES, P.O. Box 73, Warners, NY 13164. Music boxes and parts, restoration services, discs.

PLAYER PIANO REPAIR, 12 East 12th Street, New York, NY 10003 (12th floor), also pipe organs.

TREASURE ISLAND ANTIQUES (LEOPOLD AND VALERIE LYSLOFF), 378 South Country Road, Brookhaven Hamlet, NY 11719. Antique music boxes, also clocks, watches, dolls.

VICKI GLASGOW, 135 Plymouth Drive, Scarsdale, NY 10583. Mechanical musical items for sale.

WAVES, 32 East 13 Street, New York, NY 10003. Early radios and phonographs.

NORTH CAROLINA

ANTIQUE PHONOGRAPH CO., 612 South Mulberry Street, Statesville, NC 28677. Dealer of mechanical musical items.

OHIO

MUSIQUE MECHANIQUE, 2960 North High Street, Columbus, OH 43202. Music box sales.

PIANO WORKSHOP, 3166 West 33 Street, Cleveland, OH 44109. Piano and player piano restoration.

PLAYER PIANO SHOP (JAMES R. HOCKENBERGER), 776 Carlton, Toledo, OH 43609. Rebuild and sell player pianos, nickelodeons.

PENNSYLVANIA

MUSIC CURIO REPAIR SHOP, 23 N. Sycamore Street, Box 488, Macungie, PA 10862. Music boxes, small organs.

SOUTH CAROLINA

M. LYNN REID PIANOS, 110 Highway Drive, Union, SC 29379. Automatic instrument restoration.

SOUTH DAKOTA

MICHAEL V. EDWARDS, THE PIANO MAN, 2019 1st Avenue, Rapid City, SD 57701. Player piano rebuilding.

TENNESSEE

GEORGE E. KURZ, 4703-A, Sabrina Lane, Chattanooga, TN 37343. Pump organs, organettes, singing birds: repair and restoration.

TEXAS

AUTOMATIC MUSIC CO. (ED GAIDA), 600 Fredericksburg Road, San Antonio, TX 78201. Buy, sell, repair player pianos.

BEAU-DAN IMPORTS, 2040 The Promenade, Richardson, TX 75240. Music boxes.

VERMONT

PORTER MUSIC BOX CO., 5 Mound Street, Randolph, VT 05060. Make and restore music boxes, also discs for Polyphone, Regina and Porter music boxes.

REED ORGAN SERVICE, Box 3, Back Street, Jamaica, VT 05343. Reed organ parts and repair.

WASHINGTON

MUSICAL AUTOMATA OF YESTERYEAR, 1901 S.E. Sedgwick Road, Port Orchard, WA 98366. Repair and sales of mechanical musical machines.

WISCONSIN

JOHN HOVANCAK, JR., 705 N. Union, Dodgeville, WI 53533. Mechanical music repair and restoration.

AUSTRALIA

ANTIQUE CLOCK REPAIR AND ANTIQUES. 22 Ascot Blvd., Bowral, N.S.W. 2576 Australia. Music box restoration (also watches, clocks, automata).

BELGIUM

ARTHUR PRINSEN, 15 Oostjacktpack, St. Niklass, 2700 Belgium. Music boxes and organs.

CANADA

FRANKLIN H. FOLEY, Box 1476, Belleville, Ontario K8N5J2, Canada. Buy, sell, and trade mechanical musical instruments.

THE GREAT CANADIAN NICKELODEON CO. LTD., Highway 135, Industrial Park #90, Box 33, London, Ontario N6A4B8, Canada. Repair, restoration and sales of coin pianos.

PLAYER PIANO CENTRE AND MUSEUM, 3399 Dunbar Street, Vancouver, British Columbia, Canada V6S2B9. Restoration services. Specialty: Wurlitzer.

DENMARK

MEKANISKMUSIC MUSEUM (CLAES O. FRIBERG), Box 14, Rungsted Kyst DK 2960, Denmark. Automatic musical instruments, buy, sell, repair.

ENGLAND

JOHN COWDEROY ANTIQUES, 42 South Street, Eastbourne, East Sussex, England BN214X. Music boxes (restoration services).

JACK DONOVAN, 93 Portobello Road, London W11 England. Mechanical music antiques, buy and sell.

KEITH HARDING, 93 Hornsey Road, London, England N76DJ. Music boxes, parts, and publications (restoration services).

NORFOLK POLYPHONE CENTRE, Wood Farm, Baudeswell, East Dereham, Norfolk, England. Mechanical musical items buy and sell.

THE TALKING MACHINE, 30 Watford Way, Hendon, Central London, NW4 England. Buy, sell early phonographs and music boxes.

JAPAN

NOF ANTIQUES SHELLMAN, INC., (NORIO ISOGAI), 14-16 Ginza 3-chrome, Chuo-Ku Tokyo 104 Japan. Mechanical musical instruments.

NETHERLANDS

W. J. VAN OS AND H. M. G. YU, Nieuwe Spiegelstraat 68, Amsterdam, Netherlands. Antique music box sales.

SCOTLAND

MONKTON HOUSE ANTIQUES, Monkton House, Old Craig Hall, Musselburgh, Midlothian, Scotland. Buy and sell variety of mechanical antiques and curios (by appointment only).

SWITZERLAND

RETONIO'S INTERNATIONAL GALLERY, Zielstrasse 38, CH-9050 Appenzell, Switzerland. Mechanical musical items for sale.

This list of dealers and restorers has been compiled from many sources. The inclusion or exclusion from this listing of any particular company or person does not constitute a judgment about them. Each reader must make his own choice based on the guidelines previously enumerated. We know this list will be expanded in time. (Your recommendations are welcome.)

ANTIQUE RECORD DEALERS

For those with specific types of interest in the record field, there are classified sections in many of the phonograph publications listed in "Publications and Reprints" where dealers and collectors advertise their records for sale.

Listed below are just a few dealers who issue price and/or auction lists:

PAUL C. BURGESS
Box 12-A, Friendship, ME 04547
Disc and cylinder records

DENNIS DEVINE
722 Pierce Street, Council Bluffs, IA 51501
Cylinder Records

ELECTROPHONE CYLINDER RECORD COMPANY
320 Jericho Turnpike, Floral Park, NY 11001.
Newly made, prerecorded cylinder records, modern artists

MUSIQUE
1177 Bay Street, Rochester, NY 14609
Cylinder and disc record mail auctions

JOHN A. PETTY
Route 1, Box 54-A, Catawba, NC 28609
Record auction by mail

ARTHUR SANDERS, MUSICAL MUSEUM
Deansboro, NY 13328

THE 78 SHOP: DENNIS TICHY
Box 242, Murrysville, PA 15668
Sells records by artists or type by the "case."

RICHARD SIMONTON
4209 Burbank Boulevard, Burbank, CA 91602
Diamond discs

CARL A. TESSEN
1620 Columbia Avenue, Oshkosh, WI 54901
All types

VERTIGO HILL RECORDS
Vertigo Manor, 581 Arch Street, New Britain, CT 06051
Pre-1935 records, mail auctions

YANKEE RECORD CO.
39 Florence Street, Rockville, CT 06066
Mail auctions of cylinder and disc records and related items (1900–1935).

PIANO ROLL DEALERS

Player piano rolls can still be found at flea markets, auctions, and antique shops, and there are dealers who specialize in rolls. (Dealers are especially useful if one has specific artists, roll labels, or types of music in mind.) There are excellent recuts being made today, especially of hard-to-find popular artists and music styles, e.g., ragtime, Gershwin, etc.
Average 88-note roll, $1.00 and up; average reproducing roll $3.00 and up.

AMICA FOUNDING CHAPTER ROLL AUCTION
4271 N. First St., Space #1, San Jose, CA 95134. Periodic mail order piano roll auctions, extensive selection with emphasis on reproducing and expression rolls.

AUTOMATIC MUSIC ROLL CO.
P. O. Box 3194, Seattle, WA 98114. Old and new reproducing rolls and related literature.

L. CORDELL (PIANO ROLL AUCTIONS BY MAIL)
2240 Lorain Road, San Marino, CA 91108

JOHN T. DONOHUE (PIANO ROLL AUCTIONS BY MAIL)
Box 168, Southampton, NY 11968. Also has reproducing pianos for sale on consignment.

ELECTRIC PIANO ROLL CO.
Harold E. Davis, Box 1, Leslie, MI 49251

KLAVIER MUSIC ROLL (THE POWELLS)
9700 Glenoaks Boulevard, Sun Valley, CA 91352. Recuts of reproducing rolls and regular 88 note rolls.

PLAY-RITE MUSIC ROLLS, INC.
2121 S. El Camino Real, San Mateo, CA 99403. Make and sell player piano rolls.

QRS MUSIC ROLLS
1026 Niagara Street, Buffalo, NY 14213. They are the only one of the old companies still in business. Write to them for name of local dealer.

DON RAND AND ED OPENSHAW
3222 Larga Avenue, Los Angeles, CA 90039.
Old piano roll auction and collectors' classics (limited edition recuts—beautiful) by mail.

MIKE AND FRED SCHWIMMER AUCTIONS BY MAIL
241A Harbor, Glencoe, IL 60022. Monthly roll auctions.

VI & SI ANTIQUES
8970 Main Street, Clarence, NY 14031. Rolls and records (all types), auction lists (by mail).

MISCELLANEOUS ROLL DEALERS

EDWARD FREYER
Box 373 (Route 31), Flemington, NJ 08822. Recut rolls for nickelodeons (Type A, G, 4x rolls).

MUSICAL MUSEUM (ART SANDERS)
State Route 12B, Deansboro, NY 13328. Music rolls for grind organs.

SCHMIDT'S MUSIC ROLLS
Edward M. Schmidt, 5010 Elsmere Place, Bethesda, MD 20814. Manufacturer of music for organettes, paper roll and strip instruments.

AUCTION HOUSES

DON P. BRITT, Auctioneer
3125 S. Virginia, Suite #1, Reno, NV 89504. Auctioneer for the three Bellm Museum Auctions, among others.

CHRISTIE'S EAST
219 East 67 Street, New York, NY 10021. Periodic actions containing fine-quality mechanical musical machines.

CHRISTIE'S SOUTH KENSINGTON, LTD.
85 Old Brompton Road, London SW73JS England. Regular auction sales of mechanical musical items. Catalogues available, bidding by mail accepted.

DOYLE AUCTIONEERS & APPRAISERS
98 Main Street, Fishkill, NY 12524. Regular auction sales of music collectibles.

MANOR HOUSE GALLERIES
West Memorial Park Plaza, 8570 Katy Freeway, Suite 119, Houston, TX 77079. Don Mudd, Auctioneer. Occasional large auction sales of mechanical musical instruments, very entertaining.

RETONIO INTERNATIONAL GALLERY
Zielstrasse 38, CH 9050 Appenzell, Switzerland. Periodic auctions of mechanical musical machines. Illustrated catalogue issued.

SOTHEBY PARKE BERNET
1334 York Ave., New York, NY 10021. "Collector's Carrousel" auctions usually contain mechanical musical items.

SOTHEBY'S BELGRAVIA
19 Motcomb Street, London SW1S8LB, England. Auction sales of mechanical musical items. Catalogues available, bidding by mail accepted.

SOTHEBY'S LOS ANGELES
7660 Beverly Boulevard, Los Angeles, CA 90036. "Fine collectibles 'Auctions.'"

Special auctions of mechanical musical machines are widely advertised in antique publications, e.g.:
Antique and Auction News
Antique Trader
Collectors News

ANTIQUE SHOWS

SEVEN ACRES ANTIQUE VILLAGE AND MUSEUM
Route 20 and S. Union Road, Union, IL 60180. Annual antique phonograph and music box show.

TRI STATE MUSIC COLLECTIBLES SHOW
put on by Tri State Exhibitions, Inc.
P. O. Box 76, Livingston, NJ 07039. Periodic shows held in metropolitan New York area.

REPAIR AND RESTORATION GUIDELINES

In the field of mechanical musical machines, restoration is a key element. For the enterprising collector (especially one with limited financial resources) the satisfaction of restoring a potential "silk purse" is very satisfying. The prices for complete but unrestored machines are much more accessible and have not increased at a significant pace in the last few years. In fact, in some cases their value has actually gone down. Though there is the additional investment in time, expertise, and supplies required in restoring a machine expertly, it is really one of the best parts (and rewards) of collecting.

It is impossible to comprehensively describe here how to evaluate the condition one might find a particular type of machine in and what would be the best way to restore it. A machine that does not play may require only a minor adjustment, or it might need a complete overhaul.

There are some fundamental guidelines to keep in mind. First and by far the best way to evaluate the condition of a machine is to play it. One may think appearance is a more important factor, but in general it is easier to correct cosmetic problems than mechanical ones. To return to playing condition, *do not try to play the machine yourself.* Have the owner (dealer) play it for you. The old saying "you break it, you buy it" can be a costly way to satisfy your curiosity. *Be careful* of situations where the "owner" doesn't have the appropriate thing to play on the machine (piano roll, disc or cylinder record, music box disc, wooden cob, etc.) but is sure it "just needs a little adjustment to work fine." It is in your best interest to know for sure. The best way to be sure is either to prepare yourself by studying the field or to bring an expert along.

Your study should consist of visiting mechanical musical machine collections that feature demonstrations of various types of machines, learning from fellow collectors about their machines and experiences in fixing them up, attending specialized antique shows and auctions, and most important of all, reading about your area of interest (both historical treatments as well as "how to fix it" guides). With this experience you will be able to evaluate how well a machine plays, how extensive the needed repairs are going to be, and whether you are able to meet the challenge of doing the restoration yourself.

Directly related to evaluating the restorable condition of a machine is the quality of previous repairs made to it. Are they obvious, sloppy, consistent with the age, design, and type of machine, etc. Did someone, for example install an electric motor in an early model phonograph that was made only to be crank wound? You should be aware of the differences between original condition and alterations made to accommodate someone's personal needs. This is not to say that you shouldn't buy such machines, but their worth is dramatically affected by such alterations. You must know what the original condition of a machine is to know what has been done (or undone) to it and what it will take to restore it to its original condition. Some bad repairs can be undone; others may be irreversible.

The value of a mechanical musical machine is directly related to the authentic quality of the overall machine, its component parts and playing performance.

FUTURE TRENDS

While the values of mechanical musical machines enjoyed a rather rapid growth in the last few decades, recent economic conditions have checked this trend. There are many factors involved, not the least of which is a sluggish demand because of the discouragingly high prices in some circles. There is a point at which the price for a formerly popular item just reaches its peak and in some instances bottoms out. Buyers want fine-quality machines for the high prices they are paying.

There has been a very definite leveling off of prices, especially in the more common models of particular machines, e.g., Edison Homes and Standards Model B and C, Victor inside-horn table and floor models of the simple mahogany case variety, simple-tune cylinder music boxes, unrestored player pianos, etc.

Barring the improbable miracle of someone finding a warehouse full of as yet unknown mechanical musical items, the future trends seems to be for collectors to branch out into related areas of collecting. For example, a music box collector may become interested in phonographs or roller organs. A phonograph collector may become more deeply interested in records and related items.

As for new areas to conquer, the phonographs of the 1920's and 1930's are still quite reasonable, and many, especially the floor model styles, were quite elaborate in case decoration, goldplating, etc. Columbia, Brunswick, Edison, Sonora, and Victor, to name a few, manufactured lovely floor and console model disc phonographs with elaborate period decorations. There are also early electrically operated disc phonographs, notably the Victor Orthophonic table and floor models, starting to appear on the market.

Jukeboxes of the post-classic or 1950's period are physically and financially accessible, as are the pre-classic examples of the early 1930's.

MECHANICAL MUSICAL MUSEUMS AND COLLECTIONS OPEN TO THE PUBLIC

UNITED STATES

ARIZONA

ARIZONA HERITAGE CENTER, 949 East 2nd Street, Tuscon, AZ. Varied collection of mechanical musical instruments.

ARKANSAS

MILES MUSICAL MUSEUM, U.S. Highway 62 West, Eureka Springs, AR. Varied collection of 250 musical items.

CALIFORNIA

ANGELUS CLOCKWORK MUSIC, 420 Second Street, Old Town, Eureka, CA. Varied collection of musical items.

THE DIALS, 190 West J Street, Benicia, CA. Small collection of mechanical musical machines.

KNOTT'S BERRY FARM AND GHOST TOWN, Two miles south of Santa Ana Freeway on California Route #39. Thirty-five various items.

MUSEE MECHANIQUE, 1090 Point Lobos Avenue, San Francisco, CA ("Historic Cliff House"). Collection of music machines, including nickelodeons, orchestrions, and music boxes.

TOWER OF BEAUTY AT SAN SYLMAR, 15180 Bledsoe Street, San Sylmar, CA. Small collection of nickelodeons.

WELCH'S MOUNTAIN FANTASY, 23551 Highway #243, Alandale, CA.

COLORADO

PIKES PEAK GHOST TOWN, 1803 N. Cascade Avenue, Ghost Town Highway 24 West at S. 21 Street exit, Colorado Springs, CO. Small varied collection.

CONNECTICUT

THE AMERICAN MUSEUM OF MECHANICAL MUSIC, 26 Barton Hill, East Hampton, CT. Collection of music boxes, some coin-operated music machines.

MUSEUM OF THE MUSICAL BOX SOCIETY INTERNATIONAL, 295 West Avenue at the Lockwood Mathews Mansion, Norwalk, CT. Varied collection with emphasis on music boxes. Also a reference library of mechanical musical literature.

DELAWARE

DELAWARE STATE MUSEUM, Bank Lane and New Street, Dover, DE. Eldridge Johnson phonograph collection.

FLORIDA

BELLM'S CARS AND MUSIC OF YESTERDAY, 5500 North Tamiami Trail, Sarasota, FL. Very extensive collection of 1300 mechanical musical machines with demonstrations and coin-operated automatic instruments.

EDISON WINTER HOME AND MUSEUM, 2350 McGregor Boulevard, Fort Myers, FL. Large phonograph collection. Also tours of the home, garden, and laboratories.

ELLIOTT MUSEUM, 825 N.E. Ocean Boulevard, Stuart, FL. Small collection of music machines.

LIGHTNER MUSEUM, City Hall Complex 25 Granada, St. Augustine, FL. Varied collection of musical items.

ST. PETERSBURG HISTORICAL MUSEUM, 335 Second Avenue, N.E., St. Petersburg, FL. Small varied collection.

YESTERDAY IN REVIEW, Box 505, 8 miles S.W. of Kissimmee on Highway 17 and 92, Intercession City, FL. 200 mechanical musical instruments, varied collection.

GEORGIA

ANTIQUE AUTO AND MUSIC MUSEUM, Stone Mountain, GA. 35 mechanical musical instruments.

IDAHO

MANGUM'S MUSICAL ARCADE, Two miles north on Highway 91, Blackfoot, ID. Varied collection of musical items.

ILLINOIS

PEDALS, PUMPERS AND ROLLS, 675 W. Street, Elmhurst, IL. Varied collection of music machines.

RINGER AND SON MUSEUM, Broadway and Melody Lane, New Berlin, IL. Large varied mechanical musical collection.

SEVEN ACRES ANTIQUE VILLAGE AND MUSEUM, 8512 S. Union Road, Union, IL. Large collection of phonographs.

SVOBODA'S NICKELODEON TAVERN, ½ mile west of Dyer, IN, on Route 30, Chicago Heights, IL. 150 various machines.

THE TIME MACHINE, Clock Tower Inn, 7801 East State Street, Rockford, IL. Small varied collection.

INDIANA

HISTORICAL MUSEUM OF THE WABASH VALLEY, 1411 S. 6 Street, Terre Haute, IN. Small varied collection.

JULIA MEEKGAAR WAYNE COUNTY INDIANA HISTORICAL MUSEUM, 1150 North A Street, Richmond, IN. Small varied collection.

MIDWEST PHONOGRAPH MUSEUM, 2245 State Road 252, Martinsville, IN. Large phonograph collection.

IOWA

PLYMOUTH COUNTY HISTORICAL MUSEUM, U.S. Route 75 South, Le Mars, IA. 500 instruments, some mechanical.

TOM'S MECHANICAL MUSIC WONDERLAND, Highway 9 and 65, Monly, IA. 50456. Varied collection.

KANSAS

BOOT HILL MUSEUM, INC., Front Street, Dodge City, KA. Small varied collection of machines.

KANSAS MUSEUM OF HISTORY, 6425 SW Sixth, Topeka, KA. Small collection.

MAINE

MUSICAL WONDER HOUSE, 18 High Street, Wiscasset, ME. Large collection of 200 mechanical musical machines.

WELLS AUTO MUSEUM, Route 1 (Box 496), Wells, ME. Small collection, mainly nickelodeons.

MARYLAND

MARYLAND HISTORICAL SOCIETY, 201 W. Monument Street, Baltimore, MD. Small collection of music boxes.

MASSACHUSETTS

YESTERYEARS MUSEUM ASSOCIATION, INC., Main and River Streets, Sandwich, MA. 40–50 mechanical dolls and toys, some musical.

MICHIGAN

BILL'S MAGICAL MUSICAL ANTIQUES MUSEUM, 3209 Lowden, Kalamazoo, MI. Varied collection.

HENRY FORD MUSEUM, 20900 Oakwood Boulevard, Dearborn, MI. 25 musical machines.

THE MUSIC HOUSE, 7377 U.S. Route 31 North (6 miles north of Traverse City), Acme, MI. Varied collection in historic setting.

MINNESOTA

STAGE COACH MUSEUM, Route #1, Shakopee, MN. Small varied collection.

MONTANA

WORLD MUSEUM OF MINING, Box 3333, Butte, MT. Two player pianos.

NEVADA

HAROLD'S CLUB GUN COLLECTION AND MUSICAL MUSEUM, 250 North Virginia, Reno, NV. Smal varied collection, mainly nickelodeons and orchestrions.

HARRAH'S AUTOMOBILE COLLECTION, Glendale Road, Reno, NV. Varied collection of coin-operated machines.

VIRGINIA CITY MUSEUM, Virginia City, NV. Small collection of pianos and nickelodeons.

NEW HAMPSHIRE

CLARK'S TRADING POST, One mile north on Route 3, North Woodstock, NH. Small varied collection, mainly nickelodeons and orchestrions.

NEW JERSEY

ANTIQUE AUTO MUSEUM, State Highway 34 and Ridgewood Road, Wall Township, NJ. Small varied collection of mechanical musical machines.

EDISON NATIONAL HISTORIC SITE—EDISON LABORATORIES, Main Street and Lakeside Avenue, West Orange, NJ. Small phonograph collection. Walking tour of the machine shops, laboratories, library, museum exhibits, etc.

NEW YORK

MAHOPAC COUNTRY STORE, FARM AND MUSEUM, Route 6 and Baldwin Place Road, Baldwin Place, NY. Small collection of mechanical musical instruments.

MARGARET WOODBURY STRONG MUSEUM, 700 Allen Creek Road, Rochester, NY. Large varied collection, mainly music boxes and automata.

METROPOLITAN MUSEUM OF ART—ANDRE MERTENS GALLERY, Fifth Avenue at 82 Street, New York, NY. Varied collection with emphasis on musical instruments.

THE MUSICAL MUSEUM (The Sanders Family), State Route 12-B, Deansboro, NY. Large collection of mechanical musical machines, demonstrations, very pleasant atmosphere.

Q.R.S. MUSIC ROLLS, INC., 1026 Niagara Street, Buffalo, NY. Player and reproducing pianos on display, also perforating roll equipment.

NORTH CAROLINA

ANTIQUE MUSIC AND WHEELS MUSEUM, Route I-85 Exit 164, 12 miles west of Durham, NC, Daniel Boone Antique Village, Hillsborough, NC. Large variety of mechanical musical machines.

NORTH DAKOTA

STATE HISTORICAL SOCIETY OF NORTH BISMARK, North Dakota Heritage Center, Bismark, ND. Music Boxes (small collection).

OHIO

MUSIQUE MECHANIQUE, 2960 North High, Columbus, OH. Large variety of mechanical musical machines.

SNYDER'S ANTIQUE AUTO PARTS, 12925 Woodworth Road, New Spring, OH. Small collection of coin-operated machines.

OKLAHOMA

CHUCKWAGON MUSEUM, 201 S. Miss. Highway, Atoka, OK. Varied collection, mainly orchestrions.

NATIONAL COWBOY HALL OF FAME AND WESTERN HERITAGE CENTER, 1700 Northeast 63 Street, Oklahoma City, OK. Small collection, mainly nickelodeons.

PENNSYLVANIA

CAROUSEL MECHANICAL MUSIC MUSEUM, Village Mall Route 420, Morton, PA. Small varied collection.

HERSHEY MUSEUM OF AMERICAN LIFE, 300 Park Boulevard, Hershey, PA. Small collection.

INTERCOURSE MUSIC WONDER WORLD, 3457 Old Philadelphia Pike, Route 340, P.O. Box 417, Intercourse, PA 17534. Large collection of mechanical musical machines especially phonographs.

MILL BRIDGE VILLAGE, Ronk Road at Soundersburg Road, Strasburg, PA. Varied collection, Ragtime Festival July 4th.

PERELMAN ANTIQUE TOY MUSEUM, 770 S. 2nd Street, Philadelphia, PA. 50 automated toy music boxes.

SOUTH DAKOTA

OLD WEST MUSEUM, Box 275, Chamberlain, SD. Small varied collection.

PIONEER AUTO MUSEUM AND ANTIQUE TOWN, Junction of Interstate 90, U.S. 16 and 83, Murdo, SD. 50 piece collection.

TENNESSEE

HOUSTON ANTIQUE MUSEUM, 201 High Street, Chattanooga, TN. Small varied collection.

TEXAS

OLDEN YEAR MUSICAL MUSEUM, 131 Fair Meadows, Duncanville, TX. Varied collection.

VERMONT

SHELBURNE MUSEUM, ½ mile south on Route 7, Shelburne, VT. Small varied collection.

VIRGINIA

THE MARINERS MUSEUM, One mile south of Route 64 and Route 17, Newport News, VA. Very small display.

WASHINGTON STATE

BARTLESS MUSEUM, Second and Morris, La Conner, WA. Small varied collection.

MUSEUM OF HISTORY AND INDUSTRY, 2161 East Hamplin, Seattle, WA. Small collection of music boxes and phonographs.

WASHINGTON, D.C.

SMITHSONIAN INSTITUTION—NATIONAL MUSEUM OF HISTORY AND TECHNOLOGY, Varied collection.

WISCONSIN

HISTORIC CHANDLER HOUSE, 151 W. College Avenue, Waukesha, WI. Varied collection.

HOUSE ON THE ROCK, Three miles east on U.S. 14, six miles south on U.S. 23, Spring Green, WI. Small varied collection.

KALVELAGE SCHLOSS, 2432 W. Kilburn, Milwaukee, WI. Small varied collection.

FOREIGN

AUSTRIA

TECHNICAL MUSEUM FOR INDUSTRY AND COMMERCE, Mariahilferstrasse 212, Vienna, Austria. Varied collection.

THE VIENNA CLOCK MUSEUM, Schulhof 2, 1010 Vienna, Austria. Small varied collection with emphasis on music.

BELGIUM

THE INSTRUMENTAL MUSEUM OF BELGIUM, 17 Place du Petit-Sablon, Brussels, Belgium. Very large collection of musical instruments.

INSTRUMENTAL MUSEUM OF THE ROYAL CONSERVATORY OF MUSIC OF BRUSSELS, Av. Broustin 19, Brussels, Belgium. Large collection of mechanical musical machines with emphasis on music boxes.

NATIONAL MUSEUM FOR MECHANICAL ORGANS, Robert Vaudemmestrate 45, Koksijde, West Vlaanderen, Belgium. Large varied collection.

ORGAN MUSEUM ST. NIKLASS, Oostjacht Park 15, St. Niklass, Belgium. Mechanical organ collection, various types.

BRITISH ISLES

BIRMINGHAM MUSEUM OF SCIENCE AND INDUSTRY, Newhall Street, Birmingham, West Midlands, England. Small varied collection.

THE BOWES MUSEUM, Barnard Castle, County Durham, England. Small varied collection.

BRITISH MUSEUM, Great Russel Street, London, England. Small varied collection.

THE DEVON MUSEUM OF MECHANICAL MUSIC, Mill Leat, Thornbury, Nr. Holsworthy, Devonshire, England. Varied collection.

MUSEUM OF MECHANICAL MUSIC, Church Road, Portfield, Chichester, England. Varied collection.

THE NATIONAL MUSICAL MUSEUM (THE PIANO MUSEUM), Charitable Trust, 368 High Street near Kew Bridge, Brentford, Middlesex, England. Large collections, mainly keyboard mechanical instruments.

PAUL CORIN MUSIC MUSEUM, St. Keyne, Liskeard, Cornwall, England. Collection of mechanical musical items.

ST. ALBANS ORGAN MUSEUM, 326 Camp Road, St. Albans, England. Small varied collection.

SCIENCE MUSEUM, Exhibition Road, London, England. Large collection with emphasis on phonographs.

TOY MUSEUM, 18A North Parade, Matlock Bath, Derbyshire, England. Collection includes phonographs and music boxes.

VICTORIA AND ALBERT MUSEUM, South Kensington, London, England. Small collection, mainly music boxes.

WELSH FOLK MUSEUM OF MECHANICAL MUSIC, Gears Lane off North Road, Goldsithney, Penzance, Cornwall, England. Varied collection.

CANADA

EBERDT MUSEUM OF COMMUNICATIONS HISTORY, 30A Rue Principale S., Sutton, Quebec, Canada. Varied collection.

PLAYER PIANO CENTER AND MUSEUM, 3399 Dunbar Street, Vancouver, British Columbia, Canada. Large varied collection.

FRANCE

GRANDE EXPOSITION MUSEE D'INSTRUMENTS DE MUSIQUE MECHANIQUES, 13 Rue Bramtone, Paris, France. Varied collection.

MUSEE DE PHONOGRAPHE ET DE LA MUSIQUE MECHANIQUES, Parc St. Donat, Rt du Muy, Sainte-Maxime Var, Cote d'azur, France. Large collection with emphasis on phonographs.

MUSEE NATIONAL DES TECHNIQUES, 292 Rue Saint Martens. Large varied collection.

ITALY

MUSEO DI INSTRUMENTI MUSICALLI MECCANICI, S.S. Adriatica N. 16 KM 163, Savio, Italy. Varied collection.

MONACO

NATIONAL MUSEUM, Avenue Princess Grace. Collection of automatons and dolls.

NETHERLANDS

KIJK EN LUISTER MUSEUM, Verenigingsgebouw, Bennekom, Netherlands. Large music box collection.

NATIONAL MUSEUM—FROM MUSIC BOXES TO STREET ORGANS, Achter den Dom 12, Utrecht, Netherlands. Large collection of mechanical musical machines.

NORWAY

RINGVE MUSEUM, Lade alle 60, Trondheim, Norway. Varied collection with emphasis on music boxes.

SWITZERLAND

FREDY'S MECHANISCHER MUSIK SALON, Hauszur Frohburg, Lichtensteig (St. Gallen), Switzerland. Varied collection.

MUSEE D'ART ET D'HISTOIRE, Quai Leopold Robert, Neuchatel, Switzerland. Jacquet-Droz automata.

MUSEE BAUD S. A., L'Auberson, Vaud, Switzerland. Varied collection.

RETONIO'S MECHANISCHES MUSIK UND ZAUBERMUSEUM (Retonio Breitenmoser), Gerbestrasse 4, Appenzell, Switzerland. Varied collection of mechanical musical machines.

WEST GERMANY

DAS MUSEUM DER MECHANSICHEN MUSIK BRAUNSCHWEIG, Ziegenmarkt 2, Braumschweig, West Germany. Large varied collection.

DEUTSCHES MUSEUM, Museumsinsel 1, Munchen 26 West Germany. Varied collection.

DEUTSCHES UHRENMUSEUM FURTWAGEN, Gerwigstrassell, Furtwangen, Baden Wurttemberg, West Germany. Small mechanical music collection.

MECHANISCHES MUSIK MUSEUM, Kasseler Strasse 76A Fuldatal Simmershausen, Hessen, West Germany. Orchestrion collection (ten pieces).

MUSEUM FUR MECHANISCHE MUSIKINSTRUMENTE, Sofienstrasse 40, Baden-Baden, West Germany. Large varied collection.

MUSIKWISSENSCHAFFLICHES MUSEUM, Fur Selbstspielende Instrumente, Bronsart Str. 32, Hannover, West Germany. Large varied collection, by appointment.

SIEGFRIEDS MECHANISCHES MUSIKKABINETT, Ober Str 29, Rudeshiem am Rhein, Hessen, West Germany. Large varied collection.

MECHANICAL MUSICAL SOCIETIES AND THEIR PUBLICATIONS

AUTOMATIC MUSICAL INSTRUMENT COLLECTORS' ASSOCIATION
International and 10 regional (state) chapters
Write: Bobby Clark, Jr., Membership Secretary, P. O. Box 172, Columbia, SC 29202

AMICA NEWS BULLETIN
Published by Dorothy Bromage, P.O. Box 387, La Habra, CA 90631

CITY OF LONDON PHONOGRAPH AND GRAMOPHONE SOCIETY
Hillandale News, official journal
Write: B. A. Williamson, Treasurer, 157 Childwall Valley Road, Liverpool, L161LA, England.

MUSICAL BOX SOCIETY INTERNATIONAL
Bulletin published three times a year, also *MBS News Bulletin* six times a year. Write: Mrs. C. W. Fabel, Route 3, Box 202, Morgantown, IN 46160 (also local chapters).

MUSICAL BOX SOCIETY OF GREAT BRITAIN
Journal, *The Music Box,* published four times a year. 40 Station Approach, Hayes Bromley, Kent BR27EF, England.

PHONOGRAPH SOCIETY OF SOUTH AUSTRALIA
P.O. Box 253, Prospect 5082 Australia. *The Phonographic News* published six times a year.

VINTAGE PHONOGRAPHIC SOCIETY OF NEW ZEALAND
Journal, *The Phonographic Record*
Write: Mrs. L. Drummond, P. O. Box 5175, Papanui, Christ Church, New Zealand.

VINTAGE RADIO AND PHONOGRAPH SOCIETY
Write: Secretary VRPS, P.O. Box 5345, Irving, TX 75062. Monthly Journal *The Reproducer*.

PUBLICATIONS AND SOURCES FOR FACSIMILE REPRINTS

To retain the value of your machine we suggest that you acquire as much information as possible about your instrument before you attempt a do-it-yourself repair. The following are sources of printed material available to assist you.

Mechanical Musical Societies all issue their own regular bulletins and journals with historical and technical information articles. Many also issue reprinted catalogues, etc. See section on Mechanical Musical Societies for further information.

ANTIQUE PHONOGRAPH MONTHLY (APM)
Allen Koenigsberg, 502 East 17 Street, Brooklyn, NY 11226. Informative articles and classified ads relating mainly to phonographs and records. Facsimile reprints and original books on the subject also available.

AUTOMATIC MUSIC ROLL CO. (Frank Adams)
P. O. Box 3194, Seattle, WA 98114. AMR Catalog of Publications: Reprinted catalogs, manuals and other items related to pianos.

EDISON PHONOGRAPH MONTHLY
Wendell Moore, RR #, Box 4744, Sedona, AZ 86336. Reprinted bound volumes of the original monthly publication. Also phonograph related prints.

JEAN'S MUSICAL NEWS
Box 366, Mason, MI, 48854. Mainly classified advertising relating to phonographs. Some information articles.

JUKEBOX TRADER (monthly)
2545 J M S.E. 60 Court, Des Moines, IA 50317. Monthly, for collectors.

LOOSE CHANGE MAGAZINE
Mead Co., 21176 South Alameda Street, Long Beach, CA 90810. Monthly magazine, articles on coin-operated music machines, jukeboxes, etc.

CHARLES MANDRAKE
P. O. Box 955, Ashtabula, OH 44004. Facsimile catalogues, mainly phonographs.

MUSICAL MARKET PLACE
Bob Fulwider, c/o MMP 561 Washington Street, Santa Clara, CA 95050. Monthly classified ads.

TALKING MACHINE REVIEW INTERNATIONAL
19 Glendale Road, Bournemouth, England BH64JA. Bi-monthly publication dealing in all areas of the antique phonograph field, issue list of reprints and books.

ZONOPHONE NEWSLETTER
Box 955, Ashtabula, OH 44004.

FURTHER READING: A BRIEF BIBLIOGRAPHY

BAUMBACH, ROBERT W.—*Look for the Dog: An Illustrated Guide to Victor Talking Machines,* Woodland Hills, CA; Stationery X-Press (P.O. Box 207, Woodland Hills, CA 91364), 1981. Fully illustrated informative history. 326 pp.

BAYLY, ERNIE—*The EMI Collection,* Bournemouth, England; *The Talking Machine Review 1977.* 282 phonographs illustrated with photographs by Brian Willison, notes by Mr. Bayly. Many interesting European models.

BEZDECHI, ADRIAN—*Pianos and Player Pianos: An Informative Guide for Owners and Prospective Buyers.* 64 pp. 58 illustrations. Order from Player Piano House, 4001 N. Interstate, Portland, OR 97227. Basic information.

BOWERS, Q. DAVID—*Encyclopedia of Automatic Musical Instruments,* Vestal, NY; The Vestal Press, 1972. The single most important guide in the field, 1008 pages profusely illustrated. (Does not cover phonographs, jukeboxes, etc.)

BOWERS, Q. DAVID—*Put Another Nickel In,* Vestal, NY; The Vestal Press, 1966. Comprehensive illustrated history of coin-operated pianos and orchestrions.

CHEW, V. K.—*Talking Machines* 1877–1914; London, England. Her Majesty's Stationery Office, 1967. Some aspects of the early history of the gramophone, Illustrated.

DETHLEFSON, RON—*Edison Blue Amberol Recordings,* 1912–1914, Brooklyn, NY; APM Press, 1980. 206 pp.

DETHLEFSON, RON—*Edison Blue Amberol Recordings,* 1915–1929, Brooklyn, NY; APM Press, 500 pp.

DeWAARD. R.—*From Music Boxes to Street Organs,* translated from Dutch by Wade Jenkins, Vestal, NY; The Vestal Press, 1967. Mainly about pipe and reed organs, Carillon and Pierement street organs.

FROW, GEORGE and ALBERT F. SEFL—*The Edison Cylinder Phonograph: A Detailed Account of the Entertainment Models until 1929.* Kent; George L. Frow, 1978. 207 pp. Comprehensive illustrated history with detailed information about the models. George L. Frow, publisher, "Salterns," Seal Hollow Road, Sevenoaks, Kent TN13 3SH England.

FROW, GEORGE—*The Edison Disc Phonograph and the Diamond Disc,* George L. Frow, 1982, 286 pp.

FROW, GEORGE L.—*A Guide to the Edison Cylinder Phonograph: A Handbook for Collectors,* Cornwall; Francis Antony Ltd, 1970 (Mr. Frow: Sevenoaks, Kent, England). Invaluable guide to the various models of Edison cylinder phonographs.

GELATT, ROLAND—*The Fabulous Phonograph, from Edison to Stereo,* New York; Appleton-Century, 1954, 1965. Illustrated history.

GIVENS, LARRY—*Rebuilding the Player Piano.* New York; The Vestal Press, 1963. Basic guide.

GIVENS, LARRY—*Re-Enacting the Artist . . . A story of the Ampico Reproducing Piano,* Vestal, NY; The Vestal Press, 1970. Illustrated history of the Ampico.

HAZELCORN, HOWARD—*A Collector's Guide to the Columbia Spring-Wound Graphophone 1894–1910,* New York, APM (Monographs in the History of Recorded Sound No. 2), 1976. Illustrated comprehensive guide.

HOOVER, CYNTHIA—*Music Machines—American Style,* a catalogue of the exhibition, Washington, DC; Smithsonian Institution Press, 1971 (Stock No. 4700-0182), Supt. of Documents. Illustrated history.

KRIVINE, J.—*Jukebox Saturday Night,* Secaucus, NJ; Chartwell Books, Inc. 1977. Beautifully illustrated (in color) history of the jukebox.

MARTY, DANIEL—*The Illustrated History of Phonographs;* New York; Vilo, Inc. 1979. (translated from the French) 102pp.

McTAMMANY, JOHN—*The Technical History of the Player,* New York; Musical Courier, 1915 (available from the Vestal Press).

MOSORIAK, ROY—*Curious History of Music Boxes,* Chicago; Lightner Publishing Co., 1943. Interesting sections: Checklist of makers, music box related patents, etc.

MUSICAL BOX SOCIETY INTERNATIONAL—*Silver Anniversary Collection,* Summit, NJ, Musical Box Society International, 1974. Anthology of 188 articles from past issues of the Society's Bulletin, over 1,000 pp. Fully illustrated.

OBERCHAIN, ELAINE—*The Complete Catalog of Ampico Recording Piano Rolls,* Darien, CT; William H. Edgerton (Box 88, Darien, CT 06820), 1977. 197pp. Listings of titles.

ORD-HUME, ARTHUR W. J. G.—*Collecting Musical Boxes and How to Repair Them,* NY; Crown Publishers, 1967, concise history, descriptions and practical restoration techniques.

ORD-HUME, ARTHUR W. J. G.—*The Mechanics of Mechanical Music,* London; published by the author, 1973.

ORD-HUME, ARTHUR W. J. G.—*Musical Box, A History and Collector's Guide,* published by Geo. Allen and Unwin. 200 illustrations.

ORD-HUME, ARTHUR W. J. G.—*Player Piano; The History of the Mechanical Piano and How to Repair It,* NY; A. S. Barnes, 1970, comprehensive guide with illustrations.

PEARSALL, RONALD—*Collecting Mechanical Antiques,* New York; Arco Publishing Co., 1973, 197 pp. 92 illustrations. Section on mechanical musical machines.

PETTS, LEONARD (compiler)—*The Story of Nipper and the 'His Master's Voice' Picture Painted by Francis Barrard,* Bournemouth, England. 2 edition, 1982. (Published by Ernie Bayly for The Talking Machine Review International, 19 Glendale Road, Bournemouth BH64JA England). Illustrated history.

PROUDFOOT, CHRISTOPHER—*Collecting Phonographs and Gramophones,* New York, Mayflower Books, 1980. (Christie's International Collectors Series), 116 pp. Emphasis on European examples, very good color photographs.

REBLITZ, ART and Q. DAVID BOWERS—*Treasures of Mechanical Music,* New York; The Vestal Press, 1981. 630 pp., 700 illustrations, including 450 tracker scales. (Also available from the authors.)

ROEHL, HARVEY—*Player Piano Treasury; The Scrapbook History of the Mechanical Piano in America,* Vestal, NY; The Vestal Press, 1973 edition. Compilation of advertising through the years, as well as a wonderful chapter called "The Melodies Linger On," a beautifully illustrated section on musical museums.

READ, OLIVER and WELCH, WALTER L.—*From Tin Foil to Stereo: Evolution of the Phonograph,* Indianapolis; Howard Sams & Co. and Bobbs-Merrill Co., Inc., 1959–1976. Comprehensive illustrated history of the phonograph and recording industry.

SCHLICK, LAWRENCE A.—*A Portfolio of Early Phonographs,* Published by Mr. Schlick, 1966. Glossy large photographs with descriptions (50 pp).

SITTER, BOB—*Dusting Off a Little History: Spring Type Phonographs,* Yorba Linda, CA. Phonograph collectibles, (18242 Timberlane, Yorba Linda, CA 92686), 1981. 65 pp.

THOMSON, ALISTAIR G.—*Phonographs and Gramophones.* A commemorative catalogue of the exhibition held at the Royal Scottish Museum, Edinburgh 1977. Beautifully illustrated catalogue with descriptive notes.

WEBB, GRAHAM—*The Cylinder Musical Box Handbook;* London; Faber & Faber, 1968. Illustrated guide with detailed repair diagrams and descriptions.

CYLINDER MUSIC BOXES

The cylinder music box originated in the 18th century in Switzerland. The period from the mid-1800's to 1890 saw its growth and development, but by 1910 the cylinder music box's popularity was at an end, surpassed by the disc music box and other forms of home entertainment, including the Edison phonograph.

The basic mechanism is a brass cylinder with a specific arrangement of tiny steel pins protruding from it. When the cylinder revolves, these pins pluck the teeth of a tuned metal comb, which causes a specific set of notes to play. The longer and larger the cylinder and comb or combs, the more elaborate the musical arrangement. Early examples had combs of one or several teeth screwed down individually to a bedplate. These were called sectional combs.

The single most important feature of a cylinder musical box is the quality of sound it produces. The most desirable boxes sound delicate and bell-like, with every note in tune. The musical arrangements are also very important. Many of the later boxes have very simple arrangements that cause them to sound like the mass-produced items that they were. If neither good quality nor a good arrangement was present in a cylinder musical box when manufactured, no amount of restoration of repair will improve the piece. Casework or refinishing is almost always necessary since many of these boxes are over 100 years old. When the box was good to begin with, though, a competent restorer can often improve an antique piece.

The disc music box was popularly produced from the 1880's to the 1920's. Many of the manufacturers were German based firms. There were three companies that stand out in this field. Each produced a wide variety of models. They are Symphonion, Polyphone, and Regina.

The disc music box works essentially on the same principle as the cylinder box. The steel tuned comb or combs are activated by the projections in specific arrangements, on flat metal discs. As the disc turns, the projections pluck the comb creating the music.

Most models of both types of music boxes are spring wound.

Some music box terms used to describe the entries:

1. An interchangeable cylinder box has more than one cylinder, allowing for a larger selection of musical tunes. There is usually storage space for the extra cylinders.
2. A long-playing musical movement is usually found on bigger boxes; the box does not have to be wound as often because it has either a heavy-duty larger spring or several springs.
3. Manivelle is a hand-cranked musical movement (no springs), usually found in small simple boxes originally made as children's toys.
4. Sublime-Harmonie is the particular way in which double combs are tuned to create a richer, more brilliant tone.
5. Tune cards are decorated paper cards attached to the inside of the lid of the cylinder music box, listing the tunes on the cylinder.
6. There are extra devices incorporated in some boxes to enhance and vary the musical performance; for example, zither, comb, bells, drum, etc.
7. A piano-forte box plays both loud and soft by using two (or more) combs set to be plucked louder or softer.

	Price Range	
☐ **ABRAHAMS,** 6 tune 6¼″ cyl, 3 bells with butterfly strikers, grained case with transfer decoration on lid, colored tune sheet	**500.00**	**750.00**
☐ 10 tune 6½″ cyl, 3 bells with butterfly strikers, walnut veneer case with marquetry and transfer decoration, tune sheet, 18″ wide	**500.00**	**700.00**
☐ 12 tune 13″ cyl, drum, 5 bells with butterfly strikers, castanets, zither attachment, walnut veneer case, transfer decoration on lid, tune sheet, coin operated	**950.00**	**1500.00**
☐ **ALEXANDRA,** 4 tune 6″ cyl, interchangeable cyls (6), sleeve type, rosewood inlaid case, 4 bells, insect strikers, storage inside case to left of mechanism for extra cylinders, inner glass lid	**100.00**	**1400.00**
☐ 6 tune 6″ cyl, interchangeable cyls (6), c. 1890, hollow cylinders that fit over brass mandrel, single comb, inner lid of glass, two compartments on either side of mechanism with pegs for extra cylinders	**1200.00**	**1600.00**

Price Range

☐ **D. ALLARD—J. SANDOZ,** 8 tune 13″ cyl, interchangeable cyls (3), some case decoration, wide base molding hides storage drawer for extra cylinders **2000.00   3000.00**

☐ **(GEO.) BAKER & CO.,** 6 tune 11″ cyl, Sublime-Harmonie combs, tune sheet, tune indicator, and tempo control, double spring barrel, stop/start and change levers, maple case, simple case decoration, inner glass lid **1400.00   2000.00**

☐ **BAKER-TROLL,** 2 tune, crystal and gilt metal decanter, movement in base, c. 1880, 10¾″ high **200.00   400.00**

☐ 6 tune, Sublime-Harmonie Piccolo, walnut case with mother-of-pearl decoration, inner glass lid **1250.00   1800.00**

☐ 6 tune 17″ cyl, interchangeable cyls, 6 bells, bee strikers, walnut case with brass inlay decoration, matching storage table, three-part comb **2000.00   3250.00**

☐ 6 tune 19½″ cyl, interchangeable cyls (7), ornately inlaid case with brass, pewter and copper decorations, matching cabinet (wide, floor standing) for extra cylinders, decorative moldings, one large comb for cylinder and one for 10 bells, double spring drive, start/stop **4500.00   7500.00**

☐ 8 tune 13″, c. 1880, interchangeable cyls (3), early maple and ebony case with drawer for cyls, decorated tune sheet, inner glass lid, double spring, ratchet wind movement, carrying handles **3000.00   4000.00**

☐ 8 tune 15″ cyl, Sublime-Harmonie double comb, interchangeable cyls (6), c. 1870, double spring and zither attachment, tune indicator, burl walnut on ebony and rosewood case, inlaid decoration, matching table with cabriole legs, storage drawer for cylinders **6000.00   8000.00**

☐ **BENDON,** 8 tune 13″ cyl with organ, plain case **1800.00   2400.00**

Price Range

☐ **BERENS, BLUMBERG & CO.,** 6 tune 11″ cyl keywind, plain case, brass bedplate 1000.00 1400.00

☐ **BORNAND,** 6 tune 10″ cyl, simple case style, decorative tune card key wind 750.00 1200.00

☐ **BREMOND,** 4 tune 7″ cyl, simple case, tune card (92-tooth comb), case 15″ long 350.00 750.00

☐ 4 tune 9″ cyl, orchestral, 13 organ reeds ... 600.00 1200.00

☐ 6 tune 3½″ cyl, inlaid rosewood veneer case, inner glass lid, stop/start and change levers, single comb (42 teeth) 250.00 500.00

☐ 6 tune 8″ cyl, lever wind, simple fruitwood case, tune sheet, case 15″ wide 500.00 750.00

☐ 6 tune 10¾″ cyl, hidden drum and bells, inner glass lid (½ size), simple case lines with inlaid decoration on lid and front panel, tune sheet 1250.00 1800.00

☐ 6 tune 11″ cyl, tune sheet, lever wind, rosewood with floral decoration 1000.00 1500.00

☐ 6 tune 11″ cyl, 16-note organ, colored inlay, 21″ long, inner glass lid 1200.00 1800.00

☐ 6 tune 11″ cyl, drum with 8 beaters, 6 bells, 3-part comb, stop/start, rosewood case inlaid with musical motifs and other decoration 2250.00 3500.00

☐ 6 tune 13″ cyl, interchangeable cyls (6), serpentine case, burled veneer, inlays, matching table with storage drawer for extra cylinders, c. 1860 .... 3000.00 5000.00

☐ 6 tune 14″ cyl, mandolin attachment, 7 bells, stop/start and change levers, tune card, inlaid decoration on rosewood case, late 19th century 3500.00 4000.00

☐ 6 tune 16⅛″ cyl, interchangeable cyls (6), 3″ diameter (fat) cylinder, tune card, drum, 6 bells with bee strikers, castanets, 18-note organ, single massive spring, rosewood case with inlaid decorations, matching tiered table with storage drawers for extra cylinders, curved legs 3500.00 5500.00

☐ 6 tune 17¼″ cyl, mandolin attachment, tune sheet, lever wind, rosewood with floral motif 2250.00 2850.00

Price Range

☐ 6 tune 17½" cyl, (fat cyl), c. 1880, burl walnut and ebony case, tune sheet, carrying handles on sides, triple comb, double spring, lever wind, tune indicator 2100.00   2700.00

☐ 6 tune with hidden drum and bells, decorated case, floral inlay lid and on the front of case   1500.00   1750.00

☐ 8 tune 11" cyl, simple case 20" long, tune card 500.00   750.00

☐ 8 tune 13" cyl, c. 1880, mahogany case with rosewood and mother-of-pearl inlay, single comb, tune card 1000.00   1750.00

☐ 8 tune 13" cyl, interchangeable cyls (2), floral inlay design on lid and front, large inside glass lid, tune card, matching table with storage drawer for cylinders 1800.00   2700.00

☐ 8 tune 14½" cyl, c. 1870, hidden saucer bells and castanet, serpentine shaped case with inlay decoration, tune sheet inside lid 2250.00   2750.00

☐ 8 tune 15" cyl, "Piano-Forte," double comb, inner glass lid, some marquetry decoration   1500.00   2500.00

☐ 8 tune brass and pewter inlay decoration on case 1000.00   1250.00

☐ 10 tune 8" cyl, interchangeable (4) cyls, rosewood and ebony with inlaid decoration, c. 1870, double-barrel spring movement, tune indicator, organ movement 3400.00   4500.00

☐ 12 tune 13½" cyl, c. 1875, ratchet wind, rosewood and ebony case with floral marquetry on lid, tune sheet 1200.00   1800.00

☐ 14¾" cyl, interchangeable (4) cyls, organ attachment, walnut and ebony case with burl walnut trim, matching table (turned legs), storage drawer for extra cylinders, double spring tune indicator 4500.00   6000.00

☐ **CONCHON (Switzerland),** 6 tune 11" cyl, mandolin zither attachment, operatic selections, veneered and decorated case, inlaid lid, base molding, tune sheet 1200.00   1600.00

☐ 8 tune 13" cyl, interchangeable cyls (7), lever wind, double spring, zither attachment, six saucer bells, stop/start and repeat levers, tune indicator, burl walnut case with ebony

Price Range

trim on slant top (drop front) desk, four drawers on side hold cylinders, inner glass lid,
tune sheet 6000.00 8000.00

☐ 8 tune 17¼" cyl, c. 1880, double springs, 4
combs, tempo control, tune selector, tune
card, rosewood case with simple inlay decoration, inner glass lid, zither attachment
(Quatuor Expression Zither) 2750.00 4250.00

☐ Orchestra box, c. 1880, drum, bells, castanets, 16-note organ, inlaid decoration, ornate
case 2250.00 2750.00

☐ **DAWKINS,** 6 tune 13¼" cyl, interchangeable, burled walnut, gold painted decoration,
inlay on cover, tune card, one cylinder 2250.00 2500.00

☐ 10 tune 8¼" cyl, with 5 bells, walnut with inlay
decoration 1250.00 2000.00

☐ 12 tune 13" cyl, drum, bell, wood block, inlay
on cover, tune card, large case 1750.00 2500.00

☐ 8 tune 16" cyl, plain case, tune card 1500.00 2000.00

☐ **DUCOMMON GIROD,** 4 tune 8" cyl, simple
case, inlay on lid 550.00 1100.00

☐ 6 tune 6" cyl, simple case, tune sheet,
stop/start and change levers, c. 1880 ..... 500.00 1000.00

☐ 6 tune 11¼" cyl, c. 1840, walnut case, three
control levers, simple case style 700.00 900.00

☐ 6 tune 13" cyl, 7 bells, drum with eight beaters, stop/start and change levers, 123-tooth
comb, single spring barrel with crank, burl
walnut veneer with some decoration 1500.00 2000.00

☐ 8 tune 16¼" cyl, 3 bells, castanet, inlaid case,
full glass inner lid 1100.00 1700.00

☐ 12 tune 19" cyl, rosewood veneer case with
enamel and brass inlay decoration, operatic
selections, tune sheet 1500.00 2500.00

☐ **ECKARDT,** 2 tune Musical Christmas Tree
Stand, c. 1910, German, clockwork mecha-
nism, tree holder revolves and plays 300.00 500.00

Price Range

☐ **GLORIA,** 8 tune 11″ cyl, 3″ diameter cyl, zither attachment, double spring, flower inlay on lid, tune card, tune indicator, selector, 27″ long case **1000.00**   **1500.00**

☐ **J.H. HELLER (Bern, Switzerland),** 6 tune 4½″ cyl, walnut decoration, floral motifs, inner glass lid **450.00**   **650.00**

☐ 6 tune 6″ cyl, simple case, some decoration, inner glass lid, tune indicator **500.00**   **750.00**

☐ 6 tune, 13″ cyl organ box, walnut with inlay on front and lid **1500.00**   **2750.00**

☐ 8 tune 10¾″ cyl, rosewood case, simple design with inlay decoration on lid, single comb and spring, tune card, inner glass lid **800.00**   **1500.00**

☐ 8 tune 17¼″ cyl (2¼″ fat cylinder), orchestral box, drum, 6 bells, castanet, 18-note reed organ, inner glass lid, burl walnut, rosewood inlay **3500.00**   **5000.00**

☐ 8 tune 19½″ cyl, 2-piece comb tune sheet, lever wind, rosewood with fruitwood decoration, piccolo-harp, c. 1880 .... **1700.00**   **2500.00**

☐ 10 tune 13″ cyl, burled veneer walnut case with some inlaid decoration, zither attachment, decorated tune sheet **1500.00**   **2000.00**

☐ **IMHOF AND MUKLE (trade label),** 8½″ cyl, spring-driven movement, rosewood and ebony case, marquetry decoration, c. 1880 **300.00**   **500.00**

☐ **JUNOD,** 4 tune 5⅛″ cyl, inlaid rosewood case with musical motif, tune indicator, 2 bells, decorated figural tune card, inner glass lid **800.00**   **1250.00**

☐ 24 tune 13¼″ cyl, fat diameter cylinder, zither attachment, double spring, ratchet wind, decorated tune card, tune indicator, rosewood case with floral motif, inner glass lid **1250.00**   **2000.00**

☐ **KAARER,** 8 tune 11″ cyl, rosewood case with inlay, plays hymns **1100.00**   **1600.00**

Price Range

☐ **LANGDORFF & FILS (Switzerland),** 4 tune
13″ cyl (3″ diameter fat cyl), interchangeable
cylinders (2), 180-note comb, brass bedplate,
inlaid decoration on carved case 3000.00   3750.00

☐ 6 tune 10¾″ cyl, unusual inlay 1000.00   1600.00

☐ 8 tune 17¼″ cyl, three sectioned comb, zither
attachment, tune card, tune indicator, double
spring barrel, burled walnut case 2500.00   4250.00

☐ **LECOULTRE (Geneva, Switzerland),** 2
tune, snuff box, tortoiseshell case, c.
1860–1880 . . . .   1250.00   1500.00

☐ 4 tune 8¼″ cyl, key wind, early plain box, in-
stant stop and change levers 750.00   1000.00

☐ 4 tune 12″ cyl, 3″ wide diameter cyl, keywind,
pianoforte, inlaid lid, tune card, 16″ long . . .   3250.00   3750.00

☐ 6 tune 8″ cyl, keywind, simple case 750.00   1000.00

☐ 6 tune 11″ cyl, simple case, some decoration,
18″ long case, inner glass lid, lever wind . .   1000.00   1500.00

☐ 6 tune 13″ cyl, two sectioned comb, tune
sheet, stop/start, change and instant stop levers, rosewood case, inlaid lid and other dec-
oration 1000.00   1750.00

☐ 8 tune 11″ cyl, simple case 18″ long 750.00   1000.00

☐ 8 tune 13″ cyl, winding lever under inner glass
lid, 20″ long simple case 1000.00   1250.00

☐ 8 tune 13″ cyl, walnut case, with inlay 1250.00   1750.00

☐ 8 tune 14″ cyl, interchangeable cyls (6), tune
card, 9 bells struck by birds, tempo control,
stop/start levers, burl walnut with fruitwood
marquetry case, gilt metal handles, two-
tiered matching table with storage drawers
on curved legs 4000.00   6000.00

☐ 12 tune 18¼″ cyl, wide diameter cylinder,
190-tooth comb, brass bedplate, Bremond
winding handle, inlaid case with enamel dec-
oration 1250.00   2000.00

☐ **L'EPEE (France),** 4 tune 5″ cyl, simple case   300.00   500.00

☐ 6 tune 6″ cyl, inlaid floral decoration on simple
wood case, stop/start and change levers,
tune indicator, 51-tooth comb 750.00   1000.00

Price Range

☐ 8 tune 6″ cyl, single comb, operatic selections, tune indicator, inlaid wood case, ornate tune card, c. early 1900's 500.00   800.00

☐ 8 tune 9″ cyl, 6 bells, single comb, pictorial tune card, bird and flowers inlaid motif on lid, inner glass lid 1000.00   1500.00

☐ 12 tune 13″ cyl, zither attachment, simple wood case with some decoration 750.00   950.00

☐ 8 tune 15″ cyl, orchestral with drum, 6 bells and castinet, inlaid rosewood case, ornate tune card 2800.00   3400.00

☐ **MOJON–MANGER CO.,** 10 tune 13″ cyl, double spring, some inlay decoration, tune card and indicator, 28″ long case 650.00   1000.00

☐ **J. MANGER & CO. (Switzerland),** 8 tune 13″ cyl, interchangeable cylinders (10), c. 1880, 6 bells with bee strikers, 2-piece comb, 4 spring barrels, crank wind outside, speed adjustment, ornate case decoration with ebony, fruitwood and mother-of-pearl decoration, inner glass lid, matching storage table, with two drawers side-by-side for cylinder storage, turned legs 6500.00   9000.00

☐ **MERMOD FRÉRES (St. Croix, Switzerland),** 4 tune 6″ cyl, simple rosewood case, inner glass lid, ornate tune card, late 19th century 400.00   750.00

☐ 6 tune 3½″ cyl, crank wind, simple wood case with decal decoration 300.00   400.00

☐ 6 tune 7½″ cyl, simple case, inner glass lid, some decorations on case, tune card 750.00   1250.00

☐ 6 tune 7½″ cyl, interchangeable cyl, inlaid rosewood, tune indicator, Peerless Forte Piccolo 750.00   1250.00

☐ 6 tune 7½″ cyl, interchangeable cyls, zither attachment, tune selector, Jacquot safety check, single comb, oak case with base molding and case decoration, inner glass lid, ornate tune card 850.00   1400.00

☐ 6 tune 8¼″ cyl, c. 1900, tune sheet, zither attachment, lever wind, rosewood case, floral inlay, guitar zither attachment 700.00   900.00

Price Range

☐ 6 tune 9″ cyl, interchangeable cyl, zither attachment, inlaid rosewood, tune indicator, Peerless Forte Piccolo 1000.00 1800.00

☐ 6 tune 10½″ cyl, interchangeable cyl, walnut with inlay, Mandolin Piccolo, inner glass lid, 32″ long 1100.00 1900.00

☐ 6 tune 11″ cyl, Ideal Sublime-Harmonie, double comb, mahogany inlay 1500.00 2000.00

☐ 6 tune 11¼″ cyl, interchangeable cyls (2), c. 1890, burled walnut case with storage drawer in wide base molding, inner glass lid, slow/fast lever, tune indicator, zither attachment, crank wind 1700.00 2200.00

☐ 6 tune 11¼″ cyl, interchangeable cyls (4), Ideal Sublime Harmonie combs, c. 1895, original tune sheet, zither attachment, tune indicator, crank wind, oak case 2000.00 3000.00

☐ 8 tune 5½″ cyl, 3 bells, simple case, tune indicator, 16″ long case, tune skipper 800.00 1250.00

☐ 8 tune 6″ cyl, coin operated, 17″ long oak case 750.00 1250.00

☐ 8 tune 9″ cyl, inlaid rosewood, 6 bells, 19″ case, tune indicator, tune skipper 1250.00 1500.00

☐ 8 tune 9″ cyl, 2½″ diameter cyl, double springs, crank wind, inner glass cover, tune indicator, zither, inlaid rosewood 1250.00 1500.00

☐ 8 tune 11″ cyl, rosewood case with decorative molding, 6 bells, tune skipper, drum, 27″ case 1200.00 2400.00

☐ 8 tune 11″ cyl, 2¼″ diameter cyl, interchangeable cylinder, 26″ long case (called "The Concerta"), simple inlay banding decoration 3000.00 4000.00

☐ 8 tune 11¼″ cyl, coin operated, c. 1900, tune changer, slow/fast adjustment, crank wind, oak case 1500.00 2500.00

☐ 8 tune 13½″ cyl, c. 1900, crank wind at side, tune changer, zither attachment, walnut veneer case with inlay musical motifs 700.00 1500.00

☐ 8 tune 14″ cyl, simple rosewood case, inner glass lid, ornate tune card, late 19th century 900.00 1600.00

☐ 10 tune 5½″ cyl, outside crank, tune selector, simple case, 17½″ long 750.00 1000.00

Price Range

☐ 10 tune 7½" cyl, simple case, inner glass cover, crank wind, 20" case **600.00   1000.00**

☐ 10 tune 9" cyl, inlaid rosewood, crank wind, inner glass lid, tune indicator, zither attachment, 21" case **1000.00   1500.00**

☐ 10 tune 11" cyl, rosewood with decorative molding, 6 bells, coupled mainspring, large cyl, 27" case **1450.00   1950.00**

☐ 10 tune 11" cyl, carved oak case, crank wind, inner glass cover, 2½" diameter cyl, tune indicator, skipper, moderator, zither attachment **1350.00   1850.00**

☐ 10 tune 13" cyl, rosewood, drum and castanets, decorative molding, tune indicator and skipper, moderator, large cylinders, Sublime-Harmonie, double spring **2000.00   2600.00**

☐ 10 tune 13" cyl, Sublime-Harmonie, tune selector, double spring barrel, tune indicator, musical motif on inlay cover **1500.00   2000.00**

☐ 10 tune 14" cyl, piccolo, zither attachment, inner glass lid, decoration on case and lid, 27" box, original tune card **1000.00   1250.00**

☐ 10 tune 17½" cyl, 6 bells and drum, walnut case, musical instruments motif on cover (inlay) **2500.00   4000.00**

☐ 10 tune 13½" cyl, oak carved, brass handles, outside crank wind, orchestral box, bells, drums, castanets, mandolin attachment, coin op, c. 1896 . . . .   **3000.00   4000.00**

☐ 10 tune 16" cyl, 2-section comb, mandolin attachments, stop/start and change levers, burled walnut case with rosewood decoration, inner glass lid **1500.00   2000.00**

☐ 11" cyl, interchangeable cyls, zither attachment, tune selector, tempo control, rosewood case with fruitwood marquetry decoration, "ideal piccolo." **3000.00   3700.00**

☐ 11⅜" cyl, interchangeable cyls, matching table with cabriole legs, crank wind, zither attachment, slow/fast and tune indicators, carved case decoration, storage drawer in table **3500.00   5500.00**

Price Range

☐ 11¼″ cyl, interchangeable cyls, crank wind, Sublime Harmony combs, 6 bells struck by 3 automaton mandarins, single comb, simple case with some decoration 2200.00 3000.00

☐ 12 tune 10″ cyl, imitation rosewood, tune indicator, crank wind, simple case 1000.00 1500.00

☐ 12 tune 13″ cyl, carved oak case, zither attachment, inner glass lid, crank wind, tune indicator, skipper moderator 1250.00 1750.00

☐ 12 tune 16″ cyl, interchangeable cyls (4), inlay decoration, tune sheet inside lid 3500.00 5500.00

☐ 12 tune, coin operated, ornately carved, tune card, orchestral box, 6 butterflies, 6 drums, 6 bells, 6 castanets (and bee strikers) 4000.00 5200.00

☐ **H. METERT (France),** Forte-Piano cylinder box, very simple mahogany case, hinged side of case folds down for key winding, c. 1850 900.00 1400.00

☐ 4 tune, 8″ cyl, keywind, plain case, very good arrangements 800.00 1300.00

☐ **F. NICOLE,** 4 tune 8″ cyl, plain case, keywind 900.00 1400.00

☐ **NICOLE FRERES,** 2 tune snuff box, tortoiseshell case, c. 1825 .... 700.00 1200.00

☐ 3 tune 9¼″ cyl, ideal Sublime Harmonie, tune sheet, tune indicator, crank wind, oak case, zither attachment, c. 1895 .... 600.00 1000.00

☐ 4 tune 6″ cyl, double spring, inlaid case, tune card 850.00 1250.00

☐ 4 tune 8″ cyl, keywind, 15″ case with inlay and banding decoration, tune card 1000.00 1400.00

☐ 4 tune 11″ cyl, simple rosewood case with some decoration, single comb, trills 1000.00 2000.00

☐ 4 tune 11⅞″ cyl, 3¼″ diameter cyl, overture box, simple case style 1250.00 2250.00

☐ 4 tune 12″ cyl, overture box, inlaid lid, tune sheet 1500.00 2500.00

☐ 4 tune 16⅜″ cyl, fat diameter cylinder, rosewood case with mother-of-pearl and brass with enamel inlay decoration, brass tune sheet, "Overture" box, stop/start, change and instant stop levers 4000.00 5500.00

Price Range

☐ 4 tune 16½", 3½" diameter cyl, operatic overture box, piano-forte, keywind, "Grand Format," inlay 8000.00   12000.00

☐ 6 tune 11" cyl, 18" plain case, lever wind, some inlay decoration, tune card 1000.00   1500.00

☐ 6 tune 13" cyl, 3¼" diameter cyl, 24½" case, keywind, inlay, tune sheet 2000.00   2750.00

☐ 6 tune 13" cyl, interchangeable cyls (6), inlaid walnut case with decorative marquetry, matching table with storage drawer for extra cylinders, single comb, inner glass lid 4000.00   6000.00

☐ 6 tune 18" cyl, inlay brass and enamel on rosewood, mandolin attachment 2500.00   3000.00

☐ 8 tune 6 bells, double spring, rosewood case, tune card, inlaid front and lid 2000.00   2500.00

☐ 8 tune 13" cyl, inlay, lever wind, tune sheet, 20" case 1000.00   1400.00

☐ 8 tune 13" cyl, operatic selections, key wind, simple fruitwood case style 1500.00   1750.00

☐ 8 tune 17¼" cyl, interchangeable cyls (4), decorated inlaid case with matching table, drum, bells, castanet, 31-key organ, tune indicator and selector, speed control 5500.00   7500.00

☐ 8 tune 17½" cyl, "Forte-Piano," key wind, grained case with inlaid decoration on lid, inner glass lid, tune sheet 1200.00   2500.00

☐ 10 tune, wide diameter cylinder, simple case with some inlay decoration, inner glass lid 2000.00   2500.00

☐ 12 tune 12" cyl, 3" diameter cyl, floral inlay, tune card, 22" case, inner glass lid 2000.00   2500.00

☐ 12 tune 12" cyl, 3¼" (fat) diameter cylinder, Mozart opera selections, key wind, simple burled walnut veneer case with inlaid lid, ratchet crank-winder, single comb, inner glass lid 1750.00   2400.00

☐ 12 tune 13" cyl, 6 bells, drum, double spring, burled walnut, 26" case 2500.00   3750.00

☐ 12 tune 14" cyl, multiple combs, 6 bells, 3" diameter (fat) cylinder, inlaid case, "Piano-Forte," inner glass lid 3500.00   4500.00

☐ 12 tune 19½" cyl, reed organ, inlaid case, metal tune card, 34" case 2100.00   3000.00

Price Range

☐ 12 tune, Victorian Bracket Clock, ornately carved decoration and fretwork on walnut case, pianoforte movement in base 2500.00 3750.00

☐ 18 tune 19½" cyl (3⅜" diameter fat cylinder), plays two tunes per turn, lever wind, figural inlay motif 2000.00 3000.00

☐ 18 tune 3" wide cyl, 2-part comb, inlay case 1800.00 2000.00

☐ 24 tune 16" cyl, two tunes per revolution, inlaid case 1300.00 1800.00

☐ 11" cyl, keywind, simple case 1000.00 2000.00

☐ 13" cyl, keywind, sectional comb, cob organ 1500.00 2500.00

☐ 16½" cyl, simple case with floral marquetry on lid, double comb, start/stop and repeat/change levers 1000.00 1500.00

☐ **ORPHEA (American),** 6 tune 18" cyl, c. 1875, interchangeable cyls (3), walnut and ebony case with drawer for extra cyls, crank wind, double comb, tune indicator, revolving tune sheet. 3000.00 3750.00

☐ **PAILLARD,** 2 tune 1¾" cyl, Musical Photograph Album, c. 1900. Art Nouveau case decoration, single comb, album sits on ornate corner feet 100.00 300.00

☐ 4 tune 19" cyl, 3" diameter cyl, glass inner lid, Sublime-Harmonie, interchangeable cyls (2), 47" case 3500.00 5000.00

☐ 6 tune, "Amobean" interchangeable cyls (6), simple buried walnut case with some decoration, drawers open out from sides to store extra cylinders, inner glass lid, decorated tune sheet 2500.00 3500.00

☐ 6 tune 6" long cyl, 4 bells, inlay case, 18" long 1000.00 1500.00

☐ 6 tune 10½" cyl, interchangeable cyls (4), double spring, tune indicator, tune selector, zither attachment, inlaid rosewood case with matching table, storage for cylinders 2400.00 3200.00

☐ 6 tune 13" cyl, zither, pianoforte, glass inner lid, painted grain, 22" case 1500.00 2000.00

Price Range

☐ 6 tune 13″ cyl, interchangeable cyls (4), zither attachment, inlaid burled walnut veneer case with matching table with storage drawer for extra cylinders, table has carved decoration on curved legs **2500.00   3500.00**

☐ 6 tune 13″ cyl, 3″ wide cyl, 4-part spring, 2-part comb, case decoration and inlay **2250.00   2750.00**

☐ 8 tune 5½″ cyl, "Columbia," ratchet wind from the right, single comb, tune indicator, decorated tune card, inner glass lid, delicate floral and musical inlay on lid and front of box, carrying handles on sides **400.00   800.00**

☐ 8 tune 8¼″ cyl, zither attachment, simple stained-wood box, tune card **500.00   800.00**

☐ 8 tune 9″ cyl, inlay decoration, tune card ... **500.00   1000.00**

☐ 8 tune 10¾″ cyl, c. 1860, lever wind, rosewood case with floral decoration **500.00   1000.00**

☐ 8 tune 15″ cyl (3″ diameter fat cylinder), serpentine case style, elaborate metal inlay decoration, tune sheet, tune indicator **4000.00   5000.00**

☐ 10 tune 11″ cyl, bird inlay on lid, tune card, 19¾″ case **750.00   1000.00**

☐ 10 tune 13″ cyl, Sublime-Harmonie walnut inlay, pictorial lithograph, inner glass lid ... **900.00   1250.00**

☐ 10 tune 14⅛″ cyl, "Piccolo-zither," mahogany case, ebony molding with inlay decoration on lid, spring barrel, inner glass lid, decorated tune card, tune indicator, side carrying handle **1750.00   2750.00**

☐ 10 tune, 16″ cyl, large-grained case, tune card **1100.00   1400.00**

☐ 12 tune 8″ cyl, 6 bells with bee strikers, tune selector, double comb, inlaid with handles **1400.00   1800.00**

☐ 12 tune 11″ cyl, double spring, long play, tune card, walnut cabinet, inlay musical motif on lid **1000.00   1500.00**

☐ 12 tune 13″ cyl, tune card, inlay, 20″ case **1000.00   1500.00**

☐ 12 tune 13″ cyl, zither, tune card, inlay and banding, 26″ case **1000.00   1500.00**

Price Range

☐ 12 tune 15″ cyl, "Voix Celeste," 12-key double reed organ, two combs, spring barrel,
rosewood case, banded and inlay decoration
of scenes of swans and figures, inner glass
lid, tune indicator **1900.00** **2500.00**

☐ 12 tune 16¼″ cyl, zither attachment, 2-
section comb, stop/start and change levers,
rosewood marquetry case, tune card, double
spring barrel, tune indicator **1600.00** **2250.00**

☐ 24 tune 13″ cyl, zither, double spring, some
decal and inlay decoration **1250.00** **1750.00**

☐ 9″ cyl, c. 1890, interchangeable cyls (3),
crank wind, zither attachment, tune indicator,
oak case, carved decoration, drawer holds
extra cylinders **750.00** **1500.00**

☐ 11″ cyl, bells, Chinese drum, some case dec-
oration **1000.00** **1500.00**

☐ 13″ cyl, 6 bells, bird strikers, lever wind, inlaid
box **1250.00** **2000.00**

☐ 13¼″ cyl, interchangeable cyls (2), double
spring, walnut, tune sheet, storage drawer
under box for extra cylinders **2400.00** **3250.00**

☐ 15½″ cyl, 22-note organ, multiple combs,
simple case style with some decoration ... **2250.00** **3200.00**

☐ 20½″ cyl, interchangeable cyls (6), 9 bells,
58″ base matching stand with storage for
extra cylinders, tune indicator, tune selector,
inlaid and painted case decoration **5000.00** **7750.00**

☐ **PEERLESS,** 9″ cyl, interchangeable cyls (2),
"Forte Piccolo," carved decoration on ma-
hogany case, tune sheet **1000.00** **1500.00**

☐ **RIVENC,** 6 tune 13″ cyl, interchangeable cyls
(5), tune card, zither attachment, double
spring barrel, burled walnut panels on walnut
case, inner glass lid, matching table with storage drawer for extra cylinders, turned legs,
mother-of-pearl, ebony, and brass decoration **4000.00** **6000.00**

☐ 6 tune 13″ cyl, interchangeable 4″ wide (fat)
cylinders, simple case style with some deco-
ration **2750.00** **4000.00**

Price Range

□ 8 tune 6″ cyl, duplex cylinder box (cylinders placed end to end), two combs, inlaid floral decorations on lid, marquetry borders on lid and sides 2000.00 3250.00

□ 8 tune 11″ cyl, interchangeable cyls, stop/start and change levers, mandolin attachment, tune indicator, brass figures of griffons, tune card, burled walnut case inlaid with satinwood swallows 1250.00 3500.00

□ 17½″ cyl, with organ, basket case 1000.00 1500.00

□ **THIBOUVILLE-LAMY,** 6 tune 11″ cyl, long inner glass lid, winding lever under glass lid, 19″ plain case 600.00 1000.00

□ 6 tune, hidden drum and bells, plain case .. 1000.00 1500.00

□ 8 tune 12″ cyl, simple case, inner glass lid 750.00 1200.00

□ 8 tune 15″ cyl, 6 bells, drum with 9 beaters, 3-section comb, tune card, inlaid rosewood case 1250.00 2000.00

□ 10 tune 16″ cyl, 25″ rosewood inlaid case, tune card 2000.00 2500.00

□ 12 tune 15″ cyl, plain case, inlay on cover, tune card, 25″ case 1500.00 2000.00

□ **TROLL AND BAKER,** See Baker-Troll.

□ **(CHARLES) ULLMAN (Switzerland),** 8 tune 11″ cyl, tune sheet, tune indicator, rosewood case with handles, inlaid lid decoration 450.00 750.00

□ **UNIVERSALL,** 1 tune 6½″ cyl, interchangeable cyls (8), capstan wind, 3 bells, simple stained-wood case with embossed ornament on lid, single comb, c. 1891 .... 1500.00 3000.00

CYLINDER MUSIC BOXES—MAKERS UNKNOWN

□ 3 tune 4¼″ cyl, walnut, very simple, unadorned box 300.00 500.00

□ 4 tune 3⅝″ cyl, small box, mahogany (or walnut), decoration on lid, small inside glass lid, tune card, tune indicator 400.00 600.00

□ 4 tune 5″ cyl, simple case design, 11½″ long 400.00 650.00

□ 4 tune 6″ cyl, simple case, tune card, 12″ long 750.00 1000.00

Price Range

☐ 4 tune 7¾" cyl, key wind, sectional comb, single comb, simple case style **750.00** **1500.00**

☐ 4 tune 8" cyl, key wind, single comb, simple fruitwood box with some minor case decoration **500.00** **1000.00**

☐ 4 tune 8" cyl, key wind (Swiss), mahogany (or fruitwood) case with simple decoration, inner glass lid **1000.00** **2200.00**

☐ 4 tune 10¾" cyl, overture box, Swiss, c. 1850, brass plaque, tune sheet, key wind, rosewood case, boxwood brass and enamel inlay **2250.00** **3500.00**

☐ 4 tune 11" cyl, double spring, interchangeable cyls (3), inlay on lid, full inner glass lid, tune card, base molding on case **2500.00** **3500.00**

☐ 4 tune 11½" cyl, bells with butterfly strikers, simple wood case with painted decoration, ornate tune card **1000.00** **1400.00**

☐ 4 tune 12" cyl, keywind, case 20½", plain . . **2500.00** **3000.00**

☐ 6 tune 3½" cyl, simple painted-wood case with decal decoration, tune card, tune indicator **300.00** **550.00**

☐ 6 tune 3¼" cyl, zither attachment, Swiss made, spring lever movement, outside crank wind, inside glass cover, tune indicator, simple case style with some decoration **300.00** **600.00**

☐ 6 tune 4½" cyl, lever wind, grained case with inlaid decoration on lid **350.00** **600.00**

☐ 6 tune 5" cyl, inlay, painted grain, 14½" case **500.00** **750.00**

☐ 6 tune 6" cyl, 14" inlay case **450.00** **750.00**

☐ 6 tune 6" cyl, rosewood case, 16" long, some decoration **550.00** **750.00**

☐ 6 tune 6¼" cyl, simple case style with some inlaid decoration on lid, 3 bells **350.00** **600.00**

☐ 6 tune 8" cyl, plain case, 16" long, inner glass lid, floral inlay **550.00** **850.00**

☐ 6 tune 8¼" cyl, simple case with inlaid decoration on lid, tune sheet, 3 bells **600.00** **1250.00**

☐ 6 tune 8¼" cyl, c. 1900, zither attachment, rosewood case, inlaid musical motif and other simple case decorations **750.00** **1000.00**

6 Tune Swiss Cylinder Music Box, *c. 1870, maker unknown (Photo courtesy of Mechanical Center, Inc.—Darien, CT.)*

	Price Range	
☐ 6 tune 9″ cyl, interchangeable cyls (2), painted wood grain, case decoration, zither attachment, speed control, tune indicator ..	**1250.00**	**1800.00**
☐ 6 tune 9″ cyl, inlay on lid, simple case, 17″ long	**750.00**	**1000.00**
☐ 6 tune 10¼″ cyl, walnut case with bird and floral inlay on lid, tune card, stop/start, instant stop lever, hinged end flap for key wind ...	**650.00**	**1250.00**
☐ 6 tune 10¾″ cyl, lever wind, grained mahogany case with inlaid decoration on lid	**500.00**	**1200.00**
☐ 6 tune 10⅝″ cyl, c. 1860, single comb, side panel holds stop/start and instant stop levers, simple case style, key wind	**500.00**	**1500.00**
☐ 6 tune 11″ cyl, double comb, Sublime-Harmonie, inlaid rosewood, 22″ case	**1500.00**	**2000.00**
☐ 6 tune 11″ cyl, (102-tooth comb), 18″ inlaid case, zither, tune card, rosewood	**1250.00**	**1500.00**

Price Range

☐ 6 tune 13″ cyl, inlaid 21″ case, tune card, brass bedplate 1000.00 1500.00

☐ 6 tune 13″ cyl, interchangeable cyls, piccolo attachment, double spring, walnut (burled) case, matching table with storage 2000.00 3000.00

☐ 6 tune 13″ cyl, double comb, Sublime-Harmonie, key wind, simple case 1400.00 2000.00

☐ 6 tune 13″ cyl, with castanet and bells, floral inlay, inner glass lid, tune card, lever wind 1500.00 2500.00

☐ 6 tune 13½″ cyl, Swiss, c. 1885, burl walnut and ebony case with inlaid brass and mother-of-pearl, inner glass lid, tune sheet interchangeable cyls (4), ratchet wind, carrying handles 2000.00 3000.00

☐ 6 tune 16″ cyl, walnut inlay case with base molding, Sublime-Harmonie combs, tune indicator, inner glass lid 1250.00 1750.00

☐ 6 tune 19″ cyl, interchangeable cyls (3 fat cyls), Sublime Harmonie piccolo, figured walnut, ornate brass handles 2750.00 4000.00

☐ 8 tune 6″ cyl, decorative inlay on lid, inner glass lid, tune card, tune indicator, 18″ case 300.00 850.00

☐ 8 tune 5″ cyl, simple case style, some decoration, zither attachment, tune indicator, inner glass lid, outside crank, Swiss made 250.00 750.00

☐ 8 tune 6″ cyl, 3 saucer bells, walnut case with floral inlay, decorated tune card, inside glass lid 500.00 1000.00

☐ 8 tune 7″ cyl, inlay, simple case, 17″ long, inner glass lid 500.00 1000.00

☐ 8 tune 8″ cyl, floral inlay case, 17″ long 600.00 1000.00

☐ 8 tune 8″ cyl, burled walnut, decorated case, inner glass lid 600.00 1000.00

☐ 8 tune 8″ cyl, 6 bells, single comb, floral inlay, inner glass lid 1250.00 2000.00

☐ 8 tune 9″ cyl, inlaid rosewood 20″ case 600.00 1000.00

☐ 8 tune 10⅜″ cyl, 3″ wide diameter ("fat") cylinder, side panel reveals stop/start and change levers, single comb with 147 teeth, c. 1860 .... 2000.00 2500.00

Price Range

☐ 8 tune 10¾" cyl, key wind, simple rosewood case with inlaid decoration on lid, border-decorated tune sheet 650.00 1200.00

☐ 8 tune 11" cyl, walnut case with floral inlay, long play 750.00 1500.00

☐ 8 tune 11" cyl, 24" rosewood case, tune indicator, inlay 600.00 1200.00

☐ 8 tune 11" cyl, c. 1880, Guitar-tremolo, walnut case with ebony decoration, tune sheet ... 500.00 750.00

☐ 8 tune 11" cyl, 6 bells, insect strikers, tune card, inlaid decorative case, inner glass lid 1600.00 2100.00

☐ 8 tune 11" cyl, tune indicator, double spring, interchangeable cyls (3), floral inlay on cover, carrying handles, 35" long, heavy base molding hides drawer holding extra cylinders ... 2000.00 3000.00

☐ 8 tune 12½" cyl, c. 1865, ratchet wind, mahogany case, tune sheet 750.00 1500.00

☐ 8 tune 13" cyl, lever wind, tune card, 20½" case, inlay on lid 1000.00 1500.00

☐ 8 tune 13" cyl, 6 bells with bee strikers, inlay on front and cover of case, tune card 1250.00 2250.00

☐ 8 tune 13" cyl, interchangeable cyls (3), burled walnut, matching table with storage drawer 2500.00 3000.00

☐ 8 tune 13" cyl, interchangeable cyls (3), double spring barrel, stop/start and change levers, burled walnut case with fruitwood and ebony decoration, also brass, mother-of-pearl inlay, bottom half of front of box is storage space for extra cylinders 2000.00 3000.00

☐ 8 tune 13" cyl, 6 bells, burled walnut, zither attachment 1300.00 2500.00

☐ 8 tune 13" cyl, organ box (with bellows) 1500.00 2500.00

☐ 8 tune 13" cyl, 3" diameter wide ("fat") cylinder, 26-key organ, rosewood veneer case with heavy base molding, multiple combs, inner glass lid, tune sheet, inlaid motifs on lid and front, side handles 2000.00 2500.00

☐ 8 tune 13½" cyl, sublime harmony combs, rosewood case with floral marquetry, tune sheet inside lid, inner glass lid, tune indicator 1000.00 1500.00

Price Range

☐ 8 tune 15″ cyl, 2-part comb, piccolo expression, 25″ case .... | **1000.00** | **1500.00**

☐ 8 tune 15″ cyl, 9 bells with bird and bee strikers, burled walnut case with simple decoration and base molding, ornate side handles, stop/start and change levers, single comb, inner glass lid **1500.00** **2700.00**

☐ 8 tune 17″ cyl, 3″ diameter cyl, case decoration on front and lid, double comb, tune card, inner glass lid **2200.00** **2500.00**

☐ 8 tune 17½″ cyl, "Forte-Piano," operatic tunes, simple grained case with inlaid lid, single comb, tune sheet, inner glass lid **2000.00** **3000.00**

☐ 8 tune 18″ cyl, 4 combs, highly decorated lid, tune indicator, tune card, 30″ case, fancy handles on sides **1500.00** **2100.00**

☐ 10 tune 6″ cyl, bells with butterfly strikers, simple wood case with painted decoration, ornate tune card **750.00** **1250.00**

☐ 10 tune 6¼″ cyl, stencil-decorated simple wood case, tune indicator, ornate tune card, single comb, inner glass lid, late 19th century **250.00** **750.00**

☐ 10 tune 6¼″ cyl, simple wood case, three bells with butterfly strikers, 18″ wide case **350.00** **1000.00**

☐ 10 tune 7½″ cyl, zither attachment, ebony finish, gold painted decoration, tune card, tune indicator **750.00** **1000.00**

☐ 10 tune 8″ cyl, 16″ mahogany case, tune card **500.00** **1000.00**

☐ 10 tune 9″ cyl, rosewood box, drum, 4 bells, butterfly strikers, tune indicator, some inlay decoration **1100.00** **1500.00**

☐ 10 tune 9¼″ cyl, 3″ wide (fat) diameter cylinder, simple fruitwood case with some decoration, key wind side panel flap, tune sheet, single comb **1000.00** **2000.00**

☐ 10 tune 11″ cyl, inlaid case, zither, tune indicator **500.00** **650.00**

☐ 10 tune 13″ cyl, rosewood case with inlay, 23″ case, tune card **1000.00** **1500.00**

☐ 10 tune 13″ cyl, 6 bells with bird strikers, floral inlay front and top of case 23″ **2750.00** **4000.00**

Price Range

☐ 10 tune with bells, butterfly strikers, some inlay 1000.00 1500.00

☐ 12 tune 6″ cyl, c. 1860, lever wind, rosewood with inlay decoration 500.00 1250.00

☐ 12 tune 8″ cyl, zither attachment, plain case, some decorative details, inner glass lid, outside crank, tune indicator 600.00 1200.00

☐ 12 tune 8″ cyl, simple case 500.00 1000.00

☐ 12 tune 9″ cyl, nickel-plated metal parts, speed regulator, zither attachment, simple case style with some decorative details, inner glass lid, outside crank, tune indicator, tune sheet 750.00 1300.00

☐ 12 tune 11″ cyl, zither attachment, inlay decorations, tune indicator, tune card 750.00 1100.00

☐ 12 tune 13″ cyl, zither attachment, inlay case decoration, tune indicator, tune card 400.00 1000.00

☐ 12 tune 13″ cyl, 6 bells, floral inlay case 25″ long, zither, tune indicator 1250.00 1750.00

☐ 12 tune 13⅛″ cyl, 3⅛″ wide diameter (fat) cylinder, simple mahogany case with minor decoration, single comb, tune card, stop/start and change levers, single spring barrel, late 19th century 1200.00 2000.00

☐ 12 tune 15″ cyl, lever wind, rosewood with floral decoration 500.00 1500.00

☐ 12 tune 16″ cyl, 3″ diameter cyl, 2-part comb, figural inlay design on lid, 32″ case, 6 bells, drum, tune indicator, full inner glass lid 1850.00 2750.00

☐ 12 tune 16¼″ cyl, Sublime Harmonie double combs, double spring, painted black case, lever wind, tune indicator, start/stop and repeat/change levers 300.00 750.00

☐ 12 tune 16⅜″ cyl, rosewood case with inlay decoration, Swiss, Sublime Harmonie combs, inner glass lid, tune indicator and changer, speed regulator, inner glass lid 1250.00 2250.00

☐ 12 tune 17″ cyl, zither attachment, 20″ long inlaid rosewood case, tune indicator 1750.00 2250.00

☐ 12 tune 20″ cyl, 4 bells, butterfly strikers, tune indicator, plain case 1400.00 1900.00

	Price Range	
☐ 20 tune 7½″ cyl, (2 tunes per turn), simple case with gold decoration	650.00	1000.00
☐ 24 tune 13″ cyl, zither attachment, double spring, inlay floral, decoration, tune indicator, tune card, 28″ case	900.00	1200.00
☐ 24 tune 17⅜″ cyl, (fat) cylinder, side panel reveals stop/start, change and instant stop levers, simple rosewood case, inlaid musical motif on lid	1250.00	2000.00
☐ 11½″ cyl, c. 1850, French, keywind at side of case (side flips down), simple mahogany case	800.00	1000.00

Singing Bird in a Cage (Photo courtesy
of Mechanical Music Center, Inc.—Darien,
CT.)

Price Range

☐ Musical photo album, 2 tune 2½" cyl, quarto plush ornamented album, tune plays when album is opened 75.00   150.00

☐ Musical photo album, leather decorated cover, family photos, c. 1890's, 2 tune musical movement in back of album. (Many variations in photo album designs, music box essentially the same) 100.00   225.00

☐ **SINGING BIRDS IN CAGE,** One feathered bird on a branch, giltwood cage on square base 17" high 750.00   1250.00

☐ Two feathered birds on a branch (one bird seated), domed gilt metal cage on a raised circular base, 20½" high 900.00   1500.00

☐ Two feathered birds on a branch, gilt metal, domed cage on brass decorated base, 21" high 750.00   1100.00

☐ Three painted mechanical birds, gilt metal domed cage, rectangular giltwood decorated base, 23" high 900.00   1200.00

☐ Four feathered birds, square cage, 24" high   2000.00   4000.00

ORCHESTRA AND ORGAN CYLINDER MUSIC BOXES—MAKERS UNKNOWN

☐ 4 tune 9¼" cyl, drum with 10 beaters, 3 bells, walnut case with simple decoration 1250.00   2250.00

☐ 6 tune 11 cyl, 6 bells, striking clock movement on outside front which plays music on the hour, burled walnut "serpentine" shaped case with inlay decoration and wide base molding, inner glass lid 3000.00   5000.00

☐ 6 tune 11" cyl, interchangeable cyls (4), walnut decorated with inlay, corner molding, drawer in base for extra cyls, drum, 6 bells, inner glass lid, tune cards 2500.00   3500.00

☐ 6 tune 11" cyl, Duplex cylinder box (plays both side by side cylinders at the same time), 2 combs, 8 bells, 8 drum beaters (1 drum), decorative tune card, simple case style with minor decorative details 10,000.00   15,000.00

Price Range

☐ 6 tune 11″ cyl, interchangeable cyls (2), coin-operated drum, zither attachment, 6 bells, tune indicator, 4 dancing dolls viewed from front glass panel, walnut case . . . .　**2250.00**　**3250.00**

☐ 6 tune 12″ cyl, Swiss, c. 1870, lever wind spring movement, organ accompaniment, mahogany case, floral marquetry decoration on lid and front panel . . . .　**800.00**　**1400.00**

☐ 6 tune 16¼″ cyl, 2 drums with multiple beaters, 11 bells, castanets, flat-top winding lever, rosewood veneer case with inlay decoration on lid and front, operatic selections, inner glass lid, tune sheet, single comb . . . .　**2250.00**　**3000.00**

☐ 8 tune 9¼″ cyl, c. 1880, 4 saucer bells with butterfly strikers, drums, castanets, rosewood case with walnut and ebony details, floral decal on lid, tune sheet, inner glass lid, lever wind . . . .　**2000.00**　**2500.00**

☐ 8 tune 10½″ cyl, c. 1885, 6 saucer bells with bird and butterfly strikers, tune indicator, rosewood and ebony case with floral marquetry on lid, rachet wind movement, start/stop and repeat/wind levers . . . .　**500.00**　**1500.00**

☐ 8 tune 13″ cyl (2¼″ diameter fat cylinder), interchangeable cyls (3), walnut veneer, inlay rosewood and tulip, musical motif inlay on top and front . . . .　**3000.00**　**4000.00**

☐ 8 tune 14″ cyl, interchangeable cyls (4), bell, drum, castanet, bee strikers, burled walnut case 35″ long, matching table with storage for extra cylinders . . . .　**4500.00**　**6500.00**

☐ 10 tune 16″ cyl, 6 bells, drum, castanet, 26″ case, inlay, tune card . . . .　**2500.00**　**4000.00**

☐ 10 tune 16″ cyl, 17-key organ, 6 bells, burled walnut and ebony case with marquetry decoration, inner glass lid, tune sheet . . . .　**2150.00**　**3150.00**

☐ 12 tune 13″ cyl, drum with 5 bells, inlaid musical motifs on front and lid and other simple case decoration, burled walnut case, inner glass lid . . . .　**2000.00**　**2500.00**

Price Range

☐ 21 tune 14″ cyl, with organ, 6 bells, drum, castanets, 30″ burled walnut case, double spring, some inlay decoration, tune indicator   **2500.00**   **3500.00**

☐ 12 tune 16″ cyl, drum, 6 saucer bells, rosewood and ebony case with floral inlay decoration, tune sheet, lever wind start/stop and repeat/change levers **2500.00**   **3000.00**

☐ 12 tune 17″ cyl, 6 bells, 9 beaters, 8 strikers, castanets, inlay decoration on front and top, 28″ case **2500.00**   **3500.00**

☐ 12 tune 21″ cyl, c. 1870, drum, hidden bells and castanets, divided comb, tune sheet, walnut case, floral inlay decoration, lever wind, start/stop and repeat/change levers   **1650.00**   **3000.00**

☐ 12 tune 21¼″ cyl, 2 drums with multiple beaters, 6 bells, single comb, decorative inlay on case lid **2750.00**   **4000.00**

☐ 16 tune 13″ cyl, (3⅜″ diameter, fat cylinder), three governors, 41-key organ accompaniment, burl walnut with brass inlay decoration   **8000.00**   **10000.00**

☐ "Dancing Doll" Orchestra box, organ, bells, drum, castanet, ornate inlaid case decoration   **2500.00**   **3500.00**

☐ 6½″ cyl, Swiss, interchangeable cyls, 6 saucer bells in view with strikers, ratchet wind spring movement, stop/start control, rosewood and ebony case with marquetry decoration in floral motif, repeat/change lever, storage in drop front for extra cylinders **1000.00**   **1400.00**

☐ 10″ cyl, organ box, c. 1885, lever wind, divided comb, start/stop and repeat/change levers, rosewood and ebony case with floral inlay **1000.00**   **1400.00**

☐ 12½″ cyl, Swiss, c. 1880, reed organ, 9 saucer bells, bird strikers, lever wind, rosewood case with mother-of-pearl, ebony, and mahogany decoration, carrying handles **2500.00**   **3500.00**

☐ 13″ cyl, 6 bells, drum, castanets, inlay on lid, inside glass lid, tune card **2400.00**   **2900.00**

☐ 13″ cyl, 6 bells, 8 beaters, bee strikers, floral inlay front and top, base molding **2500.00**   **3500.00**

	Price Range	
☐ 13″ cyl, c. 1880, drum, 6 bells, bird, flower, and butterfly strikers, castanet, organ movement, walnut case with inlaid decoration (has fat cylinder)	3250.00	4000.00
☐ 15¼″ cyl, Swiss, organ box, lever wind spring movement, start/stop and repeat/change levers, rosewood and ebony case, floral marquetry and inlay decoration	1000.00	1400.00
☐ 24 tune 16½″ cyl, drum, castanet, 6 bells, butterfly strikers, double spring, zither attachment, tune indicator, wood box with some decoration, tune card	2000.00	3000.00

DISC MUSIC BOXES

The disc music box was produced from the 1880's until about 1920. It was developed to combat the widespread criticism of cylinder boxes that there wasn't a wide enough variety of tunes for it.

Disc boxes play interchangeable round steel discs with projections to operate each tooth of a tuned steel comb, through an intermediate star-wheel assembly. As the disc turns, the projections turn the wheels, which pluck the teeth. They were made in large numbers and were priced anywhere from 25¢ for a small disc to $2.00 for a very large one.

Disc boxes were first produced in Germany. Two of the more popular early manufacturers were Polyphon and Sumphonium. Unlike their cylinder counterparts, however, disc boxes were also made in America. The Regina Music Box Company, probably the best known manufacturer, made perhaps 100,000 disc boxes with some playing discs up to 36″ in diameter. Regina boxes are quite common today, and the firm made high-quality instruments, which accounts for the high collector interest.

The widespread popularity of the 78-rpm phonograph and the advent of movies eliminated the disc music box market. In a last effort to support lagging sales, Regina and Mira both introduced music boxes that would also play phonograph records. Their efforts were unsuccessful, and Regina switched to making vacuum cleaners, which they still manufacture today.

Price Range

☐ **ADLER (J. H. Zimmermann, Leipzig, Germany),** 7″ disc (Style #210, 18cm disc), small plain case, hand crank, 33-tooth comb, name on lid, with zither attachment (Style #210Z) 375.00   800.00

☐ 7″ disc (Style #220, 18cm disc), spring wind (lever on front), simple small case, name on lid, with zither (Style #220Z), 33-tooth comb   375.00   800.00

☐ 10½″ disc, two combs, inlaid lid, lithograph inside lid 700.00   1100.00

☐ 14¾″ disc (Style #250, 37cm), plain case, simple molding on base and lid, ball feet, crank wind, spring with zither, walnut inlay case (Style #255Z), also inner glass lid, duplex comb, lithograph inside cover: eagle and cherubs 1500.00   2200.00

Adler Disc Music Box,
table model.

Price Range

☐ 14¾" disc (Style #300Z), 77-tooth comb, upright (vertical) counter type, coin operated, zither attachment, walnut carved case, glass door, storage drawer just under mechanism (for discs) **1400.00 1750.00**

☐ 21¼" disc (54cm) large upright, walnut, highly decorated case, coin operated, double comb, zither attachment **2000.00 3000.00**

☐ **BRITANNIA DISC MUSIC BOX,** 9" disc, simple case, table model c. 1900 .... **800.00 1250.00**

☐ 9" disc, upright (vertical) counter model, double comb, simple walnut case style with transfer and inlay decoration **800.00 1500.00**

☐ 11¾" disc, c. 1905, single comb, start/stop lever, 27" high countertop vertical-style case, walnut with some case decoration, crank wind, mirrored solid front doors (coin operated) **1500.00 2000.00**

☐ 17⅛" disc, upright, carved and fretwork decoration, duplex comb **3000.00 4000.00**

☐ 19⅝" disc, upright floor model, disc storage cabinet **3000.00 4000.00**

☐ **CAPITAL SELF-PLAYING MUSIC BOXES (CUFF BOXES) F. G. OTTO & SONS, NJ,** Use interchangeable steel tune sleeves

☐ STYLE A, c. 1895, mahogany (oak), 44-tooth comb, winter scene inside lid, spring wind, simple cases, cylinders are 5½" long **1500.00 2500.00**

☐ STYLE B, mahogany (oak), 58-tooth comb, pastoral winter scene inside cover, zither attachment **2000.00 2750.00**

☐ STYLE C, mahogany (oak), 81 teeth, lithograph inside lid, simple case **2500.00 3500.00**

☐ STYLE D, same as style C, coin operated, automatic "Penny" attachment **2750.00 3250.00**

☐ STYLE F, double comb (162 teeth), oak (mahogany), lithograph inside lid **2500.00 3000.00**

☐ STYLE G, same as style B with "Penny" attachment **2500.00 3000.00**

☐ **CELESTA,** 8" disc (21cm), simple box, lever wind on front **500.00 1000.00**

Criterion Disc Music Box, *table model.*

	Price Range	
☐ 11″ disc, simple case	800.00	1400.00
☐ 15½″ disc, ornate case	1400.00	2200.00
☐ **CRITERION,** made c. 1900 by F. G. Otto & Sons, NJ, 8¾″ disc, table model, simple mahogany case with figural lithograph inside lid	500.00	750.00
☐ 11½″ disc, double comb, mahogany, lithograph inside cover, decorative molding	1000.00	1750.00
☐ 15½″ disc, table model, mahogany case with some carved decoration, double comb	2000.00	2750.00
☐ 15¾″ disc, carved oak case, double comb, lithograph inside cover	1500.00	2000.00

Price Range

☐ 15¾″ disc, mahogany simple case decoration, single comb, lithograph inside lid 1500.00 2500.00

☐ 15¾″ disc, table model, double comb, peripheral drive movement, tempo control, crank wind, carved mahogany case, trademark lithograph inside lid, matching storage cabinet has open shelf on top and front door panel, also matching case decoration 1500.00 2500.00

☐ 20½″ disc, mahogany case, simple, lithograph inside lid 2000.00 2600.00

☐ **EDELWEISS,** 4½″ disc, table model, hand crank, simple case with decoration inside lid 200.00 400.00

☐ 6½″ disc, table model, hand crank, simple beechwood case with decoration inside lid 250.00 500.00

☐ **EMPRESS (SEE MIRA, STYLE #290)**

☐ **EUPHONIA,** 15¾″ disc, large mahogany case, decorative metal corners on case, lithograph inside cover (female figure) 1000.00 1250.00

☐ **EUTERPEPHON,** 12″ disc (30.8cm), simple box, lithograph inside cover: "Goddess Euterpe," Polyphone and Regina discs will play on this music box 600.00 1500.00

☐ **FORTUNA (J. H. ZIMMERMAN, Leipzig, Germany),**

☐ 7″ disc, simple case 400.00 600.00
☐ 8¼″ disc, walnut, simple case, ratchet wind 500.00 750.00
☐ 10¾″ disc, simple case 1250.00 1600.00
☐ 16″ disc, simple case 1500.00 1850.00

☐ **HARMONIA,** 16¼″ disc, table model, single comb, burled walnut veneer case, decorative moldings and brass and ivory inlay on lid, zinc discs 1250.00 2250.00

☐ 20½″ disc table model, single comb, burled walnut case with brass and ivory inlay, zinc discs, carved corner columns 1850.00 2250.00

☐ **HELVETIA,** 8″ disc, 2 bells, black painted case, metal trim 1000.00 1250.00

☐ 8″ disc, transfer decorated case with handles, plays polyphone discs 250.00 450.00

Price Range

☐ **KALLIOPE (Leipzig, Germany),** 7″ disc (18cm), walnut case, simple case, design etched on lid, lithograph inside cover, spring wind **500.00**   **1000.00**

☐ 7″ disc (18cm), 4 bells, walnut, simple case, lithograph inside lid, zither attachment, 36-tooth comb **600.00**   **1000.00**

☐ 7¾″ disc (19.5cm), simple case, lithograph inside cover **700.00**   **900.00**

☐ 8″ disc, table model with 6 bells, simple case style **900.00**   **1200.00**

☐ 9¼″ disc (23.5cm), plain case, lithograph inside cover, 49 teeth in comb **500.00**   **850.00**

☐ 9¼″ disc with 6 bells, walnut case with floral inlay on lid, figural lithograph inside cover   **950.00**   **1250.00**

☐ 9½″ disc, table model, crank wind from center, single comb, mahogany case, simple case **500.00**   **1000.00**

☐ 9¾″ disc (25cm), simple case, lithograph inside cover, single comb (42 teeth) **600.00**   **900.00**

☐ 13½″ disc (34cm), table model, simple case, zither attachment, lithograph of lady inside cover, 61 teeth in comb **1250.00**   **1500.00**

☐ 13½″ disc with 10 bells, walnut case, decorated, ''Kalliope'' inside lid (could have lithograph) **1500.00**   **2000.00**

☐ 13½″ disc (vertical) hanging case, walnut highly decorated with gallery, glass front, coin operated, 61 teeth in comb **2000.00**   **2500.00**

☐ 17¾″ disc (45cm), carved upright case, countertop type, glass front, 106 extra-wide teeth   **2200.00**   **2600.00**

☐ 17¾″ disc, with 10 bells, otherwise same as above **2500.00**   **3000.00**

☐ 17¾″ disc, wall hanging, glass front, walnut case, coin operated, 82 teeth in comb **2750.00**   **3450.00**

☐ 17¾″ disc, table model, deluxe walnut case, carving on base molding, 82 teeth in comb, zither attachment **1500.00**   **2500.00**

☐ 17¾″ disc, table model, walnut case, double comb (164 teeth) with 10 bells, zither attachment **2650.00**   **3250.00**

Price Range

☐ 17¾" disc, "Panorama," upright (vertical) type, decorative moldings and columns on rosewood and walnut case, double comb, 53½" high, moving scene, glass door to view disc 3500.00 5500.00

☐ 20½" (52.5cm) disc, upright on storage base, walnut with decorative carving and gallery, 12 saucer bells, 120 extra-wide teeth 3500.00 5500.00

☐ 20⅝" disc, upright (vertical) model on feet with matching storage unit, 74" high simple walnut veneer case with decorative columns, glass door to view disc, double combs 4000.00 6250.00

☐ 22¾" (58cm) disc, countertop type with carved gallery, glass door, zither, 145 extra-wide teeth 2200.00 3200.00

☐ 25" disc, hanging vertical model with 12 saucer bells, some case decoration 4000.00 6000.00

☐ **KOMET (Weissbach & Co., Leipzig, Germany),** 6¾" disc (17cm) walnut, decorative inlay, figural inlay inside lid 500.00 900.00

☐ 8¾" disc, table model, simple walnut case 500.00 1000.00

☐ 10¼" disc (126cm) simple case, some decoration, figural lithograph inside lid 650.00 800.00

☐ 12" disc, upright, walnut case 800.00 1200.00

☐ 20½" disc (52cm), upright case on feet (3'3½" high) small storage drawer just under glass door, sits on base, "KOMET" etched on glass 2000.00 3000.00

☐ 20½" disc, upright counter (vertical) model, coin operated, parallel twin combs, walnut case with decorative moldings and front glass door, top wind motor 2500.00 3500.00

☐ 24½" disc, upright floor model, highly decorated case 7000.00 8000.00

☐ **LOCHMANN (Leipzig, Germany),** 10" disc, "Original," table model, plain case 500.00 750.00

☐ 15" disc, "Original," table model, scenic lithograph inside lid, simple case 1000.00 1250.00

☐ 17" disc, 8 bells, walnut case 2000.00 3000.00

☐ 21" disc, upright case, counter model 3000.00 3800.00

Price Range

☐ 24½" disc, upright case, counter model, coin operated, tubular bells, curved glass over motor, oak case, some carving, gold decoration on glass front says "Original," 45½" high, c. 1901 .... 4500.00 7500.00

☐ 24½" disc, c. 1905, upright floor model, 86" high, double comb, 12 bells, coin operated (slot in front), crank wind, glass door, walnut case, storage for discs in base 7500.00 9500.00

☐ 25¾" disc (Model 200), weight-driven motor, strings, tubular bells, walnut case with fretwork pediment, glass door, 66½" high 6000.00 7500.00

☐ **MIRA (MERMOD FRÉRES),** 6¾" disc, hand crank (manivelle), mahogany case, c. 1900   500.00 1250.00

☐ 7" disc (Style #36), straight simple lines, single comb, 34 teeth, oak (mahogany), "Mira" inside cover 750.00 1000.00

☐ 9½" disc (Style #50), single comb, 48 teeth, oak or mahogany, zither attachment, simple case, "Mira" or lithograph inside cover 800.00 1250.00

☐ 9½" disc (Style #100), oak or mahogany with case molding, duplex comb, 96 teeth, zither attachment, simple case 1000.00 1400.00

☐ 12" disc, table model, center drive movement, zither attachment, tempo control, single comb, top wind, crank inside box, mahogany case with base molding 1200.00 1500.00

☐ 12" disc (Style #132), oak or mahogany, simple case with molding on base and cover, duplex comb, 128 teeth, table model, "Mira" inside cover 1200.00 1500.00

☐ 12" disc (Style #66), 64 teeth in comb, oak or mahogany molding on base and cover, "Mira" inside cover, zither attachment 1200.00 1500.00

☐ 15½" disc (Style #79), simple oak case, molding on base and cover, zither longrunning movement, single comb, 79 teeth   1700.00 2100.00

☐ 15½" disc (Style #158), Duplex comb, 158 teeth, long-running movement, oak or mahogany, zither, case molding, "Mira" on inside of lid 2250.00 2750.00

Mira Disc Music Box, *table model.*

	Price Range	
☐ 15½" disc Miraphone, table model, music box/outside horn phonograph combination, double comb, mahogany	**4500.00**	**6000.00**
☐ 15½" disc (Style #258), floor model with storage for discs, decorative molding	**2500.00**	**3500.00**
☐ 15¾" disc, console (floor) model, lid lifts up to reveal horizontal music box, storage for discs in base, mahogany case, also made with color decal decoration on case	**3000.00**	**4500.00**
☐ 18½" disc (Style #190), simple oak or mahogany case, duplex comb, long-running movement, zither	**4000.00**	**6000.00**

Mira Disc Music Box,
style #132, table model,
mahogany.

Mira Disc Music Box,
15¾", disc console
model, storage in base.

Miraphone Disc Music Box,
console style #258.

Price Range

☐ 18½" disc (Style #290), floor model with storage, console style (sold under "Empress" label) 4500.00   7500.00

☐ 18½" disc, "Orchestral Grand," console (floor model) style, horizontal music box, lid lifts up with disc storage compartment underneath, simple mahogany case with inlay and colored decoration, 41½" high 4000.00   6000.00

☐ 18½" disc, Miraphone, music box/phonograph combination, floor model with storage for discs and records 5000.00   7000.00

☐ **MONOPOL (Leipzig, Germany),** 6" disc, plain case, lithograph inside lid 400.00   700.00

☐ 7½" disc, hand crank, walnut with transfer decoration on lid 450.00   650.00

☐ 8¼" (8¾") disc, walnut, plain case, "Monopol" lithograph inside lid 450.00   700.00

☐ 12" disc, plain mahogany case, can play Symphonion discs 500.00   700.00

☐ 13⅝" disc, plain case, lithograph inside lid   600.00   1250.00

Olympia Disc Music Box,
table model,
with drawer for extra discs.

	Price Range	
☐ 14″ disc, walnut with decorative columns, lithograph inside lid, ornamented bedplate, will play Symphonion discs	700.00	1000.00
☐ 17¼″ disc, upright counter model, carved decoration, single comb	1400.00	2000.00
☐ 20″ disc, upright with disc storage cabinet, ornate case	2000.00	3000.00
☐ **NEW CENTURY (MERMOD FRERES),** 11½″ disc, table model, mahogany or oak, simple case style, duplex comb	1800.00	2500.00
☐ 15″ disc, table model, mahogany or oak, plain case with thin molding around edges, double comb	2000.00	3000.00
☐ 18½″ disc, "Soprano," double revolution movement, duplex comb, long running on one wind, oak or mahogany	4000.00	6000.00

Price Range

☐ **OLYMPIA (F. OTTO AND SONS, NJ),** "Princess," duplex comb, winter scene lithograph, highly ornate carving all over 1000.00   1500.00

☐ 8¾" disc, c. 1905, center drive movement with single comb, crank wind at side, oak case 400.00   900.00

☐ 11¾" disc, single comb, oak case 700.00   1100.00

☐ 14" disc, single comb, simple case, storage drawer for discs 1500.00   2100.00

☐ 15½" disc, single comb, coin operated, scenic lithograph inside lid, mahogany (cherry), carved decoration 1500.00   2750.00

☐ 15½" disc, highly carved decorated case, scenic lithograph inside lid, double comb . .   1500.00   2100.00

☐ 15¾" disc, table model, mahogany, some case decoration 1750.00   2500.00

☐ 20" disc, upright, carved decorated case with storage base 4500.00   5500.00

☐ 5½" disc, manivelle 400.00   600.00

☐ **ORPHENION,** 8½" disc, table model, walnut case with simple decoration, single comb . .   750.00   1500.00

☐ 11" disc, 2 combs, ornate case 900.00   1400.00

☐ 15½" disc, 2 combs 1500.00   2200.00

☐ 16¼" disc, c. 1877, simple case style, burl walnut, crank wind, exposed spring barrel   2500.00   3500.00

☐ **ORPHEUS,** 18¼" disc, table model, multiple combs (3), decorative case and corner moldings, "Orpheus" trademark lithograph inside lid 1500.00   2250.00

☐ 22⅝" disc, upright, on legs 2500.00   3000.00

☐ **OTTO & SONS (SEE "OLYMPIA")**

☐ **PERFECTION,** 10½" disc, table model, simple mahogany case, scenic lithograph inside lid, zinc discs 1000.00   1500.00

☐ **POLYHYMNIA,** 7¾" disc, plain case 600.00   800.00

☐ **POLYPHON MUSIKWERKE (Leipzig, Germany),** 6½" disc, simple case, 30 teeth in comb, walnut, lithograph inside cover 350.00   450.00

Price Range

☐ 6½" disc, with 4 bells, spring driven, lithograph inside cover, wood case plain, decal "POLYPHONE" on lid, 30 teeth in comb .. | 400.00 | 700.00

☐ 8–8¼" disc, hand crank, walnut case, decal design on lid, lithograph, inside crank, 41 teeth in comb .... | 450.00 | 750.00

☐ 8–8¼" disc, with 4 saucer bells, lever spring wind, plain wood case, 30 teeth in music comb .... | 500.00 | 800.00

☐ 8–8¼" disc, serpentine style case, walnut, color lithograph on inside front cover, spring wind via front lever outside case, 41 teeth in comb .... | 550.00 | 850.00

☐ 9½" disc, table model, simple case style ... | 300.00 | 500.00

☐ 9½" disc, front lever, spring wind, 6 bells, simple case, 46 teeth in comb .... | 750.00 | 1500.00

☐ 9¾" disc, 6 saucer bells, some decoration simple case, pictorial lithograph inside cover, spring wind via front lever, 41 teeth in comb | 500.00 | 900.00

☐ 9⅝" disc, single comb, 6 bells, ratchet wind, grained wood case, transfer decorated lid | 500.00 | 900.00

☐ 11" disc, table model, 6 bells, simple walnut case, outside front ratchet wind, print inside lid, single comb .... | 750.00 | 1250.00

☐ 11¼" disc, walnut, some floral inlay on cover, decorative molding, 54 teeth in comb, single comb, lithograph of cherubs inside lid, plays Regina discs also .... | 750.00 | 1250.00

☐ 11¼" disc, duplex comb, 108 teeth, satinwood inlay case, decorative molding ...... | 1000.00 | 1500.00

☐ 11¼" disc, with 8 bells, walnut case .... | 1250.00 | 1750.00

☐ 14½" disc, with 12 bells, walnut, scenic lithograph inside lid, some inlay in cover, 112 notes .... | 1500.00 | 2000.00

☐ 15½–¾" disc, coin operated, single comb, 78 teeth, walnut case with some molding, lithograph inside cover, glass lid over mechanism | 1250.00 | 1750.00

☐ 15½", peripheral drive movement, 1½ combs, start/stop control, floral marquetry decoration on case, table model .... | 1750.00 | 3750.00

☐ 15½–¾" disc, single comb, 77 teeth, walnut simple case, some decoration .... | 1000.00 | 1750.00

Polyphon Disc Music Box,
walnut floor model,
with storage in base.

Price Range

☐ 15½" disc, Sublime-Harmonie Piccolo, duplex comb, 154 teeth in music comb, table
model, walnut with elaborate carving and
inlay, will play Regina discs (storage drawer
for discs) 1500.00   2250.00
☐ 15½" disc, upright (vertical) counter model,
double comb, peripheral drive movement,
crank wind, walnut case with columns and

Polyphon Upright Disc Music Box,
walnut storage base.

Price Range

deep molding, front panel is pierced with lyre design in center, drawer in bottom for extra discs, coin operated 2000.00   3000.00

☐ 15½″ disc, upright counter model, walnut, carved top gallery and front columns, 78-tooth music comb, coin operated, on feet, glass door to view disc mechanism 2250.00   3250.00

☐ 15½″ disc, twin combs, veneer case, lithograph inside lid 1000.00   1700.00

Price Range

☐ 15½″ disc, Longcase Hall Clock, weight-
driven movement, walnut case with highly
carved and turned ornaments, 91″ high ...　4750.00　　7000.00

☐ 17½″ disc, table model, 12 bells, walnut case
with inlay on lid, lithograph inside cover, 72
teeth . . . .　2800.00　　3200.00

☐ 19⅝–20″ disc, walnut case with inlay, decorative molding, lithograph inside lid, 118
teeth, table model . . . .　3500.00　　4500.00

☐ 19⅝″ disc, floor model (one whole cabinet),
highly carved case, glass front top door,
motor mechanism in glass case, coin operated, fully carved free columns between top
and bottom sections in front to form a shelf-
like section in the middle, storage of discs in
base . . . .　3800.00　　5000.00

☐ 19⅝–20″ disc, counter model, upright, front
columns, glass door, coin operated, top gal-
lery (clock), 118 teeth in music comb, walnut　2250.00　　3500.00

☐ 19⅝″ disc, floor model, carved walnut case,
glass front, storage in base, glass panel over
motor mechanism, 118 teeth in music comb　3500.00　　4500.00

☐ 22½″ disc, upright with 16 bells, on feet with
storage base, decorative molding, glass
front, walnut (Glockenspiel) . . . .　5000.00　　7000.00

☐ 22½″ disc upright (vertical) counter model,
coin operated, glockenspiel accompaniment,
glass front door, walnut case with some decorative molding, columns, and fretwork, sits
on feet, 43½″ high . . . .　3000.00　　5000.00

☐ 24½″ disc, upright floor model, carved walnut, very loud tone, large springs, 159 teeth,
storage unit for discs in base, coin operated　4500.00　　7000.00

☐ 24½″ disc, upright automatic changer, floor
model, holds 12 discs, selection indicator, or-
nate case and gallery, walnut, 159 notes ..　15,000.00　22,500.00

☐ 24⅝″ disc, upright model on feet with base
storage cabinet fretwork, gallery and finials,
glass front door, zither attachment, side wind
motor, walnut case, 92″ high . . . .　5000.00　　6000.00

Price Range

☐ 25⅝″ disc, upright coin operated, counter
model, side wind motor, double combs, wal-
nut case, glass door, on feet **5500.00   7000.00**

REGINA MUSIC BOX COMPANY (Rahway, NJ). The Regina Boxes
originally all had numerical style numbers. For easy reference they are
arranged in this order; however, this is not necessarily the order in
which they were made.
*Below are disc size and other reference guides to locating a particular
box.

DISC SIZE	STYLE
8½″ disc styles	21, 22, 91
11″ disc styles	19, 20
12¼″ disc styles	16, 17, 17a, 29, 30, 41, 141, 42, 142, 71, 171, 72, 172, 81, 116, 129
15½″ disc styles	1, 2, 3, 9–15, 35, 36 (round and flat), 40, 140, 240, 51, 251, 50, 151, 250, 55, 255, 155, 67, 113, 215, 216, 217, 246
20¾″ disc styles	24, 25, 26 (early and late), 27 (early and late), 126, 226, 28, 31, 32, 37, 38 (round and flat), 39, 139, 239, 44, 144, 61

Regina Music Box,
style #4,
Orchestral Regina,
plays 27″ discs.

27" disc styles 4, 5, 6, 7, 8, 8a, 33, 34, 45, 145

ACCORDION TOP STYLES
20¾" 26
27" 6, 7

AUTOMATIC CHANGERS
15½" 35, 36
20¾" 31, 32
27" 8, 8a, 33, 34
32" 300

CLOCKS
12¼" 81
15½" 3

COIN-OPERATED STYLES
Table models: Style #
12¼" disc .... 17 (double comb), 30 (single comb)
15½" disc .... 2, 14, 217 (single comb), 15, 51 (double comb)

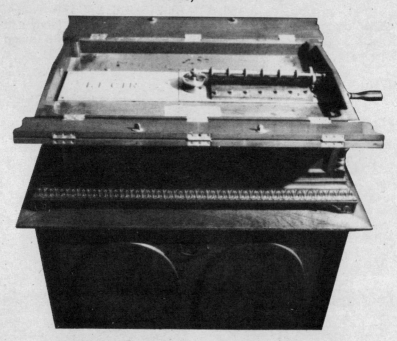

Regina Music Box, *oak accordion table model, style #6, mahogany.*

20¾" disc . . . . 27 (double comb)
27" disc . . . . 7 (double comb)
Upright floor models:
15½" disc . . . . 1, 36 (double comb)
20¾" disc . . . . 25, 38 (double comb)
27" disc . . . . 5, 34, 8 (double comb)
Vertical counter models:
12¼" disc . . . . 17a (double comb)
20¾" disc . . . . 32 (double comb)

CONSOLE (FLOOR) STYLES
12¼" 41, 42
15½" 40, 43, 67, 246
20¾" 44
27" 45

COUNTERTOP (VERTICAL) STYLES
12¼" disc . . . . 17a (coin operated)
20¾" disc . . . . 32 (coin operated)
Style 18: . . . . several disc sizes

DESK STYLE
20¾" disc . . . . 61, Reginaphone 161

GUM VENDING MACHINE
Style 18 . . . . several disc sizes

REGINAPHONE: DISC MUSIC BOX/PHONOGRAPH COMBINATION
Table models: Outside Horn (for phonograph)
12¼" disc 129, 171, 172
15½" disc 113, 150, 155
20¾" disc 126, 139

Table models: Inside Horn
15½" disc 250, 251, 255
20¾" disc 226, 239

Console (Floor) models: Outside Horn
12¼" disc 141, 142
15½" disc 140, 143
20¾" disc . . . . 144, 161 (Desk style)
27" disc 145

Console (Floor) models: Inside Horn
15½" disc . . . . 240 (Lions' heads)

TABLE STYLES
8½" disc 21, 22, 91
11" disc 19, 20
12¼" disc 16, 17, 29, 30, 71, 72
15½" disc 6, 7, 9, 10, 11, 11a, 12, 13, 14, 14a, 15, 50,
. . . . 51, 55, 215, 216, 217

Regina Disc Music Box,
upright, style, #8, automatic changer.

20¾" disc 26, 28, 27, 39
UPRIGHT (VERTICAL FLOOR) STYLES
15½" disc 1, 2, 35, 36
20¾" disc 24, 25, 31, 37, 38
27" disc 4, 5, 8, 8a, 33, 34

Price Range

☐ STYLE #1, 15½" upright coin operated, long play "Musical Automation," duplex comb, oak (mahogany)	**2700.00**	**4000.00**
☐ STYLE #2, same as above, single comb ..	**2500.00**	**3500.00**
☐ STYLE #3, 15¹/₃" disc movement musical clock (Seth Thomas), play hourly, or any time desired, grandfather style highly decorated (various case styles)	**4500.00**	**6000.00**
☐ STYLE #4, 27" disc, Orchestral Regina, oak (mahogany, walnut), large-for-home-use upright music box, storage bin in base for discs	**5000.00**	**8000.00**

Regina Disc Music Box,
style #10, oak.

Regina Disc Music Box,
style #10, mahogany.

Regina Disc Music Box,
table model, style #11.

	Price Range	
☐ STYLE #5, same as above, coin operated	5000.00	8000.00
☐ STYLE #6, 27″ disc, folding (accordion top), oak (mahogany), table model, hinged cover opens so disc can lie flat, duplex comb, long running, 172 tongues	4000.00	6000.00
☐ STYLE #7, 27″ disc, coin-operated version Style #6	7000.00	7500.00
☐ STYLE #8a, 27″ disc automatic changer, 12 discs, ornate case, floor model, carved dragons, finials on gallery	7000.00	11,000.00
☐ STYLE #8, coin-operated version Style #8a	6500.00	10,000.00
☐ STYLE #9, 15½″ disc table model, duplex comb, ornately carved paneling, walnut (oak, mahogany)	2000.00	2800.00
☐ STYLE #10, 15½″ disc table model, long-running movement, ornate case, oak (mahogany), duplex comb	2200.00	3500.00
☐ STYLE #11, 15½″ disc table model, oak, long-running movement, several case styles, some with storage drawer, basic plain straight case (see also Style #50)	1900.00	2700.00

Price Range

☐ STYLE #11a, 15½" disc, regular movement, duplex comb, REGINA lithograph inside cover 1850.00 2350.00

☐ STYLE #12, 15½" disc, table model with storage drawer in case for discs, single comb 1500.00 2250.00

☐ STYLE #13, 15½" disc, table model, plain (and decorated case styles) oak case, regular movement, single comb 1350.00 2250.00

☐ STYLE #113, Reginaphone outside-horn version #13 .... 1750.00 2500.00

☐ STYLE #14, table model 15½" disc, coin operated, single comb 1500.00 2000.00

☐ STYLE #14a, duplex version #14 .... 1600.00 2500.00

☐ STYLE #15, 15½" disc, coin operated (version #11), duplex comb, long running, oak (mahogany) 1600.00 2600.00

☐ STYLE #16, 12¼" disc table model, double comb 1000.00 1250.00

☐ STYLE #17, 12¼" disc table model, double comb, coin operated 1000.00 1250.00

☐ STYLE #17a, 12¼" disc, vertical counter style table model, double comb, coin operated 3000.00 3500.00

☐ STYLE #18, gum-vending machine, "A Musical Salesman," vertical countertop style, glass front, examples were made in 11", 12¼", 15½" disc styles. Coin operated, dispersed gum, played a tune 3500.00 5000.00

☐ STYLE #19, 11" disc, duplex comb, walnut with case decoration, 112-tooth comb 1000.00 1250.00

☐ STYLE #20, 11" disc, single comb, lever wind on front of case, lithograph inside cover, plain case, oak or mahogany, center drive 800.00 1250.00

☐ STYLE #21, 8½" disc, hand crank, single comb, oak or mahogany, 41 teeth, plain case 500.00 750.00

☐ STYLE #22, 8½" disc, single comb, spring wind, plain oak (mahogany), lithograph inside cover 500.00 750.00

Regina Disc Music Box,
*style #26, early,
table top model,
mahogany.*

Regina Disc Music Box,
*style #31,
automatic changer, oak.*

Reginaphone Disc Music Box/Phonograph, *style #255, table model, inside horn.*

Price Range

☐ STYLE #24, Regina Sublima, 20¾" disc, parlor upright long running, double comb, oak (mahogany), 71" high, carved, flat rectangular case design, openwork gallery, round glass opening the size of disc **6000.00   9000.00**

Regina Disc Music Box,
style #35, coin-op #36,
automatic changer, plays
15½" discs, leaded
glass, mahogany.

Regina Disc Music Box,
style #35, automatic
changer, plays 15½"
discs, clear glass,
mahogany.

Regina Disc Music Box, late, style #33, upright "Orchestral Corona," automatic changer.

Regina Automatic Disc Changer, mahogany, floor model, style #37.

	Price Range	
☐ STYLE #25, coin-operated version #24 ...	**6000.00**	**9000.00**
☐ STYLE #26 early, folding top (casket or accordion top), 20¾" disc, hinged cover opens out to allow for disc to lie flat, oak (mahogany), long playing, 2 combs, table model ..	**4500.00**	**6250.00**
☐ STYLE #26 late, 20¾" disc, standard straight-sided case, duplex comb, banjo attachment, oak (mahogany), speed regulator	**3000.00**	**4000.00**
☐ STYLE #126, Reginaphone outside horn, nickel Morning Glory–style "Cupola" top on lid on all models	**4450.00**	**5450.00**
☐ STYLE #226, Reginaphone with inside horn	**3500.00**	**4000.00**
☐ STYLE #27 early, coin-operated version #26	**4500.00**	**6500.00**
☐ STYLE #27 late, coin-operated version late #26	**3000.00**	**4250.00**
☐ STYLE #29, 12¼" disc, table model, single comb, various case styles	**1000.00**	**1600.00**
☐ STYLE #129, outside horn Reginaphone, nickel Morning Glory horn	**2000.00**	**2500.00**
☐ STYLE #30, 12¼" disc, table model, single comb, coin operated	**1000.00**	**1500.00**

Regina Disc Music Box,
Style #39, "Cupola."

Price Range

☐ STYLE #31, 20¾″ disc, Regina Sublima Corona, automatic disc changer, 64″ high case, top half of upright floor model case is recessed to form a narrow shelf with bottom section, glass fronts top and bottom, decorative case, long-running movement, 2 combs, oak (mahogany) **7000.00   11,000.00**

☐ STYLE #32, countertop version of #31, coin operated, 20¾″ disc **6500.00   8750.00**

☐ STYLE #33, 27″ disc, Regina Orchestral Corona, automatic changer, 2 combs, oak (mahogany), 66″ high, piano sounding board, long running, straight case, style like #31, earlier examples more ornate case design **8000.00   12,000.00**

☐ STYLE #34, 27″ disc, coin-operated version of Style #33, generally top section of case has two doors **8000.00   12,000.00**

☐ STYLE #35, 15½″ disc Corona, parlor model, automatic changer, 12 discs long-play movement, oak (mahogany) turned-wood columns on front of case, curved legs, gallery, 66″ high, tempo regulator, tune selector, bow glass front (some with art glass), banjo attachment (very few Seth Thomas clock in top gallery) **6000.00   10,000.00**

☐ STYLE #36 round, coin operated, 15½″ disc, 12 disc automatic tune changer, same style as #35 with coin mechanism **6000.00   10000.00**

☐ STYLE #36 flat, coin operated, 15½″ disc, made for arcades on cast iron legs, flat style case design, piano sounding board, long running, duplex comb, oak (mahogany), 68″ high **6000.00   10,000.00**

☐ STYLE #37, 20¾″ disc, Regina Sublima Corona, automatic changer, long play, piano sounding board, 75″ tall, two combs (130 tongues), oak (mahogany) on curved legs, case decoration (larger size version #35) **8000.00   11,000.00**

☐ STYLE #38 round, coin-operated version of Style #37, 20¾″ disc, Regina Sublima Corona, automatic changer **8000.00   11,000.00**

Price Range

☐ STYLE #38 flat, Regina Sublima Corona, coin operated, 20¾″ disc, flat glass front, spiral columns on front, carved gallery, ornate legs, solid back, open sides and front on base (casters) 8000.00 11000.00

☐ STYLE #39, table model, serpentine-style case, "Cupola" (raised ventilated section of the lid) cover, 20¾″ disc 2500.00 3500.00

☐ STYLE #139, Reginaphone with outside horn (nickel, Morning Glory style) 2500.00 3000.00

☐ STYLE #239, inside-horn Reginaphone ... 2250.00 3000.00

☐ STYLE #40, 15½″ disc, console floor model 40″ high, duplex comb, cabinet in base for disc storage (150), oak (mahogany), serpentine curved case style with carved lions' heads and paw columns on front sides, mandolin attachment 3000.00 4000.00

☐ STYLE #140, Reginaphone version with nickel Morning Glory horn, storage for discs and records 3800.00 4700.00

☐ STYLE #240, Reginaphone version with inside horn and carved lions' heads and paw columns on front sides, storage in base for discs and records 4000.00 6000.00

☐ STYLE #41, 12¼″ disc, console floor model, duplex comb, storage base, serpentine curved style, mahogany 2400.00 3500.00

☐ STYLE #141, Reginaphone version with outside horn, (Morning Glory, nickel) for phonograph, storage holds both discs and records 3500.00 4500.00

☐ STYLE #42, 12¼″ disc, console floor model, single comb, serpentine case style, mahogany, storage for discs 2200.00 3500.00

☐ STYLE #142, Reginaphone version with outside horn (Morning Glory, nickel), storage for discs and phonograph records 3000.00 4500.00

☐ STYLE #43, same as Style #40 but with storage base to the floor instead of sitting on legs (duplex comb) 3000.00 4500.00

☐ STYLE #143, Reginaphone version of Style #43, outside horn 3000.00 4700.00

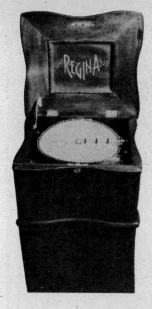

Regina Disc Music Box, style #41 or #42, console floor model.

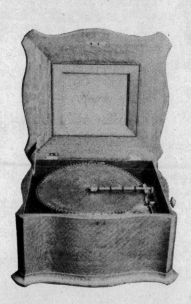

Regina Disc Music Box, style #50, table model, serpentine case, oak.

Reginaphone Disc Music Box/Phonograph Combination,
style #240, inside horn, floor model. Left: oak. Right: mahogany.

Price Range

☐ STYLE #44, floor model, simple straight-sided case, two doors in base open to store 200 discs, 20¾" disc, mahogany, 43" high 4250.00 4500.00

☐ STYLE #144, Reginaphone, outside horn, storage holds 100 discs, 200 phono records 4000.00 5000.00

☐ STYLE #45, 27" disc, same as Style #44 cabinet, mahogany only 4250.00 4500.00

☐ STYLE #145, Reginaphone with outside horn and storage 4500.00 5000.00

Regina Disc Music Box,
*style #50, table model,
serpentine case,
mahogany.*

Price Range

☐ STYLE #50, table model 15½" disc, duplex comb, serpentine curved case, banjo attachment, tempo regulator, long-running movement, oak or mahogany. A matching table was made for this model with storage for discs. 2800.00   3750.00

☐ STYLE #150, Reginaphone version of style #50, outside horn phonograph 4000.00   5000.00

☐ STYLE #250, Inside-horn version Reginaphone, table model, duplex comb, serpentine case, 15½" disc 2750.00   3500.00

☐ STYLE #51, table model, 15½" disc, duplex comb, coin operated, speed regulator, long running, plain case, short bed plate 2500.00   3600.00

☐ STYLE #251, Reginaphone, inside horn, duplex comb 2750.00   3250.00

Reginaphone Disc Music Box/Phonograph Combination,
style #150, coin operated, outside horn.

Reginaphone Disc Music Box/Phonograph Combination,
style #155, outside horn.

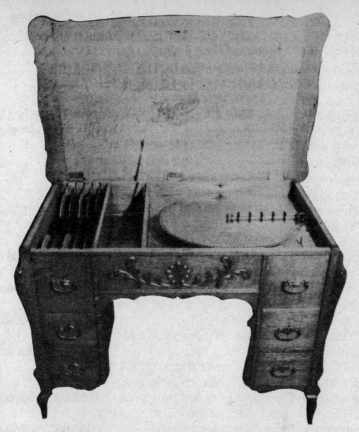

Regina Disc Music Box, style #61, "Musical Desk," oak.

	Price Range	
☐ STYLE #55, 15½" disc, single comb, tempo regulator, banjo attachment, simple case oak (mahogany), Regina trademark inside cover	1800.00	2400.00
☐ STYLE #155, Reginaphone with outside horn	3000.00	4000.00

	Price Range	
☐ STYLE #255, Reginaphone, inside horn ...	**3500.00**	**4000.00**
☐ STYLE #61, 20¾″ disc, Regina Musical Desk, kneehole style with the appearance of drawers on each side, top lifts to reveal music box and storage of discs, oak (mahogany), some decorative molding	**6000.00**	**10,000.00**
☐ STYLE #161, Reginaphone, outside horn ..	**4000.00**	**6000.00**
☐ STYLE #67, 15½″ disc, highly decorated finish (Rookwood) floor model, duplex comb, tempo regulator, upright arrangement of disc enclosed in case, two front doors open to reveal music box and storage bin	**5000.00**	**6500.00**
☐ STYLE #71, 12¼″ disc, table model, duplex comb, curved serpentine-style case, banjo attachment, oak (mahogany)	**1750.00**	**2000.00**
☐ STYLE #171, Reginaphone with outside horn	**2000.00**	**2500.00**
☐ STYLE #72, single-comb version of Style #71, REGINA inside lid	**1500.00**	**2000.00**
☐ STYLE #172, Reginaphone version of #72, outside horn	**2000.00**	**2500.00**
☐ STYLE #81, Regina Chime Clock, 12¼″ disc, Mission-style case, oak, chiming bells activated by the disc. There are no combs	**5000.00**	**9000.00**
☐ STYLE #91, 8½″ disc, single comb, oak (mahogany), some decorative molding	**500.00**	**750.00**
☐ STYLE #113, Reginaphone (see Style #13)		
☐ STYLE #126, Reginaphone (see Style #26)		
☐ STYLE #139, Reginaphone (see Style #39)		
☐ STYLE #140, Reginaphone (see Style #40)		
☐ STYLE #141, Reginaphone (see Style #41)		
☐ STYLE #142, Reginaphone (see Style #42)		
☐ STYLE #143, Reginaphone (see Style #43)		
☐ STYLE #144, Reginaphone (see Style #44)		
☐ STYLE #145, Reginaphone (see Style #45)		
☐ STYLE #150, Reginaphone (see Style #50)		
☐ STYLE #155, Reginaphone (see Style #55)		
☐ STYLE #161, Reginaphone (see Style #61)		
☐ STYLE #171, Reginaphone (see Style #71)		
☐ STYLE #172, Reginaphone (see Style #72)		

Price Range

☐ STYLE #215, with 12 bells, single comb, 15½" disc made for bell accompaniment, oak (mahogany) 4000.00   7500.00

☐ STYLE #216, duplex comb version of Style #215 .... 4000.00   7500.00

☐ STYLE #217, coin-operated version of Style #216 .... 4000.00   7500.00

☐ STYLE #226, Reginaphone (see Style #26)

☐ STYLE #239, Reginaphone (see Style #39)

☐ STYLE #240, Reginaphone (see Style #40)

☐ STYLE #246, 15½" disc console floor model, rectangular cabinet style, duplex comb, two doors in storage section 3000.00   3500.00

☐ STYLE #250, Reginaphone (see Style #50)

☐ STYLE #251, Reginaphone (see Style #51)

☐ STYLE #255, Reginaphone (see Style #55)

☐ **SIRION,** 14½" disc, shifting disc mechanism, tabletop style, walnut case with decoration, stop/start, coin operated 3000.00   4000.00

☐ 19" disc, table model, elaborate moldings and inlay decoration on fruitwood case, double comb 4000.00   5500.00

☐ 22" disc, upright, on matching disc-storage base 5000.00   8000.00

☐ **STELLA (MADE BY MERMOD FRERES),** 9½" disc, oak or mahogany, large spring motor, duplex comb, decorative molding on case, disc centered in case 900.00   1000.00

☐ 14" disc, oak (mahogany), duplex comb, some case decoration, disc placed toward left side in case 1500.00   2000.00

☐ 15½" disc, concert table model, double comb, oak (mahogany), some case decoration 2000.00   3000.00

☐ 15½" disc, oak (mahogany), duplex comb, moderator (tempo), large spring motor 2000.00   2500.00

☐ 17¼" disc, table model, peripheral drive movement, single comb tempo control, crank wind, mahogany case with carved floral decoration and base molding, storage drawer in bottom of case for extra discs 2000.00   3000.00

Stella Disc Music Box, *table model, mahogany.*

	Price Range	
☐ 17¼″ disc, Stella Grand, duplex comb, carving in front panel of base, oak (mahogany), drawer in base for 100 discs (variations in case decoration)	2500.00	3500.00
☐ 17¼″ console floor model, 36″ high, duplex comb, storage for discs, case decoration ..	3000.00	5000.00
☐ 17¼″ disc, table model, mahogany, single comb, storage drawer for discs	1900.00	2100.00
☐ 25½″ disc, upright floor model, 8′ tall, storage in base for extra discs, carved decoration and finials, glass doors	3500.00	5500.00
☐ 25½″ disc, upright floor model, highly carved and decorated, walnut and rosewood case with floral marquetry front panel in base, storage base for discs, peripheral-drive movement, single comb, stop/start button, crank	4000.00	7000.00

Stella Disc Music Box, *console model with storage in base, mahogany.*

Price Range

☐ 26″ (25¹¹/₁₆″) disc, orchestral grand (for home use), glass front doors, highly carved on top, storage in base, oak (mahogany), 6′3″ high, coin operated 5000.00   7000.00

☐ 26″ disc, Orchestral Grand, console case model, case decoration (shell and ribbon pattern), two doors in base open to reveal storage for discs, oak or mahogany, loud volume, duplex combs (some models electrically powered, Electric Orchestral Grand) 5000.00   7000.00

☐ 26″ disc, upright floor model, 81″ high, peripheral-drive wind movement, double comb, crank wind outside case, rosewood case with fluted columns, carved moldings, round glass panel in top door, carved laurel wreath motif on front door of base cabinet 4500.00   6500.00

Stella Disc Music Box, table model.

	Price Range	
☐ **SYMPHONION (Leipzig, Germany),** 4⅝″ disc, mantel clock, case decoration	1750.00	2400.00
☐ 5½″ disc, table model, simple case style . . .	450.00	750.00
☐ 5¾″ disc, plain black case with decal decorations, hand cranked (Manivelle), 40 teeth in comb (14.5 cm)	500.00	800.00
☐ 6¼″ disc, plain case, winding lever, "Symphonion" in script on cover, rosewood case, 4 bells	400.00	600.00
☐ 7½″ disc, table model, simple maple case, pictorial lithograph inside lid, single comb . .	600.00	1000.00
☐ 7½″ disc, center drive movement, single comb, stop/start control, walnut case with some decoration, colored lithograph inside lid	500.00	800.00

Price Range

☐ 7⅝" disc, simple grained case, colored lithograph inside lid, floral transfer decoration on lid 500.00   750.00

☐ 7¹¹/₁₆" (7¾") disc, walnut plain case, "Symphonion" decal on lid 500.00   700.00

☐ 7¹¹/₁₆" (7¾") disc, 3 saucer bells, zither attachment, "Symphonion" decal on lid, lithograph inside cover, crank 650.00   800.00

☐ 8⅝" disc, black plain wood case, decal design on lid, walnut, duplex Sublime-Harmonie combs, decorated card inside lid 500.00   800.00

☐ 8⅝" disc, Sublime-Harmonie, simple rectangular walnut case, monochrome print inside lid 400.00   700.00

☐ 9½" disc, black polished plain case with decal decoration "Symphonion," 72-tooth comb (case variation—walnut with base and lid molding) 650.00   750.00

☐ 10" disc, walnut, lever wind on front, duplex comb, decorative molding, lithograph inside cover, zither 700.00   900.00

☐ 10" disc, 6 bells, walnut with case decoration, lithograph inside lid, duplex comb, Sublime-Harmonie 1000.00   1500.00

☐ 10" disc, table model, lever wind, simple rosewood case, "Symphonion" trademark lithograph inside lid 650.00   1000.00

☐ 10⅝" disc, table model, spring wind movement, ratchet lever, double comb, start/stop lever, black-painted simple case 700.00   900.00

☐ 10⅝" disc, Sublime-Harmonie combs, lithograph inside cover, walnut case with base molding 700.00   900.00

☐ 10⅝" disc, black polished wood plain case with decal decoration on lid, 84 teeth in comb (also walnut, decorative molding on base and lid) 700.00   900.00

☐ 11¾" disc, Sublime-Harmonie combs, vertical cabinet counter model, walnut, gold ornamentation and lettering on glass front, coin operated, ornate carved case with gallery,

Symphonion Upright Disc Music Box.

	Price Range	
(also with painted decoration on front door instead of glass), home use model not coin operated	1500.00	3000.00
☐ 11¾″ disc, walnut case with molding on lid and base, Sublime-Harmonie combs, carrying handles on side, lithograph inside cover, 84-tooth comb	1500.00	2000.00

Symphonion Twin-Disc Music Box, *table model on storage base, plays two 11⅞" discs at the same time on separate combs, speed regulator, crank in center front of mahogany case, inlaid floral decoration on lid, carrying handles, very rare.*

	Price Range	
☐ 11¾" disc, highly ornate case, walnut, carved corner columns, moldings, brass handles, some inlay on lid, glass plate over mechanism, storage for discs, Sublime-Harmonie combs, 84-tooth comb	1300.00	1900.00
☐ 11⅞" disc, table model, coin operated, Sublime-Harmonie combs, simple walnut case, embossed name on lid	1200.00	2200.00

Symphonion Twin-Disc Music Box, *table model on storage base, plays two 11⅞" discs at the same time on separate combs, speed regulator, crank in center front of case, inlaid floral decoration on lid, carrying handles, very rare.*

Symphonion Disc Music Box, *table model, plays 11¾" discs.*

Price Range

☐ 11⅞″ disc, table model, Sublime-Harmonie combs, figural lithograph inside lid, decorative case molding with matching storage cabinet, oak **1500.00**   **3500.00**

☐ 11⅞″ disc, c. 1900, center-drive movement, Sublime-Harmonie combs, stop/start knob, detachable handle, mahogany, figural lithograph inside lid, carved corner and base moldings, inner glass lid, inlaid floral spray on lid **1500.00**   **2500.00**

☐ 11⅞″ disc, vertical counter model, coin operated, some case decoration **2000.00**   **3000.00**

☐ 11⅞″ disc table model, Twin-Discs (two discs play at the same time on separate combs), speed regulator, crank in center front of case, inlaid floral decoration on lid, carrying handles, mahogany (oak) **5000.00** **10,000.00**

☐ 11⅞″ disc, Hall Clock, style 25, highly decorated with carved ornamentation, 79″ high, walnut, storage in base for extra discs **5500.00**   **7500.00**

☐ 12″ disc, double comb (84 teeth), walnut cabinet, lithograph inside lid, table model, stop/start knob, inner glass lid, decorative corner and base molding **1500.00**   **2000.00**

☐ 13¼″ disc, single comb, walnut case, decorative molding, some inlay, 8 bells **2200.00**   **3200.00**

☐ 13¼″ disc, duplex combs, Sublime-Harmonie, walnut with base molding, figural lithograph inside cover **1000.00**   **2500.00**

☐ 13¼″ disc, vertical upright counter type, ornate case, gallery (with clock), coin operated, duplex comb **2500.00**   **3000.00**

☐ 13½″ disc, double comb, mahogany case, carved decoration, 18½″ long case, "Imperial Symphion," figural lithograph **1200.00**   **1750.00**

☐ 13½″ disc, center drive movement, table model, burled walnut case with base and corner moldings, inner glass lid, lithograph inside lid **1200.00**   **1800.00**

☐ 13⅝″ disc, combs in Sublime-Harmonie, ornate walnut case, some inlay, glass plate over mechanism **1250.00**   **2000.00**

Price Range

☐ 13⅝" disc, Sublime-Harmonie Piccolo, floor model upright case, highly decorated, gallery, walnut (oak), disc storage in base (also art glass front, or advertising on glass, or carved wood front), case variations, "Haydn" 3000.00 4000.00

☐ 13⅝" disc, vertical counter top model, Sublime-Harmonie combs, walnut case (clock in gallery), "Meteor" 1500.00 2800.00

☐ 13⅝" disc, Musical Longcase Clock, "Eroica," highly decorated, ornately carved case 6500.00 8500.00

☐ 14" disc, "Eroica," upright floor model, sets of 3 discs (A, B, C) play in harmony, three separate movements, each with 100 teeth, 2 combs in Sublime-Harmonie arrangement, oak or walnut, front panel glass or wood (art glass, coin operated) 8000.00 13,000.00

☐ 14¾" disc, table model, walnut, inlay lid, highly decorated carved panels and molding, double comb 1800.00 2200.00

☐ 14¾" disc, table model, with 10 saucer bells, duplex comb, walnut case with decoration, "Cherub" lithograph inside lid 2500.00 3500.00

☐ 15" disc, c. 1900, center drive movement, double comb, tempo control, crank wind, stop/start button outside front, mahogany case with matching storage cabinet on carved legs, beaded carved wood decoration on case and stand, trademark lithograph in-side lid 2200.00 3000.00

☐ 15½" disc, table model, simple case style, oak, some case molding at base, double comb, slow/fast lever, stop/start knob at front 1500.00 2500.00

☐ 15¾" disc, single comb, plain comb, molding on base and cover 1500.00 2000.00

☐ 15¾" disc, ornate walnut case, 10 bells, du-plex comb (156 teeth) 2500.00 3000.00

☐ 15¾" disc, walnut case, some decoration, duplex comb, lithograph inside cover 1250.00 1850.00

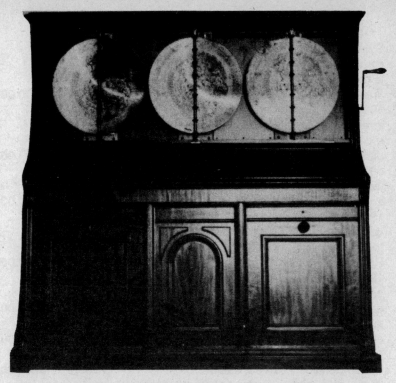

Symphonion Three-Disc Music Box, *side-by-side format, plays 17⅝" discs.*

	Price Range	
☐ 15⅝" disc, table model, single comb, zither attachment, large decorative bedplate, walnut case with simple molding, lithograph inside lid, some decoration on lid	1250.00	2250.00
☐ 17¾ (17⅝") disc, carved moulding, mahogany, "Cherub" lithograph inside lid	2500.00	3500.00
☐ 17⅝" disc, upright vertical (style 106), oak case with decorative molding, storage for discs in base	3500.00	4500.00

Price Range

☐ 17⅝" disc, 3-Disc upright floor model, A, B, C discs arranged side by side in cabinet, play same tune but each disc slightly different, large oak case, simple decoration, three separate combs, one crank 10,000.00 15,000.00

☐ 18¼" disc, floor model, upright vertical disc arrangement, two combs, top section slightly recessed from bottom, storage bin in base, glass door, openwork gallery 3500.00 4500.00

☐ 19⅛" disc, vertical upright disc arrangement, walnut ornate case on feet (no base), clock in gallery, 2 combs (106 teeth) 3750.00 4750.00

☐ 19⅛" disc, floor model glass front, highly decorated, walnut case, pull-out storage bin for extra discs, double comb in Sublime-Harmonie arrangement 4500.00 5500.00

☐ 19⅛" (19") disc, countertop, upright model, coin operated, walnut, highly carved case decoration, glass door, on feet 2000.00 3000.00

☐ 19⅛" disc, two combs, grandfather hall clock, very ornate case, music plays hourly 4000.00 5000.00

☐ 19½" disc, double comb, coin operated (uses British pennies), carved walnut 2750.00 3750.00

☐ 21¼" disc, simple walnut case, 10 saucer bells, upright vertical disc arrangement on feet, gallery, double comb (120 teeth), coin operated (also ornate case.) 5000.00 7500.00

☐ 21¼" disc, 10 saucer bells, large upright automatic disc changer, tune selector crank, ornate walnut, fully carved front legs on base, "Symphonion" on glass door (Style 100). Several case variations with and without storage 15,000.00 17,000.00

☐ 25¼" disc, upright floor model, 2 combs in Sublime-Harmonie (192 teeth), sits on storage base, ornate gallery, glass front door on top, carved decoration, 7½' high (also without storage cabinet, on feet) 6000.00 8500.00

☐ 25¼" disc, upright floor model, coin operated, Sublime-Harmonie combs, walnut case with highly carved decoration, storage base 5750.00 6750.00

Price Range

☐ 27½" disc, 12 saucer bells, walnut case, decoration and gallery, on feet, countertop, upright model .... 6000.00 ● 9000.00

☐ **TANNHAUSER,** table model, shifting disc mechanism, two tunes per disc, burled case with corner and base decorative molding .. 3500.00   4000.00

☐ **TROUBADOUR (B. GROSZ & CO., Leipzig, Germany),** 8¾" disc (22 cm), walnut, inlay on lid 600.00   900.00

☐ 8¾" disc, with 4 saucer bells, simple walnut case, figural lithograph inside lid 750.00   1250.00

☐ 9" disc (22.5 cm), simple case with gold decoration, name on cover, outside crank wind (44 teeth) 750.00   1000.00

☐ 9" disc (22.5 cm), with 4 saucer bells, simple case, figural lithograph inside cover (scenic landscape) 800.00   1500.00

☐ 11¾" disc (30 cm), single comb, table model, decorative moulding on base and cover, lithograph inside cover with "TROUBADOUR," (56 teeth), walnut with floral inlay on cover 1000.00   1300.00

☐ 20½" disc, two combs 2000.00   3000.00

MUSIC BOX DISCS

It is rare that one finds a cylinder from an interchangeable box for sale (without the music box) that will fit into a box purchased at some other time and place.

Part of the great appeal of the disc music box was its capacity for almost unlimited tune choices through its interchangeable discs. The more popular disc sizes had the widest variety of tunes. Discs are found for sale all the time. Our section on dealers and restorers is a good source.

The size of the disc and comb determine the length and complexity of the musical arrangement.

Prices for discs are subject to variables like condition, maker, size, tunes, etc. Generally they average about $5–10 each. The more common the size, the lower the value. Of course, demand also plays a big part; for example, a Polyphone 6½" disc brings around $3 each, while a 22" disc with bell accompaniment arrangement is worth around $20.

Musical Christmas Tree Stand, $500.00–$800.00 (Photo courtesy of Mechanical Music Center, Inc.—Darien, CT.)

DISCS FOR MUSIC BOXES
Sampling of current prices for discs:

	Price Range	
ADLER		
7″ disc	2.00	4.00
8¼″ disc	3.00	5.00
10½″ disc	5.00	7.00
14¼ (¾)″ disc ..	7.00	9.00
BRITANNIA		
17⅛″ disc	8.00	12.00
CAPITOL		
7¼″ cuff	15.00	25.00
CRITERION		
15¾ (½)″ disc ..	12.00	17.00
20½″ disc	18.00	24.00
EDELWEISS		
4½″ disc	2.00	4.00
6½″ disc	3.00	5.00
KALLIOPE		
7″ disc	2.00	4.00

	Price Range	
9¾″ disc	3.00	5.00
17¾″ disc	7.00	10.00
20½″ disc	8.00	12.00
KOMET		
10¼″	5.00	8.00
LOCHMAN		
25¾″ disc	17.00	24.00
MIRA		
12″ disc	9.00	13.00
15½″ disc	11.00	14.00
MONOPOL		
8¼ (¾)″ disc ...	4.00	6.00
OLYMPIA		
15¾″ disc	10.00	15.00

Price Range			Price Range		
POLYPHONE			**SYMPHONION**		
6½" disc	2.00	4.00	5¾" disc	2.00	3.00
8¼" disc	3.00	5.00	10" disc	4.00	7.00
9½" disc	4.00	6.00	10⅝" disc	7.00	10.00
11" disc	6.00	8.00	11¾" disc	5.00	8.00
14¼(½)" disc ...	7.00	10.00	13½(¼)" disc ...	6.00	10.00
19⅝" disc	10.00	13.00	20" disc	15.00	20.00
			21¼(½)" disc ...	15.00	17.00
REGINA			Eroica 3-disc sets	50.00	set
15½" disc	5.00	8.00			
20¾ disc	8.00	12.00	**TROUBADOUR**		
27" disc	17.00	24.00	8¾" disc	3.00	
			11¾" disc	6.00	
STELLA					
9¾" disc	10.00	20.00			
17¼" disc	15.00	20.00			
25½" disc	18.00	22.00			

ORGANETTES AND ROLLER ORGANS

The table model Organette industry was fully developed in the 19th century, reaching its peak in the 1880's and 1890's. By the early 20th century it had lost its popularity to other forms of mechanical music.

The organette mechanism is operated by hand cranking either a revolving wooden cob with protruding pins, paper roll (similar to a piano roll), or cardboard (sometimes metal) disc which activates organ reeds by the creation of a vacuum or wind pressure through internal bellows. There are many similar varieties of organettes.

Music for these organs ranged from patriotic to religious, with hymns being the most common. The cobs are not as difficult to locate as the paper rolls and discs. One must rely mainly on mechanical musical auctions and dealer's inventories. Prices vary from $2 each and up. (See "Auctions and Dealers" section.)

	Price Range	
☐ **AMORETTE ORGANETTE,** ebony-finish case, some decoration, plays metal discs (22.5cm) 8¾"	350.00	550.00
☐ **ARIOSA ORGANETTE (SCHMIDT & CO., Leipzig, Germany),** simple case style, ring or donut-like disc (metal or cardboard),		

Price Range

11¾", 18 brass reeds, disc placed off center and extends past case. (Other examples with centered disc, ebony finish cases.) 300.00   600.00

☐ **ARISTON ORGANETTE,** gold case decoration, carved corner decoration, 13" heavy cardboard disc, hand crank, 24 full size organ reeds 375.00   575.00

☐ **ARISTON ORGANETTE,** 22" x 22" case with some decoration, 36 reeds 600.00   1000.00

☐ **AUREPHONE,** casket-type case with cover, stencil decoration, 17 key, 9½" disc (similar to Tournaphone) 600.00   800,00

☐ **AUTOPHONE,** walnut case, bellows operated by hand, 22 reeds, music sheets 475.00   750.00

☐ **AUTOPHONE,** paper strips 5.00   10.00

Chautauqua Roller Organ *(Photo courtesy of Mechanical Music Center, Inc.— Darien, CT.)*

Price Range

☐ **BATES ORGANETTE,** American, c. 1885, plays 14-note paper roll 600.00 1000.00

☐ **BIJOU ORCHESTRONE,** walnut case, top opens to reveal roll mechanism (similar to Celestina and others in appearance), 20 key, 3⅜″ paper roll 300.00 600.00

☐ **CABINETTO ORGANETTE,** casket-style case (cover), gold stencil design, 25 reed, 13¾″ paper roll 400.00 750.00

☐ **CELESTINA ORGANETTE (WILCOX AND WHITE, CT),** walnut case, doors on top fold back to reveal roll mechanism, also control volume, 20 reeds, 5½″ wide paper roll 300.00 500.00

☐ **CHAUTAUQUA ROLLER ORGAN,** walnut case with front glass lift-up door covering cob section (same as the Concert Roller Organ made by Autophone Co., NY), 6½″ cob with metal pins 350.00 700.00

☐ **CHORDEPHON MECHANICAL ZITHER,** #15A, German, plays 14″ discs, flat rectangular base with metal strings in wooden frame on tiny turned legs, clockwork mechanism 1400.00 2500.00

☐ **CLARIONA ORGANETTE,** walnut case 13″ high, open roll assembly, reed pipe device attaches over the roll once it is put in place on top of the organ, it is then covering the roll across the middle, 14 note, 8″ wide paper roll 400.00 700.00

☐ **CONCERT ROLLER ORGAN,** related to Gem but case style different, fully enclosed organ, glass door opens at front top to show cob section, walnut case, gold stencil decoration, 6½″ cob with metal pins. (This organ was sold by many companies under many names, including Sears Roebuck) 400.00 800.00

☐ **CORONET ORGAN,** simple case, 7⅞″ paper roll 300.00 600.00

Gem Roller Organ.

	Price Range	
☐ **EUPHONIA ORGANETTE,** wood base with open roll assembly on each side, valve mechanism in center, 16 key 5¾″ paper roll	350.00	600.00
☐ **GATELY ORGAN,** square casket-style case with expression opening down middle of cover, hand crank, 14 key, 8″ wide roll (similar to Aurephone), walnut, gold decoration	300.00	600.00
☐ **GEM ROLLER ORGAN (AUTOPHONE CO., Ithaca, NY),** walnut case, gold decoration, name on top, cob exposed with valves on one side, bellows on other side, 6½″ long cob with metal pins, hand crank, 20-note organ	350.00	600.00
☐ **GEM ROLLER ORGAN,** also black painted case, sold under other names, e.g., ''Home''	250.00	600.00

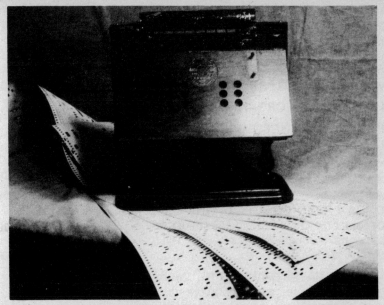

Autophone Paper Strip Organ *(Photo courtesy of Mechanical Music Center, Inc.— Darien, CT.)*

Price Range

☐ **GEM COBS,** wood cylindrical shape with tiny metal pins protruding from surface 5.00   8.00

☐ **GRAND ROLLER ORGAN (AUTOPHONE CO.),** large oak case with lift-up glass-fronted hood on top to reveal 15″ cob (with pins), wooden cylinder, 32-note scale 1200.00   2500.00

☐ **GUITAROPHONE (U.S. Guitar Zither Co.),** mechanical zither plays 14 ½″ metal discs, simple case style, c. 1890's, spring-wind, tiny hammers strike strings (also came coin operated) 1000.00   1500.00

☐ **HARMONETTE ROLLER ORGAN** 300.00   600.00

☐ **HELIKON ORGANETTE,** polished black case, gold decoration, carved corner columns, square case, 16 reeds, hand crank (examples used metal or cardboard discs), similar in appearance to Ariston 300.00   600.00

Price Range

☐ **HEROPHONE (EUPHONIKA, Leipzig, Germany),** black square case, corner decoration, name on side, 24 reeds, square disc (cardboard with metal edges), mechanism revolves under stationary disc 600.00 1000.00

☐ **HOME ROLLER ORGAN** (see "GEM")

☐ **INTONA ORGANETTE (SCHMIDT & CO., Leipzig),** ebony-finish case, "donut"-style disc, 9" hard paper disc, 16 steel reeds (variations in case and disc placement) 450.00 650.00

☐ **MANDOLINA ORGANETTE (MUNROE ORGAN REED CO.),** walnut case with gold decoration, lids on top fold out to reveal paper roll mechanism, 20 key, 5½" roll (very similar to Celestina.) 400.00 600.00

☐ **MANDOLINATA ORGANETTE,** 24 reeds, metal disc, some case decoration, name on side of ebony-finish case with gold decoration, crank operated 600.00 1000.00

☐ **MANOPAN ROLLER ORGAN (EUPHONIKA MUSIKWERKE),** black case with gold decoration, decorative molding and corner columns, cardboard music strips attached to side mechanism 650.00 850.00

☐ **MASCOTTE ORGANETTE,** walnut case, some decoration, roll mechanism in top under lid, 2½" wide roll, 14 keys 400.00 600.00

☐ **McTAMMANY ORGAN,** walnut case, decoration 7¾" continuous "roll" strip is clamped down by top mechanism holding it in place as organ is hand cranked, rollers on each end 500.00 800.00

☐ **MECHANICAL ORGUINETTE,** floor model, when shut looks like a lamp table with velvet top, 25" high, 20-note reed organ, plays 5½" wide paper roll 1000.00 1750.00

☐ **MECHANICAL ORGUINETTE,** floor model, desk shaped, walnut, decorative moldings, 47" high, plays 21½" paper roll, foot pedals 1600.00 2600.00

Price Range

☐ **MELODIA,** walnut case, whole lid lifts up to reveal roll mechanism, 14 reed notes, 7⅞″ (7¾″) paper roll 350.00   550.00

☐ **MIGNON ORGANETTE,** casket-style box with lid, paper roll inside cover, walnut with stencil decoration, hand crank on front, 22 reeds, 5¼″ paper roll 550.00   800.00

☐ **MUSETTE (MECHANICAL ORGUINETTE CO.),** walnut case with stencil decoration, 16 key, 3½″ wide paper roll (very similar to Celestina) 400.00   600.00

☐ **MUSICAL CASKET ORGANETTE (ME-CHANICAL ORGUINETTE CO.),** decorated case, front lid lifts up to reveal paper roll mechanism, 14 key, 7¾″ wide roll 300.00   500.00

☐ **ORCHESTRAL ORGANETTE,** painted case decoration, button stops, 8″ wide roll, 14 reeds 400.00   600.00

☐ **ORGANINA (MASSACHUSETTS ORGAN CO.),** rounded glass front, elaborate gold-painted decoration all over walnut case, 11″ high small box, 16 key, 8¼″ wide continuous paper strip 300.00   500.00

☐ **ORGANITA ROLLER ORGAN,** table model, walnut case with rounded segmented top, 14-note organ plays multiple tune paper strip, volume control button on top of case 300.00   550.00

☐ **ORGUINETTE PAPER ROLL ORGAN (ME-CHANICAL ORGUINETTE CO.),** long paper strips feed through a mechanism holding it in place (McTammany style), as it is cranked: there are spools on each end 350.00   600.00

☐ **ORPHEUS MECHANICAL ZITHER,** hand crank mechanism uses Ariston organette discs, ebony-finish case in shape of miniature grand piano, 34″ long, 22 strings, plays 13″ cardboard disc (24 notes) 2000.00   3500.00

Price Range

☐ **PHOENIX ORGANETTE,** decorated case with corner columns, "donut" ring type metal disc, 14½", 24 reeds, hand crank 500.00   700.00

☐ **PIANOLODEON (Child's Toy),** In the shape of a miniature upright player piano, 30 keys, plays paper rolls, plastic case (gold decoration on either red mahogany or beige plastic) 100.00   275.00

☐ **PIANO MELODICO ORGANETTE,** German, string instrument, with hand crank, ebony case, plays music books 600.00   1000.00

☐ **PLA ROLA ORGAN (Pla Rola Manufacturing Co., Easton, PA),** red and gold painted metal, 5⅛" long, plays paper rolls, 4¼" wide 50.00   150.00

☐ **Q-R-S PLAY-A-SAX (CLAROLA),** shaped like a miniature saxophone, pot metal painted gold, sounds like a harmonica, 16-note paper roll, one blows into mouth piece and cranks rolls at the same time, 1930–38 .... 100.00   250.00

☐ **ROLMONICA,** mouth organ in a bakelite case (various colors) with a paper roll mechanism, when one blows into mouthpiece and cranks roll, harmonica tunes are played, separate rewind crank, case is 4" x 3⅝", 1930–38 ... 75.00   150.00

☐ **ROLMONICA,** paper rolls 5.00   8.00

☐ **SERAPHONE,** cabinet base 11" high, center top lid lifts up to reveal roll mechanism, 20 key, 3½" paper roll 400.00   600.00

☐ **SONORA ORGANETTE (SCHMIDT & Co., Leipzig),** vertical case, carved columns with finials and gallery, decorated, "donut"-style ring discs, hand crank 700.00   1000.00

☐ **SYMPHONIA (WILCOX AND WHITE),** walnut case lid opens to reveal roll mechanism, 20 key, 5⅛" roll (similar in style to Celestina) 300.00   600.00

☐ **TANZBAR PLAYER ACCORDION (PLAYER CONCERTINA),** square ebony-finish case with decorative nickel trim (other case

Price Range

variations, some with inlay), 9″ x 11″ x 11″, concertina works manually, one end opens to reveal roll housing, plays 4¼″ wide paper rolls **475.00** **800.00**

☐ **TOURNAPHONE ORGAN,** casket-type case with expression shutter in cover, 25 reeds, 13¾″ paper roll **575.00** **675.00**

☐ **TOURNAPHONE CONSOLE,** with storage in bottom **775.00** **875.00**

☐ **TRIOLA (MECHANICAL ZITHER),** operates by a paper roll, manual bass accompaniment, some decoration on wood case **2000.00** **3000.00**

SMALL BARREL ORGANS

Small portable barrel organs were popular well into the 20th century. They had, by that time, been around for over a century, though they did show signs of decline as early as 1900.

A barrel organ operates by means of a wooden cylinder with protruding metal pins (arranged for several tunes) by activating the bank of organ pipes as the mechanism is hand cranked. There are also special effects like "piccolos," "flutes," "trumpets," etc.

The organ is carried through the streets supported by a strong shoulder strap, center support post, or moving stand.

One must rely mainly on special mechanical musical auctions and dealers, as these organs are rare.

Price Range

☐ **BACIGALUPO ORGAN,** many case variations, painted decorations, grill and cloth variations, white case, red cloth, painted flowers, decorative grill **3500.00** **6500.00**

☐ **BACIGALUPO BARREL ORGAN,** 47 key, 4 stops, plays 8 tunes, c. 1920's, ornately decorated **3750.00** **5000.00**

☐ **BACIGALUPO HARMON PAN BARREL ORGAN,** 25 keys, 8 tunes, straight wood case painted with floral decorations, view pipes from top cut out, crank wind, 17″ wide **4000.00** **6000.00**

Bacigalupo Harmon Pan Barrel Organ.

Price Range

☐ **E. BOECKER BARREL ORGAN,** Harmonipan, 33 key, 19 caned flutes on front, 8 tune barrel, decorated case, 27″ long by 26″ wide   4500.00   6500.00

☐ **BRODERIP & WILKINSON BARREL ORGAN,** c. 1825, Regency style mahogany case, simple lines, decoration on legs, 57″ high, faux giltwood pipes on decorated front panel 600.00   1000.00

☐ **BRUDER BARREL ORGAN,** 48 key, 9 tune barrel (36″ wide), trumpet pipes, case 58″ high 4000.00   5750.00

Price Range

☐ **BRUDER PORTABLE BARREL ORGAN,** 26 note, 8 tune, 4 stops, rosewood veneer case, inlaid decoration, floral marquetry, c. 1910 ... **1250.00** **2500.00**

☐ **CHIAPPA & SONS BARREL ORGAN,** table size, 36 key, 10 tune, 37″ high, brass trumpets, piccolos, flutes **3000.00** **4000.00**

☐ **ENGLISH STREET PIANO,** spring barrel operated, maple case, one cent coin operated, c. 1915, 10 tune barrel **2000.00** **2500.00**

☐ **FRATI & CO. BARREL ORGAN (Berlin),** decorated case, mirror front, copper medallions, 24″ high metal pipes, wooden roller cylinder **3000.00** **4500.00**

☐ **FRATI "MONKEY ORGAN,"** plays Mexican tunes **2500.00** **3500.00**

☐ **FRATI & CO., CORONETINA,** 2′ square "monkey" organ, 10 exposed brass coronets, 61 pipes, 33 key, hand crank barrel movement, case decoration **7500.00** **9500.00**

☐ **FRENCH BARREL ORGAN,** 15 key, 10 tune barrel (15″ wide), walnut case, 18½″ high, 53 pipes, 4 ranks **1500.00** **3000.00**

☐ **GAVIOLI BARREL ORGAN,** hurdy-gurdy type, highly decorated case with inlay **3000.00** **4000.00**

☐ **GAVIOLI & CIE (Paris) FLUTE ORGAN,** portable barrel organ, 36-key mechanism, 9 tunes, rosewood veneer case, with inlaid floral and other marquetry and painted decoration, red cloth covered openings, hand crank **6500.00** **8000.00**

☐ **GERMAN BARREL ORGAN,** c. 1866, simple grained pine case, 6-tune barrel, plays reeds and pipes **750.00** **1200.00**

☐ **J. KAMENIK–PRAHA BARREL REED ORGAN,** portable, simple wood case with fretwork panel, 17½″ wide **1500.00** **2000.00**

Price Range

☐ **G. MOLINARI & SONS (NY),** c. 1898, flute hand organ, 23 key, 7 tune, small size carried with shoulder strap, fancy front panels, inlay decoration on black walnut case (also 9 tune, 24 key with 10 tune) 2500.00   3500.00

☐ **G. MOLINARI & SONS,** flute and trumpet hand organ, flower and scroll case decoration, otherwise much like the above, 32 and 34 key, 8 tune, 8 trumpets (also 37 and 42 key, 8 tune, 12 trumpets), slightly larger case than above 4500.00   5500.00

☐ **D. POIROT OF PARIS STREET BARREL ORGAN,** 35 key, 65 flute pipes, 9 tunes, 35½″ high 3250.00   4750.00

☐ **SPANISH BARREL PIANO,** 18″ high on two-wheeled cart, 6-tune 10″ barrel, wood block, triangle, decorated case and cart, hand crank on front 500.00   800.00

☐ **WREDE VIOLINO–PAN BARREL ORGAN,** 26 key, 8 tune barrel, 14 pipes in view, floral decoration, sits on corner moldings (feet), metal trim, hand crank 5000.00   8000.00

☐ **ZIMMERMAN HURDY-GURDY (Leipzig),** some case decoration, shoulder strap, 11 brass piccolo pipes, small size 2750.00   3750.00

☐ **BARREL ORGAN,** maker unknown, 32 key portable, plays 8 tunes, green-painted case, elaborate floral and musical decoration all over case, hand crank, 20 visible flutes, 24″ wide 2000.00   3000.00

PHONOGRAPHS—CYLINDER AND DISC TYPE

The development of the tinfoil phonograph in the late 1870's by Thomas Edison was the beginning of what was to become a dynamic new home entertainment industry. Momentum grew steadily, but it wasn't until the late 1890's that the industry really got underway. In the late '20's and '30's the radio and, later, television made a real dent in its popularity. In spite of that the "record player" survives today and is a highly sophisticated machine. This guide covers the period from the 1890's to around 1930 when the phonograph was a beautiful, much simpler machine and a leader in the home entertainment field.

The capacity of the phonograph and recorded sound to entertain were unlimited, unlike any other type of mechanical machine. Everything was recorded on records quite early on, from all kinds of music and singing to speeches, vaudeville sketches, and language courses. Even blank cylinders were supplied to record your own performance.

It is a long, complex, fascinating history that requires volumes to tell. See "Further Reading," "Publications and Reprints," and "Mechanical Musical Societies" sections.

Phonographs can still be found at local sales, antique shops, flea markets, local auctions, and shows. The rarer examples are sometimes advertised for sale in the phonograph publications. (See section on "Publications and Reprints".) Occasionally they will come up for sale at special auctions when a collector sells his treasures.

Note: Many descriptions of phonograph models indicate either a metal or wood horn. Unless otherwise noted, a wood horn will increase the value of a phonograph by $175–$300. The condition of the horn is very important, especially the veneer. (These are models that came originally with either type of horn.)

AMERICAN GRAPHOPHONE CO., see COLUMBIA PHONOGRAPH CO.

	Price Range	
APOLLO		
☐ APOLLO (disc), table model, plain oak case, outside blue fluted metal (painted) horn, crank wind, plays 78rpm records, Apollo, Jr. reproducer (sound box), European maker ..	260.00	360.00
☐ APOLLO FLOOR MODEL (disc), highly styled fruitwood case, curved legs, storage for records, cover lifts to reveal turntable, nickel-plated exposed parts, European maker	285.00	385.00
APOLLOPHONE, see section on player pianos.		
ADLER		
☐ ADLER (Disc), "box camera"-style portable, tone arm fits into opening in cover, "horn" is drawer in the cover which opens out on one side to form a horn, turntable is three spokes which open out to hold record, hand crank, 7" x 4" x 7"	125.00	200.00

Price Range

ARETINO
☐ ARETINO (disc), table model, rear-mount horn bracket, 3″ spindle, Morning Glory horn   250.00   500.00

AUX-E-TO-PHONE (Auxeto-Gramophone)
☐ AUX-E-TO-PHONE, c. 1903 (disc), sold in U.S. by Victor, mahogany floor cabinet with carved and gold decoration, uncovered 12″ turntable on top with outside brass bell horn, operates on Electro-Pneumatic principle, reed sound box, motor drive, triple spring (simpler case variations) 2300.00   3600.00

BEBE JUMEAU TALKING DOLL (see "Lioret")

(EMILE) BERLINER GRAM-O-PHONES (Canada) F.L.
☐ BERLINER "STANDARD" GRAM-O-PHONE TYPE A (disc), simple oak case on wood base, top crank wind, 7″ turntable, plays 7″ and 10″ Berliner records, brass bell horn 16″ long, nickel-plated metal parts, metal horn support with wood "tone arm," reproducer attached at end of tone arm and horn (Clark/Johnson reproducer), very similar to Victor Type "B" trademark machine 1400.00   2600.00

☐ BERLINER "IDEAL" TYPE B (disc), oak case with heavy base and top molding, side crank wind, double spring, 7″ turntable, plays 7″ and 10″ records, 16″ brass bell horn, nickel-plated metal parts, wood and metal horn support and "tone arm" 1000.00   1300.00

☐ BERLINER "GRAND" TYPE C (disc), oak case with heavy base molding, double spring, side crank wind, 10″ turntable with nickel-plated exposed metal parts, 21″ brass bell horn, wood "tone arm" and metal horn support 1000.00   1350.00

☐ BERLINER "BIJOU" TYPE E (disc), small oak case, base molding, single spring, 7″ turntable plays 7″ and 10″ records, 16″ brass bell horn, nickel-plated metal parts, metal horn support and wood "tone arm" 750.00   1200.00

Price Range

BOSTON TALKING MACHINE CO.
☐ BOSTON TALKING MACHINE CO. (disc), "Little Wonder Disc Phonograph," cast iron case and horn, tone arm comes out from center of 6 sided horn, rests on rear mount bracket, 6½" turntable, single spring, records must have vertical cut grooves, plays "Little Wonder" discs, c. 1909–12 .... 125.00   200.00

BRUNSWICK-BALKE-COLLENDER CO.
☐ BRUNSWICK (disc), "The Beaux Arts," console floor model deluxe, walnut case, decorative molding, electrically powered, turntable on one side, storage for discs on the other, on legs, 45" high (Brunswick made many period cabinet styles) 325.00   475.00

☐ BRUNSWICK, c. 1921 (disc), mahogany table model, plain square-sided case, rotating reproducer plays both lateral and vertical groove records, 11¾" turntable 100.00   200.00

☐ BRUNSWICK MODEL 105 (disc), table model, c. 1921, mahogany case, 19½" high, two-headed reproducer will play both lateral and vertical cut record, 11¾" turntable, simple rectangular case style with cover, oval fretwork grill, crank wind 140.00   240.00

☐ BRUNSWICK (disc), upright model 135, 49" high, mahogany (or walnut), decorative front grill, doors beneath phonograph contain storage for discs, hand crank. (There were several similar models with varying degrees of decorative details, in oak, black lacquer, mahogany and walnut) 150.00   250.00

☐ BRUNSWICK MODEL 200, c. 1923 (disc), floor model oak (mahogany) disc phonograph, oval grill opening with fretwork, storage in base for discs, 12" turntable, reproducer head rotates to play either lateral or vertical cut records (inside horn). Case variations in floor models 75.00   200.00

Price Range

BUSY-BEE O'NEIL-JAMES (Chicago)
☐ BUSY-BEE GRAND, c. 1905 (disc), oak, simple case table model with front-mount horn support for large 8-petal Morning Glory horn (red or blue with gold), reproducer attached at end of horn (no "tone arm"), plays Busy-Bee records only. (Some variation in placement of horn and bracket and decal.) 320.00   500.00

☐ BUSY-BEE "QUEEN," c. 1906 (cylinder), oak case, plain, lyric reproducer, small ribbed horn (also front crane supported ribbed horn), Busy-Bee decal on front (see Columbia Jewel "Type BK") 320.00   420.00

☐ BUSY-BEE "NEW" (cylinder), key wind, plays Busy-Bee cylinder records, open works, small cylinder machine on small metal base, 13½″ horn with bell (see also Columbia Type "Q" first series) 160.00   310.00

CAMERAPHONE
☐ CAMERAPHONE (disc), very small portable phonograph in the shape of an old box camera, leather-covered case, simulated tortoiseshell (resonator), horn, metal spoke turntable fold out, very compact, good volume (variations in case, some wood, some covered in black material), plays 78 rpm discs 145.00   190.00

CAPITOL PHONO LAMP
☐ CAPITOL PHONO LAMP (disc), metal base large table lamp, fringed shade opens up to reveal disc turntable and tone arm 500.00   1200.00

CARYOLA HAT BOX PHONOGRAPH
☐ CARYOLA HAT BOX PHONOGRAPH (disc), flat style rounded case portable disc phonograph, small horn 65.00   125.00

COLIBRE
☐ COLIBRE "BOX CAMERA" PORTABLE (disc), black metal case 90.00   140.00

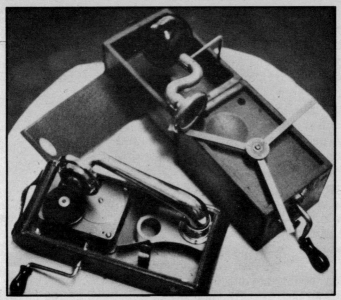

Thorens Excelda Cameraphone.

COLUMBIA DISC GRAPHOPHONE

THE TYPE YOU SEE ADVERTISED EVERYWHERE

The Columbia Disc Graphophone is an inexhaustible and universal entertainer which is particularly appropriate for

<u>A HOLIDAY</u>

<u>PRESENT</u>

It will make home delightful and afford no end of pleasure, from the coming CHRISTMAS until the next one. It is always ready; does not get out of order, and the variety of records used on it is endless— songs, instrumental solos, orchestral and band pieces, amusing stories, etc.

Columbia Disc Graphophones are superior to all others. Our FLAT, INDESTRUCTIBLE RECORDS are composed of a material controlled EXCLUSIVELY by us. They are the sweetest, smoothest and most brilliant records ever heard. Until you listen to them you can form no accurate idea of the progress that has been made in bringing the disc records to the point of perfection. Their excellence is fully equaled by their durability.

The Disc Graphophone is made in three types, selling at $15, $20, and $30
7-inch Records, 50 cents each ; $5 per dozen   10-inch Records, $1 each ; $10 per dozen

COLUMBIA HIGH SPEED MOULDED RECORDS fit all makes and all types of talking machines using cylindrical records and are superior to all others. Send for Catalogue. Sold by Dealers Everywhere and by the

COLUMBIA PHONOGRAPH COMPANY
Pioneers and Leaders in the Talking Machine Art
(GRAND PRIZE—PARIS, 1900)

NEW YORK: Wholesale and Retail, 93 Chambers St.; Retail only, 573 Fifth Ave.

BOSTON: 164 Tremont St.	SAN FRANCISCO: 125 Geary St.	BUFFALO: 645 Main St.
MINNEAPOLIS: 13 Fourth St., S.	CHICAGO: 88 Wabash Ave.	PARIS: 34 Boulevard des Italiens
BALTIMORE: 110 E. Baltimore St.	DETROIT: 37 Grand River Ave.	LONDON: 122 Oxford St., W.
PHILADELPHIA: 1609 Chestnut St.	WASHINGTON: 1212 F St., N. W.	BERLIN: 65-A Friedrichstrasse
PITTSBURG: 615 Penn Ave.	ST. LOUIS: 709 Pine St.	

Price Range

COLUMBIA PHONOGRAPH COMPANY, NY (Columbia Graphophones and Grafonolas) COLUMBIA MODELS are listed alphabetically. If a model has a name and type designation, then the name takes precedence over the type. All entries have cross references; e.g., Columbia Type BII (see Columbia Improved Sterling).

☐ COLUMBIA TYPE A, c. 1897 (cylinder), oak case and cover (plain), nickel-plated and black-painted metal parts with gold and red decoration, open-ended mandrel, small-belled horn, plays 2-minute cylinder records, "Graphophone" decal, black reproducer, early version made in Washington, later in New York 290.00   400.00

☐ COLUMBIA TYPE AA, c. 1901 (cylinder), small case, ornate moldings, oak, large ribbon decal, exposed mechanism nickel-plated, horizontally placed reproducer, 14" horn with bell, Eagle reproducer 275.00   375.00

Columbia Disc Phonograph, type AJ.

Columbia Business Cylinder Phonograph Dictaphone.

Price Range

☐ COLUMBIA TYPE AB, "McDonald Graphophone" (cylinder), open works, key wind,
mounted on oak base (fancy molding and
decoration), plays regular 2-minute cylinders
and 5″ Grand cylinders, 5″ mandrel fits over
the smaller one, nickel-plated works and
belled horn, Heavy Eagle (later Model "D" reproducer) 700.00   1200.00

Price Range

☐ COLUMBIA TYPE AD, c. 1901 (cylinder), oak "Home Grand" cabinet, plays regular 2-minute cylinders and Grand cylinders, 5" mandrel fits over 2" mandrel, nickel-plated works, six spring motor (very, very rare) (see Columbia Home Grand for case description) — **950.00 1400.00**

☐ COLUMBIA TYPE AF, (cylinder), plays concert and regular cylinders **2000.00 3000.00**

☐ COLUMBIA TYPE AG (see Grand AG and Concert Grand AG).

☐ COLUMBIA TYPE AH (disc), highly decorative case design (moldings top and bottom, corner columns, brass handles on sides), side mount detachable horn bracket, horn and reproducer attached at end of bracket, 22" brass bell horn, "analyzing" reproducer. ("Columbia" cut-out design in horn bracket.) — **575.00 900.00**

☐ COLUMBIA TYPE AJ, c. 1903–1905 (disc), fancy front-mount aluminum tone arm/horn bracket, black horn with brass bell, oak case with highly decorative moldings and rounded corner columns, side wind, carrying handles — **425.00 725.00**

☐ COLUMBIA TYPE AK (disc), oak case, heavy molding and decoration, ribbon decal, wood and metal horn bracket, reproducer and horn attached at end of bracket, 16" black bell horn, raised turntable, "analyzing" reproducer **375.00 700.00**

☐ COLUMBIA TYPE AN (cylinder), installed in a desk-style cabinet with rounded top lid which opens to reveal the phonograph set into the surface of the desk, 8 storage drawers with pegs for cylinder records (holds 200 cylinders) **2000.00 3000.00**

☐ COLUMBIA TYPE AO, c. 1902 (cylinder), highly ornate case, heavy carved moldings, triple spring, "D" type reproducer (later case variations) **350.00 450.00**

☐ COLUMBIA TYPE AQ Second Series, c. 1903 (cylinder), long tapering trivet-type base that also acts as part of horn support, small horn, key wind, simple mechanism plays 2-minute

Columbia "Baby Grand"-Shaped Disc Phonograph, floor model.

Price Range

cylinders, Model "D" reproducer (Columbia produced this for Sears Roebuck, called the "Oxford Junior") 260.00   360.00

☐ COLUMBIA TYPE AR (disc), similar to Columbia type AY but with single spring motor ... 350.00   450.00

☐ COLUMBIA TYPE AS, coin operated (see Coin Operated Phonographs).

Price Range

☐ COLUMBIA TYPE AT, c. 1898 (cylinder), oak case, decorative molding along top edge, corner columns, ribbon decal, nickel-plated mechanism (also black with gold decoration), double spring, Eagle Aluminum Reproducer, High Trunion Model c. 1903, oak case, decorative corner moldings, new style "D" reproducer, 14″ bell aluminum horn with bell, reproducer sits in horizontal position over cylinder 300.00   575.00

☐ COLUMBIA TYPE AU, c. 1903 (disc), open works mounted on base, 7″ (6¾″) turntable, 16″ metal horn with bell, horn support and metal "tone arm," reproducer attached at end of horn (see also Standard Talking Machine) 280.00   380.00

☐ COLUMBIA TYPE AW, c. 1903 (cylinder), triple spring, ornately decorated case with corner columns, 14″ aluminum horn (bell), base molding, types AO and AW are essentially the same except the AW has a different reproducer (greater volume) 575.00   1300.00

☐ COLUMBIA TYPE AZ, c. 1905 (cylinder), simple straight case style, plain base and top molding, "Graphophone" decal, lyric reproducer, plays 2-minute cylinder records 275.00   375.00

☐ COLUMBIA TYPE B, c. 1894 (see Columbia Eagle).

☐ COLUMBIA BABY GRAND (Type G) (cylinder), oak case, simple straight design, no decal, black reproducer attached from above facing down onto cylinder plays 2-minute cylinder records 575.00   750.00

☐ COLUMBIA "BABY GRAND"-SHAPED PHONOGRAPH (disc), floor model, mahogany, vertical louvered "speaker," curved Queen Anne–type legs (3), lid lifts up to reveal turntable 1800.00   2800.00

☐ COLUMBIA BABY REGENT (REGENT JR.) (disc), inside horn phonograph built into a squarish shaped mahogany table with four

Price Range

carved cabriole legs, drawer pulls out to reveal turntable, inside horn has louvered speaker 575.00   1150.00

☐ COLUMBIA TYPE BC (see Columbia Twentieth Century).

☐ COLUMBIA TYPE BD (see Columbia Majestic).

☐ COLUMBIA TYPE BE (see Columbia Leader).

☐ COLUMBIA TYPE BET (see Columbia New Invincible).

☐ COLUMBIA TYPE BF (see Columbia Peerless).

☐ COLUMBIA TYPE BFT (see Columbia New Peerless).

☐ COLUMBIA TYPE BG (see Columbia Sovereign).

☐ COLUMBIA TYPE BGT (see Columbia New Sovereign).

☐ COLUMBIA TYPE BH (see Columbia Champion).

☐ COLUMBIA TYPE BI (see Columbia Sterling).

☐ COLUMBIA TYPE BII (see Columbia Improved Sterling).

☐ COLUMBIA BIJOU (type AN, N), c. 1895–97 (cylinder), simple case style, oak, large ribbon decal, nickel-plated mechanism, black reproducer, plays 2-minute cylinders, small horn   400.00   600.00

☐ COLUMBIA TYPE BJ (see Columbia Imperial).

☐ COLUMBIA TYPE BK (see Columbia Jewel).

☐ COLUMBIA TYPE BKT (see Columbia New Leader).

☐ COLUMBIA TYPE BM (see Columbia Home Premier).

☐ COLUMBIA TYPE BN (see Columbia Improved Champion).

☐ COLUMBIA TYPE BNW (see Columbia Improved Royal).

☐ COLUMBIA TYPE BO (see Columbia Invincible).

Columbia Disc Phonograph, "Baby Regent."

Price Range

☐ COLUMBIA TYPE BQ (see Columbia Rex).

☐ COLUMBIA TYPE BS, coin operated (see Coin Operated Phonographs).

☐ COLUMBIA BUSINESS Graphophones (see Columbia Universal Type C).

☐ COLUMBIA TYPE BV (see Columbia Royal).

☐ COLUMBIA TYPE BVT, c. 1908 (cylinder), rear-mount horn and tapering tone arm (aluminum) version of Type BV (Royal). See entry on the Columbia Royal for further description. Sears Roebuck sold a model like this under the name Oxford Talking Machine 750.00   900.00

Price Range

☐ COLUMBIA TYPE BX (cylinder), c. 1897, key-wind mechanism, open works, rectangular oak base, domed lid, black painted tin horn   **400.00**   **1000.00**

☐ COLUMBIA TYPE BY (see Columbia Improved Imperial).

☐ COLUMBIA TYPE C, c. 1897, oak case, triple-spring movement with a 6¼" mandrel, amplifying reproducer, egg-and-dart decoration, domed lid, black horn **300.00**   **370.00**

☐ COLUMBIA "COLONIAL" ROUND TABLE DISC PHONOGRAPH, floor model in the shape of a round center pedestal table, pull-out drawer to reveal turntable, mahogany, c. 1912, hand crank **900.00**   **1600.00**

☐ COLUMBIA CONCERT GRAND TYPE AG (cylinder), oak case, decorative corners and top molding, plays both regular and grand cylinders, 5" diameter mandrel fits over regular 2" mandrel, nickel-plated mechanism, black and gold decorated parts, recorder. Some examples installed in desk style cabinet (See Columbia Type AN for full description) **700.00**   **1500.00**

☐ COLUMBIA DESK TABLE (see Columbia Regent).

☐ COLUMBIA DRUM TABLE (see Columbia Baby Regent).

☐ COLUMBIA EAGLE TYPE B, c. 1897, cylinder, open works mounted on oak base with cover, nickel-plated mechanism, "Graphophone" decal on cover, double spring, plays 2-minute wax cylinders, Aluminum Eagle Reproducer, small black horn (no bell) or ear tubes **225.00**   **450.00**

☐ COLUMBIA ELITE (disc), table model mahogany square shaped inside-horn style, front grill flaps forward for volume control, top cover, aluminum tone arm, plays 78rpm records **90.00**   **145.00**

☐ COLUMBIA TYPE G (see Columbia Baby Grand).

Price Range

☐ COLUMBIA TYPE GG (see Columbia Grand).

☐ COLUMBIA GRAFONOLA, c. 1920's (disc), "Jacobean style," floor model in antique oak finish, vertical louvered adjustable grill, record storage in base cabinet, decorative moldings and finish, bulbous short legs and stretchers (many period style variations) ... 160.00 250.00

☐ COLUMBIA GRAFONOLA, c. mid-1920's (disc), table model inside horn, plain mahogany (oak) case, plays 78rpm discs, louvered grill volume control, nickel-plated metal parts 90.00 180.00

☐ COLUMBIA GRAFONOLA DELUXE (disc), Regina Music Box and Columbia Disc Phonograph combination (see also Reginaphone

Columbia Granfonola, records were stored in bottom cabinet. To select a desired record, the listener pushes the correct button and the record pops out (Photo courtesy of Mechanical Music Center, Inc.—Darien, CT.)

Price Range

Style #240), floor model 48½" high, inside horn, mahogany disc phonograph with a 15½" disc music box mechanism, storage in base for discs and records, top front section is decorated with fully carved lion's head on claw-feet columns, one on each side of speaker area, aluminum tone arm, serpentine curved case style ....

no music box
175.00   2750.00
with music box
3850.00   4850.00

....

☐ COLUMBIA GRAFONOLA FLOOR MODEL (disc), inside horn, floor model disc phonograph, plain case, oak (mahogany), storage for records in base, triple spring (many case variations) 100.00   200.00

☐ COLUMBIA GRAFONOLA REGENT (see Columbia Regent).

☐ COLUMBIA GRAFONOLA TYPE A-2 (disc), table model, inside horn, horizontal louvers cover "Speaker grill" (control volume), no cover 90.00   175.00

☐ COLUMBIA GRAFONOLA TYPE C-Z & D-Z (disc), table models similar to A-2 with covers   90.00   175.00

☐ COLUMBIA GRAFONOLA TYPE L-2 (disc), upright floor model inside horn, door below turntable for record storage, mahogany (oak or walnut), record ejector system, vertical louvers over "speaker," plated metal parts, elaborate case decoration. Other Grafonola models in this series with varying degrees of case decoration and details, some without ejector system 325.00   425.00

☐ COLUMBIA GRAFONOLA TYPE #22A (disc), table model, oak, triple spring, rectangular case style of simple lines, base molding and horizontal louvered shutters over "speaker," hand crank 65.00   110.00

☐ COLUMBIA GRAFONOLA TYPE #25A (disc), c. 1920's, floor model, oak, 39½" high, triple spring, Garrand motor, 12" turntable, tone arm rotates on ball bearings, #7 repro-

Price Range

ducer, automatic brake, simple straight case lines, 5 shelf storage for discs, vertically louvered speaker grill 115.00 225.00

☐ COLUMBIA GRAPHOPHONE MODEL B 1 (disc), rear-mount outside-horn table model, 8-petal Morning Glory horn, decorative corner and base moldings, crank wind, nickel metal fittings and horn 800.00 1000.00

☐ COLUMBIA GRAPHOPHONE MODEL Bn (disc), oak outside horn table model, 11 petal Morning Glory, simple case style, rear-mount horn bracket and tone arm 600.00 925.00

☐ COLUMBIA GRAND (Type AG) (cylinder), oak case (similar to Type AT) decorative top, corner and base moldings, large ribbon decal, 5″ diameter mandrel plays Grand cylinders, black painted exposed metal parts, gold decoration, type "D" reproducer (Heavy Eagle Reproducer) 900.00 1900.00

☐ COLUMBIA GRAND (Type GG), c. 1898 (cylinder), oak, carved moldings all over base, side and top of case and cover, plays 5″ Grand cylinders, hinged front panel folds down, triple spring, black painted metal parts with gold decoration, Heavy Eagle Reproducer 700.00 1400.00

☐ COLUMBIA TYPE HG (see Columbia High Grand).

☐ COLUMBIA HIGH TRUNION (Type AT) (see Type AT).

☐ COLUMBIA HIGH GRAND (Type HG), c. 1899 (cylinders), highly decorated moldings all over base, top and sides and cover, corner columns, plays 5″ Grand cylinders, black metal exposed mechanism decorated with flowers, double spring, nickel plated metal parts, Heavy Eagle Reproducer (or Model "D" reproducer) 900.00 1800.00

☐ COLUMBIA HOME PREMIER (Type BM), c. 1906 (cylinder), in "Sovereign" mahogany case, 3″ diameter Higham Reproducer, Quadruple spring 900.00 1800.00

Price Range

☐ COLUMBIA IMPERIAL (Type BJ) (disc), single spring, 3 records on one winding. Otherwise same as Majestic Type BD 400.00   900.00

☐ COLUMBIA IMPROVED CHAMPION (Type BN) (disc), table model, simple lines, corners, base and top moldings, rear mounted horn, ribbed "floral horn," black with gold lines (nickel or wood), double spring, 10″ turntable, needle clamp, decal; profile of rear-mount outside horn phonograph with the word "Columbia" inside it 550.00   800.00

☐ COLUMBIA IMPROVED IMPERIAL (Type BY) (disc), mahogany case with curved sides and rounded corners and moldings, serpentine-style four spring motor, 12″ turntable with nickel trim edge, tone arm and elbow nickel plated, needle clamp, 23¾″ long Morning Glory nickel-plated (or mahogany) horn 900.00   1800.00

☐ COLUMBIA IMPROVED ROYAL (Type BNW) (disc), oak case with straight simple lines, heavy base with top moldings, outside horn, table model, 78rpm disc phonograph, double spring, nickel-plated tone arm, 9-petal black ribbed Morning Glory horn, black ribbed floral horn with gold lines (or nickel or wood), 10″ turntable, needle clamp, "silhouette" (profile) Columbia decal, rear-mount horn 350.00   650.00

☐ COLUMBIA IMPROVED STERLING (Type BII) (disc), table model, rear-mount outside Morning Glory horn, 78rpm disc phonograph, oak case with heavy base and top moldings, corner columns, tone arm, 9-petal ribbed oak horn, 10″ turntable, nickel-plated exposed metal parts 375.00   625.00

☐ COLUMBIA INVINCIBLE (Type BO), c. 1907 (cylinder), table model, oak, unusual case decoration (long oval cutouts in oak veneer on sides of case), ribbon "Graphophone" decal, rear-mount Morning Glory horn with tapered aluminum tone arm, plays 2-minute cyl-

Price Range

inders, 6″ long mandrel, triple spring, nickel-plated mechanism, lyric reproducer in horizontal position **625.00** **800.00**

☐ COLUMBIA JEWEL (Type BK), c. 1906 (cylinder), oak simple case, ribbon "Graphophone" decal, 14″ horn with bell (or front crane with ribbed horn), crane screws to base of case, lyric reproducer for 2-minute cylinders, exposed metal parts are either nickel plated or black with gold decoration (also made as 2- and 4-minute combination with Columbia Indestructible Reproducer for the 4-minute cylinders) **475.00** **775.00**

☐ COLUMBIA TYPE K (disc), front-mount outside horn, 10″ turntable, brass belled horn **475.00** **800.00**

☐ COLUMBIA LAMP TABLE (disc) (see Columbia Baby Regent).

☐ COLUMBIA LANGUAGE PHONE (cylinder) (see Columbia "Q" Second Series).

☐ COLUMBIA LEADER (Type BE), c. 1906 (cylinder), oak case, decorative corners, base and top moldings, triple spring, 14″ horn with brass bell, ribbon "GRAPHOPHONE" decal, lyric reproducer and recorder **230.00** **515.00**

☐ COLUMBIA MAJESTIC (Type BD) (disc), solid mahogany table model, rounded smooth case style, molding on top and base and corners, heavy-duty spring motor, aluminum tone arm, 12″ turntable, rear-mounted 23¾″ long Morning Glory horn (nickel plated), "analyzing" reproducer, automatic needle clamp **380.00** **800.00**

☐ COLUMBIA–McDONALD GRAPHOPHONE (see Columbia Type AB).

☐ COLUMBIA TYPE N (see Bijou).

☐ COLUMBIA NEW INVINCIBLE (Type BET), c. 1907 (cylinder), Case style like the "Leader Type BE" with the addition of the rear-mounted horn and tapering tone arm (aluminum), nickel plated and black with gold details, metal parts, nickel Morning Glory horn (or wood), plays 2- and 4-minute cylinders (In-

Columbia Cylinder Phonograph, type BE, "Leader."

Price Range

destructible 4-minute cylinders played with the Indestructible Reproducer, lyric reproducer for the 2-minute wax cylinders) 350.00   625.00

☐ COLUMBIA NEW LEADER (Type BKT), c. 1907 (cylinder), case like the "Jewel" Type BK but with a rear-mounted Morning Glory horn and tapered aluminum tone arm, double spring, plays 2- and 4-minute cylinder rec-

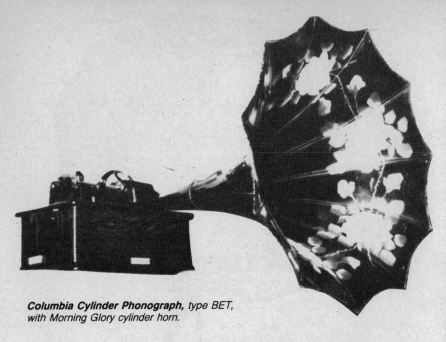

Columbia Cylinder Phonograph, type BET, with Morning Glory cylinder horn.

Price Range

ords, horn is black with gold lines, nickel or wood, ribbon decal, lyric reproducer for 2-minute wax cylinders 475.00 800.00

☐ COLUMBIA NEW PEERLESS (Type BFT), c. 1907 (cylinder), case style like the "Peerless Type BF" but with the rear-mounted Morning Glory horn and tone arm (aluminum), plays 2- and 4-minute cylinders (see Peerless for further description) 475.00 800.00

☐ COLUMBIA NEW SOVEREIGN (Type BGT), c. 1907 (cylinder), case style like the "Sovereign Type BG" mahogany case with hinged lid to reveal mechanism, quadruple spring, nickel-plated exposed parts, rear-mounted, 17½" long Morning Glory horn (nickel or wood) with tapered tone arm (aluminum), plays 2- and 4-minute cylinders with lyric and Indestructible reproducers 475.00 725.00

Price Range

☐ COLUMBIA PEERLESS (Type BF), c. 1906 (cylinder), oak case similar in style to the "Leader" but larger, quadruple spring, long play 6″ mandrel to accommodate Twentieth Century (Type BC) cylinders as well as regular 2-minute cylinders, 14″ brass bell horn, ribbon "Graphophone" decal, sapphire stylus lyric reproducer and recorder 400.00 800.00

☐ COLUMBIA PREMIER (see Columbia Twentieth Century).

☐ COLUMBIA "PRINCESS" UPRIGHT FLOOR MODEL, c. 1912 (disc), square shaped case with lid over turntable, long curved legs, open storage shelf under machine, plated metal parts 125.00 225.00

☐ COLUMBIA "Q," c. 1898 (cylinder), metal base plate, open works simple mechanism, single spring, key wind, aluminum Q reproducer, no wood base 165.00 275.00

☐ COLUMBIA TYPE QC (cylinder), open works, small table model, oak cover and baseboard (works mounted to base), plays 2-minute cylinders 175.00 300.00

☐ COLUMBIA TYPE QQ, c. 1898–1902 (cylinder), keywind, exposed works, mounted on oak base, single spring, aluminum reproducer Type Q, belled horn with nickel finish, "bent" wood oak cover with large "The Graphophone" decal 200.00 250.00

☐ COLUMBIA "Q" SECOND SERIES, c. 1903 (cylinder), black and gold base, open works, simple mechanism, plays 2-minute cylinders, key wind, type "D" reproducer 160.00 260.00

☐ Also sold as the "Languagephone" with special language cylinders (Rosenthal) 175.00 250.00

☐ COLUMBIA REGENT or GRAFONOLA REGENT (disc), floor model, mahogany "desk" style, console case style (walnut, oak), some case decoration, carved claw feet, top drawer pulls out to reveal 78rpm phonograph,

Columbia Cylinder Phonograph.

Price Range

two storage compartments for 200 12″ records, small doors on one side near top open to reveal grilled speaker (electric) **750.00**   **1400.00**

☐ COLUMBIA REGENT JR. (see Columbia Baby Regent).

☐ COLUMBIA REX (Type BQ), c. 1907 (cylinder), similar case style to "Jewel" Type BK but with rear-mounted Morning Glory horn and tapered aluminum tone arm (red horn with gold lines) plays 2-minute cylinder records with lyric reproducer, oak case **475.00**   **700.00**

☐ COLUMBIA ROYAL (Type BV), c. 1907 (cylinder), oak simple case, single spring, nickel-plated mechanism, lyric reproducer, ribbon "Graphophone" decal, ribbed Morning Glory horn with front-mounted horn crane. Sears Roebuck sold this model as the "Home Queen" **325.00**   **495.00**

☐ COLUMBIA SOVEREIGN (Type BG), c. 1906 (cylinder), mahogany case and cover, heavy base and top moldings, corner columns, nickel-plated top mechanism, quadruple spring, 14″ bell horn, long 6″ mandrel for Twentieth Century cylinders, plays regular cylinders as well, ribbon "Graphophone" decal, Sapphire lyric reproducer and recorder   **325.00**   **575.00**

Columbia Sovereign Gramaphone, *type BG.*

Price Range

☐ COLUMBIA STERLING (Type BI), c. 1906 (disc), oak case with decorative corner columns, base molding, aluminum tone arm, double spring, 10″ turntable, ribbon "Graphophone" decal, "analyzing" reproducer, 17½″ long Morning Glory horn, rear mounted **475.00   1050.00**

☐ COLUMBIA TWENTIETH CENTURY (Type BC), c. 1906 (cylinder), large oak case, hinged front panel, decorative corner columns and molding, special 6″ long mandrel for Twentieth Century cylinders, 4″ diaphragm on reproducer, also plays regular cylinders, crank wind, motor driven (Universal electric motor runs on alternating or direct current), large ribbed horn with floor stand

Price Range

	crank	
horn crane, high domed matching cover, carrying handles (also plays 4-minute Indestructible records)	750.00	1200.00
electric		
....	1250.00	1900.00
☐ COLUMBIA UNIVERSAL (Type C), c. 1897 (cylinder), oak case, front panel is hinged on the bottom, triple spring plays 6″ long cylinders, ribbon decal "Graphophone." Designed as a business machine (plays regular 2″ cylinders as well)	375.00	675.00
☐ UNIVERSAL (Type CE) (operated on a 2-volt battery electric motor)	475.00	1000.00
☐ UNIVERSAL (Type CI) (operated on 110-volt electric motor)	500.00	625.00

COLUMBIA: MISCELLANEOUS ITEMS

☐ COLUMBIA ALUMINUM HORN, 14″ long ..	75.00	125.00

Columbia 20th Century, table model, type BC.

Price Range

☐ COLUMBIA FRONT MOUNT HORNS:
☐ 19″ long with 11″ bell 50.00 75.00
☐ 21″ long with 14″ bell 75.00 125.00
☐ COLUMBIA LYRIC REPRODUCER 35.00 55.00

DAVIS CORNER PHONOGRAPH
☐ DAVIS CORNER PHONOGRAPH (disc), mahogany finish triangular shaped floor model disc phonograph, on high legs, top cover, cloth-covered speaker on one side, wood tone arm, 12″ turntable 275.00 625.00

DECCA JUNIOR PORTABLE
☐ DECCA JUNIOR PORTABLE STYLE JC (disc), leather-covered case with carrying handle, end of tone arm folds down from center of "Horn" in cover of case, 8″ turntable, exposed metal parts nickel-plated (many variations of portables by Decca and other companies) 100.00 185.00

DUPLEX PHONOGRAPH COMPANY (Kalamazoo, MI)
☐ DUPLEX PHONOGRAPH COMPANY (disc), plain oak table model case style, corner columns, "Duplex" decal, two brass bell horns coupled to one reproducer, metal horn bracket, holds both horns, small turntable 950.00 1900.00

EDISON—THOMAS A. EDISON, INC., (ORANGE, NJ) (National Phonograph Co., Orange, NJ).
There are so many models of Edison phonographs that we have listed them alphabetically for easy access. This is not their order of production.
☐ EDISON ACME (see Coin Operated Phonographs).
☐ EDISON ALVA (cylinder), mahogany table model with mahogany cygnet horn, "Edison" decal on front of wood case, Model "O" reproducer, Universal motor operates on direct or alternating current, exposed metal parts painted black with gilt decoration, Amberol and 2-minute cylinders. (Also Cygnet horn, black painted with gold trim or oak wood; gold

Price Range

plating, nickel plating or extra decoration on exposed mechanism was also used, Edison Recorder was also supplied.) 2000.00   4000.00

☐ EDISON AMBEROLA MODEL 1A, c. 1909 (cylinder), 42″ high floor model, 2- and 4-minute cylinder records, mahogany (walnut, oak), Diamond Model "M" reproducer (turn over type), exposed mechanism finished in oxidized copper gilt decoration, 4 drawers in base store 100 cylinder records, drawers hidden behind door, decorative front grill, plays 5 records on one winding of double spring, automatic stop, one of the best of the Amberola models, belt driven 2000.00   3000.00

☐ EDISON AMBEROLA MODEL 1B, c. 1911 (cylinder), floor model, 4-minute cylinder records only, mahogany (walnut) case, Diamond Model "A" reproducer (Model "L"), "Opera" motor, exposed mechanism is dark red with gilt decoration, mandrel oxidized bronze, worm and gear driven Model 1B oak case mechanism is gunmetal finish 1500.00   2500.00

☐ EDISON AMBEROLA MODEL III, c. 1912 (cylinder), 44″ high floor model with open shelf underneath, 4-minute only, oak (mahogany), Diamond Model "A" reproducer (Model "L"), deep red finish on exposed mechanism, mandrel metal gray, double spring, stationary reproducer, worm and gear drive (no belt), gilt and blue decoration on metal parts 750.00   1500.00

☐ EDISON AMBEROLA MODEL IV, c. 1913 (cylinder), floor model, Mission oak style, open shelf for storage under phonograph, single spring, traveling reproducer, belt driven, simple straight case and front grill . .   650.00   850.00

☐ EDISON AMBEROLA MODEL V, c. 1912 (cylinder), table model with cover, simple case and grill, mahogany (oak), single spring, stationary mandrel, automatic stop, traveling reproducer connected to swivel arm, Diamond Model "B" reproducer, worm and gear driven   350.00   800.00

Price Range

☐ EDISON AMBEROLA MODEL VI, c. 1913 (cylinder), table model, simple case and grill, 4-minute cylinder records, Diamond Model "B" reproducer, single spring, stationary mandrel, traveling reproducer 350.00 550.00

☐ EDISON AMBEROLA MODEL VIII, c. 1913 (cylinder), table model, simple case and grill, fireside style mechanism, "Popular Market Model," oak, single spring, swivel arm connects horn to reproducer, belt drive, Model "B" reproducer 300.00 500.00

☐ EDISON AMBEROLA X (cylinder), table model oak case, single spring, belt drive, Diamond reproducer: Model B, simple case style 250.00 450.00

☐ EDISON AMBEROLA FLOOR MODEL 30 (cylinder), floor model with cylinder record cabinet in base, table model set into a floor cabinet, front door in base opens to reveal pull-out shelves that hold cylinder records in the boxes. (See description of table model below.) 550.00 1050.00

☐ EDISON AMBEROLA MODEL 30 (cylinder), table model simple oak case, inside horn, front metal grill painted with wood grain, Diamond "C" reproducer, spring wind, 12¾" high, 3 cylinder records play on one winding, originally priced at $30, hence the model #30 .... 250.00 400.00

☐ EDISON AMBEROLA MODEL 50 (cylinder), table model, mahogany (or oak), wooden front grill, 15" case, double spring, worm and gear driven, Diamond Model "C" reproducer 225.00 400.00

☐ EDISON AMBEROLA MODEL 75 (cylinder), floor model of #50, storage shelves for cylinders (84), feed screw drive moves the reproducer across the cylinder, Diamond "C" reproducer, mahogany (oak) 300.00 465.00

☐ EDISON AMBEROLA MODEL 80, c. 1928 (cylinder), 45" high floor model in Diamond Disc case, two drawers in base hold 72 cylinder records, Model "C" reproducer 425.00 525.00

Price Range

☐ EDISON AUTOMATIC PHONOGRAPH MODEL "M" (see Edison Model "M" coin operated phonograph in the "Coin Operated Phonographs" section).

☐ EDISON "BALMORAL" (cylinder), table model, oak (mahogany), battery operated electric motor (2 volts), Model "C" reproducer, recorder, shaving device (later version of the model "M" Victor), front-mount 33" long, black-painted ribbed metal horn, exposed mechanism may be goldplated, plays 2-minute cylinder records 2500.00   3000.00

☐ EDISON "BIJOU" COIN OPERATED (see section on Coin Operated Phonographs).

☐ EDISON BUSINESS MACHINE (cylinder), table model oak case and cover, wax cylinders, recorder, dictation horn (mouthpiece), playback horn, operated by direct current (110–120 volt) electric motor 300.00   650.00

☐ EDISON "CLASS E" ELECTRIC (cylinder), early version of the Edison "Conquerer," electric motor operated, 110–120 volts 2000.00   3000.00

☐ EDISON "CLASS M" ELECTRIC ("VICTOR") (cylinder), early version of the Edison "Balmoral," 2-volt battery operated, table model, oak case, exposed metal parts finished in black with gilt decoration and nickel Edison Automatic Reproducer, recorder, shaving device, 14" brass horn or two-way hearing tube   2750.00   4100.00

☐ EDISON CLIMAX, coin operated (see section on Coin Operated Phonographs).

☐ EDISON COIN OPERATED PHONOGRAPHS (see section on Coin Operated Phonographs).

☐ EDISON "CONCERT," c. 1899–1908 (cylinder), plays 5" diameter (large) cylinder records, triple spring drive, plays 6–8 concert records on one winding (case variations), early model, oak simple case with "square" corners, no decal, exposed mechanism painted black, some gilt decoration, front drawer, 24" brass belled horn with floor

Price Range

stand, shaving device, automatic reproducer, recorder. Later models: Triumph type case, "Edison" decal (may have Model "D" reproducer and repeating device) 1800.00 2500.00

☐ EDISON CONCERT, with Polyphone attachment (see Polyphone Talking Machines).

☐ EDISON "E" CONCERT, operated by direct current electric motor (110–120 volts), otherwise same as "Concert" description above 2000.00 2600.00

☐ EDISON "M" CONCERT, c. 1900 (cylinder), battery operated (2 volts) 2000.00 2500.00

☐ EDISON CONQUERER (cylinder), table model (later version of the Model "E," see "Class E," "Class M"), oak (mahogany), operated by direct current (110–120 volt) electric motor, front-mount horn crane, 33" long ribbed black horn, recorder, shaving device, Model "C" reproducer, plays 2-minute cylinder records (also came with nickel- or gold-plated exposed mechanism) 2500.00 3000.00

☐ EDISON DIAMOND DISC MODEL A-80, c. 1913–15, table model, oak (mahogany) simple case with cover, base molding, 12" turntable, Diamond reproducer, nickel-plated metal parts, turntable stop 200.00 400.00

☐ EDISON DIAMOND DISC MODEL A-100 ("MODERNE"), c. 1915–19, floor model, mahogany, open storage shelf under phonograph, tapered legs, Sheraton style, 12" turntable, nickel-plated parts, automatic stop Diamond reproducer 250.00 375.00

☐ EDISON DIAMOND DISC MODEL A-150, c. 1915, floor model, oak (mahogany), open shelf storage under phonograph, case decoration, tapered legs, shelf will hold 6 Edison record portfolios, 12" turntable, Diamond reproducer, metal parts oxidized bronze, automatic stop, 44" high 200.00 325.00

☐ EDISON DIAMOND DISC MODEL A-200, c. 1915, floor model, oak (mahogany), simple lines, curved legs (on wheels), large storage

Edison Diamond Disc,
table model,
style #A-80.

Edison Diamond Disc,
floor model,
stlye #A-100,
"Moderne."

Price Range

drawer under phonograph grill holds 36 discs, 12″ turntable, automatic stop, gold plated exposed metal parts, 47″ high **235.00** **385.00**

☐ EDISON DIAMOND DISC MODEL A-250, c. 1915, floor model, mahogany (oak), two large storage drawers behind a door hold 72 discs, decorative grill, 51½″ high (Amberola IA case), goldplated exposed metal parts, volume control, Diamond reproducer, automatic stop **350.00** **500.00**

☐ EDISON DIAMOND DISC MODEL A-290, basically Model A-275 with marquetry decoration **375.00** **500.00**

☐ EDISON DIAMOND DISC MODEL A-300, same as Model A-250 in Circassian walnut **400.00** **600.00**

☐ EDISON DIAMOND DISC MODEL A-375, c. 1912–14, Louis XV style case floor model, mahogany, highly decorative case, curved legs, ornate grill, case molding, storage drawer for 36 discs, 12″ turntable, Diamond reproducer, goldplated metal parts, automatic stop, 50″ high **400.00** **650.00**

☐ EDISON DIAMOND DISC MODEL A-400, c. 1912–14, Louis XVI style case, floor model, mahogany, highly stylized case decoration, decorative molding, fluted decoration, tapered legs, storage drawer for 36 discs, 12″ turntable, Diamond reproducer, goldplated exposed metal parts, automatic stop, 48″ high **375.00** **675.00**

☐ EDISON DIAMOND DISC MODEL A-425, same style in Circassian walnut **400.00** **650.00**

☐ EDISON DIAMOND DISC MODEL A-450, same style in Circassian walnut as above .. **400.00** **650.00**

☐ EDISON DIAMOND DISC MODEL B-60, c. 1913–14, table model, oak simple case and grill, no cover, 12″ turntable, nickel plated exposed parts (turntable, "arm" and reproducer head), single spring, turntable stop, plays Edison Diamond Disc records, Diamond reproducer **150.00** **260.00**

Price Range

☐ EDISON DIAMOND DISC MODEL B-80 (disc), c. 1915, table model, simple grill, mahogany case, 12″ turntable, single spring.   200.00   250.00

☑ EDISON DIAMOND DISC MODEL C-150, c. 1915–19, floor model, straight lines, stylized grill design, storage for discs under grill, oak (mahogany), Diamond reproducer, automatic stop, 12″ turntable 200.00   365.00

☐ EDISON DIAMOND DISC MODEL C-200, c. 1915–19, floor model, straight lines, decorative grill, storage drawer in base holds 36 discs, Diamond reproducer, mahogany, single spring, 12″ turntable 250.00   470.00

☐ EDISON DIAMOND DISC MODEL C-250, "Official Laboratory Model" Chippendale style floor model, oak case with decorative "speaker" grill and trim, gold metal fittings, storage in base for records, 49¾″ high . . .   250.00 —— 450.00

☐ EDISON DIAMOND DISC MODEL S19, floor model, goldplated metal parts, oak case with fretwork grill, flap-down bottom door conceals record storage space, 43½″ high . . .   250.00   450.00

☐ EDISON DIAMOND DISC MODEL, Adams 18th-century English, c. 1918–22, console floor model cabinet, mahogany, decorative double grill front, on tapering legs, double spring, goldplated trim and hardware. By 1922 equipped for long playing records . . .   350.00   650.00

☐ EDISON DIAMOND DISC MODEL, Chalet table model gumwood case, very simple design, lattice-like grill design, nickel-plated parts, single spring, automatic stop, 12″ turntable, 20″ high (also called Bungalow, Style B-19) 250.00   350.00

☐ EDISON DIAMOND DISC MODEL, Chippendale (CC-32), c. 1922, console model disc phonograph, basically simple lines, two compartments for record storage (64 discs), grill same as C-19 and C-250, somewhat oriental, double spring, some decorative molding along top and grill, 12″ turntable 450.00   775.00

Edison Diamond Disc,
floor model,
style #C-250.

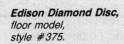

Edison Diamond Disc,
floor model,
style #375.

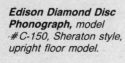

Edison Diamond Disc Phonograph, model #C-150, Sheraton style, upright floor model.

Price Range

☐ EDISON DIAMOND DISC MODEL, Hepplewhite, c. 1919–1926, floor model, mahogany (oak), simple case style, highly carved grill, storage in base for discs, 12″ turntable, tone modulator, Diamond reproducer, automatic stop, single spring, gold trim, 41½″ high (Model H-19) **400.00**   **650.00**

☐ EDISON DIAMOND DISC MODEL, Jacobean, c. 1919–27, floor model, oak, simple lines, some case decoration, decorative grill, horizontal supports between legs, storage beneath phonograph for discs, 12″ turntable, Diamond reproducer, automatic stop, single spring. By 1927 equipped to play long playing discs **350.00**   **525.00**

Edison Diamond Disc Phonograph *"Chalet,"* also called Bungalow, style #B-19.

Edison Diamond Disc Phonograph, *model #CC-32, Chippendale-style console.*

Price Range

☐ EDISON DIAMOND DISC MODEL, London No. 1 (L35), c. 1922, table model made for export market, equipped with reproducer to play 78rpm records as well 275.00 425.00

☐ EDISON DIAMOND DISC MODEL, London Upright (LU 37), brown mahogany floor model, fretwork grill, simple case, storage for discs, 43½" high (export item) 475.00 650.00

☐ EDISON DIAMOND DISC MODEL, Louis XIV, c. 1919–27, floor model, Louis XIV stylized case design, walnut, case molding and decoration, rounded cover, 50" high, storage for discs, 12" turntable, tone modulator, Diamond reproducer, automatic stop, double spring, by 1927 equipped for long playing records 325.00 575.00

Edison Diamond Disc,
London upright model,
style #LU-37.

Price Range

☐ EDISON DIAMOND DISC MODEL, Sheraton, floor model, oak, straight lines, decorative grill and molding, goldplated metal parts, automatic stop, Diamond reproducer, storage in base **200.00**   **350.00**

☐ EDISON DIAMOND DISC MODEL, William and Mary, period art case, floor model, goldplated metal parts, automatic stop, Diamond reproducer, disc storage in base **250.00**   **350.00**

Edison Diamond Disc,
oak, floor model,
"Sheraton."

Price Range

☐ EDISON DISC, table model, outside-horn disc phonograph, oak simple large case, rounded corners, base and top molding, Morning Glory-type horn, tapered end curves down and around to form tone arm in one piece, reproducer attached at end of it, rear-mounted special horn support, plated metal parts ...　400.00　650.00

☐ EDISON DISC, Army and Navy table model, c. 1917, single spring, painted wood case, metal grill inside protective front flap, reinforced case construction, storage for 10 discs ....　1000.00　2000.00

☐ EDISON DOLL (see Edison Talking Doll).

☐ EDISON DUPLEX (cylinder), table model simple oak case, plays regular cylinders and concert cylinders by means of a slip on concert mandrel and automatic reproducer ....　650.00　1050.00

☐ EDISON FIRESIDE MODEL A, c. 1909 (cylinder), compact table model, oak cabinet, rounded corners and cover, "Edison" decal

Edison Disc Phonograph, "Army and Navy," table model, c. 1917.

Price Range

on front of case, single spring belt drive, 2- and 4-minute, Model "K" reproducer, 19" long two piece ribbed metal horn (maroon, blue, or black) 350.00 600.00

☐ c. 1910, Cygnet horn also (black ribbed, mahogany, spruce, oak) 450.00 675.00

☐ MODEL B, c. 1912–14, 4-minute only, improved spring motor, variety of horns: Cygnet wood or metal, blue flowered horn, two part Fireside Horn, Model "N" or Diamond "B" reproducer 475.00 775.00

☐ EDISON GEM MODEL A, c. 1898 (cylinder), table model, key wind, 2-minute wax cylinder records, metal case black with gold decoration, knob to control speed and moves in and out to stop or start, 10" black horn (no bell), with gold band, single spring, one cylinder on one wind 215.00 400.00

☐ EDISON GEM MODEL A, c. 1901 (cylinder), table model, metal case on wooden base, gold-painted decoration, improved stop and start mechanism and speed control, black horn (no bell), key wind 250.00 375.00

☐ EDISON GEM MODEL B, c. 1905 (cylinder), table model, black metal case on wooden base, gold-painted decoration, 2-minute cylinder records, crank permanently placed in machine, slot in cover to accommodate crank, Model "C" reproducer, plain black horn 300.00 400.00

☐ EDISON GEM MODEL C, c. 1905 (cylinder), table model, black metal case on an oak base with domed lid, slot in cover to accommodate crank, brass horn 250.00 300.00

☐ EDISON GEM MODEL D, c. 1909, maroon (cylinder), table model, metal case finished in maroon, gilt decoration, oak base and cover, 2- and 4-minute combination, single spring, Model "H," Model "R" reproducers, 2-piece crane (or Model "K" combination reproducer) 450.00 750.00

Edison Gem Cylinder, phonograph.

Edison Gem Phonograph, model D.

Price Range

☐ EDISON GEM MODEL E, c. 1912, maroon (cylinder), maroon finish metal case, maroon ribbed horn, 4-minute only, Model "N" reproducer, oak base and cover ....   1000.00 · 1400.00

☐ EDISON GEM WITH POLYPHONE ATTACHMENT (see Polyphone Talking Machine).

☐ EDISON HOME MODEL A, c. 1896–1901 (cylinder), suitcase model, clip-type cover, oak case, ribbon decal on cover, black painted mechanism, single spring, starting lever, speed control, 14″ brass bell horn, slotted crank, shaving device found on some early models 350.00   625.00

☐ EDISON HOME MODEL A, c. 1901 (cylinder), table model, rounded "new style" case and cover, ribbon decal on base, Model "C" reproducer, 2-minute cylinder records, 14″ polished brass horn (also 30″ ribbed horn, with rear-mount crane) 18″ case 275.00   375.00

☐ EDISON HOME MODEL B, c. 1906 (cylinder), table model, oak "new style" case, shorter than Model "A," 16½″ wide, single spring,

Edison Home Cylinder Phonograph.

Price Range

Model "C" reproducer, threaded crank, 14" bell horn (brass), 19" ribbed black horn with front mount crane (repeat mechanism)	250.00	425.00
☐ EDISON HOME MODEL C, c. 1908, table model, oak, plain case, push button lift to carrier arm, Model C reproducer, plays 2 minute cylinders, 10-petal ribbed cygnet horn	350.00	475.00
☐ EDISON HOME MODEL D, c. 1908 (cylinder), table model, short oak case, 2- and 4-minute cylinder records, used Model "C" and "H" reproducers, 19" horn and crane, "Edison" decal on front of case (also cygnet horn and crane in black metal or oak)	300.00	400.00
☐ EDISON HOME MODEL E, c. 1911 (cylinder), oak case, plays 2- and 4-minute cylinder records, Model "O" reproducer, cygnet horn, open-ended mandrel	400.00	675.00
☐ EDISON HOME MODEL F, c. 1911 (cylinder), very similar in all respects to Model "E" and "D"	275.00	400.00
☐ EDISON HOME MODEL G, c. 1912 (cylinder), oak case table model, plays 4-minute cylinders only, Diamond Model "B" reproducer, metal cygnet horn (painted oak finish)	325.00	450.00
☐ EDISON HOME MODEL H, coin operated (see Coin Operated Phonographs).		
☐ EDISON HOME WITH POLYPHONE ATTACHMENT (see Polyphone).		
☐ EDISON IDEAL (see Edison Idelia).		
☐ EDISON IDELIA MODEL D1, c. 1907 (cylinder), originally called "Ideal" table model, mahogany case, heavy moldings, rounded cover, decorative carrying handles on sides, 2-minute cylinders, triple spring, "Edison" decal on front of base, horn, crane, reproducer (Model "C") recorder, all oxidized bronze finish, also mahogany horn	4000.00	6000.00
☐ EDISON IDELIA MODEL D2, c. 1908 (cylinder), table model, mahogany case, combination 2- and 4-minute, Model "C" and Model "H" reproducers, recorder, triple spring	3750.00	5750.00

Edison Home Cylinder Phonograph, *horizontally mounted reproducer for cygnet horn.*

Price Range

☐ Later Model, c. 1910–11, exposed metal parts enameled maroon instead of oxidized, mahogany finish cygnet horn, nickel-plated crane, Model "O" reproducer, double spring. May be fitted with a repeating attachment which allowed a cylinder to be played over and over automatically (other Edison models could be fitted with this device) 3500.00   5000.00

☐ EDISON "LANGUAGE" PHONOGRAPH (see Edison Standard Model "B").

☐ EDISON LONG PLAYING CONSOLE, Model No. 1, c. 1920's (disc), two-speed gearing for 12" long-play discs and Diamond discs, two front doors on cabinet, one for record storage, one for speaker, turned legs, some applied case decoration on front doors 225.00   450.00

Price Range

☐ EDISON LONG PLAYING CONSOLE, Models No. 2, 3, and 4, c. 1920's (disc), simple brown mahogany case with center grill, classical-style decoration, turned legs (all three models differ only slightly in size not style), two-speed gearing for 12″ long play and Diamond discs, double spring 275.00   500.00

☐ EDISON OPERA, c. 1911–13 (cylinder), table model, mahogany case also in oak, exposed mechanism in enameled maroon, sliding mandrel automatic stop, self-supporting cygnet type wood horn ("Music Master"), oxidized bronze crank, reproducer and carrying

Edison Long Playing Disc Console, model 2, 3, or 4.

Price Range

handles, Model "L" reproducer and Diamond Model "A" reproducer, 4-minute wax and blue Amberol Cylinder records 2500.00 3450.00
☐ with matching cylinder cabinet 3200.00 4200.00
☐ EDISON POLYPHONE CYL PHONOGRAPH (see EDISON TRIUMPH Phonograph with Polyphone attachment).
☐ EDISON SCHOOL PHONOGRAPH, c. 1912 (cylinder), table model, metal case fits into metal floor stand, on wheels with four storage boxes for 96 cylinders (Blue Amberol), self-supporting cygnet-type black metal horn, Diamond Model "A" reproducer (Opera mechanism) 1500.00 2500.00
☐ EDISON SPRING MOTOR PHONOGRAPH (see Edison Triumph Model "A").

Edison Opera Cylinder Phonograph,
with oak cygnet horn.

Price Range

☐ EDISON STANDARD MODEL A, c. 1897 (cylinder), oak case, "suitcase"-style model with metal clips to hold cover, plays 2-minute cylinders, slotted crank, plays 3 cylinders on one winding, squared-off corners on base of case, 14″ brass belled horn, shaving device, single spring 325.00 425.00

☐ EDISON STANDARD MODEL B, c. 1905 (cylinder), oak case and rounded cover, base molding, mechanism screwed to lid of base, Model "C" reproducer, ribbon decal, speed control, screw on crank, single spring, plays 2-minute cylinder records (no shaving device), 14″ brass belled horn, may be fitted with manual language repeater mechanism operated by pressing on lever attached to front of mechanism. The reproducer is set back several grooves to repeat last phrases, usually accompanied by a small plate on front of machine, e.g., "International Textbook Co." Special language cylinders were made with a whole course of instruction 260.00 360.00

☐ With language repeat (International Correspondence School) 350.00 500.00

☐ EDISON STANDARD MODEL C (see Model "B").

☐ EDISON STANDARD MODEL D, c. 1908 (cylinder), oak case and cover, combination 2- and 4-minute gearing, single spring, Model "C" and Model "H" reproducers, flowered ribbed horn and crane, exposed metal parts black with gold decoration and nickel plated 350.00 500.00

☐ EDISON STANDARD MODEL E, c. 1911 (cylinder), oak case with cover, plays 2- and 4-minute cylinder records, reproducer carriage arranged horizontally to accommodate a cygnet horn (ribbed black metal with gold decoration), combination Model "S" or "O" reproducer (Model "C" and Model "H" reproducers) 300.00 625.00

Edison Triumph, *with polyphone attachment.*

Price Range

☐ EDISON STANDARD MODEL G, c. 1912 (cylinder), oak case and cover, plays Blue Amberol cylinders only (4-minute), cygnet horn, Diamond Model "B" reproducer (flowered horn) 350.00   600.00

☐ EDISON STANDARD WITH POLYPHONE ATTACHMENT (see Polyphone).

☐ EDISON TALKING DOLL, c. 1890 (Edison Phonograph Toy Manufacturing Co.), female doll with bisque head, wood and plaster limbs, metal body with grill holes in front for sound, back panel of body comes off to expose cylinder record mechanism, hand crank, cylinder was permanently placed in

Edison Triumph Cylinder Phonograph,
horizontally mounted reproducer for cygnet horn.

Price Range

doll, 3″ diameter cylinder plays ½ minute. There were a variety of tunes available. One tune per doll 1750.00   2500.00

☐ EDISON TREADLE PHONOGRAPH, foot-powered cylinder phonograph mounted on a sewing machine base with drawers, originally conceived for both commercial and household use. **Rare** (confined mainly to museum examples) 5000.00   7000.00

☐ EDISON TRIUMPH MODEL A, c. 1895–1900 (cylinder), Edison spring motor, simple oak case with small front drawer, no decals, triple spring, 2-minute cylinder records, 14″ brass horn, square winding crank, Edison Automatic Reproducer and Recorder (shaving device) 500.00   1050.00

Price Range

□ (Later Model), c. 1900, oak "new style" case, case molding, ribbon decal on front, exposed mechanism painted black with gold decoration, nickel plated, triple spring, 14" brass horn, Edison Automatic Reproducer and Recorder (Model "C" reproducer c. 1902), other horns of various sizes also supplied) 600.00 800.00

□ EDISON TRIUMPH MODEL B, c. 1906 (cylinder), oak case with raised panels on sides, "Edison" decal, triple spring, plays 2-minute cylinders, screw on crank, 14" brass horn, Model "C" reproducer (triumph horn) 625.00 725.00

□ EDISON TRIUMPH MODEL D, c. 1908 (cylinder), oak (mahogany) case and cover, decorative base molding and raised panels on all sides of base, "Edison" decal, plays 2- and 4-minute cylinder records, Model "C" and Model "H" reproducers, 33" long ribbed black horn, speed control, triple spring (cygnet horn) 700.00 1000.00

□ EDISON TRIUMPH MODEL E, c. 1910 (cylinder), oak (mahogany), triple spring, speed regulator, plays 2- and 4-minute cylinder records, Model "O" combination reproducer with sapphire stylus, cygnet, or straight ribbed horn 800.00 1300.00

□ EDISON TRIUMPH MODEL F, c. 1911 (cylinder), case style slightly different, corner columns, no raised panels. Otherwise description is same as Model "E," oak cygnet horn 800.00 1300.00

□ EDISON TRIUMPH MODEL G, c. 1912 (cylinder), oak case, corner pillars, no raised panels, "Edison" decal, plays 4-minute cylinders only (Blue Amberol), Diamond Model "B" reproducer, oak cygnet horn 600.00 1000.00

□ EDISON TRIUMPH CYLINDER PHONOGRAPH WITH POLYPHONE ATTACHMENT, machine has a special double reproducer which holds two small belled horns, this unit played on one cylinder. (Edison offered this attachment as an option.)

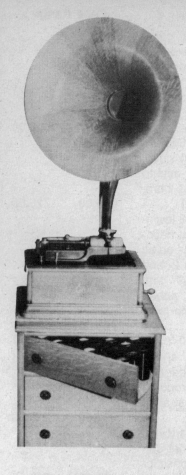

*Edison Triump
Cylinder Phonograph.*

	Price Range	
☐ EDISON WINDSOR, coin operated (see section on Coin Operated Phonographs).		

EDISON: MISCELLANEOUS PHONOGRAPH ITEMS

☐ EDISON AMBEROLA MODEL "B" REPRODUCER, 4-minute diamond stylus	50.00	95.00
☐ EDISON BLUE AMBEROL 4-minute wax ...		2.00 & up
☐ EDISON CONCERT CYLINDER RECORDS, 5" diameter	10.00	25.00
☐ EDISON CYLINDER RECORDS, 2-minute wax		3.00 & up

Price Range

☐ EDISON CYLINDER (AMBEROL), 4-minute wax		3.00 & up
☐ EDISON DIAMOND DISCS		1.00 & up
☐ EDISON FIRESIDE MORNING GLORY HORN, two-piece metal, painted	150.00	225.00
☐ EDISON LONG PLAYING DISCS		10.00 & up
☐ EDISON MODEL C REPRODUCER	35.00	75.00
☐ EDISON MODEL H REPRODUCER	45.00	75.00
☐ EDISON MODEL K REPRODUCER	60.00	125.00
☐ EDISON MODEL N "RED GEM" REPRODUCER	80.00	175.00
☐ EDISON MODEL O REPRODUCER	75.00	95.00
☐ EDISON DIAMOND B REPRODUCER	75.00	95.00
☐ EDISON DIAMOND DISC REPRODUCER	25.00	50.00
☐ EDISON HOME SHAVER, c. 1912, oak case, shave off previous recordings on 4-minute wax cylinders, 4-minute recorder and blanks came with the shaver	50.00	75.00
☐ EDISON FLOOR MODEL SHAVER, black metal	35.00	65.00
☐ EDISON 78rpm PHONOGRAPH HEAD, nickel plated	45.00	65.00
☐ EDISON RECORD CABINET (cylinder records), doors open to reveal five pull-out shelves, simple case style, holds 75 cylinders	175.00	350.00
☐ CYLINDER RECORD CABINET, oak, 5 drawers, holds 75 cylinders, decorative molding, brass pulls (many variations, some holding well over 100 cylinders)	200.00	400.00
☐ EDISON, 4-minute recorder	50.00	75.00
☐ EDISON, mahogany cygnet horn	100.00	200.00

EXCELDA (see Thorens "Excelda").

EXCELSIOR

☐ EXCELSIOR (cylinder), key wind motor, vertical crank wind, aluminum reproducer and belled horn (one-piece horn), machine mounted on oak base, curved cover with Excelsior decal	300.00	450.00

Price Range

FAIRY PHONOGRAPH LAMP

☐ FAIRY PHONOGRAPH LAMP, c. late 1930's (disc), "Copper" metal base, wood grain finish, cloth shade (quite elaborately decorated), 35″ high, center section of lamp base holds turntable, Eagle on cover of phonograph section, plays 78rpm records 500.00   1000.00

FERN-O-GRAND PHONOGRAPH

☐ FERN-O-GRAND PHONOGRAPH (disc), small "Baby Grand" piano-style floor model phonograph case, lid lifts to reveal turntable, tone arm, etc., plays 78rpm records (see Phonogrand) 575.00   775.00

GRAM-O-PHONES (see Berliner Gram-O-Phones).

GUITAROPHONE (see Organettes and Roller Organs).

Fairy Phono Lamp, plays disc records.

HARMONY

☐ HARMONY, c. 1906 (disc), rear-mount outside horn, painted Morning Glory horn (blue, 8 petals), oak case some decoration, rounded column at corner, single spring motor, plays large holed records **450.00   600.00**

☐ HARMONY (disc), outside-horn, front-mount, painted Morning Glory horn, oak case, rounded column at corner, large spindle, single spring motor **325.00   425.00**

HIS MASTER'S VOICE GRAMOPHONE CO. (British company related to the Victor Talking Machine Co.) ("H.M.V.").

☐ H.M.V. JUNIOR GRAND, c. 1910 (disc), oak floor model, inside horn, exhibition reproducer, gooseneck tone arm, two front doors open to reveal "Speaker Horn," grill, storage in base for disc records, 45¾" high **165.00   215.00**

☐ H.M.V. LUMIERE PHONOGRAPH MODEL #460, c. 1924–26 (disc), plain large rectangular table model case with cover, oak veneer, 14" pleated gold paper diaphragm which folds down parallel to the turntable when not in use (Louis Lumiere Patent), gold-plated exposed metal parts and trim, double spring, 12" turntable **850.00   1250.00**

☐ H.M.V. LUMIERE CABINET GRAND MODEL #510, c. 1926 (disc), floor model, straight case style with storage for discs, mahogany (oak), curved legs, 14" pleated gold paper diaphragm (see last entry for further description), quadruple spring motor **1250.00   1750.00**

☐ H.M.V. MODEL 32, c. 1927 (disc), table model, outside horn, mahogany case, some decoration, quadruple-spring motor, black ribbed Morning Glory horn **200.00   300.00**

☐ H.M.V. MODEL 102C PORTABLE (disc), black cloth-covered carrying case, suitcase style, #5B reproducer (also came in blue leather-like cloth, with #5A reproducer, storage for records) **75.00   150.00**

Price Range

☐ H.M.V. MODEL 110 (disc), inside-horn table model, oak, gooseneck tone arm, door covered louvered horn grill **75.00** **150.00**

☐ H.M.V. MODEL 126, c. 1925–26 (disc), inside-horn table model, #4 Reproducer, louvered grill over horn with doors, shaped bracket feet, oak **75.00** **150.00**

HOME QUEEN
☐ HOME QUEEN (Sears Roebuck) (see Columbia Royal).

EIDRIDGE JOHNSON GRAM-O-PHONES
☐ ELDRIDGE JOHNSON GRAM-O-PHONES (see Victor Type A, B, C).

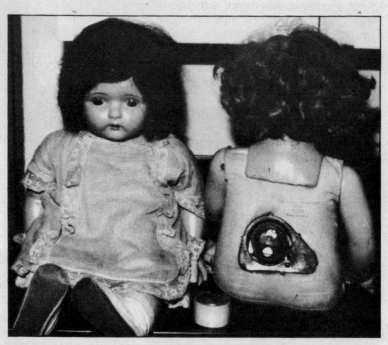

Madame Hendren Talking Doll.

Price Range

JUNOPHONE
☐ JUNOPHONE (disc), table model, plain oak case, rear-mount metal horn in simulated woodgrain finish, horn is outside, Junophon Reproducer (case variations and different horns, e.g., red fluted metal horn with pressed design) 175.00   275.00

KAMERAPHONE
☐ KAMERAPHONE PORTABLE DE LUX (disc), "Box Camera" style, 5″ x 6″ x 7″, 5″ turntable, tone arm fits into a ring inside the lid, crank wind 100.00   200.00

KLINGSOR
☐ KLINGSOR TABLE MODEL (disc), simple rectangular case style with cover, small front doors open to reveal horn (speaker) opening, crank wind 200.00   300.00
☐ KLINGSOR TABLE MODEL WITH "ZITHER" STRINGS, c. 1908 (disc), 38″ high case contains two leaded glass doors on top which open to reveal internal horn with zither-like piano strings on a metal frame, turntable located beneath this section, acoustic reproducer 1500.00   2000.00
☐ KLINGSOR PHONOGRAPH WITH ZITHER STRINGS, upright floor model, storage cabinet for disc records in base, 60″ high (phonograph sits on storage cabinet) 1750.00   2500.00

LAKESIDE PHONOGRAPH
☐ LAKESIDE PHONOGRAPH (cylinder), sold by Montgomery Ward, oak case, plain style, plays 2- and 4-minute cylinder records, 14″ horn with brass bell, rear horn crane 150.00   325.00
☐ LAKESIDE PHONOGRAPH (cylinder), table model, inside horn 125.00   270.00

LANGUAGE PHONE
☐ LANGUAGE PHONE, c. 1903 (cylinder), open works, simple mechanism, black and gold base, plays 2-minute cylinders, type "D" reproducer, key wind 175.00   250.00

Price Range

LANGUAGE PHONE COMPANY
☐ LANGUAGE PHONE COMPANY (disc), table model outside horn, rear-mount horn bracket and tone arm, 8-petal Morning Glory horn, decal on front of case 750.00   1100.00

LARK PORTABLE
☐ LARK PORTABLE (disc), wood case, nickel-plated metal parts 65.00   140.00

MADAME HENDREN
☐ MADAME HENDREN TALKING DOLL (cylinder), child's doll 26″ long, stuffed cloth body, metal horn in chest is open and goes through to mechanism in back where cylinder record is placed, crank on right side of body, light blue celluloid type cylinders are 2″ diameter by 1½″ long and are interchangeable, name stamped on metal end of cylinder: "Averill Manufacturing Company, N.Y." Variety of children's tunes and verses were available all sounding like a little girl, e.g., "Mary Had a Little Lamb," "Now I Lay Me Down to Sleep." 125.00   235.00

MAE STARR
☐ MAE STARR TALKING DOLL, c. 1930's (cylinder), child's doll 29″ long, 2″ (2⅛″) diameter celluloid cylinders, phonograph in the doll's back, horn grill in chest, wound with a handle, plays nursery rhymes 250.00   425.00

MARKSMAN PHONOGRAPH
☐ MARKSMAN PHONOGRAPH (disc), rear-mount disc phonograph with cygnet-type horn and Marksman Reproducer (European) 275.00   400.00

McDONALD GRAPHOPHONE
☐ McDONALD GRAPHOPHONE (cylinder), open works, mounted on an oak base, plays 2-minute cylinders (see Columbia type AB) 700.00   1200.00

MIGNONPHONE (Paris)
☐ MIGNONPHONE PORTABLE (disc), flat "box camera"-type case, 8¾″ x 5½″ x 2¾″, collapsible hexagonal cardboard horn, cloth-

Price Range

covered octagonal reproducer will play both lateral and vertical cut records, 4⅜" turntable, crank wind 100.00 200.00

MIKIPHONE
☐ MIKIPHONE POCKET PORTABLE, c. 1924–25 (disc), "Pocket Watch"-style phonograph, black (celluloid) composition resonator, "Mikiphone" sound box, 4" diameter turntable, metal tone arm plays 1½" to 10" records, key wind 175.00 325.00

MIRAPHONE (Germany)
☐ MIRAPHONE (disc), outside-horn phonograph, c. 1905, oak case, 7" turntable, green-painted flowered horn, Exhibition reproducer (see also "Mira" listing in "Metal Disc Music Box" section) 500.00 1100.00

MODERNOLA
☐ MODERNOLA PHONOGRAPH LAMP (disc), floor model disc phonograph with a fringed lamp coming out of the top of the console cabinet, walnut, decorated grill, highly embellished lampshade 750.00 1650.00

MUSIC MASTER
☐ MUSIC MASTER HORN, mahogany, Morning Glory style, used on outside-horn disc phonographs 175.00 350.00

ODEON TALKING MACHINE CO. (London, England)
☐ ODEON TALKING MACHINE CO. (disc), table model, simple case lines, base molding, crank wind, brass belled horn, straight tone arm 375.00 550.00

OXFORD
☐ OXFORD JR. (see Columbia Type AQ Second Series).

OXFORD
☐ OXFORD TALKING MACHINE (Sears Roebuck) (see Columbia Type BVT).

Price Range

PAILLARD PORTABLE
☐ PAILLARD PORTABLE, c. 1920's (disc), "suitcase" style, spring wind, thin rectangular case 100.00 200.00

PARLOGRAPH
☐ PARLOGRAPH (cylinder), black metal painted case, 14″ brass bell horn, name in large script gold letters on side of case ... 150.00 250.00

PARLOPHON (German)
☐ PARLOPHON (disc), table model outside horn, oak case, rear-mounted horn bracket and tone arm, 30″ long brass bell horn with 17½″ bell, free-standing column at the four corners of the case, wide column at the four corners of the case, wide base molding, straight tone arm, crank wind, large single spring, 11¾″ turntable 325.00 475.00
☐ PARLOPHON (disc), table model, outside horn, Morning Glory horn (fluted, painted), rear-mounted horn bracket and tone arm, crank wind, simple plain case style with wide base molding, oak, 10″ turntable 350.00 450.00
☐ PARLOPHON (disc), inside-horn table model, simple straight case with cover over turntable, horizontal grill louvers, crank wind, mahogany, 11¼″ turntable 50.00 125.00

PATHE (Paris, France).
☐ PATHE ACTUELLE (disc), outside-horn, disc table model, rear mount, tapering tone arm, simple case with some corner decoration, Morning Glory horn with gold decoration ... 300.00 550.00
☐ PATHE "AIGLON" (cylinder), open works on flat metal base, "bent" wood oak cover with large decal, plays 2-minute wax cylinders, key wind on right side, curved bell horn 27″ long with 10″ bell, table model 200.00 325.00
☐ PATHE "CONCERT A", c. 1908–11 (disc), outside-horn table model, single spring, speed regulator, brake lever, rear-mounted horn support and tone arm connection, 11¼″

Price Range

turntable, highly decorated case and molding, 12-petal (ribbed) Morning Glory horn (later known as "Majestik") .... | 375.00 | 500.00

□ PATHE COQUET (cylinder), simple walnut case, Orpheus attachment, Bakelite reproducer and recorder, slip-on Salon mandrel, aluminum horn, plays both 2″ diameter and 4″ diameter Salon cylinders, shallow cover | 450.00 | 665.00

□ PATHE "DUPLEX" GRAND CONCERT (cylinder), simple oak case, carrying handles, small aluminum bell horn, plays both regular and Salon size cylinders, slightly smaller than the Concert Cylinder, Orpheus attachment | 225.00 | 475.00

□ PATHE "ELF," c. 1915 (disc), table model, "horn" built into the cover of the machine and finished to match the oak case, the tone arm comes down from the center of the "horn," hand crank wind, simple lines .... | 200.00 | 350.00

□ PATHE MODEL B (disc), table model, outside horn, simple case with base and top molding, reproducer attached to end of horn, 9¾″ turntable, single spring, small ribbed horn supported by rod-type horn support .... | 350.00 | 525.00

□ PATHE "EXCELSIOR" (cylinder), walnut case and cover, double spring, slip-on Salon mandrel .... | 250.00 | 350.00

□ PATHE "REFLEX," c. 1912 (disc), oak table model, inside horn, disc phonograph, tone arm folds down from center of cover, the horn is in the cover as well, speed control (case variations, e.g., wood base with metal cover painted to simulate wood base) .... | 225.00 | 325.00

□ PATHE MODEL 175 (disc), inside horn, upright floor model, 12″ turntable, turn-over diaphragm reproducer, mahogany, record storage compartment in base, 47½″ high ..... | 275.00 | 375.00

□ PATHE (disc), table model, rear-mount Morning Glory–type ribbed horn (painted), some case decoration (many variations), single spring, metal tone arm, outside horn in oak or mahogany, 11″ turntable .... | 375.00 | 700.00

Price Range

☐ PATHE (disc), table model, simple case with cover, some case decoration (many variations), metal tone arm, inside horn, simple front grill, 11″ turntable 175.00   275.00

PETER PAN CAMERAPHONE
☐ PETER PAN CAMERAPHONE, c. 1924 (disc), "box camera"-style portable disc phonograph, gooseneck tone arm, bellows horn in lid, leather-covered case (variations in case covering) 110.00   210.00

PET-O-FONE
☐ PET-O-FONE (disc), "box camera" portable style 110.00   210.00

PHONOGRAND
☐ PHONOGRAND PHONOGRAPH, c. 1920's (disc), floor model in shape of baby grand piano, lid lifts up to reveal turntable, crank wind, case is almost 3′ deep, 35″ high 750.00   1250.00

PHONOGRAPH DOLLS (see Edison Talking Doll, Lioret's Bebe Jumeau, Madame Hendren).

POLLY PHONOGRAPH CO. (New York)
☐ POLLY PHONOGRAPH CO., c. 1922 (disc), flat portable with cover, paper folding horn, 9″ turntable, tone arm, crank wind 50.00   150.00

POLYPHONE TALKING MACHINE CO.
☐ POLYPHONE CYLINDER PHONOGRAPH, c. 1898, simple oak case, cylinder phonograph with polyphone special attachment that allowed two reproducers each with their own small bell horn playing at the same time on one cylinder record. This produced an echo effect with a louder tone than one reproducer 750.00   1500.00
☐ T. Edison Co., Orange, NJ, advertised this attachment with some of their models:
☐ EDISON GEM with Polyphone attachment 400.00   600.00
☐ EDISON HOME with Polyphone attachment 475.00   675.00
☐ EDISON STANDARD with Polyphone attachment 450.00   650.00

Price Range

☐ EDISON CONCERT with Polyphone attachment 2000.00   2750.00

REGINA HEXAPHONE (See Coin Operated Phonographs).

REGINAPHONE
☐ REGINAPHONE (disc), many outside- and inside-horn styles with disc music box and disc phonograph combination mechanisms (see Disc Music Boxes—Regina for descriptions).

SILVERTONE (Sears Robeuck Co.)
☐ SILVERTONE, c. 1914 (disc), table model, serpentine-style case, oak, interesting fretwork grill, 10″ turntable, two reproducers for lateral and vertical cut records 100.00   200.00

SONORA DISC CONSOLE PHONOGRAPHS c. 1920's. Many period style variations were made and were quite expensive at the time.
☐ "CANTERBURY," walnut or mahogany, nickel-plated exposed parts, double spring, auto stop, storage for 60 records 150.00   250.00
☐ ISLINGTON, disc floor model phonograph similar in style to the above but has no disc storage 100.00   200.00
☐ "LUZERNE," without storage, otherwise companion style case (English Renaissance case style quite similar with storage for 80 records) 100.00   175.00
☐ "NOTRE DAME" style, no storage for discs 175.00   250.00
☐ SONORA DUNCAN PHYFE DELUXE "FULTON" style, mahogany (oak), triple spring, goldplated, tone modifier, automatic stop, stores 100 records, simple case lines with delicate trim decoration 175.00   300.00
☐ SONORA GOTHIC DELUXE, c. 1920's, "NORMANDY" console case style, walnut, triple spring, goldplated metal parts, automatic stop, storage for 80 records, gothic junior 200.00   350.00

Talk-O-Phone,
"The Herbet," disc.

**Sonora Inside-Horn
Console Disc
Phonograph,** *with
record storage.*

Price Range

☐ SONORA HEPPLEWHITE DELUXE "TRAY-MORE," mahogany console with graceful delicate case decoration, basically simple case style, gold trim automatic stop, storage for 80 records 175.00   300.00

☐ SONORA INVINCIBLE (disc), floor model, mahogany (or walnut) cabinet, 50" high, gold-plated exposed metal parts and trim, 12" turntable, triple spring, plays 45 minutes on one winding, automatic stop, holds 80 records in base, curved (bowed) case lines, decorative corner details, fancy front speaker grill, front doors open to reveal record storage 250.00   350.00

☐ SONORA ITALIAN RENAISSANCE "MI-LANO" style, walnut case, turned legs, some case decoration, triple spring, goldplated, automatic stop, storage for 100 discs 275.00   400.00

☐ SONORA MELODIE (disc), table model, 16" high, straight simple case style and grill, nickel-plated trim, double spring, automatic stop, separate record cabinet with slightly curving corner decoration on legs, front doors open to reveal storage for 80 discs   75.00   150.00

SPRANGOPHONE (German)

☐ SPRANGOPHONE PORTABLE (disc), "box camera" style, oak case, 6½" x 5" x 7¼", telescopic tone arm, fixed into the lid, 4½" diameter turntable, crank wind 100.00   200.00

STANDARD TALKING MACHINE CO. (related to Columbia Phonograph Co.)

☐ STANDARD TALKING MACHINE, c. 1903–05 (disc), small metal open works machine on wood base, 6¾" (7") turntable, all black bell horn, large spindle ($^9/_{16}$") requires special disc records with large hole made by Standard, metal front "tone arm" and horn brackets (see also Columbia Type "AU") . .   250.00   420.00

☐ STANDARD TALKING MACHINE MODEL A, c. 1902–05 (disc), oak table model, outside horn, disc phonograph, rear-mount Morning

Price Range

Glory horn (red with gold lines), ½" (⁹/₁₆") spindle for special standard discs, some case decoration 350.00   525.00

☐ STANDARD TALKING MACHINE MODEL X, c. 1902–10 (disc), outside horn, table model, disc phonograph, front-mount Morning Glory–style horn, 10" turntable, oak case, ½" (⁹/₁₆") wide spindle for special standard discs (nickel ribbed horn) 450.00   750.00

STUART PHONOGRAPH

☐ STUART PHONOGRAPH (disc), table model, inside horn, round metal small case style with grill in base 65.00   145.00

TALKING DOLLS (see Edison Talking Doll, Lioret's Bebe Jumeau, Madame Hendren).

TALK-O-PHONE COMPANY (Toledo, Ohio)

☐ TALK-O-PHONE "THE BROOKE," c. 1904 (disc), table model, oak case with decorative base molding, nickel-plated exposed metal parts, front-mount brass bell horn (16" long), single spring, 10" turntable, exhibition concert Talk-O-Phone reproducer, metal detachable front-mount bracket, metal horn support "tone arm," brake and speed regulator 400.00   550.00

☐ TALK-O-PHONE "THE CLARK," c. 1904 (disc), oak table model with beading decoration along top, bottom, and sides of case, triple spring, 10" turntable, detachable metal front-mount horn bracket and "tone arm" horn support for 30" steel horn with brass bell, Talk-O-Phone Exhibition Concert Reproducer, combination brake and speed regulator 400.00   550.00

☐ TALK-O-PHONE "THE ENNIS," c. 1904 (disc), oak table model with base molding and decorative corner carving, nickel-plated exposed parts, double spring, 10" turntable, Talk-O-Phone Exhibition Concert Reproducer, 21" front-mount horn with brass bell

Talk-o-phone

THE PERFECT
TALKING
MACHINE

$15 to
$40

"ABSOLUTELY NATURAL"
describes the sound re-
production of the Talk-o-phone.
Whether vocal or instrumental, this wonderful machine,
when used with the Talk-o-
phone records, reproduces
every delicate shading of tone,
harmony and technique exactly
as the artist produced it. If
you are accustomed to hearing
other talking machines you
cannot realize just how perfect
the Talk-o-phone is until you
have listened to it.

Let us send you the name of nearest agent.

THE TALK-O-PHONE CO.
TOLEDO, O.
244 West 23d Street, New York.
San Francisco, Cal., Pacific Coast Distributing Point.

	Price Range	
detachable metal front-mount horn bracket and "tone arm" horn support, combination brake and speed regulator	400.00	550.00
☐ TALK-O-PHONE "THE HERBERT," c. 1904 (disc), simple oak case style, base molding, front-mount 16" horn with brass bell, detachable metal horn bracket and support, Talk-O-Phone Exhibition Concert Reproducer, single spring, 9" turntable, combination speed and brake regulator	400.00	500.00
☐ TALK-O-PHONE "THE SOUSA," c. 1904 (disc), oak table model, highly carved decoration on sides, nickel- or goldplated exposed metal parts, triple spring, 10" turntable, Talk-O-Phone Exhibition Concert Reproducer, 30" horn with bell (all brass) detachable metal horn bracket and support, combination brake and speed regulator	475.00	625.00

Price Range

THORENS

☐ THORENS "EXCELDA," c. 1930's (disc), portable phonograph in metal case made to look like Kodak Folding Camera, nickel-plated metal parts, screw-on nut holds disc in place (tiny turntable). Case comes in several colors: red, green, brown, and black .. **140.00** **250.00**

☐ THORENS PORTABLE (disc), small rectangular box (somewhat like "box camera") 8¼" x 6" x 4", 6½" tone arm attaches inside of lid, trademark inside lid, 4¾" turntable, (another model with slightly larger model 8⅝" x 6½" x 5½") **65.00** **115.00**

☐ **THORNWARD CYLINDER PHONOGRAPH,** c. 1895 (cylinder), sold by Montgomery Ward, made by Columbia **260.00** **310.00**

☐ **UNIVERSAL PHONOGRAPH CO.** See Zon-o-Phone.

VICTOR TALKING MACHINE CO. (Camden, NJ). All Victor models were disc machines.

☐ VICTOR, c. 1900, Eldridge R. Johnson (toy), simple mechanism, 7" table, top wind, small horn 10" metal, no bell, hand cranked, open works, horn rests on support, no tone arm, reproducer attached at end of horn, children's model, special 7" discs were sold that played children's tunes **270.00** **360.00**

☐ VICTOR TYPE A, c. 1900, Eldridge Johnson, simple metal mechanism mounted on wood base, spring wind top crank wind, 16" black metal bell horn, small turntable plays 7" and 10" discs, uses the Victor Standard (or Victor Concert) sound box reproducer, changeable steel needles, reproducer attached to horn at horn support bracket, wood and metal horn support **340.00** **475.00**

☐ VICTOR AUX-E-TO-PHONE (see Aux-E-To-Phone).

☐ VICTOR TYPE B, c. 1900, Eldridge Johnson ("Trademark"), oak case table model with some decorative trim molding, top wind

Price Range

crank, metal and wood horn support, metal bell horn, Victor Standard (or Victor Concert) Reproducer (Eldridge Johnson Reproducer). This model was used in the "HIS MASTER'S VOICE" trademark with the dog "Nipper." It is also like the Berliner Type A Gram-O-Phone. Plays 7" discs 1400.00   2800.00

☐ VICTOR TYPE C, c. 1900, Eldridge Johnson, oak case, table model, decorative fluted corner columns, base and top moldings, wood "tone arm," wood and metal horn support, reproducer attached to the end of the horn, Victor Standard (or Victor Concert) Reproducer, brass bell horn, crank on side, plays 7" and 10" discs. Another case design also identified as an Eldridge Johnson Model "C" has what appears to be a "Royal Type R" case with metal corner decorations but with a horn bracket support like the above Victor Model "C" 800.00   1,500.00

☐ VICTOR TYPE D (disc), c. 1893–1907, table model, large oak case with decorative corner columns and base, rear-mount horn bracket, 12" turntable, triple spring, tapering metal tone arm, concert reproducer 1400.00   1900.00

☐ VICTOR TYPE E, c. 1901 (Monarch Junior), oak case with fluted corner columns, metal horn bracket, belled horn, 7" turntable, slotted crank, Concert or Exhibition reproducer   375.00   675.00

☐ Front-mount horn bracket 575.00   775.00

☐ Rear-mount horn bracket 450.00   650.00

☐ VICTOR JUNIOR, c. 1910–11 (toy), oak case with simple molding top and base, front-mount Morning Glory horn (dark red with gold trim); decorative horn bracket support, combination brake and speed regulator, 8" turntable, plays all sizes of records 300.00   400.00

☐ VICTOR MONARCH, c. 1901, table model with heavy base molding, corner columns, 21" brass bell horn, 7" turntable, wood "tone

Price Range

arm," horn support and metal bracket, "Concert" reproducer attached at end of horn, plays 10″ Monarch discs 675.00 1400.00

☐ VICTOR "IMPROVED" MONARCH, c. 1902, oak table model with heavy base molding, corner columns, 10″ turntable, larger case than the "Special," brass bell horn, metal "tone arm." 425.00 575.00

☐ VICTOR MONARCH JUNIOR (see Victor Type E)

☐ VICTOR MONARCH M, c. 1902–03, rear-mount table model, oak case, fluted corner columns, decorative moldings, slotted crank, double spring, black metal horn with brass bell, tapered tone arm 650.00 1150.00

☐ VICTOR MONARCH SPECIAL TYPE MS, c. 1901, highly decorated table model, corner columns, 10″ turntable, heavy spring motor, wood tone arm on metal front mount bracket, black metal brass bell horn, reproducer attached on end of horn 800.00 1800.00

☐ VICTOR TYPE O, c. 1907–1908, plain case, threaded crank, rear mount, 8″ turntable, Morning Glory–type horn, tapering tone arm, brake, speed regulator, mahogany case, single spring, Exhibition Reproducer, horn painted in amber shading, 16″ long 400.00 700.00

☐ VICTOR TYPE P (disc), c. 1902–1906, table model, front-mount horn bracket, hinged to wood tone arm, Concert reproducer, 10″ turntable, single spring, oxidized copper hardware, 18″ black horn with brass bell, simple oak case style 550.00 750.00

☐ VICTOR TYPE R, c. 1901–02 ("Royal"), front-mount table model, black horn with brass bell, 7″ turntable, wood "tone arm" support with metal bracket, simple case design with metal corner decoration, Exhibition or Concert Reproducer, 7″ discs 450.00 750.00

☐ VICTOR SCHOOL HOUSE VV–XXV, floor model, outside horn, golden oak case and horn, straight simple case design, nickel-

Price Range

plated exposed metal parts, phonograph has a top cover and storage shelf underneath that folds up to make space to store horn, pull-out writing tray, triple spring Exhibition Reproducer **1250.00   1900.00**

☐ VICTOR I, c. 1902–08, plain oak case, 8″ turntable, slotted crank, rear mount, Exhibition Reproducer, heavy base molding, tapering arm, brake, speed control, fluted black horn with gold decoration (20″ brass bell horn, oak horn) also Concert Reproducer (later examples had 10″ turntable, Exhibition reproducer) **450.00   650.00**

☐ VICTOR II, plain oak case with heavy base molding, rear-mount ribbed horn (black with gold decoration) 23″ long, Exhibition Repro-

Victor School House Disc Phonograph, floor model VV–XXV.

Price Range

ducer, tapering tone arm, brake speed regulator, 10″ turntable, single spring (also brass belled horn or oak wood horn) 450.00 675.00

☐ VICTOR III, oak case, fluted corner columns, heavy base molding, Exhibition Reproducer, tapering tone arm, brake, speed regulator, 10″ turntable, double spring, 23″ long ribbed horn (black metal with gold decoration) rear mount. (Also brass belled horn, oak wood horn or flowered horn) 650.00 1250.00

☐ VICTOR IV, mahogany case with rounded corner columns, base and top molding, rearmount 24″ ribbed horn (black metal with gold decoration), tapering tone arm, brake, speed control, 10″ turntable, heavy double spring, Exhibition Reproducer (also black tapered horn with brass bell, flowered horn or mahogany horn) 675.00 1200.00

☐ VICTOR V, oak case, corner columns, heavy base and top molding, triple spring, tapering tone arm, brake, speed control, 12″ turntable, 26″ black ribbed horn (flowered or oak) Exhibition Reproducer 850.00 1400.00

☐ VICTOR VI, c. 1906, mahogany case with fluted Corinthian corner columns, with carved capitals, gold decoration on columns, 14 karat triple goldplated Exhibition or Concert reproducer and tone arm, triple spring, 24″ bell brass Morning Glory horn or mahogany horn, 12″ turntable ....: 1200.00 2000.00

☐ VICTOR XXV (see Victor School House VV–XXV).

☐ VICTOR VICTROLA (disc), floor model, inside horn, straight style case lines, storage for 10 albums arranged on each side and below centered speaker doors (doors are cut out forming an "L" shape around speaker doors, no grill over speaker, storage drawer in center bottom of cabinet, triple spring, goldplated exposed metal parts, Exhibition or Concert reproducer, 12″ turntable, mahogany, ma-

Price Range

roon cloth covered record albums, 48″ high, speed regulator (also came in several case finishes including painted decoration) 175.00 275.00

☐ VICTOR VICTROLA (VV–IV), oak inside horn, table model, plain case, two front doors open to reveal louvered speaker, rear-mount tone arm, Exhibition sound box (no cover), 10″ turntable, single spring, metal parts nickel-plated, brake, speed control 100.00 150.00

☐ VICTROLA VI, oak, inside horn, table model, case essentially the same as IV, slightly larger with double spring 100.00 150.00

☐ VICTROLA VIII, oak, inside horn, table model with cover and two doors in front covering louvered speaker, 10″ turntable, Exhibition Reproducer, double spring, nickel-plated metal parts 100.00 150.00

☐ VICTROLA IX (VV–IX), mahogany (oak), inside horn, table model with cover, two doors over speaker, double spring, 12″ turntable, nickel-plated Exhibition Reproducer (case variations) 75.00 125.00

☐ VICTROLA X, mahogany, inside horn, table model (oak), with cover, some case decoration, tapered nickel-plated tone arm, Exhibition Reproducer, two doors in front cover speaker, 12″ turntable 100.00 150.00

☐ VICTROLA X (floor model), mahogany (oak), inside horn, floor model on slightly curved legs with shelf for storage underneath, two doors cover speaker, nickel-plated Exhibition Reproducer, double spring, all metal parts nickel plated, brake, speed regulator and indicator 100.00 200.00

☐ VICTROLA XI, mahogany (oak), inside horn, table model with cover, decorative gold decoration on case, goldplated tone arm, reproducer and metal trim, heavy double spring, two doors in front cover louvered speaker, lock for cover 100.00 150.00

Victrola Disc Queen Anne Console, floor model.

Price Range

☐ VICTROLA XI (floor model), mahogany (oak) floor model, inside horn with cover, plain case, 43″ high, slightly curving corner moldings down to legs, two doors over speaker, storage in base for records, nickel-plated metal parts, Exhibition Reproducer, brake, speed regulator and indicator, double spring 100.00   200.00

☐ VICTROLA XII, mahogany, inside horn, table model with cover, two small doors on front open to reveal louvered speaker, goldplated metal parts 65.00   115.00

Price Range

☐ VICTROLA XIV, mahogany (oak), inside horn, floor model, simple case lines, curved legs, goldplated (nickel-plated) exposed metal parts, tapered tone arm, Exhibition Reproducer, trim, storage in base for 6 record albums holding 102 records, triple spring, 45″ high, two doors cover front speaker **110.00   200.00**

☐ VICTROLA XVI (floor model), mahogany (oak, walnut) 50″ high floor model, inside horn, cabinet with some case decoration along front corners (slightly carved with gold decoration), two doors cover speaker, storage in base for 14 Victor record albums for a total of 231 records, goldplated exposed metal parts, Exhibition Reproducer, triple spring, many case finishes including painted decorations **125.00   225.00**

☐ VICTROLA XVII (disc), c. 1916, floor model, triple spring motor, goldplated exposed metal parts, automatic speed indicator, Exhibition (Victor #2) reproducer, storage in base for 16 record albums (160 records), mahogany (oak painted, or walnut), slightly curved case lines, some decorative details **100.00   200.00**

☐ VICTROLA XVIII (disc), c. 1915, floor model, bowed front and sides, mahogany (walnut), triple spring (also electrified), fancy veneer work and decorative details, Exhibition reproducer, speed indicator, semiautomatic stop, 12″ turntable, goldplated exposed metal parts, 48″ high **150.00   250.00**

☐ VICTROLA XX (disc), c. 1908, floor model, very similar to Victor Victrola with additional elaborate case decoration, mahogany veneers with gilded applied decoration **225.00   325.00**

☐ VICTROLA MODEL #1–1 (disc), table model, inside horn, open turntable (no cover), mahogany case, very simple grill work over "horn," crank wind **65.00   140.00**

☐ VICTROLA MODEL #1–2 (disc), same as Victrola #1–1 except case painted with color decorations for children **75.00   135.00**

Price Range

☐ VICTROLA MODEL #1–70 (disc), table model, inside horn rectangular cabinet 12½" high x 17½" wide x 14" deep, grill cloth over speaker ("horn"), mahogany with maple inlay, No. 4 reproducer, spring motor, crank wind 125.00   200.00

☐ VICTROLA PORTABLE MODEL #2–30 (disc), rectangular "suitcase" style straight case, black cloth with nickel fittings, 7¾" high x 11¾" wide x 14" deep, storage for six 10" disc records, No. 4 reproducer, crank wind 65.00   115.00

☐ VICTROLA PORTABLE MODEL #2–60 (disc), slightly larger case than #2–30 with "safety" record holder inside lid for 12 records, gold-finished fittings inside and out, dark blue or brown textured cloth covered case 100.00   125.00

☐ VICTROLA 125 (disc), floor model, inside horn, disc storage in base under phonograph, graceful case style and decorative details, two doors cover speaker ("horn"), mahogany (walnut), crank or electric. There were several models of similar case style 200.00   285.00

☐ VICTROLA 130, oak (mahogany), painted decoration, inside horn, floor model, serpentine curved case style, some corner decorations, goldplated metal parts, storage in base, two doors cover speaker 300.00   400.00

☐ VICTROLA 215 (disc), console floor model, mahogany case, turntable on right side, storage for record discs on left, Victrola #2 reproducer, replaceable needles, automatic brake, crank wind 135.00   185.00

☐ VICTROLA 220 (disc), console floor model, lid on right lifts to reveal turntable, left side holds disc records, mahogany (oak, walnut) crank or electric 135.00   185.00

☐ VICTROLA 300 (disc), console floor model, lid covering turntable in center of cabinet, center front doors open for speaker (inside "horn"), storage on each side of speaker,

Victrola (X, XI, XII) Table Model inside-Horn Disc Phonographs *on record storage cabinets.*

Victrola Model #300 Console Disc Phonograph *with record storage.*

Price Range

some case decoration, mahogany (also oak, walnut), crank or electric. There were several models similar in style to the Model 300 . . .   **200.00**   **350.00**

☐ VICTROLA PERIOD CASE STYLE, Queen Anne stye (disc), console cabinet, phonograph set in center of case, small double doors open to reveal louvered inside horn, long doors on right and left and compartment under phonograph allow for storage of many albums, "pear drop door pulls, cabriole leg" (many period styles similar to this with minor case variations) **230.00**   **275.00**

VICTOR ORTHOPHONIC PHONOGRAPH was an acoustic system with improved tonal quality.

☐ ORTHOPHONIC VICTROLA 1–90 (disc), portable mahogany veneer with overlay rectangular mahogany table cabinet, grill cloth over speaker (inside "horn"), automatic stop without pre-setting, similar in appearance to the Victrola #1–70 . . . .   **180.00**   **230.00**

☐ ORTHOPHONIC VICTROLA 4–3, console "Hepplewhite Colonial" style mahogany veneer, straight lines, some maple overlay, 36½" high and 19⅛" wide, automatic stop, holds 24 discs, plays 10 minutes on one winding of spring motor (also Induction Disc or Universal Electric Motor) **225.00**   **450.00**

☐ ORTHOPHONIC VICTROLA 4–7, simple mahogany veneer console case in "Italian Renaissance" style, 38" high and 21¾" wide, automatic stop, holds 30 records, spring motor runs 10 minutes on one wind (also Induction Disc or Universal Electric Motor) **200.00**   **300.00**

☐ ORTHOPHONIC VICTROLA 4–40, console cabinet, simple case lines, mahogany veneer, raised panels, 37¾" high and 37" wide, tapered legs with stretchers, automatic stop, plays 10 minutes on one wind, holds 72 records (also Induction Disc or Universal Electric Motor) **380.00**   **550.00**

Price Range

☐ ORTHOPHONIC VICTROLA 8–12, console, walnut veneer case on curved legs in "French Renaissance" style, 45″ high and 30½″ wide, some case decoration, automatic stop, holds 96 records, spring motor plays 20 minutes on one winding (also Induction Disc or Universal Electric Motor) 375.00 525.00

☐ ORTHOPHONIC VICTROLA 8–30, console-type cabinet in walnut (mahogany), Italian Renaissance decoration on low round feet, 46″ high and 31″ wide automatic stop, spring motor runs 20 minutes on one winding, storage for 80 records (also Induction Disc or Universal Electric Motor). Case variation came with tooled leather paneling 480.00 670.00

☐ AUTOMATIC ORTHOPHONIC VICTROLA 1050, "French Renaissance" cabinet style in walnut veneer, highly decorative carving, goldplated, 48″ wide and 49″ high, changes its own records (12), automatic stop. Induction Disc or Universal Electric Motor 750.00 1400.00

WIZARD PHONOGRAPH

☐ WIZARD PHONOGRAPH (cylinder), oak table model, plain case, the mechanism is attached to the underside of the cover, when flipped over and clamped down the whole mechanism is exposed, a horn elbow holds the Morning Glory horn in position. (Other examples have been identified by labels "Champion" and "Ellisdon.") 450.00 900.00

ZON-O-PHONE (Universal Talking Machine Co., NY)

☐ ZON-O-PHONE TYPE A, c. 1899 (disc), table model, outside horn, oak case, corner columns, beveled glass sides on case, black metal horn with brass bell (or all brass horn), metal horn bracket support and "tone arm," front mounted horn 750.00 2000.00

Price Range

☐ ZON-O-PHONE TYPE B (disc), oak case table model with raised decorated side panels, corner columns, brass bell horn, metal horn bracket and "tone arm" horn support, "V" sound box, reproducer 400.00 800.00

☐ ZON-O-PHONE TYPE C (disc), oak table model, some decoration, small raised turntable, base molding, front horn bracket and support, "V" sound box, reproducer 400.00 750.00

☐ ZON-O-PHONE TYPE D (disc), oak table model, simple case, front horn bracket and support, small turntable, "V" reproducer ... 400.00 750.00

☐ ZON-O-PHONE "CHAMPION," c. 1910 (disc), table model, rear mount, oak case, double spring, tapering tone arm, ribbed brass horn 400.00 750.00

☐ ZON-O-PHONE "CONCERT" (disc), table model, oak case, simple lines, tapering tone arm, 9″ turntable, 27″ Morning Glory horn (red, blue, or green), double spring, rear mount 500.00 1000.00

☐ ZON-O-PHONE "CONCERT GRAND" c. 1901–04 (disc), oak case, ornate front-mount horn support, all-brass belled horn, reproducer attached to horn at tapered end, 10″ turntable 750.00 1250.00

☐ ZON-O-PHONE "GRAND OPERA" (disc), table model oak case, rounded corner columns and heavy base molding, triple spring, tapering tone arm (nickel plated), rear-mount 27″ wood-ribbed horn, Morning Glory painted horn, or brass horn, 10″ turntable 650.00 1250.00

COIN-OPERATED PHONOGRAPHS

CYLINDER AND MULTIRECORD PHONOGRAPHS

The "One-Record" coin operated cylinder phonograph was the first attempt at charging the public to hear a recorded voice. They were found largely in arcades and similar places. Later came multi-tune cylinder mechanisms, the Multiphone being a real forerunner of the jukebox.

Jukeboxes are coin operated disc phonographs with elaborate record changing devices that allow the listener to choose from several selections. Several companies made many case variations culminating in what was the "Classic Period" in case styles from 1939 to 1950. Few jukeboxes are still made today.

For information and history see "Further Reading" section. For sources see "Dealers and Restorers" and "Publications and Reprints" sections.

Price Range

☐ **AUTOPHONE,** c. 1912, floor model 200, holds 12 Edison Blue Amberol records on a large wheel, one full winding will play all 12, console mahogany cabinet, front top panel folds down to expose the whole wheel mechanism, decorative grill in front under mechanism on curved legs **3500.00   4750.00**

☐ **COLUMBIA TYPE AS,** c. 1897, coin operated cylinder phonograph, one 2-minute cylinder plays on machine at a time, basically type "A" machine with curved glass top, hand crank, bottom of case drops down to reveal inner mechanism **1500.00   2600.00**

☐ **COLUMBIA TYPE BS,** c. 1898, coin operated "Eagle," with curved glass top, mechanism mounted on a board, horn attached at top outside, oak, ribbon decal, 2-minute cylinder record **1800.00   2600.00**

☐ **COLUMBIA TYPE S** (cylinder), table model phonograph, curved glass top cover, motor in cabinet below **2000.00   2500.00**

☐ **COLUMBIA TYPE SG** (cylinder), coin operated, curved glass cover on top, oak case, listening tubes, electrified **2250.00   3000.00**

☐ **EDISON ACME,** coin operated floor model cylinder phonograph, 46" high (with advertising sign, 72" high) operating on alternating electric current, oak, cabinet, square top fitted with beveled glass, top and three sides, mirror in back section, rubber hearing tubes

Columbia, Type BS, cylinder.

	Price Range	

or 24″ horn with crane, some case decoration, Model "B" reproducer, Model "D" return attachment **2000.00** **3500.00**

☐ **EDISON AUTOMATIC PHONOGRAPH MODEL M** (see Edison Model "M")

☐ **EDISON BIJOU,** c. 1901–08, table model, plain Edison phonograph base cabinet with curved glass top cover over phonograph, coin operated, spring wind once coin is inserted, plays one 2-minute cylinder, Gem mechanism, 14″ black bell horn attached outside top of glass, Model "B" reproducer, oak, "Bijou" decal on front base **1500.00** **2100.00**

Price Range

☐ **EDISON CLASS M ELECTRIC** (see Edison Model M)

☐ **EDISON CLIMAX,** c. 1901–03, floor model with curved glass top covering phonograph mechanism, oak case, door in bottom, plays large Concert cylinder record, 24″ brass horn and crane attached at top of glass cover, coin operated, hand crank, Model "B" reproducer (there are battery operated and electrically wound versions, too) 3000.00   5000.00

☐ **EDISON ECLIPSE,** operates on 125-volt direct current, electrically controlled governor, otherwise description the same as for the "Acme." 2500.00   3700.00

☐ **EDISON EXCELSIOR,** c. 1901–08, table model, oak base cabinet with high curved glass cover over phonograph (Edison Standard mechanism), coin operated, 14″ brass bell horn attached at top of glass cover, plays 2-minute cylinder record, spring wind after coin is inserted, "Excelsior" decal on base front of case, Model "B" reproducer, Model "D" return attachment 2750.00   3850.00

☐ **EDISON MODEL H ("Domestic"),** table model coin operated phonograph (uses Edison "Home" mechanism), oak base with decorative molding with a curved glass cover, plays 2-minute cylinder record, automatic reproducer 1250.00   1750.00

☐ **EDISON MODEL M COIN SLOT PHONOGRAPH,** floor model 53″ high, automatic reproducer plays 2-minute cylinder records, automatic coin slot, 2-volt battery operated, no winding necessary, oak case, curved glass top section, case decoration, 24″ brass horn attached by elbow and support on the top of glass top 2250.00   4250.00

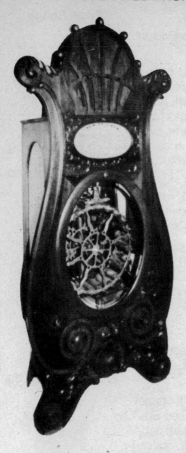

Multiphone Lyre,
floor model.

	Price Range	
☐ **EDISON MODEL E COIN SLOT PHONO-GRAPH,** the same as above only electric motor wound on direct current—110–120 volt	2500.00	5500.00
☐ **EDISON MODEL M CONCERT COIN OPER-ATED PHONOGRAPH,** same as model "M" above but plays 5″ diameter concert cylinder records (Model "E" Concert same difference as above)	3500.00	6000.00
☐ **EDISON STANDARD,** suitcase style, mahogany table model with curved glass cover, coin operated	1500.00	2500.00

Price Range

☐ **EDISON WINDSOR,** operates on a 2-volt battery, governor electrically controlled, otherwise description is the same as for the "Acme" 2500.00   3700.00

☐ **MANHATTAN PHONOGRAPH CO. (NY),** coin operated one-cylinder phonograph (similar to Edison Excelsior), oak case on cast iron curved legs, sign on top 2750.00   3500.00

☐ **MULTIPHONE (Kalamazoo, MI),** c. 1900, tall rectangular case of simple lines with large brass horn extending out of top, on legs, oak case, 24 2-minute cylinders on a wheel, hand crank tune selector, coin operated, large glass front exposing record, some case decoration, fluted columns on sides (case variations) 4000.00   6000.00

☐ **MULTIPHONE "LYRE,"** c. 1905–08, large floor model, decorative lyre-shaped case, speaker on top, carvings and moldings (very impressive appearance), 24 cylinders on a large wheel, large oval glass front panel to view the wheel, coin operated, spring motor crank 6000.00   9000.00

☐ **MULTIPHONE,** c. 1913, tall thin basically rectangular case 6'2½" high, plays 12 cylinders on a revolving mechanism (4-minute cylinders), coin operated, long glass viewing panels, some decorative fretwork and molding on case top 5000.00   10,000.00

☐ **REGINA HEXAPHONE,** c. 1909–21, console cabinet, oak, wood horn in front section of cabinet open, tilted glass top covering phonograph mechanism, large mandrel 6 selections, 4-minute cylinder records, coin operated, diamond stylus reproducer (several case style variations over a 10-year period) 4500.00   6500.00

☐ **ROSENFIELD AUTOMATIC TALKING MACHINE,** Columbia "AZ" works, simple rectangular case on feet, square glass top and

Price Range

sides cover the phonograph mechanism, electric motor winds the main spring after each play, one 2-minute cylinder, lyric reproducer, nickel play 2000.00   3700.00

JUKEBOXES

AUTOMATIC MUSICAL INSTRUMENT CO.

☐ AMI MODEL A, c. 1946–48, 40 tune selections, large case with a lot of plastic ("Mother of Plastic"), window in center front to view record mechanism, grill on top lights up different colors, "jewels" in metal sitting down front 1250.00   2250.00

☐ AMI MODEL B, c. 1947–49, 40 tune selections, large case, grill front, tune card in top front panel, large crown top plastic, plastic side panels, metal trim, simple lines, actually holds 20 records but has flipping device so both sides can be played, color wheel in upper case 800.00   1700.00

☐ AMI MODEL C 800.00   1400.00

☐ AMI MODEL FR, c. 1932, simple wood case in an Art Deco style, 20 tunes, top glass panel is record mechanism and tune cards 300.00   500.00

☐ AMI "SINGING TOWER," c. 1941, 10 tunes, 78rpm, 6′ high, looks like an Art Deco skyscraper, colored panels with pressed designs, lights behind 2500.00   3100.00

☐ AMI "STREAMLINER," c. late 1930's, 20 tune selections, narrow glass panel near top to view mechanism, colored plastic along corners and top, decorative metal grill, lights up 350.00   600.00

☐ AMI "TOP FLIGHT," c. 1936, 20 tune selections, straight rectangular case, metal trim, rounded speaker opening, lights up 400.00   800.00

CAPEHART

☐ CAPEHART DELUXE, c. 1930's, two horizontal record stacks, automatic changer 500.00   1000.00

Price Range

☐ CAPEHART JUKEBOX, early example, oak rectangular cabinet, some decoration but basically simple case, large three-part glass panel in top speaker with decorative grill in base 500.00   800.00

CARRYOLA (Allen H. Carryola Co., Milwaukee, WI)
☐ CARRYOLA "CABARET" JUKEBOX, c. 1930's, coin operated, electrically amplified, 3'6½" high wood case, large front grill, top lifts to reveal turntable 700.00   1100.00

FILBEN
☐ FILBEN "MAESTRO," c. 1940's, 30 tune selections, push buttons, very space age design, long front aluminum metal grill looks like a locomotive, orange plastic top, front panels, metal trim 1000.00   1600.00

GABEL'S
☐ GABEL'S CHARME, c. 1936, all-wood rectangular case, 18 tune selections, selection dial, some case decoration, tune cards inside clear glass window 275.00   525.00
☐ GABEL'S JR., simple rectangular case, case decoration, beveled glass panels on top to view mechanism, grill in front 250.00   550.00

MILLS NOVELTY CO.
☐ MILLS AUTOMATIC PHONOGRAPH, 12 disc "Ferris Wheel" record changer mechanism (10" size disc), 61" high burled walnut case, simple rectangular case, some decorative case details on legs, two glass panels in top front to view "Ferris Wheel," selector dial tune cards 650.00   1350.00
☐ MILLS "EMPRESS" MODEL 910, c. 1939, 20 tune selections, push buttons, small glass panel to view tune cards, large decorative metal front section, large rounded case corners, orange plastic panels, mechanism unusual in that the rack moves to the record position but the changer remains stationary, lights up 1250.00   1850.00

Price Range

☐ MILLS JUKEBOX, early 1930's, 12 selections (78rpm), arranged in a "Ferris Wheel" effect, wood case, some decoration, fluted columns on sides, dial tune selector, volume control, doors open on front top of case, speaker grill in bottom. (many case variations) **650.00** **1250.00**

☐ MILLS "THRONE OF MUSIC," 20 tune selections, push buttons, large orange plastic panels, wood trim and base (similar in appearance to "Empress"), tune selections behind small glass panel in front top, lights up **1000.00** **1800.00**

PACKARD

☐ PACKARD "MANHATTAN," c. 1946, burled wood cabinet, "cylinder" front edged window, glass window panel, 24 tunes, chromed mechanism, large front open grill design. Tune selection cards on revolving wheel on top, open fretwork decoration **750.00** **1350.00**

☐ PACKARD PLA-MOR (CAPEHART), 24 selections, plastic and wood, large viewing window in top front to view mechanism, decorative grill in base, tune selection cards on top on a wheel, plastic on top and sides, coin mechanism in top center **900.00** **1500.00**

ROCK-OLA (arranged alphabetically by model name)

☐ ROCK-OLA "COMET," c. 1953, 120 selections, modern case design, curved glass top section, multicolored base side panels, compact console model **1100.00** **1600.00**

☐ ROCK-OLA "COMMANDO," c. 1942, high wood case, no viewing window, large glass panels along sides and top, 20 tune selections, smaller panels (plastic) in base **1100.00** **1600.00**

☐ ROCK-OLA "FIREBALL" MODEL 1436, c. 1950's, 120 selections, push button, wood case, dome glass top, colored plastic panels on front corners **1000.00** **1500.00**

☐ ROCK-OLA "LUXURY LIGHT-UP," 20 tune selections, large rounded corners case, orange and green plastic panels throughout

Price Range

front of case, push button tune selector in center of front, tune cards just under the plastic panel, decorative grill panel and trim ...   2000.00   2600.00

☐ ROCK-OLA "LUXURY LIGHT-UP SUPER," c. 1939, 20 tune selections, simpler case style than "Luxury Light-up," large plastic panels, rounded case, metal grill in center, two vertical panels, tune selections and push buttons, mechanism cannot be seen 1850.00   2750.00

☐ ROCK-OLA "MONARCH," c. 1938, 20 tune selections, push-button panel in center of case, clear viewing window to see record mechanism, two-tone wood case, metal grill   500.00   900.00

☐ ROCK-OLA "MULTI-SELECTOR," c. 1935, 12 tune selections, clear glass, top front panel to view mechanism, push-button tune selection, simple wood case and front grill (walnut) 400.00   800.00

☐ ROCK-OLA "RHYTHM KING," c. 1937, 12 tune selections, wood case (walnut), simple style, decorative grill, push buttons, viewing window 720.00   1250.00

☐ ROCK-OLA "ROCKET" MODEL 1434, early 1950's, 50 tune selections, push button, simple grill, colored panels, dome top covers record mechanism, colored corner panels 650.00   1250.00

☐ ROCK-OLA "COMMANDO," c. 1942, high wood case, no viewing window, large glass panels along sides and top, 20 tune selections, smaller panels (plastic) in base 1000.00   1600.00

☐ ROCK-OLA "SPECTRAVOX," 1941, 7′ high, golden bowl on top with lights 1000.00   2000.00

☐ ROCK-OLA STYLE 1422, "MAGIC GLO," c. 1946, center front grill of wood, fluted plastic panels on sides and top, multicolored, first in the series, see also 422 and 1426 ....   1400.00   2000.00

☐ ROCK-OLA STYLE 1426, c. 1947, 20 tune, "Classic Style," push buttons, revolving lights, large front metal grill work, plastic behind grill and around top and sides, speaker in bottom, viewing window, wood case (1422)   1650.00   2250.00

Rock-Ola,
style #1422,
"Magic Glo,"
c. 1946.

Rock-Ola,
style #1426,
"Classic Style,"
c. 1947.

Price Range

☐ ROCK-OLA STYLE 1428, same basic lines of 1422 and 1426, fluted side and center plastic panels with raised patterns, decorative chrome trim, patterned front grill, wood case, viewing window 1750.00   2250.00

SEEBURG (arranged alphabetically)
☐ SEEBURG, early model, c. 1934, 10 tune selections, very simple rectangular case, clear glass panel to view records, tune cards, selector dial 350.00   550.00
☐ SEEBURG AUDIOPHONE, c. 1928, 8 disc records, plain rectangular case, oval glass opening on top front to view mechanism and discs, "Ferris Wheel" type mechanism with 8 turntables (one for each disc as it comes into play), speaker on door in front 450.00   750.00
☐ SEEBURG AUDIOPHONE MODEL E, c. 1931, wood case with decorative grill over speaker in base, selector dial, tune cards inside glass panel 350.00   550.00
☐ SEEBURG AUDIOPHONE SENIOR, c. 1928, 8 disc selections, rectangular wood case, decorative grills over speakers on either side of glass panel on top, moldings on bottom of case, small glass panel on top front to view records, tune cards over panel, selector dial   350.00   550.00
☐ SEEBURG "COMMANDER," c. 1940, 20 selections, "Space Age" 1930's look, plastic front, sides, top, decorative trim moldings, button next to each tune card 800.00   1500.00
☐ SEEBURG "ENVOY," c. 1940's, hidden mechanism, large red panels at sides and top, a lot of wood trim, decorated panels, 20 tune selections 900.00   1300.00
☐ SEEBURG "HI TONE," WW II, unusual case style, rounded simple lines, tune card selection area slopes down, rounded speaker enclosure above, mechanism in base, lighted columns, revolving color wheel, science fiction robot shape and appearance, wood and plastic 400.00   800.00

Price Range

☐ SEEBURG P146 .... 800.00 1200.00

☐ SEEBURG P147 P148, c. 1947, 20 tune selections, "Washing Machine" rounded shape, tapering slightly down, plastic top, wood with plastic panels on sides, large decorative grill on front 750.00 1200.00

☐ SEEBURG SYMPHONOLA, c. 1936, 12 tune selections, selector dial, (case variations), decorative grill, rectangular wood case, simple lines, glass window to view mechanism 600.00 1250.00

☐ SEEBURG "SYMPHONOLA CLASSIC," c. 1938, 20 tune selections, push button, mainly wood and red plastic panels in front and top corners, decorative trim, lights up 600.00 1000.00

☐ SEEBURG "SYMPHONOLA REGAL," c. 1940, 20 tune selections with push buttons, rounded sides and top, orange plastic panels along corners and top, tune cards in top (no viewing of mechanism), wood case and trim, green plastic on front grill area 1000.00 1500.00

☐ SEEBURG MODEL 9800, c. 1940's, rounded shape with "tower" effect on top, plastic panels, front panel lighted to give multicolor effect, hidden mechanism 750.00 1000.00

WURLITZER (arranged by model number)

☐ WURLITZER MODEL P 10, c. 1934, 10 selections, rectangular wooden case, simple lines, glass window to view record changer mechanism, tune selector dial, simple front grill on bottom, early version of "Simplex" 250.00 500.00

☐ WURLITZER MODEL P 12, c. 1935, 12 tunes, similar to style P 10, front speaker grill larger with decorative fretwork, tune selector dial 250.00 500.00

☐ WURLITZER MODEL P 20, c. 1934, 10 selections, slight case difference, otherwise very like P 12................................. 250.00 500.00

☐ WURLITZER MODEL 24, c. 1938, 24 tunes, floor model, Art Deco style, tune selector dial in center with tune cards on either side under glass viewing panel 250.00 500.00

Price Range

☐ WURLITZER MODEL P 30, c. 1935, 12 tune selections, simple wood case, Art Deco lines, decorative grill, tune selector dial 300.00 500.00

☐ WURLITZER MODEL 35, c. 1930's, 12 tune selections, more elaborate walnut case, Art Deco style, clear glass front window to view mechanism 350.00 550.00

☐ WURLITZER COUNTER MODEL 41, c. 1940, 12 tune selections, metal and wood veneer trim, rounded case style, plastic sides, some on top front, small open window to view record 1250.00 2250.00

☐ WURLITZER MODEL 50, c. 1937, 12 tune selections, floor model, simple rectangular lines, wood case, glass window to view mechanism (changer), oval shaped grill in base with decorative fretwork, push button tune selector 300.00 500.00

☐ WURLITZER COUNTER MODEL 51, c. 1937, 12 tune selections, push buttons, very modernistic wood case, rectangular with speaker on left side and small glass panel on right 500.00 800.00

☐ WURLITZER COUNTER MODEL 61, c. 1938–39, 12 tune selection, wood base and sides, some plastic and metal decoration (came with matching floor stand) 1000.00 2000.00

☐ WURLITZER COUNTER MODEL 71, c. 1940–41, 12 tune selections, graceful decoration of metal and plastic sides, front and top, larger than Style 41, wood areas 1500.00 3000.00

☐ WURLITZER COUNTER MODEL 81, c. 1940's, 12 tune selections, wood base and sides, curving plastic panels, graceful front grill, small viewing window with tune selection cards, push buttons directly under window 1000.00 2000.00

☐ WURLITZER MODEL 312, c. 1936, 12 tune selections, early 275.00 400.00

☐ WURLITZER SIMPLEX "MODERNISTIC" 316, c. late 1930's, 16 tune selections, case mainly wood with fluted plastic frontside panels, tune selection dial, clear glass front panel to view record mechanism 500.00 800.00

Price Range

☐ WURLITZER (P) 400, c. 1935–36, similar in design to the P-12, rectangular wood case, simple lines, dial indicator, glass viewing window, tune cards inside window, simple decorative grill over speaker **275.00** **400.00**

☐ WURLITZER MODEL 412, c. 1936, 12 tune selections, 78rpm, early **750.00** **1600.00**

☐ WURLITZER MODEL 416, mid-1930's, 16 tune selections, simple wood case, tune selector dial, rounded front corner columns, decorative front grill over speaker **325.00** **475.00**

☐ WURLITZER MODEL 500, c. 1938–39, 24 selections, very similar case design to Model 600, plastic panels on corners, front and along sides of grill, decorative grill, push buttons, wood case **800.00** **1600.00**

☐ WURLITZER MODEL 600, c. 1938–39, 24 selections, rectangular case, plastic panels, top, front corners, sides and on either side of metal grill, wood case, tune indicator dial in center front, clear glass front panel to view tune cards and record mechanism **1000.00** **2000.00**

☐ WURLITZER MODEL 616 SIMPLEX, c. late 1930's, 16 tune selections, wood case, rounded rectangular style, simple lines, clear glass top front viewing panel, tune selector dial, decorative grill, tune cards on top of case above viewing window **750.00** **1750.00**

☐ WURLITZER MODEL 616A, c. late 1930's, 12 tune, walnut case, rounded simple lines, Art Deco feeling, viewing window tune cards on top above window, tune selector dial **250.00** **500.00**

☐ WURLITZER MODEL 700, c. 1940, 24 selections, wood case, plastic panels on front corners and top, push-button tune selections, decorative metal grill **1000.00** **2500.00**

☐ WURLITZER SIMPLEX "MODERNISTIC" 716, c. 1937, 16 tune selections, multicolor wood case, simple lines in Art Deco style, tune selector dial, clear glass viewing window to see record mechanism (some variation in case design) **400.00** **650.00**

Price Range

☐ WURLITZER MODEL 750, c. 1937–40's, "Classic Style" 24 tune selections, large rounded case style, plastic panels down sides, up and around front top of case, large oval center section of case contains half circle glass panel on top to view record mechanism and tune cards, push buttons directly under viewing panel, coin mechanism in center of case, decorative speaker grill in base 2000.00 3250.00

☐ WURLITZER MODEL 780, c. 1941, 24 tune selections, "Colonial Style" model, decorative molding on side (corner), front panels and grill, push-button tune selector, viewing windows 500.00 700.00

☐ WURLITZER MODEL 800, c. 1940, 24 selections, wood trim and base, large orange and red plastic corner sides and top panels, decorative grill, clear glass panel to view mechanism and tune selections, lights up, wood case 1500.00 3000.00

☐ WURLITZER MODEL 840 "PEACOCK," c. 1941, "Classic Style," 24 tune selections, highly styled case, large plastic panel along rounded side corners and up around top front of case, center panel "peacock" design, stylized grill section U-shaped around "peacock" panel, half circle glass viewing panel on top, tune selector cards in rows under glass panel, push buttons, lights up, wood case 5000.00 7000.00

☐ WURLITZER MODEL 850, "PEACOCK," polarized film unit created prism effect behind plastic panels (looks like Model 840) 4750.00 6750.00

☐ WURLITZER MODEL 850A, c. 1941 .... 4750.00 6750.00

☐ WURLITZER MODEL 950, c. 1942, "Classic Model," 24 tune selections, curved top, large corner plastic panels, also on top front and sides of speaker, grill decorated with Art Deco motifs of animals and satyrs, half circle glass panel on top to view record mechanism, tune cards and buttons just below window, wood sides and base 7000.00 11,000.00

Price Range

☐ WURLITZER "VICTORY," c. 1942–43, 24 selections, distinctive design, wood case with angular straight lines on top, decorated multicolored glass panels along front top and down front sides with musical instruments, harlequins, etc., small half circle viewing window, push buttons, decorative grill with colored panels behind 2000.00   2750.00

☐ WURLITZER MODEL 1015, c. 1946–47, 24 tune selections, "Classic Style," revolving lights in plastic "bubble tubes" all around top front and down front sides of case, U-shaped plastic tubes in middle around decorative grill half circle viewing window in top front of case, tune cards with push buttons just under glass viewing window, metal trim 4000.00   6500.00

☐ WURLITZER MODEL 1050, c. 1974, nostalgia model, 100 tune selections, similar in style to the 1015 "Classic Style," this model turns up in sales with older models but it does not really compare in design quality at all .. 2000.00   4000.00

☐ WURLITZER MODEL 1080, c. 1947–49, 24 tune selections, "Classic Model," graceful curving contours with decorated mirrored panels along front sides and around top, large lyre-shaped grill, glass panel to view mechanism, tune selection cards in front above speaker grill 4000.00   6000.00

☐ WURLITZER MODEL 1080A, c. 1946, "Colonial," lyre grill 3000.00   4000.00

☐ WURLITZER MODEL 1100, c. 1948–49, 24 tune selections, space age look, large pointed half dome top provides full view of record mechanism, tune selection push buttons, tune cards are on a roller type mechanism with 8 cards showing at one time, swirl design large front side panels with multicolors, metal grill with decorative grate on bottom 2250.00   3500.00

☐ WURLITZER MODEL 1200 (see Model 1100).

Price Range

☐ WURLITZER MODEL 1250, c. 1950, 48 tune selections, wood case rounded top clear plastic dome, decorative multicolored panels along front sides of speaker, metal grill, push buttons 1100.00   1750.00

☐ WURLITZER MODEL 1400, c. 1951–52, 48 selections, can play 45, 78, and 33$\frac{1}{3}$rpm discs, see also Model 1450 .... 750.00   1750.00

☐ WURLITZER MODEL 1450, c. 1951–52, 48 tune selections, push buttons, dome top to view mechanism, wood case, multicolored front panels, decorative metal grill 600.00   1000.00

☐ WURLITZER MODEL 1500, c. 1952, 104 tune selections, wood case, rounded top to view mechanism, colored corner front panels, push buttons, twin stacks of discs, either 78, 45, or 33$\frac{1}{3}$rpm 400.00   800.00

☐ WURLITZER MODEL 1600, 48 selections, simple lines, large dome top, push buttons, 78rpm (Model 1650 looks the same) 500.00   800.00

☐ WURLITZER MODEL 1700 .... 750.00   1100.00
☐ WURLITZER MODEL 1800 .... 750.00   1100.00
☐ WURLITZER MODEL 1900 .... 750.00   1100.00

☐ WURLITZER "AMBASSADOR," c. 1947, cosmetic change in Model 1015. No bubble tubes, large red curved top plastic multi-tone side panels, red U-shaped center panels, window to view mechanism, 24 tune selections 2000.00   3000.00

PIANOS (SELF-PLAYING)

The push-up piano player came into general prominence in the 1890's. By the early 1900's the player piano (inner player) took over the industry. Between the turn of the century and the early 1930's there were literally hundreds, if not thousands, of piano companies in this country. Quite a number of them ventured into the player piano field. Some companies made player mechanisms for their own pianos exclusively, but most used mechanisms made by companies specializing in the field. The Standard Pneumatic Action Co. and the Simplex Player Action Co. are two well-known examples.

The player piano is a self-playing piano that uses a vacuum that is controlled by a paper roll passing over a tracker bar to activate valves and then pneumatics (little bellows), which operate the piano action and cause the notes to play. This type of mechanism was made by many companies. The original concept was a push-up piano player mechanism, which was housed in a free-standing floor cabinet that sat in front of the keyboard of a regular piano and when a roll was inserted and the player was foot-pumped, the mechanism acted on the tops of the keys like little fingers.

While the regular player piano plays its music with basically the same degree of force and volume, the reproducing expression piano has a much more elaborate mechanism, which produces a human-like master performance by varying the amount of suction, thereby causing the notes to play louder and softer.

The three reproducing mechanisms that dominated the field through the 1930's are Welte-Mignon, Duo-Art, and Ampico. Welte produced push-up players as well.

Except for early foot-pumped transitional models, the reproducing players were built with electric motors that controlled their playing speed more efficiently.

When sales in pianos and players began to decline in the 1920's, companies were bought up and consolidated into other companies. This has led to some confusion over the years. Needless to say, only a handful of companies still exist from those days.

The following compilation is an effort to identify some of the better known company names and indicate what type of player mechanism was used in their pianos.

When evaluating a player or reproducing expression piano, the main points are

1. The overall reputation of the piano company.
2. The type of player mechanism used in the piano.
3. Related to #2 is whether the piano and player mechanism have been expertly restored and how well the piano plays.

It must be noted here that it is quite rare that one comes upon a player in "original unrestored" condition, that is to say, playing as it was meant to. Time and temperature have dried and worn it out. Most require restoration.

4. Case styles—while most players, especially upright models, are basically straight simple styles in mahogany or oak, there are many exceptions. When a piano has an "art case," it is decorated with fancy moldings, carvings, inlay or veneer work, or all of these. Generally, the more elaborate a model is, the more valuable.

There are more examples of this in reproducing pianos than the regular players. (For specific examples see "Reproducing Expression Pianos.")

For history and detailed information see "Further Reading" section.

In some parts of the United States, players are still quite common. House sales, antique shops, local auctions are all good sources. (See "Dealers and Restorers.")

Restoration encompasses three main elements:

1. Rebuilding of the pneumatic mechanism with new materials.
2. Regulating or rebuilding the piano action, and often repinning and refringing the piano.
3. Refinishing of the case.

Prices for restored player pianos in the following section assume complete rebuilding of the pneumatic system, but only minor piano work and no refinishing. Prices for reproducing pianos assume a complete job, including refinishing.

	Unrestored	Restored

PUSH-UP PIANO PLAYERS

	Unrestored	Restored
☐ **AEOLIAN,** 65-note Push-Up Player, some case decoration	250.00	1000.00
☐ **AEOLIAN METROSTYLE PIANOLA,** 65-note Push-Up Player	150.00	1250.00
☐ **AEOLIAN METROSTYLE-THEMODIST,** Push-Up Piano, 65-note and 88-note combination player	750.00	1500.00–2500.00
☐ **AEOLIAN STECK,** 65-note Push-Up Player	250.00	1000.00
☐ **ANGELUS,** Push-Up Player, 65-note, some case decoration	250.00–500.00	1750.00–2750.00
☐ **ANGELUS REED ORGAN,** Push-Up Player	300.00	1000.00
☐ **APPOLLO,** 58-note, auto rewind, made by Clark	250.00	1000.00
☐ **ARTEMIS (Krell),** 65-note Push-Up Player	275.00	1250.00
☐ **CECILLIAN Push-Up Player,** 65-note, paneled case in ebony finish, foot pump, plays Cecillian rolls and has an adaptor for regular 65-note rolls	200.00–250.00	1350.00–2000.00
☐ **CHASE AND BAKER,** 65-note Push-Up Player	250.00	1000.00

Angelus Push-Up Player, 65 note (Photo courtesy of Mechanical Music Center, Inc. —Darien, CT.)

	Unrestored	Restored
☐ **HUPFELD,** 65-note Push-Up Player	500.00	1250.00
☐ **KRELL,** Auto Push-Up Player, 65-note, foot pump, simple case decoration, c. 1900–05	225.00–300.00	1250.00–2000.00
☐ **ROTH AND ENGLEHARDT,** Piano Player, mahogany case with some decoration, 35″ high	200.00–250.00	1350.00–1950.00
☐ **SIMPLEX** (early), Push-Up Player, rosewood, fluted legs	250.00	1250.00
☐ **STERLING CABINET PLAYER,** oak console	250.00	1250.00
☐ **WELTE-MIGNON VORSETZER,** Push-Up Player, cabinet on legs	1200.00	2750.00
☐ **WELTE-MIGNON VORSETZER,** Push-Up Player, console, "Red" Welte Rolls	1500.00	2750.00

	Unrestored	Restored
☐ **WELTE VORSETZER,** "Red Welte," Push-Up Player, simple cabinet, style down to floor, factory painted, raised border panel decoration	1000.00–1500.00	2500.00–3000,00
☐ **WILCOX & WHITE, ANGELUS,** 65-note (with reeds), Push-Up Player	300.00	1000.00
☐ **WILCOX & WHITE,** Push-Up Player, 65-note, with two ranks of organ reeds	200.00–350.00	1000.00–2250.00

Many 65-note push-up players use special 65-note player rolls (with pin ends). These rolls were made by Aeolian, Angelus, Universal, Connorized, Chase and Baker, and others. The musical selections were somewhat limited, and they cannot be played on regular 88-note players.

PLAYER PIANOS

Unless otherwise described, the values given are for upright regular player pianos.

☐ **ACKERMAN AND LOWE PIANO CO. (OH),** used foot pump regular player mechanism made by Amphion 250.00   2500.00

    ADAPTO, Player mechanism used in upright pianos made by the Lindenberg Piano Co. (Columbus, OH).

☐ **ADLER MANUFACTURING CO. (Louisville, KY),** used the Amphion Player mechanism   250.00   2500.00–3000.00

☐ **AEOLIAN COMPANY (NY) and the AEOLIAN WEBER PIANO & PIANOLA CO. (NY),** controlled the production of the Pianola Players, Duo Art Reproducing Player mechanism and the following piano companies: Weber, George Steck & Co., Wheelock, Stuyvesant, Chilton, Technola, and others. They produced players known as the Weber Pianola, George Steck Pianola, Wheelock Pianola, Stuyvesant Pianola, and Stroud Pianola. They also manufactured the Aeolian Orchestrelle and the Aeolian Pipe Organ, and con-

	Unrestored	Restored

trolled the Melodee and Universal Music Companies which produced piano rolls. The Aerolian Player mechanism is identified by a name plate above the tracker bar. (See "Reproducing Expression Pianos" section for examples, and see individual listings for values.) Regular Pinaolas 250.00– 2250.00–
                                                                400.00   2750.00

□ **AERIOLA PLAYERS,** made by Aeolian 150.00– 2500.00–
                                                                250.00   2750.00

□ **ALDRICH PIANO CO.,** used the Aeolian Player mechanism or the Simplex Player mechanism 250.00   2000.00

Apollophone Upright Player, with built-in disc phonograph.

Unrestored   Restored

☐ **AMERICAN PIANO CO. (NY).** By the mid-1920's this company was the affiliation of several well-established piano companies: Chickering and Sons (Boston), William Knabe and Co. (Baltimore, MD), Mason and Hamlin Co. (Boston), Foster-Armstrong (Rochester, NY), Haines Bros., Marshall and Wendell Piano Co., Franklin Piano Co., Brewster Piano Co., The Ampico Co., Armstrong Piano Co., The Amphion Co. (See "Reproducing Expression Pianos" section for examples, and see individual listing for values.)

☐ **AMERICAN PLAYER PIANO** (see Bjur Bros. of N.Y.)

☐ **AMPHION PIANO PLAYER CO. (Syracuse, NY),** maker of regular player actions found in numerous pianos, e.g., Ackerman and Lowe, Adler, Baumeister, Claredon, Emerson, R. S. Howard, Krakauer, Laffargue, and others. (See also American Piano Company and see individual listings for values.)

☐ **AMPICO** (American Piano Co., NY), maker of reproducing expression player actions found in many good pianos, e.g., Chickering, Marshall & Wendell, Fischer, Knabe, Steck, Franklin, Haines Bros., Steinway, and others. The Ampico mechanism can be identified in many ways, the most obvious is a name plate. (For examples and values see section on "Reproducing Expression Pianos.")

☐ **ANGELUS,** player action affiliated with the Premier Grand Piano Corp. It used what was called the "Artistyle" system of expression and is found in many pianos, e.g., Wilcox and White, Emerson, Lindemann, George Norris. Early examples were push-up players. (See sections on "Reproducing Expression Pianos" and "Push-Up Players" for examples, and see individual listings for values.)

Unrestored   Restored

☐ **APOLLO PIANO CO. (IL),** used foot pump player actions made by Melville and Simplex in their pianos 175.00–   2000.00–
                                                      265.00   2600.00

☐ **APOLLOPHONE,** upright player piano, foot pump, with built-in disc phonograph inside front left panel next to paper roll assembly 1150.00–   3500.00–
                                                      2450.00   5000.00

☐ **AUTO ART PIANO CO. (NY),** used Standard player mechanism 140.00–   2500.00–
                                                      240.00   2750.00

☐ **AUTO PLAYER** (see Werner Industries)

☐ **AUTO PNEUMATIC PLAYER,** regular player mechanism used in Kohler Pianos, NY. (see Horace Waters.)

☐ **ARTEMIS (KRELL),** player action used in Thompson, Steger, Reid and Sons, Krell, and other pianos 175.00–   1500.00–
                                                      275.00   2000.00

☐ **ARIA DIVINA,** reproducing player mechanism by M. Schulz (see M. Schulz Co.)

☐ **ARTISTANO,** player pianos made by A. B. Chase Co. (see A. B. Chase Co.)

☐ **ARTISTYLE,** player system (see Angelus)

☐ **ARTRONOME,** made by Straube Piano Co. (Hammond, IN). Player mechanism that had a "Penulum Valve" (see Straube Piano Co.)

   AUTOLA, trade name for players made by the Horace Waters Co. piano company of NY (see Horace Walters)

☐ **AUTOPIANO COMPANY (NY),** maker of a player piano mechanism used in many pianos, e.g., Symphotone, Peck & Sons, Jacob Bros., Cunningham, and others. Also produced the Autopiano Grand, Welte-Mignon, The Autopiano Electric Self-Expression Piano, and the Pianista Player 210.00–   1500.00–
                                                      280.00   2500.00

☐ **WELTE** 450.00–   2750.00–
                                                      950.00   3000.00

   AUTOSTYLE, player affiliated with John Church Company Cincinnati, OH (see John Church Co.)

	Unrestored	Restored
☐ **AUTOTONE PIANO CO.,** used the Hardman Peck player mechanism, it was also used in Harrington pianos (made by Hardman Peck)	250.00	2100.00–2600.00
☐ **FRANCIS BACON PIANOS (NY),** used the Standard player mechanism	240.00 375.00	2000.00 2500.00
☐ **BACHMAN PIANO COMPANY,** used the Standard player mechanism	140.00–240.00	1900.00–2500.00
☐ **BAILEY PIANO COMPANY (NY),** used the Bjur Bros. player mechanism	140.00–240.00	1900.00–2500.00
☐ **BALDWIN PIANO MANUFACTURING CO. (Cincinnati, OH),** controlled the manufacture of the following piano companies: Ellington, Hamilton, Howard, Monarch, St. Regis. They produced the Manualo player for their pianos, also used the Welte-Mignon reproducing player mechanism (see "Reproducing Expression Pianos-Welte" for examples)	250.00–350.00	2250.00–2750.00
☐ **BARKLAY PIANO,** used the Aeolian pianola mechanism	140.00–240.00	2000.00–2500.00
☐ **BAUMEISTER PIANO,** used the Amphion player mechanism	200.00–250.00	2000.00–2500.00
☐ **BAUS PIANO CO. (NY),** controlled by and used the Jacob Doll player mechanism	190.00–240.00	1500.00–2500.00
☐ **H. C. BAY (Chicago, IL and Bluffton, IN),** made their own player action, also used in other pianos, e.g., Harmony, Strauss, Walters, Wegman	190.00–240.00	1850.00–2600.00
☐ **BECHWITH PIANOS,** sold by Sears Roebuck only; used the Standard, Simplex, and Beckwith's own player mechanisms	190.00–240.00	2000.00–2500.00

	Unrestored	Restored
☐ **BECKER BROS. (NY),** Standard or Amphion player, mechanisms were used in their pianos. They also produced the Bennington, Playernola, and Mell-O-Tone pianos and players	190.00– 240.00	2000.00– 2250.00
☐ **BEHNING & SONS PIANOS CO. (NY),** used the Behning or Standard player mechanisms	215.00– 265.00	2250.00– 2750.00
☐ **BEHR BROS. AND CO. (NY),** used their own player mechanism, also the Standard player mechanism and the Auto deluxe Welte-Mignon Reproducing mechanism	200.00– 400.00	2000.00– 3000.00
☐ With Welte mechanism	400.00– 600.00	2750.00– 4000.00
☐ **BENNINGTON PIANOS,** made by Becker Bros., NY, with a Standard player mechanism	200.00– 260.00	2000.00– 2500.00
☐ **BILLINGS AND CO.,** used the Standard player mechanism	200.00– 250.00	1950.00– 2500.00
☐ **BJUR BROS. CO.,** made their own player mechanism, and Bjur mechanism was also used in Bailey, Craighead, Stultz & Co. pianos	200.00– 250.00	1750.00– 2500.00
☐ **BLASIUS AND SONS,** used the Pratt & Read player mechanism in their pianos	200.00– 260.00	2250.00
☐ **BOARDMAN AND GRAY,** used the Standard player action in their pianos	200.00– 250.00	2000.00– 2500.00
☐ **BOUDOIR PIANO COMPANY,** used the Amphion player action in their pianos	150.00– 220.00	2000.00– 2500.00
☐ **BRADLEY PIANO COMPANY (MA),** used the Simplex player action	200.00– 250.00	2000.00– 2500.00
☐ **BRAMBACH PIANO CO. (NY),** used the Standard player action, also the Auto deLuxe Welte-Mignon in their grand pianos	210.00– 260.00	2000.00– 2750.00

	Unrestored	Restored
☐ With Welte mechanism	500.00–750.00	3000.00–4500.00
☐ **BREWSTER PIANOS,** used the Standard player action in their pianos	210.00–260.00	2500.00
☐ **BRIGGS PIANO CO. (Boston, MA),** used the Simplex or National Air-O-Player mechanisms in their pianos	270.00–320.00	2500.00
☐ **BRINKERHOFF PIANO CO. (Chicago, IL),** used the Schulz player action. This company also made the Schriver & Sons piano	170.00–220.00	2500.00
☐ **BUSH AND GERTS PIANOS (Chicago, IL),** used Simplex, Standard, Amphion, Gulbransen, Pratt Read, Autopiano, and Otto Higel player mechanisms	250.00–400.00	2750.00–4000.00
☐ **BUSH AND LANE (MI),** manufacturer of the Cecilian player action mechanism. The Welte-Mignon reproducing mechanism was used in upright and grand models as well ..	210.00–260.00	2500.00–2750.00
☐ **BUTLER BROS. (Cincinnati, OH),** used the H. C. Bay, Simplex and Gulbransen player mechanisms in their pianos	200.00–250.00	2500.00–3000.00
☐ **CABLE CO. PIANOS (Chicago, IL),** made their own regular player action (usually trademark found on harp of piano), this mechanism was used in other Cable Company pianos, Conover, Kingsbury, and Wellington pianos.................................	210.00–260.00	2000.00–2500.00
☐ **HOBART M. CABLE (IN),** associated with Story and Clark Co., used player actions made by Standard, Simplex, Amphion, Pratt and Read, Stauch Bros	250.00–300.00	2500.00–3000.00
☐ **CABLE-NELSON (MI),** used several different player mechanisms in their pianos, e.g., Standard, Simplex, Amphion mechanisms.		

	Unrestored	Restored
They also made the Radcliff Piano (Boston)	250.00–300.00	2500.00–3500.00

☐ **CAMBRIDGE PIANO CO. (NY),** made small players, e.g. Style "O" is 3'9", Style "F" is 4'3" 600.00–900.00   2750.00–3750.00

☐ **CAMP AND CO. PIANOS,** made by Henry G. Johnson Piano Manufacturing Co. (Bellevue, IA), made a line of players 200.00–250.00   2000.00–2750.00

CAROLA INNER PLAYER, player mechanism used in Cable Co. Pianos, e.g., Conover.

☐ **CECILIAN PLAYER ACTION by FARRAND (MI),** pianos are usually marked "Cecilian," some grands are labeled "Farrand" 200.00–280.00   2500.00–3500.00

☐ **CELLOTONE PIANOS,** sold by S. A. Hawke & Co. (Mass.), a line of players was sold under the name Cellotone 240.00–275.00   2500.00

☐ **A. B. CHASE (ALLEN B. CHASE, OH),** used Chase's own player mechanism, also the Standard and Amphion 210.00–260.00   2500.00–3000.00

☐ **CHASE AND HACKLEY CO. (MI),** used Standard and Otto Higel player mechanisms   175.00–275.00   2500.00–3000.00

☐ **CHICKERING AND SONS (NY),** used a regular Gulbransen player mechanism, also the Ampico reproducing player mechanism. (See "Reproducing Expression Pianos—Ampico" section for examples) 300.00–400.00   2500.00–5000.00

☐ **CHRISTMAN PIANO CO. (NY),** used their own player mechanism and the Welte-Mignon reproducing player mechanism 210.00–260.00   2000.00–2500.00

☐ With Welte mechanism 500.00–1000.00   3000.00–5000.00

☐ **CHUTE AND BATLER (IN),** used the Standard player mechanism 200.00–250.00   1750.00–2500.00

	Unrestored	Restored
☐ **CLARENDON PIANO CO. (Rockford, IL),** used the Amphion and Pratt and Read player mechanism	210.00–260.00	2500.00
☐ **MELVILLE CLARK (Chicago, IL),** used their own player action, also used in Appollo pianos	210.00–260.00	2500.00
☐ **CONCERTONE,** player made by Mansfield Piano Co. (NY) for their pianos	220.00–265.00	2500.00
☐ **CONOVER CABLE CO.,** used the Cable Co. player mechanism and the Welte-Mignon reproducing mechanism. (See "Reproducing Expression Pianos" section for examples)	250.00–300.00	2500.00–3000.00
☐ With Welte mechanism	500.00–1000.00	
☐ **CONREID (KOHLER & CAMPBELL),** used the Standard player mechanism	220.00–265.00	2500.00–3000.00
☐ **CONWAY (Boston, MA),** used the Simplex player mechanism and Angelus reproducing grands	200.00–500.00	2000.00–4000.00
☐ **COPLEY PIANOS (Chicago, IL),** made a line of players	225.00–250.00	2500.00–2750.00
☐ **CUNNINGHAM PIANO CO. (Philadelphia, PA),** used the Standard and Autopiano player mechanisms	250.00	2000.00–2500.00
☐ **DAVENPORT AND TREACY (NY),** used the Standard player mechanism and the Welte reproducing mechanism	200.00–250.00	2000.00–2500.00
☐ With Welte mechanism	500.00–1000.00	3000.00–5000.00
☐ **DERIVAS AND HARRIS (NY),** used Standard and Simplex player mechanisms	150.00–250.00	2500.00–2750.00

	Unrestored	Restored
☐ **DETMER, HENRY (Chicago, IL)**, used the Amphion action	250.00	2500.00–2750.00
☐ **JACOB DOLL & SONS (NY)**, used their own player mechanism. This mechanism was also used in the Gabler, Hudson, Lakewood, Mason, Stodart, Victor, and Wellsmore pianos. Doll pianos also used the Welte reproducing mechanism	320.00–370.00	2500.00–3500.00
☐ With Welte mechanism	500.00–1000.00	3000.00–5000.00
☐ **DOLL AND SON** (see also Jacob Doll), used Standard, Simplex, and Jacob Doll mechanisms	175.00–275.00	2500.00–3250.00
DRACHMAN PLAYER PIANO, made by H. C. Bay.		
☐ **DUCHESS PIANOS,** trade name of line of players by Werner Industries Corp	220.00–260.00	2100.00–2600.00
☐ **DUNBAR PIANOS,** used the Kimball Player mechanism	220.00–260.00	2100.00–2600.00
☐ **DUO ART,** reproducing player action made by Aeolian (NY) used in many makes of pianos. (See "Reproducing Expression Pianos" section for examples)		
DYNACORD, trademark name used by the Amphion Piano Player Co.		
☐ **EBERSOLE PIANO,** made by Smith & Nixon (Cincinnati), used Standard, H. C. Bay, and Krell player mechanisms	150.00–250.00	2500.00–2750.00
☐ **ELBURN MUSIC CO. (Kansas City, MO),** used the Aeolian player mechanism	220.00–260.00	2500.00–2750.00
☐ **ELECTROVA CO. (NY),** controlled by Jacob Doll & Sons. This company made automatic electric instruments (coin operated).		
☐ **ELLINGTON PIANO CO. (Cincinnati, OH),** used the Baldwin Player mechanism	230.00–280.00	2500.00–3000.00

	Unrestored	Restored
EMERSON PIANO CO. (Boston, MA), used the Standard, Simplex, Amphion, and Angelus player mechanisms	250.00–400.00	2500.00–5000.00
ESTEY PIANO CO. (NY and Bluffton, IN), made a line of upright and grand pianos, also used the Welte reproducing mechanism. (See "Reproducing Expression Pianos" for examples)	220.00–260.00	3000.00–6000.00

EUPHONA REPRODUCING INNER PLAYER, mechanism made by Cable Co.

	Unrestored	Restored
EUPHONOLA (Jesse French), used the Amphion Player mechanism	240.00–290.00	2000.00–2500.00
EVERETT PIANO CO., used the John Church player mechanism	170.00–225.00	1650.00–2250.00
EXCELTONE PLAYER PIANO, manufactured by Chase-Hackley Piano Co. (Muskegon, MI)	200.00–250.00	2000.00–2500.00
FABER PIANO CO. (NY), controlled by Jacob Doll (also used Welte Reproducing mechanism)	250.00–300.00	2500.00–3000.00
With Welte mechanism	500.00–750.00	2750.00–4000.00
FARRAND PIANO CO. (Holland, MI), maker of the Cecilian player mechanism, also made Farrand reproducing grands	250.00–300.00	2500.00–3000.00
J & C FISCHER (NY), used the Standard and Amphion player mechanisms. Also used the Ampico reproducing player mechanism. (See "Reproducing Expression Pianos" for examples)	400.00–500.00	3000.00–5000.00
FOSTER-ARMSTRONG (Rochester, NY), affiliated with the American Piano Co. (NY)	200.00–250.00	2250.00–2500.00

	Unrestored	Restored
☐ **FRANKE PIANOS (NY),** made by Baldwin. Used Autopiano and Baldwin player mechanisms	250.00–350.00	2500.00–3500.00
☐ **FRANKLIN PIANO CO. (NY),** used the Ampico reproducing player mechanism. (See "Reproducing Expression Pianos" for examples)	250.00–400.00	3000.00–5500.00
☐ **JESSE FRENCH & SONS,** used the Standard, Simplex, and Amphion player mechanisms	250.00–500.00	2500.00–3000.00
☐ **E. GABLER BROS.,** used the Jacob Doll player mechanism	220.00–260.00	2500.00–3000.00
☐ **A. B. GARDNER (Los Angeles, CA),** used the Amphion player mechanism	220.00–265.00	2500.00–3000.00
☐ **GODFREY PIANOS (New York),** melodic upright, 88-note regular players	220.00–265.00	2500.00–2750.00
☐ **GORDON & SONS (KOHLER & CAMPBELL),** used the Standard and Pratt and Read player mechanisms	210.00–265.00	2500.00–2750.00
☐ **GRINNELL BROS. (Detroit, MI),** used the Aeolian and Lester player mechanisms	250.00–300.00	2500.00–3000.00
☐ **GRUNET-HUPFELD SOLOPHONOLA,** regular upright player, foot pump (see also Hupfeld, Ludwig)	350.00–450.00	3500.00–4500.00
☐ **GUEST PIANO CO. (Burlington, IA),** made a line of players	220.00–260.00	2250.00–2750.00

☐ **GULBRANSEN (Chicago, IL),** made their own player mechanisms. They made what they called a "Registering Piano" player mechanism. Early model was screwed together, later the stack was glued together and is much more difficult to restore. Gul-

	Unrestored	Restored
bransen player mechanisms found in many pianos	200.00–250.00	2250.00–2750.00
☐ **GULBRANSEN-DICKINSON (Chicago, IL),** used their own player mechanism	220.00–260.00	2500.00–2750.00
☐ **HADDORF PIANO CO. (Rockford, IL),** used the Amphion player mechanism	220.00–260.00	2500.00–3000.00
☐ **HAINES BROS. (NY),** used the Pratt and Read player mechanism and also used the Ampico reproducing mechanism	220.00–265.00	2500.00
☐ **HALLET AND DAVIS (Boston, MA),** used the Simplex Player mechanism and Angelus reproducing grand	250.00–350.00	2500.00–3500.00
☐ **HAMILTON PIANO CO. (IL),** used the Baldwin player mechanism	220.00–260.00	2500.00–3000.00
☐ **HAMMOND PIANOS,** made by Straube (IN), used the Standard, Simplex, Pratt-Read, and Straube player mechanisms	250.00–350.00	2500.00–3500.00

HARDMAN, Autotone and Playotone mechanisms found in Harrington, Hensel, Minipiano, and Playotone Pianos and others.

	Unrestored	Restored
☐ **HARDMAN PECK CO. (NY),** made their own player mechanism. It was used in other pianos as well. (See "Reproducing Expression Pianos" for examples)	300.00–500.00	3000.00–5000.00
☐ **HARMONIST PLAYERS,** made by the Peerless Player Co.		
☐ **E. G. HARRINGTON AND CO. (NY),** used the Hardman player mechanism	250.00–300.00	2250.00–2750.00
☐ **HARRISON PIANO,** used the Kimball Regular player mechanism	220.00–260.00	2000.00–2500.00
☐ **HAYES PIANO,** used the Lester player mechanism	200.00–250.00	2500.00–2750.00

	Unrestored	Restored
☐ **HAZELTON BROS. (KOHLER & CAMPBELL, NY)**, used the Standard player mechanism and the Welte-Mignon reproducing player mechanism	250.00	2500.00
☐ With Welte mechanism	500.00– 1000.00	3000.00– 4000.00
☐ **HEINTZMAN AND CO. (Toronto, Canada)**, used the Otto Higel player mechanism	220.00– 260.00	2000.00– 3000.00
☐ **HENSEL PIANOS**, made by Hardman, Peck and Co. Used regular and Welte reproducing player mechanisms	250.00	2500.00
☐ With Welte mechanism	500.00– 1000.00	3000.00– 4000.00
☐ **OTTO HIGEL PLAYER ACTION**, used in Bond, Lindsay and Worthington pianos and others	250.00	2500.00– 2750.00
☐ **HINZE PIANO (Chicago, IL)**, made by Kimball with Kimball player mechanism	250.00	2500.00
☐ **HOLLAND PIANO CO.**, used the Simplex player mechanism	350.00	3500.00
☐ **HOWARD PIANO CO. (Cincinnati, OH)**, made by Baldwin with Baldwin player mechanism (Manualo)	250.00	2500.00
☐ **R. S. HOWARD (NY)**, used the Amphion and Pratt and Read Player mechanism	220.00– 265.00	2200.00– 2600.00
HUMANA, (See Lauter)		
☐ **HUNTINGTON PIANOS (CT)**, made by Sterling. Used Standard or Sterling player mechanisms	220.00– 260.00	2500.00– 2750.00
☐ **HUPFELD, LUDWIG INC.**, BLUTHNER-HUPFELD SOLOPHONOLA, regular upright and grand player foot pump piano	350.00– 450.00	3500.00– 4500.00
☐ GRUNET-HUPFELD SOLOPHONOLA, regular upright player, foot pump	350.00– 450.00	3500.00– 4500.00

	Unrestored	Restored
☐ LANGHAM-HUPFELD SOLOPHONOLA, upright foot-pump player piano	350.00–450.00	3500.00–4500.00
☐ RONISCH-HUPFELD SOLOPHONOLA, upright foot-pump player piano	350.00–450.00	3500.00–4500.00
☐ HUPFELD GOTHA SOLOPHONOLA, Upright foot-pump player piano	350.00–450.00	3500.00–4500.00

INVISIBLE PLAYER PIANOS, name used by the Milton Piano Co. (NY)

	Unrestored	Restored
☐ **IRVING PIANOS,** made by the M. Schulz Co. (Chicago), used the Schulz player mechanism	200.00–300.00	2500.00–3000.00
☐ **IRVINGTON PIANOS,** made by Story and Clark (Chicago). Used their own player mechanism	200.00–300.00	2500.00–3000.00
☐ **IVERS AND POND (MA),** made a line of players	200.00–300.00	2500.00–3000.00
☐ **JAMES AND HOLSTROM (NY),** used Standard and Autopiano player mechanisms	175.00–300.00	2500.00–3200.00
☐ **JANSSEN PIANO CO. (NY),** made a line of players	200.00–300.00	2500.00–3000.00
☐ **JARRETT PIANOS,** used the Lester player mechanism	200.00–300.00	2500.00–3000.00
☐ **E. P. JOHNSON (IL),** used the Standard, Simplex, Pratt and Read player mechanisms ..	200.00–250.00	2500.00–3000.00
☐ **HENRY G. JOHNSON (Bellevue, IA),** Player De Luxe Piano Co	250.00–300.00	2000.00–3000.00
☐ **GEORGE F. KELLER PLAYER PIANOS,** made by Laffargue Co. (NY)	200.00–250.00	2000.00–2500.00

	Unrestored	Restored
☐ **W. W. KIMBALL CO. (Chicago, IL),** made several variations in their player mechanism. Used in the following pianos: Kimball, Hinze, Whitney, Harrison, Dunbar. Also used Welte reproducing mechanism	220.00– 260.00	2500.00
☐ **KINGSBURY (CABLE PIANO CO.) (Chicago, IL),** used the Cable player mechanism	220.00– 260.00	2500.00– 3000.00
☐ **KINGSTON PIANOS,** made by Wurlitzer. Used Wurlitzer, Simplex, H. C. Bay, and Standard player mechanisms	150.00– 250.00	2500.00– 2750.00
☐ **WM. KNABLE & CO. (Baltimore, MD),** used the Standard and Angelus player mechanisms and the Ampico reproducing player mechanism. (See "Reproducing Expression Pianos" section for examples)	400.00– 750.00	3000.00– 7000.00
☐ **KNIGHT-BRINKERHOFF (IN),** used the Standard Player mechanism	250.00	2500.00– 2750.00
☐ **KOHLER & CAMPBELL (NY),** used the Standard player mechanism and the Welte reproducing player mechanism. This company made many pianos, notably The Autopiano, Artistyle, Peterpan, Soloist, Solostyle, Symphonia, Symphotone, Tom Thumb, Waldorf. (See "Reproducing Expression Pianos" section for examples)	250.00– 350.00	2500.00– 3500.00
☐ **KRAKAUER BROS. (NY),** used the Amphion Player mechanism	250.00– 300.00	2500.00– 3500.00
☐ **KRANICH AND BACH (NY),** used their own regular player mechanism and the Welte reproducing player mechanism. (See "Reproducing Expression Pianos" section for examples)	250.00– 350.00	2500.00– 3500.00

	Unrestored	Restored
☐ **KRELL AUTO-GRAND PIANO CO. (IN) (ARTEMIS-KRELL)**, used their own player mechanism	200.00– 300.00	2500.00– 3000.00
☐ **KROEGER PIANO CO. (CT)**, used the Otto Higel Player mechanism	250.00– 275.00	2500.00
☐ **KURTZMANN (Buffalo, NY)**, used the Standard or Pratt and Read player mechanism, also the Welte	250.00	2500.00
☐ With Welte mechanism	500.00– 1000.00	3000.00– 5000.00

LAFAYETTE, trade name used by H. Lehr & Co. (Easton, PA) Players.

	Unrestored	Restored
☐ LAFFARGUE PIANO CO. (NY), used the Amphion player mechanism	220.00– 260.00	2500.00
☐ **LAGONDA PIANO CO. (IN)**, made by Krell-French and Jesse French. Used Simplex and Amphion player mechanisms	150.00– 250.00	2500.00– 2750.00
☐ **LAKESIDE PIANOS**, made by Cable Nelson (Chicago). Made a line of players	250.00	2500.00
☐ **LAUTER-HUMANA CO. (Newark, NJ)**, used their own player mechanism	250.00– 350.00	2750.00– 3500.00
☐ **LAWRENCE PIANO**, used the Lester player mechanism	250.00	2500.00
☐ **LEITER PIANOS**, used the Aeolian player mechanism	250.00	2500.00– 2750.00
☐ **LENOX PIANO MANUFACTURING CO.**, made by and used the Lauter Player mechanism	250.00	2500.00
☐ **LEONARD & CO. (LESTER)**, used the Standard, Simplex, and Lester player mechanisms	250.00	2500.00
☐ **LESTER PIANO CO. (Philadelphia, PA)**, used their own, the Standard, and Simplex player mechanisms. The Lester mechanism was also used in the Hayes, Jarrett, Lawrence, Leonard, and other pianos	250.00	2500.00– 3000.00

	Unrestored	Restored
☐ **LEXINGTON PIANO CO. (Boston, MA),** used the Simplex player mechanism	250.00	2500.00–2750.00
☐ **LINDEMAN PIANO CO. (NY),** used the Standard and Amphion player mechanisms	250.00–300.00	2500.00–2750.00
☐ **LINDEMANN AND SONS,** used the Angelus player mechanism	250.00–350.00	2500.00–3500.00
☐ **LINGARD PLAYER PIANO,** made by Rudolf Wurlitzer Co	250.00	2500.00–2700.00
LINK PIANO CO. (see section on "Nickelodeons")		
☐ **LIVINGSTON PIANOS,** controlled by Weaver Piano Co. (York, PA). Made a line of players	220.00–260.00	2500.00–2700.00
☐ **LORRAINE PIANOS,** made for the Field-Lippman Piano Stores (St. Louis, MO). Sold a line of popular-priced player pianos	250.00	2500.00
☐ **LUDWIG AND CO. (NY),** used the Standard player mechanism	200.00–250.00	2500.00–3000.00
☐ **LYON AND HEALY PIANO CO. (Chicago),** used the Amphion player mechanism in their players. (See also "Nickelodeon" section)	250.00–350.00	2500.00–3500.00
MANUALO, player mechanism made by Baldwin (See "Baldwin" for further information)		
☐ **MARQUETTE PIANO CO. (Milwaukee, WI),** made player mechanism for their own pianos. (See also "Nickelodeon" section)	220.00–260.00	2500.00–3500.00
☐ **MARSHALL AND WENDELL PIANO CO. (NY),** used the Standard and Aeolian player mechanisms and also the Ampico reproducing player mechanism. (For example, see the section on "Reproducing Expression Pianos—Ampico")	250.00–500.00	3500.00–5000.00
☐ **MASON AND HAMLIN PIANO CO. (NY),** used the Aeolian Player and Ampico Reproducing Player mechanisms. (See section on		

	Unrestored	Restored
"Reproducing Expression Pianos—Ampico" for examples)	350.00–1000.00	3250.00–6000.00
☐ **MASON AND RISCH (Toronto, Canada),** used their own player mechanism	200.00–250.00	2500.00
☐ **MASTER PLAYER PIANO,** made by Winter & Co. (NY)	250.00	2500.00
☐ **MATHUSHEK PIANO CO. (NY),** used the Auto Piano Player mechanism, also Welte reproducing player mechanism	250.00	2500.00
☐ With Welte mechanism	350.00–750.00	3500.00–5500.00
☐ **MEHLIN AND SONS (NY),** used the Standard player mechanism and the Welte-Mignon reproducing player mechanism. (See section on "Reproducing Expression Pianos—Welte")	220.00–260.00	2500.00–3000.00
☐ **MELBOURNE PIANO,** used the Baldwin player mechanism	220.00	2500.00
☐ **MELODIGRAND,** made by Lindeman. Used Standard and Otto Higel player mechanisms	200.00–275.00	2500.00–3250.00
☐ **MELOSTRELLE PIANOS,** made by Steger and Sons Piano Manufacturing Co. (Chicago)	200.00–250.00	2500.00–2750.00
☐ **MENDELSSOHN PIANOS,** made by Winter, later Aeolian. Used Simplex, Pratt-Read, Standard, Higel, and Sterling player mechanisms	225.00–300.00	2500.00–3500.00
☐ **MERCER PLAYER PIANOS,** controlled by Weaver Co. (York, PA)	250.00	2500.00–2750.00
☐ **MERRILL PIANO MANUFACTURING CO. (MA),** used several player mechanisms in their pianos: The Simplex, Jacob Doll, Angelus "Reproducing" Grand, and National Air-O-Player	250.00	2500.00–2750.00

Unrestored Restored

METROSTYLE PIANOLA, made by Aeolian. This mechanism also found in early 65-note push-up players.

☐ **MIESSNER PIANO CO. (Milwaukee, WI),** made small upright players less than 4' high — 750.00–1250.00 — 3000.00–4750.00

☐ **HENRY F. MILLER (MA),** made their own player mechanism .... — 250.00 — 2500.00–2750.00

☐ **MILTON PIANO CO. (NY),** used the Standard player mechanism .... — 250.00 — 2500.00–2750.00

☐ **MODELLO PLAYER PIANO,** made by Baldwin and used the Manualo player mechanism — 250.00 — 2500.00

☐ **MONARCH PIANO CO. (IL),** used the Baldwin Manualo player mechanism .... — 250.00 — 2500.00

☐ **NATIONAL AIR-O-PLAYER,** player mechanism used in the Merrill, Briggs, Norris and Hyde Pianos .... — 250.00 — 2500.00

☐ **H. P. NELSON (Chicago, IL),** used their own player mechanism. It was also used in the Stanley & Sons and Weiler pianos .... — 250.00 — 2500.00

☐ **NETZOW PIANO CO. (Milwaukee, WI),** used the Simplex and Gulbransen player mechanisms .... — 200.00–300.00 — 2500.00

☐ **NEWBY AND EVANS (NY),** used the Simplex, Standard, Amphion, and Pratt and Read player mechanisms .... — 250.00–300.00 — 2500.00–3000.00

☐ **NORRIS AND HYDE,** used the National Air-O-Player mechanism .... — 250.00 — 2500.00

OPERATORS' PIANO CO. (Chicago, IL) (See section on "Nickelodeons")

☐ **PACKARD PIANO CO. (IN),** used the Standard, Simplex, Pratt and Read Player mechanisms and the Welte-Mignon Reproducing Player mechanism. (See also section on "Reproducing Expression Pianos-Welte") ..... — 250.00–350.00 — 2500.00–4250.00

☐ **PEASE PIANO CO. (NY),** used the Standard player mechanism .... — 250.00 — 2500.00

	Unrestored	Restored
☐ **PERRYOLA PLAYER PIANOS,** made by Ludwig & Co., NY	250.00	2500.00
☐ **PHILHARMONIC PLAYER PIANOS,** affiliated with Paul G. Mehlin & Sons	250.00	2500.00
☐ **H. L. PHILLIPS PIANOS,** made for Knight-Campbell Music Co., Denver, CO by Cable-Nelson Piano Co	250.00–350.00	2500.00–3500.00
☐ **PIANISTA PLAYER PIANO (NY),** made by Auto Piano later Kohler and Campbell. Used Autopiano Standard player mechanism	200.00–300.00	2500.00–3250.00
☐ **PIANOLA,** trade mark name used by Aeolian for their player pianos	200.00–250.00	2500.00–2750.00
☐ **PLAYERNOLA,** player made by Becker Bros	250.00	2500.00
☐ **PLAYOTONE,** player made by Autotone of Hardman Peck	250.00	2750.00–3000.00
☐ **PLAYTONA,** player made by Grinnell Bros	250.00	2500.00

PRATT AND READ, player mechanism used in many pianos. Many examples have a nameplate with a "9R" trademark in tracker bar area.

	Unrestored	Restored
☐ **PREMIER GRAND PIANO CORP. (NY & Los Angeles, CA),** maker of the Premiera "reproducing" grand. They also used the Welte reproducing player mechanism in many different case styles	750.00–1500.00	3750.00–4500.00
☐ **PRICE AND TEEPLE (Kankakee, IL),** used their own player mechanism and the Standard player mechanism	250.00	2500.00
☐ **PRIMATONE,** small players made by Foster-Armstrong (NY)	250.00–300.00	2500.00–3000.00
☐ **PUTNAM PIANOS,** made by Wissner & Sons (NY)	250.00	2500.00
☐ **F. RADLE CO. (NY),** used the Auto Piano player mechanism	250.00	2500.00–2750.00
☐ **REGAL PIANOS (NY),** used the Standard player mechanism	250.00	2500.00

	Unrestored	Restored
☐ **REMINGTON,** made by Starr with the Starr player mechanism	250.00	2500.00
REPRO-PHRASO, Player mechanism made by Story and Clark.		
☐ **RICCA & SON (NY),** used the Standard player mechanism	250.00	2500.00– 2750.00
☐ **RICHMOND,** made by Starr with the Starr player mechanism	250.00	2500.00
☐ **RIDGEWAY PLAYERS,** made by O. K. Houck Piano Co. (Memphis, TN)	200.00– 250.00	2500.00
☐ **ROTHCHILD OR ROTHSCHILD PIANOS (Chicago),** used Simplex and Amphion player mechanisms	200.00– 300.00	2500.00– 3250.00
☐ **ROYAL PIANOS,** made by Krell and used the Artemis (Krell) player mechanism	200.00	2500.00
☐ **RUDOLF PIANO CO. (NY),** used the Winter and Co. player mechanism	250.00	2500.00
☐ **SALYER AND SALYER,** used the Amphion player mechanism	250.00	2500.00– 2750.00
☐ **SARGEANT PIANOS,** used the Baldwin Manualo player mechanism	250.00	2500.00
☐ **ADAM SCHAAF (Chicago, IL),** used the Simplex and Amphion player mechanisms	250.00– 300.00	2500.00– 3500.00
☐ **SCHOMAKER PIANO CO. (Philadelphia, PA),** used the Angelus player mechanism . .	250.00– 350.00	2500.00– 4000.00
☐ **SCHROEDER PIANO,** used the Baldwin Manualo player mechanism	300.00	3000.00
☐ **SCHUBERT PIANO CO. (NY),** used the Schumann player mechanism	250.00	2500.00

☐ **M. SCHULZ CO. (Chicago, IL),** used their own regular player mechanism. In Grand Models their "Aria-Divina" mechanism and also the Welte-Mignon reproducing player mechanism was used. Their regular player mechanism is also found in the Irving, Griggs, Bradford, Walworth, Werner, Meyers,

Unrestored Restored

Brinkerhoff and George Allen pianos. (See "Reproducing Expression Pianos" section for specific examples) 250.00 2500.00

☐ ARIA-DIVINA 500.00 5000.00

☐ **SCHUMANN PIANO (Chicago, IL),** used their own player mechanism, also found in other pianos 250.00 2500.00

☐ **J. P. SEEBURG PIANO CO. (Chicago, IL)** (See section on "Nickelodeons")

☐ **SHERMAN CLAY CO. (San Francisco, CA),** used Amphion and Aeolian player mechanisms 250.00– 2750.00–
350.00 3500.00

SIMPLEX PLAYER ACTION COMPANY (Worcester, MA), very popular player mechanism used in many pianos.

☐ **SOHMER AND CO., INC. (NY),** made a line of upright players and used the Welte-Mignon reproducing player mechanism in their player grands. (See "Reproducing Expression Pianos" section) 250.00– 2500.00–
400.00 5000.00

☐ **SMITH AND BARNES (Chicago, IL),** installed Standard 88-note player action 250.00 2500.00

STANDARD PNEUMATIC ACTION CO. (NY), maker of one of the most popular regular player mechanisms found in many pianos.

☐ **P. A. STARCK (Chicago, IL),** used the Standard and Simplex player mechanisms 240.00– 2350.00–
290.00 2850.00

☐ **STARR PIANO CO. (IN),** made many variations of their own Starr player mechanism, also found in other pianos, e.g., the Remington, Maxwell, Zimmermann, and others 200.00– 2500.00
250.00

☐ **GEORGE STECK & CO. (NY),** related to the Aeolian Co. Used the Duo-Art reproducing player mechanism. (See section on "Reproducing Expression Pianos—Duo-Art.")

☐ **STEGER AND SONS (Chicago, IL),** made a line of player pianos 220.00– 2500.00–
270.00 3000.00

	Unrestored	Restored
☐ **M. STEINERT (GA)**, used the Simplex player mechanism	220.00–280.00	2500.00–2750.00

STEINWAY & SONS (NY), used the Welte, Duo-Art, and Ampico reproducing player mechanisms in upright and grand models. (See "Reproducing Expression Pianos" section for numerous examples.)

	Unrestored	Restored
☐ **Some upright examples had Aeolian Themodist 65/68-note foot-pump mechanisms**	500.00–1000.00	3500.00–4750.00
☐ **STERLING PIANO CO. (CT)**, used their own and the Standard player mechanisms. The Sterling mechanism also found in Harvey, Huntington, Mendelssohn, and other pianos	220.00–260.00	2500.00–3250.00
☐ **STORY AND CLARK PIANO CO. (Chicago, IL)**, used their own player mechanism. Also made miniature upright players. Their mechanism also used in Gibbs, Irvington, Iverson, and other pianos	275.00–325.00	2500.00–3000.00
☐ **STRAUBE PIANO CO. (Chicago, IL)**, made their own player mechanism and also used the Standard mechanism. Straube mechanism also used in Woodward, Hammond, and Gilmore pianos	220.00–260.00	2500.00–2750.00
☐ **STROUD PIANOS (AEOLIAN)**, used the Aeolian and Duo-Art reproducing player mechanism. (See "Reproducing Expression Pianos—Duo-Art")	320.00–360.00	3500.00
☐ **STULTZ AND BAUER (NY)**, used the Standard player mechanism	250.00	2500.00
☐ **STUTZ AND CO. (NY)**, used the Bjur Bros. player mechanism	200.00–250.00	2500.00–2750.00
☐ **STUYVESANT PIANOS (NY)**, used the Aeolian player mechanism	220.00–260.00	2500.00
☐ **SYMPHONOLA PLAYER PIANO**, made by Price and Teeple Piano Co	275.00	2750.00

	Unrestored	Restored
☐ **SYMPHONY PLAYER,** made by Paul G. Mehlin & Sons	275.00	2750.00
☐ **TECHNOLA PLAYER PIANO,** made by Aeolian	250.00–275.00	2500.00–2750.00
☐ **TEMPLE PIANO,** used Simplex and Aeolian player mechanism	250.00–300.00	2500.00–3000.00
☐ **WILLIAM TONK & BRO. INC. (NY),** maker of players, Triplex Electric Player, and reproducing uprights and grands	250.00	2500.00
☐ **GEORGE TRAYSER (IN),** used the Starr player mechanism	200.00–250.00	2500.00–2750.00
☐ **VAN DYCK PIANO CO. (Scranton, PA),** made a line of players	220.00–260.00	2500.00
☐ **VICTOR PIANO & ORGAN CO. (Chicago, IL),** used the Bush and Lane (Cecilian) player mechanism	250.00–350.00	2500.00–2750.00
☐ **VIRTUOLO PLAYER,** made by Hallet and Davis Piano Co., later affiliated with Jacob Doll and Premier Grand Piano Co	300.00–400.00	2500.00–4000.00
☐ **VOSE AND SONS (Boston, MA),** used their own player mechanism	250.00–300.00	2500.00–3000.00
☐ **WALDORF PIANO CO.,** controlled by Autopiano Co. Made a line of players	250.00–275.00	2500.00–3000.00
☐ **WALTERS PIANO CO. (Long Island, NY),** made pianos under several names, among them Bloomingdale Bros. Used Standard, H. C. Bay, and Strauch Bros. player mechanisms	250.00–350.00	2750.00–3500.00
☐ **WASHBURN (LYON AND HEALY) (Chicago, IL),** used the Amphion player mechanism	295.00–345.00	2750.00–3000.00

	Unrestored	Restored
☐ **HORACE WATERS & CO. (NY)**, made the Autola Player and also used the Pratt and Read player mechanism	250.00–300.00	2500.00–3000.00
☐ **WEAVER PIANO CO. (York, PA)**, used the Standard player mechanism	250.00–350.00	2500.00–3500.00
☐ With Welte mechanism	500.00–1000.00	3500.00–4500.00
☐ **WEBER & CO. (NY)**, used the Aeolian and the Duo-Art reproducing player mechanism. (See "Reproducing Expression Pianos—Duo-Art" section.) Regular player	300.00–600.00	3000.00–5500.00
☐ **WEBSTER PIANO CO. (MA)**, used the Pratt and Read player mechanism	220.00–260.00	2500.00–3250.00
☐ **WEGMAN PIANOS (NY)**, used the Standard and H. C. Bay player mechanisms	250.00–300.00	2500.00–3000.00
☐ **WELLSMORE PIANO CO. (NY)**, used the Simplex and Jacob Doll player mechanisms	220.00–260.00	2500.00
☐ **WERNER INDUSTRIES CO. (Chicago, IL)**, affiliated with Krell, Auto-Player, Royal, and Duchess pianos. Made their own player mechanism	250.00	2750.00
☐ **WESER BROS. (NY)**, used their own player mechanism	250.00–400.00	2500.00–3750.00
☐ **WESER PIANO CO.** (also Weser Bros., NY), used the Standard, Simplex, Amphion, Aeolian, and their own player mechanisms	250.00–400.00	2750.00–3750.00
☐ **CALVIN WESER MONARCH UPRIGHT SELF PLAYING PIANO**, oak, some case decoration	750.00–1250.00	2750.00–4500.00
☐ **WEYDIG PIANO CORP. (NY)**, used the Standard and Simplex player mechanisms	250.00–350.00	2500.00–3500.00

	Unrestored	Restored
□ **WHEELOCK PIANO CO. (NY),** used the Aeolian and Duo-Art reproducing player mechanism. (See "Reproducing Expression Pianos" section.) Regular player	250.00– 350.00	2500.00– 3750.00
□ **WILCOX AND WHITE (CT),** used the Angelus mechanism	350.00	3750.00
□ **WINTER AND CO. (NY),** used their own player mechanism. Winter mechanism also found in Heller & Co., Andrus, Rudolf, Reinhardt, and other pianos	320.00– 365.00	3500.00
□ **WISSNER AND SONS (NY),** used the Stauch Bros. player mechanism	250.00– 300.00	2350.00– 2950.00
□ **WONDERTON PLAYER PIANOS,** made by Lindenberg Piano Co. (Columbus, OH)	220.00– 260.00	2200.00 2800.00
□ **WOODBURY PIANOS,** used the Simplex and Pratt and Read player mechanisms	250.00	2750.00
□ **WRIGHT AND SONS CO.,** used their own player mechanism	250.00– 275.00	2500.00– 3000.00
RUDOLF WURLITZER CO. (IL), used the Apollo reproducing mechanism (see "Nickelodeon" section)		
□ **YORK PLAYER PIANOS (York, PA),** made by Weaver Piano Co	225.00– 265.00	2500.00– 2750.00

PLAYER ORGANS AND ORCHESTRELLES

The rise in popularity of the player piano directly related to the short-lived market for player organs for home use. In America their popularity spanned from the mid-1880's to the first decade of the 20th century.

These organs look like large upright keyboard pianos with highly ornate fretwork decoration.

A paper roll activated by foot pumping operates the mechanism; there are many manually controlled stops that create special effects: harp, oboe, viola, flute, etc. Knee-operated swell levers control the volume. Their popularity peaked in the 1890's.

These machines are difficult to find and are most commonly seen for sale in dealer catalogues. (See "Dealers and Restorers" section.)

	Unrestored	Restored
☐ **AEOLIAN DUO ART PLAYER AND PIPE ORGAN,** 13 ranks	1000.00– 2500.00	5500.00– 7500.00
☐ **AEOLIAN DUO ART ORCHESTRELLE PLAYER REED ORGAN,** breakfront style when closed, keyboard folds down when in use, mahogany cabinet, uses Duo Art organ rolls	1500.00– 3000.00	8000.00– 12000.00
☐ **AEOLIAN GRAND PLAYER ORGAN,** c. 1900–1910, 58-note, 73 keys, 20 stops, red mahogany, 5 fretwork panels, carved columns, high-back keyboard upright piano style, foot pump, 60″ high	750.00– 1750.00	2250.00– 4500.00
☐ **AEOLIAN HAMMAND PLAYER ORGAN,** walnut case, plays Aeolian-Skinner Duo-Art Semi Automatic Player organ rolls	750.00– 1500.00	3000.00– 4000.00
☐ **AEOLIAN-SKINNER DUO-ART,** semi-automatic player, organ rolls	20.00	30.00
☐ **AEOLIAN ORCHESTRELLE,** 18 stops, mahogany, upright style, 58-note	500.00– 1000.00	2500.00– 4500.00
☐ **AEOLIAN ORCHESTRELLE STYLE F,** 116-note, mahogany case, electric or foot pump, plays 116-note solo and 58-note rolls interchangeably	2250.00– 3250.00	12500.00– 20000.00
☐ **AEOLIAN ORCHESTRELLE STYLE V,** 5′6″ high, fretwork panels, decorative moldings, upright piano style	1500.00– 3000.00	7500.00– 10000.00
☐ **AEOLIAN ORCHESTRELLE STYLE Y,** 58-note player organ, golden oak case, plays Aeolian Grand rolls, 8′4″	1500.00– 3000.00	8000.00– 10000.00
☐ **AEOLIAN PLAYER ORGAN,** 5′ high, 5′2″ wide upright, 3 panels of fretwork on front, roll in center just above keyboard, front legs fully		

	Unrestored	Restored
carved, foot pump, 46-note 9½″ (9⅝″) music roll, 17 stops. Rolls $8.00 and up	500.00–1500.00	2750.00–4500.00
☐ **AEOLIAN ORGAN STYLE 1500,** ebony-finish upright piano style, three fretwork panels, plays Aeolian 46-note organ rolls	1000.00–1600.00	3750.00–5000.00
☐ **AEOLIAN SOLO ORCHESTRELLE,** mahogany, 6′7″ high upright style, plays Aeolian Grand 58-note rolls and Aeolian pipe organ 116-note rolls. Rolls $5.00 and up	2000.00–3000.00	7000.00–9000.00
☐ **AEOLIAN STYLE 1050 PLAYER REED ORGAN,** 12 stops	1250.00–1500.00	3000.00–4500.00
☐ **ANGELUS ORCHESTRAL PLAYER ORGAN,** 58-note organ piano, mahogany, 7 stops	500.00–850.00	2000.00–3500.00
☐ **C.A.V. LUNDHOLM (Stockholm) REED ORGAN,** upright piano style, 51½″ high, bellows pumped by piano-type pedals, knee swells, ebony-finished case, plays Ariston organette discs, mechanism is situated on outside side end of case	500.00–1000.00	2400.00–4000.00
☐ **ORCHESTRONE STYLE 441 B PAPER ROLL ORGAN,** c. 1880's, 55″ high (made by Munroe Organ Reed Co.), ornately carved walnut case with fretwork decoration, bowed front section houses roll assembly, storage for extra rolls on either side	3000.00–4000.00	8000.00–12000.00
☐ **ORCHESTRONE PAPER ROLL ORGAN,** 47″ high, walnut case, carved decoration, foot pedals create vacuum, roll operates by hand crank, 48-note organ, 8½″ wide paper roll	750.00–1500.00	2750.00–4000.00
☐ **REPRODUCO (OPERATOR'S PIANO CO.) PIPE ORGAN,** three ranks of pipes, coin operated, combination mechanism plays 88-		

	Unrestored	Restored
note piano rolls as well as "OS" and "NOS" rolls	3000.00–4000.00	6500.00–7500.00
☐ **REPRODUCO PIANO PIPE ORGAN,** made by Operator's Piano Co., Chicago, double keyboard upright piano style, mahogany, rank of pipes, uses "OS" and "NOS" rolls	2000.00–3000.00	6000.00–7500.00
☐ **SEEBURG MORTUARY ORGAN MODEL H-O,** 61-note, all pipes, plays H-O rolls, also Seeburg XP and regular 88-note piano rolls, double keyboard, simple lines, case cabinet comes up and around keyboard and pipes, leaving a wide curved opening in front	3500.00–4500.00	7500.00–9500.00
☐ **SEEBURG THEATER PIANO/ORGAN,** 4'10½" high upright keyboard piano style, simple case with candle holders on front side panels, mahogany, blower, pseudo-organ pipes	3750.00–4500.00	7500.00–9500.00
☐ **STORY AND CLARK "ORPHEUS" PARLOR PLAYER ORGAN,** c. 1898, single keyboard, 61-note, two sets of reeds, plays 58-note rolls, decorative embossed and colored panels on top front, middle panel contains roll box, 9 stops, walnut case, plays "Orpheus" grand $10^{7/16}$" rolls	1500.00–2000.00	3000.00–5000.00
☐ **VICTOLIAN PLAYER ORGAN,** 46-note, oak plain case, tempo and re-roll stops, knee swells, 59-key, roll placed just above keyboard in center	1600.00–2000.00	3000.00–5000.00
☐ **WELTE PHILHARMONIC PIPE ORGAN,** 8 ranks, fully automatic roll playing mechanism, harp and chimes	3000.00–4000.00	6500.00–9500.00
☐ **WELTE PLAYER ORGAN,** 8 rank organ, player cabinet, harp, chimes	1500.00–2000.00	6500.00

Unrestored   Restored

☐ **WILCOX AND WHITE PLAYER ORGAN,** 44-note piano keyboard style, three elaborately designed front panels (pressed wood), roll assembly just above keyboard, foot pedals, 57½" high .... | 500.00– | 2250.00–
900.00 | 3750.00

☐ **WILCOX AND WHITE PNEUMATIC SYM-PHONY,** Reed organ, upright piano style, oak, fretwork center panel, some case decoration, roll mechanism just above keyboard, 22 stops .... | 1000.00– | 2500.00–
1500.00 | 4000.00

☐ **WURLITZER RESIDENCE (OR MORTU-ARY) ORGAN,** c. 1930, 4'11" high, double keyboard, "Gothic"-style case decoration, 4 ranks of pipes, one metal, swell shutters, 61-note organ, 88-note piano, remote suction motor, walnut case .... | 4000.00– | 10,000.00–
4500.00 | 13,000.00

☐ **WURLITZER THEATER PIPE ORGAN STYLE 135,** console piano style, twin roll player, 88-note rolls, two keyboards, 5 ranks of pipes, drums, xylophone, bells .... | 3000.00– | 8000.00–
4000.00 | 10,000.00

REPRODUCING AND EXPRESSION PIANOS

See introduction to Player Piano section for brief history and description.

Welte-Mignon was the first well-known reproducing and expression system in the United States, though it originated in Germany. Duo-Art and Ampico developed their mechanisms here.

Reproducing and expression mechanisms were installed in the usual upright piano styles most people associate with the player piano. They were also installed in many sizes and makes of baby and full grand pianos. The Ampico system was installed in a "drawer" horizontally placed beneath the keyboard. One pulls the drawer outward to reveal the tracker bar/roll assembly with the tempo, play/rewind, and other controls. The Ampico "B" system is later than the "A" system. In the open-drawer position there are dials instead of sliding controls for the tempo, etc.

In grand-style pianos, the Duo-Art piano roll housing is located above the keyboard, just below and slightly in front of the music desk. The center section lifts up to reveal the tracker bar. The tempo, play/rewind, etc., controls are located in the key slip in front of the keys. In later examples the controls are up near the tracker bar.

The Welte piano roll housing is placed like the Duo-Art above the keyboard. The Welte Licensee system is in a drawer beneath the keyboard like the Ampico.

The Recordo system is housed in a drawer beneath the keyboard also.

Except for early examples most reproducing pianos were originally powered electrically. This is true of the upright models as well.

All reproducing mechanisms require especially arranged piano rolls to produce the proper "expressive" performance desired. Each company made rolls for their mechanism that would not work on any other make.

Regular 88-note rolls will play on these pianos; however, they will sound much as they do on a regular player piano.

Reproducing Expression mechanisms were made for all types and sizes of pianos, from a tiny Kohler and Campbell Tom Thumb Recordo upright with 61 notes to the large Steinway Duo-Art Grands.

(See "Piano Rolls" section for further information about reproducing rolls. Also "Dealers and Restorers—Piano Roll Dealers.")

Unlike the previous section, the following values are for specific piano styles in either restored or unrestored condition: Unrestored (complete but not working), Restored (completely, inside and out, to "original working condition").

These values are subject to the variables described in the introduction to the "Player Piano" section and the "Determining Values" explanation in the front of the book.

	Unrestored	Restored
AMPICO "A"		
☐ CHICKERING AMPICO "A", upright, simple lines	1000.00–2000.00	4000.00–7000.00
☐ CHICKERING AMPICO "A" GRAND, art case, Italian Renaissance, ornately carved, matching bench	3800.00–4500.00	10,000.00–15,000.00
☐ CHICKERING AMPICO "A" GRAND, c. 1930, simple case style in mahogany, 5'2"	1600.00–2000.00	5000.00–8000.00

Unrestored Restored

☐ CHICKERING AMPICO "A" GRAND, c. 1927, painted art case with floral and figural decoration, triple legs with fancy moldings, 5'2" .. 2000.00– 10,000.00–
3500.00 15,000.00

☐ CHICKERING AMPICO "A" GRAND, art case, William and Mary case style, 5'3½", mahogany (walnut) bulbous legs, scalloped molding 4200.00– 8000.00–
4900.00 12,000.00

☐ CHICKERING AMPICO "A" GRAND, 5'4", c. 1924, walnut with maple burl decoration ... 2000.00– 10,000.00–
3500.00 15,000.00

Chickering Ampico "A", Louis XV Case (Photo courtesy of Mechanical Music Center, Inc.—Darien, CT.)

	Unrestored	Restored
☐ CHICKERING AMPICO "A" GRAND, c. 1925, simple mahogany case style, 5'4"	1500.00– 3000.00	8000.00– 11,000.00
☐ CHICKERING AMPICO "A" GRAND, art case style decoration, Louis XVI, 5'4"	1500.00– 3000.00	8000.00– 10,000.00
☐ CHICKERING AMPICO "A" GRAND, art case, Louis XV, 5'8" carved legs and trim	4600.00– 5300.00	13,500.00– 15,000.00
☐ CHICKERING AMPICO "A" GRAND, simple style, 5'9", ebony case finish	1500.00 2000.00	5000.00– 7000.00
☐ CHICKERING AMPICO "A" GRAND, simple lines (Style #65), 6'5", mahogany or walnut	3300.00– 3900.00	8000.00– 12,000.00
☐ CHICKERING AMPICO "A" GRAND (Style #52), simple case, double legs	1500.00– 3000.00	8000.00
☐ CHICKERING AMPICO "A" GRAND (Style #58), straight lines, double legs, 5'8" grand	2500.00– 3500.00	7000.00– 11,000.00
☐ CHICKERING AMPICO "A" GRAND, art case, florentine, walnut with gold decoration especially on fluted legs, 5'3½"	5000.00– 7000.00	13,000.00– 15,000.00
☐ CHICKERING AMPICO "A" GRAND, simple mahogany case style, 6'0"	1700.00 2200.00	6500.00 7500.00
☐ CHICKERING AMPICO "A" GRAND, 9', simple lines, mahogany	8500.00– 10,000.00	17,500.00– 22,500.00
☐ CHICKERING AMPICO "A" GRAND, 5'4", simple case, fruitwood	2500.00– 3500.00	6500.00– 7000.00
☐ CHICKERING AMPICO STUDIO CABINET PIANO, keyboardless, carved walnut case in Italian Renaissance style, very rare, c. 1927	2500.00– 3500.00	10,000.00– 14,000.00
☐ CHICKERING AMPICO "A", SQUARED OFF GRAND, cabinet style ("coffin case," 8 legs, Jacobean-style decoration	3000.00– 5000.00	8000.00– 12,000.00

	Unrestored	Restored
☐ FISCHER SPINET AMPICO "A", c. late 1930's, top loading	1500.00– 2000.00	3500.00– 4000.00
☐ FISCHER AMPICO "A" GRAND, 5'2", simple case style	1500.00– 2000.00	8000.00– 9000.00
☐ FISCHER AMPICO "A" GRAND, 5'3", mahogany, Louis XV art case, single legs, matching bench	2500.00– 3500.00	8500.00– 9500.00
☐ FISCHER AMPICO "A" GRAND, 5'4", simple case, mahogany, matching bench	2000.00– 3000.00	7500.00– 9000.00
☐ FISCHER AMPICO "A" GRAND, Louis XV, walnut art case, decorative moldings	1500.00– 3000.00	8000.00– 12,000.00
☐ FISCHER AMPICO A/B GRAND, c. 1929, rosewood case, 5'7", some decoration	1500.00– 1750.00	7500.00– 10,000.00
☐ FISCHER STUDIO UPRIGHT, c. 1930's, top loading, Ampico "A," 3'10"	2000.00– 3000.00	3500.00– 7000.00
☐ FISCHER AMPICO "A" GRAND, c. 1923, simple case style	1500.00– 1750.00	6500.00– 10,000.00
☐ FRANKLIN AMPICO "A" GRAND, c. 1923, 5', simple case style	1500.00– 2000.00	5000.00– 7000.00
☐ FRANKLIN AMPICO "A," upright, simple case, mahogany	1000.00– 2000.00	4000.00– 5000.00
☐ FRANKLIN MARGUE AMPICO UPRIGHT, c. 1923, simple mahogany case style, foot pump	750.00– 1500.00	3500.00– 4500.00
☐ HAINES BROS., upright Ampico "A"	700.00– 1200.00	3750.00– 4750.00
☐ HAINES BROS. MARQUE AMPICO UPRIGHT, c. 1920, mahogany case, simple straight style, foot pump	1000.00– 1500.00	3000.00– 4000.00

	Unrestored	Restored
☐ HAINES BROS. AMPICO "A" GRAND, 5'1", c. 1925, mahogany simple case	1750.00–2500.00	6000.00–8000.00
☐ HAINES BROS. AMPICO "A" GRAND, c. 1922, Louis XV mahogany art case, 5'4" ..	2500.00–3400.00	8500.00–9500.00
☐ HAINES BROS. AMPICO "A" EXPRESSION (Model "B" Drawer), c. 1930, Semi-art case	3500.00–4000.00	7500.00–8500.00
☐ KNABE AMPICO PARLOR GRAND, 6'5", c. 1928, black walnut, cabriole legs with carving	2500.00–3500.00	7000.00–9000.00
☐ KNABE AMPICO "A" GRAND, 5'2", simple case style	1500.00–2500.00	6500.00–10,000.00
☐ KNABE AMPICO "A" GRAND, 5'3", walnut art case (style A-GE)	2600.00–4400.00	6750.00–8200.00
☐ KNABE AMPICO "A" GRAND, 5'4", plain case	2600.00–3400.00	6700.00–8500.00
☐ KNABE AMPICO "A" GRAND, 5'4", Louis XVI art case style, 9 legs, with stretchers, decorative moldings	3000.00–5000.00	8000.00–12,000.00
☐ KNABE AMPICO "A" GRAND, 5'8", simple case, heavy legs	3000.00–3900.00	10,000.00–12,500.00
☐ KNABE AMPICO "A" GRAND, c. 1921, 5'8", Louis XV case style, graceful curved legs with decoration, mahogany	3000.00–5000.00	8000.00–12,000.00
☐ KNABE AMPICO "A" GRAND, 6', c. 1925, Louis XV style case, walnut, cabriole legs	3500.00–4500.00	8000.00–10,000.00
☐ KNABE AMPICO "A," upright, 4'8¾", plain case	750.00–1750.00	4500.00–6000.00
☐ KNABE AMPICO, "A", upright, 4'4¼", plain case	750.00–1750.00	4500.00–6000.00

	Unrestored	Restored
☐ KNABE AMPICO "A" SPINET, c. late 1930's, top loading	2200.00– 2700.00	5000.00– 6000.00
☐ KNABE AMPICO "A" GRAND, 7"7½", three sets of double-width legs, ornate decoration, gilded painted panels and carved moldings	7500.00– 10,000.00	20,000.00– 30,000.00
☐ KNABE AMPICO "A" GRAND, 9', rosewood, decorative music stand and trim	3500.00– 4500.00	10,000.00– 12,000.00
☐ MARSHALL AND WENDELL AMPICO "A," 4'8", mahogany grand	2500.00– 3500.00	6500.00– 7500.00
☐ MARSHALL AND WENDELL AMPICO "A" GRAND, 5'0", c. 1930, simple mahogany	2500.00– 3000.00	6500.00– 8000.00
☐ MARSHALL AND WENDELL AMPICO "A" GRAND, c. 1925, 5", Louis XVI art case style	2000.00– 3000.00	6500.00– 7500.00
☐ MARSHALL AND WENDELL AMPICO "A" GRAND, c. 1924, 5'1", mahogany simple case	2500.00– 3500.00	7000.00– 8500.00
☐ MARSHALL AND WENDELL AMPICO "A" GRAND, 5', walnut	2000.00– 3000.00	7000.00– 8000.00
☐ MARSHALL AND WENDELL AMPICO "A" GRAND, c. 1927, 5'4", Spanish-style art case, wrought iron decoration (also called "Mediterranean" style)	3000.00– 5000.00	8600.00– 12,000.00
☐ MARSHALL AND WENDELL AMPICO "A" GRAND, 5'5", mahogany art case, carved floral moldings, 3 "triple" legs with carved fretwork (center leg), stretchers connecting legs	3000.00– 5000.00	10,000.00– 15,000.00
☐ MARSHALL AND WENDELL, upright, 46", mahogany	1500.00– 2250.00	4000.00– 6000.00

	Unrestored	Restored
☐ MARSHALL AND WENDELL AMPICO "A", upright, 55" high, c. 1922, Circassian walnut	1750.00–2250.00–3000.00	4500.00–6500.00–6500.00
☐ MARSHALL AND WENDELL AMPICO "A," upright, 5'3", mahogany, simple case style	1000.00–1500.00	3000.00–4000.00
☐ MARSHALL AND WENDELL, studio upright, Ampico "A," simple case	1250.00–2250.00	5000.00–6500.00
☐ MARSHALL AND WENDELL AMPICO "A" SPINET (BABY AMPICO), 37"	2000.00–2500.00	6750.00–8200.00
☐ MASON AND HAMLIN AMPICO "A" GRAND, 5'4", plain mahogany case	4500.00	8500.00
☐ MASON AND HAMLIN AMPICO "A" GRAND, 6'4", c. 1928, simple mahogany case	3000.00–4000.00	9000.00–12,000.00
☐ MASON AND HAMLIN AMPICO "A" GRAND, 5'9", Style AR, simple mahogany case	3200.00–3600.00	8500.00–10,000.00
☐ MASON AND HAMLIN AMPICO "A" GRAND, 6'2", figural walnut	3500.00–5000.00	14,000.00–18,500.00
☐ MASON AND HAMLIN AMPICO "A" GRAND, c. 1926, 6'2", "Colonial" style art case	3500.00–5000.00	8000.00–12,000.00
☐ MASON AND HAMLIN AMPICO "A" GRAND, 7', c. 1925, plain case	4000.00–7500.00	15,000.00–25,000.00
☐ MASON AND HAMLIN AMPICO "A" GRAND, Style AA, ebony finish, simple case style	2750.00–4500.00	7500.00–9000.00
☐ STECK AMPICO "A" SPINET, c. late 1930's, top loading roll mechanism	2300.00–2700.00	6000.00

	Unrestored	Restored

AMPICO "B"

☐ CHICKERING AMPICO "B" GRAND, walnut case with some maple decoration 3000.00– 10,000.00– 4500.00 15,000.00

☐ CHICKERING AMPICO "B" GRAND, c. 1940, 5', mahogany 4000.00 10,500.00

☐ CHICKERING AMPICO "B" GRAND, c. 1930, 5'4", Sheraton art case style 2750.00– 7500.00– 4000.00 9500.00

☐ CHICKERING AMPICO "B" GRAND, c. 1934, 5'10", walnut 4500.00 12,500.00 5300.00

☐ FISCHER AMPICO "B" SPINET STYLE, c. 1930's, some case molding and decoration 1500.00– 4000.00– 2500.00 6000.00

☐ FISCHER AMPICO "B" GRAND, 4'10", walnut case finish with single "french" leg 2000.00– 5500.00– 2750.00 7500.00

☐ FISCHER AMPICO "B" GRAND, 5'4", c. 1930, mahogany, simple case style 2500.00– 7000.00– 3150.00 9000.00

☐ HAINES BROS. AMPICO "A/B" GRAND, 4'8", Louis XV art case 2000.00– 5500.00– 2900.00 7500.00

☐ HAINES BROS. AMPICO "B" GRAND, 4'8", simple case, turned legs 2000.00– 7500.00– 2900.00 8500.00

☐ HAINES BROS. AMPICO "B" GRAND, 5', art case 2000.00– 5500.00– 3000.00 7500.00

☐ KNABE AMPICO "B" GRAND, c. 1926, 5', simple case style 1750.00– 7000.00– 2000.00 8000.00

☐ KNABE AMPICO "B" GRAND, 5'4", Queen Anne single leg, figured walnut with decorative details 3000.00– 13,500.00– 6000.00 17,000.00

☐ KNABE AMPICO "B" GRAND, Style #406, 5'8", mahogany with Ampichron unit 5000.00– 12,000.00– 6000.00 15,000.00

	Unrestored	Restored
☐ KNABE AMPICO "B" GRAND, 5'3", Louis XV art case, walnut	4000.00	8000.00–10,000.00
☐ KNABE AMPICO "B" GRAND, c. 1933, walnut, 5'4", simple case	2800.00–3300.00	8500.00–9500.00
☐ KNABE AMPICO "B" GRAND, c. 1941	2000.00–3000.00	14,000.00–16,900.00
☐ MARSHALL AND WENDELL AMPICO "B" GRAND, c. 1931, 5'2", mahogany, simple case style	2200.00	8500.00
☐ MARSHALL AND WENDELL AMPICO "B" GRAND, 5'2", Mediterranian art case style	2600.00–2900.00	9000.00–11000.00
☐ MARSHALL AND WENDELL AMPICO "B" GRAND, 4'8", simple mahogany case	2500.00–3400.00	7500.00–9500.00
☐ MARSHALL AND WENDELL AMPICO "B" GRAND, c. 1931, 4'8", William and Mary art case style	2000.00–3000.00	7500.00–8500.00
☐ MARSHALL AND WENDELL AMPICO "B" GRAND, c. 1930's, 4'10"	2200.00–2800.00	7500.00–9500.00
☐ MASON AND HAMLIN AMPICO "B" GRAND, c. 1933, plain case	2500.00–3000.00	5000.00–7000.00
☐ MASON AND HAMLIN AMPICO "B," Louis XV art case, painted decoration	5000.00–7000.00	13,500.00–17,500.00
☐ MASON AND HAMLIN AMPICO "B" GRAND, c. 1930, 5'8", Florentine art case, walnut	5000.00–7000.00	25,000.00–35,000.00
☐ MASON AND HAMLIN AMPICO "B" GRAND, c. 1942, 5'8", art case	5000.00–7000.00	25,000.00–35,000.00
☐ MASON AND HAMLIN AMPICO "B" GRAND, c. 1930, 5'8", brown mahogany, simple style	3000.00–5000.00	15,000.00–20,000.00

	Unrestored	Restored
☐ MASON AND HAMLIN AMPICO "B" GRAND, 7', simple case style	3000.00–5000.00	15,000.00–20,000.00
☐ STECK AMPICO "B" GRAND, 5', mahogany, matching bench, jumbo rolls	2500.00–3500.00	6000.00–8500.00
☐ STEINWAY AMPICO "B" GRAND, c. 1930's, simple case, pull-out drawer	10,000.00	20,000.00

ANGELUS EXPRESSION PIANOS

	Unrestored	Restored
☐ CHICKERING ANGELUS GRAND, 6'6", foot pump, simple mahogany case style	1000.00–1500.00	4000.00–7000.00
☐ EMERSON ANGELUS, 65-note player	750.00–1500.00	3500.00–6000.00

APOLLO EXPRESSION PIANOS

	Unrestored	Restored
☐ APOLLOPHONE UPRIGHT PLAYER/PHONOGRAPH COMBINATION, 57½", simple case style phonograph installed on upper left side of piano above keyboard	2000.00–2500.00	5000.00–7500.00
☐ MELVILLE CLARK APOLLO GRAND, simple case style	1000.00–1500.00	5000.00–7000.00
☐ WURLITZER APOLLO GRAND, 4'9", mahogany, simple case style	1500.00–2000.00	4500.00–6500.00

DUO-ART

	Unrestored	Restored
☐ AEOLIAN DUO-ART GRAND, Style RR, 5'2½", mahogany	3000.00	8000.00
☐ AEOLIAN DUO-ART GRAND, 5'6", mahogany case, simple style	1500.00–2000.00	5000.00–7000.00
☐ LYON AND HEALY DUO-ART GRAND, 5'4", c. 1928, simple case style	1500.00–2000.00	5000.00–7000.00
☐ MASON AND RISCH DUO-ART GRAND, c. 1930, 6'1", mahogany	5000.00	10,000.00
☐ **GEORGE STECK DUO-ART GRAND,** 5', plain case	1500.00–2500.00	4500.00–5500.00

	Unrestored	Restored
☐ GEORGE STECK DUO-ART GRAND, 5'4", c. 1920's, plain mahogany case	2000.00–3000.00	5000.00–7500.00
☐ GEORGE STECK DUO-ART GRAND, 5'7", walnut	1000.00–2000.00	6000.00–7500.00
☐ GEORGE STECK DUO-ART GRAND, c. 1922, 5'8", mahogany	1000.00–2000.00	6000.00–8000.00
☐ GEORGE STECK DUO-ART GRAND, Style HR	1000.00–2000.00	6000.00–7500.00
☐ GEORGE STECK DUO-ART GRAND, Style MM, 6'½", mahogany plain	1000.00–2000.00	7000.00–8500.00
☐ GEORGE STECK DUO-ART, c. 1922, upright, walnut	750.00–1000.00	4000.00–5000.00
☐ GEORGE STECK DUO-ART, upright, 4'4¾", mahogany (oak), foot pump, early	500.00–1000.00	3700.00–4700.00
☐ STECK-GOTHA DUO-ART GRAND, pump pedals enclosed in case under keyboard at pedal lyre, triple legs, inlaid garlands, oval scenes in medallions along body of case (art case), early Duo-Art	2250.00–3250.00	8000.00–12,000.00
☐ STEINWAY DUO-ART GRAND, 6'1", c. 1920, walnut case	3500.00–4500.00	10,500.00–15,000.00
☐ STEINWAY DUO-ART, Style XR, 6'1", mahogany	5000.00–7000.00	13,000.00–15,000.00
☐ STEINWAY DUO-ART GRAND, Model OR, Italian Renaissance art case style, c. 1929	8500.00–10,500.00	15,000.00–20,000.00
☐ STEINWAY DUO-ART, c. 1922. Style OR, 6'6", turned double legs, matching bench ..	6000.00–7000.00	13,000.00–16,000.00
☐ STEINWAY DUO-ART, upright, Style "S," c. 1920. mahogany case	2500.00–3000.00	6000.00–9000.00

	Unrestored	Restored
☐ STEINWAY UPRIGHT DUO-ART, simple case	3000.00	8000.00
☐ STEINWAY DUO-ART GRAND, Style AR, 6′11½″, mahogany	5000.00–6000.00	13,000.00–15,000.00
☐ STEINWAY DUO-ART GRAND, art case, Italian-style fluted, tapered double legs, decorative moldings	10,000.00	20,000.00
☐ STEINWAY DUO-ART MODEL SALON GRAND, 6′6″, Spanish Renaissance, highly carved, turned legs	10,000.00	20,000.00
☐ STEINWAY DUO-ART GRAND, Model OR, mahogany	3500.00–4400.00	10,000.00–15,000.00
☐ STEINWAY DUO-ART GRAND, Model OR, art case, Louis XVI, fluted carved legs, 6′5″	10,000.00	20,000.00
☐ STEINWAY VERTIGRAND, c. 1911, Aeolian player	1500.00–2000.00	4000.00–5000.00
☐ STEINWAY DUO-ART GRAND, Style XR, Louis XV art case, 6′2″, matching bench	4000.00–5000.00	15,000.00–20,000.00
☐ STEINWAY DUO-ART GRAND, c. 1918, ebony, 6′4″	4000.00–5000.00	10,000.00
☐ STEINWAY DUO-ART GRAND, Model D, 9′6″, extra-braced double legs	4500.00–5500.00	20,000.00–30,000.00
☐ STROUD DUO-ART GRAND, c. 1932, 5″, walnut case	1500.00–2500.00	5250.00–6000.00
☐ STROUD UPRIGHT DUO-ART, c. 1928	1000.00–1500.00	3000.00–4500.00
☐ STROUD UPRIGHT DUO-ART, 4′7″, mahogany	1000.00–1500.00	3000.00–4500.00
☐ STROUD DUO-ART UPRIGHT, foot pump, 4′6″, early	750.00–1500.00	3750.00–5000.00
☐ STROUD DUO-ART GRAND, 5′2″, simple case style, some decoration	3000.00–4000.00	6000.00–7500.00

	Unrestored	Restored
☐ STROUD DUO-ART GRAND, 5'3", art case style, decorative details and molding	3000.00–4000.00	6000.00–7500.00
☐ STROUD DUO-ART, c. 1932, 5'4", fruitwood, (brown mahogany)	3000.00–4000.00	6000.00–8000.00
☐ STROUD DUO-ART GRAND, c. 1928, 5'8", gold and white painted case decoration ...	3000.00–4000.00	6500.00–8000.00
☐ WEBER DUO-ART GRAND, 5'9"	3000.00–9000.00	6500.00–
☐ WEBER DUO-ART GRAND, Style FR, 5'11½", mahogany	3700.00–4300.00	8000.00–9000.00
☐ WEBER DUO-ART GRAND, 5'8", inlaid art case	5700.00–6200.00	10,000.00–12,000.00
☐ WEBER DUO-ART GRAND, 5'8", walnut art case	4000.00–5000.00	8000.00–10,000.00
☐ WEBER DUO-ART GRAND, fruitwood finish, 5'8", matching bench and roll cabinet	2700.00–3300.00	8500.00–12,000.00
☐ WEBER DUO-ART GRAND, 5'8", burled oak, gothic style case, 10 legs	6000.00–8000.00	15,000.00–17,500.00
☐ WEBER DUO-ART GRAND, 6'1", painted case	4000.00	8000.00
☐ WEBER DUO-ART GRAND, c. 1921, 6'3", walnut	3500.00–4500.00	7500.00–9500.00
☐ WEBER DUO-ART GRAND, c. 1924, 6'2", walnut case with some simple decoration ..	3500.00–4500.00	7500.00–9000.00
☐ WEBER DUO-ART GRAND, c. 1920, 5'10", Style WR, brown mahogany	3000.00–3400.00	6000.00–8000.00
☐ WEBER DUO-ART GRAND, c. 1929, 5'6", inlaid medallions on case, bench	1500.00–3000.00	9000.00–12,000.00

	Unrestored	Restored
☐ WEBER DUO-ART GRAND, c. late 1920's, Louis XVI art case, scroll details	4000.00–5000.00	8000.00–12,000.00
☐ WEBER DUO-ART UPRIGHT, c. 1915, flame-grain mahogany	1500.00–2000.00	4000.00–5000.00
☐ WEBER UPRIGHT DUO-ART, foot pump (and electric), 4'5", plain case, mahogany	750.00–1250.00	3500.00–4500.00
☐ WEBER UPRIGHT DUO-ART, oak, 4'5", plain case	1000.00–1500.00	3750.00–5000.00
☐ WHEELOCK DUO-ART UPRIGHT, early, 4'6¾", mahogany case, foot pump	750.00–1000.00	3250.00–4500.00

HUPFELD EXPRESSION PIANOS

	Unrestored	Restored
☐ HUPFELD (BLUTHNER) THIPHONOLA GRAND, 6'3", rosewood, foot pump with electric expression, simple case lines, double leg	5000.00–6000.00	10,000.00–12,000.00
☐ HUPFELD-DEA GRAND, 6'1", ebony finish, foot pump and electric expression, simple case lines, double leg	4500.00–5000.00	7500.00–10,000.00
☐ HUPFELD-DEA (RONISH) UPRIGHT, c. 1905, mahogany with some case decoration, electric drive	2500.00–3500.00	6000.00–7000.00
☐ HUPFELD PHONOLA UPRIGHT, 65-note, foot pump, ebony case finish, mother-of-pearl decoration	1200.00–1500.00	6000.00–7000.00
☐ HUPFELD PHONOLA UPRIGHT, 73-note, pedal operated, decorated walnut case with brass and mother-of-pearl inlays, candle holders on sides of top front panels	1200.00–1500.00	6000.00–7000.00

	Unrestored	Restored
☐ HUPFELD (RONISCH) TRIPHONOLA UPRIGHT, 4'4", mahogany case, foot pump and electric expression mechanism, simple case style	2500.00–3500.00	6000.00–7000.00

RECORDO

	Unrestored	Restored
☐ APOLLO RECORDO GRAND, simple case style	750.00–1250.00	3750.00–5000.00
☐ H. C. BAY, 5'3", baby grand with bench	500.00–1000.00	3500.00–4750.00
☐ BRINKERHOFF RECORDO, small grand	750.00–1100.00	3500.00–5000.00
☐ BUSH AND LANE RECORDO GRAND, c. 1924, 5", simple case style	800.00–1100.00	3500.00–4750.00
☐ CABLE-NELSON RECORDO, upright, 4'10" high, plain case	2000.00–3000.00	5500.00–7500.00
☐ CHOPIN RECORDO GRAND, c. mid-1920's, 5'2", mahogany, simple case style	500.00–1000.00	3500.00–5000.00
☐ CUNNINGHAM RECORDER GRAND, c. 1927, 5', Auto De Luxe, Circassian walnut, single cabriole legs	750.00–1250.00	3500.00–5500.00
☐ JACOB DOLL, c. 1928, 4'8", baby grand, drawer under keyboard	500.00–1000.00	3000.00–3500.00
☐ KOHLER & CAMPBELL "TOM THUMB," c. 1926, 61-note upright Chinese art case and bench, rare	1500.00–2500.00	4000.00–4500.00
☐ LINGARD (WURLITZER) RECORDO GRAND, 5', "A" expression mechanism, mahogany case	1800.00–2500.00	4500.00–5500.00
☐ MEHLIN & SONS, c. 1934, 4'9", baby grand, walnut	1500.00–2000.00	4000.00–4500.00

	Unrestored	Restored
☐ RECORDO PIXIE-DAVENPORT & TREACY PIANO CO., 41″, 40½″ wide, 61-note, mahogany, matching bench	750.00– 1500.00	3000.00– 4000.00
☐ STUYVESANT UPRIGHT, simple case, mahogany	500.00– 1000.00	3500.00– 4000.00
☐ WALTHAM GRAND, 5′1″, mahogany	1000.00– 1500.00	3000.00– 4000.00
☐ WURLITZER 4′10″, mahogany, art case (9 legs)	1500.00– 2000.00	4000.00– 5750.00

WELTE, WELTE-MIGNON, WELTE LICENSEE

	Unrestored	Restored
☐ BALDWIN WELTE GRAND, art case, Louis XIV	2500.00– 3500.00	7000.00– 9000.00
☐ BALDWIN WELTE GRAND, art case, Louis XVI	2500.00– 3500.00	7000.00– 9000.00
☐ BALDWIN WELTE GRAND, art case, Jacobean	2500.00– 3500.00	7000.00– 9000.00
☐ BECHSTEIN WELTE GRAND, 7′, ebony finish	3500.00– 4500.00	10,000.00– 15,000.00
☐ BECHSTEIN WELTE MIGNON GRAND, Model 98, plays green Welte rolls, simple case style	1000.00– 2000.00	7000.00– 9000.00
☐ BRAMBACH WELTE LICENSEE GRAND, 4′10″, brown mahogany, simple case style	1000.00– 1750.00	3500.00– 5000.00
☐ BUSH AND LANE WELTE GRAND, c. 1923, 6′, art case style with decorative moldings	1000.00– 1500.00	5000.00– 6500.00
☐ BUSH AND LANE WELTE GRAND, 6′6″, walnut art case	1250.00– 1750.00	6000.00– 7000.00
☐ CABLE (HOBART M.) WELTE GRAND, 4′10″, mahogany, simple case	1000.00– 1500.00	5500.00– 7500.00

	Unrestored	Restored
☐ CABLE NELSON WELTE LICENSEE, art case upright, turned front legs, decorative molding, inlay	1500.00–2000.00	4500.00–5000.00
☐ CHICKERING WELTE ACOUSTIGRANDE	1500.00–2000.00	7000.00
☐ CONOVER WELTE UPRIGHT, simple case	500.00–1000.00	3500.00–4750.00
☐ ELLINGTON WELTE MIGNON LICENSEE GRAND, c. 1914, 5′6″, brown mahogany ...	1000.00–1500.00	5000.00–7000.00
☐ ESTEY WELTE-MIGNON 5′3″, grand, walnut	1500.00	6800.00
☐ ESTEY WELTY MIGNON GRAND, 5′7″, burled mahogany case, some decoration ..	1000.00–1250.00	4500.00–6500.00
☐ FARRAND WELTE GRAND, c. 1926, 5′2″, Jacobean case style, decorative moldings	500.00–1000.00	3000.00–4000.00
☐ FEURICH WELTE UPRIGHT, mahogany, 5′ high	1850.00–2250.00	4500.00–5500.00
☐ FEURICH WHITE CABINET KEYBOARD-LESS UPRIGHT PIANO (oak) mahogany, "Red" Welte System, 5′	2000.00–3000.00	7000.00–10,500.00
☐ HARDMAN WELTE-MIGNON, 5′10″, grand, Jacobean art case, mahogany with burled walnut inlay, matching bench	1500.00–2000.00	7500.00–9500.00
☐ HARDMAN WELTE UPRIGHT, simple lines, mahogany	750.00–1000.00	3500.00–4750.00
☐ HOWARD (BALDWIN) WELTE GRAND, simple case	750.00–1000.00	3000.00–4000.00
☐ KIMBALL WHITE GRAND, 5′9″, simple case style	500.00–1250.00	4500.00–5500.00
☐ KIMBALL WELTE GRAND, 6′, simple case	500.00–1250.00	4500.00–5500.00

	Unrestored	Restored
☐ KRANICH AND BACH BABY GRAND, c. 1924, Welte-Mignon, 5', grand	2000.00–2500.00	3500.00–4500.00
☐ KRANICH AND BACH WELTE, c. 1928, art case, Louis XV, walnut	4000.00	10,000.00
☐ LESTER WELTE GRAND, 5'7", simple case style	1500.00–2000.00	4500.00–6500.00
☐ MASON AND HAMLIN WELTE UPRIGHT, c. 1913, simple case style	1000.00–2000.00	7500.00–9500.00
☐ MATHUSHEK WELTE GRAND, c. 1935, 5'3", action in drawer	1500.00–1800.00	2700.00–3400.00
☐ MEHLIN AND SONS, WELTE UPRIGHT, simple case style, mahogany	500.00–1000.00	3000.00–4750.00
☐ PACKARD WELTE UPRIGHT, plain case style, mahogany	500.00–1000.00	3000.00–4750.00
☐ SCHULZ WELTE GRAND, 5'1", plain case	1000.00–2500.00	4500.00–6500.00
☐ SCHULZ WELTE, art case, Bardini Italian Renaissance, carved double legs, decorative molding, action in drawer	1500.00–2500.00	4000.00–6500.00
☐ SCHULZ WELTE, art case, French style (also Spanish style), action in drawer	1500.00–2500.00	4000.00–5000.00
☐ SOHMER WELTE UPRIGHT, simple case . .	500.00–1000.00	2000.00–2500.00
☐ SOHMER WELTE, art case, Queen Anne style	750.00–1500.00	4000.00–6000.00
☐ SOHMER WELTE GRAND, art case, Jacobean	1000.00–2500.00	4000.00–6000.00
☐ SOHMER WELTE GRAND, art case, Italian Renaissance style	1500.00–3500.00	6000.00–8500.00

	Unrestored	Restored
☐ SOHMER WELTE GRAND, 6', walnut case, simple lines	2000.00–3000.00	5500.00–7500.00
☐ STEINWAY WELTE GRAND, simple case style with large single leg supports, top front roll loading mechanism (13½" roll)	2000.00–4000.00	8000.00–12,000.00
☐ STEINWAY WELTE MIGNON GRAND, Model 100, 6'10", plays Red Welte rolls, simple case style in ebony finish	3500.00–4500.00	9000.00–11,000.00
☐ STEINWAY WELTE UPRIGHT, c. 1910, 13½" roll, play action in top only, 6', upright	3500.00–4400.00	9000.00–11,000.00
☐ STEINWAY WELTE GRAND (Red and Green rolls), c. 1913. 6'11" (German), inlaid case decoration, remote pump	4000.00–6000.00	9000.00–12,000.00
☐ STEINWAY "RED" WELTE VERTIGRAND, c. 1908, 6' upright style, birds-eye maple ..	6000.00–7000.00	9000.00–12,000.00
☐ STEINWAY GREEN WELTE UPRIGHT, ebony finish, large simple case (German made)	4000.00–6000.00	9000.00–11,000.00
☐ (CHARLES M.) STIEFF WELTE LICENSEE GRAND, 4'8" (drawer), dark mahogany, delicate case decoration	500.00–1000.00	3500.00–6500.00
☐ STIEFF WELTE MIGNON GRAND, c. 1928, 5', walnut case, graceful Louis XV art case style, curved legs with carved decoration (drawer)	750.00–1250.00	4000.00–6500.00
☐ WEISER & SONS WELTE GRAND, 5'4", walnut, some simple case decoration	750.00–1500.00	4000.00–6500.00
☐ WELTE LICENSEE GRAND, Louis XV art case	2500.00–3500.00	7000.00–10,000.00

	Unrestored	Restored
☐ WELTE GRAND, 5'3", mahogany, some case decoration	1500.00– 2500.00	7000.00– 8000.00
☐ WELTE UPRIGHT (with Red Welte Mechanism), simple case style	500.00– 1250.00	3750.00– 6500.00
☐ "RED" WELTE, cabinet-style keyboardless upright piano, oak, 5'3"	2500.00– 3500.00	7000.00– 9000.00
☐ "RED" WELTE GRAND, 6'4", ebony finish	2000.00– 2500.00	9000.00– 10,000.00

MISCELLANEOUS EXPRESSION PLAYER PIANOS

	Unrestored	Restored
☐ A. B. CHASE ARTECHO GRAND, c. 1921, 5'8", ebony finish, simple case style	1000.00– 2000.00	4500.00– 6500.00
☐ EMERSON ANGELUS, 65-note player	750.00– 1000.00	3500.00– 5000.00
☐ MERRILL ARTRIO-ANGELUS, c. 1928	750.00– 1500.00	3500.00– 5000.00
☐ J. D. PHILLIPS & SONS DUCA GRAND, c. 1923 (German), 7'10", some case decoration	2500.00– 3500.00	12,000.00– 15,000.00
☐ SCHULTZ MARIONETTE ARIA DIVINA GRAND, miniature 3'8" size, walnut art case, 73 note	1500.00– 2500.00	5500.00– 7000.00
☐ SHIEDMAYER-PHONOLA UPRIGHT, c. 1912, 73-note player, walnut, inlaid decorative panels (German)	2000.00– 2500.00	4750.00– 5500.00
☐ WILCOX AND WHITE ANGELUS UPRIGHT, "Artistyle" expression system, 88-note player, could also play 65-note Angelus rolls	1500.00– 2000.00	3750.00– 5000.00

PIANO ROLL PRODUCERS

During the height of the player piano's popularity there were hundreds of companies producing rolls. Some of the better known and easier to find labels are as follows:

AMPICO CORP. (American Piano Co., NY)
ARTEMPO WORD ROLLS (Bennett & White, Buffalo)
ARTISTYLE MUSIC ROLL (Wilcox & White, CT)
ATLAS WORD ROLL (Newark, NJ)
CAPITOL ROLL & RECORD CO. (Chicago)
CECILIAN PIANO ROLL (The) (Detroit)
CHASE AND BAKER MUSIC ROLLS (Buffalo)
COLUMBIA WORD ROLL CO. (Chicago)
CONNVORIZED PLAYER ROLL CO. (NY)
DELUXE (WELTE) REPRODUCING PLAYER ROLL CORP. (NY)
DUO-ART (Aeolian Company, NY)
ELECTRA MUSIC ROLLS (Standard Music Roll Co., NY)
GLOBE MUSIC ROLLS (Phila.)
IDEAL MUSIC ROLLS (Rose Valley Co., Media, PA)
IMPERIAL PLAYER ROLL CO. (Chicago)
INTERNATIONAL PLAYER ROLL CO. (NY and Phila.)
KEYNOTE SONG ROLLS (Music Note Roll Co., Illinois)
KIBBEY MUSIC ROLLS (Chicago)
LANDAY WORD ROLL (Atlas Player Roll Co., Newark, NJ)
MEL-O-ART (Baltimore)
MEL-O-DEE MUSIC CO. (Chicago)
MELOGRAPHIC ROLL CO. (Buffalo)
MENDELSSOHN PERFORATED MUSIC ROLL (Boston)
PARAMOUNT MUSIC ROLL (NY)
PERFECTION MUSIC ROLL (NY)
PIANOSTYLE WORD ROLL (Brooklyn, NY)
Q. R. S. (Buffalo)
REPUBLIC PLAYER ROLLS (NY)
ROYAL MUSIC ROLLS (Buffalo)
RYTHMODIK RECORD MUSIC ROLLS (Belleville, NJ)
STANDARD MUSIC ROLL (Orange, NJ)
UNITED STATES MUSIC CO. (Chicago)
UNIVERSAL MUSIC ROLL (Chicago)
VOCALSTYLE MUSIC CO. (Cincinnati, OH)
WELTE-MIGNON REPRODUCING (RECORD) (NY)

As in all things, condition of roll and box, rarity of music, and artist govern value. Most of the above piano roll companies made 88-note regular rolls that play on any regular player action piano. (See section on "Dealers and Restorers—Piano Roll Dealers.")

Reproducing Rolls (Ampico, Duo-Art, Welte-DeLuxe) express only on the piano equipped with that particular reproducing mechanism. These pianos can also play regular 88-note rolls.

PLAYER PIANO ROLLS

Sampling of current prices for Reproducing and Expression Piano Rolls.

	Price Range	
☐ AEOLIAN GRAND ROLLS	4.00	6.00
☐ AMPICO "A" ROLLS	3.00	8.00
☐ AMPICO "B" ROLLS	5.00	12.00
☐ AMPICO JUMBO ROLLS	10.00	25.00
☐ ANGELUS ROLLS	3.00	5.00
☐ APOLLO CONCERT GRAND ROLLS	2.00	3.50
☐ APOLLO SOLO ROLLS	2.00	3.50
☐ ART-ECHO ROLLS	10.00	15.00
☐ CECILIAN 65-NOTE ROLLS	2.00	3.00
☐ DE LUXE (for use on Welte)	3.00	6.50
☐ DUO ART ROLLS	3.00	6.00
☐ DUO ART AUDIOGRAPHIC	15.00	20.00
☐ ELECTROVA ROLLS (88-note)	3.00	6.00
☐ HUPFELD DEA ROLLS	10.00	14.00
☐ HUPFELD "T" ROLLS (for Tri-Phonola) ...	8.00	10.00
☐ HUPFELD 73-NOTE ROLLS	8.00	10.00
☐ RECORDO ROLLS	3.00	5.00
☐ SIMPLEX ROLLS	2.00	3.00
☐ WELTE MIGNON ("RED") ROLLS	12.50	20.00
☐ WELTE MIGNON ("GREEN") ROLLS	15.00	25.00
☐ WELTE LICENSEE ("PURPLE")	10.00	12.00
☐ WELTE LICENSEE	3.00	7.00
☐ WURLITZER AUTOMATIC PLAYER ROLLS	15.00	20.00
☐ 58-NOTE ROLLS	2.00	4.00
☐ 65-NOTE ROLLS	1.00	3.00

NICKELODEONS AND SMALL ORCHESTRIONS

A coin-operated piano can simply be defined as basically an upright player piano that is electrically activated by the insertion of a coin. There are differences from the home player piano, however. Generally, the roll mechanism is a larger multi-tune system that rewinds automatically after the last tune on the roll is played. It is then ready to begin again. Depending on the maker, there are many places, the "roll" may be located inside and outside the piano. Most coin-operated pianos were originally designed for public places, and the cases may be elaborate with clear, leaded, or art glass panels. They usually had a mandolin attachment if nothing else.

The term nickelodeon in this instance can be defined as a coin-operated piano as described above, though it might have one or two more instruments in addition to the piano. Basically, it is a semantic difference used by the makers.

Orchestrions go back to the 19th century in Europe. Their production there and in America essentially came to an end with the depression in 1930. Orchestrions (sometimes referred to as nickelodeons, as well) are coin-operated upright piano or cabinet-case mechanisms with a piano sounding board and other instruments and effects. Cases can be quite large and elaborate with highly decorative art glass panels.

All of the above-described types are basically related to the player piano in their pneumatically operated mechanisms. When pipes are part of the instrumentation, they work on wind pressure.

These machines are the most difficult to come by. (See sections on "Auctions," "Dealers and Restorers," and "Mechanical Musical Societies.")

Price Range

AMERICAN PIANO PLAYER
☐ UPRIGHT PIANO, plays 5-tune Wurlitzer paper rolls, coin operated 4000.00   4500.00

BERRY-WOOD PIANO PLAYER CO. (Kansas City, MO)
☐ BERRY-WOOD AUTO ELECTRIC PIANO PLAYER, upright keyboard piano case style, endless roll mechanism (large container attached to rear of piano to catch roll), 88-note and 65-note mechanism, vacuum pump, coin

Price Range

operated, examples have large oval or rectangular clear glass panel in top front section of piano (art glass, also), oak case, plain .. **5000.00 7500.00**

☐ BERRY-WOOD STYLE AOH ORCHESTRION, high-back upright piano style, leaded art glass panels, case decoration, hanging lamps, front top panels open to reveal mechanism, 88-note player action, violin, flute pipes, bass and snare drums, cymbal, triangle (variations in instrumentation: mandolin attachment, tympani, wood block tambourine, xylophone), endless roll (also came in rewind roll type: AOHR) **10,000.00 20,000.00**

☐ BERRY-WOOD STYLE AOE: AUTO ORCHESTRA ORCHESTRION, high upright piano style, art glass, hanging lamps, 88-note player, flute or violin pipes, bass and snare drum, cymbal, triangle, 5-tune endless roll, coin operated (Style AOSR: rewind roll with 8 tunes) **10,000.00 20,000.00**

☐ BERRY-WOOD STYLE C-B, upright keyboard piano with art glass front panels, 25 orchestra bells, endless roll **5000.00 10,000.00**

☐ BERRY-WOOD STYLE AOW (Auto Orchestra, Style W), high-back upright keyboard style, art glass panels, lamps, piano, flute, pipes, violin pipes, orchestra bells, xylophone, snare, kettle and bass drums, castanets, crash cymbal, tambourine and mandolin, rewind roll **7500.00 15,000.00**

☐ BERRY-WOOD STYLE F, upright piano style, teakwood finish, art glass leaded panels (three), violin and flute pipes, 88-note player action, coin operated **7500.00 10,000.00**

☐ BERRY-WOOD STYLE 15, upright piano style with high back, flute pipes, mandolin attachment, art glass, front panels, mission oak case style, hanging lamps on front side panels **7500.00 12,500.00**

CAPITOL PIANO AND ORGAN CO. (North Tonawanda Musical Instrument Works, NY)

Price Range

☐ CAPITOL NICKELODEON, oak upright piano style case, simple lines, three art glass panels on top front, center panel is clear glass (shows roll mechanism). Piano, mandolin attachment, xylophone (usually has violin or flute pipes), A-roll: 10 tunes. (Variations in number and design of art glass panels.) ...   4000.00   8000.00

CHICAGO ELECTRIC PIANOS
☐ CHICAGO ELECTRIC PIANO, upright piano model, art glass panels, coin operated, regular A-roll (10 tunes), mandolin attachment, 4'7" high 6000.00   8000.00
☐ CHICAGO ELECTRIC PIANO WITH XYLOPHONE, coin operated, rectangular case style, art glass, mandolin attachment, A-roll   5000.00   10,000.00

COINOLA (OPERATORS' PIANO COMPANY, Chicago, IL)
☐ COINOLA MIDGET STYLE A, console-style case, 5'4" high, leaded art glass panel in top, coin operated, piano, mandolin, plays 65-note rolls, piano action on top, motor and roll mechanism on bottom 3750.00   5500.00
☐ COINOLA MIDGET ORCHESTRION STYLE K, cabinet style, small art glass panel in center top, coin operated, instruments in top, roll mechanism in bottom, volume control behind cloth covered grill in bottom (louvered shutters), metal violin and wood flute pipes, oak case, Style O roll (all models have piano, mandolin attachment) 4000.00   6000.00
☐ COINOLA MIDGET ORCHESTRION STYLE F, same description as Style K but only flute pipes 3750.00   4750.00
☐ COINOLA MIDGET ORCHESTRION STYLE O, c. 1920's, cabinet style, grill work, bottom doors, 10 tune "O" roll, piano mandolin effect, orchestra bells, and drums 4000.00   6000.00
☐ COINOLA MIDGET ORCHESTRION STYLE V, same description as Style K but with violin pipes 4000.00   6000.00

Price Range

☐ COINOLA MIDGET ORCHESTRION STYLE
X, same description as Style K but with xylophone or bells 4000.00   6000.00

☐ COINOLA "CUPID" (DUPLEX), cabinet style,
4½" high, piano, mandolin (xylophone), two
10-tune A-roll mechanisms side by side in top
section of cabinet, glass panel 4500.00   6500.00

☐ COINOLA STYLE C, upright piano style, mandolin attachment, A-roll 10 tunes, 65-note, art
glass, case decoration, oak, high front posts   3500.00   4750.00

☐ COINOLA STYLE C, reproducing piano, man-
dolin, use 88-note expression rolls 3250.00   4500.00

☐ COINOLA STYLE CF, description same as
Style C with flute pipes, O-roll 3750.00   5000.00

☐ COINOLA STYLE CX, description same as
Style C but with xylophone mechanism, O-roll   3750.00   5000.00

☐ COINOLA STYLE CK, upright piano style similar to other Style C models but with solo vio-
lin pipes and flute pipes, O-roll 3900.00   6500.00

☐ COINOLA STYLE C2, upright piano style,
leaded art glass, oak, mandolin attachment,
bass and snare drums, cymbal 5500.00   8500.00

☐ COINOLA STYLE CO, high upright keyboard
piano style, 3 art glass panels, hanging
lamps, instruments in top section of case,
tambourine, mandolin attachment, bass and
snare drums, tympani, cymbal, xylophone,
flute pipes, Indian block triangle 7000.00   10,000.00

☐ COINOLA STYLE J, upright piano style, simple lines, small leaded glass panel in top front
center section, hanging lamps, coin operated, 65-note player piano with mandolin attachment, A-roll 4000.00   6500.00

☐ COINOLA STYLE JF, same description as
Style J but with flute pipes added, O-roll ... 4750.00   7000.00

☐ COINOLA STYLE JK, same description as
Style J but with violin pipes added, O-roll .. 4750.00   8000.00

☐ COINOLA STYLE JX, same description as
Style J but with xylophone added, O-roll ... 4750.00   7000.00

☐ COINOLA STYLE X, upright piano style case,
high front posts, rounded glass sections in
front top section, instruments in base, O-roll,

Price Range

oak, instrumentation: piano, mandolin attachment, xylophone, bass, plus snare drums, tympani, cymbal, triangle, wood block 7500.00 15,000.00

☐ COINOLA PUSH-UP ORCHESTRA, cabinet style (full height of an upright piano) when pushed up against front of piano keyboard plays piano with instrument accompaniment (Style X instruments) 5000.00 7500.00

CREMONA (MARQUETTE PIANO COMPANY, Chicago, IL)

☐ CREMONA STYLE 2, upright piano style, art glass panels in top front section, oak simple lines, 57″ high, coin operated, mandolin attachment, 10-tune rolls 4500.00 6750.00

☐ CREMONA STYLE 3, upright piano style, clear glass panels on top front (art glass examples), A-roll. Reginapiano same model made by Marquette 3000.00 4500.00

☐ CREMONA STYLE 4 and STYLE 5, upright piano style, oak (mahogany, walnut), art glass, coin operated, A-roll 3750.00 5750.00

☐ CREMONA STYLE 20, 30, upright piano style, art glass, hanging lamps, oak, coin operated, tune selector device, M-roll (allowed patron to choose the tune he wanted, otherwise the tunes played in order) paper M-roll, mandolin attachment, 88-note roll 5000.00 7500.00

☐ CREMONA STYLE A, upright piano style, 57″ high, large art glass panels across front top section, hanging lamps, coin operated, 10-tune roll, oak 6000.00 9000.00

☐ CREMONA STYLE G WITH FLUTE PIPES, high-back upright piano, art glass panels, hanging lamps, oak (walnut) 10-tune A-roll piano, mandolin, flute or violin pipes 7500.00 13,000.00

☐ CREMONA STYLE J, 80″ high upright piano style, art glass panels (case variations), piano, mandolin, flute (violin), bass and snare drums, cymbal, triangle, xylophone, tympani, coin operated, special 88-note (M-roll) orchestral music roll 10,000.00 20,000.00

Price Range

☐ CREMONA STYLE K, 67″ high upright piano style, "Grecian" design case, oak, front legs extend up from floor to top of piano and form a narrow open archway on each side for hanging lamps, 4 large leaded glass panels in front, flute pipes, piccolo, violin pipes, piano, mandolin, triangle, tambourine, castanets. 88-note orchestral music rolls (M-roll) **15,000.00 20,000.00**

☐ **EMPRESS ELECTRIC PIANO (Sold by Lyon and Healy),** keyboard upright piano style, small art glass panel in top front section, coin operated, piano, mandolin attachment, xylophone (or bell unit), O-roll. (Coinola mechanism made by Operators Piano Co.) **3900.00 6250.00**

☐ **ENCORE AUTOMATIC BANJO,** coin-operated automatic 4-string banjo (plays by means of tiny hook-like steel fingers through pneumatically operated fret buttons activated by a paper roll mechanism. Case resembles an upright disc music box. Display case–type top section houses the banjo, roll in bottom section. Oak simple case (must be restored, tuned and regulated expertly to be appreciated). (Some case variations.) Plays 5-tune endless roll **8000.00 15,000.00**

ENGELHARDT & SONS PIANO CO., (ST. JOHNSVILLE, NY) (Peerless Piano Player Co.)

☐ ENGELHARDT CABINET NICKELODEON (Peerless), 4′10″ high, plain cabinet-style case, large art glass panel in front section, oak, piano, mandolin attachment, A-roll **5000.00 7500.00**

☐ ENGELHARDT NICKELODEON (Peerless), upright piano-style case, with xylophone, mahogany finish, coin operated **6000.00 8000.00**

☐ ENGELHARDT NICKELODEON (Peerless), with flute pipes, upright piano case, large art glass panel, piano, mandolin, flute pipes in top section, roll and motor mechanisms in bottom, coin operated **5750.00 8500.00**

Interior View of the Seeburg "KT" Special.

Price Range

LUDWIG HUPFELD, INC. (Leipzig, Germany)
☐ HUPFELD CLAVIMONIUM, upright piano with harmonium effects, walnut case, 4'7" high, two glass windows on top front 3750.00   5900.00
☐ HUPFELD CLAVITIST UNIVERSAL, piano, mandolin, xylophone 6000.00   7500.00
☐ HUPFELD KONZERTIST UNIVERSAL OR-CHESTRION, upright keyboard piano style, 8' high, painted scene on three large glass panels, piano, mandolin, bass and snare drum, xylophone, crash cymbal 8500.00 14,000.00
☐ HUPFELD ANIMATIC CLAVITIST PIANO, up-right piano, light walnut, 4'5" high, electric 2850.00   4250.00

Price Range

☐ HUPFELD HELIOS ORCHESTRION, keyboardless-style piano mandolin, bass and snare drums, violin and cello pipes, cymball, bells **14,500.00 47,500.00**

☐ HUPFELD PHONOLISZT VIOLINA, MODEL A, duplex 6 roll automatic changer **65,000.00 95,000.00**

☐ HUPFELD PHONOLIZST VIOLINA, MODEL B, upright expression autograph piano, hanging lamps on front of piano, three violins placed vertically in section above piano, rotating circular bow (many case variations) **25,000.00 30,000.00**

IMHOF AND MUKLE (Germany)

☐ IMHOF AND MUKLE "LUCIA" ORCHESTRION, c. 1900, 10'7" high, three large floral art glass front panels, violin and cello pipes, orchestra bells, bass and snare drums, tympani, cymbals, mandolin accompaniment, keyboardless piano, elaborate case decoration **12,500.00 23,000.00**

☐ IMHOF AND MUKLE ORCHESTRION, c. 1908–14, keyboard style, louvered swell shutters, pipes high back upright style, pictorial scene, hanging glass lamps **10,000.00 20,000.00**

☐ IMHOF AND MUKLE "RAMONA" VIOLIN PIANO, upright keyboard piano case with high back (6' high), oak case, mandolin, violin pipes, plays 88-note rolls and Imhof and Mukle rolls **7500.00 15,000.00**

KREITER NICKELODEON

☐ KREITER NICKELODEON PIANO, oak keyboard style, coin operated, three glass panels on top front, 10 tune roll mechanism in base **7500.00 15,000.00**

LINK PIANO CO., INC. (Binghamton, NY)

☐ LINK STYLE A ORCHESTRION, large keyboard-type piano case, 6' high, art glass front panels (Chaddorff Piano), mandolin attachment, metal violin, wood flute pipes, wood block, snare drum, triangle, tom tom, tambourine, continuous roll on top **6500.00 12,000.00**

Price Range

☐ LINK STYLE C, c. 1915–20, high-back upright keyboard-style case, 28 flute pipes, oak, several art glass panels, coin operated lamps, RX endless rolls 15,000.00 20,000.00

☐ LINK STYLE E, upright keyboard piano style, high back, art glass panels and lamps, mandolin, xylophone, oak 10,000.00 15,000.00

☐ LINK STYLE 2E, cabinet-style (plain, rectangular case), clear glass panels on top and bottom for viewing "continuous" endless roll, coin operated, xylophone 5500.00 7500.00

☐ LINK STYLE R, upright keyboard-style piano with art glass panels, and hanging lamp, piano, mandolin, violin or flute pipes, continuous roll 4000.00 7500.00

☐ LINK RELIABLE, upright piano style, coin operated, mandolin attachment, continuous roll feed into a bin attached to the front under the keyboard but outside the case, beveled oval mirror in top section, bin slides out to change roll. The model sold under other company names, e.g., Majestic by Lyon and Healy .. 4500.00 6900.00

☐ LINK NICKELODEON, upright keyboard style, 6'5" high, simple oak case lines with hanging lights, four large leaded glass panels with folding doors covering top glass panels 4500.00 6500.00

PAUL LOSCHE (Leipzig Orchestrion Works)

☐ LOSCHE "JAZZBAND" ORCHESTRION, c. 1920's, piano, mandolin attachment, 4 beater bass drum, triangle, 3-beater wood block, 3-beater cymbal, snare drum 10,000.00 15,000.00

☐ LOSCHE NICKELODEON, upright keyboard piano style, plain case, roll in center, mandolin attachment, oak case 3500.00 6000.00

☐ LOSCHE ORCHESTRION (FLUTE AND VIOLIN SOLO PIANO), high keyboard style, 7½' high, beveled mirrors and hanging lamps, oak case, flute and violin pipes, piano, mandolin attachment (also xylophone and clarinet pipes) 4500.00 7500.00

Price Range

LYON AND HEALY (Chicago, IL), sold machines made by other companies.

☐ LYON AND HEALY EMPRESS ELECTRIC PIANO (see Empress Electric Piano)

☐ LYON AND HEALY LITTLE EMPRESS ELECTRIC CABINET PLAYER (made by Operators' Piano Co.), coin-operated cabinet-style case sits on or up against keys, plain case (also came fitted with all the instruments of a COINOLA X) 4000.00   6500.00

☐ LYON AND HEALY MAJESTIC (see Link Reliable)

☐ LYON AND HEALY MAJESTIC JUNIOR, cabinet style, glass top, 44-note piano, coin operated, endless roll in bottom section 4000.00   6250.00

☐ LYON AND HEALY PIANETTE (made by F. G. Otto & Sons, NJ), cabinet-style piano operated by a metal disc, 39 notes, long running, 75″ high, coin operated, oak (mahogany), glass panels in front doors 5000.00   6750.00

MARQUETTE PIANO CO. (see Cremona)

MILLS NOVELTY CO. (Chicago, IL)

☐ MILLS VIOLANO-VIRTUOSO, GRAND MODEL, sometimes referred to as "Single Mills," the roll-activated mechanism plays a real violin and a real piano by means of electric magnets and switches. Magnets press the bow onto the string, magnets finger the string just as a violinist does, and there are even magnets to effect a vibrato. Other magnets operate the piano mechanism. These parts were housed in a roughly square oak or mahogany case 5 or 6 feet tall. Four beveled glass paneled doors allow viewing in the top section, and the roll machinery in the lower part was behind solid doors. Uses a 5-tune roll, usually coin operated, the piano plays 44 notes. This machine dates from 1912 .... 7700.00   13,000.00

☐ MILLS VIOLANO VIRTUOSO, CONCERT GRAND, just slightly larger cabinet size ... 7000.00   10,000.00

Price Range

☐ MILLS VIOLANO-VIRTUOSO, DELUXE MODEL, referred to as "Double Mills," slightly taller than the "Single Mills," usually about 6'; machine has two violins, both play the same tune, greater volume, harder to find than the single 12,500.00 25,000.00

☐ MILLS VIOLANO VIRTUOSO, EARLY COMMERCIAL MODEL, Art Nouveau–style curved case, bowed with carving and decoration, single violin, piano action, glass front and side panels on top 7000.00 12,500.00

☐ MILLS MAGNETIC EXPRESSION PIANO, straight plain rectangular cabinet style, oak (mahogany), 65-note piano, 5'5" high, whole front opens like a door, piano action attached to the door, also pneumatic action (very compact), roll mechanism in base of cabinet, plays Mills Electric Piano Rolls, art glass panels 4000.00 6000.00

NATIONAL AUTOMATIC MUSIC CO. (see NATIONAL PIANO MANUFACTURING CO.)

NATIONAL PEERLESS PIANOS (see PEERLESS PIANO PLAYER CO.)

NATIONAL PIANO MANUFACTURING CO. (Grand Rapids, MI)

☐ NATIONAL NICKELODEON PIANO, upright piano style, mandolin, large rectangular glass panel in top front, oak case, 10-tune A-roll 3750.00 6250.00

☐ NATIONAL NICKELODEON PIANO WITH AUTOMATIC CHANGER, upright piano style case (keyboardless), coin operated, clear glass top front panel, 8-roll automatic changer, tune selector, one tune per roll, roll assembly housed in wooden case below "keyboard" area 4000.00 7500.00

NELSON-WIGGEN PIANO CO. (Chicago, IL)

☐ NELSON-WIGGEN BANJ-O-GRAND, cabinet style, art or clear glass, mandolin attachment, A-roll (gambling devices on this model) 5000.00 7000.00

Price Range

☐ NELSON-WIGGEN CASINO X, 5½' high cabinet style, simple case, glass panel on top, piano, coin operated, A-roll (gambling devices added) **3700.00   6700.00**

☐ NELSON-WIGGEN STYLE 3 PIANOGRAND, walnut case, three large art glass panels, with mandolin and xylophone, coin-operated keyboard piano style, 4'6" high, 5'3" wide, c. 1920 .... **7000.00 10,000.00**

☐ NELSON-WIGGEN STYLE 4, cabinet style, contains the following instrumentation, piano, mandolin, xylophone, snare drum, triangle, cymbal **6000.00 12,000.00**

☐ NELSON-WIGGEN STYLE 4X, cabinet style, three glass sections on top, decorative columns on corners, two doors in base, piano, mandolin trap effects, G and 4X rolls, 10 tunes **5000.00   7000.00**

☐ NELSON-WIGGEN STYLE 5X, 5½' high cabinet style, three glass panels in top front (art or clear glass), walnut (mahogany), contains piano, banjo (mandolin) attachment, set of marimbas, snare drum, triangle, plays standard orchestral 10-tune roll, G-rolls, 4X rolls, xylophone **10,000.00 15,000.00**

☐ NELSON-WIGGEN STYLE 6 ORCHESTRA, cabinet style, columns on front, simple console case, glass section on top, curtains behind, double doors on bottom, roll mechanism in bottom, piano, mandolin, xylophone, bass plus snare drum, cymbal, triangle, tympani, castanets, wood block, tambourine, 5½' high, walnut, 10-tune 4X and G-roll ... **12,000.00 20,000.00**

☐ NELSON-WIGGEN STYLE 7 FULL ORCHESTRA KEYBOARD PIANO, upright piano style, art glass in top front section, walnut, roll mechanism in top, piano, xylophone, banjo (mandolin), bass and snare drum, tympani, cymbal, triangle, castanets, Indian block **14,000.00 20,000.00**

Mills Violano Virtuoso Grand Model, doors open to reveal roll mechanism in base.

Price Range

☐ NELSON-WIGGEN STYLE 8, cabinet style, some decoration, art glass panels, oak, mahogany, walnut, 4½' high, roll in base section, piano, mandolin, xylophone, bells, special "G" roll 6000.00   8000.00

Price Range

☐ NELSON-WIGGEN SELECTOR DUPLEX (DUAL KEYBOARD) PIANO ORGAN, upright piano style, full piano, organ 10-tune roll, mechanism plays 5 tunes forward then 5 tunes in rewind position 6000.00   9000.00

NORTH TONAWANDA MUSICAL INSTRUMENT WORKS, (NY)

☐ NORTH TONAWANDA PIANOLIN, cabinet style, beveled glass top section, protruding base section holds endless roll mechanism, 44-note piano action, violin and flute pipes, coin operated 6000.00   9500.00

☐ NORTH TONAWANDA AUTOMATIC KEYBOARD PIANO STYLE L, upright keyboard style, two art glass panels in top front, hanging lamps, oak, 4½' high, piano, mandolin attachment, violin or flute pipes, coin operated, roll in top center, 14-tune L-roll, later 10-tune A-roll 5000.00   8500.00

OPERATORS' PIANO CO. (See COINOLA).

PEERLESS PIANO PLAYER CO. (NATIONAL "PEERLESS" PIANOS)

☐ PEERLESS "ARCADIAN" ORCHESTRION STYLE O, high upright keyboard piano style, high front posts with globes on top, leaded glass front and panels 6500.00   12,500.00

☐ PEERLESS ART CABARET STYLE A, upright piano keyboard case, art glass panel in top front, piano, mandolin, roll on top 3000.00   5000.00

☐ PEERLESS ART CABARET STYLE B, 5'1" high, oak upright keyboard case, 24 flute pipes, large art glass panel in top front, lamps on either side of front 4750.00   7500.00

☐ PEERLESS ART CABARET STYLE C, instrumentation: piano, mandolin, bass and snare drums, cymbal, triangle (semi-orchestrion) 6000.00   8000.00

☐ PEERLESS ART CABARET STYLE D, instrumentation: piano, mandolin, bass and snare drums, cymbals, triangle, violin and flute pipes (called Theatre or Peerless Orchestrion) 7000.00   8500.00

Price Range

☐ PEERLESS STYLE D NICKELODEON PIANO, keyboard upright style, oval beveled glass in top section, endless roll mechanism in cabinet in back of piano, coin operated, oak **2750.00   4750.00**

☐ PEERLESS STYLE 44, cabinet style, clear beveled glass top section (oval or scalloped), endless roll, 44-note piano, coin operated **3000.00   5000.00**

☐ PEERLESS NICKELODEON PIANO, upright keyboard style, three art glass panels in front, oak, coin operated, 10-tune A-roll **3000.00   6000.00**

PHILIPPS AND SONS (Frankfurt, Germany)

☐ PHILIPPS DUCA PIANO REPRODUCING, high-back upright reproducing piano, with (or without) roll changer, coin operated, simple case, some decoration **3750.00   6000.00**

☐ PHILIPPS PIANELLA NICKELODEON STYLE C, upright keyboard piano style, mandolin attachment, oak case, coin operated **3000.00   5750.00**

☐ PHILIPPS PIANELLA PIANO STYLE PC 3, upright piano style with hanging lamps, piano, mandolin (roll changer) type PM rolls, 4 tunes **4000.00   6750.00**

☐ PHILIPPS PIANELLA MODEL #15, upright cabinet, keyboardless style cabinet, elaborate case decoration including three large art glass panels, 6 hanging lamps, instrumentation includes piano, mandolin, xylophone, bell, bass and snare drums, tambourine, cymbal, castanettes, triangle, automatic six roll changer mechanism **50,000.00   75,000.00**

☐ PHILIPPS STYLE PC-7, ornate decorated high-back upright piano turned front legs and other case decoration, also large top panel with scenic panel "motion picture." Uses Philipps PM rolls **9000.00   13,000.00**

☐ PHILIPPS STYLE PC-10 ORCHESTRION, upright keyboard style high back (7½' high), beveled mirror and some case decoration, piano, mandolin, violin pipes, snare and bass drums, xylophone, crash cymbal **9000.00   13,000.00**

Price Range

POLYPHONE COIN PIANOS (Leipzig, Germany)
☐ POLYPHONA I, keyboard-style case, high upright, hanging lamps, case decoration, pneumatically operated, piano, mandolin, xylophone, bells 4000.00   6250.00

☐ POLYPHONA II, upright keyboard style, high back, hanging lamps, decoration, piano, mandolin attachment 4000.00   6000.00

☐ POLYPHONA IV—DUX, high upright piano case, art glass lamps on high front posts, piano, mandolin, xylophone 4500.00   7000.00

POPPER AND CO. (Leipzig, Germany)
☐ POPPER "HAPPY JAZZBAND," upright piano orchestrion, 6′ high, drums, wood block, triangle, cymbal, mandolin attachment, oak case, bracket lamps, circular "jazzband" painted picture on drum, coin operated 7500.00   15,000.00

☐ POPPER JAZZ BAND, upright keyboard piano, high back, some case decoration, instrumentation in top section. Piano, mandolin, bass and snare drums, tympani, wood block, triangle 5000.00   7500.00

☐ POPPER REPRODUCING PIANO, upright, "Stella" (many case variations), hanging lamps, leaded glass panels, coin operated (wall boxes) 3750.00   5250.00

☐ POPPER NICKELODEON, upright keyboard piano, simple lines, hanging lamps, mandolin attachment, 5′ high, coin operated 3750.00   5500.00

☐ POPPER "ROLAND" (WITH SWANEE WHISTLE) ORCHESTRION, tall case upright keyboard style, simple lines (Art Deco style) with Swanee whistle attachment 15,000.00   20,000.00

☐ POPPER "WELT" PIANO, upright high back piano case, art glass, hanging lamps, case decoration (variations in case design), coin operated, piano, mandolin, xylophone, drums 3500.00   5500.00

☐ **REGINAPIANO** (see Cremona, Style #3), upright keyboard piano, three glass panels, mandolin attachment, 10-tune A-roll (made by Marquette) 3500.00   5750.00

Price Range

☐ **REGINA SUBLIMA (MANDOLIN QUARTETTE) (MANDOLIN ORCHESTRA),** chunky-style 5′ tall stepped-back cabinet with glass in top section to show the 20″ wide heavy paper music roll that operates this instrument. The sound is much like a dulcimer, with rapidly beating hammers striking the strings. Coin operated, usually electrically powered, though some had spring wind mechanisms 4000.00   8000.00

☐ **REGINA SUBLIMA PIANO STYLE 302,** cabinet style over 7′ high, oak, mandolin attachment, coin operated 3500.00   7500.00

☐ **ROLAND BARREL ORCHESTRION,** c. 1900, 7′6″ high rectangular case style, some decoration, two front doors, glass windows reveal barrel (8-tune) and other instruments, piano, bass and snare drums, crash cymbal   5500.00   7500.00

J. P. SEEBURG PIANO CO. (Chicago, IL)
☐ SEEBURG STYLE A NICKELODEON, upright keyboard piano, simple lines, coin operated, art and clear glass, front panel, mandolin attachment, plays A-roll, 10 tunes, 65-note piano, automatic rewind, oak (mahogany) case and glass variations 3750.00   7000.00
☐ SEEBURG STYLE B, more elaborate art glass and case details 4500.00   6000.00
☐ SEEBURG STYLE C, upright keyboard style, five arched sections in top front of piano with a continuous scene in leaded art glass, lamps on front posts, A-roll coin operated 5000.00   7500.00
☐ SEEBURG STYLE E, keyboard piano, oak, art glass on top front doors, hanging lamps, 65-note, 10-tune selections, automatic rewind, violin or flute pipes, mandolin attachment, coin operated 8000.00   11,000.00
☐ SEEBURG STYLE E SPECIAL, same case style with piano, mandolin, xylophone, bass and snare drum, tympani, cymbal, triangle, castanets, tambourine, Chinese block, coin operated 6750.00   20,000.00

Price Range

☐ SEEBURG STYLE G, high-back upright keyboard piano style (6'7½" high), 4 large art
glass panels, oak case, violin and flute pipes,
mandolin attachment, bass and snare drum,
tympani, cymbal, triangle, 65-note, 10-tune
rolls, coin operated **15,000.00 23,000.00**

☐ SEEBURG STYLE H SOLO ORCHESTRION,
high keyboard upright piano style, two fully
carved figures on side posts, three leaded art
glass shades along top front of case, 4 large
art glass panels in front top section, piano,
flute, violin pipes, piccolo and clarinet, mandolin attachment, bass and snare drums,
tympani, cymbal, triangle, castanets, oak
case, H-roll, instruments in top section, coin
operated **30,000.00 50,000.00**

☐ SEEBURG STYLE J SOLO ORCHESTRION,
upright keyboard style case, high back, large
elaborate art glass, decorated case, walnut
(mahogany), 6' high, piano, mandolin attachment, pipes for flute, violin, oboe, clarinet, triangle, castanets, xylophone, coin operated,
H-roll **17,500.00 21,000.00**

☐ SEEBURG STYLE K "MIDGET" ORCHEST-
RION "EAGLE," cabinet-style case, 5'2"
high, simple style, some case decoration,
gold trimming, oak, art glass panel in top section, half circle with eagle design (other designs used). Piano, mandolin, xylophone,
coin operated, 65-note, 10 tune selection, A-
roll **9000.00 11,500.00**

☐ SEEBURG STYLE KT ORCHESTRION
"EAGLE," same description with added instrumentation: castanets, triangle, tambou-
rine, G-roll **9000.00 15,000.00**

☐ SEEBURG STYLE KT SPECIAL, cabinet-
style case, 5'5½" high, simple lines, Oriental-
design art glass panel on top, oak with gold
trim, piano, mandolin attachment, xylophone,
bass and snare drums, tympani, cymbal, tri-

Price Range

angle, castanets, tambourine, Chinese block, G-roll, 10-tune, rewind device to shut off all instruments but piano, coin operated **13,000.00 19,000.00**

☐ SEEBURG KT SPECIAL (EDGERTON REPLICA) **12,500.00 14,000.00**

☐ SEEBURG STYLE L NICKELODEON "SEEBURG JUNIOR," cabinet style, art glass panels on top, piano, mandolin, mahogany (oak), 51½" high, roll in top center of cabinet, A-roll, 10-tune, 65-note (also known as "Lilliputian"), coin operated **4000.00 6500.00**

☐ SEEBURG STYLE L ORCHESTRION, oak case, 10-tune "G" rolls, piano, mandolin, flute pipes, bass and snare drums, tympani, triangle, cymbal, art glass **25,000.00 40,000.00**

☐ SEEBURG STYLE P-G-A, console style, leaded art glass top front panel, coin operated, 10-tune A-roll **4500.00 7000.00**

☐ SEEBURG STYLE X ELECTRIC EXPRESSION PIANO, upright piano, reproducing expression mechanism, coin operated, (oak) mahogany plain case, X-P roll (4–6 selections per roll), 88-note roll also plays, 4'9½" high **4500.00 6500.00**

VIOLANO VIRTUOSO (See MILLS NOVELTY CO.)

WEBER (GEBRUDER WEBER)
☐ WEBER MAESTRO ORCHESTRION, c. 1920's, oak case, 9'3" high, piano, mandolin, xylophone, violin, cello, flute, saxophone, clarinet, oboe, trumpet, drums, castanets, full rounded columns on front, other case decoration mirrors, hanging lamps, expression devices **50,000.00 85,000.00**

☐ WEBER "UNIKA" PIANO ORCHESTRA, c. 1920's, high-back keyboard style, approximately 6½' high, mandolin, violin pipes, oak case, mirrored doors, two double brass lamps on each side front panel, some case decoration, roll is housed behind mirrored doors well above keyboard **8000.00 12,000.00**

Price Range

WESTERN ELECTRIC PIANO CO. (J. P. SEEBURG)

☐ WESTERN ELECTRIC SELECTRA MODEL B, console cabinet style, 5'2" tall, oak, simple case, simple decorative glass panels in top section, piano, mandolin, xylophone, Selectra tune selecting mechanism, tune card, indicator dial, coin operated **4500.00   8000.00**

☐ WESTERN ELECTRIC STYLE X, cabinet style, doors on top and bottom, simple case, glass panels in top, roll mechanism in top, piano, mandolin, xylophone, oak **3000.00   6000.00**

☐ WESTERN ELECTRIC "DERBY" RACE HORSE PIANO, console cabinet, oak, simple case, glass front on top to view diorama of racing horses, coin operated, A-roll, piano (mandolin attachment), 4'4" high, 3'0" wide, and 2'3" deep **7000.00   9000.00**

RUDOLPH WURLITZER CO. (North Tonawanda, NY)

☐ WURLITZER AUTOMATIC PLAYER PIANO, upright piano case style, 65-note player, mandolin attachment, three beveled glass panels, in top front, case decoration, oak, coin operated (early example c. 1907), plays 10-tune A-roll **2700.00   4500.00**

☐ WURLITZER STYLE A AUTOMATIC PLAYER PIANO, upright piano case style, 65-note, one rank of pipes violin or flute, mandolin attachment, 4'10" high, electric, 5-tune roll, beveled clear (or art) glass panel in top front of piano, oak **3750.00   6500.00**

☐ WURLITZER STYLE AX, c. 1920, 5' high, oak case, 6-roll mechanism **7500.00   12,000.00**

☐ WURLITZER STYLE AX AUTOMATIC PLAYER PIANO, upright piano, 65-note, mandolin attachment, flute or violin pipes, art glass panels in top front, automatic roll changer plays 65-tune rolls **3500.00   6500.00**

☐ WURLITZER STYLE B ORCHESTRION, high-back upright piano case style, three art glass panels, piano, mandolin, flute pipes, bass and snare drum, cymbal, triangle, panel

Price Range

just above center of keyboard for roll: Wurlitzer automatic player piano 10-tune rolls, coin operated 10,000.00 19,500.00

☐ WURLITZER STYLE BX ORCHESTRION WITH "WONDER LIGHT," high-back upright piano case, three large art glass panels, case decoration (many variations in case and glass designs), violin or flute pipes, automatic roll changer, "wonder" light in top gallery (rotating "jeweled" light) 18,000.00 28,000.00

☐ WURLITZER STYLE BX, 7' high, plays six 5-tune rolls, bass and snare drums, triangle, 38 flute pipes 15,000.00 21,000.00

☐ WURLITZER STYLE CX ORCHESTRION, automatic roll changer (similar to Style BX), high-back oak case, several art glass panels, keyboard style, instruments, flute pipes 18,000.00 29,000.00

☐ WURLITZER BIJOU ORCHESTRA, large 8½' tall cabinet, galleries, lamps, art glass panels, roll in center front section, automatic roll changer, 44-note piano, mandolin attachment, violin pipes, xylophone, snare drum, pianino roll 13,000.00 17,000.00

☐ WURLITZER CALIOLA, oak case, 44 flute pipes, base and snare drums with cymbal, will play from roll or attached keyboard, 5'4" high, 3'8" wide, 3'0 deep 25,000.00 30,000.00

☐ WURLITZER AUTOMATIC HARP (J. W. Whitlock & Co., Rising Sun, IN), Style A, straight rectangular case 6'6" high, automatically activated by a 8½" wide perforated paper roll, 6 tunes per roll, automatic rewind, coin operated 7500.00 17,500.00

☐ STYLE B, decorative case design, curved top section and carved post (looked more like a harp)

☐ WURLITZER STYLE LX ORCHESTRION, high-back upright piano style, leaded art glass panels, oak, 2 ranks of pipes, bells, 2 drums, triangle, instruments in top section, roll changer over keyboard, 7½' high 17,000.00 22,000.00

Wurlitzer Automatic Roll Changer Mechanism.

Price Range

☐ WURLITZER ELECTRIC PIANO AUTO-
GRAPH STYLE, upright keyboard piano, 4′9″
high, plain simple case, coin operated, automatic roll changer, plays special expression
rolls: autograph reproducing piano rolls **2500.00**   **5750.00**

☐ WURLITZER ELECTRIC PIANO STYLE IXB,
upright keyboard style, three art glass front
panels, mandolin attachment, automatic roll
changer, 65-tune rolls, coin operated (or-
chestra bells) **6000.00**   **8500.00**

☐ WURLITZER MANDOLIN QUARTETTE, 5′
high rectangular case, some decoration, beveled glass sections in top, oak (mahogany,
many finishes), 34-note piano and 27-note

Price Range

mandolin attachment, 5-tune rolls, coin operated, roll mechanism in top middle section behind glass door 5000.00 10,000.00

☐ WURLITZER PHOTOPLAYER PIANO STYLE G, upright piano case, 4'10" simple case, double- roll mechanism (automatic player piano rolls), 65-note Wurlitzer rolls, piano, mandolin attachment, storage chest situated next to piano held instrumentation: violin, flute pipes, drums, sound effects 6000.00 9000.00

☐ WURLITZER PIANINO, console case style, 5' high, 44-note electric piano, protruding middle section for roll mechanism, leaded art glass on top front, oak case, coin operated, mandolin attachment (late models, case variations) 4000.00 8000.00

☐ WURLITZER SOLO VIOLIN PIANO, upright keyboard piano, plain case, 88-note player, violin pipes, automatic roll changer ("violin" can play solo), 4'10½" high 5000.00 8000.00

☐ WURLITZER TONOPHONE, upright piano case style, large oval beveled glass panel in top front, with or without keyboard, coin operated, 10-tune wooden cylinder 3500.00 6000.00

☐ WURLITZER STYLE W ORGANETTE, upright piano style, two keyboards, pipe organ, walnut, two roll mechanisms side by side in top front 4000.00 6000.00

☐ WURLITZER VIOLIN-FLUTE PIANINO, keyboardless cabinet, 4'8" high, fancy decorative details, 21 flute pipes and violin pipes 9500.00 12,500.00

☐ WURLITZER #146 BAND ORGAN, "Carouselle Organ," simple case ivory painted trimmed in black and gold, three front panels (painted silk), 6'7" high, drums mounted outside, cymbal on top, pipes on center front panel, plays paper roll, instrumentation effects: trombones, basses, trumpets, flute pipes, violin pipes 8000.00 15,000.00

Price Range

☐ WURLITZER #148 MILITARY BAND
ORGAN, duplex roll mechanism, exposed
belled horns (18), drums and cymbal
mounted at sides on top, plays paper rolls   **6500.00**   **9500.00**

NICKELODEON, ORCHESTRION, AND BAND ORGAN ROLLS

☐ **NORTH TONAWANDA,** one tune endless roll	8.00	10.00
☐ **NICKELODEON "A" ROLLS,** recuts	10.00	20.00
☐ **PEERLESS** 65-note endless roll, multitone	7.50	15.00
☐ **PEERLESS** 44—note endless roll	7.50	15.00
☐ **PIANOLIN** 6-tune endless roll	12.00	17.00
☐ **WURLITZER CONCERT PIANO ORCHESTRA ROLLS**	10.00	20.00
☐ **WURLITZER BAND ORGAN ROLLS**	7.50	15.00

MUSICAL INSTRUMENTS

Musical instruments, being native to nearly all races and societies and having primitive origins dating to prehistoric times, exist in vast varieties and offer the collector wide choice. It would be very mistaken to believe, however, that all classes of instruments are to be found in profuse quantities on the antique market, or that the finest examples of noted instrument manufacturers can be easily obtained. The sort of instruments available in the greatest quantity as antiques are those that enjoyed extensive popularity in the age of classical instrument making, especially violins and pianos. Antique wind instruments are less common, if one speaks of specimens of 200 or 300 years ago.

The approach to collecting antique instruments may be either from a musical point of view or with regard to styling and ornamentation or, in the case of very early specimens, as historical pieces. A *specialized* collection may deal with instruments of one given sort, such as mandolins or flutes or harps. But as even this is rather broad territory, the collector is likely to specialize still further, confining himself to German flutes of the 19th century or Italian harps of the 18th or, very likely, examples of the work of a single manufacturer. In violin collecting, the traditional approach has long been to concentrate on the work of one craftsman or family of craftsmen. As instruments are not the sort of articles of which large collections can be easily made, this is probably the wisest course to follow.

It is not only the collector who seeks out antique instruments, however. There are other buyers and potential buyers, whose activities in the market have an influence on both the availability of specimens and their price. First is the musician. It is difficult to state what proportion of antique instruments that pass through the hands of dealers, auctioneers, etc., are purchased by musicians, but it is unquestionably a fact that sales of antique instruments to musicians have increased over the past 10 to 15 years. Violins and stringed instruments in general head the list; though there are many instruments sought by collectors who are of the opinion (right or wrong) that a certain manufacturer, perhaps long deceased, made his instruments to a standard not found in current examples. The musician is a powerful force in the market, as he buys perhaps one instrument to last a lifetime and thus can expend a great amount of money on it, rather than making the frequent purchases of a collector.

Investors also account for a certain measure of sales. As with any commodity that shows a history of gaining steadily in value, there will be individuals who may have little love or knowledge of the item but will buy on speculation. This is true of instruments more than many other articles, as they are interesting as well as attractive items in addition to their value.

So far as the advisability of investing in musical instruments is concerned, this is a complex matter. Certain instruments gain more steadily in value than others, depending on the strength of demand. Usually, the more suitable the instrument is for modern use, especially concert use, the greater its demand and the more steady its rise in value will be. Museum-type instruments that have no place in the modern concert hall, such as the spinet or certain kinds of obsolete horns, may be quite valuable, but the demand over a long period of time is difficult to forecast. Auctioneers, who have the task of estimating prices only two or three months in the future, are hard pressed on occasion when faced with the task of evaluating "offbeat" instruments or unusual models of standard instruments, and frequently guess wrong. Instruments are one class of collectors' item for which past sales records cannot be relied upon too faithfully in determining what the next sale will bring. Obviously, there will always be buyers for $20,000 antique harpsichords, even should the bottom totally fall out of the instrument market; but at what price, no one can predict.

The investor who purchases only "top of the market" items may be interested to know that instruments of somewhat less reputation, but of nearly as fine quality, have advanced more sharply in price over a period of years. It is really not difficult to see why. The world supply of fine instruments is not inexhaustible, and while some reach peaks of price, going beyond the range of all but the wealthiest buyers, others suddenly become attractive. The musician of 1900 who saved or borrowed to buy a genuine Amati or Stradivari violin, stubbornly believing these the only violins of worthy quality, now contents himself with a 17th- or 18th-century instrument by a lesser-known maker. The fact that Strads and Amatis are out of reach for most buyers has opened up demand for the works of many other makers, which, in due time, will probably also become prohibitively costly. Then buyers will turn to still lesser known names, and so on, until (though this should be a long distance off) every violin dated before 1800 is cherished and fought over in the salesrooms.

The following may better illustrate this point.

	Average price, 1930	Average price mid-1980's	% of increase
Stradivarius	$10,000.00	$55,000.00–125,000.00	550–1250
Fabris	600.00	3500.00–4500.00	c. 600–750
Meloni	480.00	4000.00–6000.00	c. 800–1200

For an instrument to be a good investment, it must be a good instrument. It must be identifiable to a maker. It must have a reputation, even if only locally. It must be an instrument that a musician can play and would use professionally. It should, preferably, be representative of the better class of work produced by its maker. Factory products, as opposed to instruments made and signed by craftsmen, are generally not as good investments.

After all this talk of "antique instruments," it may be well to define or attempt to define what is meant by this expression. Technically, there is no satisfactory definition that can be applied to all classes (or even to most classes) of instruments. The usual standard for antiques—anything 100 or more years old—does not suit instruments, as some instruments have much earlier origins than others, and some fell into the class of factory or commercial work earlier than others. It might, for example, be proper to term a Sears Roebuck violin of 1895 an antique, but it is neither desirable nor valuable on that account. Nor is it entirely proper to class a 1720 and an 1890 piano under the heading of "antique" without making any further distinction. This is why the term (loose though it may be) "classical instruments" has been adopted, to signify instruments that, in addition to merely being old, are noteworthy on other grounds; or, if merely old, are sufficiently old to be valuable for that reason alone.

BUYING ANTIQUE MUSICAL INSTRUMENTS

A number of possible sources of supply exist for the collector, the principal ones being retail dealers who make a specialty of musical instruments, auction houses, musicians, private parties, exchange clubs, advertisements in collector magazines, and various others. It is impossible to state that any single source is preferable to others, as this depends very much on the individual collector and his circumstances. First (and foremost) it should be borne in mind that a buyer who is not an authority on the material he buys leaves himself at the seller's mercy, and really has no alternative—unless he enjoys risks—but to rely on competent dealers.

BUYING FROM DEALERS SPECIALIZING IN ANTIQUE INSTRUMENTS

There are a fair number of full-time dealers both here and abroad (more in Europe than the United States) who make a specialty of antique musical instruments. Some of them deal in just one variety of instrument, others in miscellaneous instruments, while still others also sell general musicana as well (sheet music, phono records, record players, and the like). Some issue catalogues or price listings. Others do not prepare lists, stating as their reason for not doing so the fact that merchandise moves too quickly and prices rapidly become outdated. Most do, however, sell by mail in addition to making shop sales. The usual method in selling by mail is either through advertisements in the collector press or individual quotations to interested parties. The collector should be aware that items offered to him by mail are seldom held in reserve pending a reply but have been (or will be) offered to others as well, on a first-come basis.

Are dealers' prices fair? This is a question that could be discussed at great length. Because the musical instrument market is not regulated by standard catalogue prices—such as exist for stamps, coins, and many kinds of collectors' items—there is opportunity for the dealer to make somewhat freer evaluations. However, it is not in the best interest of any dealer to attempt selling a $200 instrument for $1000, or to overprice at all, as most of his customers are well aware of values, and an overpriced item is not likely to sell. The fact that dealers' prices run higher on average than auction sale prices is undeniable, but this is likewise true of most kinds of antiques. The dealers do a great deal of their buying at auctions, and when you buy from them you must pay the auction price plus their margin of profit. There is really no substitute for buying from an experienced, responsible professional dealer, however. You have the option of keeping or returning the item (within a specified time limit), personal attention, and someone to ask questions of and obtain advice from. Not every dealer is in this lofty category, but we do have in this country a number of professionals in whom the trade can take pride and without whom the activities of collectors might not be so successful.

When buying by mail, it is wise to ask that a photograph be sent of any item that you seriously contemplate buying. A slight charge might be made for this, as the dealer is not likely to have photos on hand unless he issues catalogues, and he may have to take the picture especially for you. It will most likely be a Polaroid in color.

BUYING FROM AUCTIONS

Good buys can be made at auctions, but there is somewhat more uncertainty than in purchasing through retail channels. Auctions are not advisable as a source of supply for the beginning collector, unless he has an agent to advise and act for him.

Antique instruments turn up at all classes of auctions, from those conducted by prestigious international houses to local estate sales. Sometimes the larger galleries hold sales devoted entirely to instruments, but such sales are rare, especially in the United States, as few private collections of instruments are large enough to warrant an auction of their own. More commonly, instruments are included in general sales of "Western art" or "European art." In an estate sale there may be just a single instrument among 400 or 500 miscellaneous lots, but this is where some of the best opportunities occur. At the average estate sale, there are few bidders who have knowledge of antique instruments and, usually, no dealers who specialize in them. Therefore, an informed buyer is likely to have the chance at purchasing material well below its actual value. The problem is that many estate sales are unaccompanied by catalogues or listings, and the majority of those issuing catalogues provide inadequate information; it is impossible to know from their descriptions whether an instrument being sold is modern or old. Unless one attends the sale, it is very difficult to make intelligent purchases.

A certain share of open-mindedness is necessary at country or estate auctions. Do not prejudge the quality of instruments being sold by the quality of other items in the sale. An estate may consist of mediocre furnishings, pictures, etc., but contain a really good antique guitar, mandolin, or other instrument. The item itself must be examined before reaching any conclusion.

ANTIQUE SHOPS AND OTHER NONSPECIALIST DEALERS

Musical instruments are very frequently offered by general dealers in antiques. A nonspecialist dealer will not often place a large investment in valuable instruments, but specimens of ordinary variety are acquired in the normal course of business, from estate purchases and the like. These are more likely to be smaller wind instruments and guitars rather than anything of substantial proportions. Sometimes violins will turn up, and a good quantity of harmonicas, accordions, and banjos. The dealer's geographical location plays some part in the sort of instrument he is apt to acquire, certain instruments being more popular in one part of the country than another (banjos in the southern states, for example).

There is no harm in buying antique instruments from antique shops if you have a fair knowledge of the material purchased and an eye for quality. To build a collection via such purchases is difficult, though, because of the uncertainty of what will be available from one shop to another and from one moment to the next. Usually, the instruments sold in American antique shops are of late 19th- or 20th-century manufacture, the kind sold by mail-order firms or otherwise widely produced and distributed and not too highly respected as antiques. They are apt to be in somewhat less than good condition and on occasion are badly damaged, as antique dealers are not, on the whole, as discriminating in their acquisitions as are the specialist dealers in antique instruments. They will buy an old banjo with a string missing for $5 or $6, feeling that some customer capable of making the necessary repair will be willing to buy it for $10. On occasion an 18th-century violin or something similar will turn up, but this is far more likely to occur in foreign shops.

BUYING FROM PRIVATE COLLECTORS

This is not a bad source, if the seller is a responsible party and a fair price can be agreed upon. Often, however, private owners overvalue their instruments and do not back up the sale with a guarantee of satisfaction. When private owners ask for "offers" on instruments they have for sale, this can be taken as an indication that they have little or no knowledge of values and probably also have little knowledge of instruments. What they are selling is, most likely, some item discovered in the attic, which may generously be worth $40 or $50 but which they fondly hope will bring them untold riches.

GARAGE SALES, FLEA MARKETS, ETC.

Well worth looking into, if just for entertainment. The chance of finding a desirable instrument exists, but it is small.

VALUES OF ANTIQUE MUSICAL INSTRUMENTS

There are no hard and fast rules about the values of instruments. The prices presented in this section are merely a guide to general values. Any given instrument may sell higher or lower, depending on quality and circumstances of sale. Naturally, there is a greater variation in values of the more costly specimens than of modestly priced items. A Stradivari violin that might normally carry an evaluation of $75,000 could easily fetch double that amount in a hotly contested international sale, especially if such a sale occurs during a market peak. Also, it should be understood that these prices do not represent forecasts or predictions of future values, but rather the values current at the time of compiling. Conditions change, sometimes rapidly, and demand for instruments of any given type could force prices beyond the levels shown here. Barring events of a very extreme nature, however, we feel that these prices should be valid for at least one year following publication.

The prices stated are retail selling prices, not wholesale prices or prices at which a dealer would buy from a private owner. We have not attempted to give "average buying prices," in the belief this would only lead to confusion. But it can be pretty safely assumed that the average or fair buying price on most instruments will run from 40 to 50 percent of the sums indicated, for specimens in good playable condition.

BOOKS ON INSTRUMENTS

Price Range

ACCOUSTICS

☐ **CULVER, C. A.,** *Musical Acoustics,* Philadelphia, 1947 . . . . 9.00   12.00

☐ **LLOYD, L. S.,** *Music and Sound,* London, 1937 . . . . 10.00   14.00

☐ **MILLER, C. D.,** *The Science of Musical Sounds,* New York, 1922 . . . . 15.00   20.00

☐ **OLSON, HARRY F.,** *Musical Engineering,* New York, 1952 . . . . 9.00   12.00

☐ **SEASHORE, C.,** *The Psychology of Music,* New York, 1938 . . . . 13.00   18.00

Price Range

☐ **VON HELMHOLTZ, H.,** *The Sensations of Tone,* London, 1875. . . . .   18.00   24.00

☐ **WOOD, ALEXANDER,** *The Physics of Music,* London, 1944 . . . .   10.00   14.00

ANCIENT AND FOLK

☐ **ANDERSSON, O.,** *The Bowed Harp,* London, 1930 . . . .   15.00   20.00

☐ **BAINES, A.,** *Bagpipes,* Oxford, 1960 . . . . . .   7.00   10.00

☐ **FARMER, H. G.,** *The Minstrelsy of the Arabian Nights,* Glasgow, 1945 . . . .   10.00   14.00

☐ **PANUM, H.,** *Stringed Instruments of the Middle Ages,* London, 1940 . . . .   11.00   15.00

☐ **SACHS, CURT,** *The Rise of Music in the Ancient World,* New York, 1943 . . . .   10.00   14.00

CLAVICHORDS

☐ **NEUPERT, H.,** *Das Klavichord,* Kassel, Germany, 1950 . . . .   11.00   15.00

ELECTRONIC

☐ **DORF, R. H.,** *Electronic Musical Instruments,* New York, 1954 . . . .   15.00   20.00

☐ **DOUGLAS, ALAN,** *The Electronic Musical Instrument Manual,* London, 1949 . . . .   25.00   32.00

GENERAL

☐ **BESSARABOFF, N.,** *Ancient European Musical Instruments,* Cambridge, 1941 . . . .   15.00   20.00

☐ **BOYDEN, DAVID D.,** *The Hill Collection of Musical Instruments,* London, 1969 . . . .   30.00   40.00

☐ **BUCHNER, A.,** *Musical Instruments through the Ages,* London, 1956 . . . .   13.00   18.00

Price Range

☐ **CARSE, ADAM,** *The Orchestra from Beetho-ven to Berlioz,* London, 1948 . . . . 11.00 15.00

☐ **DONINGTON, R.,** *The Instruments of Music,* London, 1949 . . . . 14.00 19.00

☐ **DURFEY, THOMAS,** *Wit and Mirth—or Pills to Purge Melancholy, Being a Collection of the Best Merry Ballads and Songs, Old and New,* 6 volumes, London, 1719–20 . . . . 175.00 250.00

☐ **GALPIN, F. W.,** *Old English Instruments of Music,* London, 1910 . . . . 40.00 55.00

☐ **GEIRINGER, K.,** *Musical Instruments,* London, 1943 . . . . 15.00 20.00

☐ **KINSKY, G.,** *History of Music in Pictures,* Leipzig, 1929 . . . . 30.00 40.00

☐ **MALCOLM, ALEXANDER,** *A Treatise of Musick—Speculative, Practical and Histori-cal, full calf, 4to,* London, Osborn & Long-man, 1730 . . . . 300.00 400.00

☐ **TERRY, C. S.,** *Bach's Orchestra,* London, 1932 . . . . 13.00 17.00

HARPSICHORD AND RELATED

☐ **BOALCH, DONALD,** *Makers of the Harpsi-chord and Clavichord, 1440–1840,* London, 1956 . . . . 23.00 30.00

☐ **RUSSELL, RAYMOND,** *The Harpsichord and Clavichord,* London, 1959 . . . . 10.00 14.00

HORNS (BRASS)

☐ **COAR, B.,** *The French Horn,* Ann Arbor, MI, 1947 . . . . 17.00 23.00

☐ **FARKAS, P.,** *The Art of French Horn Playing,* Chicago, 1956 . . . . 13.00 18.00

☐ **MORLEY-PEGGE, R.,** *The French Horn,* London, 1960 . . . . 11.00 15.00

	Price Range	

LUTES

☐ **BOETTICHER, W.,** *Studien zur soloistischen Lautenpraxis der 16ten und 17ten Jahrhunderte,* Berlin, 1943 . . . .   15.00   20.00

PIANOFORTES

☐ **HARDING, ROSAMUND,** *The Pianoforte, Its History Traced to the Great Exhibition,* 1851, Cambridge, 1933 . . . .   30.00   40.00

☐ **HIPKINS, A.J.,** *The Story of the Pianoforte,* London, 1896 . . . .   7.00   10.00

☐ **HIPKINS, E.,** *How Chopin Played,* London, 1937 . . . .   9.00   12.00

PRIMITIVE

☐ **IZIKOWITZ, K. G.,** *Musical and Other Sound Instruments of the South American Indians,* Goteborg, 1935 . . . .   22.00   30.00

☐ **KIRBY, P. R.,** *The Musical Instruments of the Native Races of South Africa,* London, 1934   35.00   45.00

VIOLINS

☐ **BACHMANN, ALBERTO,** *An Encyclopedia of the Violin,* New York, 1929 . . . .   15.00   20.00

☐ **BODA, JOSEPH,** *Bows for Musical Instruments of the Violin Family,* limited edition of 3000 copies, numerous plates, 4to, Chicago, 1959 . . . .   400.00   500.00

☐ **DORING, ERNEST N.,** *The Guadagnini Family of Violin Makers,* limited edition of 1500, numerous plates, cloth, Chicago, 1949 . . . .   500.00   600.00

☐ **DUBORG, G.,** *The Violin,* London, 1836 . . . .   55.00   70.00

☐ **HILL, W. HENRY, ARTHUR F., & ALFRED E.,** *Antonio Stradivari—His Life and Work,* first edition, quarter calf, folio, W. E. Hill & Sons, 1902 . . . .   450.00   550.00

Price Range

☐ **JALOVEC, KAREL,** *Encyclopedia of Violin Players,* two volumes, illustrated, cloth, dust-jackets, slip-case, 4to, London, 1968 . . . . . .   350.00   450.00

☐ **JALOVEC, KAREL,** *Italian Violin Makers,* numerous plates, cloth, 4to, London 175.00   250.00

☐ **OTTO, J. A.,** *Treatise on the Structure and Preservation of the Violin,* London, 1848 . . .   80.00   100.00

☐ **SANDYS, W. and FORSTER, S. A.,** *History of the Violin,* London, 1864 . . . .   55.00   70.00

☐ **VAN DER STRAETEN, E.,** *The History of the Violin,* two volumes, London, 1933 . . . .   70.00   90.00

☐ **WERRO, HENRY,** *"Ole Bull" Joseph Guarnerius Del Gesu, 1744,* limited edition of 400, signed by author, quarter calf, slip case, 8vo, Berne, 1971 . . . .   85.00   95.00

WOODWINDS

☐ **BAINES, A.,** *Woodwind Instruments and Their History,* London, 1957 . . . .   18.00   23.00

☐ **BATES, P.A.,** *The Oboe,* London, 1956 . . . .   9.00   12.00

☐ **BOEHM, THEOBALD,** *The Flute and Flute-Playing,* Cleveland, 1922 . . . .   14.00   19.00

☐ **CARSE, ADAM,** *Musical Wind Instruments,* London, 1939 . . . .   17.00   13.00

☐ **CHAPMAN, F. B.,** *Flute Technique,* London, 1936 . . . .   11.00   15.00

☐ **LANGWILL, L. G.,** *The Bassoon and Double Bassoon,* London, 1948 . . . .   10.00   14.00

☐ **LORENZO, L. DE,** *My Complete Story of the Flute,* New York, 1951 . . . .   12.00   17.00

☐ **RENDALL, F. G.,** *The Clarinet,* London, 1954   12.00   17.00

☐ **ROCKSTRO, R. S.,** *A Treatise on the Flute,* London, 1890 . . . .   23.00   30.00

	Price Range	
☐ **ROTHWELL, E.,** *Oboe Technique,* London, 1953	12.00	17.00
☐ **THURSTON, F.,** *Clarinet Technique,* London, 1955	12.00	17.00
☐ **WELCH, C.,** *History of the Boehm Flute,* London, 1883	16.00	22.00
☐ **WILLAMAN, R.,** *The Clarinet and Clarinet Playing,* New York, 1949	10.00	14.00

AMERICAN FOLK

American folk instruments are a category unto themselves. In many instances it is difficult to draw a clear distinction between folk and non-folk work, but even when instruments of this class are put aside, a great deal remains that can unquestionably be labeled "native art."

What is a folk instrument? The best and most universally understood definition is an instrument not commercially produced but made for use by its manufacturer, his family, or someone in the local community. The term "commercially produced" should not be interpreted too literally, however. It is certainly conceivable that some folk instruments were made with the intent of selling them, but they were not made by persons who manufactured instruments as a livelihood, and therein lies the difference.

Why were folk instruments made in America? A good question. It is readily understandable why Africans, South Sea Islanders, South American Indians, etc., made their own instruments—because no other source of supply was available. In America, where professionally manufactured instruments could be purchased, why did some persons take the trouble of making them? For several reasons. In the first place, "store-bought" instruments were not accessible in some parts of the country until the late-19th-century mail-order boom. Where they were available, they were often more expensive than many people could afford. Also, in many areas, especially rural, there was a taste for certain varieties of instruments that factories did not offer. Also, many local craftsmen thought their efforts to be well above the quality of commercial output.

The 19th century was the prime era for American folk instruments, though a good many were produced before and after—and continue to be today. They were of many sorts, some in imitation of standard instruments, others bearing no resemblance to them. Many were made of odd materials and were played in ways that could only be termed bizarre. Their designation as musical instruments might well be challenged by some persons, on the basis that anything that makes noises could be termed an instrument—even beating on a table with a hammer. However, folk instruments seldom originated out of a quest for novelty. Strange though some may be, they were designed and created to be used either as part of a band or by a lone performer, and this would seem sufficient to declare them instruments.

The study of American folk instruments is no cakewalk. Dates and points of origin are rarely known for sure and must be estimated. This is often difficult. Just because a particular sort of instrument was common to a given locality is no reason to conclude that every specimen originated there. Values are equally hard to fix. They depend on a variety of considerations, including (but not necessarily in this order) age, type of instrument, styles, quality, decoration, materials, and state of preservation. Rarity, of course, enters the picture but is not generally the deciding factor. A freak instrument may be very rare insofar as few or no others quite like it are known to exist, but it will not necessarily realize a high price.

Some folk instruments—it is not easy to estimate the proportion—are unquestionably within the class of "tramp art," i.e., items fashioned out of driftwood and throwaway materials by itinerants, who sought to exchange them for food or drink. These can reasonably be dated in the 1870–1930 era. Others are the work of children. They are no less highly regarded on this account, assuming they meet the standards of desirability that would be applied to any folk instruments.

A few words to the prospective buyer of folk instruments. This is a "collectible" found in diverse places, to put it mildly. Some of the best specimens have come to light in junkshops, at rummage sales, and, literally, in garbage dumps. The proportion handled by recognized dealers is very small compared to those changing hands "at the source." Not too many persons can recognize the value of a folk instrument or distinguish between old and new. A great deal of personal initiative is necessary in this hobby as well as a level of expertise that might not be required when collecting certain types of commercially made instruments. Inspect all components. A genuinely old instrument is not made partially from old and partially from recent materials.

Note: Many folk instruments do not have accepted names. In these cases we have described the instrument rather than attempting to name it.

Price Range

BANJO

- ☐ Made from a tambourine to which a length of mahogany is attached, backed in sheet tin, painted, damaged, Southern U.S., pre-Civil War **210.00** **250.00**
- ☐ Made from a barrel stave with skin stretched over, hardwood neck, strings missing, skin broken, probably Arkansas or Kentucky, c. 1870 .... **125.00** **150.00**
- ☐ Made from sheet zinc, 28″ long, maple neck, eastern U.S., c. 1890 .... **65.00** **80.00**

FLUTE

- ☐ Carved from a solid piece of walnut, 16½″ long, probably Pennsylvania, c. 1780 ...... **575.00** **650.00**
- ☐ Carved from a solid piece of ebony wood, whalebone mouthpiece, possibly sailor-made, thought to be of New England origin, early c. 1800's **480.00** **535.00**
- ☐ Carved from maple, 12⅝″ long, five holes, mouthpiece broken, place of origin not known, early 19th century **210.00** **250.00**
- ☐ Carved from whalebone, silver mouthpiece and decoration, size not stated, Massachusetts(?), c. 1840 .... **1750.00** **2250.00**
- ☐ Carved from pine, 13¼″ long, eastern U.S., c. 1850 .... **250.00** **275.00**
- ☐ Carved from rosewood, 18″ long, mouthpiece missing, eastern U.S. or possibly foreign (England or Wales), c. 1950 .... **315.00** **350.00**
- ☐ Carved from white ash, painted (paint decayed), 15″ long, possibly Pennsylvania, c. 1850–70 .... **315.00** **350.00**
- ☐ Carved from elephant tusk, 11½″ long, several cracks, ivory discolored, eastern U.S., third quarter of the 19th century **1400.00** **1800.00**
- ☐ Carved from cedar, boxwood mouthpiece, 21½″ long, seven holes, place of origin unknown, name "K. Brown" carved in wood, c. 1880 .... **400.00** **450.00**

Price Range

☐ Carved from oak, 15¼″ long, nickel mouthpiece, place of origin unknown, possibly foreign, c. late 1800's 250.00 300.00
☐ Made from bronze plumbing pipe with holes
bored in, size not stated, possible southern
U.S., c. early 1900's 85.00 100.00
☐ Made from galvanized steel tubing, 20″ long,
place of origin unknown, c. early 1900's ... 60.00 80.00
☐ Made from heavy rolled cardboard, painted,
19″ long, possibly New England, age uncer-
tain 65.00 80.00

ONE-MAN BAND

☐ Contraption containing a harmonica, zither,
small trumpet, ocarina, chimes, bells and
other instruments, attached to several
leather-covered lengths of wood, straps broken, used by a vaudeville performer who did
a one-man act, eastern U.S., c. 1900 ..... 210.00 240.00

STRINGED INSTRUMENT

☐ Wooden cigar box attached to broom handle,
37″ long, three strings, painted, southern
U.S.(?), second half of the 19th century ... 55.00 70.00
☐ Sawn barrel bottom with hardwood neck, repaired, two strings (three others missing),
eastern U.S., second half of the 19th century 70.00 90.00
☐ Instrument resembling mandolin, oval body
carved from sandalwood, walnut neck,
strings missing, decorated with shallow line
incising, traces of old paint, Virginia or Kentucky, late 19th century 285.00 350.00
☐ Instrument constructed from flat wooden
board, 12″ x 16″, oval cut in center, eight
strings running across from top to bottom,
board painted with floral design, worn, Penn-
sylvania(?), late 19th century 150.00 175.00

WASHBOARD INSTRUMENT

Price Range

☐ Metal washboard, wooden frame, mounted on a larger wooden plank measuring overall 22″ x 34″, painted dark brown with eagle head and other decorations, name "L. Cotter" painted at foot, rusted, worn, Appalachia, c. 1870–1890 .... **95.00** **110.00**

☐ Metal washboard, wooden frame (broken), size not stated, to one side is attached a length of thin chain with a wooden stick at the end, Appalachia, c. 1890 .... **80.00** **100.00**

☐ Metal, washboard, 29″ x 41″, narrow home-made wooden frame, two bells attached, southern or southeast U.S., c. 1880–1900 **80.00** **100.00**

☐ Metal washboard with pine frame, 32″ x 51″, with a leather strap attached so musician could wear it over his body, painted dull green, name "Mulvey's Minstrels" in silver letters, worn, partially damaged, probably eastern U.S., c. 1880–1900 .... **200.00** **240.00**

INDIVIDUAL INSTRUMENTS

ACCORDIONS

The most popular of the bellows-type instruments, in which sound is produced by aspiration and expiration (sucking in and pushing out air), the accordion is of rather modern invention. It was developed in 1822 by a German named Friedrich Buschmann, who invented the mouth organ a year earlier. It was termed the Ziehharmonika. The earliest models not only operated on the bellows principle but closely resembled a bellows. The accordion gained almost instant acceptance, though its use was restricted mainly to folk and popular music. Rarely was it used as a classical orchestral instrument. Later it saw even wider use in vaudeville and music halls, both in Europe and America. Improvements in design were made throughout the 19th century and into the 20th. By the late 19th century, accordions were being manufactured in a number of localities in Europe, though Germany held the lead in production, and German accordions were considered the most desirable.

Accordions were manufactured in a great variety of styles, sizes, and quality of materials. There were cheap models imported from Europe into the American market that retailed at as little as $2.25 around 1900. At the same time, a top-quality accordion could be had for $10 to $15. Retail prices rose sharply during the 1920's.

Price Range

☐ **"Accordeon"** (so marked), molded frame, enameled cloth trimmed bellows, nickel key cover, 10 keys, one stop, two sets of reeds, American, c. 1895 .... 150.00   175.00

☐ **American,** 1906 .... 375.00   425.00

☐ **Concertone,** marked "Nicolo Salanti", 21 pearl keys, 12 basses, four sets of steel reeds, 18-fold bellows, leather covered, rosewood finish frames, made in Italy for sale in U.S. by Montgomery Ward, c. early 1920's   250.00   300.00

☐ **Concertone,** 10 keys, two long spoon basses, 10-fold bellows, nickel corner protectors, enameled, mahogany finish pearls, ebonized moldings, size 10¼" x 5½" (closed)   120.00   150.00

☐ **Concertone,** 10 keys, four basses, metal valves and two sets of steel bronze reeds, rosewood finish with white enameled pressed borders, 14-fold bellows, 10" x 5½"   135.00   170.00

☐ **Concertone,** 31 pearl keys, 12 basses, metal valves, six sets of steel reeds, 18-fold cloth-covered leather bellows, rosewood finish frames, inlaid fingerboard and front edge, 12½" x 8¾" 275.00   335.00

☐ **Concertone,** two stops, two sets of reeds, 10 keys, gilt valves, 9-fold bellows, ebonized panels and frames, 12" x 6" 100.00   125.00

☐ **Concertone,** German model, 10 keys, two basses, three sets of reeds, three ebonized wooden stops, gilt valves with brass basses, 8-fold bellows with three middle partitions, 11⅛" x 6" 130.00   150.00

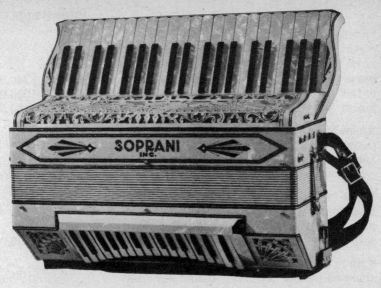

Accordion Italian, *c. 20th century. Courtesy: The Metropolitan Musuem Of Art, gift of Mrs. Margaret Gatz Werner, 1969.*

Price Range

☐ **Concertone,** 10 keys, gilt valves, four sets of steel bronze reeds, four enameled wooden stops, ebonized enamel woodwork, gilt embossing, 12⅞″ x 7″ 150.00 175.00

☐ **Concertone,** marked "Corelli," 21 keys, metal valves, four sets of steel bronze reeds set on lead plates, 14-fold bellows, rosewood finish frame, enameled embossings, oak finish panels, 11″ x 5¾″ 185.00 225.00

☐ Ebonized molding, nickel edges, open keyboard, 10 nickel keys ornamented with gilt stars, panels, corners and clasps bronzed, two stops, two sets of reeds, double bellows, c. 1890's 185.00 225.00

☐ German, c. 1860 .... 725.00 1100.00

☐ Imitation oak, hand carved molding, corners and clasps heavily nickel-plated, double bellows, 10 keys, two stops, two sets of reeds, late 19th century 210.00 250.00

Price Range

☐ Imitation oak, open keyboard, corners and clasps nickel-plated, double bellows, 10 keys, two stops, two sets of reeds, German-made (marketed in America), c. 1890 . . . . .   210.00   240.00

☐ Italian, third quarter of the 19th-century 750.00   1000.00

☐ Italian, 1891 . . . .   650.00   850.00

☐ **Kalbe Imperial,** ebonized moldings, sunken panels, twin bellows, nickel-plated clasps and corners, 10 nickel-plated keys, two stops, two sets of reeds 425.00   550.00

☐ **Kalbe Imperial,** medium size, bellows frame silver-stamped, corners and clasps nickel-plated, 10 keys, two basses, two stops, two sets of broad reeds 475.00   600.00

☐ **Kalbe Imperial,** ebonized moldings, gilt-stamped panels, ten nickel-plated keys and two basses, leather-bound bellows with nickel protectors, bellows frame silver-stamped, two stops, two reed sets 500.00   650.00

☐ **Kalbe's Improved Accordion,** 12 keys, ebonized moldings, hand-painted bellows frame, open keyboard, nickel-plated corners and clasps, double leather bound bellows, two stops, two sets of reeds, c. late 1800's 375.00   450.00

☐ Miniature accordion, hand-painted, panels and moldings ebonized, 10 nickel-plated keys, clasps and corners nickel-plated, double bellows, two stops, two sets of reeds, about ¾ full size, c. 1890–1900 . . . .   375.00   450.00

☐ Molded frame, open keyboard, 10 nickel-plated keys, double bellows, two stops, two sets of reeds, made in Germany for the American market, c. 1890–1900 . . . .   250.00   300.00

☐ Molded frames, panels nickel-ornamented, mirrored nickel round rings, double leather-bound bellows, 17 keys, two stops, four sets of reeds 475.00   600.00

☐ **Pitzchier Accordion,** fluted moldings in imitation mahogany, mahogany panels, sunken open-action keyboard, 19 nickel keys, heavy

Price Range

twin bellows with nickel protectors, nickel-plated corners and clasps, four stops, four sets of reeds, made in Germany (sold in America), c. late 1800's 550.00 700.00

☐ **Pitzschier Accordion,** identical to above except has 21 keys instead of 19 .... 600.00 750.00

☐ 10 nickel-plated keys, nickel-plated corners and clasps, ornamented panels, 16 trumpets in molding and 10 trumpets in key cover, triple bellows, two stops and two sets of reeds 425.00 475.00

☐ **"Tuxedo," with "Vox Humana" or Tremola attachment,** may be Kalbe, ebonized moldings and panels, open keyboard with 10 nickel-plated keys and two basses, leather-bound twin bellows, two stops, two sets of reeds 440.00 490.00

APOLLO HARPS

The Apollo Harp was a harp with a keyboard; or, it might be better put, an instrument with a keyboard, as it bore only slight resemblance to a harp. It originated in the late 1800's, at a time when instrument manufacturers (and novelty manufacturers) strove to place on the market a variety of musical devices that could be played with little practice or talent—items whose appeal would not be to the serious musician but to the general public.

☐ Imitation rosewood, 33 strings, sliding four-bar keyed bridge, produces 32 chords 100.00 125.00

☐ Imitation rosewood, 34 strings, five-bar sliding keyed bridge which produces five chords in every key, overall size 12½" x 21" 130.00 160.00

☐ Imitation rosewood, 36 strings, six-bar sliding keyed bridge, American, c. 1890's 170.00 210.00

☐ Imitation rosewood, six-bar sliding keyed bridge 215.00 300.00

☐ 33 strings, three-bar keyed sliding bridge, bridge can be adjusted to play in keys of C, C sharp, D, E flat, E or F, produces 18 chords, American, c. 1890's 60.00 80.00

BAGPIPES

The principle of the bagpipe is simple. Air is blown into a large bladder, then forced out through pipes. As it passes through the pipes, it creates various musical tones which can be shortened or lengthened depending on the rate of air escape. The bagpipe is among the most historically important of instruments and surely one of the most varied, if one takes into account the geographical area in which it has been produced and the many designs of bagpipes. It might also be mentioned that the bagpipe is one of very few instruments that can have considerable value as a collector's item even in deteriorated condition.

Bagpipe collecting, as opposed to the purchase of a single second-hand instrument to play, is a complex endeavor whose techniques we could hardly hope to explore here at any length. The advanced specialist seeks not only the earliest obtainable examples but those of especially fine workmanship, or from territories that have yielded few antique bagpipes. As the manufacturers of early bagpipes have left behind far scantier records of their activities than makers of, say, violins or pianos, it is often difficult or impossible to determine the origin of any given specimen.

Bagpipes of a primitive form were in use by the 3rd or 4th century A.D. in the Near East, from whence they appeared in Europe, but it was not until late in the Middle Ages that the instrument became really widespread. Scotland has had a reputation for bagpipe making (and playing) from at least as early as the 15th century. Unknown to most people, however, many other nations and peoples have adopted bagpipes as a national instrument, including the Irish, Slavic and Turkish.

	Price Range	
☐ French, early 18th-century	3000.00	5000.00
☐ French, Louis XV	2800.00	4500.00
☐ Scottish, walnut chaunters, 16th-century ...	6200.00	10500.00
☐ Scottish, early 17th-century	4800.00	7200.00
☐ Scottish, c. 1630	4500.00	6500.00
☐ Scottish, rosewood chaunters, late 17th-century	3700.00	5700.00
☐ Scottish, c. 1710	3500.00	5000.00
☐ Scottish, mid 18th-century	2900.00	4000.00

Bagpipe, *Italian, c. 19th century. Courtesy: The Metropolitan Museum of Art, gift of Burt Ives, 1963.*

BANJOS

The banjo is most familiar as the chief instrument of old-time minstrel shows. It has had a revival today in the folk music field, where it is almost as widely used as the guitar. Its origins are obscure. Apparently, a primitive type of banjo was played in Africa in the 17th and 18th centuries and was taken to America by slaves. Much easier to construct and to play than most other stringed instruments, it became a favorite in this country. By the time of the Civil War, the banjo was clearly the leading "folk" instrument of the southern and southwestern states. Though not extensively used north of Virginia, its influence extended into New England and even Canada.

	Price Range	
☐ American, Trap door style, snakehead, no logo, straight neck, 1920's	200.00	270.00
☐ American, Hutchins 5-string, maple neck, 11½″ rim, abalone-shell pattern on peghead and fingerboard, steel rod inlaid underneath the fingerboard to prevent warping	300.00	400.00
☐ American, maple shell with nickel band, neck finished in imitation cherry, 10″ calfskin head with six screw brackets, c. 1895–1905	200.00	250.00
☐ American, S. S. Steward, "Wondertone," walnut, marketry inlay, no case, 1920's	150.00	240.00

Price Range

☐ American, Gibson Tenor, snakehead, "The Gibson" logo, 17-fret neck, hardshell case, 1920's 250.00   350.00

☐ American, nickel shell, wood lined, neck stained in imitation cherry, with seven nickel-plated hexagon brackets, calfskin head, c. 1895–1905 .... 210.00   260.00

☐ American, imitation mahogany head, raised frets, nine nickel-plated hexagon brackets, calfskin head, c. 1895–1905 .... 225.00   300.00

☐ American, calfskin head, heavy strainer hoop, 21 nickel-plated brackets with protection nuts, polished cherry neck, ebony fingerboard inlaid with pearl position dots, ebony pegs, c. 1900 .... 325.00   400.00

☐ American, Bacon Banjo Co., "Style C," open back, 17-fret neck, hardshell case 150.00   225.00

☐ American, Regent Tenor, "Conqueror" model, solid celluloid inlays, rosewood resonator, maple neck 50.00   90.00

☐ American, nickel shell, maple rim, wired edges, 25 nickel-plated brackets with rabbeted stainer hoop, solid birch neck, ebony fingerboard inlaid with pearl and metal, ebony pegs, c. 1900 .... 375.00   450.00

☐ Banjo-ukelele, Waverly-baritone, maple body, 12 brackets, 1920's 40.00   70.00

Banjo,
American, Metal, 2' 11" L.
Courtesy: The Metropolitan
Museum of Art, The Crosby Brown
Collection of Musical
Instruments, 1889.

Price Range

☐ **Edgemere Banjo,** nickel shell, wood-lined, 17 nickel-plated hexagon brackets, raised frets, birch neck finished in imitation mahogany, c. 1900 .... 260.00   320.00

☐ Five-string, wood rim, 11″ rim, 12 nickel-plated brackets, birch neck, three pearl position dots, celluloid pegs, c. 1920's 70.00   90.00

☐ **Leader Banjo,** nickel shell, calfskin head, wired edges, nickel-plated strainer hoops, 21 nickel-plated brackets, fretted fingerboard, raised frets, inlaid with pearl position dots, birch neck 275.00   350.00

☐ **Piccolo Banjo, 13″ scale model, 7″ rim** .. 75.00   120.00

☐ Tenor banjo, maple rim, four strings (A, D, G, C), 20 nickel-plated brackets, pearl position dots 120.00   160.00

BASSOONS

The bassoon, firmly entrenched in orchestras since the Baroque age though never a widely popular instrument, underwent major alterations in the 19th century to arrive at its present design and performance. Early bassoons were attacked for unevenness of notes. In the 1820's Carl Almenraeder designed a new bassoon with realigned fingerholes and keys. Though a substantial technical improvement rendered the bassoon easier and more practical to play, Almenraeder's instrument was greeted with reservations by purists, who felt the tone was not equal to that of old bassoons. Later in the same century, another German, Wilhelm Heckel, succeeded in producing a bassoon that combined the best features of the old and new types. Bassoons manufactured today are essentially identical to Heckel's.

☐ **Buffet-Crampon** model, Paris, 20th century 1600.00   2100.00

☐ English, pearwood, 8-keyed, by William Milhouse, branded Milhouse/London; brass mounts, brass keys, F key with fishtail touchpiece, length 48¼″ 450.00   650.00

☐ **Heckel** model, Biebrich, 20th century 1500.00   1850.00

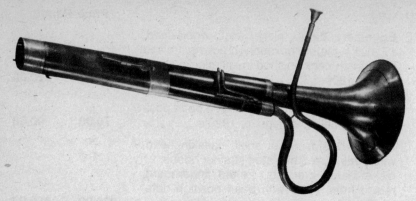

Bassoon in B Flat, French, c. 1800, wood and brass, 3' 3" L. Courtesy: The Metropolitan Museum of Art, The Crosby Brown Collection of Musical Instruments, 1889.

BONES

Bones, normally made of wood, derive their name from the practice in primitive cultures of making clappers from actual bone. It is quite likely that bones are the oldest of all musical instruments; their use may well date before recorded history. The principle by which they produce sound—one object striking another—is not unlike the drum's. They are, even today, an integral ingredient in the native folk music of many lands. Their popularity in America occurred in the late 1800's and early 1900's, when vaudeville and sideshow entertainers employed them.

	Price Range	
☐ Ebony, 5½", set of four	20.00	25.00
☐ Ebony, large size, 7", set of four	22.00	30.00
☐ Hardwood, 5½", set of four, American made, sold in the period c. 1890–1900	18.00	23.00
☐ Ivory, 5½", set of four, carved decor, c. 1910	65.00	95.00
☐ Ivory, 6", set of four, etched designs, probably New England	200.00	250.00
☐ Rosewood, 5½", set of four	20.00	25.00
☐ Rosewood, large size, 7", set of four, c. late 1800's	23.00	30.00

BOWS

It is hardly surprising that the bows made for playing certain stringed instruments (violin, viola, cello, etc.) have become collectible in themselves. For centuries the art of bow making has been an important phase of the musical instruments trade. It was well known even before the days of Stradavari and Amati that the best violin would not perform up to its potential if played with a lesser-quality bow. Of course this is true of all instruments employing a bow. Not only has technical precision gone into the crafting of fine bows over the years, but lavish materials including gold, silver, ivory, tortoiseshell, pearls, and occasionally even platinum. The finest bows are acknowledged to be works of art, and a selection of them is generally included in every major sale of collectible musical instruments. Prices have advanced steadily to the point where, today, it is by no means easy to purchase a high-quality antique bow for less than four figures. Some are commanding as much as $5000 and occasional specimens go even higher. Of course, the collecting appeal of bows is quite obvious, insofar as they display magnificently and consume very little space compared to most instruments. They were made all over the world, with Europe reigning as the chief production center. While most of the fine violins on the antiques market are Italian, this is not the situation with bows, where one finds a predominance of French specimens along with many of English, German, and miscellaneous origins. The American makers did not really compete on a level with those of Europe, but some domestic manufacturers did gain a reputation for their bows, notably John Norwood Lee of Chicago.

In purchasing antique bows it is advisable to make a thorough examination, or have this done by a competent expert if you are not confident of your own skills. Some have replacement parts.

	Price Range	
☐ Cello, English by James Tubbs of London, round stick mounted with silver, ebony frog, pearl dots, ebony adjuster	2500.00	3300.00
☐ Cello, French, by Adam of Paris, octagonal stick mounted with silver, ebony frog, pearl dots, ebony adjuster	2100.00	2450.00
☐ Cello, silver-mounted, by Fonclause, unbranded; round stick with an ivory face, mounted with a silver and ebony replacement frog, French silver and ebony adjuster, wt. 78 grams	2000.00	2500.00

Price Range

☐ Cello, silver-mounted, branded Bazin; round stick with an ivory face, mounted with a silver and ebony frog with pearl eye, silver-sheathed adjuster, wt. 74 grams 300.00 400.00

☐ Cello, French, by an unidentified maker, round stick mounted with silver, ebony frog, pearl dots, ebony adjuster, c. 1840–1860 .. 3200.00 3700.00

☐ Cello, French, by Fand Freres of Paris, round stick mounted with silver, ebony frog, pearl dots, ebony adjuster, c. 1860–1880 .... 2275.00 3000.00

☐ Cello, silver-mounted, English, by W. E. Hill & Sons; branded W. E. Hill & Sons; octagonal stick with a silver face, mounted with a silver and ebony frog with Paris eye, silver-sheathed adjuster, wt. 72 grams 1000.00 1400.00

☐ Cello, French, by Jean Dominique Adam of Paris, octagonal stick mounted with gold, ebony frog, pearl dots, ebony adjuster, c. 1830–1840 .... 6200.00 7500.00

☐ Cello, French, by Charles Jean Baptise Collin-Mezin of Paris, round stick mounted with silver, ebony frog, pearl dots, ebony adjuster 1700.00 2200.00

☐ Cello, French, by Gand of Paris, round stick mounted with silver, ebony frog, pearl dots, ebony adjuster 2100.00 2375.00

☐ Cello, French, by Eugene Sartory of Paris, octagonal stick mounted with silver, ebony frog, pearl dots, ebony adjuster 3800.00 4600.00

☐ Cello, German, by Sigfried Finkel with no place of residence given, octagonal stick mounted with gold and ivory, ivory frog, pearl dots, ivory adjuster 1600.00 1900.00

☐ Viola, silver-mounted, French, branded G. A. Chanot; round stick mounted with a silver and ebony frog with pearl eye, silver-sheathed adjuster, wt. 69 grams 450.00 550.00

☐ Viola, silver-mounted, French, faintly branded; round stick with an ivory face, mounted with a silver and ebony frog with Paris eye, silver-sheathed adjuster, wt. 67 grams 210.00 310.00

Price Range

☐ Viola, silver and tortoiseshell-mounted, by Vidoudez, branded Vidoudez Geneva; octagonal stick with a silver face, mounted with a silver and tortoiseshell frog with Paris eye, silver-sheathed adjuster, wt. 69 grams **800.00**   **1200.00**

☐ Viola, silver-mounted, by Albert Nurnberger, branded Albert Nurnberger; octagonal stick with an ivory face, mounted with a silver and ebony frog with Paris eye, silver-sheathed adjuster, wt. 65 grams **800.00**   **1200.00**

☐ Viola, gold-mounted, English, unbranded; round stick with an ivory face, mounted with a replacement ivory frog with gold ferrule, gold and ivory adjuster, wt. 72 grams **400.00**   **500.00**

☐ Viola, gold and ebony-mounted, by Bernard Ouchard, Geneva, stamped Vidoudez Geneve on either side of the butt; octagonal stick, ebony frog with pearl eye, ebony adjuster with two gold rings, wt. 69 grams . . .   **1000.00**   **1500.00**

☐ Viola, American, by Emile A. Ouchard of New York, round stick mounted with silver, ebony frog, pearl dots, ebony adjuster mounted in silver **2100.00**   **2350.00**

☐ Viola, English, by Stephen Bristow of London, round stick mounted with silver, ebony frog, pearl dots, ebony adjuster **700.00**   **850.00**

☐ Viola, French, by Roger Gerome, octagonal stick mounted with gold, ebony frog, pearl dots, ebony adjuster **2250.00**   **2875.00**

☐ Viola, Swiss, by Bernard Ouchard of Geneva, octagonal stick mounted with gold and ebony, ebony frog, pearl dots, ebony adjuster   **1600.00**   **1850.00**

☐ Violin, American, by John Norwood Lee of Chicago, round stick mounted with gold and tortoiseshell, tortoiseshell frog, pearl dots, ebony adjuster **2200.00**   **2850.00**

☐ Violin, American, by John Norwood Lee of Chicago, octagonal stick mounted with gold and tortoiseshell, tortoiseshell frog, pearl dots, ebony adjuster **2200.00**   **2850.00**

Price Range

☐ Violin, English, by C. E. Tubbs of London, round stick mounted with silver, ebony frog, pearl dots, ebony adjuster **1600.00** **1800.00**

☐ Violin, silver and ivory-mounted, English, by W. E. Hill & Sons, branded W. E. Hill & Sons; octagonal stick with a silver face, mounted with an ivory frog, plain sides, silver ferrule and silver-sheathed adjuster, wt. 59 grams **1200.00** **1600.00**

☐ Violin, English, by Arthur Bultitude of London, octagonal stick mounted with gold and tortoiseshell, tortoiseshell frog, gold flower ornaments **2100.00** **2450.00**

☐ Violin, English, by W. E. Hill of London, octagonal stick mounted with silver and tortoiseshell, tortoiseshell frog with silver decorations, tortoiseshell adjuster **1750.00** **2175.00**

☐ Violin, English, by W. E. Hill of London, round stick mounted with silver, ebony frog, pearl dots, ebony adjuster **1100.00** **1350.00**

☐ Violin, by C. Sartory, French, by E. Sartory à Paris; round stick with an ivory face, mounted with a silver and ebony frog, pearl eye and silver-and-ebony adjuster, wt. 57 grams ... **1700.00** **2300.00**

☐ Violin, silver-mounted, French, by J. Voirin à Paris; round stick with an ivory face, mounted with a silver-and-ebony frog with silver-and-pearl eye, silver-and-ebony adjuster, wt. 60 grams **600.00** **800.00**

☐ Violin, French, by Eugene Sartory of Paris, round stick mounted with silver, ebony frog, pearl dots, ebony adjuster **3200.00** **3675.00**

☐ Violin, silver-mounted, French, by J. S. Rameau; round stick with a silver face, mounted with a silver-and-ebony frog with Paris eye, silver-and-ebony adjuster, wt. 64 grams **200.00** **300.00**

☐ Violin, French, by C. Bazin, branded Bazin on the stick and frog; round stick with an ivory face, mounted with a silver-and-ebony frog, pearl eye, silver-and-ebony adjuster, wt. 56 grams **475.00** **575.00**

Price Range

☐ Violin, French, by J. B. Vuillaume with no place of residence given, round stick mounted with silver, ebony frog, pearl dots, ebony adjuster **2600.00** **2850.00**

☐ Violin, French, by Emile A. Ouchard with no place of residence given, round stick mounted with silver and tortoiseshell, tortoiseshell frog, pearl dots, silver-capped adjuster **1400.00** **1700.00**

☐ Violin, French, by Alfred Lamy of Paris, octagonal stick mounted with engraved silver, ebony frog, pearl dots, ebony adjuster capped in silver **1900.00** **2375.00**

☐ Violin, French, by Charles Peccatte of Paris, round stick mounted with silver, ebony frog, pearl dots, ebony adjuster, c. 1860–1880 .. **2100.00** **2375.00**

☐ Violin, French, by Alfred Lamy of Paris, round stick mounted with silver, ebony frog, pearl dots, ebony adjuster **1800.00** **2150.00**

☐ Violin, French, by Alfred Lamy of Paris, round stick mounted with silver, ebony frog, pearl dots, ebony adjuster **2300.00** **2800.00**

☐ Violin, French, by Paul Simon of Paris, octagonal stick mounted with silver, ebony frog, pearl dots, ebony adjuster, c. 1840–1860 .. **4200.00** **5500.00**

☐ Violin, French, by Claude Thomassin of Paris, octagonal stick mounted with silver, ebony frog, pearl dots, ebony adjuster **1800.00** **2250.00**

☐ Violin, French by Marcel Lapierre, round stick mounted with gold and ivory, ivory frog, pearl dots, gold rings, ivory adjuster **1175.00** **1400.00**

☐ Violin, French, by Joseph Henry of Paris, round stick mounted with gold and tortoiseshell, tortoiseshell frog, pearl dots, ebony adjuster, c. 1850 .... **3200.00** **3750.00**

☐ Violin, French, by Guillaume Maline of Paris, round stick mounted with silver, ebony frog, pearl dots, ebony adjuster, c. 1830–1840 .. **4300.00** **5600.00**

Price Range

☐ Violin, gold-mounted, probably French, branded Geo. Withers & Sons; round stick with an ivory face, mounted with a gold-and-ebony frog with Paris eye, gold-sheathed adjuster, wt. 60 grams 1000.00 1500.00

☐ Violin, German, by Ludwig Bausch, round stick mounted with silver, ebony frog, pearl dots, ebony adjuster 1100.00 1425.00

☐ Violin, silver-mounted, German, by W. A. Pfretzschner, branded W. A. Pfretzschner, round stick with an ivory face, mounted with a silver-and-ebony frog with pearl eye, silver-and-ebony adjuster, wt. 53 grams 100.00 150.00

☐ Violin, silver-mounted, German, by F. R. Wunderlich, branded F. R. Leipzig; octagonal stick with an ivory face, mounted with a silver-and-ebony frog, plain sides, silver-sheathed adjuster, wt. 60 grams 500.00 600.00

☐ Violin, by Otto Hoyer, branded Otto A. Hoyer, round stick with an ivory face, mounted with a silver-and-ebony frog, plain sides, silver-sheathed adjuster, wt. 57 grams 275.00 350.00

☐ Violin, silver mounted, by J. Knopf, branded J. Knopf; round stick with ivory face, mounted with silver-and-ebony frog with Paris eye, silver-sheathed adjuster, wt. 65 grams 500.00 600.00

☐ Violin, by James Tubbs, branded Jas. Tubbs; round stick with a silver face, mounted with a silver-and-ebony frog with pearl eye, silver-sheathed adjuster, wt. 60 grams 2600.00 3300.00

☐ Violin, ivory-mounted, by Dodd, branded Dodd on the stick and frog; round stick mounted with carved-ivory open frog, ivory adjuster, wt. 54 grams 700.00 1000.00

☐ Violin, silver-mounted, by M. Fleury, branded M. Fleury; round stick with an ivory face, mounted with silver-and-ebony frog with Paris eye, silver-sheathed adjuster, wt. 58 grams 600.00 800.00

BUGLES

	Price Range	
☐ American, c. 1878	160.00	200.00
☐ American, artillery bugle, brass, c. 1900	130.00	160.00
☐ American, artillery bugle, nickel-plated, c. 1900	185.00	225.00
☐ American, cavalry bugle, brass, c. 1900	150.00	185.00
☐ American, cavalry bugle, nickel-plated, c. 1900	160.00	200.00
☐ American, Civil War	325.00	450.00
☐ American, infantry bugle, brass, c. 1900	125.00	175.00
☐ American, infantry bugle, nickel-plated, c. 1900	160.00	190.00
☐ American, officer's bugle, c. 1900	80.00	110.00
☐ American, officer's bugle, nickel-plated, c. 1900	100.00	130.00
☐ English, by Metzler of London, six keys, copper mounted with brass, white metal keys, 16¼", c. 1840–1850	800.00	1000.00

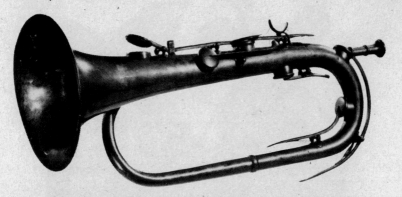

Bugle, keyed, Belgium, c. 19th century, brass, 1' 9" L. Courtesy: The Metropolitan Musuem of Art, The Crosby Brown Collection of Musical Instruments, 1889.

CASTINETS (ALSO SPELLED CASTANETS)

Castinets are known as a Spanish or Latin American instrument only because the Latin peoples have preserved its use in their folk music. It was not their invention or exclusive property, as castinet-type instruments (consisting of two lengths of wood, bone, or other material clapped together to produce clicking sounds) are both ancient and universal. Castinets are ideal collectors' items; old specimens do not get "out of order" and often are splendidly decorated or made from exotic materials. Unfortunately, not too many good specimens are available on the American market. The traveler in Mexico, Brazil, Argentina, or Spain stands a better chance of encountering fine examples if he hunts the music shops and secondhand markets.

	Price Range	
☐ American, early 20th century	35.00	40.00
☐ Argentinian, early 19th century	170.00	215.00
☐ Mexican, 1890	70.00	90.00
☐ Portuguese, c. 1830	150.00	185.00
☐ Spanish, late 18th century	200.00	250.00
☐ Spanish, c. 1810	160.00	200.00
☐ Spanish, mid-19th century	140.00	175.00
☐ Spanish, c. 1860	80.00	110.00

Castinets, Spanish, c. 19th century hardwood, 2" x 2¾". Courtesy: The Metropolitan Museum of Art. The Crosby Brown Collection of Musical Instruments, 1889.

Violincello, Italian, Gioffredo Cappa, Mandovi 1697, length of back 29" (Photo courtesy of Christie's, New York).

CELLOS

The cello, or violoncello as it was originally and still correctly called, has long been an important orchestral and solo instrument, first in classical music and more recently in jazz, rhythm and blues, and rock. The cello provided the "beat" on rock recordings of the 1950's. But there is considerable difference in the manner of play between classical and nonclassical cello, one played with a bow, the other with fingers.

The cello became a standard orchestra instrument in the 17th century, though developed earlier. The first solo pieces for cello were composed by an Italian named Gabrielli (1659–1690), who is generally credited with bringing it to a level of attention it had not previously attained. Various modifications and improvements were made to the cello in the following century and a half.

Cellos of the 17th century are rarely on the market. When sold, their price is well into the four-figure and often five-figure range if the specimen is decently preserved. Those of the 18th century are more plentiful, but fine ones are very expensive.

	Price Range	
☐ American, inlaid edges, sold by Sears Roebuck, c. 1900	420.00	525.00
☐ American, peg head, pegs and fingerboard of ebony, c. 1895–1900	475.00	600.00
☐ American, ebony fingerboard, ebony tailpiece, solid ebony trimmings	610.00	760.00
☐ Double bass, half-size, dark red wood, American, c. 1900	630.00	800.00
☐ Four-string bass, American, iron head, c. 1895–1905	700.00	800.00
☐ Three-quarter size double bass, four strings, iron head, American, c. 1900	850.00	1100.00
☐ Three-quarter size, four strings, ebony fingerboard, American, c. 1895–1905	900.00	1250.00
☐ Czech, violoncello by Bohuslav Lantner of Prague, back in two sections, broad-grain table, burnt orange varnish, back measures 29¼", c. 1920	3275.00	3850.00
☐ English, unlabeled, one-piece back of faint small curl, similar ribs and head, open-grain table, dark red varnish, in case with two bows, one bow is silver mounted, back measures 29$^{1}/_{16}$"	2000.00	2600.00
☐ English, labeled Willm. Forster 1790, also Forster on inside of right C bout, two-piece back of narrow curl descends from joint, similar ribs and head, fine-grain table, red-brown varnish, in case with silver-mounted bow stamped August Rau, back measures 28$^{15}/_{16}$"	7000.00	10,000.00
☐ French, maker and city of origin unidentified, single-piece back, medium-grain table, burnt orange varnish, back measures 29½", c. 1820–1840	1750.00	2250.00

Price Range

☐ French, first half of 19th century, unlabeled, one-piece back of medium curl, similar ribs and head, medium-grain table, red orange-brown varnish, in case with bow, back measures $29^{5}/_{16}$" 2000.00   3000.00

☐ French, inscribed Repare par Salf a Toulon 1847; two-piece back of faint horizontal narrow curl, similar ribs and head, fine-grain table widens toward flanks, dark golden orange-brown varnish, measures 29¼" 700.00   1000.00

☐ German, violoncello by Leopold Widhalm of Nuremberg, single-piece back, fine-grain table, burnt rust-red varnish, back measures 29½", dated 1768 .... 1100.00   1425.00

☐ German, violoncello by Johann Lippold of Neukirchen, back in two sections, medium-grain table, burnt orange varnish, back measures 29⅞", dated 1823 .... 2175.00   2825.00

☐ Italian, Naples, early 19th century, unlabeled, two-piece back of narrow irregular curl, similar ribs and head, fine-grain table, orange-red varnish, in case with bow, back measures 29¼" 4000.00   6000.00

☐ Italian, violoncello by Ettore Soffritti of Ferrera, back in two sections, medium-grain table, pale orange-hued varnish, back measures 29¾", dated 1923 .... 7500.00   10000.00

☐ Italian, modern, labeled Antoniazzi Romeo Cremonese / fecit Cremona l'anno 1910; bears the label Benito Saccani, one-piece slab-cut back, similar ribs and head, medium-grain table, golden orange varnish, in case with bow, measures 29" 12,000.00   16,000.00

☐ Italian, violoncello by Niccolo Gagliano of Naples, back in two sections, plain head, medium-grain table, inlaid with gold leaf, orange-brown varnish, back measures 29¼", dated 1774 .... 65,000.00   75,000.00

☐ Japanese, violoncello by Hajime Nakamura of Tokyo, back in two sections, fine-grain table, red-brown varnish, back measures 29½", dated 1981 .... 3500.00   4500.00

Price Range

☐ Swiss, violoncello, maker and city of origin un-identified, back in two sections, broad-grain table, reddish brown varnish, back measures 28½", date undetermined	900.00	1150.00
☐ Cello with expert's certificate attributing it to be Italian, unlabeled, two-piece back of narrow curl, similar ribs and head, medium-grain table, red orange-brown varnish, in case with two bows, back measures 29¾", c. 1850 ..	900.00	1300.00

CLARINETS

☐ Austrian, high A, stained maple, stamped F. Muss / Wien; brass mounts, 10 brass keys, length 11½"	400.00	550.00

Laube clarinets, 13 keys, two rings, Grenadilla wood, nickel silver keys and trimming cork joints, graduated bore, c. 1920.

☐ B-flat, low pitch	300.00	375.00
☐ A, low pitch	300.00	375.00
☐ C, low pitch	300.00	375.00
☐ E-flat, low pitch	300.00	375.00
☐ **Laube clarinet,** B-flat, low pitch, 15 keys, four rings, four rollers	450.00	600.00
☐ A, low pitch, 15 keys	450.00	600.00
☐ C, low pitch, 15 keys	450.00	600.00
☐ E-flat, low pitch, 15 keys	450.00	600.00

CONCERTINAS

☐ American, late 19th century	135.00	175.00
☐ American, child's toy, c. 1900	100.00	130.00
☐ American, child's toy, c. 1920	70.00	90.00
☐ American, child's toy, c. 1940's	35.00	50.00
☐ French, c. 1830	400.00	500.00
☐ French, mid-19th century	375.00	475.00
☐ French, c. 1871	275.00	360.00
☐ Mahogany tops, decorated with German-silver edges and inlaying, double bellows ..	85.00	110.00
☐ Mahogany tops, 20 keys, nickel ornaments and sound rings, large bellows, c. 1890–1900	100.00	130.00

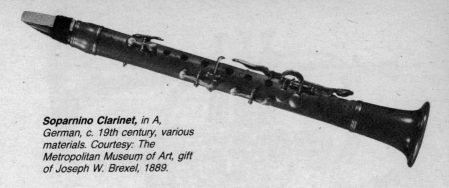

Soparnino Clarinet, in A, German, c. 19th century, various materials. Courtesy: The Metropolitan Museum of Art, gift of Joseph W. Brexel, 1889.

	Price Range	
☐ Mahogany with German-silver inlayings, leather bound bellows, 20 keys, broad reeds, figure of dog on top	150.00	175.00
☐ Mahogany, 20 keys, leather-bound bellows with five folds, made in England, in the original wooden case, 1897	225.00	300.00
☐ Mahogany, 20 keys, bone buttons, nickel sound rings, c. 1895	75.00	100.00
☐ Rosewood tops, figured moldings, 20 bone keys, large bellows	140.00	170.00

CORNETS

☐ **Artists' B-Flat,** brass, polished, before 1910	235.00	280.00
☐ **Artists' B-Flat,** nickel-plated	275.00	335.00
☐ **Artists' B-Flat,** silverplated, satin finish, gold-lined bell	325.00	425.00
☐ **Artists' B-Flat,** silverplated, polished, gold-lined bell	350.00	450.00
☐ **Concertone,** one water key, pearl buttons, nickel silver mouthpiece, 16½″ long, brass, c. 1920's	125.00	175.00
☐ **Concertone,** as above, nickel-plated	130.00	180.00
☐ **Concertone,** as above, silverplated, satin finish, goldplated bell	200.00	250.00

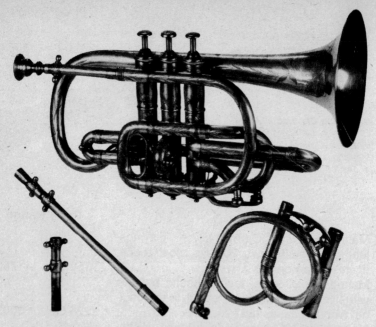

Cornet in B-Flat, American, 20th century, silverplated brass. Courtesy: The Metropolitan Museum of Art, The Crosby Brown Collection of Musical Instruments, 1889.

	Price Range	
☐ **Dupont B-Flat,** single water key, brass finish	120.00	150.00
☐ **Dupont B-Flat,** single water key, burnished nickel plate	130.00	160.00
☐ **Dupont B-Flat,** single water key, triple silver-plate, satin finish	160.00	200.00
☐ **Dupont B-Flat,** single water key, triple silver-plate, burnished	200.00	250.00
☐ **Dupont B-Flat,** double water key, highly polished brass	150.00	185.00
☐ **Dupont B-Flat,** double water key, burnished nickel plate	175.00	225.00
☐ **Dupont B-Flat,** double water key, triple silver-plate	225.00	275.00

Price Range

☐ **Dupont B-Flat,** double water key, triple silver-plate, burnished 285.00 350.00

☐ **Dupont B-Flat,** double water key, ornamental trimmings, heavily braced, highly polished brass 210.00 250.00

☐ **Dupont B-Flat,** double water key, ornamental trimmings, heavily braced, burnished nickel plate 210.00 250.00

☐ **Dupont B-Flat,** double water key, ornamental trimmings, heavily braced, triple silverplate, satin finish 250.00 320.00

☐ **Dupont B-Flat,** double water key, ornamental trimmings, heavily braced, triple silver finish, burnished 300.00 350.00

☐ **Dupont C,** highly polished brass 125.00 160.00

☐ **Dupont C,** burnished nickel plate 135.00 170.00

☐ **Dupont C,** triple silverplate, satin finish 160.00 210.00

☐ **Dupont C,** triple silverplate, burnished 180.00 230.00

☐ **Dupont E-Flat,** highly polished brass finish 100.00 140.00

☐ **Dupont E-Flat,** burnished nickel plate 125.00 160.00

☐ **Dupont E-Flat,** triple silverplate, satin finish 145.00 170.00

☐ **Dupont E-Flat,** triple silverplate, burnished 160.00 200.00

☐ **Leaders' B-Flat,** double water key, brass, polished, c. 1905–1910 .... 225.00 280.00

☐ **Leaders' B-Flat,** double water key, nickel-plated 250.00 320.00

☐ **Leaders' B-Flat,** silverplated, satin finish ... 285.00 350.00

☐ **Leaders' B-Flat,** silverplated, polished 300.00 400.00

☐ **Marceau B-Flat,** brass, highly polished 85.00 115.00

☐ **Marceau B-Flat,** nickel-plated 100.00 125.00

☐ **Marceau B-Flat,** double water key, brass, highly polished 140.00 180.00

	Price Range	
☐ **Marceau B-Flat,** double water key, nickel-plated	150.00	190.00
☐ **Marceau C,** brass	100.00	125.00
☐ **Marceau C,** nickel-plated	110.00	140.00
☐ **Marceau E-Flat,** brass, highly polished, c. 1905–1910	80.00	110.00
☐ **Marceau E-Flat,** nickel-plated	95.00	120.00

CYMBALETS

The cymbalet was a novelty instrument never really taken seriously and rarely, if ever, played professionally. It made a moderate splash on the American market late in the 1800's, about the time that many other novelty music-making contrivances were put out. The public of that era had a remarkable appetite for small instruments which, according to the ads, could be played by young and old with little practice or skill. The cymbalet was something in the nature of a tambourine.

☐ Made of two pieces of bent wood, fastened together, with two loose brass jingles at each end, c. 1897	12.00	16.00

CYMBALS

Cymbals are concussion instruments; that is, they produce sound not by being struck by something (as with percussion instruments) but by being struck against each other. The cymbal's heritage is Near Eastern, and it remains today more popular and widely produced in that part of the world than in the West. Cymbals have made themselves known in Europe and America, however, in classical, swing, jazz, and rock music—in fact in nearly all forms of music, with the exception of country and western.

Turkey has been headquarters of the cymbal for well over a century, supplying this instrument to distributors in all corners of the globe. Cymbals have been made elsewhere, including America, but the reputation for Turkish-made specimens has been such that others, no matter of what quality, receive little notice. It is believed that cymbals were first used in a presentation of Western classical music in Germany in 1680, in a not-too-well-remembered opera entitled *Esther* by Nicolaus Strungk. From Germany the employment as an orchestral accessory spread into neighboring lands. The big wave of commercial success came in the American marching band era (1880–World War I). Since then they have been included in nearly every street parade, football "half-time" show, and other public amusements.

	Price Range	
☐ American, 10″, leather handles, c. 1900 ...	80.00	110.00
☐ American, 11″, leather handles, c. 1900 ...	95.00	120.00
☐ American, 12″, leather handles, c. 1900 ...	110.00	145.00
☐ American, 13″, leather handles, c. 1900 ...	130.00	160.00
☐ Chinese, late 19th century	80.00	110.00
☐ Dutch, late 19th century	95.00	120.00
☐ English, c. 1800	140.00	175.00
☐ French, late 18th century	200.00	250.00
☐ French, c. 1800	160.00	215.00
☐ French, first quarter 19th century	150.00	200.00
☐ Italian, brass mid-19th century	120.00	160.00
☐ Turkish, 10″, leather handles, c. 1900	100.00	135.00

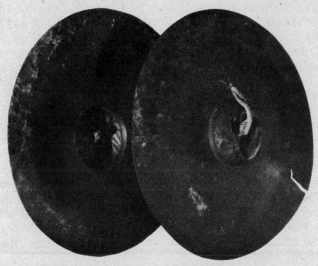

Cymbals, *European, brass, 1' 3". Courtesy: The Metropolitan Museum of Art, The Crosby Brown Collection of Musical Instruments, 1889.*

DRUMS

Drums are of ancient origins and are to be found among the native culture of almost all peoples. Their variety—in size, design, and materials—is undoubtedly greater than of any other instrument.

Primitive drums are known to have been made and used as long ago as 1500–2000 B.C. by the Mesopotamians and were likely in use by other ancient civilizations at this same time. To place a date on the invention of drums, or even to name their place of origin, is impossible, as the first drums or drum-like instruments were hollow logs of wood on which prehistoric men beat with their fists or sticks.

One type of Mesopotamian drum is known today as a friction drum. It differs from the traditional variety in that it was not struck to produce sound. Instead, it consisted of a bowl with animal hide stretched across the top, with a stick running up through the bottom. Upon rubbing the stick, the instrument gave forth a sort of groan. Needless to say, these specimens are not available to collectors.

By the 4th or 5th century B.C., drums of one kind or other were known to the Persians, Asian Indians, Greeks, and probably Chinese. The Romans used drums extensively at a somewhat later period. It was during the Middle Ages that the kettledrum was introduced into Europe. Returning Crusaders brought specimens back from the eastern battlefronts, probably just as curiosities at first, but the kettledrum became popular in the West. The English named it "nakers," a not-too-successful attempt to phonetically translate its Arabic name *naqqara.* From the kettledrum evolved all subsequent European (and American) drums, though later models bore little resemblance to the *naqqara.*

Antique and semi-antique percussion instruments are found on the market in enormous quantity and variety. Many were not designed as orchestral instruments but for marching bands, fife and drum corps, etc. Their military connection lends value to certain specimens over and above their interest as antique instruments. Normal signs of use are to be expected on the skins of early drums; this does not detract from the value. However, drums on which the skin is split or otherwise defective, or the stringing damaged, are worth considerably less than the prices indicated here.

	Price Range	
☐ **Acme Professional Bass,** 24″ diameter, c. 1900	175.00	200.00
☐ **Acme Professional Bass,** 26″ diameter, c. 1900	200.00	250.00
☐ **Acme Professional Bass,** 28″ diameter, c. 1900	200.00	270.00

Price Range

☐ **Acme Professional Bass,** 30″ diameter, c.
1900 . . . . 220.00 275.00

☐ **Acme Professional Snare,** 14″ diameter, c.
1900 . . . . 160.00 200.00

☐ **Acme Professional Snare,** 16″ diameter, c.
1900 . . . . 170.00 220.00

☐ **Acme Professional Snare,** 16″ diameter, 8
rawhide snares, c. 1900 . . . . 185.00 240.00

☐ American, painted with scenes of firefighting,
inscribed "32nd Battalion," some damage,
early 19th century 1100.00 1500.00

☐ American, War of 1812 vintage, 16″ diameter 1000.00 1400.00

☐ American, 15½″ diameter, c. 1788 . . . . 850.00 1100.00

☐ American Revolutionary field drum 1300.00 2000.00

☐ American, mounted on wooden trestle, 29″
diameter, second quarter of 19th century . . 1400.00 2100.00

☐ American, painted with stars and stripes, per-
haps New England origin, c. 1820 . . . . 1100.00 1400.00

Bass Drum, *American, double head, wood, parchment, leather, brass.
Courtesy: The Metropolitan Museum of Art, The Crosby Brown Collection
of Musical Instruments, 1889.*

Price Range

☐ American, band instrument, second quarter of 19th century	900.00	1175.00
☐ American Civil War military drum, c. 1860's	800.00	1050.00
☐ American toy, 12½" diameter, c. 1850's ...	475.00	625.00
☐ American toy, 14" diameter, c. 1860	475.00	625.00
☐ American toy, painted with figures of wild animals, paint chipped, c. 1860–70	500.00	650.00
☐ American toy, 11¾" diameter, leather strap, c. 1870's	400.00	500.00
☐ American toy, c. 1890's	160.00	210.00
☐ American toy, tin, cord strap, c. 1920's	75.00	100.00
☐ American toy, Mickey Mouse, c. 1930's	300.00	375.00
☐ American toy, the Beatles, c. 1960's	80.00	110.00
☐ Bass, American, c. 1900	300.00	375.00
☐ Bass, English, mid-19th century	350.00	460.00
☐ Bass, English, late 19th century	230.00	300.00
☐ Bass, French, c. 1790	1250.00	1600.00
☐ Bass, German, silver mountings, early 19th century	725.00	900.00
☐ Bass, German, c. 1830	550.00	700.00
☐ Bass, German, foot pedal, c. 1860	500.00	650.00
☐ Bass, German, third quarter of 19th century	450.00	600.00
☐ Bass, Italian, wooden mountings, 18th century	900.00	1200.00
☐ Bass, Italian, Roman, 1791	800.00	1100.00
☐ Bass, Portuguese, purple membranes, silver chased, c. 1810	1200.00	1600.00
☐ Bass, Russian, 19th century	550.00	750.00
☐ Bass, Swiss, ivory inlays, early 19th century	700.00	900.00
☐ English, 13½" diameter, leather straps, 18th century	625.00	800.00
☐ English, 14" diameter, painted with figural subjects, c. 1760	700.00	900.00
☐ English, 16½" diameter, restored, leather straps renewed, c. 1800	500.00	600.00

FANFARES

This was a name applied to a special kind of brass horn, similar to a bugle. It was supposedly easier to play than either a bugle or trumpet. But it never attained much popularity.

	Price Range	
☐ Eight reed valves, c. 1890–1900	40.00	45.00
☐ Six reed valves, c. 1890–1900	30.00	35.00
☐ 10 reed valves, c. 1890–1900	45.00	55.00

FIFES

☐ "Acme Hand Made," metal, nickel-plated, c. 1900	150.00	200.00
☐ American, early 19th century	475.00	600.00
☐ Cocoa wood, c. 1900	50.00	70.00
☐ **"Crosby Model,"** ebony, c. 1900	110.00	150.00
☐ Ebony, nickel-plated ferrules, c. 1900	90.00	120.00
☐ French, "Atlas," cast metal, nickel-plated, c. 1900	45.00	60.00
☐ Irish, c. 1725	450.00	600.00
☐ Irish, c. 1820	300.00	400.00
☐ Rosewood, brass ferrules, c. 1900	50.00	65.00
☐ Scottish, c. 1680	600.00	750.00
☐ Scottish, c. 1710	550.00	700.00
☐ Scottish, ivory, silver mountings, c. 1740 ...	550.00	700.00
☐ Scottish, last quarter of 18th century	400.00	525.00

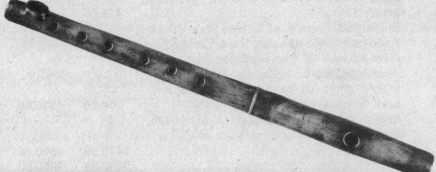

Fife In B-Flat, Austria, c. 1880, light wood, 1' 1¼" L. Courtesy: The Metropolitan Museum of Art, The Crosby Brown Collection of Musical Instruments, 1889.

FLUTES

Price Range

- [ ] American, cocuswood, 5-keyed, stamped E. Riley/N-YORK; ivory mounts, 5 silver saltspoon keys, in original case, sounding length 23⅞″ .... 150.00 | 250.00
- [ ] American, 8-keyed, c. 1920's .... 125.00 | 150.00
- [ ] Bavarian, c. 1805 .... 5200.00 | 7000.00
- [ ] Cherrywood, American, first quarter 19th century .... 3000.00 | 3200.00
- [ ] Ebony, Italian, length 27″, in a leather-covered, fleece-lined case, 18th century ... 4600.00 | 5500.00
- [ ] Ebony, Prussian, length 26¼″, c. 1800 .... 2000.00 | 2400.00
- [ ] Ebony, Scottish, late 18th century .... 2600.00 | 3700.00
- [ ] English, ivory, 8-keyed, stamped Patent/Clementi & Compy/No. 26 Cheapside/London; silver keys with pewter plugs, graduated tuning slide, in mahogany box, sounding length 23½″ .... 500.00 | 700.00
- [ ] English, silver, inscribed Rudall, Carte & Co. / 23 Verners Street / Oxford Street / London 1867 Patent and D.S.D.; engraved band-lip plate, silver keywork, in case, sounding length 23¹³/₁₆″ .... 475.00 | 625.00
- [ ] English, silver, inscribed Council Prize Medals / 1851 and 1862 / Rudall, Rose, Carte & Co. / Patentees / 20 Charing Cross / London / Boehm's Patent / Carte's Mechanism / M.S.A.; engraved band-lip plate, silver keywork, in case, sounding length 23¼″ ..... 200.00 | 300.00
- [ ] English, by Thomas Stanesby, Jr. of London, ivory with silver mountings, silver key, 21½″, c. 1740 .... 3475.00 | 4600.00
- [ ] Flemish, walnut, 18th century .... 2000.00 | 2600.00
- [ ] French, one-keyed, ivory, 22⅜″, mid-18th century .... 6500.00 | 8000.00
- [ ] French, by Claude Laurent of Paris, glass with silver mountings, silver keys and key covers, 24½″, dated 1838 .... 4650.00 | 5450.00
- [ ] German, mid-18th century .... 6250.00 | 7500.00
- [ ] German, cocoa wood, silver-trimmed, one-keyed, late 19th/early 20th century .... 55.00 | 75.00

Flute, *German, c. 18th century, wood, 10" L. Courtesy: The Metropolitan Museum of Art, The Crosby Brown Collection of Musical Instruments, 1889.*

	Price Range	
☐ Grenadilla wood, 8-keyed, tuning slide, c. 1900	100.00	130.00
☐ Hardwood, English, early 19th century	1000.00	1300.00
☐ **Henry Hill,** carved ivory, 6-keyed	550.00	700.00
☐ Italian, length 25¾", c. 1781	3000.00	4000.00
☐ Italian, Milan, in carry box, c. 1786	3300.00	4500.00
☐ Ivory, 7-keyed, by Goulding & Co., London, silver mounts and keys, long "F" with pewter plugs, 23³/₁₆", c. 1800	2600.00	3150.00
☐ **Meyer Model,** 8-keyed, c. 1900	175.00	210.00
☐ **Meyer Model,** 10-keyed, c. 1900	250.00	325.00
☐ Rosewood, Italian, late 18th century	3475.00	4250.00
☐ Russian, silver mountings, in case, c. 1790	6200.00	9000.00
☐ Russian, silver mountings, c. 1807	6000.00	8000.00
☐ Six-keyed, ivory, Goulding & Co., London, silver mounts and keys, c. 1815	800.00	1100.00

FLUTE ACCORDIONS

Flute accordions are a novelty instrument played mostly by amateurs and manufactured mainly in the late 1800's and early 1900's.

☐ Nickel-trimmed, 10 keys, two basses	32.00	42.00
☐ 10 bone keys, nickel-covered case, projecting metal bell, American made	35.00	45.00
☐ 10 bone keys, two basses, reeds, with original wooden case, c. 1895	40.00	55.00

Price Range

☐ 10 patent nickel keys, two basses, ebonized sides and keyboard with gilt ornaments, nickel-plated corners, trumpet and mouthpiece 65.00   85.00

FLUTE HARMONICAS

Flute harmonicas are among those instruments readily found as antiques but for which the customer will search long and hard in the shops of dealers in newly made instruments. A popular novelty for awhile, its popularity did not last a very long time.

The flute harmonica belongs to the era (1880–1920 or thereabout) of vaudeville entertainment and traveling shows, when many bizarre instruments came and went. It was the sort of thing a "one-man-band" performer used and children enjoyed as a gift. A cross between flute and harmonica, is was not the musical equal of either but it was fun to fool with, and this undoubtedly accounted for its brief success.

☐ Eight long keys, gilt trumpets, gilt mouthpiece, sold by mail-order houses in the 1890–1900 era 13.00   18.00
☐ Nickel-plated frame with 10 keys, two basses and bell 15.00   20.00
☐ Wooden case with nickel and paper cover, 8 round keys 10.00   15.00

GUITARS

The guitar is one of those instruments of vast antiquity whose history is enveloped with much legend and whose actual inventor is unknown. That it even had an inventor cannot be stated with certainty. Like man himself, the guitar very likely evolved gradually from lower forms, changing a bit here and there as it passed through the hands of various groups. It is without argument one of the most universal of instruments, having achieved popularity on all continents and among musicians of all sorts from classical to folk to rock.

Guitars, or their close ancestors, are definitely known to have existed in Spain in the 12th century A.D., to which they had apparently come via Asia. They were widely used in late medieval Europe by court musicians, troubadors, wandering minstrels, and balladists. The poems of Chaucer and other early poets were originally recited to music, and frequently guitarists and other independent musicians contrived their own lyrics. By the 15th century, guitars were being manufactured not only in Spain but France, Portugal, and elsewhere. They became extremely widespread in the 16th century. Henry VIII of England, who died in 1547, owned 21 guitars (which he did not play; he was a collector of instruments and boasted some 381 of various types).

The six-string or standard guitar familiar today belongs to the late 18th century. It is not known who made the first "modern" six-string guitar nor where it originated. It might possibly have been an Italian innovation. This advance brought the instrument even greater popularity. Soon afterward, guitar makers sprang up in many areas where none had previously been active, including a number of U.S. towns.

	Price Range	
☐ American, Civil War era	2000.00	2800.00
☐ American, "The Troubadour," c. 1900	95.00	115.00
☐ American, "The Edgemere," c. 1900	120.00	160.00
☐ American, "The Marlowe," c. 1900	140.00	180.00
☐ American, "The Acme," c. 1900	150.00	200.00
☐ American, "The Kenmore," c. 1900	160.00	210.00

Guitar, French, c. 1770, made by Guillaume. Courtesy: The Metropolitan Museum of Art, Gift of Mrs. Lucy W. Drexel, 1889.

	Price Range	
□ American, "The Aron," c. 1900	160.00	220.00
□ American, "The Julien," c. 1900	185.00	240.00
□ American, "The Richard," standard size, c. 1900	235.00	300.00
□ American, "The Richard," concert size	265.00	350.00
□ American, "The Richard," grand concert size	275.00	375.00

Construction of "The Richard": mahogany neck, rosewood veneer on front and back, convex ebony fingerboard, inlaid with pearl position marks. Bone nut and saddle.

□ American, "The Seroco," standard size, c. 1900	300.00	400.00
□ American, "The Seroco," concert size	325.00	425.00
□ American, "The Seroco," grand concert size	375.00	500.00

□ Austrian, modern, by Johann Staufer, labeled Nach dem Modell / Langi Legnani 1955/Johann Georg Staufer / Juni (1) 830 in Wien No. 480; one-piece back of faint medium figure, similar ribs, even-grain table, soundhole surrounded by inlaid mother-of-pearl, detachable neck, s-shaped head with metal tuners, in case, length of back 16" **1100.00** **1500.00**

□ **"The Cambridge,"** rosewood back and sides, spruce top, inlaid around sound hole with colored wood and celluloid, ebony fingerboard, nickel-plated head, c. 1905–1910 **130.00** **160.00**

□ **"The Columbia,"** back and sides made of quarter-sawn oak, inlaid with vari-colored woods, spruce top, inlaid around sound hole with colored woods and celluloid, c. 1905–1910 . . . . **100.00** **130.00**

□ **"The Cornell,"** rosewood sides and back, spruce top, sound hole inlaid with vari-colored woods and celluloid, mother-of-pearl inlays on front **175.00** **220.00**

□ English, mid-19th century	1500.00	1900.00
□ English, third quarter of 19th century	1000.00	1300.00

□ French, unlabeled, one-piece back of small figure, similar ribs; back, front, and soundhole edged with bone and ebony purfling, head

Price Range

with machine-geared tuners, 12 metal frets on fingerboard, 5 on table, in leather case, overall length $35^{13}/_{16}''$	350.00	475.00
☐ French, labeled Jerome Thibouville-Lamy; rosewood back and ribs, edge of the front and soundhole inlaid with mother-of-pearl, machine-geared tuners, in case, $17^{15}/_{16}''$ ..	130.00	215.00
☐ French, unlabeled, unusual form, upper body with pointed corners, two-piece back, rosewood ribs, soundhole surrounded by inlaid chevrons and checkered design, head with machine-geared tuners, c. 1870, length of back $17^3/_{16}''$	225.00	350.00
☐ **"The Harvard"**, rosewood back and sides, back inlaid down the center with mother-of-pearl, spruce top, mahogany neck, brass head, c. 1905–1910	250.00	310.00
☐ Hawaiian Guitar, spruce top, basswood neck, celluloid-bound ebonized fingerboard, colored cut-block inlay around sound hole and top edge, white celluloid binding around top edge, six strings	150.00	200.00
☐ Italian, by Matteo Sellas of Venice, five course, arched back, lavishly decorated with ivory, overall 38″, c. 1620–1640	11,000.00	14,250.00
☐ Italian, c. 1800	2100.00	2500.00
☐ Italian, c. 1840	1600.00	2000.00
☐ Koa wood, birch top, back and sides, metal tailpiece, steel strings. (This was an inexpensively produced guitar sold on the American market for under $5 in the 1920's)	50.00	65.00
☐ Mahogany back and sides, spruce top, imitation pearl and cut block inlay with celluloid binding around sound hole and top edge, pearl inlaid fingerboard, ebonized pin bridge, steel strings	135.00	170.00
☐ Mexican, c. 1880	475.00	600.00
☐ Mexican, early 20th century	235.00	300.00

Price Range

☐ **"The Oakwood,"** imitation quarter-sawn oak, spruce top, edges inlaid with wood of varying shades, bound with white celluloid, brass head, metallic frets, nickel-plated tailpiece, c. 1905–1910 .... 50.00   65.00

☐ **"The Oxford,"** back and sides mahogany, spruce top, colored woods inlaid around sound hole, head inlaid with rosewood, metallic frets on fingerboard, c. 1905–1910 ... 125.00   160.00

☐ Portuguese, c. 1860 .... 1100.00   1500.00

☐ **"The Princeton,"** rosewood back and sides, inlaid down the middle with colored wood, spruce top, head inlaid on front and back with rosewood, raised frets, pearl position dots, c. 1905–1910 .... 170.00   225.00

☐ Rosewood, birch back and sides, vertical grained spruce top, inlays around sound hole, consisting partly of celluloid, basswood neck, ebonized bridge, c. 1920 .... 80.00   100.00

☐ Spanish, mid-17th century 7500.00   16000.00

☐ Spanish, early 18th century 4000.00   11000.00

☐ Spanish, c. 1740 .... 3350.00   8500.00

☐ Spanish, late 18th century 2300.00   5000.00

☐ Spanish, c. 1800 .... 2075.00   4500.00

☐ Spanish, mid-19th century 2000.00   3000.00

☐ Spanish, by Antonio de Torres of Seville, rosewood back composed of triple sections, rose hole, mahogany neck, back measures approximately 19", c. 1860 .... 3500.00   4500.00

☐ **"The Stanford,"** hardwood sides and back, finished in imitation rosewood, spruce top, brass head, rosewood fingerboard, nickel-plated tailpiece 85.00   110.00

☐ **"The University,"** rosewood back and sides, heavily ornamented with vine and leaf patterns, spruce top, ebony guard plate, mahogany neck, trimmed in mother-of-pearl, c. 1905–1910 .... 225.00   300.00

HARMONICAS

Though it would appear from their vastly dissimilar size and design that no connection could exist between the organ and harmonica, the latter came into being as an attempt to create a small, easily handled, cheaply produced instrument that would approximate the musical virtuosity of an organ.

Harmonicas have received, over the years, what might be termed a "bad press," to the degree that many histories of musical instruments fail even to take any note of them—as if they do not deserve classification as true instruments but rather as novelties or curiosities. This results from (a) their modern origin, (b) lack of use in performance of classical music, (c) the great proliferation of badly made, near-worthless models that have flooded the market. From as long ago as the late 1800's, cheap harmonicas—and there is no reason to presume that an *old* bad harmonica is better than a *new* bad harmonica—were being given away as prizes at amusement parks and sold as souvenirs at seaside resorts. Today there are conservatively a thousand poorly made harmonicas on the market for every one that could be said to claim some musical quality. In the face of these odds, it should not be surprising that the instrument has gained a less-than-enviable reputation. But decent harmonicas are to be found. They will never, perhaps, end up as valuable as other instruments, but they are still highly collectible.

	Price Range	
☐ **Angel's Clarion,** made by Weiss, 28 holes, brass reed plates, c. 1900	35.00	50.00
☐ **Babe's Musical Bat,** 5 holes, 10 reeds, a small wooden bat fitted with a 5-hole miniature harmonica. Sold as a souvenir at Yankee Stadium when Babe Ruth was playing baseball there, c. 1930	1500	25.00
☐ **Bell Harmonica (Richter),** 10 single holes, brass reed plates, German-silver covers, extended ends, one bell	30.00	40.00
☐ As above, with two bells	35.00	45.00
☐ **Bohm's Jubilee Harmonica,** 10 single holes, 20 brass reeds, brass reed plates, c. 1900	22.00	28.00
☐ **The Brass Band Clarion,** by Weiss, 10 single holes, 20 reeds, c. 1900	25.00	35.00
☐ **Cartridge** by Hohner, 10 single holes, 20 brass reeds and plates, nickel covers attached to attractive colored cartridge shell which is detachable, c. 1903	20.00	30.00

The Trumpet Call, by M. Hohner.

Price Range

☐ **Chimewood** by Hohner, 10 single holes, 20 reeds, brass plates to the rear of the harmonica are attached a wooden device called a resonater into which the tone passes and responds to give a violin effect. Came in three sizes—above and 10 double holes, 40 reeds, and 28 double holes, 56 reeds, c. 1907 ...   30.00   50.00

☐ **Chromatic Harmonica,** 40 reeds, brass plates, heavy nickel-plated covers, fitted with a special wind-saving device (leather), has outside shuttle spring and is Richter tuned, such as the 10-hole Marine Band, packed in wood box, c. 1912 ....   35.00   50.00

☐ Concert harmonica with two bells, 10 double holes, with 40 reeds, brass reed plates, engraved German-silver covers 30.00   50.00
Bell harmonicas are collected as interesting fossils of the music instrument world; they are seldom played any longer.

☐ **Doerfel's International,** made of celluloid, 10 double holes, 40 reeds, brass reed plates   12.00   20.00

Price Range

☐ **Doerfel's New Best-Quality Harmonika,** 48 steel-bronze reeds, brass reed plates, in original box (also known as "Nero Mouth-Organ".) 12.00   17.00

☐ **Doerfel's Patent Universal Harp,** made of celluloid, 10 single holes, 20 reeds, brass reed plates, one of the earliest celluloid harmonicas (introduced 1890's) 20.00   30.00

☐ **Duss Band Harmonica,** 14 double holes, 28 metal reeds set on brass plates, nickel covers, 4¾" long, c. 1920's 15.00   20.00

☐ **Duss Band Tremelo,** three-in-one harmonica, each tuned to a different key (the instrument was rotated, as if the player were eating an ear of corn). 32 double holes, 96 reeds, brass plates, nickel covers, 8¾" long, post-World War I 20.00   25.00

☐ **Duss Full Concert Harmonica,** 10 double holes, 40 reeds on brass plates, nickel covers, 4½" long 12.00   16.00

☐ **Echo Lux** by Hohner, 48 double holes, 96 reeds, brass plates. The cover plates were nickled and enameled in contrasting colors. This is one of many models, c. 1936 . . . . . . 20.00   40.00

☐ **Carl Essbach's French Harp # 44,** 10 single holes, 20 German-silver reeds, brass reed plates, nickel covers 14.00   20.00

☐ **Carl Essbach's Richter Harmonica,** 10 single holes, 20 reeds, brass reed plates, nickel cover, marked "French Harp #22" 12.00   16.00

☐ **European, "Brass Band Harmonica,"** 10 double holes, 40 reeds, brass reed plates 20.00   30.00

☐ **"High Art,"** 16 double holes, 32 reeds, brass plates, curved mouthpiece, nickel covers, 4" long 10.00   15.00

☐ **Hohner Auto Harmonica,** shaped like auto (late version, sold in 1920's), 14 double holes, 28 reeds, metal cover 50.00   75.00

☐ **Hohner,** concert harmonica, marked "Ulm 1871–Philadelphia 1873", actually made in c. 1890's, 20 double holes, 80 reeds, brass reed plates, nickel covers 25.00   30.00

Price Range

☐ **Hohner,** "Grand Auditorium," 16 double holes, 32 reeds, brass reed plates, nickel covers 30.00   42.00

☐ **M. Hohner Harmonica,** 10 single holes, brass reed plates, c. 1900 .... 20.00   30.00

☐ **Hohner Harmonica,** 20 double holes, 80 reeds, brass reed plates, nickel covers, c. 1900 .... 25.00   30.00

☐ **Hohner,** harp-shaped, 14 double holes, 28 tremolo reeds, brass plates, nickel-plated covers, 4⅝" long 20.00   30.00

☐ **M. Hohner's Newest and Best Full Concert Harmonica,** 10 double holes, 40 reeds, brass reed plates, nickel covers 30.00   40.00

☐ **Hohner's Organola,** 10 single holes, 8 keys. Consists of a solo mouth organ specially tuned, comprising 2½ octaves and several half-tones, which makes it nearly chromatic. This enables the performer to produce practically any music correctly, as well as to modulate from one key to another. The second part of the instrument contains 2 sets of reeds controlled by a double row of valves, which are pressed by the fingers and render chords and bass notes, both major and minor, that accurately harmonize with the solo organ. By changing from one key to another, the chords and basses can be rendered in any variety, so giving the same effects as the different stops of a church organ. For playing this accompaniment, the wind is supplied through the small nickeled tube held in the mouth; blowing and drawing have the same effect, c. 1903 .... 50.00   75.00

☐ **Loud Speaker,** 10 holes, 20 reeds, one long horn attached to back; horn is detachable; c. 1927 .... 30.00   45.00

☐ **Ludwig Harmonica,** double sided with 10 holes and 20 reeds on each side, c. 1890's 35.00   40.00

☐ **Ludwig Harmonica,** Richter Pattern, 10 single holes, 20 reeds, c. 1890's 30.00   40.00

Price Range

☐ **Ludwig Harmonica,** 20 double holes, 40 brass reeds, heavy brass reed plates and nickel covers, c. 1900 . . . .   20.00   35.00

☐ **Gebruder Ludwig's "Professional Concert (mouth) Organ,"** 10 double holes, 40 reeds, brass reed plates, German-silver covers . . .   20.00   35.00

☐ **Marine Band** with bell by Hohner, 10 single holes, 20 reeds, brass plates, heavy convex nickel covers, with one improved patent bell, red hinged case with gilt lettering, c. 1903   24.00   35.00

☐ **Pipeolion** by Weiss, 10 single holes, 20 brass reeds, in pipes, fan-shaped body fitted with 10 pipes, blow and draw reeds in each pipe, c. 1908 . . . .   50.00   75.00

☐ **"The Prairie Queen,"** 10 single holes, steel-bronze reeds, nickel-plated reed plates and covers 45.00   60.00

☐ **"The Quadruple Reed Mouth Organ,"** 160 reeds, 7¼″ long, inscribed "House Music, Best Harp for Artists from Ocean to Ocean"   15.00   20.00

☐ **"Radio Band Jazz Mouth Organ,"** novelty harmonica in shape of flashlight with horn at end, 11″ long, sold in U.S., 1929 . . . .   15.00   20.00

☐ **"Reveille Mouth Organ,"** nickel-plated covers, c. 1925 . . . .   7.00   10.00

☐ **Rolmonica,** automatic harmonica that plays a music roll just like a player piano. All you have to do is insert a roll and turn the handle while you blow; rolls are made in many songs (2.00 each); c. 1925 . . . .   35.00   60.00

☐ **Sacramento Triller,** 10 single holes, 20 reeds, nickel covers with patent slide for trilling, c. 1903 . . . .   30.00   40.00

☐ **Sousa's Band Harmonica,** 4x1″, 10 holes, 20 brass reeds, c. 1900 . . . .   25.00   35.00

☐ **Sousa's Band Harmonica,** 4¾″x1¼″, 20 holes, 40 brass reeds, c. 1900 . . . .   35.00   50.00

☐ Wilhelm Thie, four harmonicas in box, all identical with 10 single holes, brass reed plates, nickel covers, but in different keys. This set

Price Range

was made in the c. 1890's in Germany for export and sale in America, price given is for a set in the original box 55.00   75.00

☐ **Trumpet Call** by Hohner, 10 double holes, 40 reeds, brass plates, similar to the Chimewood but fitted with 5 trumpet horns that point upward in a fan shape. Most impressive looking and probably one of the most sought after harmonicas ever made, c. 1907 .... 50.00   75.00

☐ **Tuckaway** by Hohner, 10 single holes, 20 reeds, brass plates, cover plates form a complete housing to cover harmonica holes while not in use. A slight pressure on the corners automatically brings the harmonica into playing position, c. 1933 .... 35.00   45.00

☐ **Up To Date Siamese Twins,** 2–14 double holes, 28 reeds, brass plates, nickel cases. Two Up To Date Harmonicas joined together at the ends, forming a V shape, c. 1907 ... 24.00   30.00

☐ **"World's Fame,"** 10 single holes, 20 reeds, brass plates, nickel covers, 4" long 7.00   10.00

☐ **Zobo Harmonophone** by Clover, 10 single holes, 20 reeds, brass reed plates, nickel-plated cover of one solid piece. This instrument is a combination of a Clover harmonica, Metal Phone, and Zobo. The player produces tremolo effects by placing the right hand over the phone and the Zobo effects by humming or singing through the Zobo mouthpiece, which is at small end of cone; c. 1903 .... 30.00   50.00

HARPS

Harps have been in use since as early as 3000 B.C. They were played in Egypt at the time of the Pharaohs, in Mesopotamia, Babylonia, and throughout most of the ancient world. Harp playing was popular even in India, in Alexander the Great's time. Each nation designed its harps somewhat differently, as we know from representation in art (sadly, few ancient specimens survive), and styles changed periodically within given localities. Basically, though, the ancient-world harp was a much smaller instrument than its modern descendant, some small enough to be easily carried about and played in the road by itinerant musicians. China had harps at least as early as the 4th century A.D.; how much earlier it is impossible on strength of present evidence to speculate. The harp was one of the few popular classical instruments that remained in use throughout the European Middle Ages; though, of course, it, like others, became more or less limited to the realm of church music. It is believed that harps were played in England from the eleventh century and possibly even earlier. Their use in Ireland is probably of earlier beginnings. Irish harps were generally regarded as superior to English. They were mostly made of willow and would often be richly ornamented.

During the European Renaissance, with the revival of secular interest in music, harps regained the prominence they had enjoyed in Greek and Roman times. A number of fine specimens from this era and shortly afterward survive today, the majority in museums or churches. Only a small percentage of European harps made before 1650 have reached the American trade. They are held in high regard and seldom have any difficulty realizing prices of five digits.

	Price Range	
☐ English, maple base, 4'7", c. 1650	1200.00	1500.00
☐ English, three strings lacking, wood split, Restoration	1100.00	1400.00
☐ English, 6'5", mid-18th century	1900.00	2750.00
☐ English, polished walnut, late 18th century	1150.00	1500.00
☐ French, by Cousineau of Paris, painted and gilded with a pattern of floralwork and insects, 64", c. French revolutionary era	2300.00	2750.00
☐ Italian, Renaissance, polychromed wood with cherubic figures, carved acanthus leaf designs at base, portions of original gilding with red paint showing through, partially restored, restrung, 6'7" tall, c. 1580	5500.00	7000.00
☐ Italian, walnut, carved base, traces of old gilding, partially restored base, restrung, c. 1620	3175.00	3750.00
☐ Italian, carved rosewood, 5'2½" tall, possibly Naples, third quarter of 17th century	3175.00	3750.00
☐ Italian, gilded and polychromed wood, base replaced in 19th century, restrung, 6' tall, c. 1680	2600.00	3000.00
☐ Italian, Milan, late 17th century	1500.00	2000.00
☐ Italian, Turin, 7'8", c. 1700	2150.00	2700.00
☐ Italian, mahogany, 2'11", early 18th century	1650.00	1875.00

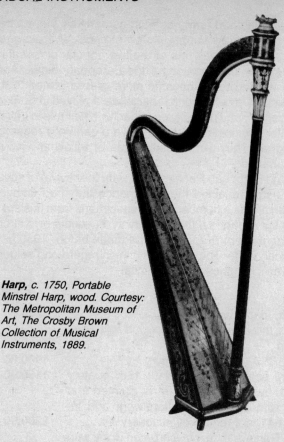

Harp, c. 1750, Portable Minstrel Harp, wood. Courtesy: The Metropolitan Museum of Art, The Crosby Brown Collection of Musical Instruments, 1889.

HURDY-GURDIES

Price Range

☐ French, maker unidentified, guitar shape, maple, stamped pegbox, black painted wheel cover, iron handle, 25″, c. 1790–1810 . . . . . **2200.00** **2750.00**

JEWS' HARPS

The Jews' harp, also known as jaws-harp or juice-harp, is strictly an instrument for close-range audiences. It produces a sound that can be heard distinctly no further than a few feet from the performer. Thus, it is unsuitable for orchestral or concert use, if indeed anyone would conceive of using a Jews' harp for such purposes. But it also has many advantages. It is easily handled, mastered without painstaking effort, and adaptable to music of every kind—as well as to improvisational creations.

It is a very small instrument held to the mouth while playing, but is not a wind instrument in the sense of a harmonica or flute. Rather it is played by plucking and vibrates between the player's teeth. Among the most primitive of instruments, its close relatives or ancestors can be found in use by primitive peoples in various parts of the world. The belief that it originated in ancient Israel and thereby obtained its name is probably incorrect; in fact, it is likely that the name was at first jaws-harp, which eventually came to be corrupted into the present form thanks to cheap versions being sold by street peddlers, most of whom were Jewish.

The Jew's harp is an excellent instrument to collect because of the many types that can be found and their relative cheapness compared to many other instruments.

	Price Range	
☐ American, 2″ frame, c. 1900	9.00	12.00
☐ American, 2¼″ frame, c. 1900	12.00	17.00
☐ American, 2½″ frame, c. 1900	12.00	17.00
☐ American, 2¾″ frame, c. 1900	73.00	18.00
☐ American, 3¼″ frame, c. 1900	15.00	20.00
☐ American, 3½″ frame, c. 1900	17.00	23.00
☐ American, 3¾″ frame, c. 1900	20.00	25.00
☐ American, 4¼″ frame, c. 1900	30.00	40.00

"KAZOO BAND" INSTRUMENTS

"Kazoo Band" instruments are a class of small-size versions of (in most cases) standard band instruments, designed for use in a "kazoo" or mini-orchestra. They were sold extensively in the 1920's and '30's and aimed partly to juveniles and partly to persons who had musical ambitions but could not afford or perform on instruments of full size. They have some appeal today as collectors' items; as musical instruments, though, most were not of high quality.

	Price Range	
☐ Baby Jazz Kazoo Clarinet, 6½″, brass finish	5.50	7.50
☐ Baby Jazz Kazoo Saxophone, 6½″, brass finish	5.50	7.50
☐ Bugle, 20″ long, brass finish, combination bugle, kazoo, and blow-horn (sold in large numbers to Boy Scout troops)	7.00	10.00

	Price Range	
☐ Clarinet, 18″, brass finish, 8 plungers	11.00	15.00
☐ Cornet, 15″, 3 plungers	9.00	12.00
☐ Cornet, 11″, 3 plungers	5.50	8.50
☐ Cornet, 12″, flaring bell end (a real "piece of tin" that gave a sound no better than a party noisemaker)	7.50	6.00
☐ Saxophone, 20″, brass finish, 8 plungers ...	11.00	15.00
☐ Saxophone, 9″	7.00	10.00
☐ Trombone, 27″ closed, about 38″ extended	10.00	15.00
☐ Trombone, 11″ closed, 15″ extended	5.00	7.00
☐ Trumpet, also called "musical submarine," c. 1920's	3.50	5.00

LUTES

If the lute was not the first stringed instrument of the Western world, it was certainly one of the first and became the inspiration for many related instruments that followed. It was known in primitive forms, perhaps as early as 2500 B.C. Its use in the ancient world extended into Persia, Mesopotamia, India, China, and elsewhere. Surprisingly, it never became popular in the two chief centers of European culture, Greece and Rome, for reasons that have yet to be explained. There is no doubt that the Greeks and Romans knew of lutes, however. In India the lute developed into the modern sitar.

Widespread use of the lute in Europe dates from the 13th century A.D., when Crusaders introduced it (reintroduced might be a better word) from the East. It soon became one of the favorite instruments of the time and is represented in numerous drawings, sculpture, and other art of the late Middle Ages. Very few lutes of this era still exist but they do occasionally turn up.

Lutes were manufactured in a range of sizes and many kinds of wood, according to local taste or the availability of materials. During the 16th century, a time of immense popularity for this instrument, the favorite woods were cypress, sandalwood, and sycamore, with the "belly" made of common pine. There is every reason to believe that good lutes cost a rather substantial sum of money then, more so, proportionately, than the present-day cost. Decoration at this period was minimal in most specimens. Lutes were in favor until well into the 18th century. They were especially well suited as accompaniment instruments for madrigal singers.

	Price Range	
☐ Balkan, early 19th century	1000.00	1300.00
☐ English, Tudor	11,000.00	15,000.00
☐ English, late 17th century	6500.00	8200.00
☐ English, Restoration	4000.00	7000.00
☐ English, Georgian	1800.00	4000.00
☐ Flemish, c. 1470	20,000.00	25,000.00
☐ Flemish, mid-16th century	16,000.00	21,000.00
☐ French, c. 1350	27,500.00	37,500.00
☐ French, c. 1480	21,000.00	25,000.00
☐ French, early 16th century	16,000.00	21,000.00
☐ French, c. 1570	15,000.00	20,000.00
☐ French, mid-17th century	13,000.00	17,000.00
☐ French, Louis XIV	12,500.00	16,500.00
☐ French, Louis XV	8000.00	11,000.00
☐ French, Louis XVI	5200.00	7200.00
☐ Genoese, early 18th century	5000.00	7000.00
☐ Hungarian, c. 1800	1100.00	1400.00
☐ Italian, 15th century	30,000.00	35,000.00
☐ Italian, mid-16th century	15,000.00	20,000.00
☐ Italian, mid-1700's	2600.00	3500.00
☐ Italian, c. 1800	1500.00	2000.00
☐ Spanish, first quarter 17th century	10,000.00	14,000.00
☐ Spanish, late 17th century	6000.00	9000.00
☐ Swiss, c. 1750	3150.00	3750.00

MANDOLINS

☐ **"Ballinger,"** nine ribs of alternating mahogany and maple with strips of black wood between, rosewood cap, imitation tortoiseshell guard plate, c. 1905–1910	45.00	60.00
☐ **"Challenge,"** 15 ribs of mahogany with strips of black wood between, rosewood cap, sound hole inlaid with ring of colored wood, imitation tortoiseshell guard plate	65.00	80.00
☐ **"Competition,"** nine ribs of alternating mahogany and maple with strips of black wood between, rosewood cap and top of silver spruce, mahogany neck, rosewood fingerboard	45.00	60.00

Lute, European, 2' 11" x 11"
Courtesy: The Metropolitan
Museum of Art, The Crosby Brown
Collection of Musical
Instruments, 1889.

Price Range

☐ **"Concertone,"** flat back (similar to guitar), birch back and sides, spruce top, basswood neck, ebonized fingerboard, black-and-white inlay around sound hole, tortoise celluloid guard plate, c. 1920 . . . .   65.00   80.00

☐ **The Edgemere,** 13 ribs of mahogany with black inlay between the, rosewood cap, edges bound with celluloid and wood inlaying, imitation tortoiseshell guardpiece, nickel-plated tailpiece 275.00   325.00

☐ English, medieval 31,000.00 42,000.00

☐ English, c. 1650 . . . .   14,000.00 19,000.00

☐ English, early 18th century 6100.00   9000.00

☐ English, mid-1700's 3200.00   4800.00

Mandolin, Italian, c. 1781,
1' 11" x 7½". *Courtesy:
The Metropolitan Museum of Art,
The Crosby Brown Collection of
Musical Instruments, 1889.*

	Price Range	
☐ English, c. 1800	1400.00	1800.00
☐ Flemish, c. 1500	40,000.00	50,000.00
☐ French, 14th century	45,000.00	70,000.00
☐ French, first quarter of 16th century	32,000.00	52,000.00
☐ French, c. 1550	27,000.00	42,000.00
☐ French, late 16th century	22,000.00	40,000.00
☐ French, early 17th century	15,000.00	26,000.00
☐ French, Louis XIV	7500.00	14,000.00
☐ French, Louis XV	3200.00	8500.00
☐ French, Louis XVI	3000.00	6000.00
☐ French, early 19th century	2000.00	3200.00
☐ **The Glencoe,** 13 ribs of rosewood and ma-hogany, redwood strips inlaid between, rose-wood cap and sides, spruce top, celluloid imi-tation tortoiseshell guardplate, c. 1900	300.00	375.00

Price Range

☐ **The Illinois,** nine mahogany ribs, alternating with maple, rosewood fingerboard with inlaid position dots, fretted with raised frets, imitation mahogany neck, c. 1900 . . . . 200.00   250.00

☐ Italian, Renaissnce 35,000.00   50,000.00

☐ Italian, first quarter of 17th century 27,500.00   42,000.00

☐ Italian, mid-1600's 20,000.00   35,000.00

☐ Italian, c. 1700 . . . . 10,000.00   20,000.00

☐ Italian, first quarter of 18th century 8000.00   17,000.00

☐ Italian, third quarter of 18th century 3300.00   8500.00

☐ **"New Departure",** 13 ribs of rosewood with white holly between, rosewood cap, inlaid with vari-colored woods, c. 1905–1910 . . . . 80.00   125.00

☐ Nine figured hardwood ribs, hardwood top, basswood neck, ebonized fingerboard, black celluloid binding around top edge, c. 1920's 85.00   125.00

☐ Rosewood, 16 ribs, inlaid white lines between, mahogany-finished neck, tortoise celluloid side guard plate, colored block inlay around top and edge 150.00   200.00

☐ **The Royal,** 11 ribs of rosewood with white holly inlaid between strips, inlaid guard plate, c. early 1900's 400.00   500.00

☐ **The Senora,** 15 ribs of rosewood with white holly between strips, rosewood cap and sides, celluloid binding, American made, c. 1900 . . . . 475.00   575.00

☐ **"20th-Century,"** 21 ribs of rosewood, spruce top inlaid with pearl, mahogany neck, rosewood-veneer head, c. 1900 . . . . 425.00   500.00

MIDWAY MUSETTE

The Columbian Exposition of 1892–93 featured Oriental music played at the Midway. New at the time to most Americans visiting the fair, it caused a temporary fad for instruments that could produce Oriental-sounding tones. The Midway Musette was heralded by its manufacturers and retailers as the perfect instrument for this purpose. It looked something like the long, narrow tin horns used as noisemakers at parties. The assertion that "anyone can play it" was true insofar as everyone, whether musically skilled or not, got about the same results—disappointing. As an example of musical instrument fadism, it rates high.

	Price Range	
☐ Nickel-plated, with reed, manufactured shortly after the Columbian Exposition	**55.00**	**75.00**

MUSICAL SLEIGH BELLS

The playing of bells as musical instruments originated in ancient times. It is beyond the scope of this book to enter into bells and their musical properties, but we have included musical sleigh bells on grounds that they were retailed strictly as musical instruments with no other purpose. They consisted of a set of bells attached to straps, the straps being strung on a vertical frame. Though never really popular, musical sleigh bells reached the point of being featured in a number of dealer catalogues of the late 19th and early 20th centuries. They have more interest as a curiosity than an instrument.

Colonial Sleigh Bell, American, 2" Dia. Courtesy: The Metropolitan Museum of Art, The Crosby Brown Collection of Musical Instruments, 1889.

Price Range

☐ Mounted on frame made of oak, measuring 30"x24", eight straps with six bells attached, keys represented are B-flat, C, D, E-flat, F, G, A and B-flat in that order, American made, c. 1890's 95.00   120.00

NOSE FLUTES

The lowly nose flute probably rates as the least glamorous of musical instruments. Whether it can properly be termed an instrument is open to debate; but a great many were manufactured and sold in the U.S., especially during the period 1920–1940. A contemporary advertisement stated "the tone is very musical and flute-like. It is capable of the most charming modulations, and the most popular melody or the most elaborate operatic air can be played ..." It was a small metal object shaped roughly like a figure eight, with a wind-hole and air passage similar to a whistle. It was played by holding it to the nose and exhaling.

☐ "The Magic Nose Flute," 1920's 3.00   5.00

OBOES

☐ English, early 18th century 8000.00   10000.00
☐ English, third quarter of 18th century 5000.00   7000.00
☐ English, first quarter of 19th century 4375.00   6000.00
☐ English, early Victorian 1100.00   1500.00
☐ English, late Victorian 700.00   900.00
☐ German, 17th century 22000.00   30000.00
☐ German, first quarter of 18th century 5000.00   7000.00
☐ German, mid-18th century 4250.00   6000.00

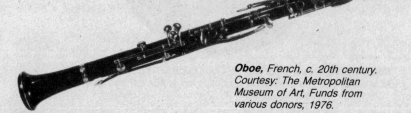

Oboe, French, c. 20th century. Courtesy: The Metropolitan Museum of Art, Funds from various donors, 1976.

	Price Range	
☐ German, c. 1770	3175.00	4000.00
☐ Italian, mid-18th century	1600.00	2000.00
☐ Italian, c. 1790	1600.00	2000.00
☐ Italian, c. 1840	550.00	700.00
☐ Italian, third quarter of 19th century	500.00	650.00
☐ Three-keyed, by Thomas Stanesby, Sr., London, 23^{3}/$_{16}$″ long, c. 1700	17,500.00	22,500.00

OCARINAS

These small instruments, never highly regarded by professional musicians, were sold in great quantities to the American public in the period from about 1880 to 1930. They were advertised in nearly every mail-order catalogue, including the famous Johnson Smith, as well as in comic books. Most sold originally for under $1 or could be obtained free by sending in coupons or cereal box lids. The majority of purchasers were children, or parents who hoped that by introducing their child to the ocarina, he might develop a taste for music. In the early days of vaudeville they became a standard in music shows, especially minstrel shows, along with various other nonconcert instruments. They were used even by country and western artists occasionally.

☐ European, A, alto, c. 1900	28.00	35.00
☐ European, A, bass, c. 1900	55.00	80.00
☐ European, A-flat, alto, c. 1900	30.00	40.00
☐ European, A-flat, bass, c. 1900	75.00	95.00
☐ European, A, soprano, c. 1900	15.00	20.00
☐ European, B-flat, alto, c. 1900	25.00	35.00
☐ European, B-flat, bass, c. 1900	60.00	80.00
☐ European, B-flat, soprano, c. 1900	15.00	20.00
☐ European, C, alto, c. 1900	25.00	35.00
☐ European, C, bass, c. 1900	50.00	70.00
☐ European, C, soprano, c. 1900	15.00	20.00
☐ European, D, bass, c. 1900	42.00	55.00
☐ European, E, alto, c. 1900	42.00	55.00
☐ European, E, soprano, c. 1900	22.00	33.00
☐ European, E-flat, alto, c. 1900	42.00	55.00
☐ European, E-flat, soprano, c. 1900	22.00	32.00
☐ European, F, alto, c. 1900	40.00	55.00
☐ European, F, soprano, c. 1900	20.00	25.00
☐ European, G, alto, c. 1900	40.00	55.00
☐ European, G, bass, c. 1900	90.00	175.00

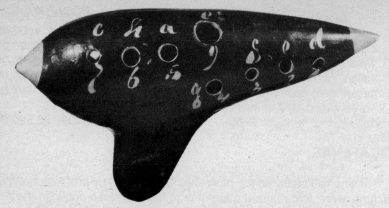

Ocarnia, Austrian, c. 19th or 20th century, clay. Courtesy: The Metropolitan Museum of Art, The Crosby Brown Collection of Musical Instruments, 1889.

PIANOS

Private collections of pianos are few, not so much because of their price (antique violins, which fall more or less within a comparable price range, are collected) but the space necessary for storage. Nevertheless, there are many devotees of antique pianos, who, even though they may wish to own just one single specimen, will pay dearly for the piano that appeals most to them. In fact it is collectors—or, maybe more accurate to say, those who take an interest in pianos from a historical and artistic point of view—who account for the majority of sales, as few musicians seek out antique pianos. This is quite a different situation than with violins.

The musical merits of antique pianos is a subject too complex to enter into in this book. The claim of some experts is that old pianos, especially those of noted manufacturers, produce a finer tone than any currently offered. Others feel quite the opposite, that antique pianos are splendid museum pieces but not so desirable from a musician's point of view. Probably the real answer lies in the sort of music being played. French harpsichords and pianos of the later 17th and 18th centuries, with their sweet sugary tones, are not likely to be matched by modern instruments for playing French compositions of that era. Ditto for Wagnerian scores played on old German pianos. Today's pianos are, if not so perfectly suited to any one type of music, at least more versatile.

Of course, it must be understood that any piano of 200 years age has been restrung, retuned, and otherwise serviced innumerable times, so that its performance may no longer be an exact duplication of the original, even though it appears "like new" visually. The tonal character of a piano is subject to all manner of influences, from heat, cold, being moved about, carelessly played, improperly cleaned, etc. If maintained at regular intervals from time of manufacture to the present, its sound may approximate the original; but any piano neglected for 20, 50, or more years, then serviced, is apt to end up sounding very different than it did originally. Thus, by playing an antique piano you do not necessarily hear 200-year-old scores as the composer intended them to be heard. The odds that they will sound as the composer intended, even with a $100,000 instrument, are not high.

The survival rate of antique pianos is not especially high. It would be expected, by someone unaware of all circumstances involved, that old pianos should exist today in numbers close to the original output. Representing sizable investments, they were well cared for by the original purchasers. However, being difficult to move about, pianos were frequently abandoned when fires broke out, and left behind when European towns had to be evacuated during time of war. Rather than being taken as war spoils, as were valuable small articles, they were generally destroyed by the enemy. The number of pianos that perished during the Napoleonic Wars (to name one of many) must have been enormous. Thus, the present-day existing totals of pianos once manufactured are roughly as follows:

16th century, 5–8%, of which 70% or more are in museums
17th century, 10–15%, of which 50–70% are in museums
18th century, 25–40%, of which less than 50% are in museums
19th century, 40–60%, of which less than 20% are in museums

Of very early pianos that do exist, many are no longer in a condition approximating the original, either structurally or musically.

Piano making (and we are talking of all piano-like instruments collectively, as the first true piano was not brought out until 1709) did not become an industry in the accepted sense of the term until the last quarter of the 18th century. Prior to that time, piano-making studios were small, on the same order as violin shops, and, because of the greater length of time needed to produce each specimen, turned out fewer instruments than violin makers. Production was stepped up around 1780, to satisfy a more affluent ready market, but still the output lingered well behind that of most smaller instruments. "A piano in every home" became a popular advertising slogan of three generations ago, but not only was this far from realized then, it certainly did not reflect the situation of 1700 or 1800. European noble families were the chief owners of piano-like instruments up to about 1720. Private ownership was uncommon in the 17th century. In America there were very few pianos in the colonial era, though the proportion owned by private individuals, per capita, was probably as great as in Europe. During the first and second quarters of the 19th century many French and English pianos were imported into this country. The second half of the 19th century witnessed extensive piano manufacture in the United States.

Buying Antique Pianos. While the reputation of manufacturers may mean less with pianos than violins, the careful buyer will generally seek out a respected name and purchase the best piano by that manufacturer he can afford. Unfortunately, much antique piano buying is done for the wrong reasons, by persons who, though wealthy enough to afford fine material, are not equipped with the knowledge or connoisseurship to buy intelligently.

Antique pianos may be acquired through instrument dealers, auctions, or from private parties. Unless you have the knowledge to make accurate on-the-spot appraisals, buying from private sources is the least favorable. Many estate sales include pianos. They are well worth watching, as good-quality antique pianos can often be bought at these sales at prices under the market value.

When buying from foreign dealers or auctioneers, keep in mind that the cost of transporting a piano overseas is very high and that there is risk of it arriving damaged. The auctioneers will not perform the actual crating; this is done by private contractors, who charge for their service in addition to transportation.

Values of Antique Pianos. The value of any antique piano, whether made by a celebrated manufacturer or a second-rater, depends very much on design and casework. Almost every manufacturer offered various grades of pianos, from rather plain and inexpensive to "art grands" that were lavishly sculptured, painted, or otherwise decorated. The artwork on art grands of the 17th and 18th centuries is often remarkable and would be worth fair sums in itself beyond the value of the instrument.

Listed below are representative examples of pianos of various ages and grades, ranging from highly desirable to quite ordinary. This is but a mere sampling of the available specimens that pass through the market; many others are to be found, in all ranges of price.

	Price Range	
☐ **Baldwin Art Grand,** Cincinnati, painted scenes on sides, otherwise modest design, c. 1900	11,000.00	16,500.00
The Baldwin factory, not as renowned as Steinway, produced some exceptional work.		
☐ **Baldwin Baby Grand,** 5′3″, c. early 1900's	500.00	700.00
☐ **Baldwin Concert Grand,** Cincinnati, 9′	9100.00	14,000.00
☐ **Baldwin Upright,** rebuilt, c. early 1900's ...	550.00	750.00

Price Range

☐ **Beckwith Acme Cabinet Grand,** upright
model 775.00   1175.00

☐ **Beckwith Artists' Cabinet Grand** 700.00   1100.00

☐ **Beckwith Cabinet Grand,** upright model, c.
early 1900's 1100.00   1600.00

☐ **Beckwith Home Favorite,** upright model .. 550.00   700.00

☐ **Beckwith Palace Grand,** upright model ... 700.00   1000.00

☐ **Blasser, Thomas, Harpsichord,** London,
two manual, inscribed on name board
"Thomas Blasser fecit Londini 1744," 8'1½",
1744 .... 22,000.00   28,750.00

☐ **Bluthner, Julius, Art Grand,** Leipzig, Egyp-
tian motifs, late 19th-century 25,000.00   30,000.00
The styling of piano cases to suit contempo-
rary fads of interior decor was common
throughout almost the whole history of piano
making. As styles changed so rapidly during
the Victorian era, many variations of piano
cases are to be found from that period. The
Egyptian style is not one of the more heralded today.

☐ **Bosendorfer, Ludwig, Art Grand,** Vienna,
second quarter of the 19th century 33,000.00   40,000.00

☐ **Broadwood, John, and Sons, Art Grand,**
featuring various colored inlays, late 18th
century 70,000.00   90,000.00

☐ **Broadwood Grand,** 7½' 2750.00   3775.00

☐ **Broadwood Grand, Pianoforte,** marquetry
by A. Morris & Company, 7'6", late 19th cen-
tury 15,000.00   20,000.00

☐ **"Chang,"** made in Korea, 6'2" 6000.00   7500.00

☐ **Chickering Ampico-A Grand,** 5'4" 5750.00   7500.00

☐ **Emerson Oak Grand,** new strings and ham-
mers 5000.00   6250.00

☐ **Erard, Sebastian, Art Grand,** London, exqui-
sitely decorated with carved and gilded cherubs in the Louis XVI fashion (Erard was a
Frenchman), c. 1800 .... 35,000.00   45,500.00

☐ **Fisher Grand,** 5'1", ebony 4000.00   4500.00

Honduras Mahogany Piano, Mason & Hamlin.

	Price Range	
☐ **Fritz, Johann, square,** Vienna, 65½″	2750.00	3500.00
☐ **Ganer, Christopher, square,** London, 59½″, c. 1781	2000.00	2750.00
☐ **Hallet and Davis Baby Grand,** 5′2″	4200.00	5200.00
☐ **Kimball Grand,** 5′3″, mahogany	3950.00	4575.00
☐ **Kimball Grand,** 5′8″, walnut	4800.00	5600.00
☐ **Kirkman, Jacob, Harpsichord,** London, two manual, c. 1760	2500.00	3200.00
☐ **Kirkman, Jacob, Harpsichord,** London, two manual, inscribed "Jacobus Kirckman Londini fecit 1767," mahogany case, 7′9″, c. 1767	40,000.00	50,000.00

The difference in value between these two specimens from the same studio is attributable mostly to case decoration. Kirkman's name is often spelled Kirckman.

Price Range

☐ **Kirkman, Jacob and Abraham, Harpsichord,** London, single manual, inscribed "Jacobus and Abraham Kirckman Londini fecerunt 1774," 7'3", c. 1774 .... **20,000.00 23,750.00**

☐ **Kirkman, Jacob and Abraham, square,** London, 4'8¾", c. 1775 .... **4500.00 6000.00**
The Kirkmans were the most prolific English piano and related-instrument makers of their time. Their pianos are still rather common on the market, even at a distance of 200 years. Their musical quality is considered less than brilliant.

☐ **Player, John, Spinet,** London, inscribed "Johannes Player, Londini, fecit," walnut body on oak trestle stand, 5'1½", undated, third quarter of the 17th century **22,000.00 27,500.00**
This fine spinet dates from the time of Samuel Pepys and the Restoration. At about this time, "popular" music—that is, ballads and poems that could be set to simple music—was gaining great favor in Britain. There were music masters who could be hired to teach spinet playing, singing, etc. The spinet was often called a virginal. Pepys owned one of these instruments; his would be worth at least five times the value shown, for association interest.

☐ **Pleyell-Lyon Gothic Upright,** Paris, c. 1900 **11,500.00 14,000.00**
A well-designed case with motifs borrowed from gothic choir stalls of the 15th century. In workmanship it was perhaps the finest piano that could be bought at the time; but gothic design soon fell out of favor in pianos, tallcase clocks, and just about everything else.

☐ **Pleyell-Lyon Renaissance Art Grand,** Paris, an admixture of styles (really more Louis XIV) that would not readily be recognized as Renaissance by most persons, c. 1900 .... **20,000.00 25,000.00**

Price Range

The Pleyell-Lyon factory was the French equivalent of Steinway. It turned out some very handsome pianos that won high favor among French musicians. Its instruments gained only limited popularity elsewhere in Europe.

☐ **Rucker, Hans, Double Spinet,** Antwerp, Flanders, a specimen designed to suit the decor of a lavish 16th-century interior, well carved and featuring a large mural painting on the underside of lid, c. 1560 .... 165,000.00 225,000.00

The double spinet was a variety of harpsichord in use before introduction of the piano. It remained popular thereafter but gradually lost favor during the latter part of the 18th century.

☐ **Schiller Cabinet Grand,** upright model, c. 1890's 1500.00 2000.00

☐ **Schiller,** seven and one-third octaves, double veneered case, double roll fall-board, ivory keys, ebony sharps, double repeating action, sostenuto pedal, upright model 1650.00 2000.00

☐ **Schiller,** seven and one-third octaves, iron frames and continuous hinge on fall-board, ivory keys, ebony sharps, double repeating action, nickel-plated rail, upright model 1275.00 1800.00

☐ **Schmahl Portable Pianoforte,** Ulm, Germany, case painted with vines and rose, 46¾", probably third quarter of the 18th century 11,500.00 16,000.00

☐ **Sears Roebuck American Home Parlor Grand,** upright piano measuring 4'7" tall, 61" wide, 2'3" deep, mahogany finish 1500.00 2000.00

☐ **Sears Roebuck Home Favorite piano-organ,** upright, 4'10½" long, 4'7½" high, 2'1½" deep, seven and one-third octaves of keys and four sets of reeds, 176 reeds in all, walnut, c. 1900 .... 750.00 975.00

☐ **Sears Roebuck Home Favorite,** as above, mahogany 725.00 950.00

Price Range

☐ **Sears Roebuck Home Favorite,** an improved version of the above with 214 reeds, walnut case 750.00   1100.00

☐ As above, 214 reeds, mahogany case 950.00   1400.00

☐ **Sears Roebuck New American Home,** upright grand piano, 4′7″ high, 61″ long, maple with walnut finish, c. 1900 .... 1000.00   1300.00

☐ **Steinway and Sons Art Grand,** New York, a massive and richly ornamented instrument, manufactured at an original cost of $40,000 as a "special order," late 19th century 65,000.00   87,500.00
The American Art Grand of this era sometimes became very grand indeed, as American millionaires wished to own pianos that equaled the finest obtainable in Europe. Tonally they were superior to the average run of instruments, but their huge prices went mostly for casework. Collectors view them with mixed feelings.

Steinway Grand Piano, rosewood, 1973.

Price Range

☐ **Steinway Grand,** Model "L," 5′10½″, ebony
body, c. 1935 ....   7000.00   9000.00

☐ **Trasunti, Alessandro, Art Harpsichord,**
Italy, an elaborate early specimen, probably
commission work for the apartment of a no-
bleman, decorated with a series of inset
paintings, c. 1531 ....165,000.00 190,000.00
Harpsichords of this age, well over 400 years
old, are very uncommon. Not made for general sale, they were almost exclusively com-
missioned work. Those who had the commis-
sions were as concerned with the
instrument's decor as with its musical qualities, perhaps more so. They generally reach
the market only through the sale of old European estates.

☐ **Waverly,** burled walnut, seven and one-third
octaves, double roll fall-board, ivory or celluloid keys (found with either; does not affect
value), carved trusses, upright model, made
in Oregon, Illinois, c. 1890–1900 ....   900.00   1200.00

☐ **Weber Louis XIV Art Grand,** New York,
sculptured, gilded case, late 19th century ..   8000.00   9500.00

PICCOLOS

The piccolo is a close relative to, and offshoot of, the flute. It is
in reality a small flute and plays at one octave higher than do most
flutes. It is not an instrument to which great attention has been given
by composers, but it has, gradually become accepted in the world of
classical music. It is also used by jazz musicians. Because of its ease
of handling, compared to a standard flute, and its lower price, piccolos
became quite popular as an instrument by which children could be introduced to music. Many students primed for an eventual career as flutists
started on the piccolo.

☐ **"Atlas Piccolo,"** cast metal, c. 1900 ......   40.00   55.00
☐ Cocoa wood, one key, c. 1900 ....   65.00   85.00
☐ Cocoa wood, one key and tuning slide, c.
1900 ....   85.00   110.00
☐ Grenadilla wood, four keys and tuning slide,
c. 1900 ....   120.00   150.00

Harpsichord, *Italian, c. 17th century. Courtesy: The Metropolitan Museum of Art, The Crosby Brown Collection of Musical Instruments, 1889.*

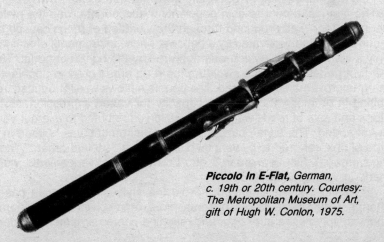

Piccolo In E-Flat, *German, c. 19th or 20th century. Courtesy: The Metropolitan Museum of Art, gift of Hugh W. Conlon, 1975.*

	Price Range	
☐ Grenadilla wood, six keys, c. 1900	160.00	200.00
☐ Italian, c. 1730	675.00	850.00
☐ Italian, hardwood with silver trimming, enclosed in a finely decorated walnut box lined with plush, c. 1742	800.00	1100.00
☐ Italian, c. 1761	475.00	625.00
☐ Italian, c. 1800	365.00	450.00
☐ Italian, early 19th century	325.00	400.00
☐ Meyer, grenadilla wood; ivory head, six keys, c. 1900	250.00	300.00
☐ **Piccolo-Flageolet** (combination), boxwood, c. 1900	110.00	135.00
☐ **Piccolo-Flageolet,** grenadilla wood, c. 1900	125.00	150.00

REED ORGANS

During the last half of the 19th century, the reed organ was a popular instrument and could be found in lodge halls, churches, chapels, schools, and the home. One of the more successful instruments was invented by Alexander Debaine of Paris about 1840. Unfortunately, when he secured letters-patent for his invention, he patented too much and included in his claim the name Harmonium. This prevented other makers of similar instruments from using the name, and as a result the name of the most dignified of all instruments, *organ,* was applied to a class of instruments that were in reality not organs at all. Hence, men who appropriated the name *organ* for their new production not only sinned against etymology but really were not true to their own cause.

The first instrument to gain popularity in this country was the melodeon. Its tone was produced through the vibration of reeds caused by a current of wind generated by a bellows. These instruments contained only a single bellows, which was operated by the right foot pedal. The left foot pedal operated a swell. As the reed organ grew in popularity, many improvements appeared. The double bellows was introduced, resulting in greater volume and a capacity for varied expression. More stops and sets of reeds were added, which contributed to a larger variety of sound. The style changed and the instrument was housed in a type of box, referred to by various builders as a "cabinet organ," "cottage organ," "flat top organ," etc. From here, advancements were made in various directions.

As furniture styles changed, so did the style of reed organ cases change. The simple cases became more ornate, with mirrors, lamp shelves, spindles, embossing, and machine-carved ornaments added.

These instruments functioned as much as a piece of furniture for the Victorian parlor as a musical instrument. For the more serious musician or a small church, the chapel organ was designed. These instruments had less attention given to case style and more emphasis placed on being musical instruments. The chapel organ contained several sets of reeds that gave a variety of tones and had a well-built mechanical action. For the church organist in need of a practice instrument or for a moderate-size church, two-manual (keyboards) with pedal-board (keyboard played with the feet) organs were built. These had a wide variety of sound, and much of the standard organ literature could be performed on organs of this type.

The lowly reed organ soared to swift popularity during the 19th century but began to dwindle in esteem by the first decade of the present century. Within living memory of some of us, the reed organ was relegated to the attic, made into other pieces of furniture, such as a liquor cabinet or a desk, or worse still, banished to the local dump. More recently, interest in the reed organ has once more begun to increase. A good supply of literature concerning the reed organ—how to rebuild it and where to purchase replacement parts—is available. Persons knowledgeable about repair and restoration of the reed organ can be found in several locations. Occasionally, it is possible to purchase a recording on which a reed organ can be heard. An international Reed Organ Society has been formed with headquarters at The Musical Museum in Deansboro, New York 13328. The popular National Public Radio show *A Prairie Home Companion* has featured the reed organ on several of its programs. Compared to other antiques from the Victorian era, the price for a reed organ is still a bargain. With increasing popularity, these instruments will disappear from the marketplace, be more difficult to find, and cost more. Consider the low price of many antiques and collectibles twenty years ago—this process will always continue to evolve.

Note: The value of a reed organ depends on its condition. Definition of terms used for value of reed organs are as follows: *poor condition*—instrument does not play, parts missing, case needs to be refinished; *good condition:* instrument playable, needs only minimal work to return to good playing condition, no parts missing, original finish still in good condition; *fully restored:* wind system re-covered with new bellows cloth and rebuilt, mechanical action cleaned, felts and leathers replaced where necessary and adjusted, reeds cleaned and tuned, case refinished (this would require many of hours of careful work for the hobbyist or cost somewhere between $400 for a simple melodeon to $2000 for a two-manual with pedal-board church organ if done by a professional.)

Price Range

☐ **Alexandre Pere et Fils Harmonium,** c. 1890, 10 stops, two sets of reeds, rosewood veneer case, good condition 250.00   400.00

☐ **Barnard and Prior Harmonium,** c. 1835, one set of reeds, mahogany veneer case, fully restored 1250.00   1500.00

☐ **Carhart & Needham Portable Melodeon,** c. 1866, one set of reeds, rosewood veneer case, good condition 250.00   400.00

☐ **Beatty Golden Tongue Organ,** c. 1891, 10 stops, two ranks of reeds, octave coupler, ornate walnut case with pipe-top, good condition 500.00   800.00

☐ **Burdett "Wagner" Parlor Organ,** c. 1887, 10 stops, two sets of reeds, octave coupler, walnut case with high back missing 200.00   450.00

☐ **Chicago Cottage Organ,** style 40, c. 1894, 12 stops, two sets of reeds, octave coupler, ornate walnut case, good condition 500.00   800.00

☐ **Cornish Parlor Organ,** c. 1890, 18 stops, six octaves, 257 reeds, ornate walnut case, good condition 500.00   750.00

☐ **Crown Parlor Organ,** c. 1891, 10 stops, two sets of reeds, octave coupler ornate walnut case with high top, good condition 400.00   650.00

☐ **Estey Portable Melodeon,** c. 1862, one set of reeds, rosewood veneer case, poor condition 70.00   150.00

☐ **Estey Cottage Organ,** style 17, c. 1871, 6 stops, two and three-fifths sets of reeds, walnut case with flat top, good condition 250.00   500.00

☐ **Estey "New Parlor Model,"** style 1520, c. 1890, 9 stops, two sets of reeds, walnut case with restrained design, good condition 400.00   750.00

☐ **Estey "Style S" Parlor Organ,** c. 1903, 11 stops, two sets of reeds, octave coupler, very ornate walnut case with beveled glass mirror in high back, good condition 750.00   1250.00

☐ **Estey "Piano Cased" Organ,** style X case, c. 1903, seven and one-third octave compass, two full sets of reeds, oak case resembling upright piano, good condition 200.00   450.00

Price Range

☐ **Estey Chapel Organ,** style H97, c. 1903, 16 stops, four sets of reeds with sub-bass and octave coupler, Philharmonic reeds, oak case, finished back with grill, good condition   **300.00**   **500.00**

☐ **Estey Philharmonic Organ,** case design O, Action 81, c. 1920, 16 stops, four sets of Philharmonic reeds plus 17 sub-bass reeds and octave coupler, oak case, fully restored ...   **1500.00**   **1750.00**

☐ **Estey Duo-Manual Organ,** style T without pipe-top, c. 1920, 15 stops, 10 sets of reeds (548 total) plus couplers, oak case, bench and electric suction unit included, good condition **800.00**   **1500.00**

☐ **Estey Duo-Manual Organ,** same as style T above except fully restored **3000.00**   **3500.00**

Estey Duo-Manual Organ (Photo courtesy of the Reed Organ Society).

Price Range

☐ **Estey Folding Organ,** c. 1940, 4 octaves, two sets of reeds, solid oak case, good condition 300.00   500.00

☐ **Farrand Organ Company,** style S 3-B, 12 stops, two sets of reeds plus sub-bass and octave coupler, restrained oak case with low back, good condition 300.00   450.00

☐ **William Hastings Chamber Organ,** c. 1873, 11 stops, four and three-fifths sets of reeds plus sub-bass, burl walnut-veneer case with gold-leafed pipe screen, fully restored 2750.00   3500.00

William Hastings Chamber Organ (Photo courtesy of the Reed Organ Society).

Price Range

☐ **Isaac Bradley Seraphine,** c. 1835, one set of 58 reeds, painted and grained base with rosewood veneer top, fully restored 950.00   1495.00

☐ **J. Foster Elbow Melodeon** with table, c. 1840, rosewood case, good condition 500.00   800.00

☐ **Palace Organ,** style 20, c. 1891, 11 stops, two sets of reeds plus octave coupler, ornate walnut case with high back, good condition   425.00   800.00

☐ **Mason & Hamlin Portable Melodeon,** c. 1857, one set of reeds, walnut veneer case, good condition 225.00   450.00

☐ **Mason & Hamlin Piano Style Melodeon,** c. 1857, rosewood case with octagonal legs ... good condition 450.00   750.00

☐ **Mason & Hamlin Cabinet Organ,** c. 1876, 5 stops, two sets of reeds, walnut case with flat top, poor condition 100.00   175.00

☐ **Mason & Hamlin Parlor Organ,** case 93 with extended top A, c. 1880, 10 stops, two sets of reeds, walnut case with gold bronze ornamentation, good condition 375.00   750.00

☐ **Mason & Hamlin Liszt Organ,** style 523, c. 1895, 15 stops, 281 reeds plus octave coupler and pedal point, oak case with polychrome pipe top, good condition 1500.00   2000.00

☐ **Mason & Hamlin** two-manual and pedal Liszt organ, c. 1895, 19 stops, twelve and three-fifths sets of reeds, oak case including bench and electric suction blower, good condition   850.00   1500.00

☐ **Mason & Hamlin** three-manual and pedal organ, c. 1899, 24 stops, oak case with pipe-top, bench, and electric suction blower included, good condition 2500.00   4000.00

☐ **Miller Parlor Organ,** c. 1885, 10 stops, two ranks of reeds plus octave coupler, ornate walnut case with high back containing beveled glass mirror, good condition 450.00   750.00

☐ **New England Parlor Organ,** c. 1884, 9 stops, two sets of reeds, ornate walnut case with high back, good condition 350.00   600.00

Price Range

☐ **Packard Organ,** case 310, action 43, c. 1890, 11 stops, two sets of reeds plus octave coupler, walnut case with restrained design, high back containing beveled glass mirror, good condition 400.00   650.00

☐ **Packard Organ,** case 580, action 51, c. 1892, 12 stops, two sets of reeds plus sub-bass and octave coupler, very ornate walnut case with high back containing three beveled glass mirrors, good condition 750.00   1250.00

☐ **Packard New Combination Chapel Organ,** case 480, action 80, c. 1890, 14 stops, four sets of reeds plus sub-bass and octave coupler, oak case, good condition 350.00   600.00

☐ **Prince Portable Melodeon,** c. 1855, one set of reeds, rosewood veneer case, good condition 275.00   450.00

☐ **Prince Two-Manual Melodeon,** c. 1865, two sets of reeds plus manual couplers, rosewood veneer case with octagon legs, good condition 1000.00   1500.00

☐ **Prescott Bros. Portable Melodeon,** c. 1862, one set of reeds, rosewood veneer case, good condition 225.00   400.00

☐ **Prescott Bros. Cabinet Organ,** c. 1867, 5 stops, two sets of reeds, walnut case with flat top, finished all four sides, good condition   300.00   450.00

☐ **S. D. & H. W. Smith American Cabinet Organ,** style #10, c. 1868, 5 stops, two sets of reeds, oak finish with paneling and black walnut moldings on all sides, flat top, good condition 400.00   550.00

☐ **Smith American Parlor Organ,** c. 1885, 11 stops, two sets of reeds plus octave coupler, walnut case with high back, good condition   400.00   750.00

☐ **Smith American Parlor Organ,** c. 1885, 11 stops, two sets of reeds plus octave coupler, walnut case with high back missing, poor condition 75.00   150.00

☐ **Spang Melodeon,** c. 1865, one set of reeds, ornate rosewood case with cabriole legs, good condition 500.00   800.00

Price Range

☐ **Story & Clark Parlor Organ,** style 690, c. 1890, 15 stops, three sets of reeds plus octave coupler, very ornate walnut case, good condition 500.00   850.00

☐ **Taylor & Farley National Organ,** style 14, c. 1869, 5 stops, two sets of reeds, walnut case with flat top, good condition 300.00   500.00

☐ **Tobin & Company Standard Melodeon,** c. 1865, 4 stops, two sets of reeds, rosewood veneer case with painted and grained top, completely restored 1250.00   1500.00

☐ **Williams Organ Co. Epworth Organ,** c. 1890, 13 stops, two and three-fifths ranks of reeds plus octave coupler, oak case, finished back with grill, good condition 350.00   600.00

☐ **Vocalion,** two-manual with pedal, c. 1890, 14 stops, nine sets of reeds plus couplers, oak case with carved oak screen, including bench and electric blower, good condition 1750.00   2500.00

☐ **Vocalion,** two-manual with pedal, c. 1885, 20 stops, eight sets of reeds plus couplers, cherry case with polychromed pipe screen including bench, fully restored, including releathering bellows and reservoir plus new silent Ventus blower 8000.00   10,000.00

☐ **George Woods and Company Organ,** c. 1865, 6 stops, two and three-fifths sets of reeds plus sub-bass, walnut case finished four sides with flat top, good condition 350.00   500.00

SAXOPHONES

☐ **Bantone,** bell front, three valves, lacquer bore 1000.00   1350.00

☐ **Bantone,** same as above, upright bell 950.00   1250.00

☐ **Dupont Alto–Solo,** bell front, highly polished brass 150.00   200.00

☐ **Dupont Alto–Solo,** bell front, burnished nickel plate 150.00   200.00

☐ **Dupont Alto–Solo,** bell front, triple silver plate, satin finish 200.00   250.00

Saxophones, French, c. 1867. Courtesy: The Metropolitan Museum of Art, The Crosby Brown Collection of Musical Instruments, 1889.

	Price Range	
☐ **Dupont Alto–Solo,** bell front, triple silver-plate, burnished	265.00	315.00
☐ **Dupont Alto–Solo,** bell upright, highly polished brass	150.00	185.00
☐ **Dupont Alto–Solo,** bell upright, burnished nickel plate	160.00	210.00
☐ **Dupont Alto–Solo,** bell upright, triple silver-plate, satin finish	180.00	225.00
☐ **Dupont Alto–Solo,** bell upright, triple silver-plate, burnished	200.00	250.00
☐ **Dupont Alto,** French Horn model, highly polished brass	275.00	350.00

Price Range

☐ **Dupont Alto,** French Horn model, burnished nickel plate	325.00	400.00
☐ **Dupont Alto,** French Horn model, triple silverplate, satin finish	400.00	500.00
☐ **Dupont Alto,** French Horn model, triple silverplate, burnished	450.00	600.00
☐ **Dupont B-Flat Tenor,** highly polished brass	190.00	240.00
☐ **Dupont B-Flat Tenor,** burnished nickel plate	225.00	275.00
☐ **Dupont B-Flat Tenor,** triple silverplate, satin finish	225.00	300.00
☐ **Dupont B-Flat Tenor,** triple silverplate, burnished	275.00	350.00
☐ **Dupont B-Flat Baritone,** highly polished brass	300.00	400.00
☐ **Dupont B-Flat Baritone,** burnished nickel plate	325.00	425.00
☐ **Dupont B-Flat Baritone,** triple silverplate, satin finish	375.00	475.00
☐ **Dupont B-Flat Baritone,** triple silverplate, burnished	400.00	500.00
☐ Double French horn, mechanical valve linkage, ball-bearing suspension, bronze bell ..	3000.00	3600.00
☐ **Holton,** double French horn, lacquer bore ..	1400.00	2000.00
☐ **Holton,** double "Farkas," nickel silver	1500.00	1800.00
☐ **Holton,** double "Farkas," nickel silver, screw bell	2150.00	2675.00
☐ **Holton,** double "Farkas," brass, screw bell	2150.00	2675.00
☐ **Holton,** double "Farkas," lightweight brass	2150.00	2675.00
☐ **Holton,** "Hand horn"	2300.00	2800.00
☐ **Holton,** Double "Farkas" hand horn, lightweight brass, screw bell	2200.00	3000.00
☐ **Marceau E-Flat** alto, brass, polished, c. early 1900's	110.00	150.00
☐ **Marceau E-Flat** alto, nickel, polished	125.00	160.00
☐ **Marceau E-Flat** alto, silver-plated, satin finish	150.00	200.00
☐ **Marceau B-Flat** tenor, brass, polished	125.00	160.00
☐ **Marceau B-Flat** tenor, nickel, polished	130.00	170.00
☐ **Mellophonium,** bell forward, lacquer bore ..	1100.00	1400.00
☐ Single French horn in key of F	900.00	1150.00
☐ Single French horn, B-flat	1000.00	1500.00
☐ **Tourville & Co.** alto, brass, polished, c. early 1900's	200.00	265.00

	Price Range	
☐ **Tourville & Co.** alto, nickel-plated	175.00	225.00
☐ **Tourville & Co.** alto, silver, satin finish	225.00	280.00
☐ **Tourville & Co.** alto, silver, polished	250.00	350.00
☐ **Tourville & Co.** B-flat baritone, brass, polished	225.00	280.00
☐ **Tourville & Co.** B-flat baritone, nickel-plated	250.00	330.00
☐ **Tourville & Co.** B-flat baritone, silverplated, satin finish	325.00	425.00
☐ **Tourville & Co.** B-flat baritone, silverplated, polished	325.00	425.00
☐ **Tourville & Co.** tenor, nickel-plated	275.00	350.00
☐ **Tourville & Co.** tenor, silver, satin finish . . .	275.00	350.00
☐ **Tourville & Co.** tenor, silver, polished	300.00	375.00

SERPENT

☐ English, by Thomas Key, London, c. 1820, leather-bound wood tube, brass and nickel mountings, four brass keys, brass crook and bit with ivory mouthpiece, length of tube 7'11½"	1900.00	2400.00

(On strength of rarity, this imposing wind instrument, an ancestor of the tube, deserves a higher price. Its value is low because it is not suitable either as a concert or orchestral instrument and is really only in the category of a museum piece.)

TAMBOURINES

☐ Albanian, c. 1860	70.00	100.00
☐ Albanian, silver jingles, third quarter of 19th century	100.00	125.00
☐ Brazilian, second quarter of 19th century . . .	125.00	180.00
☐ Czech, 19th century	110.00	150.00
☐ English, 1860	115.00	160.00
☐ English, third quarter of 19th century	90.00	120.00
☐ English, c. 1895	75.00	100.00
☐ Irish, 19th century	95.00	125.00
☐ Italian, mid-19th century	100.00	125.00
☐ Mexican, c. 1890–1900	70.00	100.00

Serpent in C, *English, c. 1820, wood and leather, 2' 4" L. Courtesy: The Metropolitan Museum of Art, The Crosby Brown Collection of Musical Instruments, 1889.*

	Price Range	
☐ Polish, early 19th century	**165.00**	**215.00**
☐ Polish, c. 1840	**150.00**	**225.00**
☐ Polish, third quarter of 19th century	**90.00**	**125.00**
☐ "Salvation Army" model, c. 1900	**60.00**	**90.00**
☐ "Salvation Army" model with 32 sets of jingles, c. 1900	**60.00**	**100.00**
☐ Spanish, c. 1870	**85.00**	**110.00**
☐ Spanish, late 19th century	**70.00**	**100.00**

TRIANGLES

It is very likely that the average public estimation of the triangle is no higher than of the kazoo or Jews' harp, that it represents someone's slightly strange notion of what ought to be included in an orchestra. But the simple little triangle—just a length of bent metal—is a bona fide instrument with a long, well-documented history in the performance of classical and semiclassical music. It would be impossible without the triangle to produce certain notes necessary for the correct rendering of many scores. They vary quite a bit in quality, too, and it would not be an exaggeration to state that a triangle player values a fine instrument almost to the degree that a violinist does, despite its lesser versatility.

	Price Range	
☐ Four inches, nickeled steel, with hammer, c. 1890's	8.00	11.00
☐ Six inches, nickeled steel, with hammer	9.00	13.00
☐ Seven inches, nickeled steel, with hammer, American made, c. 1890–1900	10.00	15.00
☐ Eight inches, nickeled steel, with hammer ..	12.00	17.00
☐ 10 inches, nickeled steel, with hammer	15.00	20.00
☐ 12 inches, nickeled steel, with hammer	22.00	30.00

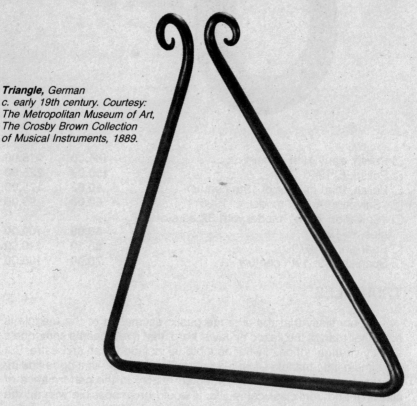

Triangle, German
c. early 19th century. Courtesy:
The Metropolitan Museum of Art,
The Crosby Brown Collection
of Musical Instruments, 1889.

TROBONES

Price Range

☐ **Concertone B-Flat Tenor Slide,** low pitch, nickel silver mouthpiece and music rack, 42½" long, c. early 1920's 200.00   265.00

☐ **Concertone,** as above, nickel-plated 210.00   270.00

☐ **Concertone,** as above, silverplated, satin finish, goldplated bell 275.00   335.00

☐ **Dupont B-Flat Baritone Valve,** highly polished brass 500.00   625.00

☐ **Dupont B-Flat Baritone Valve,** burnished nickel plate 625.00   750.00

☐ **Dupont B-Flat Baritone Valve,** triple silverplate, satin finish 750.00   950.00

☐ **Dupont B-Flat Baritone Valve,** triple silverplate, burnished 800.00   1000.00

☐ **Dupont B-Flat Tenor Slide,** highly polished brass................................. 400.00   500.00

☐ **Dupont B-Flat Tenor Slide,** burnished nickel plate 425.00   550.00

☐ **Dupont B-Flat Tenor Slide,** triple silverplate, satin finish 600.00   725.00

☐ **Dupont B-Flat Tenor Slide,** triple silverplate, burnished 750.00   1000.00

☐ **Dupont B-Flat Tenor Valve,** burnished nickel plate 550.00   625.00

☐ **Dupont B-Flat Tenor Valve,** triple silverplate, satin finish 575.00   650.00

☐ **Dupont B-Flat Tenor Valve,** triple silverplate, burnished 600.00   775.00

☐ **Dupont B-Flat Tenor Valve,** highly polished brass................................. 525.00   650.00

☐ **Dupont E-Flat Alto Slide,** highly polished brass................................. 525.00   650.00

☐ **Dupont E-Flat Alto Slide,** burnished nickel plate 525.00   650.00

☐ **Dupont E-Flat Alto Slide,** triple silverplate, satin finish 600.00   775.00

☐ **Dupont E-Flat Alto Slide,** triple silverplate, burnished 700.00   900.00

☐ **Dupont E-Flat Alto Valve,** highly polished brass................................. 300.00   375.00

Trombone, *American, c. 19th century, brass, 3' 10½" L. Courtesy: The Metropolitan Museum of Art, The Crosby Brown Collection of Musical Instruments, 1889.*

	Price Range	
☐ **Dupont E-Flat Alto Valve,** burnished nickel plate	325.00	400.00
☐ **Dupont E-Flat Alto Valve,** triple silverplate, satin finish	400.00	525.00
☐ **Dupont E-Flat Alto Valve,** triple silverplate, burnished	400.00	525.00
☐ **Lamoreaux Freres Slide,** ornamented bell, brass, polished, c. 1905	250.00	300.00
☐ **Lamoreaux Freres,** nickel-plated	325.00	425.00
☐ **Lamoreaux Freres,** silverplated, satin finish	325.00	425.00
☐ **Lamoreaux Freres,** silverplated, polished	300.00	375.00
☐ **Marceau Slide,** leaf-work ornament, brass, polished, c. 1905	200.00	250.00
☐ **Marceau,** nickel-plated, polished	275.00	350.00
☐ **Marceau,** silverplated, satin finish, gold-lined bell	300.00	370.00

Price Range

☐ **Marceau,** silverplated, burnished gold-lined bell 260.00 300.00

TRUMPETS

☐ **Concertone B-Flat,** high pitch with low-pitch slide, quick-change slide to A, medium bore and bell, one water key, nickel-silver mouthpiece, pearl buttons, 20⅝" long, 4¾" bell, brass, sold in the 1920's 160.00 200.00

☐ **Concertone,** as above, nickel-plated 175.00 225.00

☐ **Concertone,** as above, silverplated, satin finish, goldplated bell...................... 250.00 300.00

☐ **Holton B-Flat Bass,** lacquer 1200.00 1400.00

☐ **Holton B-Flat,** "Maynard Ferguson Firebird," slide valve combination, lacquer 1600.00 1850.00

☐ **Holton B-Flat,** lacquer bore 300.00 400.00

☐ **Holton B-Flat,** red brass bell, "U" hook third valve 375.00 450.00

☐ **Holton B-Flat,** nickel finish 500.00 625.00

☐ **Holton B-Flat,** "Al Hirt Special," lacquer ... 750.00 900.00

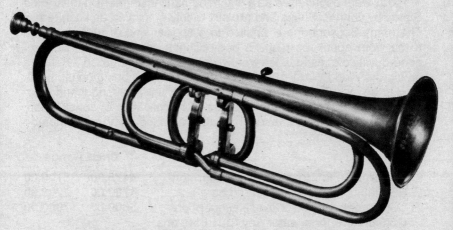

Trumpet in E-Flat, English, c. 19th century, brass. Courtesy: The Metropolitan Museum of Art, The Crosby Brown Collection of Musical Instruments, 1889.

	Price Range	
☐ **Holton B-Flat,** "Maynard Ferguson"	1000.00	1200.00
☐ **Holton E-Flat/D**	950.00	1200.00
☐ **Holton E Alto,** with E-flat slide	1500.00	1800.00
☐ **Holton,** four-valve trumpet	1400.00	1700.00
☐ **English slide trumpet,** Richard John Bilton engraved 93 Westminster Ridge Road / Bilton / London; embossed with musical instruments and foliage, crook socket mount decorated with foliage and spiral twisting, slide designed for watch spring operation, length 23⅛"	1200.00	1700.00

TUBAS

The tuba, the largest brass in general use as an orchestral instrument, is closely related to the cornet and the old European "post horn," a horn of circular body sounded by post riders. Compared to many other instruments, it is of rather modern origin, the first tuba having been constructed in 1835. It is seldom used in solo recitals, being of limited musical flexibility, but is indispensable to the orchestration of many operatic scores.

Tubas were popularized as a marching-band instrument in the United States by John P. Sousa and are still widely employed as such today. The name Sousaphone is applied to a special kind of tuba designed to be worn about the player's body. Cheap commercial versions of good-quality orchestra tubas were widely marketed in the United States during the World War I–1930's era. All other things being equal, tubas tend to be more expensive, whether bought new or secondhand, than other brasses. This is due to its size and complication of construction, also because tubas are made in relatively limited numbers compared to other instruments.

	Price Range	
☐ **Holton BB-Flat,** four valves, lacquer bore ..	4475.00	5700.00
☐ **BB-Flat,** upright bell, lacquered bore	1700.00	2200.00
☐ **CC,** upright bell, four valves, lacquer bore ..	5500.00	7000.00
☐ **Concertone,** one water key, pearl buttons, nickel silver mouthpiece, music rack, engraved bell, 28" long, 14" bell, brass	210.00	260.00
☐ **Concertone,** as above, nickel-plated	240.00	310.00
☐ **Concertone,** as above, silverplated, satin finish, goldplated bell	360.00	425.00

Price Range

☐ **Dupont B-Flat Bass,** highly polished brass	385.00	450.00
☐ **Dupont B-Flat Bass,** burnished nickel plate	415.00	500.00
☐ **Dupont B-Flat Bass,** triple silverplate, satin finish	465.00	575.00
☐ **Dupont B-Flat Bass,** triple silverplate, burnished	520.00	625.00
☐ **Dupont E-Flat Bass,** highly polished brass	415.00	500.00
☐ **Dupont E-Flat Bass,** burnished nickel plate	435.00	525.00
☐ **Dupont E-Flat Bass,** triple silverplate, satin finish	490.00	575.00
☐ **Dupont E-Flat Bass,** triple silverplate, burnished	540.00	650.00
☐ **Dupont E-Flat Contra Bass,** highly polished brass	435.00	525.00
☐ **Dupont E-Flat Contra Bass,** burnished nickel plate	445.00	500.00
☐ **Dupont E-Flat Contra Bass,** triple silverplate, satin finish	560.00	700.00
☐ **Dupont E-Flat Contra Bass,** triple silverplate, burnished	575.00	725.00
☐ E-flat, upright bell, lacquered bore	1675.00	2000.00
☐ **Marceau B-Flat Bass,** brass, polished, pre-World War I	220.00	300.00
☐ **Marceau B-Flat Bass,** nickel-plated, polished	195.00	250.00
☐ **Marceau E-Flat Bass,** brass, polished	230.00	275.00
☐ **Marceau E-Flat Bass,** brass, polished	275.00	350.00
☐ **Marceau E-Flat Bass,** nickel-plated, polished	325.00	400.00
☐ Recording model, BB-flat, three valves	5000.00	7000.00
☐ As above, four valves	5500.00	7500.00
☐ **Sousaphone, BB-Flat,** fiberglass white bore	1750.00	2200.00
☐ BB-flat, upright bell, four valves, lacquer bore	2300.00	3000.00
☐ **Sousaphone BB-Flat,** brass, lacquer bore	2500.00	3100.00
☐ BB-flat, upright bell, three valves	4000.00	5500.00
☐ **Tourville & Co. B-Flat Bass,** brass, polished	300.00	400.00
☐ **Tourville & Co. B-Flat Bass,** nickel-plated	325.00	425.00
☐ **Tourville & Co. B-Flat Bass,** silverplated, satin finish	350.00	450.00
☐ **Tourville & Co. B-Flat Bass,** silverplated, polished	430.00	525.00
☐ **Tourville & Co. E-Flat Bass,** brass, polished	410.00	475.00

	Price Range	
☐ **Tourville & Co. E-Flat Bass,** nickel-plated	400.00	500.00
☐ **Tourville & Co. E-Flat Bass,** silverplated, satin finish	525.00	650.00
☐ **Tourville & Co. E-Flat Bass,** silverplated, polished	550.00	700.00

UKELELES

☐ Banjo, 7″ maple shell, birch neck, rosewood fingerboard, nickel-plated straining hoop and tailpiece, three pearl position dots	80.00	115.00
☐ Birch body, black rings around sound hole, white celluloid binding, c. 1920's	35.00	50.00
☐ Koa wood, black and white inlay around sound hole, brass pegs, violin gut strings, koa wood bridge	80.00	100.00
☐ Mahogany body, brass peds, block inlay around sound hole	50.00	65.00

VIOLINS

In terms of their antiquity, craftsmanship, and reputation for musical quality, old violins are unquestionably the premier collectors' items among instruments. It is impossible in the limited space available here to enter fully into the background of violin making or collecting, or to render extensive advice on the purchase of antique violins. A few words only for the beginner can be given, summed up with this standard but still wise advice: entrust your purchasing to an expert and go to the experts for answers to any questions or problems you have. Antique violins are very complex "collectibles." To know them thoroughly and buy them intelligently, one must have an ear for tonal quality, coupled with the experienced collector's knowledge of fine workmanship.

Why an old violin? Why are antique violins so highly respected by musicians? It is natural enough that collectors, museums, and others whose interest lie with historical objects prefer early violins to those manufactured recently. Buy why does a violinist prefer to play a 250-year-old Stradivarius rather than the best current models?

First, it should be understood that violins are not automatically valuable or desirable (either as antiques or instruments) merely on grounds of being old. Any skilled violinist will agree that the *majority* of antique specimens, even those dating back 200 years or more, are in no way superior to the best modern violins. Many are inferior, in fact; not because of decay or damage but simply because they were not first-rate when manufactured. The violin-maker geniuses of olden days were comparatively few, matched against the thousands of independent violin makers who flourished in the 17th, 18th, and 19th centuries. But there *were* geniuses, here and there, who produced instruments that no modern artisan has been successful in duplicating. It is these instruments—not "old violins" as a lot—that are sought by concert musicians and that sell for high sums on the antiques market. If one wishes simply to own a product of 18th-century violin making, it can be had pretty cheaply (they turn up in antique shops that do not even specialize in instruments), but for a "Strad" or an Amati you will be asked to pay a sum of at least five and possibly six figures.

Whether or not a fine old violin, like wine, improves with age is a point on which the authorities do not agree; but it certainly loses nothing with age, and properly cared for will retain its tonal qualities for an indefinite period of time, very likely a thousand years or more.

Values. Violins are really the only antique musical instruments in which the maker's fame or reputation serves as the basis for price. Yes, it is true that a piano by Erard will be worth more than another made at approximately the same time by a less celebrated manufacturer, but the difference in price is not so great. An "Art Grand" piano of 1800, well preserved, cannot help but be expensive, no matter its maker. With violins you have a situation where the best are valued 20 or 30 times higher than the run-of-mill.

The best antique violins are costly for a variety of reasons. Rarity in itself is not a prime factor. One often reads, in the comments of uninformed writers, of "rare Stradivarius." In fact, the products of this extremely long-lived manufacturer (93 years) are among the most plentiful violins of their time. Somewhere between 500 and 600 original "Strads" exist, or about one-third of the total that left his factory. This is a very hefty supply, compared to the extant number of other costly collectors' pieces: the 1856 British Guiana one-cent postage stamp, 1804 silver dollar, Gutenberg Bible. Of course, many are in museums, but several hundred remain "in circulation," that is, in the hands of musicians, collectors, dealers, and (increasingly these days) investors. They are well distributed, too, throughout many parts of the world, with U.S. owners possessing their share of Strads.

One thing to realize is that good violins were expensive from the beginning. The 1856 postage stamp mentioned above cost its original purchaser a penny. Volume one, number one of *Action Comics*—now worth many thousands—cost just a dime when issued. But violin makers, especially those of reputation, did not give away their products. Even during Stradivari's lifetime, owners of violins made by him 20 or

30 years earlier were selling them for considerable prices. They were not collectors' items or museum pieces, but musicians knew their worth and paid dearly for them.

Also, the collecting of violins as a hobby is quite old, going back at least to 1800. As soon as collectors entered the market, competing against musicians for the better examples, prices rose sharply, and continued more or less to rise ever since. As a "blue-chip" collectible, one with a good long track record of increased valuations and demand, violins have few equals. Even during the depression of 1930–38, Strads were fetching in the neighborhood of $10,000; cheap compared to their present prices, but very strong for a buyer's market.

Some hints for violin buyers. As stated earlier, trust the experts rather than your own taste or judgment unless you have more than a basic knowledge of violins. There are no "bargains" to be had, except for the occasional (now almost unheard-of) discovery of valuable violins in junk shops, etc. It is very rare for any dealer or private party who does not know the value of antique violins to come into possession of a valuable specimen, more rare for it to be offered for sale. You may sometimes get a slight price break on violins by makers whose names are not known to the general public, but whose instruments might be worth more than garden-variety violins of their time. Some antiques dealers, if they do not find the name Stradivari or Amati or something else they recognize in a violin, price the item by age or appearance. This of course is very foolish, as the violins of one maker can be worth much more than of another, even if both worked at the same time, in the same place and turned out instruments similar in appearance.

Normally, it is more sensible for the collector to purchase from dealers or auction houses than from musicians. The relationship between collectors and musicians has never been the best, from the earliest days of violin collecting. It is undeniable that musicians often place a higher cash value on their instruments than they would actually be worth on the market. It has been suggested that the reason for this may be the fact that a musician thinks in terms of the profits from performing that an instrument earns him.

Do not buy violins on the basis of beauty of design. Some manufacturers who produced handsome cases did not take such care with the tonal quality of their instruments.

A violin must be played (not necessarily by yourself but by a skilled musician in your presence) before purchase. No amount of visual examination can take the place of hearing the instrument being played.

Fakes and counterfeits (and "ghosts"). Faked specimens of violins by most of the celebrated makers exist and are a plague to the market. They do not often fool the experts, but unwary buyers frequently purchase them, in the belief they are "getting the best of the seller" by paying 30 percent or 40 percent less than the market price.

Fakes are produced in various fashions, by manufacturing violins in the style of old masters, by taking unimportant old violins and changing varnish, label, etc., to give the impression that they were made by noted craftsmen, and in other ways. Labels are easy to fake, for someone expert in the practice.

"Ghosts" are violins bearing labels of makers who never existed. This is not a study for the amateur. It is sometimes impossible, because of lack of evidence, to prove whether a particular maker actually existed. The fact that one violin bearing his label has been found is not proof of a "ghost," nor even reason to suspect one; there are many instances of manufacturers leaving behind just one specimen.

Care of violins. It should be needless to point out that violins, whether antique or modern, should not be subjected to sudden changes in temperature or humidity if possible, should be kept in a proper case, made for a violin, and should be attended to by a competent restorer when in need of repair.

The following pages give approximate values for violins by manufacturer. When dealing with violins made before 1900, and especially before 1800, this is the chief point on which values are based and the only way in which values can be sensibly arrived at. *It must be understood,* however, that values vary from one specimen to another even on violins made by the same hand, depending on when it was made and other considerations. For examples the products of Stradivari dating after 1700 are considered superior to his earlier efforts.

The place of sale plays a part in price. Generally, fine violins (say, those in the $10,000-up category) fetch higher sums in the salesrooms of New York and London than elsewhere. It should also be taken into account that advertised prices at which dealers are offering antique violins are not necessarily the figures at which sales are finally made.

Prices of antique violins do fluctuate. Though the overall trend is up (by about 8–10% per year in a normal nonrecession year), you cannot take a list of prices from ten years ago, multiply them by a certain figure, and hope to arrive at figures that would be fair in today's market. The violins of some makers rise in price and demand faster than others. There are fads in this field, though nobody cares to admit it (classical violins are supposed to be above fads). The fact is that violin collectors are very much influenced by circumstances and opinion. When a book is published praising the violins of a given maker, his work is sure to increase in price; while a sour word from an expert can damage the market for violins of any but the most outstanding names. Perhaps this should not be, especially as opinion varies from one book to another and one expert to another, but it is. Investors are constantly watchful for things of this sort.

In the following list, the arrangement is as follows: name of maker, city of occupation (which may or may not be birthplace), years of life or activity, value. Date of birth and death are stated when known; otherwise the dates are those during which the maker was active.

It is important to note that the range of prices has nothing to do with condition, unlike the situation with price ranges in most sections of this book. Rather, it reflects the scope of values for different violins by the same maker and for identical violins sold under different sale conditions.

	Price Range	
☐ **Abbati, Giambattista,** Modena, 1755–1795	7500.00	10500.00
☐ **Adani, Pancrazio,** Modena, 1770–1830 . . .	6500.00	8500.00
☐ **Albanesi, Sebastiano,** Cremona, 1720–1762	4000.00	5500.00
☐ **Albani, Paolo,** various cities, 1630–1695 . . .	7000.00	10,000.00
☐ **Amati, Jerome,** Cremona, 1649–1740	25,000.00	37,000.00
☐ **Amati, Nicolo,** Cremona, 1596–1684	55,000.00	80,000.00

Nicolo Amati was the teacher of Stradivari. It is not for this reason that his violins are highly prized, but on their own merit. He was indisputably the supreme violin maker of the middle part of the 17th century.

☐ **Baldantoni, Guiseppi,** Ancona, 1784–1873	4000.00	5200.00

Baldantoni, a not-very-remarkable artisan, made violins of average quality for their time. He had a habit of using old labels, thus fooling purchasers into believing his violins are rather more antique than they really are.

☐ **Balestrieri, Pietro,** Cremona, 1725–1740 . .	9500.00	12,000.00

Balestrieri was active at Cremona at the same time as Stradivari, the "golden age" of Italian violin making.

☐ **Balestrieri, Tommaso,** Mantua, 1720–1795	25,000.00	34,000.00
☐ **Barbanti, Silvio,** Corregio, mid-1800's	3000.00	4000.00
☐ **Barnia, Fedele,** Venice, 1745–1780	5500.00	7500.00
☐ **Barzellini, Aegidius,** Cremona, 1670–1720	4750.00	6000.00
☐ **Belveglieri, Gregorio,** Bologna, 1742–1772	5750.00	8000.00

Violin, Italian, c. 1690, by Antonio Stradivari, known as the "Leopold Auer," sold at Christie's East in 1984 for $308,000 (Photo courtesy of Christie's, New York).

Price Range

☐ **Benedetti, Giuseppi,** Piacenza, early 18th century 3700.00   5000.00

☐ **Bergonzi, Carlo,** Cremona, 1676–1747 . . . . 55,000.00 76,000.00

Bergonzi, a contemporary of Stradivari, was thought by some to be if not the equal of the maestro, at least next to him in skill among makers of that time. His instruments have exceptional tonal quality and deserve, perhaps, to sell for even higher prices; they bring on average only half the sums of Stradivari's and are certainly better than half as good.

Price Range

☐ **Bergonzi.** In addition to the above-named Carlo, at least a dozen members of this family were active as violin makers from the 17th to 19th centuries. Their instruments are generally of above average quality, with prices ranging from $10,000 to $50,000.

☐ **Bertolotti, Gasparo,** Brescia, 1540–1609 .. 40,000.00 55,000.00
The instruments of this pioneer violin maker are well respected and rare. Brescia was an important center of violin making for about 200 years, gaining a reputation for its violins before Cremona.

☐ **Cabroli, Lorenzo,** Milan, 1716–1720 ...... 4000.00 5375.00
Cabroli's violins are not the best musically but very handsomely finished.

☐ **Camilli, Camillus,** Mantua, 1704–1754 .... 19,000.00 24,000.00
☐ **Casini, A.,** Modena, 1630–1710 .... 6500.00 8000.00
☐ **Cosetto, Guiseppi,** Venice, 1760–1790 .... 5750.00 7500.00
☐ **Danieli, Giovanni,** Padua, 1745–1785 ..... 4000.00 5000.00
☐ **Eberle, Tommaso,** Naples, 1760–1792 .... 15,000.00 20,000.00
☐ **Emiliani, Francesco,** Rome, 1704–1736 ... 16,500.00 22,000.00
Rome was significant as a center for violin production only for a brief time in the 18th century. Even then, it boasted no makers to equal those of Cremona, a much smaller town.

☐ **Fabris, Luigi,** Venice, 1838–1873 .... 4750.00 6000.00
One of the outstanding makers of the 19th century, whose violins would undoubtedly bring higher prices if there were greater collecting enthusiasm for instruments of the mid- to later 19th century.

☐ **Farinato, Paola,** Venice, 1695–1725 ...... 5000.00 6500.00
☐ **Filano, Donato,** Naples, 1763–1783 .... 3600.00 4200.00
☐ **Gabrielli, Giovanni,** Florence, 1739–1770 15,000.00 20,000.00
☐ **Gagliano, Alessandro,** Naples, 1660–1725 37,000.00 45,000.00
One of the foremost Neapolitan violin makers.

☐ **Gibertini, Antonio,** Parma, Genoa, 1797–1866 .... 4150.00 5300.00
☐ **Gigli, Giulio,** Rome, 1721–1762 .... 19,000.00 25,000.00
☐ **Jorio, Vincenzio,** Naples, c. 1780–1849 ... 4500.00 6000.00

Price Range

☐ **Landolfi, Carlo,** Milan, 1714–1787	28,000.00	32,500.00
☐ **Lanza, Antonio,** Brescia, 1650–1715	6500.00	8500.00
☐ **Leb, Matthias,** Piacenza, third quarter of 18th century	9500.00	13,000.00
☐ **Maggini, Giovanni,** Brescia, 1580–1632 . . .	60,000.00	85,000.00

A legendary violin maker, who gave Brescia a reputation for fine instruments nearly a century before Cremona attained one.

☐ **Mantegazza, Pietro,** Milan, 1750–1760	9750.00	12,500.00
☐ **Meloni, Antonio,** Milan, late 17th century . .	5750.00	7750.00
☐ **Montaganna, Domenico,** Venice, 1690–1750	67,000.00	130,000.00

The greatest Venetian violin maker. Also spelled Montagnana.

☐ **Nadotti, Joseph (Guiseppi),** Piacenza, 1757–1789	10,000.00	12,500.00
☐ **Pazzini, Giovanni,** Brescia, Florence, 1630–1666	7000.00	10,000.00
☐ **Pressenda, Gian,** various cities, 1777–1854	24,000.00	30,000.00
☐ **Rinaldi, Gofredo,** Turin, 1850–1888	4000.00	5000.00
☐ **Rogeri, Giovanni,** Brescia, 1650–1730	16,000.00	20,000.00
☐ **Ruggeri, Francesco,** Cremona, 1645–1700	45,000.00	60,000.00
☐ **Soliani, Angelo,** Modena, 1752–1810	19,500.00	25,000.00
☐ **Stradivari, Antonio,** Cremona, 1644–1737	125,000.00	200,000.00
☐ **Tanegia, Carlo,** Milan, 1725–1731	4000.00	5000.00
☐ **Tassini, Bartolomeo,** Venice, 1740–1756 . .	12,000.00	16,000.00
☐ **Valenzano, Giovanni,** various cities, 1771–1825	7500.00	10,000.00
☐ **Zanotti, Antonio,** Lodi and Mantua, 1709–1745	12,000.00	15,000.00

EXAMPLES OF VALUES OF INDIVIDUAL SPECIMENS

The following is a brief presentation of the value ranges of antique violins based on individual specimens, rather than the ranges given above for makers.

☐ American, by John Justice Hull, Kingston, Pennsylvania, 1934, labeled Made by / John Justice Jull / in Kingston Pa. 1934 / U.S.A.; two-piece back of narrow curl, similar ribs and

Price Range

head, medium-grain table narrows towards flanks, red-orange varnish, back measures 14⅛" **1300.00** **1700.00**

☐ American, by John Justice Hull, Kingston, Pennsylvania, 1926, labeled Made by / John Justice Jull / in Kingston, Pa. 1926 / U.S.A.; two-piece back, medium-grain table, orange-brown varnish, back measures 14¹/₁₆" **650.00** **850.00**

☐ American, labeled George Gemunder fecit / Astoria, L.I. Anno 1894; one-piece slab-cut back of broad curl, similar ribs and head, medium to broad grain table, golden orange-brown varnish, in oblong case, back measures 14⅛" **1400.00** **2000.00**

☐ American, branded on inside back J. ALBERT / MANUFACTURER / AMERICAN VIOLINS / PHILA.; two-piece back of nearly horizontal narrow curl, similar ribs and head, fine-grain table, reddish-brown varnish, shaped case, back measures 14¹/₁₆" **550.00** **750.00**

☐ American, labeled No. 321 / made by / A.W. White / Boston Oct. 1883; two-piece back of medium curl descends from joint, similar ribs and head, mostly fine-grain table, orange-red varnish, with two nickel-mounted bows, shaped case, back measures 14⅛" **475.00** **600.00**

☐ Bohemian, by Joannes Udalricus Eberle, labeled Joannes Udalricus Eberle / Fecit Pragae 17; one-piece back of faint medium curl, ribs are more prominently figured, plain head, open-grain table, dark golden varnish, in case, back measures 14" **700.00** **900.00**

☐ Czech, viola by Bohuslav Lantner of Prague, back in two sections, medium-grain table, orange brown varnish, back measures 15⅞", dated 1882 .... **3300.00** **3750.00**

☐ Czech, viola d'amore by Joannes Guidantus of Prague, back in two sections, pegbox topped by carving of female mask, back measures 15½", dated 1740 .... **5300.00** **6700.00**

Price Range

☐ English, by David Lindsey, labeled David Lindsey ... Gateshead; one-piece back of medium curl, similar ribs and head, medium-grain table, dark golden varnish, in case with two bows, back measures 14³/₁₆" **250.00**   **350.00**

☐ English, viola by John Betts of London, back in two sections, maple with geometrical motif, maple ribs, broad-grain table, reddish maroon varnish, back measures 15½", c. 1780–1790 .... **3300.00**   **3775.00**

English musicians of that era were well acquainted with the superiority of Italian violins. However, the cost of Italian violins plus their importation made them very expensive on the London market and gave an incentive for local makers to compete.

☐ English, modern, Paul Bickle, London, labeled Antonio Gagliano; two-piece back of faint medium curl, similar ribs, plain head, broad-grain table, golden-brown varnish, back measures 14¹/₁₆" **900.00**   **1150.00**

☐ English, modern, by A. Warwick, labeled A. Warwick / Pupil of Canot / Leeds Anno 1913; two-piece back of medium curl, similar ribs and head, medium-grain table, red color over a golden ground varnish, in case with bow, back measures 14¹/₁₆" **700.00**   **900.00**

☐ English, by John Johnson of London, back in two sections, fine-grain table, burnt orange varnish, back measures 14", dated 1753 .. **1000.00**   **1300.00**

☐ English, modern, by John Jackson, labeled John S. Jackson ... 1974; one-piece back of broad curl, plain ribs and head, medium-grain table, light golden varnish, back measures 14" **80.00**   **120.00**

☐ Flemish, by Ambroise DeComble of Tournai, back in two sections, medium-grain table, reddish brown varnish, back measures 14¼", dated 1772 .... **2500.00**   **3375.00**

Price Range

☐ French, modern, labeled Leon Paroche ... 1927; one-piece back of medium curl, similar ribs, plain head, open-grain table, orange varnish, in case with bow, back measures 14¼″   160.00   260.00

☐ French, Salomon School, unlabeled, two-piece back of medium curl, similar ribs and head, open-grain table, deep golden varnish, in case, back measures 14″, c. 1780 ......   1700.00   2200.00

☐ French, branded Duke / London on the back, one-piece back of plain wood, similar ribs and head, open grain table, golden brown varnish, in case with two bows, back measures 14¼″ 190.00   260.00

☐ French, labeled Lutherie Artistique ... 1896; two-piece back of medium curl, similar ribs and head, medium-grain table, dark golden varnish, in case, back measures 14⅛″ 500.00   700.00

☐ French, by Chappuy, branded Chappuy / à Paris beneath the back button; two-piece back of medium curl, similar ribs, plain head, medium grain table, dark golden-brown varnish, in case, back measure 14³/16″ 1300.00   1800.00

☐ French, attributed to Pierre Silvestre, labeled Pierre Silvestre / à Lyon 1840; one-piece back of broad curl, similar ribs and head, medium-grain table, varnish is red color over a golden ground, in case, back measures 14″   2800.00   3300.00

☐ French, modern, labeled Marcel Roux / Luthier à Lyon / Anno 1922 B&S; two-piece back of small curl, similar ribs and head, fine-grain table, golden-orange varnish, in case with bow, back measures 14⅛″ 500.00   650.00

☐ French, Mirecourt, labeled Spiritus sorsano; two-piece back of plain wood, similar ribs and head, open-grain table, golden-brown varnish, in case with bow, back measures 14″   75.00   95.00

☐ French, labeled Bergonzi; one-piece back of medium curl, similar ribs, plain head, open-grain table, dark golden varnish, in case, silver-mounted bow branded C. Buthod à Paris, back measures 14″ 250.00   300.00

Price Range

☐ French, Francesco Ruggeri, two-piece back of medium curl descends from joint, similar ribs, plain head, table of fine to medium grain table, golden-brown varnish, back measures 14½″ **150.00** **300.00**

☐ French, modern, by Caressa & Francais, labeled Caressa & Francais / Luthiers du Conservatoire de Musique / No. 78 Paris, 1903; two-piece back of broad curl, similar ribs and head, medium-grain table, dark red varnish over a golden ground, two bows, in case, back measures 14¹/₁₆″ **3200.00** **3900.00**

☐ French, copy of a Stradivarius, unknown maker, back in two sections, medium-grain table, reddish brown varnish, back measures 14¼″, c. 1870 .... **1600.00** **1850.00**

If today's collector thinks he has problems with reproductions, think of the musicians who have been confronted for 300 years with reproductions of Stradivarius violins. Most of these copies, like the one listed here, bore Stradivari's name, and it was by no means easy to tell the difference unless one had intimate knowledge of violins.

☐ French, copy of a Maggini, labeled Giovan Paolo Maggini / brescia; two-piece back of medium curl descends from the joint, similar ribs and head, fine-grain table widens toward flanks, golden-brown varnish, back measures 14⁹/₁₆″ **300.00** **450.00**

☐ French, modern, Amédèe Dominique Dieudonne, Mirecourt, labeled Amédèe Dieudonne / No. 313 Mirecourt Anno 1928 / à Rudolphe Wurlitzer e Cie, Cincinnati; two-piece back of medium curl descends from the joint, similar ribs and head, medium-grain table widens toward flanks, orange-brown varnish, in case, back measures 14⅛″ **700.00** **1000.00**

☐ German, labeled Berini Violin / B. & S.L.; two-piece back of plain wood, similar ribs and head, medium-grain table, dark golden-brown varnish, in case, back measures 14⅛″ **110.00** **180.00**

Price Range

☐ German, labeled Frid. Aug. Glass; one-piece
back of medium curl, similar ribs and head,
medium-grain table, golden-brown varnish, in
case with two bows, back measures 14³/₁₆",
c. 1880 ....   **160.00**   **260.00**

☐ German, by Joseph Kloz . . . Anno 1791; two-
piece back of small curl, similar ribs and
head, medium-grain table, red-gold varnish,
in case with silver-mounted bow, back meas-
ures 13" **600.00**   **800.00**

☐ German, child's model, labeled Dearlove &
Flyer; two-piece back of faint figure, plain ribs
and head, open-grain table, orange varnish,
in case, back measures 12½" **100.00**   **175.00**

☐ German, labeled Josephus Strnad / me fecit
Prague Ao 1817; one-piece back of medium
curl descends from left to right, similar ribs
and head, mostly fine-grain table, orange-
brown varnish, measures 14" **900.00**   **1350.00**

☐ German, second half of 18th century, labeled
Aegidus Klaz in Mitten / wald an der Ifer
1780; one-piece back of bird's-eye maple,
similar ribs, fine-grain table widens toward
flanks, faint irregular curl on head, toast-
brown varnish, in case with two bows, back
measures 13¹⁵/₁₆" **500.00**   **800.00**

☐ Italian, Camillo Camilli, Mantua, first half of
18th century, labeled Camillus Camilli Fecit
/ Mantua 1742; two-piece back of medium to
broad curl, similar ribs, faint irregular curl on
head, medium-grain table, orange-brown var-
nish, in case, back measures 13⅞" **30,000.00**   **40,000.00**

☐ Italian, modern, labeled Azzo Rovescalli Cremonese / fece l'anno 1932; two-piece back
of narrow curl descends from joint, similar
ribs and head, medium-grain table, orange-
red varnish, back measures 14" **1400.00**   **2000.00**

☐ Italian, modern, labeled Caciano Sderci di
Igino / fece in Firenze, Anno 1968; two-piece
back of narrow curl descends from joint, ribs

Price Range

of medium curl, fine-grain table widens toward the flanks, orange-brown varnish, shaped case, back measures 14^1/$_{16}$" 2600.00 3100.00

☐ Italian, viola by Vincenzo Cavani of Modena, single-piece back, medium-grain table, pale golden honey varnish, back measured 16½", dated 1958 .... 3800.00 4700.00

A fine violin need not be an antique to command a price in this range. When sold to a musician (rather than a collector), it is the musical capability of the instrument that sets the price. A new or recent violin may well be on a par musically with one of two centuries earlier.

☐ Italian, viola by Enzo Barbieri of Mantua, single-piece back, medium curl ribs, yellow beige varnish, back measures 16½", dated 1983 .... 3000.00 3750.00

☐ Italian, viola, maker and city of origin unidentified, single-piece back, broad-grain table, golden brown varnish, back measures 15½", c. late 1700s 2000.00 3500.00

Unidentified violins were seldom issued anonymously. In most instances it is simply a case of the maker's label becoming detached and lost.

☐ Italian, by Guilio & Eugenio Degani, faintly labeled, one-piece back of irregular curl, similar ribs and head, open grain table, dark golden varnish, in case with two bows, back measures 14" 5100.00 7000.00

☐ Italian, modern, labeled ANTONIO LEDRI / FECE CREMONA 1922; two-piece back of medium curl descends from joint, similar ribs, plain head, fine-grain table widens toward flanks, orange-red varnish, back measures 14^5/$_{16}$" 375.00 525.00

☐ Italian, viola by Guiseppi Borona of Bologna, back in two sections, medium-grain table, burnt orange varnish, back measures 16½", dated 1896 .... 4800.00 5700.00

Price Range

☐ Italian, viola by Loveri Fratelli of Naples, back in two sections, maple, medium-grain table, burnt orange varnish, back measures 15¾", c. World War II era **2250.00   2800.00**

☐ Italian, by Gaetano Antoniazzi, labeled Antoniazzi Gaetano Cremonese / fece à Milano l'anno 1889; two-piece back of small curl, ribs of medium curl, the head is not original, medium-grain table, light-red varnish, in case, back measures 14" **3000.00   3800.00**

☐ Italian, viola d'amore by Leandro Bisiach of Milan, single piece arched back, cupid head, ivory inlaid tuning pegs, back measures approximately 14¼", dated 1904 .... **3200.00   4800.00**

☐ Italian, by Francesco Ruggieri of Cremona, back in two sections, medium-grain table, reddish brown varnish, back measures 14", dated 1696 .... **25000.00   30000.00**

☐ Italian, br Francesco Grancino of Milan, back in two sections, medium-grain table, honey brown varnish, back measures 14", dated 1740 .... **6000.00   8000.00**

☐ Italian, by Antonio Pedrinelli of Crespano, back in two sections, fine-grain table, reddish brown varnish, back measures 14", dated 1828 .... **5375.00   6750.00**

☐ Italian, modern, by Archimede Orlandini, labeled Archimede Orlandini / Fecit in Parma anno 1976; signed by maker, one-piece back of broad curl, similar ribs, plain head, medium-grain table, golden-red varnish, in case with bow, back measures 14¹/₁₆" **1100.00   1700.00**

☐ Italian, by Antonio Stradivari of Cremona, back in two sections, medium-grain table, burnt orange varnish, back measures 14", dated 1712 ....**150,000.00 180,000.00**

☐ Italian, by Joannes F. Pressenda of Torino, single-piece back, medium-grain table, burnt orange varnish, back measures 14", c. 1835–1845 .... **32,000.00   36,000.00**

Price Range

☐ Italian, by Gasparo de Salo of Brescia, back in two sections, broad-grain table, burnt orange and red varnish, back measures 14", c. 1580 .... 25,000.00 30,000.00
Specimens this early are very scarce on the market, yet they generally fall far short in price of the Cremona masterpieces of the 1700s.

☐ Italian, modern, labeled Umberto Lanaro / fece in Padova / anno 1971; two-piece back of narrow curl descends from joint, similar ribs, head of broader curl, medium-grain table, light orange-brown varnish, back measures 14^1/$_{16}$" 750.00 1200.00

☐ Italian, by Gennaro Gagliano of Naples, back in two sections, medium grain table, burnt orange varnish, back measures 13⅞", mid-1700s 37,000.00 46,000.00

☐ Italian, labeled Januarius Gagliano Filius/Alexandri fecit Neap. 1763; two-piece slab-cut back of irregular narrow curl, ascends from joint, similar ribs and head, medium to broad grain table, dark golden brown varnish, in case, back measures 14^1/$_{16}$" ... 3600.00 4200.00

☐ Italian, by Tommaso Carcassi of Florence, back in two sections, fine grain table, burnt orange varnish, back measures 14", dated 1749 .... 9000.00 11,500.00

☐ Italian, by Camillus Camilla of Mantua, single-piece back, fine-grain table, honey brown varnish, back measures 13⅞", dated 1730 ... 1000.00 1400.00

☐ Italian, by Alessandro d'Espine of Torino, single-piece back, fine-grain table, honey brown varnish, back measures 14", c. 1830 16,000.00 18,500.00

☐ Scottish, modern, labeled James W. Briggs/Glasgow 1909; two-piece back of medium to broad curl ascends from joint, ribs and head are medium curl, medium-grain table, golden-brown varnish, in case with two bows, back measures 14^1/$_{16}$" 900.00 1300.00

Price Range

☐ Tyrolean, labeled Jacobus Stainer; two-piece slab-cut back of irregular medium curl, ribs of narrow curl, plain head, medium-grain table, golden-brown varnish, in case, back measures 13⅞" **375.00** **500.00**

☐ Viennese, probably by Johann Georg Thir, mid-18th century, labeled Joannes Georgius Thir, fecit/Viennae Anno 1768,; two-piece back of medium curl, similar ribs and head, medium-grain table widens toward flanks, red-brown varnish, in case, back measures 13¾" **400.00** **700.00**

SEMI-ANTIQUE COMMERCIALLY MADE VIOLINS

Beginning in the later 19th century, cheap violins made for sale to students, amateur musicians, and others who could not afford (or who perhaps did not appreciate) the work of masters came on the market in very large numbers. They were sold by variety houses, department stores, music shops and by mail order. Numerous different models were offered, mostly named after noted makers, but bearing little resemblance (especially in tonal quality) to the originals. They were advertised in such a fashion as to suggest that, by spending just a few dollars (some cost as little as $2.50), the purchaser could have an instrument equal or nearly equal to the antique. But they did serve a purpose; they encouraged violin practice, and undoubtedly some of their purchasers went on to bigger and better things.

These violins, like their more illustrious predecessors, were "hand made," the difference being that they were produced in large commercial factories in a sort of assembly-line process rather than in the studio of a master craftsman who gave each instrument his personal attention.

Semi-antique violins are not usually sought by musicians, but they do have a modest collector appeal. Prices given are for specimens in good condition, but without carrying cases. They were not usually sold with cases.

Price Range

☐ **Amati Model,** curly maple back and sides, maple neck and scroll, the top was said to be made from old wood **125.00** **150.00**

☐ **Amati Model,** maple (grained) back, spruce top, ebony pegs with gold mountings, ebony fingerboard, c. early 1920's **285.00** **375.00**

Price Range

☐ **Caspar DaSalo Model,** reputedly made from choice old wood, European manufacture, sold for $14.25 .... 150.00 200.00

☐ **Concert Strad,** spruce top, full-lined shell, ebony pegs 200.00 250.00

☐ **Conservatory Model,** Reddish brown, with ebony fingerboard and tailpiece, original price $3.45 .... 100.00 125.00

☐ **Duerer Model,** these violins were bought in wholesale quantities for the American mail-order market from the Duerer factory of Germany. They were facsimiles of Stradivari .. 175.00 225.00

☐ **"Genuine" Stradivarius Model,** European, somewhat superior to the $2.45 model, maple, spruce and ebony, this sold originally for $6.95 .... 125.00 175.00

☐ **Guarnerius Model,** grained maple back and sides, spruce top, full-lined shell, first quarter of the 20th-century 140.00 175.00

☐ **Guarnerius Model,** Amber varnish, ebony trimmed 150.00 190.00

☐ **Imperial Amati,** one of the better semi-antique violins, made by Wilhelm Duerer ... 170.00 210.00

☐ **Maggini Model,** advertised as "a direct copy of violins by that great maker". It was, in fact, a fair visual facsimile; its tone was another matter 100.00 125.00

☐ **Paganini Model,** made by Lowendall (Germany), amber varnish, label with signature of Louis Lowendall, original price $19.95 ..... 195.00 240.00

☐ **Stainer Model,** maple (grained), name "Stainer" stamped on back, ebony fingerboard and tailpiece 200.00 230.00

☐ **Stainer Model,** mediocre tone, ebony trimmings, original price $5.65 .... 110.00 135.00

☐ **Stainer Model,** mediocre tone, this Stainer Model was supplied with a case 150.00 200.00

☐ Spruce back, full-lined shell, maple neck, ebonized fingerboard, tailpiece and pegs, c. 1920 .... 125.00 160.00

	Price Range	

☐ **Stradivarius Model,** briar brown finish, maple back, spruce top, ebony pegs and fingerboard, c. 1920's **250.00 300.00**

☐ **Stradivarius Model,** "specially selected wood, beautifully varnished, reddish color, highly finished", manufactured in the tens of thousands and sold originally for $2.45 .... **65.00 90.00**

☐ **Stradivarius Model,** two-piece maple back, spruce top, ebonized fingerboard, post-World War I.................................... **160.00 200.00**

VIOLIN OUTFITS

Department stores and mail-order houses did a brisk business in "violin outfits" in the 1890–1910 era. The outfits usually consisted of a carrying case, instructional book, rosin, strings, fingerboard chart and a very cheap violin. Occasionally these outfits are still found with the original accessories. Prices are for complete outfits.

☐ **Sears Roebuck Violin Outfit #12R300,** Stradivarius model violin, Brazil wood bow, case, set of strings, piece of rosin, instruction book, lettered fingerboard chart **100.00 125.00**

☐ **Sears Roebuck Violin Outfit #12R304,** Maggini model violin, Brazil wood bow, case, set of strings, piece of rosin, instruction book, fingerboard chart **140.00 175.00**

☐ **Sears Roebuck Violin Outfit #12R308,** Stradivarius model violin (better grade), Brazil wood bow, case made of wood, strings, rosin, instruction book, fingerboard chart, tuning pipe...................................... **150.00 200.00**

☐ **Sears Roebuck Violin Outfit #12R316,** Stradivarius violin, "Vuillaume" model bow, wood case, rosin, instruction book (a better one than provided with the above sets), strings, fingerboard chart, tuning pipes, book of "choice violin music", sold originally for $15 .... **250.00 325.00**

Price Range

☐ **Sears Roebuck Violin Outfit #12R318,**
Lowendall violin, "Tourte" bow, wood case,
rosin, instruction book, strings, chin rest, fingerboard chart, tuning pipes, violin mute,
book of violin music 250.00   325.00

XYLOPHONES

The modern xylophone evolved slowly during a period of many centuries from an instrument that, though played in essentially the same
fashion, bore only slight resemblance to its present physical state. It
won favor only after a very lengthy trial during which time its enthusiasts
had no success convincing professional musicians, composers, or critics of its musical possibilities. Perhaps the simplicity of its appearance
counts against it as it has all the look of a plaything for children to bang
on. It is, in fact, while perhaps not a sophisticated apparatus, an instrument that can produce very effective and pleasing music in the hands
of a skilled performer. Because of its close similarity to primitive and
native instruments of various parts of the world, it can be adapted to
music of many kinds and is equally at home in a classical or a jazz orchestra.

Xylophones are of Asian origin and have been played there, in one
form or another, since antiquity. The earliest European or Western xylophones date from the late 15th century or beginning of the 16th. At this
time it was merely a curiosity in the West and retained that status for
quite a long while. Records of xylophone makers during the 16th, 17th,
and even the 18th centuries, are scant, and the likelihood is that few
specimens were produced. It was in the class of a gypsy instrument
during that time, played by persons who learned it as children but were
otherwise musically uneducated. During the 19th century its fortunes
improved considerably. Felix Mendelssohn witnessed the concert of a
xylophonist in 1836 and was struck with the instrument's capabilities
and the performer's virtuosity (the musician was a Russian named Gu-
sikov). He wrote favorably of it, and this brought it to attention. By the
third quarter of the 19th century it was firmly entrenched as a concert
instrument and was widely used in orchestras. Around 1900 it was riding
a crest of popularity, with xylophones in the tens of thousands being
manufactured annually by commercial factories and sold to the public
as well as to musicians. Since then its appeal has waned somewhat—probably because of the introduction of electronic instruments,
which have turned attention away from many standard nonelectric instruments.

	Price Range	
☐ American, 15 maple bars, c. 1900	100.00	130.00
☐ American, 25 maple bars, c. 1900	275.00	335.00
☐ Eastern European, c. 1830	225.00	300.00
☐ German, mid-1800's	275.00	375.00
☐ German, c. 1870	230.00	295.00
☐ Italian, c. 1810	300.00	395.00
☐ Italian, mid-19th century	240.00	325.00
☐ Polish, late 19th century	175.00	225.00

ZITHERS

The Egyptians, Greeks, and other early civilizations had zithers among their ample storehouses of musical instruments—a supply that, even matched against the variety available in today's market, was formidable indeed. Two types of zithers came from the ancient world—the plucked and struck varieties. Both spread out over the European continent in the Middle Ages and were firmly established in most countries of the west by 1500. Since then the zither's popularity has risen and fallen many times. Zithers were known by various names in different areas of Europe, and generally each nation or region had its favorite design. Plucked zithers were traditionally, at least in early times, the general choice in southern Europe. Cheap zithers of various sizes, often stunted, poured upon the American market in the late 19th century and continued to be sold in remarkable numbers well into the 20th. It was considered an instrument that anyone, with or without musical aptitude, could learn to play as well as a professional. This resulted in many zithers landing in the hands of not very musically inclined children, who played them to the utter distraction of everyone within earshot. But anyone who has heard a zither played well could hardly fail to agree that it is a worthy instrument.

☐ Autoharp, 20 strings, three bars, pre-World War I....................................	25.00	32.00
☐ Autoharp, 23 strings, five bars	37.00	45.00
☐ Autoharp, 32 strings, eight bars	50.00	65.00
☐ Autoharp, 37 strings, 12 bars	60.00	75.00
☐ Autoharp, six bars, 16 chords, pine sounding board, edges inlaid with white marble, bars and supporters enameled in black, celluloid finger buttons	70.00	90.00

	Price Range	
☐ **Columbia,** 19½″, maple, c. 1900	135.00	175.00
☐ **Columbia,** same as above but imitation ebony, 31 strings, c. 1900	175.00	225.00
☐ **Columbia,** 14″x20″, 38 strings, c. 1900	190.00	235.00
☐ **Columbia,** 16″x21½″, 47 strings, c. 1900 ..	265.00	350.00
☐ **Deweylin Harp,** three instruments in one, 31 strings, four chords, c. 1900	165.00	210.00
The Deweylin Harp never achieved much popularity. Its interest today is basically as a curiosity.		
☐ Guitar, 31 strings, four chords, c. 1905–1910	22.00	30.00
☐ Guitar, 31 strings, four chords, maple body, ebonized, sound hole ornamented	35.00	45.00
☐ Guitar, 41 strings, five chords	40.00	55.00
☐ Guitar, 51 strings, six chords	55.00	70.00
☐ Harp, 21 melody strings, five groups of chords, size 25″x23″	45.00	65.00
☐ **Marx Harp Piano,** 23 strings, seven hammers, 11″x20″	35.00	45.00

MUSIC RACKS

Racks or holders are designed to hold music scores so they can be referred to by the musician. They are not to be confused with **music stands,** which are mounted generally on tripod legs and rest on the floor. Racks are normally attached to the instrument itself or, in cases where this is not practical, to the musician's arm or other part of his body. Music racks had their beginnings with marching bands, which could not, for obvious reasons, employ stands. Since then they have also been used by jazz, swing, and various orchestral musicians.

The following racks are all of American manufacture and date from 1890 to the early 1900's. They are quite easy to find, not only in music shops but wherever antiques are sold.

	Price Range	
☐ Brass, square wire shank, three separate prongs, for band instruments	15.00	20.00
☐ Brass, three separate prongs, with plate for bass drums	20.00	25.00
☐ Brass, three separate prongs, with plate for snare drums	25.00	33.00

Double Zither, *German, wood, metal, bone. Courtesy: The Metropolitan Museum of Art, The Crosby Brown Collection of Musical Instruments, 1889.*

Price Range

☐ Brass, three separate prongs, with arm-strap (for use when playing instruments to which rack cannot be mounted) 22.00   30.00

☐ Brass, similar to above but with long shank for trombones 25.00   35.00

☐ Nickel-plated, adjustable ring, for clarinets . .   20.00   25.00

☐ Nickel-plated, three separate prongs, for trombones 30.00   40.00

☐ Nickel-plated, square wire shank, three separate prongs, for band instruments 20.00   25.00

MUSIC STANDS

Music stands are one of the few items in this book collected by persons with no special interest in music; they appeal to antique lovers because of their age or beauty or simply as an antique. Over the years, they have been fashioned of almost every conceivable variety of wood, as well as other materials, and have been styled to suit various decors. The handsomest ones likely to be encountered by the average collector are of Victorian origin. These, while factory products, are still held in high regard. Earlier examples tend to be costly. Places of origin of early music stands are often difficult to judge with accuracy.

It should be pointed out to buyers that so-called "classic" designs of early periods were frequently imitated at later dates (many Victorian stands are in Louis XIV to Louis XVI style), often very convincingly, and if one is not well versed in antiques, it is quite easy to be confused. Music stands in styles of 100 to 200 years ago are still in fact being produced, mainly in France and Italy.

Restorations and repairs. As with the purchase of any antiques, potential buyers should take care to note whether restorations or repairs have been made and, if so, whether this is reflected in the price. Minor repairs have little effect on value, especially in a very rare or elegant stand. But occasionally examples will be found in which the neck, feet, or other components are modern replacements, and in this instance the value is considerably reduced. In the cases of painted, gessoed, or gilded stands, the paint or other surface coating should be original or at least closely contemporary with the date of manufacture. A modern refinishing job ruins, or at the least seriously reduces, the desirability of a fine old specimen.

	Price Range	
☐ English, early Victorian duet stand, turned finial, pierced lyre-shaped splats, ring-turned and ribbed vase-shaped shaft and molded scrolled tripartite base	600.00	850.00
☐ French, mid-height, bronze, tapered neck, last quarter of the 18th century	3000.00	4200.00
☐ Italian, carved walnut, finished with gesso and gilt (peeling), the legs in the form of cherubs, one with head missing, late 16th/early 17th century	3200.00	4500.00
☐ Umbrella pattern, made of iron, japanned, folds up, American, c. 1890's	9.00	12.00

	Price Range	
☐ Same as above, nickel-plated	**15.00**	**20.00**
☐ Rosewood Duet Music Stand, mid-19th-century desk pierced with lyres, brass candleholders, adjustable baluster support on trefoil base, raised on ball shaped feet, 50¼" high	**1600.00**	**1900.00**

ACCESSORIES

In the early days of musical instruments (European Renaissance/Baroque eras) it was usually necessary, when one needed a certain attachment or accessory, to have it custom manufactured. When large-scale commercialization of instruments began, factories produced accessories to be sold separately. By the mid-1800's it was possible to buy ready-made accessories of all types for every kind of instrument, just as today.

While old accessories are not necessarily collectors' items in themselves (though they could possibly be), they are frequently sought by owners of antique instruments in cases where replacements or alterations must be made.

BANJO

	Price Range	
☐ Bag, canvas, fleece-lined, for 10–13" banjo	**11.00**	**14.00**
☐ Bag, green cloth, buttoned, for 10–13" banjo	**8.00**	**11.00**
☐ Bracket, globe pattern, brass, polished, bolt and nut	**7.00**	**9.00**
☐ As above, nickel-plated	**9.00**	**12.00**
☐ Bracket, hexagon pattern, brass, turned and polished, with bolt and nut	**9.00**	**12.00**
☐ As above, nickel-plated	**11.00**	**14.00**
☐ Bracket, leaf pattern, brass, cast with bolt and nut, c. 1890–1900	**9.00**	**12.00**
☐ As above, nickel-plated, c. 1890–1900	**12.00**	**15.00**
☐ Bridge, celluloid, "professional model," imitation tortoiseshell	**6.00**	**8.00**
☐ Bridge, ebony, American made	**5.00**	**7.00**
☐ Bridge, maple, American made, c. late 1800's/early 1900's	**5.00**	**7.00**
☐ Case, brown canvas, edges leather-bound, flannel-lined	**14.00**	**19.00**

Price Range

☐ Case, russet leather, embossed, flannel-lined, with strap and buckle, for 10 or 11″ instrument, c. 1900	28.00	35.00
☐ As above, for 12–13″ instrument	30.00	40.00
☐ Case, wood, black varnished, flannel-lined, lock and hooks, for 11″ banjo, late 1800's	18.00	24.00
☐ Head, nickel-plated, engraved sides, bone buttons, good quality, c. 1895	9.00	12.00
☐ Peg, celluloid, imitation amber, Greek cross design	5.00	7.00
☐ Peg, celluloid, imitation ebony, nickel-mounted, "Champion" patent	5.00	7.00
☐ As above, white, nickel-mounted	5.00	7.00
☐ Peg, ebony, hollow shape, pearl dot in each end	3.00	5.00
☐ Peg, imitation ebony, hollow shape, pearl dot on handle, American made	2.50	4.00
☐ As above, with side pegs	2.50	4.00
☐ Peg, same as above but side peg	3.00	5.00
☐ Tailpiece, brass, nickel-plated	5.00	7.00
☐ Tailpiece, celluloid, imitation ivory, solid heel piece	5.00	7.00
☐ Tailpiece, ebony, c. late 1800's	3.00	5.00
☐ Tailpiece, walrus ivory, engraved, "Artist model"	10.00	13.00
☐ Thimble, made of German silver, c. 1890's	3.00	5.00
☐ Wrench, brass, key shape, nickel-plated . . .	5.00	7.00
☐ Wrench, cast brass, ground and lacquered, for ¼″ or ⁵/₁₆″ nut	7.00	10.00

GUITAR

☐ Bag, cloth, with buttons, late 19 century	9.00	12.00
☐ Bag, canvas, fleece-lined	11.00	14.00
☐ Bridge, celluloid, imitation amber	6.00	8.00
☐ Bridge, ebony, American made, late 1800's	6.00	8.00
☐ Bridge, ebony, pearl inlaying, American made, c. 1895	12.00	14.00
☐ Bridge, pearl inlaid at each end, c. 1890–1900	8.00	11.00
☐ Bridge-pin, celluloid, imitation amber	2.50	4.00
☐ Bridge-pin, celluloid, imitation tortoiseshell . .	2.50	4.00

	Price Range	
☐ Bridge-pin, ebony, polished pearl inlaying ..	4.00	6.00
☐ Bridge-pin, ivory, polished pearl inlaying, c. 1895	6.00	8.00
☐ Bridge-pin, maple, black finish, polished head, c. 1890–1900	2.50	4.00
☐ Capo d'Astro, brass, nickel-plated, rubber-covered clamps, vest pocket model	6.00	8.00
☐ Capo d'Astro, brass, lacquered, cork-lined clamps	6.00	8.00
☐ As above, nickel-plated	8.00	11.00
☐ Capo d'Astro, nickel-plated, spring action, felt covered clamps	8.00	11.00
☐ As above but made of aluminim, c. 1895 ...	9.00	12.00
☐ Case, American made, wood, half-lined, with lock, handle, and hooks, c. 1890's	25.00	32.00
☐ Case, brown canvas, leather-bound edges, open end, with strap, buckle, and handle, c. 1890–1900.............................	14.00	18.00
☐ Same as above, larger size (for concert model guitar)	20.00	25.00
☐ Case, hand-sewn leather, embossed, sold by Sears Roebuck in c. 1890's	42.00	55.00
☐ As above, concert size	55.00	70.00
☐ End-pin, ebony, polished head, American made, late 19th century	3.50	5.00
☐ End-pin, ebony, pearl dot inlaid	5.00	8.00
☐ Fingerboard, ebony, plain (without frets), American, c. 1895	12.00	17.00
☐ Fingerboard, ebony, with frets, c. 1895	14.00	19.00
☐ Fret, brass, c. 1895	2.50	4.00
☐ Patent head, brass, engraving on sides, bone buttons, c. 1895	14.00	19.00
☐ Patent head, nickel-plated, engraved, bone buttons	16.00	20.00
☐ Patent head, polished and lacquered, while celluloid buttons	22.00	25.00
☐ Tailpiece, celluloid, imitation ivory, c. 1890's	8.00	11.00
☐ Tailpiece, nickel-plated brass	10.00	14.00

MANDOLIN

Price Range

☐ Bag, canvas, fleece-lined, c. 1890's 14.00 18.00
☐ Bag, green cloth, buttons, American made 15.00 17.00
☐ Bridge, ebony, ivory inlaid 7.00 10.00
☐ Bridge, ebony, plain finish 5.00 8.00
☐ Case, black leather, hand-sewn, flannel-lined, leather carrying strap 55.00 70.00
☐ Case, brown canvas, leather bound edges, flannel-lined, sold by Sears Roebuck in c. 1890's 24.00 33.00
Note: Prices on cases that are defective in any respect, such as having the carry-strap missing, are considerably lower. It is to be expected, however, that specimens of 75–100 years age will show moderate wear.
☐ Head, brass, nickel-plated, white celluloid buttons 20.00 25.00
☐ Head, German-silver, full plate style, engraved 27.00 35.00
☐ Pick, gutta-percha, oval shape 3.50 4.50
☐ Pick, similar to above but large size 3.50 4.50
☐ Pick, tortoiseshell, oval shape, c. 1895 ..... 3.50 4.50
☐ Pick, tortoiseshell, triangular shape, c. 1890–1900 .... 3.50 4.50
☐ Tailpiece, brass, nickel-plated, c. 1890's ... 8.00 11.00

VIOLIN

☐ Becker's chin rest, ebonite and nickel, pre-1900 .... 22.00 28.00
☐ Bridge, "Panpi" model, maple, three scrolls, c. 1895 .... 5.00 8.00
☐ Bridge, "Vuillaum" model, maple, three scrolls 8.00 11.00
☐ Case, papier-mache, "French" shape, lined with baize, nickeled lock 40.00 50.00
☐ Case, varnished black wood, "exposition" shape, flannel-lined, with nickeled lock, handle and spring clasps, American, c. 1890's 42.00 53.00
☐ Case, varnished wood, flannel-lined, nickel-plated lock, hook clasps 37.00 45.00

	Price Range	
☐ Case, varnished wood, half-lined with flannel, turn of the century	28.00	35.00
☐ Case, varnished wood, half-lined with flannel, without lock	26.00	30.00
☐ Case, wood covered in leather, velvet-lined, leather handles, plated lock	70.00	90.00
☐ Chin rest, ebony, nickel-plated double screw fastenings	12.00	16.00
☐ Chin rest, gutta-percha, nickel-lated mountings	20.00	25.00
☐ Chin rest, velvet covered, German-silver double screw fastening	20.00	25.00
☐ Fingerboard, ebony, c. 1890's	8.00	11.00
☐ Fingerboard, maple, imitation ebony finish ..	6.00	8.00
☐ Head, nickel-plated, engraved sides, bone buttons	14.00	18.00
☐ Head, solid brass, engraved on sides, bone buttons, c. 1895	9.00	12.00
☐ Mute, ebony, c. 1890–1900	5.00	8.00
☐ Mute, German-silver, c. late 1800's	5.00	8.00
☐ Mute, German-silver, with tuning pipe	9.00	12.00
☐ Screw, ebony and German-silver button, octagon shape, inlaying in end	5.00	7.00
☐ Tailpiece, celluloid, imitation amber, decorated in relief	16.00	20.00
☐ Tailpiece, ebony, inlaid with colored pearl flower and two leaves	14.00	18.00
☐ Tailpiece, imitation ebony finish, inlaid with fancy colored pearl flowers and leaves	6.00	8.00
☐ Tailpiece, maple, black stained, plain pearl inlaying	3.00	4.00
☐ Tailpiece, solid ebony, c. 1890–1900	6.00	8.00

ZITHER

☐ Brush, bone handle, 19th century	6.00	8.00
☐ Case, wood, black varnish, flannel-lined, with lock	20.00	25.00
☐ Duster, bone handle, American made, late 19th century	8.00	11.00
☐ Head, nickel-plated, engraved	20.00	25.00
☐ Ring, made of German silver	1.00	3.00

	Price Range	
☐ Ring, made of horn	2.50	4.00
☐ Ring, nickel-plated steel	2.50	4.00
☐ Tuning hammer, black handle, c. 1890's ...	2.50	4.00
☐ Tuning hammer, ivory handle, early 1900's	7.00	10.00

The quantity of old zither accessories found on the market bears testimony to the popularity this instrument once enjoyed.etch rather high prices.

BOOKS AND SHEET MUSIC

BOOKS ON MUSIC

Music literature is a huge and varied subject for the collector, ranging from choir books of the Middle Ages to books of psalms published in colonial America to a vast array of semi-modern and modern works in every field of music. In this section, ''Books on Music,'' we have included general reference titles as well as a number of rare works that fetch rather high prices.

COLLECTING MUSIC LITERATURE

Generally, the approach is to specialize in some way or other, either by author, date, place of origin, or (more usually) the specific field of music to which the book relates. The possibilities are limitless, the only restriction being those imposed by the collector's budget. Even a relatively obscure topic, such as the history of a given instrument, could be the basis for a library of several hundred titles, with rarities included.

The prime sources for rare and out-of-print musicana are specialist dealers. These are antiquarian booksellers, some with shops and some who deal out of their homes, who normally offer not only books but music memorabilia, posters, sometimes autographs and other material. Desirable items are also likely to be found on the shelves of general ''used'' bookshops, at prices lower than the specialists charge. Music books also turn up in antiques shops, at auctions, garage sales, and the like. Collectors make a practice of following the auction schedules and attending sales in which an array of musical instruments are offered, on the chance that anyone who had owned instruments might also have possessed a reference library of musical literature. Usually the auction lists are not very thorough in giving titles or other information, so a trip to the sale (or the presale exhibition) is mandatory to really discover what is being offered.

VALUES

The cash value of out-of-print musical literature is set on the same basis as that of other collector's items: supply and demand. Age alone is not the determining factor, though any book strictly on music (as opposed to an encyclopedia with just a section on the subject) that is over 100 years old will have some collector value. **Song books** tend not to be as valuable as works on instruments, music history, opera librettos, and the like. This is largely because early song books carried only lyrics without musical notations; therefore, they are considered by many collectors to be in the category of poem books. Even where noted authors are involved, the value can be rather low.

Any title may be scarce or even rare without having more than a minimal value, if not in demand. On the other hand, a much-sought work will carry a high price even if in more or less plentiful supply. The more desirable early histories of music, such as Hawkins' *A General History of the Science and Practice of Music* (London, 1776), five volumes, sells in the neighborhood of $750 for a decently preserved set, yet is not rare. Most specialist dealers sell several copies of Hawkins every year, but the price is high because of the work's reputation and its appeal to buyers.

CHOIR BOOKS

We have not listed choir books within the main listings because, as manuscripts, no two are quite alike and it is, therefore, impossible to arrive at standard values. A few words on the subject here will not, however, be out of place.

There are few collectors of choir books or hymnals; that is, few persons who make a specialty of collecting them to the exclusion of other musical literature. Many collectors, however, especially those whose interests run to the history of music, choose to purchase one or two specimens of these impressive volumes just as examples of their species. It could almost be said that no library of music history is complete without at least one good choir book, regardless its age or origin or even (if you can't afford a really prime specimen) condition. Failing this, individual leaves can be easily had, at prices ranging from $3 upward, which make excellent decorations when matted and framed. These can be bought from dealers in prints as well as from specialists in musical literature, as well as, sometimes, general dealers in rare books.

Choir books were very large collections of chants or other works sung at church service. Beginning collectors often wonder about their huge sizes; why was it necessary to design them so large? For the simple reason that the entire choir, which might have comprised 50 or more voices, all read from the same book, which stood open on a lectern across the choir stall. Some members of the choir might be 20 or 30 feet from the book and could not easily read it if the writing were small. Thus you have leaves of double folio or elephant folio size—sometimes even larger (the Escorial in Spain has choir books five feet high). Each letter is usually about the size of an egg. There are, however, smaller choir books to be found, often referred to as antiphonals.

The range in price of early choir books is just as varied as their size and composition. Contrary to the belief of some beginners, they are not uniformly expensive. Many can be had at rather reasonable prices, in light of their age, history, and workmanship. A good price break can be had, too, on specimens that are handsome and essentially complete but have several leaves lacking and/or a defective binding.

Manuscript choir books were almost always (and in the case of specimens dating to the 16th century and earlier, without exception) written on vellum rather than paper; not because paper was unobtainable, but vellum afforded more durability. Choir books received a lot of heavy handling. For this reason, even though vellum was used and stout, sturdy bindings applied, it is not to be expected that their present-day condition be as fresh and blemish-free as a book designed for occasional use.

The average choir book consisted of no more than 100 leaves, often much fewer, but this was sufficient, with the thickness of vellum as opposed to paper, to make a book of considerable width. Their bindings were sometimes elegant and highly decorated, but more often designed to withstand wear and tear rather than for visual attractiveness. The usual binding consisted first of wooden planks or boards of ¼- to ½-inch thickness, oak being the preferred variety. These were sanded, then covered over in a good strong leather, such as calf or pigskin; for a volume of major proportions, a whole animal hide was used. Then, various metal attachments would be added: clasps (two for smaller volumes, four for larger—two at the fore-edge and one each at top and bottom) to keep the volume tightly shut while not in use and prevent the vellum from curling or becoming unduly soiled; brass or iron corner-pieces to keep the corners from bruising; centerpieces so the leather at the sides of the binding would not be scratched or torn; and, sometimes, a chain and staple to keep the book attached to its stand and reduce the risk of theft (this being, of course, a problem, as choir books, like most manuscript volumes, had a rather high value). It is not often, however, that copies are discovered with all of these accessories still intact, nor does it detract very much from their value when any are missing.

Most choir books found on the market are not as early as might be believed. The popular concept is that choir books, being manuscripts, antedate the invention of printing in c. 1450 A.D. Some of them, of course, do, but these are rarely offered for sale and, when found, are in the upper price bracket ($1,000 and upward, with prices of $50,000 not unusual for brilliantly decorated examples). Those on the market are basically of Spanish or Italian origin and date from the 16th, 17th, and 18th centuries. It may seem odd that manuscript choir books were still in production as late as the 1700's, with printing 300 years old by then, but this was done simply because the scribe, using a brush, could draw letters much larger than a printer could print with the equipment then available.

PRICES OF CHOIR BOOKS

The values hinge on size, age, place of origin (where known, which it frequently is not; the language is not a clue, this being always in Latin), decoration and various other considerations. A specimen of Spanish origin, dating from 1650–1750, measuring 14x20 inches and containing 75 leaves, would have a retail value of from $500 to $750. With a really handsome binding, and if the volume could be reasonably shown to be complete (it is not always easy to prove a choir book either complete or incomplete), the figure might be pushed up to $1,000. On the other hand, this same volume, with somewhat smaller measurements, and containing 50 instead of 75 leaves, would fall in the $250–$400 territory. The leaf count is important because many choir books, especially those which are incomplete or have a damaged binding, *are bought by dealers for the purpose of breaking them up and selling the leaves individually.* As leaves will retail usually for $3–$5, a dealer will seldom pay more than $2 per leaf for a choir book unless the leaves are exceptionally large or very well decorated.

Choir books of English origin are not frequently found on the market. They are worth more than continental specimens, all other things being equal. Many English churches apparently imported their service books from abroad.

BUYING TIPS FOR OUT-OF-PRINT AND RARE MUSICAL LITERATURE

First of all, know what you're buying! A set of three volumes worth $100 may be worth only $30 if a volume is missing. A book normally valued at $75 could bring just $20 or even less if several text or illustration pages are lacking. A $200 first edition might be worth $50 or $20 or less in a second or later edition. You must be aware of these things to buy intelligently, and you must know enough of the physical anatomy of books, especially old ones, to determine their condition. Normally, when buying from specialist dealers through catalogues or price listings, a full description will be provided for each item, giving the condition, etc., and the price will be adjusted accordingly. This is not the case when making purchases from the shelves of bookshops, however. It is uncommon for a bookseller to make a notation of defects in his books, and in fact he may be unaware of defects until brought to his attention by a customer. You cannot just assume that because a volume is being offered by a reputable bookseller, it must be complete and in good condition. Every bookshop has among its stock a certain number of volumes that are defective in some way or other; this is not considered a black blot on the shop, because these books, even while defective, do have *some* value and are desirable to some people.

When inspecting an old book, it will (or should) be obvious whether the binding is well or poorly preserved. Volumes bound in calf—those dating from the early 19th century and before—will sometimes show peeling or, if dry, flaking of leather at the sides or spine. The spine labels, if any, may be missing. Check the hinges—the juncture at which the covers meet the spine—for possible wear. They may be weak or even completely broken, in which case the cover(s) will be detached or on the verge of becoming detached. It is not too expensive a task for a professional binder to reattach the covers, but on a book worth only $10 or $15 this is hardly worthwhile. Are the blank endleaves present? Very often on old books they are not. Their lack is not a matter of great concern, certainly not so important as if text leaves are missing, but the value may be brought down by 10 percent or so. Inspect the title page. Are corners torn away? Is it wrinkled or otherwise damaged? Moreover, is it present at all? Nearly all books published from the mid-16th century onward have a title page. When no title page is present, it can be assumed that this is missing, and that the volume is worth *considerably less* than if intact. A missing title page will normally result in a price reduction of at least 30 percent and up to 50 percent. In a cheap book it will entirely destroy the value. A $5 book without title page is usually placed in the bookseller's "grab-'em" tray at 25¢ or 35¢ each.

Determining whether *plates of illustration are lacking,* in illustrated books, can be difficult if no list of plates is provided. This can be accomplished easily if the plates are numbered in series; all you need do is check the numbers to see if they run consecutively. It will *not* tell you, however, if additional plates should be present *after* those found in the book. A clue can possibly be found by carefully running through the text for references to plates. The matter of missing plates is of no small consequence in early books, especially those with colored or steel-engraved plates, as the original owners quite often cut up books and framed the plates.

VALUES OF SPECIAL COPIES

Just as defective copies are worth less than the normal prices, there are many situations in which a book, by virtue of a fine binding or otherwise, carries a value higher than is normal for that particular edition. In the case of books dating from the era of cloth bindings (the third quarter of the 19th century to today), most copies that exist will be in similar bindings—those applied by the publisher—except those in which the binding became so damaged that a rebinding was necessary. However, early books, which did not carry cloth bindings, may be found in a variety of coverings. It was usual in the pre-cloth era to issue books in a very cheap unsubstantial kind of binding, such as strawboards backed with leather or merely paper, so that the book would be inexpensive enough to market to a wide audience. Some buyers chose to leave them "as they came," but others preferred to ship them off to a bindery to be encased in leather, half-leather, or whatever appealed to them. The fashion in some countries, at certain times, was for the owners of fine libraries to have their initials or heraldic shield appear in gilt on the upper cover of each volume. Other book collectors had very elaborate gold or silver tooling applied to the covers and spines of their books. Some had the covers set with ivory miniatures, etc., These special copies, when found, are naturally in a different category from ordinary specimens and generally command much higher prices. A really exquisite binding on a $50 book can result in a $200 or $300 price—more for binding than contents. Old music books are sometimes found with gilt stampings of instruments on the covers, or figures of nymphs playing harps. These are very desirable copies. It is impossible to set price guidelines because every "deluxe" binding is different from others and must be appraised in light of the age, workmanship, originality, and the quality of leather. Full morocco is the most respected and, in most circumstances, most valuable of binding leathers. Books bound in full morocco will normally carry the title and author in gilt on labels attached to the spine, and the spine will be "compartmented," that is, divided up into sections via raised bands.

TERMINOLOGY

The terms used in book collecting are far more numerous to attempt listing here in anything approaching completeness, but we herewith present a brief sampling of some of the more often encountered words and expressions. (For further information, consult *The Official Price Guide to Old Books & Autographs,* published by The House of Collectibles.)

Anonymous. This can mean either of two things, that the author is not named in the book but his identity is known, or the author is unnamed and unknown. When the former is the case, a catalogue will state "ANONYMOUS (Bartolin, Edward)" or simply "(BARTOLIN, Edward)." Whenever anything appears in brackets in a bookseller's catalogue, this means the information is deduced rather than stated in the book. The same is true of a date. "(1769)" means the work is known to have been published then but is undated. If the cataloguer is simply making an estimate, it appears as "(c. 1769)" or "(1769 ?)". The authorship of anonymous books is sometimes guessed at, too.

Association Copy. A book that once belonged to someone noteworthy, often a relative or close associate of the author, and bears evidence of having done so. The most valuable association copies are those that belonged to the author and carry his corrections or other notations.

Binder's Cloth. A cloth binding that was not applied by the publisher when the book was issued but by a bindery at a later date. It is always worth less than a copy in the publisher's binding. Nor can you tell, from a catalogue description that merely states "binder's cloth," whether the volume was bound recently or ages ago.

Boards. This can mean wooden boards, stiff paper, strawboards, or boards covered in linen, buckram, canvas, etc. Generally, though, when a book is said to be bound in boards, paper boards—either bare or covered in thin paper—can be expected. Boarded books date mostly from 1750 to 1820, the era just before cloth bindings.

Calf. A leather used in binding. The natural color is light tan to medium brown. It is rarely dyed. Calf is a good-quality leather, durable if properly cared for, but not as good-looking (in traditional opinion) as morocco.

Cheap Copy. A defective book, which the bookseller is offering at a discount and wants to be sure everybody realizes it.

Collated Perfect. The volume has been inspected page by page and come through with flying colors—everything supposed to be present is. However, the book could still be stained, mutilated, foxed, or otherwise undesirable.

Contemporary Binding. Not the original binding probably, but one applied before the book got very old. When used on books printed before 1700, it can be taken to mean no more than 25 years after publication. But, of course, it represents only an estimate, as the exact dating of bindings, in the absence of real evidence, is impossible.

Cropped. Margins cut so close by the binder that text or illustrations are shaved. This occurs mostly in old books that have been rebound several times.

Cuts. Illustrations of any kind, including photographic.

Deckle Edges. Rough page-ends, untrimmed.

Disbound. This does not mean a volume lacking its binding, but rather an unbound pamphlet or other brief work that once was part of a larger one. Values are hard to fix.

Dust Jacket (or Wrapper). Experiments with dust jackets began in the early 1800's, but they did not become common until around 1910. Even then, many volumes were without them. Their importance is greater with first editions of novels than with music books or most non-fiction.

First Edition. Ideally, the first appearance of that book. But it isn't always so simple. When a book has been published in England and America in the same year, it can be difficult or impossible to tell which came first. Also, there are many instances of writings serialized in newspapers or periodicals before appearing in book form. The term "first collected edition" refers to matter published in dribs and dribbles over the years, in various periodicals or even other books, before collected into a book of its own.

Folio. A book of large size, ranging from about 12 inches up. A royal folio stands about 18 inches, an atlas folio 24, an elephant folio 30, a double elephant folio 36.

Foxed. Brownish spots on old (sometimes not so old) paper are known as foxing. It's caused by lice, which have a particular craving for moist paper. When light it can be overlooked, but heavy foxing is a defect in most books, unless printed on paper of such poor grade that heavy foxing was inevitable. It tends to be strongest on endleaves and plates of illustrations.

Half Morocco (or Half Calf, Vellum, etc.). A binding in which the spine and an inch or two of the sides are leather, the remainder of the covers buckram or plain boards. In a quarter binding only the spine is leather, and in a three-quarter binding the corners are also leather.

Half Title. The page before the actual title page, which states the book's title but nothing else. Sometimes the reverse side of the half title carries the dedication. The lack of a half title, if the book was published with one, is a serious defect (deduct about 20 percent from the value).

Imperfect. A defective book, which could be missing just one leaf or a hundred (and the binding, too).

Large-Paper Copy. Large-paper copies had their origins in the 18th century, as a way of satisfying collectors and ordinary readers. When issuing a book of some importance, publishers were torn between putting out a really deluxe edition or keeping the price low enough to attract a wide circle of buyers. This was solved by issuing a part of the edition on small paper in a cheap binding and a limited number on large paper in a better binding. Usually the text was identical and printed from the same type. The only difference was that large-paper copies had wider margins. Additional illustrations were sometimes included, or impressions of the plates in two states. They always command a higher price than small-paper copies, sometimes much higher depending on circumstances.

Library (or Ex-Library) Copy. Books that have been in public libraries are considered less desirable by collectors than those that haven't, up to about 50 percent less desirable. Exceptions are made in the case of rare volumes.

Limited Edition. A book issued in a certain number of copies and no more, after which the type is broken up and illustration plates destroyed. To be recognized as bona fide, the number of copies must be stated in the book and each copy numbered. This is the only guarantee against the limitation number being overstepped.

Morocco. The most luxurious leather used in bookbinding. It is known in a variety of types: niger, levant, straight-grained, etc. and is made from goathide. Morocco takes a fine polish, has a wonderfully mellow glow, but does not always hold its color well. Green morocco fades to purple, and purple morocco deteriorates into a sort of mud color.

N.D. No date.

N.P. No place (of publication).

Octavo. The size of standard-format books, about 8½x6 inches. Abbreviated as 8vo.

Out of Print. No longer obtainable from the publisher. It is not so cut-and-dried as that seems to suggest, though. An edition can be out of print without a book being out of print.

Privately Printed. Financed by the author, as in subsidy publishing. Some privately printed books are offered for sale, others are just given away by the author to his friends or to libraries (which usually toss them into waste cans).

Provenance. The history of a book's ownership; a kind of family tree of the book's past owners. A book owned by famous collectors tends to be more respected than an identical copy with unpedigreed background.

Publisher's Cloth. Cloth binding (or buckram) applied by the publisher to a trade edition.

Quarto. A book format in which the size varies from 8x10 to 7x9 inches. A "small quarto" is around 6½x8.

Reading Copy. A damaged book suitable only for reading.

Remainder. When a book seems to have run its course on the market and sales are dwindling down, the publisher may dispose of unsold copies in his warehouse at a sharply reduced price. These are sold as "remainders."

Roan. A cheap grade of leather that looks like imitation leather.

Rubbed. Leather bindings on which the surface is worn or scratched are said to be rubbed. Any book handled often over a long stretch of time is sure to get rubbed.

Shaken. The book is pulling loose from the spine.

Spine. The backstrip or shelfback of a binding.

Trade Binding. A binding applied by the publisher to a trade edition, usually in cloth or buckram on books dating from the mid-1800's onward.

Unbound. Properly, this means a book issued in a binding but now lacking it. A work issued in wrappers is described as "softbound" or "stitched" or simply "wrappered".

Uncut. The edges of the leaves are untrimmed.

Unopened. The leaves have not been cut apart—sure proof the book was never read.

Vellum. Degreased calfskin, sometimes called parchment. Being white or yellowish, vellum bindings do not take gilding too well but can be decorated by blind stamping or in other fashions.

THE CARE AND REPAIR OF BOOKS

Books are not really difficult to care for. They tend to suffer more from improper handling and storage, not to mention simple neglect, than from accidents. A normal book, printed on decent paper with rag content, will survive in good condition for hundreds of years if properly looked after. Proper care means shelving in a case that is not so over-crowded that the books must be squeezed in tightly; not leaving books lying about in heaps; dusting them periodically with a feather-duster; not exposing them to moisture; holding them carefully while reading, especially books with valuable or delicate bindings. Books bound in leather, with the exception of vellum, should be dressed with an oil prep-aration twice a year. This is very simple to do. Most bookbinders sell leather dressing. A small amount on a swab of cotton, worked into the leather with a circular motion, does the trick. This renews the natural grease content of the skin, which dries out in the same fashion as does a leather handbag or pair of shoes (but do not polish books with shoe polish unless nothing better is available).

Repairs to valuable books should not be attempted by an amateur. With inexpensive books, there is no reason why a collector cannot do the job himself. Paste does the job nicely in most cases; always use either standard library paste or a polyvinyl acetate, such as "Elmer's Glue-all," rather than a clear glue. Use less than seems to be neces-sary; an excess of paste can cause soiling or other problems.

If you own valuable books in a delicate condition, or fine bindings that should not be subjected to rubbing against neighboring volumes on the shelf, you may want to consider having slipcases or boxes made for them. This is, however, rather costly.

VALUES

So far as the values stated in the following pages are concerned, it should be borne in mind that, because of the many varied factors in-volved, old books are among the most difficult of collectors' items to place price guidelines on. Aside from differences in binding, condition, and the like, one must take into account regional price differences. These do not come into play so much with the prices charged by catalogue-issuing dealers, who distribute their catalogues nationwide and make sales around the country, but are definitely a factor when buying off the shelf from local bookshops. Prices are higher in New York and Los Angeles because more book collectors are located in these cities; also, there are many dealers, and the dealers have each other

as potential customers, whereas in a smaller town there are few secondhand bookshops and not as many local collectors. A $20 book in
New York may be considerably less in the Midwest.

Price Range

BOOKS

☐ **AITKEN, ANNA LAETITIA,** *Poems, including Poem to the Origin of Song.* London, 1773	**20.00**	**25.00**
☐ **AITKEN, JOHN,** *Essays on Song-Writing* with a collection of such English Songs as are most eminent for poetical merit, to which are added some original pieces. London, n.d. c. 1770	**30.00**	**37.00**
☐ **ALBYN'S ANTHOLOGY,** or a Select Collection of the Melodies and Vocal Poetry Peculiar to Scotland and the Isles hitherto unpublished. Volume One only, Edinburgh, 1816	**37.00**	**45.00**
☐ **ALCOCK, JOHN,** *Harmonia Festi,* or a collection of canons; cheerful and serious glees and catches . . . Oblong folio, 59 pp, privately printed. Lichfield, 1791	**145.00**	**180.00**
☐ **ARNOLD, BARTHELEMON, CARTER & SHIELD,** *A Selection of the most favorite Scots Songs* chiefly pastoral, adapted for the harpsichord with an accompaniment for a violin by masters. London, n.d. c. 1780	**120.00**	**150.00**
☐ **ATHOLE COLLECTION** *of Dance Music of Scotland* compiled and arranged by James Stewart-Robertson. Two volumes, London, 1883	**23.00**	**30.00**
☐ **ATTWOOD . . . ,** *The Curfew.* A Glee for three voices. London, n.d. c. 1810	**110.00**	**135.00**
☐ **AYRES & SONGS, CHOICE,** *To Sing to the Theorbo, Lute or Bass* . . . composed by several Gentlemen of His Majesty's Musick and others. The Fourth Book, London, 1683 . . .	**375.00**	**450.00**
☐ **BATEMAN, S.,** *The Strange evolution of our illiterate National Anthem from a Rebel Song.* London, 1902	**8.00**	**11.00**

Price Range

☐ **BEAUTIES OF MELODY, THE,** *A collection of the most popular Airs, Duets, Glees, etc., of the most esteemed authors, also a selection of the most admired Irish melodies.* London, 1827 . . . .   12.00   15.00

☐ **BELLAMY, T.,** *Lyric Poetry of Glees, Madrigals, Catches, Rounds.* Performed in the Noblemen's and Gentlemen's Catch Club. London, 1840 . . . .   9.00   12.00

☐ **BORREN, C. VAN DEN,** *The Sources of Keyboard Music in England.* London, 1914 . . . .   13.00   17.00

☐ **BOSSI, C.,** *Irza. A Favourite Ballet as performed at the Kings Theatre, Haymarket.* London, n.d.c. 1805 . . . .   10.00   14.00

☐ **BOULTON, H.,** *Songs of the Four Nations; England, Scotland, Ireland, Wales.* For the most part never before published with complete words. London, 1893 . . . .   13.00   17.00

☐ **BREMNER, ROBERT,** *Thirty Scots Songs.* Adapted for a voice and harpsichord. The words by Allen Ramsey. London, n.d.c. 1770   60.00   80.00

☐ **BRITISH ORPHEUS, THE,** *Being a selection of 270 Songs and Airs adapted for the Voice, Violin, German Flutes, Flageolet, etc., with Jigs, Dances.* London, n.d.c. 1805 . . . .   20.00   25.00

☐ **BULL, HENRY L.,** *Dr. John Bull, the Queen's Master of Musicke.* London, 1937 . . . .   20.00   25.00

☐ **BUNTING . . . ,** *A General Collection of the Ancient Music of Ireland,* arranged for the piano-forte. London, 1809 . . . .   90.00   120.00

☐ **BURGH, A.,** *Anecdotes of Music,* historical and biographical in a series of letters. Three volumes, London, 1814 . . . .   80.00   110.00

☐ **BURNS, ROBERT,** *The Songs of Robert Burns.* Now first printed with the melodies for which they were written. Edited by J. C. Dick. Glasgow, 1903 . . . .   20.00   25.00

☐ **BUTLER, T. H.,** *A Select Collection of original Scottish Airs* arranged for one and two voices with Introductory and Concluding Symphonies. Glasgow, 1790 . . . .   25.00   32.00

Price Range

☐ **CALLCOTT, J. W.,** *A Musical Grammar.* London, 1806 . . . .   **100.00**   **130.00**

☐ **CHETHAM, JOHN,** *A Book of Psalmody.* Leeds, 1787 . . . .   **60.00**   **80.00**

☐ **CHRISTIE, W.,** *Traditional Ballad Airs* arranged and harmonized for the Piano-forte, from copies procured in the counties of Aberdeen, Banff and Moray, with illustrative notes. Edinburgh, 1876–81 . . . .   **110.00**   **145.00**

☐ **CLARK, R.,** *God Save the King.* An account of the National Anthen entitled "God Save the King." Folding plates, London, 1822 . . .   **30.00**   **40.00**

☐ **CLIFFORD, JAMES,** *The Divine Services and Anthems usually sung in His Majesties Chapell.* London, 1664 . . . .   **100.00**   **130.00**

☐ **COX, JOHN EDMUND,** *Musical Recollections of the Last Half-Century.* Two volumes, London, 1872 . . . .   **100.00**   **125.00**

☐ **CROSBY . . . ,** *English Musical Repository.* A choice selection of esteemed English Songs adapted for the Voice, Violin and German Flute. Edinburgh, 1811 . . . .   **20.00**   **25.00**

☐ **CROWEST, F.,** *The Story of British Music* from the earliest times to the Tudor Period. London, 1896 . . . .   **23.00**   **30.00**

☐ **CUMMINGS, W.,** *God Save the King,* origin and history of the music and words. London, 1902 . . . .   **10.00**   **13.00**

☐ **CURWEN, J. S.,** *Music at the Queen's Accession.* A paper read before the Society of Arts. London, 1897 . . . .   **6.00**   **9.00**

☐ **DAVEY . . . ,** *History of English Music.* London, 1895 . . . .   **10.00**   **13.00**

☐ **D'EGVILLE . . . ,** *Barbara and Allen.* A Favorite Ballet including the Celebrated Pas Seul. London, n.d.c. 1800 . . . .   **10.00**   **13.00**

☐ **DERMODY, T.,** *The Harp of Erin.* Two volumes, London, 1807 . . . .   **15.00**   **20.00**

☐ **DIBDIN, CHARLES,** *Six Songs* written and composed by the late celebrated Mr. Dibdin of Sans Souci, Strand and Leicester Place.

Price Range

Published by subscription for the benefit of his widow and daughter. 18 pp., London, 1816 . . . .   **13.00**   **18.00**

☐ **DIBDIN, CHARLES,** *The Songs of Charles Dibdin,* chronologically arranged with notes, biographical and critical, and the music for the best and most popular of the melodies, with new pianoforte accompaniments. Two volumes, London, 1842 . . . .   **30.00**   **38.00**

☐ **D'URFEY . . . ,** *Wit and Mirth or Pills to Purge Melancholy. Songs Compleat, Pleasant and Diverting, set to Musick by Dr. John Blow, Mr. Henry Purcell and other excellent Masters of the Town.* Three volumes. Facsimile of an 1876 facsimile of a work originally published in London, 1719–20. New York, 1959 . . . . .   **55.00**   **75.00**

☐ **ENGEL, CARL,** *The Music of the Most Ancient Nations,* particularly the Assyrian, Egyptian and Hebrew. London, n.d. 1909 . . . . . .   **45.00**   **60.00**

☐ **FAIRBURN'S EVERLASTING SONGSTER,** *being an Extensive Collection of One Thousand Naval, Love, Comic, Hunting, Bacchanalian, etc.* Songs. London, n.d. early 1800's   **100.00**   **130.00**

☐ **FITZGERALD, S. J. A.,** *Stories of Famous Songs.* The history of such well-known songs as Home Sweet Home, Auld Lang Syne, Yankee Doodle. London, 1898 . . . .   **20.00**   **25.00**

☐ **FOUNDING HYMNS,** *Psalters, Hymns and Anthems for the Foundling Chapel.* London, 1809 . . . .   **50.00**   **65.00**

☐ **FRAZER, CAPT. SIMON,** *The Airs and Melodies peculiar to the Highlands of Scotland and the Isles,* communicated in an unusual pleasing familiar state. London, 1874 . . . . . .   **50.00**   **65.00**

☐ **FULL & BY,** *Being a Collection of Verses by Persons of quality in Praise of drinking here.* London, 1920 . . . .   **13.00**   **18.00**

☐ **GAY . . . ,** *Polly, with the music prefixed to the songs. Limited to 350 copies.* London, 1923   **13.00**   **18.00**

☐ **GIBBON, J. M.,** *Melody and the Lyric from Chaucer to the Cavaliers.* London, 1930 . . .   **20.00**   **25.00**

	Price Range

☐ **GILLMAN, F.,** *Evolution of the English Hymn.* An historical survey of the origins and development of the hymns of the Christian Church. London, 1927 .... **13.00**   **18.00**

☐ **GOW . . . ,** *The Vocal Melodies of Scotland,* arranged for the pianoforte or harp, violin and violincello by Nathaniel Gow. Folio, Edinburgh, 1822 .... **45.00**   **60.00**

☐ **GRAVES, A. P.,** *The Celtic Song Book.* Representative folk songs of the six Celtic Nations. London, 1928 .... **15.00**   **20.00**

☐ **HAGUE, CHARLES,** *A Collection of Songs, Moral, Sentimental, Instructive and Amusing.* The words selected and revised by Rev. James Plumptree. The music adapted and composed by Charles Hague. London and Cambridge, 1805 .... **25.00**   **32.00**

☐ **HANDEL, GEORGE FREDERIC,** *Flavius an Opera,* as it was Perform'd at the Kings Theatre for the Royal Academy. London, n.d. 1723 .... **450.00**   **600.00**

☐ **HANDEL, GEORGE FREDERIC,** *Six Concertos for the Harpsichord or Organ (Opus 4).* London, n.d. 1738 .... **130.00**   **165.00**

☐ **HANDEL, GEORGE FREDERIC,** *The Occasional Oratorio* as it was Perform'd at Theatre Royal in Covent Garden. Second edition, London, n.d.c. 1747 .... **200.00**   **250.00**

☐ **HANDEL, GEORGE FREDERIC,** *Israel in Egypt,* an oratoria, in score, as it was originally composed by Mr. Handel. Large folio, London, n.d. 1771 .... **325.00**   **425.00**

☐ **HANDEL, GEORGE FREDERIC,** *Messiah,* an oratorio in score as it was originally perform'd. London, n.d.c. 1803 .... **210.00**   **265.00**

☐ **HANNAGAN, M. and CLANDILLON, S.,** *Songs of the Irish Gaels* with the music and English metrical translation. London, 1927 **15.00**   **20.00**

☐ **HAWKINS, JOHN,** *A General History of the Science and Practice of Music.* Five volumes, originally bound in calf. The most comprehensive history of music published in the

Price Range

English language up to that time, and the most historically valuable sourcebook of 17th- and 18th-century English music history. London, 1776 .... 1100.00   1500.00

☐ Bound in full gilt morocco 1650.00   2000.00

☐ **HAYDN and MOZART,** *The Lives of Haydn and Mozart,* translated from the French. Second edition, London, 1818 .... 60.00   80.00

☐ **HIPKINS, A. J.,** *Musical Instruments, Historic, Rare and Unique.* Illustrated by a series of 50 plates in colors, by William Gibb. Atlas folio, Artist's proof copy, one of 50. Edinburgh, 1888 .... 1600.00   2150.00

☐ **HONNEYMAN, WILLIAM C.,** *The Violin: How to Master It.* Boston, n.d.c. 1895 .... 50.00   65.00

☐ **HULLAH, JOHN,** *The History of Modern Music.* London, 1896 .... 55.00   70.00

☐ **JACKSON, V.,** *English Melodies from the 13th to the 18th Centuries.* London, 1910   20.00   25.00

☐ **JACOBS, B.,** *National Psalmody.* A collection of tunes with appropriate symphonies set to a course of psalms selected from the new version by J. T. Barrett for the services of the United Church of England and Ireland. London, 1819 .... 25.00   33.00

☐ **JEBOULT, H.,** *Somerset Composers, Musicians and Music.* London, 1923 .... 4.00   6.00

☐ **JENKINS, JOHN,** *Fancies and Ayres.* For 4 or 5 viols, two trebles and bass violin. Wellesley, 1950 .... 20.00   25.00

☐ **JONES, EDWARD,** *Musical and Poetical Relicks of the Welsh Bards,* preserved by Tradition and authentic manuscripts from very remote antiquity to the bardic times. London, 1805 .... 100.00   130.00

☐ **KIDSON ... ,** *Old English Country Dances.* London, 1890 .... 18.00   23.00

☐ **LEVERIDGE, RICHARD,** *A Collection of Songs,* with the Music. Two volumes, London, 1727 .... 425.00   550.00

Price Range

☐ **LOGIER, J. B.,** *A System of the Science of Music and Practical Composition.* London, 1827 .... 120.00 150.00

☐ **MAITLAND, J. FULLER.,** *English Music in the 19th Century.* London, 1902 .... 15.00 20.00

☐ **MAY, PHIL,** *Songs and their Singers from "Punch."* London, 1898 .... 13.00 18.00

☐ **MEE, J.,** *The Oldest Music Room in Europe.* The Oxford Music Room, its history and that of the Society, with list of music in the library. London, 1911 .... 13.00 18.00

☐ **MEYER, E.,** *English Chamber Music,* the history of a great art from the Middle Ages to Purcell. London, 1946 .... 12.00 16.00

☐ **MUSICAL CABINET,** *The New Musical and Vocal Cabinet* comprising a selection of the most favorite English, Scotch and Irish melodies. Volume one only. London, 1820 ..... 13.00 18.00

☐ **MUSICAL GOLCONDA, THE,** *Or Beauties of Melody.* A collection of the most popular airs, duets, glees of the most esteemed author ancient and modern, comprising those of Arne, Handel, Mozart, Winter . . . to which is prefixed observations and instructions on music. London, 1827 .... 15.00 20.00

☐ **NAYLOR, E. W.,** *An Elizabethan Virginal Book.* Being a critical essay on the contents of a MS. in the Fitzwilliam Museum. London, 1905 .... 20.00 25.00

☐ **NAYLOR, E. W.,** *The Poets and Music.* London, 1928 .... 12.00 16.00

☐ **NEALE, RICHARD,** *A Pocket Companion for Gentlemen and Ladies'* being a collection of the finest opera songs and airs in English and Italian. Two volumes, London, n.d. 1724 ... 375.00 475.00

☐ **NIGHTINGALE, THE,** *A Collection of Songs Set to Music.* London, n.d.c. 1825 .... 9.00 12.00

☐ **PALGRAVE, F. T.,** *The Treasury of Sacred Song.* Limited to 600 copies, Oxford, 1889 9.00 12.00

☐ **PURCELL,** *The Beauties of Purcell,* dedicated by permission to Miss Susan Beckford in two volumes Consisting of the most favor-

Price Range

ite songs, duets, trios, etc., selected from the
various works of the Great Master. Two vol-
umes, London, 1819 . . . .   35.00   45.00

SHEET MUSIC

One of the most popular fields of music-related collectibles, sheet
music—or "song sheets"—offer limitless possibilities. While space pro-
hibits us from listing the very earliest specimens, music sheets as old
as 200 years and even older exist. Probably close to a million have been
published. They can be collected by song type, by composer, by era
(such as swing-age sheets), or by the cover art. Those carrying photos
of top celebrities on the cover are always worth a premium. If the star
is someone like Al Jolson and the sheet dates to the early part of his
career (say before 1920), you have a very in-demand item. Many hobbyists like to frame their song sheets. For a large collection, storage in
file folders or boxes is most logical. Valuable specimens can be stored
in mylar envelopes to guard against deterioration, and an indexing system can be set up to help you find any desired sheet.

As with paper collectibles in general, those with frayed edges, stain-
ing, or other damage have less value than well-preserved examples.
Reprints—which are common—are also of less value. Some reprints
are included below to give an idea of their value—they are clearly indicated in the listings. But please note that a reprint is different from a
facsimile or reproduction. A reprint of a song sheet was issued by a
music publisher and sold in the same fashion as any other song sheet.
Therefore, it certainly ranks as "collectible," even though its value is
not as high as the original's. A facsimile is a reprint made by someone
other than a music publisher and is not desirable to collectors.

Price Range

☐ **After I've Called You Sweetheart (How
Can I Call You Friend),** words by Bernie
Grossman, music by Little Jack Little, pub.
Milton Weil, inset Little Jack Little, © 1927   3.00   5.00
☐ **Alexander's Ragtime Band,** by Irving Berlin,
pub. Standard Music (reprint) 2.25   3.00
☐ **All I Want Is You,** lyric and music by Benny
Davis, Harry Akst and Sidney Clare, Starmer
cover, inset Corinne Arbuckle, © 1927 . . . .   3.00   5.00

Price Range

☐ **All or Nothing at All,** Lawrence/Altman; photos of Harry James and Frank Sinatra on cover, Leeds Music Corp, ⓒ 1940 . . . .   2.00   5.00

☐ **America Forever March,** by E. T. Paull, large-format color litho of Columbia with prominent figure of eagle, flag and shield, ⓒ 1898 . . . .   12.00   18.00

☐ **Among My Souvenirs,** words by Edgar Leslie, music by Horatio Nicholls, ⓒ 1927 . . . .   2.25   3.00

☐ **Annie Doesn't Live Here Anymore,** lyric by Joe Young and Johnny Burke, music by Harold Spina, inset Guy Lombardo, ⓒ 1933 . . .   2.25   3.00

☐ **Arm in Arm,** words by Ned Washington, music by Frances Zinman and Victor Young, inset Arthur Tracy, the Street Singer, ⓒ 1932   2.25   3.00

☐ **The Army Air Corps,** words and music by Robert Crawford, pub. Carl Fischer, 1942 edition 2.25   3.00

☐ **As You Desire Me,** words and music by Allie Wruble, inset Morton Downey, pub. Keit Engel, ⓒ 1932 . . . .   3.00   4.00

☐ **Away Down South in Heaven,** words by Bud Green, music by Harry Warren, Barbelle cover, ⓒ 1927 . . . .   2.00   3.00

☐ **Battle of the Nations,** by E. T. Paull, large-format color litho of war scene, horse-drawn artillery, zeppelin in sky, bombs exploding, ⓒ 1915 . . . .   12.00   18.00

☐ **(Dance) Ballerina (Dance),** lyric by Bob Russell, music by Carl Sigman, inset Vaughn Monroe, pub. Jefferson Music, ⓒ 1947 . . . .   2.00   3.00

☐ **Bebe,** lyric by Sam Coslow, music by Abner Silver, pub. W, inset Bebe Daniels, ⓒ 1923   2.25   4.00

☐ **Because I Love You,** by Irving Berlin, Leff cover, ⓒ 1926 . . . .   2.25   3.00

☐ **Because of You,** lyric by Walter Hirsch, music by Ted Fiorito, pub. Feist, ⓒ 1925 . .   3.00   4.00

☐ **Beside a Babbling Brook,** lyric by Gus Kahn, music by Walter Donaldson, inset Karyl Norman, ⓒ 1923 . . . .   2.25   3.00

Price Range

☐ **Blue Flame,** lyric by Leo Corday, music by James Noble and Joe Bishop, nice photo Woody Herman, his theme song, recorded on Decca Record No. 3643, pub. Charling Music, blue printing of cover shows through on inside pages, © 1943 . . . .   **3.50**   **5.00**

☐ **Blue Grass,** by B. G. DeSylva, Lew Brown and Ray Henderson, © 1928 . . . .   **2.25**   **4.00**

☐ **(I've Got The) Blue Ridge Blues,** lyric by Chas. A. Mason, music by Chas. S. Cooke and Richard Whiting **2.25**   **4.00**

☐ **Breeze (Blow My Baby Back to Me),** by Ballard MacDonald, Joe Goodwin and James F. Hanley, small inset Owsley and O'Day, black face, © 1919 . . . .   **3.50**   **5.00**

☐ **Broken Blossoms,** lyric by Ballard MacDonald, music by A. Robert King, © 1919 . . . . .   **3.50**   **5.00**

☐ **Budweiser's A Friend of Mine,** Bryan/Furth, photo Chas. J. Ross, decorative writing on cover, from Ziegfeld's Review "Follies of 1907," Shapiro pub., © 1907 . . . .   **4.00**   **8.00**

☐ **Burgundy,** by Tommy Malie, Jimmy Steiger, Jimmy Steiger and Harry Richman, inset Albert E. Short, Musical Director Capitol Theatre, Chicago, pub. Frank Clark, Inc., Barbelle cover, © 1925 . . . .   **2.25**   **3.00**

☐ **Burning of Rome,** by E. T. Paull, large-format color litho of Rome in flames, vivid fire scene, small figure of Nero fiddling, © 1903 . . . . . .   **10.00**   **15.00**

☐ **Bye Bye Blackbird,** by Dixon/Henderson; strolling boy and girl, large photo of Gus Edwards on cover, Jerome Remick & Co., © 1926 . . . .   **2.00**   **4.00**

☐ **Bye Lo,** words and music by Ray Perkins, © 1919 . . . .   **2.25**   **3.00**

☐ **By the Campfire,** lyric by Mary Elizabeth Girling, music by Percy Wenrich, pub. Feist, © 1919 . . . .   **2.25**   **3.00**

☐ **Carnival King,** by Elicker, arr. Paull, large-format color litho, front of parade scene, people in vivid costumes, king above the crowd, © 1911 . . . .   **17.00**   **22.00**

**All the King's Horses,
A Little White Gardenia,**
words and music by Sam Coslow,
pub. Famous Music Corp.,
$3.00–$5.00.

**Artists and Models,
Whispers in the Dark,**
words and music by Leo Robin
and Frederick Hollander,
pub. Famous Music Corp.,
$2.50–$5.00.

Price Range

☐ **Carolina in the Morning,** lyric by Gus Kahn, music by Walter Donaldson, inset Mildred Patrick, penciled number on cover, © 1922   2.25   3.00

☐ As above, inset Maurice Sherman 2.25   3.00

☐ **(I Am Always Building) Castles in the Air,** words by Ted Garton, music by A. Fred Phillips, pub. Garton music, M. M. Fisher cover, © 1919 . . . .   4.50   6.00

☐ **Catch a Falling Star,** words and music by Paul Vance and Lee Pockriss, photo Perry Como, © 1954 . . . .   2.25   3.00

☐ **Charge of the Light Brigade,** by E. T. Paull, large-format color litho, reproduction of famous painting connected with the charge of the 600, © 1896 . . . .   15.00   20.00

☐ **Chariot Race, or Ben Hur March,** by E. T. Paull, large-format color litho, depicts violent chariot race in Roman arena, one down, two trying to get around, © 1894 . . . .   10.00   15.00

☐ **Cinna Mon Sinner (Selling Lollipop Lies),** inset Tony Bennett, pub. Raleigh Music, © 1954 . . . .   2.25   3.00

☐ **Circus Parade,** by E. T. Paull, large-format color litho, vivid parade of animals and circus acts around the center ring, © 1904 . . . . . .   22.00   28.00

☐ **Collegiate,** words and music by Moe Jaffee and Nat Bronx, pub. SB, inset Fred Damons Greenwich Villagers, © 1925 . . . .   3.00   4.00

☐ **Come in Out of the Draft; or, the Disconsolate Conscript,** Rossiter/Walters; title and six verses printed on cover, Civil War comic song, Lee & Walker pub., © 1863 . . . .   10.00   15.00

☐ **The Creaking Old Mill on the Creek,** by Al Lewis, Larry Stock and Vincent Rose, nice photo Sammy Kaye, © 1940 . . . .   2.25   3.00

☐ **Croon a Little Lullaby,** lyric by Harry D. Kerr, music by Chris Schonberg and Clyde Baker, pub. Sherman Clay, inset Jack Coakley and his Cabirians, © 1925 . . . .   2.25   3.00

☐ **Crying For You,** by Ned Miller and Chester Cohn, inset Moher and Eldridge, pub. Feist, © 1923 . . . .   2.25   3.00

Price Range

☐ **Danube Waves,** by J. Ivonovici, pub. Morris, Key of "C" EXC 1.25   2.00

☐ **The Dardanella Blues,** words by Fred Fisher, music by Johnny Black, Wohlman cover, pub. Fred Fisher, © 1920 . . . .   3.00   4.00

☐ **Dashing Cavaliers,** by Braham and Paull, large-format color litho, galloping horse and rider cover, fancy armor and helmets, © 1911 . . . .   18.00   22.00

☐ **Dawn of the Century,** by E. T. Paull, woman with light bulb on her headband stands on a winged wheel above the earth, turn-of-the-century inventions float in the sunrise behind her, large-format color litho, © 1900 . . . . . .   25.00   35.00

☐ **Dawn of Tomorrow,** words by Jeanne Gravelle, music by Joe Green, pub. Henry Waterson, © 1927 . . . .   1.25   2.00

☐ **Dear Heart,** words by Jean LeFavre, music by W. C. Polla, beautiful colored cover, pub. by Church, © 1919 . . . .   3.00   4.00

☐ **Dearie,** by Bob Hilliard and Dave Mann, pub. Laurel, © 1950 . . . .   3.00   4.00

☐ **Dinah,** Lewis/Young; drawing of a girl with fan, photo of Rube Wolf on cover, Henry Waterson Inc. © 1925 . . . .   2.00   4.00

☐ **Don't Go To Sleep,** lyric by Arthur Freed, music by Oscar Levant, inset John L. Fogarty, © 1932 . . . .   2.25   3.00

☐ **Down by the Meadow Brook,** words by Edgar Leslie, music by Pete Wendling, Barbelle cover, © 1919 . . . .   2.25   3.00

☐ **Don't Let the Stars Get in Your Eyes,** by Alan Qillwt, star Sales, inset Perry Como, inked and pencilled instructions inside, © 1952 . . . .   1.50   2.50

☐ **Do You Ever Think of Me,** lyric by Harry D. Kerr, music by Earl Burtnett, © 1920 . . . . .   2.00   3.00

☐ **Down the Trail to Home Sweet Home,** by Ernest R. Ball, © 1920 . . . .   2.00   3.00

☐ **Dream Train,** words by Charles Newman, music by Billy Baskette, photo Guy Lombardo, pub. M. Weil, © 1928 . . . .   2.00   3.00

Broadway Rhythm,
Irresistible You,
words and music by Don Raye
and Gene DePaul,
pub. Leo Feist, Inc.,
$1.50–$3.00.

Carefree,
I Used to be Color Blind,
words and music by Irving Berlin,
pub. Irving Berlin, Inc.,
$3.00–$5.00.

Price Range

☐ **Dreamy Melody,** words and music by Ted Koehler, Frank Magine, and C. Naset, inset The Misses Dennis: Ruth, Ann, and Cherie, © 1922 .... **2.50** **3.50**

☐ **(You Know I Know) Ev'rything's Made for Love,** by Howard Johnson, Charles Tobias and Al Sherman, Aileen Stanley photo on cover, © 1926 .... **2.75** **3.50**

☐ **Falling in Love with You,** lyrics by Benny Davis, music by Joseph Meyer, © 1926 ... **2.75** **3.50**

☐ **Feather Your Nest,** by Kendis and Brockman and Howard Johnson, inset Anna Chandler, pub. Feist, © 1920 .... **2.75** **3.50**

☐ **Flashlight,** by Edwin Ellis, arr. Paull, large-format color, night scene of boats on a stormy sea being guided by large lighthouse, © 1909 .... **20.00** **30.00**

☐ **Flat Foot Floogee,** Gaillard, Stewart & Green; busy cover with sketches of dancers and musicians, Green Bros. & Knight, © 1938 .... **3.00** **6.00**

☐ **(That's Just My Way of) Forgetting You,** by DeSylva, Brown and Henderson, Pud Lane cover, © 1928 .... **2.75** **3.50**

☐ **Forgive Me,** words by Jack Yellen, music by Milton Ager, inset Grace Hayes, Barbelle cover, © 1927 .... **3.00** **4.00**

☐ **Four Horsemen of the Apocalypse,** by E. T. Paull, standard format color cover by Starmer, picturing four end-of-the-world horsemen as described in the Bible, © 1924 ... **22.00** **28.00**

☐ **Franklin D. Roosevelt,** Caesar/Woodin, "Dedicated to the 32nd President of the United States of America," large photo of F.D.R. on red, white, and blue cover, Miller Music Inc. pub., © 1933 .... **10.00** **15.00**

☐ **(On the) 'Gin 'Gin 'Ginny Shore,** words by Edgar Leslie, music by Walter Donaldson, pub. SB, inset Adele Rowland, cover is southern scene with river boat, © 1922 .... **3.00** **4.00**

Price Range

☐ **Girls,** lyric by Alfred Bryan, music by Harry Carroll, Starmer cover, photos Five Geo White Girls, © 1919 . . . . 4.00 6.00

☐ **Give Me a Ukelele (And a Ukelele Baby),** by Lew Brown and Gene Williams, Starmer cover, © 1926 . . . . 2.25 3.25

☐ **Give My Regards to Broadway,** by George M. Cohan, reprint 2.25 3.25

☐ **The Glory of Love,** by Billy Hill; large photo of Bing Crosby set against sketch of boy and girl on cover, Shapiro, Bernstein & Co. © 1936 . . . . 2.00 4.50

☐ **Good Night, Wherever You Are,** photo Ginny Sims on cover, S-VG, © 1944 . . . . . . 2.25 3.25

☐ **Granny,** words by L. Wolfe Gilbert, music by Alex Belledna, pub. Gilbert & Freidland, De-Tacaks cover, © 1929 . . . . 2.25 4.00

☐ **Granny (You're My Mammy's Mammy),** music by Harry Akst, © 1921 . . . . 3.00 6.00

☐ **The Gypsy,** words and music by Billy Reid, pub. Leeds, © 1946 . . . . 2.50 4.00

☐ **Hands Across the Table,** lyrics by Mitchell Parish, music by Dean DeLettre, photo Lucienne Boyer, pub. Mill, © 1934 . . . . 2.50 4.00

☐ **Happiness (Where Are You),** by L. Wolfe Gilbert and Leon Flatow, pub. Gilbert & Friedland, © 1919 . . . . 4.50 6.00

☐ **(There's a) Harbor of Dream Boats (Anchored on Moonlight Bay,** by Nat Burton, Al Sherman, and Arthur Altman, inset "The Townsmen," © 1943 . . . . 2.00 3.00

☐ **He,** lyric by Richard Mullan, music by Jack Richards, inset McGuire Sisters, pub. Avas, © 1954 . . . . 3.00 4.00

☐ **Heaven's Artillery,** March and Two-Step, by Harry J. Lincoln, W. J. Dittmar (?) cover, pub. Vandersloot, © 1904 . . . . 5.00 7.00

☐ **He's My Uncle,** lyric by Charles Newman, music by Lew Pollack, introduced by Dick Powell on the "Maxwell House Coffee Time" with special version for schoolchildren, © 1940 . . . . 4.00 5.50

Price Range

☐ **He She and Me,** by Carmen Lombardo and Charles Newman, inset "Cookie" and his Ginger Snaps, pub. M. Weil, © 1929 ......   3.00   4.00

☐ **Hillbilly Fever,** by George Vaughn, inset Kenny Roberts, pub. Forrest Music, © 1950   2.25   3.00

☐ **Home Again Blues,** by Irving Berlin and Harry Akst, © 1920 ....   2.25   3.00

☐ **Home Coming March,** by E. T. Paull, large-format color litho, large crowds watch a parade marching through a large bunting-decorated arch, insert scenes at corners depict different types of homecomings, © 1908   15.00   20.00

☐ **Home Sweet Home Polka,** words by Leni Mason, melody by Arthur Berman, pub. Central Music, inset Texas Jim Robertson, © 1948 ....   3.00   4.00

☐ **Honey Hula,** Hawaiian Waltz Song, words and music by Fred Fisher, pub. Fred Fisher, © 1921 ....   3.00   4.00

☐ **Hop Scotch Polka,** words and music by William Whitlock, Carl Sigman and Gene Rayburn, inset Gene Rayburn and Dee Finch with mike from WNEW, pub. Cromwell Music, © 1949 ....   3.00   4.00

☐ **Hot Lips,** words and music by Henry Busse, Henry Lange, and Lou Davis, photo Henry Busse, pub. Feist, penciled numbers on cover, © 1922 ....   3.00   4.00

☐ **How Do You Do,** as introduced by Phil Fleming, Harry Geise, and Vernon Rick, inset Carl Caul, special verses by Charlie Harrison and Cal De Voll, pub. Ted Browne, © 1924 ....   2.25   3.00

☐ **(I'm Tellin' the Birds—Tellin' the Bees) How I love You,** by Cliff Friend and Lew Brown, © 1926 ....   2.25   3.00

☐ **Hummingbird,** words and music by Don Robertson, photo Les Paul and Mary Ford, pub. Ross Jungnickel, © 1955 ....   2.25   3.00

☐ **The Hurricane,** by S. L. Alpert, arr. E. T. Paull, large-format color litho, men cling to mast of sinking ship, another troubled ship in the distance, © 1906 ....   22.00   28.00

The Dolly Sisters,
I Can't Begin to Tell You,
words by Mack Gordon,
music by James Monaco,
pub. BVC, Inc.,
$3.00–$7.00.

The Gay Bride,
Mississippi Honeymoon,
words by Gus Kahn,
music by Walter Donaldson,
pub. by Robbins Music Corp.,
$2.50–$4.50.

Price Range

☐ **I Ain't Nobody's Darling,** words by Elmer Hughes, music by Robert King, Wohlman cover, pub. Skidmore Music, © 1921 ..... 2.25 3.00

☐ **I Love You All the More,** words by Darl Mac-Boyle, music by Nat Vincent, E. E. Walton cover, pub. George T. Worth, © 1919 ..... 4.00 5.50

☐ **I Love You So,** lyric by Gus Kahn, music by Ted Fiorito, pub. Feist, © 1930 .... 3.00 4.00

☐ **I Said My Pajamas (And Put on My Prayers),** words and music by Eddie Pola and Geo. Wyle, insets Fran Warren and Ton Marin, pub. Leeds, © 1950 .... 3.00 4.00

☐ **I Wanna Go Home (with You),** words and music by Jack Joyce and Joe Cancullo, pub. Paxton, inset Perry Como, © 1945 .... 3.00 4.00

☐ **I Wouldn't Change You for the World,** words by Charles Newman, music by Isham Jones, inset Tom Brown, pub. Olman, © 1931 .... 2.25 3.00

☐ **Ida I Do,** words by Gus Kahn, music by Isham Jones, pub. IB, Perret cover, © 1925 ..... 3.00 4.00

☐ **I Love to Fall Asleep and Wake Up in My Mammy's Arms,** words by Sam Lewis and Joe Young, music by Fred E. Ahlert, © 1920 2.25 3.00

☐ **(I'd Climb the Highest Mountain) If I Knew I'd Find You,** words and music by Lew Brown and Sidney Clare, inset Grace Aldrich, Leff cover, © 1926 .... 2.25 3.00

☐ **I'll Be Happy When the Preacher Makes You Mine,** words by Sam M. Lewis and Joe Young, music by Walter Donaldson, © 1919 3.00 4.00

☐ **I'll Be With You When the Clouds Roll By,** by the Three White Kuhns: Robert, Paul, and Charles, inset Joe Whitehear "A Fool There Was," Starmer cover, © 1922 .... 3.00 4.00

☐ **I'm A Dreamer That's Chasing Bubbles,** words by Geo. A. Little, music by Frank Magine, Wohlman cover, pub. Jack Mills, © 1919 .... 2.25 3.00

It's Love Again,
I Nearly Let Love Go
Slipping Through My Fingers,
words and music by Harry Woods,
pub. Chappell & Co.,
$1.50–$3.00.

Johnny Doughboy
Found a Rose in Ireland,
words and music by Kay Twomey
and Al Goodhart,
pub. Crawford Music Corp.,
$2.00–$3.50.

Price Range

☐ **I'm Bringing a Red, Red Rose,** Kahn/Donaldson; drawing of cowgirl on bronco on cover, from Ziegfeld's production "Whoopee" with Eddie Cantor, Walter Donaldson Pub. © 1928 . . . .   2.00   4.00

☐ **I'm Glad There Is You,** words and music by Paul Madeira and Jimmy Dorsey, inset Dorsey, pub. Mayfair, © 1942 . . . .   2.25   3.00

☐ **I'm In Heaven (When I'm In My Mother's Arms),** by Howard Johnson, Cliff Hess, and Milton Ager, pub. Feist, © 1920 . . . .   3.00   4.00

☐ **I'm On My Way Home,** by Irving Berlin, Leff cover, © 1926 . . . .   2.25   3.00

☐ **I'm Sorry Sally,** words by Gus Kahn, music by Ted Fiorito, pub. Feist, © 1928 . . . .   2.25   3.00

☐ **In a Shanty in Old Shanty Town,** words and music by Joe Young, John Siras, and Little Jack Little, inset Abe Lyman, © 1932 . . . . .   2.25   3.00

☐ **In a Little Garden (You Made Paradise),** words by Earl Whittemore, music by Felice S. Iula, Starmer cover, © 1926 . . . .   2.25   3.00

☐ **I Found a Rose (In the Devil's Garden),** words and music by Willie Raskin and Fred Fisher, pub. Fisher, Goldbeck cover, © 1921   2.25   3.00

☐ **Indian Dawn,** poem by Charles O. Roos, music by J. S. Zamecnik, pub. Fox, © 1924   2.25   3.00

☐ **Indianola,** by S. R. Henry and D. Onivas, pub. Jos. Stern, Starmer cover (Indian with head dress, blue and white), © 1918 . . . .   2.00   3.00

☐ **It Is No Secret (What God Can Do),** words and music by Stuart Hamblen, pub. Duchess, © 1950 . . . .   2.00   3.00

☐ **It's All Over Now,** words and music by Sunny Skylar and Don Marcotte, photos 12 recording artists, © 1946 . . . .   4.00   5.50

☐ **It's A Long Way to Berlin But We'll Get There,** Fields/Flatow; drawing of marching soldiers, photo of Maurice Burkhart inset, Feist pub., © 1917 . . . .   2.00   5.00

☐ **It's Been a Long Long Time,** lyric by Sammy Cahn, music by Jule Styne, photo Stan Kenton, pub. Morris © 1945 . . . .   2.25   3.00

Price Range

☐ **It's Never Too Late to Be Sorry,** words by J. E. Dempsy, music by Jos. A. Burke, pub. Stasney, © 1918 ....   2.25   3.00

☐ **I've Made Up My Mind to Forget You (But I Can't Let You Out of My Heart),** words and music by May Tully and Martin Broones, Perret cover, © 1923 ....   2.25   3.00

☐ **Ivory Tower,** words and music by Jack Fulton and Lois Steele, inset Cathy Carr, pub. Melrose, © 1956 ....   2.25   3.00

☐ **Johnny Doughboy Found a Rose in Ireland,** Twomey/Goodhart; large photo of Kate Smith on cover, Crawford Music Corp. © 1942 ....   2.00   4.00

☐ **Johnny Is the Boy for Me,** lyrics by Marcel Stillman and Paddy Roberts, music by Les Paul, photos Les Paul and Mary Ford, pub. Iris Music, © 1953 ....   2.25   3.00

☐ **The Jolly Blacksmiths,** by Braham and E. T. Paull, large-format color litho of smithing scene, E. T. Paull himself is the head smith, also pictured are two strikers and a boy outside the shop holding a horse, © 1905 ...   15.00   20.00

☐ **Just a Little Drink,** words and music by Byron Gay, comical cover, © 1925 ....   2.25   3.00

☐ **Just a Little Fond Affection,** by Elton Box, Desmond Cox, and Lewis Ilda, pub. Skidmore, © 1944 ....   2.25   3.00

☐ **Just a Little Longer,** by Irving Berlin, Leff cover, pub. IB, © 1926 ....   2.25   3.00

☐ **Just Around the Corner (May Be Sunshine for You),** lyric by Dolph Singer, music by Harry Von Tilzer, inset Ted Lewis, © 1925   2.25   3.00

☐ **Just a Prayer Away,** words by Charles Tobias, music by David Kap, inset Mel Cooper, © 1944 ....   2.25   3.00

☐ **Just Between Friends,** words and music by Robert Mellin and Gerald Rogers, pub. Mellin, © 1955 ....   3.25   4.50

Price Range

☐ **Just Say I Love Her** (Dicitencello Fuie), lyric by Martin Kalmanoff and San Ward, music by Jack Val and Jimmy Dale, pub. Larry Spier, © 1950 .... 3.25 4.50

☐ **Kaiser Jubilee March,** by E. T. Paull, large-format color litho, cover pictures E. T. Paull in elaborate uniform offering a rose to a medallion carved with the image of William II of Germany, © 1913 .... 28.00 35.00

☐ **Keep It a Secret,** by Jessie May Robinson, inset Jo Stafford, Nick cover 2.00 3.00

☐ **Kiki,** words and music by George A. Little, Paul Hosang, and Art Sizemore, pub. Harold Rossiter, © 1928 .... 2.00 3.00

☐ **Kiss Me Goodnight,** words by Archie Gottler, music by Horatio Nicholls, photo Morton Downey, © 1931 .... 3.00 4.00

☐ **La Cucarachua,** English text by Stanley Adams, with guitar chords, inset Don Pedro, pub. Calumet 2.25 3.00

☐ **The Lady from 29 Palms,** words and music by Allie Wrubel, pub. Martin Music, © 1947 2.25 3.00

☐ **Lady of Spain,** words by Erell Reaves, music by Tolchard Evans, photo Eddie Fisher, pub. Fox, © 1944 .... 2.25 3.00

☐ **Land of Dreams,** lyrics by Norman Gimbel, music by Eddie Heywood, inset Hugo Winterhalter, pub. Meridian, © 1954 .... 2.25 3.00

☐ **Last Night I Dreamed You Kissed Me,** lyric by Gus Kahn, music by Carmen Lombardo, pub. Feist, © 1928 .... 2.25 3.00

☐ **Laughing at Life,** lyric by Nick and Chas. Kenny, music by Cornell and Bob Todd, inset Bert Lown, © 1930 .... 3.00 4.00

☐ **Laura,** lyric by Johnny Mercer, music by David Raksin, © 1945 .... 2.25 3.00

☐ **Lay My Head Beneath a Rose,** words by W. Madison, music by G. Falkenstein, Cameron covern, inset Ernest Morrison 2.25 3.00

☐ **Let Me Know,** words and music by Slim Willet, inset Willet, pub. 4 Star Sales, © 1953 2.25 3.00

	Price Range	

☐ **Let the Rest of the World Go By,** lyric by J. Kiern Brennan music by Ernest R. Ball **2.25** **3.00**

☐ **Lisbon Antigua (In Old Lisbon),** lyric by Harry Dupree, music by Raul Portela, J. Galhardo, and A. do Vale, pub. Southern Music, inset Nelson Riddle, © 1954 reprint **2.25** **3.00**

☐ **Little Curly Hair in a High Chair,** words by Charles Tobias, music by Nat Simon, pub. Leo Feist, © 1940 reprint **2.25** **3.00**

☐ **(Watch, Hope and Wait) Little Girl (I'm Coming Back to You),** words by Lew Brown, music by Will Clayton, © 1918, near mint **2.25** **3.00**

☐ **Little Grass Shack (In Kealakekua),** words and music by by Bill Cogswell and Johnny Noble, inset Ted Fiorito, © 1934 .... **3.00** **4.00**

☐ **Little Log Cabin of Dreams,** words and music by James F. Hanely and Eddie Dowling, © 1927 .... **2.25** **3.00**

☐ **A Little on the Lonely Side,** music and lyric by Dick Robertdon, James Cavanaugh, Frank Weldon, inset George Olsen, pub. Advanced, © 1944 .... **2.50** **3.75**

☐ **Little White Lies,** by Walter Donaldson, inset red photo Rudy Vallee, pub. W. Donaldson, © 1930 .... **2.50** **3.75**

☐ **Lonesome and Sorry,** by Benny Davis and Con Conrad, pub. Henry Waterson, inset Lou Raderman, Barbelle cover, © 1926 .... **2.50** **3.75**

☐ **Those Lonesome Nights,** by Gus Kahn, Harry Akst, and Richard Whiting, © 1931 .. **2.50** **3.75**

☐ **Looking at the World (Thru Rose Colored Glasses),** by Tommie Malie and Jimmy Steiger, inset Jack Osterman, pub. Weil, © 1926 .... **2.25** **3.00**

☐ **Lost (A Wonderful Girl),** words by Benny Davis, music by James Hanley **2.25** **3.00**

☐ **The Love Bug Will Bite You (If You Don't Watch Out),** words and music by Pinky Tomlin, photo Pinky Tomlin, © 1937 .... **2.25** **3.00**

☐ **Love Every Moment You Live,** by Bennie Lowe, Kal Mann, and Art Singer, inset June Valli, pub. Meridian, © 1953 .... **2.25** **3.00**

The Little Cherub,
My Irish Rosie,
words by W.M. Jerome,
music by Jean Schwartz,
$3.50–$5.00.

Marianne,
Hang on to Me,
words by Raymond Klages,
music by Jesse Greek,
pub. Robbins Music Corp.,
$2.50–$4.00.

Price Range

☐ **Love Is a Melody,** words and music by David Sokoloff and Charles F. Shisler, photo Patti Clayton, pub. J. W. Pepper, © 1947 ......   2.25   3.00

☐ **Mama Don't Want No Peas an' Rice an' Coconut Oil,** by L. Wolfe Gilbert and L. Charles, pub. Marks, © 1931 ....   3.00   4.00

☐ **Mambo Italiano,** by Bob Merrill, inset Rosemary Clooney, pub. Ryan Music, © 1954 ..   2.25   3.00

☐ **The Man Upstairs,** by Dorinda Morgan, Harold Stanley, and Gerry Manners, inset Kay Starr, pub. Vesta Music, © 1954 ....   2.25   3.00

☐ **Managua Nicaragua,** lyric by Albert Gamse, music by Irving Fields, photo Guy Lombardo, pub. Encore, © 1946 ....   2.25   3.00

☐ **Manhattan Serenade,** music by Louis Alter, lyric by Harold Adamson, photo Guy Lombardo 2.25   3.00

☐ **Many Happy Returns of the Day,** lyric by Al Dubin, music by Joe Burke, inset Russ Columbo, © 1931 ....   2.25   3.00

☐ **Masquerade,** by C. F. Krell, arr. E. T. Paull, large-format color litho, colorful scene of masked ball, with party favors in the border graphics, © 1907 ....   18.00   23.00

☐ **Maybe It's Because,** lyric by Harry Ruby, music by Johnny Scott, inset Andy and Della Russell, © 1949 ....   2.25   3.00

☐ **Meadow-Lark,** by Ted Fiorito and Hal Keidel, © 1926 ....   2.25   3.00

☐ **Mellow Mountain Moon,** by Fred Howard and Nat Vincent, pub. Calument, inset Herbie Kay, © 1930 ....   1.50   2.00

☐ **The Melody That Made You Mine,** words by Cliff Friend, music by W. C. Polla, inset Vincent Lopez, © 1925 ....   2.25   3.00

☐ **Memories of France,** words by Al Dubin, music by Russell Robinson, pub. WBS, © 1928 ....   2.25   3.00

☐ **Memories of Virginia,** pub. Weile Pub. St. Louis, © 1918 ....   2.25   3.00

Price Range

☐ **The Merry-Go-Round Broke Down,** words and music by Cliff Friend and Dave Franklin, inset Guy Lombardo, © 1937 . . . .   2.25   3.00

☐ **Midnight Fire Alarm,** by Harry J. Lincoln, arr. E. T. Paull, large-format color litho of old three-horse fire engine charging down a street, belching smoke and fire from its boiler, © 1900 . . . .   12.00   18.00

☐ **Midnight Flyer,** by Frederick Hager, arr. E. T. Paull, large-format color litho, remarkable detailed picture of Colorado Express pulling out of the station, © 1903 . . . .   22.00   28.00

☐ **Midnight Rose,** lyric by Sidney Mitchell, music by Lew Pollack, inset Friend and Sparling, Barbelle cover, © 1923 . . . .   2.25   3.00

☐ **Midnight Waltz,** lyric by Gus Kahn, music by Walter Donaldson, inset Bernie Cumming's Recording Orchestra, pub. Feist, © 1925 . .   2.25   3.00

☐ **Moments to Remember,** lyric by Al Stillman, music by Robert Allwn, insets Four Lads, pub. Beaver Music, © 1955 . . . .   2.25   3.00

☐ **Moonbeam Kiss Her for Me,** lyric by Mort Dixon, music by Harry Woods, inset Geo. Lipschultz, Leff cover, © 1927 . . . .   2.25   3.00

☐ **Moonlight and Roses,** by Edwin H. Lemare and Neil Moret, pub. Moret, B&W, inset Nell Gwynn, © 1925 . . . .   2.25   3.00

☐ **Moonlight Down in Lover's Lane,** words by George Pitman and Bartley Costello, music by Max Kortlander, pub. Joe Davis, © 1933   2.25   3.00

☐ **Moonlight on the Ganges,** words by Chester Wallace, music by Sherman Myers 2.25   3.00

☐ **Moon Love,** by Mack David, Mac Davis, and Andre Kostelanetz, Glenn Miller with trombone on back cover, © 1939 near mint . . .   5.00   7.00

☐ **Moon Melody,** by Martin Broones, pub. Schirmer, © 1935 . . . .   2.25   3.00

☐ **Muddy Water (A Mississippi Moan),** words by "Jo" Trent, music by Peter DeRose and Harry Richman, inset Nora Bayes 2.25   3.00

Price Range

☐ **(Put Another Nickel In) Music! Music! Music!,** words and music by Stephan Weiss and Bernie Baum, inset Teresa Brewer, pub. Cromwell, © 1950 . . . .   2.25   3.00

☐ **My Blue Heaven,** words by George Whiting, music by Walter Donaldson, pub. Feist, © 1927 reprint 2.25   3.00

☐ **My Blue Ridge Mountain Home,** words and music by Carson Robison featured by Vernon Dahlhart, both photos on cover, pub. Triangle Music, © 1927 . . . .   2.25   3.00

☐ **My Cabin of Dreams,** by Nick Kenny, Al Frazzini, and Nat Madison, inset Nano Rodrigo, © 1937 . . . .   2.25   3.00

☐ **My Castles in the Air Are Tumbling Down,** words by Arthur J. Lamb, music by W. C. Polla, pub. Church, beautiful colored litho by The Knapp Co., © 1919 . . . .   2.25   3.00

☐ **My Dream Christmas,** by Nancy North and Stan Hadley, pub. Life Music, Barbelle cover, nice winter scene, © 1950 . . . .   2.25   3.00

☐ **My Dreams Are Getting Better All the Time,** lyrics by Mann Curtis, music by Vic Mizzy, inset Marion Hutton, pub. SJ 2.25   3.00

☐ **My Gal Is a High-Born Lady,** by Fagan; black couple strolling, red background, M. Witmark & Sons Pub., © 1896 . . . .   15.00   21.00

☐ **My Heart Cries For You,** by Carl Sigman and Percy Faith, inset Dinah Shore, pub. Massy, © 1950 . . . .   2.25   3.00

☐ **My Hindoo Queen,** by Frederick Seymour and Fred W. Pike, pub. Waldorf, P. Hubbard cover, © 1920 . . . .   2.25   3.00

☐ **My Ohio Home,** lyric by Gus Kahn, music by Walter Donaldson, pub. Feist, © 1927 . . . .   1.75   2.50

☐ **My Mammy Knows,** by Harry DeCosta and M. K. Jerome, shows steam train 2.00   3.00

☐ **My Mother's Evening Prayer,** by Bud Green, Charlie Pierce, and Al Dubin, © 1920 . . . . .   2.00   3.00

☐ **My Sin,** by DeSylva, Brown and Henderson, inset Jack Osterman, © 1929 . . . .   2.00   3.00

Price Range

☐ **My Sister and I,** by Hy Zaret, Joan Whitney and Alex Kramer, Im-Ho cover, ⓒ 1941 ...   2.00   3.00

☐ **My Thoughts Are You,** words by John Steel, music by Charles Wakefield Cadman, pub. Harold Flammer, ⓒ 1923 ....   1.50   2.00

☐ **My Twilight Dream,** lyric and adaption by Lew Sherwood and Eddie Duchin, (based on Chopin's Nocturne in E-Flat), photo Duchin, ⓒ 1939 ....   2.25   3.00

☐ **My Wishing Song,** lyric by Irving Kahal, music by Joe Burke, inset Mark Fisher 2.25   3.00

☐ **Napoleon's Last Charge,** by Edw. Ellis, arr. E. T. Paull, large-format color litho, Blue sky, horses and riders falling into bottomless pit, bomb exploding behind lead horse and rider, ⓒ 1910 ....   22.00   28.00

☐ **Napoleon's Last Charge,** by Edw. Ellis, arr. E. T. Paull, large-format color litho, yellow-pink sky, exciting cover of horses and riders falling into rock-strewn ditch, battle parapher-nalia at the sides, ⓒ 1910 ....   12.00   18.00

☐ **Naturally,** words and music by George and Bert Clarke and Ben Kruger, inset Guy Lom-bardo, pub. Olman, ⓒ 1934 ....   2.00   3.00

☐ **The Naughty Lady of Shady Lane,** by Sid Tepper and Roy C. Bennet, inset the Ames Bros., pub. Paxton, ⓒ 1954 ....   2.25   3.00

☐ **Nelly Bly,** by Stephen Foster; black and white decorative lettering on cover, Firth, Pond & Co., 4th edition, ⓒ 1850 ....   8.00   12.00

☐ **Nestle in Your Daddy's Arms,** by Lou Hers-cher and Joe Burke, pub. Feist, ⓒ 1921 ...   2.25   3.00

☐ **Never a Day Goes By,** words and music by Walter Donaldson, Peter De Rose and Mitch-ell Parish, inset Guy Lombardo, pub. Miller, ⓒ 1943 ....   2.25   3.00

☐ **Night and Day,** words and music by Cole Por-ter, inset Frank Sinatra, pub. Harms, ⓒ 1932   3.25   5.00

☐ **(Give Me) A Night in June,** by Cliff Friend, Starmer cover, ⓒ 1927 ....   2.00   3.00

Price Range

☐ **No! No! A Thousand Times No!,** by Al Sherman, Al Lewis, and Abner Silver, pub. Feist, inset Milton Ebbins, © 1934 . . . .   1.75   2.50

☐ **Normandy,** by Nelson Ingham, Frank Kienzle and Charles Smith, inset Sophia Kassmit, pub. Mills, Barbelle cover, © 1920 . . . .   1.50   2.50

☐ **Normandy,** by Russell Robinson, Jack Little and Addy Britt, pub. Henry Waterson, © 1925   2.00   2.75

☐ **No Stone Unturned,** photo June Hutton, pub. Miller, © 1953 . . . .   1.50   2.50

☐ **Now and Then,** lyric by Joe McKiernan, melody by Norman Spencer, pub. Richmond, © 1920 . . . .   2.00   2.75

☐ **Now-I-Know,** music by S. R. Henry and D. Onivas, lyric by H. Warren, pub. Stern, colored litho cover by Knapp, © 1919 . . . .   1.75   2.50

☐ **Oceana Roll,** words by Roger Lewis, music by Lucien Denni, pub. Jerry Vogel, reprint, © 1938 . . . .   1.50   2.00

☐ **O Dio Mio,** words and music by Al Hoffman and Dick Manning, large photo Annette, pub. Topper, © 1959 . . . .   2.00   3.00

☐ **Oh, How I Love You,** words by Joe Larkin, music by Ted Johnson, pub. Spitzer, inset Evelyn Knight, © 1951 . . . .   3.00   4.25

☐ **Oh! How I Wish I Could Sleep Until My Daddy Comes Home,** words by Sam M. Lewis and Joe Young, music by Pete Wendling, inset Al Jolson, Barbelle cover, © 1918   3.00   4.25

☐ **An Old Guitar and an Old Refrain,** words and music by Gus Kahn, Ben Black, and Neil Moret, pub. Villa Moret, © 1927 . . . .   2.25   3.00

☐ **The Old Master Painter,** lyric by Haven Gillespie, music by Beasley Smith, inset Richard Hayes, © 1949 . . . .   2.25   3.00

☐ **Old Pal,** lyric by Gus Kahn, music Egbert Van Alsyne, Med. Key of F 2.25   3.00

☐ **The Old Refrain,** words by Alice Mattullath, Viennese popular song, arr. Fritz Kreisler, pub. Fischer, key of F 2.25   3.00

☐ **On a Dreamy Night,** by Walter Smith, Stainford cover, © 1920 . . . .   2.25   3.00

Price Range

☐ **On the Campus,** from "Memories of Mt. Gal-
litzin," composed by a Sister of St. Joseph
(Baden, PA) **2.25**   **3.00**

☐ **On Treasure Island,** by Edgar Leslie and Joe
Burke, pub. Morris, Cliff Miska cover, © 1935   **1.50**   **2.00**

☐ **One Minute to One,** words by Sam M. Lewis,
music by Fred Coots, inset Ted Fiorito, pub.
Feist, © 1933 .... **2.00**   **2.50**

☐ **Only You,** by A. H. Eastman and Fred Heltman, pub. Heltman, © 1919 .... **1.75**   **2.50**

☐ **The Oregon Trail,** words by Billy Hill, music
by Peter DeRose, photo Fred Waring, ©
1935 .... **2.25**   **3.00**

☐ **Our Bungalow of Dreams,** by Tommie Malie,
Charlie Newman, and Joe Verges, pub. Ted
Browne, inset Baby Dorothy Johnson, ©
1927 .... **1.25**   **1.75**

☐ As above, inset Norma Leslie and Monte
Vandergrift (The California Poppy and the
Sap) **2.25**   **3.00**

☐ **Our Love,** words and music by Larry Clinton,
Buddy Bernier, and Bob Emmerich, pub.
Chappe, © 1929 .... **1.50**   **2.00**

☐ **Out of Nowhere,** lyric by Edward Heyman,
music by John W. Green, inset Seger Ellis,
pub. Famous, © 1931 .... **2.00**   **3.00**

☐ **Out Where the West Begins,** words by Arthur Chapman, music by Estelle Philleo, ©
1917 .... **2.00**   **3.00**

☐ **Pagan Moon,** by Al Bryan, Al Dubin and Joe
Burke, © 1931 .... **2.00**   **3.00**

☐ **Pale Moon (Indian Love Song),** lyric by
Jesse M. Glick, music by Frederic Knight
Logan **1.50**   **2.00**

☐ **Pal of My Cradle Days,** lyric by Marshall
Montgomery, music by Al Piantadosi, inset
Franklyn Baur, pub. Feist **2.25**   **3.00**

☐ **Pals,** lyric by Gilbert Wells, music by Lynn
Cowan, © 1919 .... **2.25**   **3.00**

☐ **Paradise Lane,** words and music by Charles
O'Flynn, Charlie McCarthy, and Mickey Addy,
inset Frankie Master, pub. Feist, © 1933 .. **2.50**   **3.50**

	Price Range	

☐ **Paper Doll,** by Johnny Black, inset Bing Crosby, pub. Marks, © 1943 . . . .   2.50   3.50

☐ **Paradise Isle,** words by Ray Klages, music by Al Goering and Jack Pettin, pub. Harms, © 1927 . . . .   2.25   3.00

☐ **Parlez Moi d'Amour (Speak to Me of Love),** words and music by Jean Lenoir, American version by Bruce Siever, pub. Harms 1.50   2.00

☐ **Patsy,** lyric by Dick Coburn, music by Earl Burtnett and Dick Winfree, inset Art Landry and his Orchestra, Griffith cover, © 1924 . .   1.25   1.75

☐ **Paul Revere's Ride,** by E. T. Paull, large-format color litho, Revere on a galloping horse warning the townspeople, night scene, © 1905 . . . .   12.00   18.00

☐ **Peace of Mind,** lyric by James Dyrenforth, music by Carrill Gibbons, pub. Gene Austin, © 1929 . . . .   2.25   3.00

☐ **Penny Serenade,** words by Hal Hallifax, music by Melle Weersma, inset Guy Lombardo, © 1938 . . . .   2.25   3.00

☐ **Pershing's Crusaders,** by E. T. Paull, large-format color litho, General Pershing on horseback leading thousands of troops, ghosts of the Crusaders float behind, © 1918   18.00   22.00

☐ **Play to Me, Gypsy (The Song I Love),** English version by Jimmy Kennedy, original lyrics by Beda, music by Karel Vacek, © 1934 . .   2.00   3.00

☐ **Poor Little Butterfly Is a Fly Girl Now,** lyric by Sam M. Lewis and Joe Young, music by M. K. Jerome, © 1919 . . . .   2.00   3.00

☐ **The Poor People of Paris,** by Marguerite Monnot, pub. Reg Connelly, © 1954 . . . . . .   3.00   4.00

☐ **Poor Papa (He's Got Nothing at All),** words by Billy Rose, music by Harry Woods, inset Bob Cause and his Collegians, © 1926 . . .   3.00   4.00

☐ **Poppy,** words by Phil Roy, music by Isabel Mayer, pub. Mayer, Portland, OR, inset Mildred Fields (The Texas Belle), © 1947 . . . .   2.00   3.00

Price Range

☐ **Powder Your Face with Sunshine, Smile! Smile! Smile!,** words and music by Carmon Lombardo and Stanley Rochinski, inset Lebert, Carmen and Guy Lombardo, pub. Lombardo Music, © 1948 . . . .   3.00   4.00

☐ **Practice Makes Perfect,** by Don Roberts and Ernest Gold, © 1940 . . . .   2.25   3.00

☐ **Praise the Lord and Pass the Ammunition,** words and music by Frank Loesser, pub. Famous, © 1942 . . . .   3.00   4.00

☐ **Precious,** words by Raymond B. Egan, music by Stephen Pasternacki and Richard Whiting, pub. Feist, © 1926 . . . .   3.00   4.00

☐ **Pretend,** by Lew Douglas, Cliff Parman and Frank Lavere, inset Ralph Marterie, pub. Brandom, © 1952 . . . .   1.50   2.00

☐ As above, inset Nat "King" Cole 3.00   4.00

☐ **Pretending,** words by Marty Symes, music by Al Sherman, inset Andy Russell, pub. Capitol, © 1946 . . . .   1.50   2.00

☐ As above, Bing Crosby on cover 3.00   4.00

☐ **Pretty Baby,** words by Gus Kahn, music by Tony Jackson and Egbert Van Alstyne, © 1916 . . . .   2.25   4.00

☐ **Pretty Cinderella,** words and music by Will J. Harris, pub. IB, Left cover, © 1926 . . . .   2.25   4.00

☐ **Pretty Kitty Blue Eyes,** lyrics by Mann Curtis, music by Vic Mizzy, inset Joan Brooks, © 1944 . . . .   1.50   2.00

☐ **Pretty Kitty Kelly,** words by Harry Pease, music by Ed Nelson, pub. A. J. Stasney, colored litho cover, © 1920 . . . .   2.00   2.75

☐ **Pretty Little Thing,** words and music by Tommy Malie and Little Jack Little, pub. Feist, inset Evelyn Wilson 3.00   5.00

☐ **Prisoner of Love,** words and music by Leo Robin, Clarence Gaskill and Russ Columbo, inset Perry Como, pub. Mayfair, © 1931 . . .   2.25   3.00

☐ **The Prisoner's Song,** words and music by Guy massey 2.25   3.00

Price Range

☐ **Profecia (Bolero),** (Cuban) words by Francisco Llorens, music by Rodriguez Fiffe, pub. Pan American, © 1941 ....   2.25   3.00

☐ **Pua Kona,** in C Sharp Minor, professional arr. for Hawaiian guitar, inset Sol Hoopii, pub. Ball Music, © 1940 ....   2.50   3.50

☐ **Pucker Up and Whistle ('Til the Clouds Roll By),** words and music by Blanche Franklyn and Nat Vincent, inset Yvette Rugel, Barbelle cover, pub. Fred Fisher, © 1921 ....   2.25   3.00

☐ **Puddin' Head Jones,** lyric by Al Bryan, music by Lou Handman, inset Ozzie Nelson, Harris cover, © 1933 ....   3.00   4.25

☐ **Pu-Leeze! Mister Hemingway!,** words and music by Milton Drake, Walter Kent, and Abner Silver, inset Guy Lombardo, pub. Olman, © 1932 ....   3.00   4.25

☐ **Put Away a Little Ray of Golden Sunshine,** words by Sam M. Lewis and Joe Young, music by Fred E. Ahlert, pub. Waterson, inset Underhill Macy and J. William Scott, © 1924   2.25   3.00

☐ **Put on an Old Pair of Shoes,** by Mr. and Mrs. Billy Hill, inset Ozzie Nelson and Harriet Hilliard, © 1935 ....   4.00   6.00

☐ **Put Your Arms Where They Belong (For They Belong to Me),** words and music by Lou Davis, Henry Santly, and Herman Ackman, inset Nick Lucas, © 1926 ....   2.25   3.00

☐ **Put Your Hand in the Hand,** words and music by Gene MacLellan, pub. Beechwood, inset Anne Murray, © 1970 ....   2.25   3.00

☐ **The Race Course,** by J. Glogau, arr. E. T. Paull, large-format color litho, racing scene in a rondelle, reproduction of 19th-century piece, grandstand and people cheering, © 1910 ....   28.00   34.00

☐ **Rain,** words by Billy Hill, music by Peter De-Rose, inset Henry King 1.75   2.50

☐ **Rain,** lyrics and music by Eugene Ford, inset Brooke Jones, © 1927 ....   2.25   3.00

Red River Valley,
insets of Gene Autry,
pub. Calumet Music Co.,
1935, **$3.00–$5.00.**

Revenge,
words by Lewis and Young,
music by Harry Akst,
pub. by Remick Music Corp.,
$3.00–$6.00.

Price Range

☐ **Red Sails in the Sunset,** lyric by Jimmy Kennedy, music by Hugh Williams, inset Fred Waring, Barbelle cover, pub. SB, from Prindetown Follies, © 1935 .... 2.00   3.00

☐ **Ring Out Wild Bells,** by E. T. Paull, large-format color litho, wonderful night sky, full moon, and Father Time flying by large church steeple with ringing bells, © 1912 .... 25.00   30.00

☐ **Rio Nights,** words and music by Elmer Vincent and Fisher Thompson, pub. Fisher Thompson, © 1920 .... 2.00   3.00

☐ **Roaring Volcano,** by E. T. Paull, large-format color litho, vivid scene of Mt. Vesuvius erupting, belching fire, and raining rocks and burning cinders, Pompeii in flames below, people running across bridge to escape, © 1912   22.00   28.00

☐ **Rock-A-Bye Land,** words and music by W. C. Weasner, pub. Weasner, © 1921 .... 2.00   3.00

☐ **Rock-A-Bye to Sleep in Dixie,** words and music by Sylvester L. Cross, inset Clyde Kittell, WGY's Singing Announcer, pub. S. L. Cross, © 1929 .... 2.00   3.00

☐ **Roll Along Prairie Moon,** by Ted Fiorito, Harry MacPherson and Albert Von Tilzer, photo Ted Fiorito, © 1935 .... 2.00   3.00

☐ **Rolling the Moon,** words by Donald Hutton and Rholin Cooley, music by Vernon Suckow, pub. Madrona Music, Portland, OR, © 1920   2.00   3.00

☐ **Rose O'Day (The Filla-ga-du-sha Song),** by Charlie Tobias and Al Lewis, pub. Tobias-Lewis, © 1941 .... 1.50   2.25

☐ **The Rose of No Man's Land,** Caddigan/Brennan; nurse on cover, small WWI format, 7" x 10½", Feist pub., © 1918 ...... 2.00   5.00

☐ **Roses of Picardy,** words by Fred E. Weatherly, music by Haydn Wood, pub. Chappell Harms, Medium in C, © 1916 .... 1.75   2.75

☐ **Rosette,** lyric by Charles Newman, music by Carmen Lombardo, Ransley Studio cover, pub. M. Weil, © 1928 .... 2.25   3.00

Price Range

☐ **Rudolph the Red Nosed Reindeer,** lyric and music by Johnny Marks, pub. St. Nickolas Music, © 1949 . . . .   **2.00**   **3.00**

☐ **Rumors Are Flying,** words and music by Bennie Benjamin and George Weiss, inset Perry Como, © 1946 . . . .   **2.25**   **3.00**

☐ As above, inset Margie Hughes, pub. Oxford   **2.25**   **3.00**

☐ **Sam the Old Accordion Man,** words and music by Walter Donaldson, inset Joe Mace   **1.50**   **2.00**

☐ **Santa Claus is Comin' to Town,** words by Haven Gillespie, music by Fred Coots, pub. Feist, © 1934 . . . .   **2.50**   **3.50**

☐ **Satisfied with You,** words by Harold Dixon, music by Sam H. Stept, inset The Record Boys: Sammy Stept, Si Bernard, and Frank Kamplain, pub. Jack Mills, © 1926 . . . .   **2.25**   **3.00**

☐ **Scatter Brain,** lyric by Johnny Burke, music by Keen-Bean and Frankie Masters, inset Masters **1.25**   **1.75**

☐ **Sentimental Journey,** by Bud Green, Les Brown, and Ben Homer, inset Les Brown, pub. E. H. Morris, © 1944 . . . .   **2.25**   **3.00**

☐ **(When You and I Were) Seventeen,** words by Gus Kahn, music by Chas Rosoff, Shea's Hippodrome Symphony Orchestra, © 1924   **2.50**   **3.50**

☐ As above, inset Mack Davis and his Paradise Orchestra **2.50**   **3.50**

☐ **Shadows of Love,** lyric by Annelu Burns, music by Madelyn Sheppard, pub. Geo Friedman, © 1920 . . . .   **2.25**   **3.00**

☐ **Shanghai Dream Man,** by Benny Davis and Harry Akst **1.50**   **2.00**

☐ **She Didn't Say Yes,** Kern/Harbach; Art Deco design on cover, Pierrot and dancers, from "The Cat and the Fiddle," T. B. Harms pub, © 1931 . . . .   **2.00**   **4.00**

☐ **Sheridan's Ride,** by E. T. Paull, standard format color litho, Sheridan on horseback leading troops, waving to large group of soldiers, © 1922 . . . .   **15.00**   **20.00**

Price Range

☐ **She's a Cornfed Indiana Girl,** lyric and music by Fran Frey, Eddie Killfeather and George Olsen, pub. Feist, inset Geo. Olsen, © 1926   2.25   3.00

☐ **Shine on Harvest Moon,** words and music by Nora Bayes and Jack Norworth 2.25   3.00

☐ **The Shrine of St. Cecilia,** words by Carroll Loveday, music by Jokern, pub. Braun, © 1940 ....   2.50   3.00

☐ **A Signal from Mars,** by Raymond Taylor, arr. E. T. Paull, large-format color litho, two Martian astronomers observe the earth from Mars, large red Mars, and stars on a field of blue, © 1901 ....   12.00   18.00

☐ **Silver Sleigh Bells,** by E. T. Paull, large-format color litho, winter night scene of troika sleigh, bells and holly in border graphics, © 1906 ....   12.00   18.00

☐ **The Singing Hills,** by Mack David, Dick Sanford, and Sammy Mysels, inset Blue Barron, © 1940 ....   2.25   3.00

☐ **Sing Me a Baby Song,** words by Gus Kahn, music by Walter Donaldson, pub. Feist, © 1927 ....   2.25   3.00

☐ **Sing Me "O Sole Mio,"** lyrics by Gus Kahn, music by Egbert VanAlstyne, © 1924 .....   3.00   4.00

☐ **Sing Me To Sleep,** words by Clifton Bingham, music by Edwin Greene, pub. Boston Music, © 1902 ....   2.25   3.00

☐ **Siren of a Southern Sea,** by Abe Brashen and Harold Weeks, © 1920 ....   2.25   3.00

☐ **Sitting by the Window,** by Paul Insetta, © 1949 ....   2.25   3.00

☐ **Sleepy Head,** words and music by Benny Davus and Jesse Greer, © 1926 ....   2.50   3.00

☐ **So Blue,** by B. G. DeSylva, Lew Brown, Ray Henderson, based on a theme by Mrs. Jesse Crawford, inset Henri Garden, © 1927 ....   2.50   3.50

☐ **Soldier's Chorus from the Opera "Faust,"** by Charles Gounod, pub. Jack Mills 1.00   1.50

☐ **Somebody Else Is Taking My Place,** by Dick Howard, Bob Ellsworth and Russ Morgan, inset Vaughn Monroe, © 1937 ....   3.00   4.25

1935 Scandals,
It's an Old Southern Custom,
words by Jack Yellen, Cliff Friend
and Herb Magidson,
music by Joseph Meyer,
pub. Movietone,
$3.00–$5.00.

Oklahoma,
The Surrey with
the Fringe on Top,
words by Oscar Hammerstein,
music by Richard Rodgers,
pub. Williamson Music, Inc.,
$2.50–$5.00.

Price Range

☐ **Some Day You'll Want Me Back (Maybe I Won't Want You),** by Carey Morgan and Wel Retrop (Lew Porter?), pub. Stern, inset Fred Freddy, Gus Hill's Minstrels, © 1919 . . . . . .   2.25   3.00

☐ **Some Day (You'll Want Me To Want You),** words and music by Jimmy Hodges, inset Vaughn Monroe, pub. Duchess, © 1940 . . .   2.25   3.00

☐ **Somewhere,** lyric and music by L. Earl Abel, Barbelle cover, © 1922 . . . .   2.25   3.00

☐ **Songs My Mother Taught Me,** by Anton Dvorak, inset Gale Page, pub. Calumet 1.00   1.50

☐ **The Song of Songs,** words by Clarence Lucas, music by Moya, © 1914 . . . .   2.25   3.00

☐ **Southern Dreams,** slow melody waltz, words by Charles L. Browne, music by Geo Hamilton Green, pub. Daniels & Wilson, WR Campbell cover, © 1919 . . . .   2.25   3.00

☐ **Someone is Losin' Susan,** by Roy Turk, Geo W. Meyer and Paul Ash, inset Bob Blake, pub. H. Waterson, Barbelle cover, © 1926 . . . . .   2.00   3.00

☐ **Springtime,** lyric by Gus Kahn, music by Anatol Friedland, © 1920 . . . .   2.00   3.00

☐ **(When It's) Springtime in the Rockies,** by Mary Woolsey, Robert Sauer and Milt Taggart, inset Rudy Vallee, © 1929 . . . .   2.00   3.00

☐ **Star Dust,** words by Mitchell Parish, music by Hoagy Carmichael, pub. Mills, © 1929 . . . .   3.00   4.00

☐ **A Star Fell out of Heaven,** words and music by Mack Gordon and Harry Revel, inset Johnny Johnson, pub. Crawford, © 1936 . .   2.50   3.50

☐ **The Stars and Stripes Forever,** by John Phillip Sousa, pub. Church, © 1897 . . . .   2.25   3.00

☐ **The Statue of Liberty is Smiling,** words by Jack Mahoney, music by Halsey K. Mohn, © 1918 . . . .   2.25   3.00

☐ **Stolen Kisses,** words by Francis Wheeler, music by Ted Snyder, Barbelle cover, © 1921 . . . .   2.25   3.00

Price Range

☐ **Storm King,** by E. T. Paull, large-format color litho, Neptune-like god rides in a sky chariot drawn by four white horses, lightning bolts in their nostrils, and in the stormy sky behind, stormy sea below, © 1902 .... **12.00** **18.00**

☐ **Stumbling,** words and music by "Zez" Confrey, pub. Feist, © 1922 .... **2.25** **3.00**

☐ **Suez,** words by Will Pancoast, music by Ferdie Grofe and Peter DeRose, inset Waring's Pennsylvanians, pub. Triangle, © 1922 .... **2.25** **3.00**

☐ **Sunshine Rose,** words by Jean Lefavre, music by W. C. Polla, Rolf Armstrong cover, pub. Church, © 1920 .... **2.50** **3.50**

☐ **Sweet and Low,** words by Stanley Royce, music by Charles L. Johnson, pub. Forster, © 1919 .... **2.00** **2.75**

☐ **Sweet Child (I'm Wild About You),** by Richard A. Whiting, Al Lewis and Howard Simon, inset Boyd Senter, © 1935 .... **2.00** **2.75**

☐ **The Sweetest Story Ever Told (Tell Me Do You Love Me),** by R. M. Stults, pub. Ditson, © 1920 .... **2.00** **2.75**

☐ **Sweetheart,** words by Benny Davis, music by Arnold Johnson, pub. Feist, © 1921 ...... **2.25** **3.00**

☐ **(I Love You, I Love You) Sweetheart of All My Dreams,** by Art Fitch, Kay Fitch, and Bert Lowe, inset Wm. Stamm with the Kit Kat Boys, © 1928 .... **2.25** **3.00**

☐ **Sweetheart of My Dreams,** by Al Jacobs and Al Pearce, photo Al Pearce and his Gang, © 1933 .... **2.00** **2.75**

☐ **Sweethearts on Parade,** words by Charles Newman, music by Carmen Lombardo, © 1928 .... **2.00** **2.75**

☐ **Sweetie Please Tell Me,** by Will R. McDowell, pub. McDowell, cover with apple blossoms and bluebirds, mint, © 1921 .... **2.50** **3.50**

☐ **Sweetness,** lyric by Gus Kahn, music by Marie Dodge, B&W, © 1920 .... **1.50** **2.00**

☐ **Sweet Indiana Home,** lyric and music by Walter Donaldson, inset Aileen Stanley, © 1922 .... **2.25** **3.00**

Price Range

☐ **Sweet Jennie Lee,** by Walter Donaldson, photo Guy Lombardo, pub. Donaldson, ©
1930 . . . . **2.25** **3.00**
☐ **Sweet Little You,** by Irving M. Bibo, pub. Maurice Abrahams **1.75** **2.75**
☐ **Sweet Violets,** by Cy Coben and Charles Grean, photo Dinah Shore **1.25** **1.75**
☐ **Sweet Violets,** novelty song by Benny Samberg, pub. Southern, inset Gene Kardos, ©
1932 . . . . **1.75** **2.25**
☐ **The Sweetest Rose of All,** lyric by O. Abbey, music by Wm. Witol, pub. American Music Pub., Leff cover, © 1923 . . . . **2.00** **3.00**
☐ **The Sweetheart of Sigma Chi,** lyric by Byron Stokes, music by Dudleigh Vernor, pub. Melrose Bros., 28th ed., © 1927 . . . . **3.00** **4.00**
☐ **Swinging Down the Lane,** lyric by Gus Kahn, music by Isham Jones, pub. Feist, inset Isham Jones, © 1923 . . . . **2.25** **3.00**
☐ **Swingin' in a Hammock,** words by Tot Seymour and Chas O'Flynn, music by Pete Wendling, inset Eddie Lane, © 1930 . . . . **2.25** **3.00**
☐ **Symphony,** words by Andre Tabet and Roger Bernstein, American version by Jack Lawrence, music by Alstone, inset Johnny Desmond, © 1945 . . . . **2.25** **3.00**
☐ **Syncopated Clock,** words by Mitchell Parish, music by Leroy Anderson, pub. Mills, © 1950 **2.25** **3.50**
☐ **Take It Easy,** words and music by Albert De Bru, Irving Taylor and Vic Mizzy, © 1943 . . **2.25** **3.50**
☐ **Take Me Back to My Boots and Saddle,** words and music by Walter Samuels, Leonard Whitcup and Teddy Powell, inset Buddy Clark, pub. Schuster & Miller, © 1935 . . . . . **2.50** **3.50**
☐ As above, inset Dick Gasparre **2.25** **3.00**
☐ **Take Me Back to Your Heart,** lyric by Billy Rose, music by George W. Meyer, inset Harry Meyer, conductor, Stanton Symphony Orchestra, Philadelphia, Starmer cover, © 1924 **3.00** **4.00**
☐ **Take Me to the Land of Jazz,** words by Bert Kalmar and Edgar Leslie, music by Pete Wendling, © 1919 . . . . **3.00** **4.00**

Second Fiddle,
Back to Back,
words and music by Irving Berlin,
pub. Irving Berlin, Inc.,
$3.00–$6.00.

Second Fiddle,
I Poured My Heart Into a Song,
words and music by Irving Berlin,
pub. Irving Berlin, Inc.,
$3.00–$6.00.

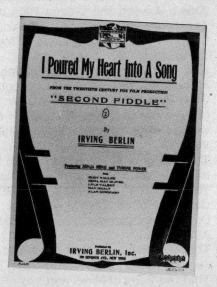

Price Range

☐ **A Taste of Honey,** words by Ric Marlow, music by Bobby Scott, pub. Songfest Music, ©️ 1962 . . . .   2.25   3.00

☐ **Tea Leaves,** by Morty Berk, Frank Capano and Mac C. Freedman, inset Geo. Olsen, ©️ 1948 . . . .   1.75   2.50

☐ **Tears Tell (the Story to Me),** by C. & F. Wilson Armstrong; cover with pretty girl holding armful of roses, Stasny Music Co. ©️ 1919   4.00   8.00

☐ **Teddy Bear's Picnic,** words by Jimmy Kennedy, music by John W. Bratton, ©️ 1947 . .   2.00   3.00

☐ **Tell Me,** lyric by J. Will Callahan, music by Max Kortlander, ©️ 1919 . . . .   2.00   3.00

☐ **Tell Me Why,** lyric by Richard Coburn, music by Vincent Rose, ©️ 1919 . . . .   2.00   3.00

☐ **Temptation,** lyric by Arthur Freed, music by Nacio Herb Brown, ©️ 1933 . . . .   2.00   3.00

☐ **Ten Little Miles From Town,** words by Gus Kahn, music by Elmer Schoebel, ©️ 1928 . .   2.50   3.50

☐ **Tennessee Waltz,** by Redd Stewart and Pee Wee King, inset Patti Page, pub. Acuff Rose   2.50   3.50

☐ **(Down Among the Sleepy Hills of) Ten-Ten-Tennessee,** words by Joe Young and Sam M. Lewis, music by Geo W. Meyer, Perret cover, ©️ 1923 . . . .   2.25   3.00

☐ **(Did You Ever Get) That Feeling in the Moonlight,** by James Cavanaugh, Larry Stock and Ira Schuster, inset Gene Krupa   1.50   2.00

☐ **(You're the Only Girl) That Made Me Cry,** words and music by Fred Fisher, pub. Fisher, Wohlman cover, ©️ 1920 . . . .   2.25   3.00

☐ **That Naughty Waltz,** lyric by Edwin Stanley, music by Sol. P. Levy, ©️ 1920 . . . .   2.25   3.00

☐ **That Old Fashioned Mother of Mine (An Old Fashioned Lady),** words by Worton David, music by Horatio Nicholls, medium in A-flat 1.50   2.50

☐ **That Old Irish Mother of Mine,** lyric by Wm. Jerome, music by Harry Von Tilzer, ©️ 1920   1.50   2.50

☐ **That Old Gang of Mine,** words by Billy Rose, music by Ray Henderson, blue and white, reprint 2.50   3.50

Price Range

☐ **That's How I Believe in You,** lyric by Al. Dubin and Paul Cunninghamm, music by Bert Rule, © 1921 . . . .   2.25   3.00

☐ **That's My Desire,** words by Carroll Loveday, music by Helmy Kresa, inset Alvino Rey, pub. Mills, © 1931 . . . .   2.25   3.00

☐ **That's My Mammy,** words by Harry Pease, music by Abel Baer and Ed Nelson, pub. Feist, inset Harry Richman, © 1928 . . . .   3.00   4.00

☐ **That's The Way I've Missed You,** lyric by Gus Kahn, music by Egbert VanAlstyne, inset Mabel Juliene Scott, Lumiere Studios, photo   2.50   3.50

☐ **That's Why I Love You,** words and music by Walter Donaldson and Paul Ash, photo Paul Ash, pub. Feist, © 1926 . . . .   2.25   3.00

☐ **That's Your Mistake,** words and music by Rudy Toombs, inset The Crew Cut, © 1955   2.50   4.00

☐ **(I Wanna Go Where You Go, Do What You Do) Then I'll Be Happy,** words by Sidney Clare and Lew Brown, music Cliff Friend, inset Crafts and Sheehan, Leff cover, © 1925 . . . .   2.50   4.00

☐ **There I Go,** words by Hy Zaret, music by Irving Weiser, pub. BMI, © 1940 . . . .   2.25   3.00

☐ **There Must Be a Way,** lyric and music by Sammy Gallop, Davis Saxon and Robert Cook, inset Charlie Spivak, pub. Stevens Music, © 1945 . . . .   2.25   3.00

☐ **There's a Star Spangled Banner Waving Somewhere,** by Paul Roberts and Shelby Darnell, pub. Bob Miller, Barbelle cover, © 1942 . . . .   1.75   2.50

☐ **There's Something Nice About Everyone "But" There's Everything Nice About You,** words by Alfred Bryan, Arthur Terker, music by Pete Wendling, Barbelle cover, inset Lou Calabrese 1.75   2.50

☐ **There's No You,** lyric by Tom Adair, music by Hap Hopper, pub. Barton, inset Eileen Barton   2.25   3.00

Swing Symphony,
Cow Cow Boogie,
pub. Leeds Music,
$1.00–$2.50.

The Time,
the Place and the Girl,
Oh, But I Do,
words by Leo Robin,
music by Arthur Schwartz,
pub. M. Witmark & Sons,
$3.00–$7.00.

Original Manuscript of "Dixie," by its composer Daniel D. Emmett.

Price Range

☐ As above, inset Frank Sinatra **3.00**   **4.25**

☐ **There's Something About a Rose (That Reminds Me of You),** words by Irving Kahal and Francis Wheeler, music by Sammy Fain, inset Nick Romano, © 1928 ....   **2.25**   **3.00**

☐ **These Things I Offer You (For a Lifetime),** words and music by Mort Nevins, Bennie Benjamin, and George Weiss **2.50**   **3.50**

☐ **They Were Doin' the Mambo,** words and music by Sonny Burke and Don Ray, pub. Mayfair, inset Vaughn Monroe, © 1954 ...   **2.25**   **3.00**

☐ **The Thing,** words and music by Charles R. Grean, inset Phil Harris, pub. Hollis Music, © 1950 ....   **2.25**   **3.00**

☐ **The Things I Love,** words and music by Harold Barlow-Lewis Harris, inset Jimmy Dorsey, pub. Campbell, © 1941 ....   **2.50**   **3.50**

☐ **The Things We Did Last Summer,** words by Sammy Cahn, music by Jule Styne, inset Joe Stafford, pub. Ed Morris, © 1946 ....   **2.50**   **3.50**

☐ **The Things You Left in My Heart,** by Buddy Kaye, Hugo Taiani and Herb Leighton, photo Freddy Martin, pub. Lewis, © 1947 ....   **2.50**   **3.50**

☐ **This is No Laughing Matter,** lyric by Van Loman and Martin Block, music by Al Frisch, pub. Martin Block, © 1941 ....   **2.25**   **3.00**

☐ **This is Worth Fighting For,** words and music by Edgar DeLange and Sam H. Stept, © 1942 ....   **2.25**   **3.00**

☐ **(Somewhere) This Side of Heaven,** words and music by Chick Adams and Bert Reisfeld, pub. Yankee Music, Barbelle cover, © 1943   **2.25**   **3.00**

☐ **A Thousand Good Nights,** by Walter Donaldson, inset Lebert Lombardo, © 1934 ...   **2.25**   **3.00**

☐ **The Three Bells** (The Jimmy Brown Song), inset The Browns, pub. Southern Music, © 1945 ....   **2.50**   **3.50**

☐ **The Little Fishies (Itty Bitty Poo),** by Saxie Dowell, © 1939 ....   **2.50**   **3.50**

☐ **Three Little Sisters,** lyric by Irving Taylor, music by Vic Mizzy, © 1942 ....   **2.50**   **3.50**

Price Range

☐ **The Three Caballeros,** Gilbert/Esperon from the Disney movie "The Three Caballeros," drawing of Donald Duck, Panchito, and Jose Carioca; photos of Aurora Miranda, Carmen Molina, and Dora Luz on cover, Peer International Corp. © 1944 (Mexican copyright 1941) 4.00   7.00

☐ **Three O'Clock in the Morning,** words by Dorothy Teriss, music by Julian Bobledo, © 1922 .... 2.25   3.00

☐ **Three Little Maids From School,** from "The Mikado," by Gilbert & Sullivan, pub. Calumet 1.25   2.00

☐ **Three on a Match,** words by Raymond B. Egan, music by Ted Fiorito, photo Fiorito, © 1932 .... 2.25   3.00

☐ **Through the Years,** words by Edward Heyman, music by Vincent Youmans, medium in E-flat, © 1931 .... 1.50   2.00

☐ **Throw Another Log on the Fire,** by Charles Tobias, Jack Scholl, Murray Mencher, inset Sam Robbins, pub. Feist, © 1933 .... 2.25   3.00

☐ **Throwing Stones at the Sun,** by Nat Simon, Billy Hueston and Sammy Mysels, inset Larry Siry, © 1934 .... 2.50   3.00

☐ **Thru the Night,** words by Virginia K. Logan, music by Frederic Knight Logan, Van Doorn cover, © 1922 .... 1.25   1.75

☐ **Tie Me to Your Apron Strings Again,** words by Joe Goodwin, music by Larry Shay, pub. M. Weill, © 1925 .... 2.00   3.00

☐ **Till,** words by Carl Sigman, music by Charles Danvers, inset Tony Bennett 2.25   3.00

☐ **Till the End of Time,** based on Chopin's "Polonaise," by Buddy Kayw and Ted Mossman, © 1945 .... 1.50   2.25

☐ **Till the Heavens Roll Away,** words and music by John R. Nelson, pub. Seliladean 2.00   3.00

☐ **Till Then,** words and music by Eddie Seiler, Sol Marcus and Guy Wood, pub. Sun, sung by the Mills Bros. on Decca Record #18599, © 1944 .... 1.50   2.25

Price Range

☐ **The Shadows Have Flown,** lyric by Haven Gillespie and Lee Onidas, music by Egbert VanAlstyne, pub. VanAlstyne & Curtis, cover by C. T. Agnew, © 1919 .... 1.50   1.75

☐ **Till We Meet Again,** lyric by Raymond B. Egan, music by Richard Whiting 1.50   2.00

☐ **'Til Reveille,** words and music by Stanley Cowand and Bobby Worth, inset Rudy Vallee, pub. Melody Lane, © 1941 .... 2.50   4.00

☐ As above, inset Diane Courtney with large NBC mike 2.50   4.00

☐ **Time on My Hands,** words by Harold Adamson and Mack Gordon, music by Vincent Youmans, pub. Miller, © 1930 .... 2.00   3.00

☐ **Tipperary Guards,** by E. T. Paull, large-format Starmer 2-color, soldiers with guns and drums marching below, narrow band of fighting soldiers above, © 1915 .... 15.00   20.00

☐ **Ti-Pi-Tin,** music and Spanish lyrics by Maria Grever, English lyrics by Raymond Leveen, photo Horace Heidt, pub. Feist, © 1938 ... 2.00   3.00

☐ **To Be Worthy of You,** words by Benny Davis, music by J. Fred Coots 2.00   3.00

☐ **Tomorrow Begins Another Year,** by Webb Pierce and Harmie Smith, pub. Leeds, photo Smith, © 1945 .... 2.50   3.50

☐ **Tomorrow Land,** by H. J. Tandler, Griffith cover, © 1921 .... 2.25   3.00

☐ **Too Many Kisses in the Summer (Bring Too Many Tears in the Fall),** words by Billy Rose and Al Dubin, music by Harry Warren, Barbelle cover 1.50   3.00

☐ **The Touch of Your Lips,** by Ray Noble, Leff cover, © 1936 .... 2.25   3.00

☐ **To You,** words and music by Benny Davis, Tommy Dorsey, and Ted Shapiro, inset Harry Richman, © 1939 .... 2.25   3.00

☐ **Tricks,** by "ZEZ" Confrey, pub. Feist, © 1922 2.50   3.50

☐ **Triumphant Banner,** by E. T. Paull, large-format color litho, nice large 45-star flag, sunrise, and large eagle/shield, buntings, olive branches, © 1905 .... 15.00   20.00

Price Range

☐ **Trust in Me,** by Ned Wever, Jean Schwartz and Milton Ager, inset Pete Pontrelli, © 1936   2.50   3.50

☐ **(Tuck Me to Sleep in my Old) 'Tucky Home,** words by Joe Young and Sam M. Lewis, music by Geo W. Meyer, © 1921 . . . .   2.00   2.75

☐ **Two in a Dream,** by Al Sherman, Al Lewis and Abner Silver, inset Wayne King, pub. Feist, © 1934 . . . .   2.50   3.50

☐ **Ukelele Lady,** words by Gus Kahn, music by Richard A Whiting, inset Gendron Orchestra, © 1925 . . . .   1.75   2.50

☐ **The Umbrella Man,** words and music by James Cavanaugh, Larry Stock, and Vincent Rose, inset Dorothy Rochelle 2.50   3.50

☐ **Undecided,** words by Sid Robin, music by Charles Shavers, inset Ames Bros., pub. Leeds, © 1939 . . . .   2.25   3.00

☐ **Underneath Hawaiian Skies,** lyrics by Fred Rose, music by Ernie Erdman, pub. Feist, © 1920 . . . .   2.50   4.00

☐ **Underneath the Arches,** by Bud Flanagan, inset Sammy Kaye, © 1932 . . . .   2.00   2.75

☐ **Underneath the Stars with You,** words and music by Sam Stept and Nick Lucas, early B&W printing, © 1927 . . . .   2.25   3.00

☐ **Under the Willow Tree,** words and music by Billy Reid, pub. Peter Maurice Music, © 1945   2.25   3.00

☐ **The Utah Trail,** words ad music by "Bob" Palmer, pub. Palmer, © 1928 . . . .   2.25   3.00

☐ **(It Will Have to Do) Until the Real Thing Comes Along,** words and music by Mann Holiner, Alberta Nichols, Sammy Cahn, Saul Chaplin and L. E. Freeman, © 1936 . . . . . .   5.00   7.00

☐ **Under Western Skies,** by James W. Casey, Harold Weeks and Henry Murtagh, inset Monte Austin, pub. Echo, © 1920 . . . .   1.75   2.50

☐ **Valley of Broken Dreams,** poem by Baron Keyes, music by Leigh Harline, pub. Campbell, © 1930 . . . .   2.25   3.00

Price Range

☐ **Velvetone,** The Heart of the Radio, pub. Velvetone Corp., inset Elinor Fairfax, "The Original Velvetone Girl," lyric by Fred D. Moore, music by Chas. Caldwell 2.50 3.50

☐ **Venetian Love Boat,** by Frank Magine and Ted Koehler, pub. Feist, © 1922 . . . . 2.50 3.50

☐ **Vict'ry Polka,** words by Samuel Cahn, music by Jule Styne, © 1943 . . . . 2.50 3.50

☐ **The Voice in the Old Village Choir,** words by Gus Kahn, music by Harry Woods, inset Ted Fiorito 2.25 3.00

☐ **Wait For Me Mary,** by Charlie Tobias, Nat Simon, and Harry Tobia, Harris cover, pub. RE, © 1942 . . . . 2.50 3.50

☐ **Waitin' for the Train to Come In,** by Sunny Skylar and Martin Block, insets Jo Stafford, Johnny Johnson, pub. Martin Block Music, © 1945 . . . . 2.50 3.50

☐ **Waiting,** by Harold Lawrence, Jay Milton and Carl Ravazza, Barbelle cover, © 1944 . . . . 2.50 3.50

☐ **Waiting (When I Hear the Gate A-Swinging),** words by Reginald Rigby, music by Leo C. Croke 1.75 2.25

☐ **Waiting at the End of the Road,** by Irving Berlin, photo Kate Smith, from movie "Hallelujah," © 1929 . . . . 4.50 6.50

☐ **Waiting for the Rainbow,** words by Billy Rose and Benny Davis, music by Harry Akst, pub. M. Weill, © 1927 . . . . 2.50 3.50

☐ **Waiting for the Robert E. Lee,** Gilbert/Muir; silhouetted figures on levee watching approach of paddle-wheeler, photo of Jack Manion inset, F. A. Mills pub., © 1912 . . . . 6.00 10.00

☐ **Wait Till You Get Them up in the Air Boys,** Brown/Von Tilzer; girls in plane cockpit on cover, Broadway Music Corp. pub., © 1919 3.00 6.00

☐ **(Wait Till You Get Them) Up In the Air Boys,** words by Lew Brown, music by Albert Von Tilzer, pub. BDW, © 1919 . . . . 5.00 7.00

Price Range

☐ **We Three (My Echo, My Shadow and Me),** by Dick Robertson, Nelson Cogane and Sammy Mysels, pub. Mercer & Mercer, Im-Ho cover, © 1940 . . . . 2.50   3.50

☐ **We'll Gather Lilacs,** words and music by Ivor Novello, © 1945 . . . . 2.00   3.00

☐ **Were You Sincere,** lyrics by Jack Meskill, music by Vincent Rose, inset Leo Reisman, © 1931 . . . . 2.25   3.00

☐ **The West a Nest and You,** by Larry Yoell and Billy Hill, Griffith cover, © 1923 . . . . 2.25   3.00

☐ **We've Come a Long Way Together,** lyric by Ted Koehler, music by Sam H. Stept, pub. Feist, © 1939 . . . . 2.00   2.75

☐ **What Could Be Sweeter Than You?,** lyric by Lew Brown, music by Cliff Friend, inset Stanley Cable, Leff cover, © 1925 . . . . 2.00   2.75

☐ **What Do We Do On a Dew-Dew-Dewy Day,** by Howard Johnson, Charles Tobias and Al Sherman, © 1927 . . . . 2.00   3.00

☐ **What'll We Do On a Saturday Night (When the Town Goes Dry),** by Harry Ruby, Barbelle cover, © 1919 . . . . 3.00   4.00

☐ **What's the Use of Crying,** lyric by Verdi Kindel, music by Lou Forbes, inset Lou Forbes, pub. Jenkins, © 1926 . . . . 2.00   3.00

☐ **The Wheel of the Wagon is Broken,** words and music by Box & Cox and Michael Car, pub. Feist, © 1935 . . . . 2.25   3.00

☐ **When a Gypsy Makes His Violin Cry,** words by Dick Smith and Jimmy Rogan, music by Emery Deutsch, inset Emery Deutsch, pub. Donaldson, Douglas & Gumble, © 1935 . . . 1.75   2.50

☐ **When Did You Leave Heaven?,** lyric by Walter Bullock, melody by Richard A. Whiting, photo Tony Martin, from "Sing Baby Sing," © 1936 . . . . 5.00   7.00

☐ **When Ireland Comes into Her Own,** words by Jeff Branen, music by Jack Stanley, © 1919 . . . . 3.00   4.00

☐ **When It's Sunset in Sweden,** lyric by Dave Morrison, music by Earl Burtnett, © 1919 3.00   4.00

Price Range

☐ **When My Ships Come Sailing Home,** words
by Reginald Steward, music by Francis Dorel,
pub. Boosey, © 1903 . . . .   2.25   3.00

☐ **When That Midnight Choo-Choo Leaves of
Alabam!** by Irving Berlin, drawing of locomotive, photo of Al Warren and Bert Starkey
inset, Ted Snyder Co. pub., © 1912 . . . . . .   5.00   9.00

☐ **When the Autumn Leaves Begin to Fall,**
words by Neville Fleeson, music by Albert
Von Tilzer, © 1920 . . . .   2.25   3.00

☐ **When the Dew Is Falling,** words by Fiona
MacLeod, music by Edwin Schneider, pub.
Boosey, © 1915 . . . .   2.25   3.00

☐ **When the Leaves Bid the Trees Goodbye,**
lyric by Tot Seymour, music by Vee Lawn-
hurst, © 1935 . . . .   2.25   3.00

☐ **When the Leaves Come Tumbling Down,**
words and music by Richard Howard, pub.
Feist, © 1922 . . . .   1.75   2.25

☐ **When the Lights Are Low,** words by Gerald
M. Lane, music by Burton Arant, inset Avalon
Male Quartet, pub. Arant Music, © 1924 . .   2.50   3.50

☐ **When the Lights Go On Again (All Over the
World),** by Eddie Seiler, Sol Marcus, Bennie
Benjemen, © 1942 . . . .   2.00   3.00

☐ **When the Lusitania Went Down,** McCar-
ron/Vincent; photos of full ship and two par-
lors on cover, Feist pub., © 1915 . . . .   17.00   22.00

☐ **When the Morning Glories Wake Up In the
Morning (Then I'll Kiss Your Two Lips
Good-Night),** words by Billy Rose, music by
Fred Fisher, pub. Weill, © 1927 . . . .   2.25   3.50

☐ **When They Ask About You,** words and
music by Sam H. Stept, inset Joan Brooks,
© 1943 . . . .   2.25   3.50

☐ **When They Played the Polka,** words by Lou
Holzer, music by Fabian Andre, inset Ozzie
Nelson, Sorokin cover, © 1938 . . . .   3.50   5.50

☐ **When Times Get Better,** lyric by Irving
Kahal, music by Sammy Fain, © 1932 . . . .   2.50   3.50

☐ **When Will the Sun Shine for Me,** lyric by
Benny Davis, music by Abner Silver, © 1923   1.75   2.50

Price Range

☐ **When You Come Back to Me,** music by Neil Moret, words by Harry Williams, pub. Daniels and Wilson, © 1919 .... 1.25   1.75

☐ **When You Look in the Heart of a Rose,** lyric by Marian Gillespie, music by Florence Methven, pub. Feist, © 1918 .... 2.00   3.00

☐ **When Your Lover Has Gone,** words and music by E. A. Swan, Ben Harris cover, © 1931 .... 2.50   3.50

☐ **Where the Lazy Daisies Grow,** by Cliff Friend, inset The Ross Girls, © 1924 ..... 2.50   3.50

☐ **Wild Cherries** by Ted Snyder; drawing of girl sitting in a cherry tree, photo of Amy Butler inset, "Characteristique Rag," Ted Snyder Co. pub., © 1908 .... 6.00   10.00

☐ **Wing Lee's Ragtime Clock,** by Al Trahern; photo of performers, title is in mock Chinese lettering on cover, supplement to New York Journal & Advertiser, September 2, 1900 .. 4.00   6.50

☐ **Witch's Whirl Waltzes,** by E. T. Paull, large-format color litho, scene pictures a witch stirring up a spell from a large cauldron, devils and faeries spin in the cyclone spell, © 1901 22.00   28.00

RECORDINGS AND MEMORABILIA

CLASSICAL

COMPOSER MEMORABILIA

Thanks to at least 200 years of active collecting, memorabilia relating to most composers of classical and semiclassical music is well preserved. Due to heavy institutional buying and more interest internationally, these items are much more expensive than a similar item would be for a jazz or rock personality.

One generally thinks of autographs, but many other varieties of "collectible" items can be found, including (in the case of composers who lived from the mid-19th century onward) photographs, personal items, posters, etc. The fame or importance of the composer has little relation to the cash value of his memorabilia. It is mainly a question of what has been preserved, and the significance of the individual item. Verdi, perhaps the most celebrated operatic composer, lived a long life and was a voluminous letter-writer; hence, his letters, excepting those of really worthy content, sell rather cheaply. Handwritten letters in this section are designated by the heading AL. The manner in which an item has been preserved also enters into the picture. An autograph that has been framed along with a photo, which is often done with composers' autographs, is sure to bring a higher price than if unframed.

The European dealers are the best sources for memorabilia of European composers. However, their prices are frequently higher than those charged by U.S. dealers, because of the overwhelming foreign demand for composers' autographs and other items. Auction sales both here and abroad are another prime source for this material

	ALs	Signed Photo	Plain Signature
☐ Albeniz, Isaac	40.00–50.00	75.00–100.00	5.00–8.00
☐ Bach, C. P. E.	1100.00–2200.00		120.00–150.00
☐ Bach, Johannes Sebastian ..	12,000.00–16,000.00		1100.00–1300.00
☐ Barber, Samuel	100.00–125.00	50.00–70.00	7.00–12.00

	ALs	Signed Photo	Plain Signature
☐ Bartok, Bela	180.00–265.00	100.00–135.00	7.00–12.00
☐ Beethoven, Ludwig von	11,750.00–15,500.00		1100.00–1300.00
☐ Bellini, Vincenzo	505.00–800.00		20.00–25.00
☐ Berg, Alban	200.00–265.00	75.00–100.00	7.00–12.00
☐ Berlioz, Hector	355.00–600.00	450.00–750.00	15.00–20.00
☐ Bernstein, Leonard	25.00–40.00	6.00–9.00	3.00–4.00
☐ Bizet, Georges	305.00–450.00	375.00–550.00	15.00–20.00
☐ Bloch, Ernest	120.00–175.00	65.00–85.00	7.00–10.00
☐ Boieldieu, Francois	38.00–45.00		
☐ Boito, Arrigo	50.00–70.00	55.00–75.00	4.00–7.00
☐ Borodin, Alexander	450.00–600.00	300.00–400.00	13.00–17.00
☐ Brahms, Johannes	300.00–500.00	450.00–600.00	45.00–65.00
☐ Britten, Benjamin	40.00–60.00	43.00–60.00	4.00–6.00
☐ Bruch, Max	67.00–110.00	35.00–50.00	4.00–6.00
☐ Bruckner, Anton	93.00–158.00	105.00–165.00	6.00–10.00
☐ Busoni, Ferruccio	70.00–95.00	60.00–80.00	4.00–7.00
☐ Cage, John	97.00–155.00		4.00–6.00
☐ Chabrier, Alexis	67.00–105.00	100.00–150.00	4.00–7.00
☐ Charpentier, Gustave	37.00–55.00	53.00–75.00	3.00–5.00
☐ Chopin, Frederic	2000.00–2600.00		70.00–100.00

	ALs	Signed Photo	Plain Signature
☐ Copland, Aaron	27.00–43.00	15.00–20.00	3.00–4.00
☐ Debussy, Claude	300.00–370.00	195.00–270.00	13.00–20.00
☐ Delibes, Leo	250.00–315.00	275.00–335.00	12.00–17.00
☐ Dello Joio, Norman	15.00–20.00	6.00–9.00	3.00–4.00
☐ Donizetti, Gaetano	300.00–400.00		15.00–23.00
☐ Dukas, Paul	25.00–35.00	24.00–35.00	4.00–6.00
☐ Dvorak, Antonin	125.00–165.00	155.00–225.00	6.00–9.00
☐ Elgar, Sir Edward	155.00–215.00	95.00–135.00	6.00–9.00
☐ Falla, Manuel de	45.00–60.00	65.00–85.00	5.00–6.00
☐ Faure, Gabriel	40.00–55.00	50.00–75.00	4.00–6.00
☐ Flotow, F. von	120.00–165.00	300.00–425.00	6.00–9.00
☐ Franck, Cesar	105.00–145.00	115.00–160.00	5.00–8.00
☐ Gershwin, George	600.00–850.00	105.00–105.00	6.00–9.00
☐ Giordano, Umberto	35.00–50.00	33.00–43.00	3.00–5.00
☐ Glazunov, Alexander	95.00–135.00	105.00–150.00	6.00–9.00
☐ Glinka, Mikhail	75.00–115.00	115.00–165.00	6.00–9.00
☐ Gounod, Charles	60.00–90.00	105.00–150.00	4.00–6.00
☐ Grieg, Edvard	175.00–250.00	190.00–235.00	6.00–9.00
☐ Handel, Georg F.	8000.00–12000.00		400.00–555.00
☐ Hanson, Howard	30.00–35.00	27.00–35.00	3.00–4.00

	ALs	Signed Photo	Plain Signature
☐ Harris, Roy	20.00–28.00	20.00–28.00	3.00–4.00
☐ Haydn, Joseph	3000.00–4000.00		80.00–120.00
☐ Hindemith, Paul	25.00–34.00	28.00–35.00	3.00–4.00
☐ Holst, Gustav	70.00–100.00	75.00–120.00	4.00–6.00
☐ Honegger, Arthur	32.00–40.00	43.00–55.00	3.00–4.00
☐ Hovhannes, Alan	11.00–17.00	9.00–13.00	2.00–3.00
☐ Humperdinck, Engelbert	120.00–150.00	155.00–200.00	7.00–10.00
☐ Ives, Charles	95.00–125.00	35.00–55.00	7.00–10.00
☐ Khachaturian, Aram	70.00–115.00	60.00–85.00	5.00–7.00
☐ Kodaly, Zoltan	75.00–120.00	40.00–60.00	5.00–7.00
☐ Kreisler, Fritz	50.00–75.00	50.00–75.00	3.00–4.00
☐ Kreutzer, Rudolphe	150.00–200.00		8.00–12.00
☐ Lalo, Edouard	75.00–115.00	175.00–225.00	5.00–7.00
☐ Leoncavallo, R.	75.00–115.00	90.00–120.00	5.00–7.00
☐ Liszt, Franz	350.00–525.00	350.00–470.00	8.00–13.00
☐ MacDowell, Edward	115.00–160.00	85.00–120.00	4.00–6.00
☐ Mahler, Gustav	500.00–700.00	250.00–320.00	8.00–12.00
☐ Mascagni, Pietro	60.00–80.00	35.00–48.00	3.00–4.00
☐ Massenet, Jules	75.00–120.00	100.00–130.00	5.00–7.00
☐ Mendelssohn-Bartholdy	300.00–400.00		8.00–12.00

	ALs	Signed Photo	Plain Signature
☐ Menotti, G. C.	35.00– 50.00	26.00– 35.00	3.00– 4.00
☐ Monteverdi, Claudio	6750.00– 11000.00		450.00– 650.00
☐ Mozart, Wolfgang A.	17500.00– 25000.00		1250.00– 1600.00
☐ Offenbach, Jacques	160.00– 220.00	335.00– 435.00	7.00– 10.00
☐ Orff, Karl	25.00– 35.00	20.00– 26.00	3.00– 4.00
☐ Paderewski, Ignace	70.00– 110.00	55.00– 70.00	4.00– 6.00
☐ Paganini, Niccolo	320.00– 460.00		7.00– 10.00
☐ Palestrina, G. P.	4000.00– 5500.00		175.00– 230.00
☐ Ponchielli, A.	225.00– 280.00	250.00– 320.00	7.00– 10.00
☐ Poulenc, Francis	35.00– 40.00	30.00– 38.00	3.00– 4.00
☐ Prokofieff, Serge	320.00– 420.00	110.00– 160.00	7.00– 10.00
☐ Puccini, Giacomo	300.00– 400.00	170.00– 230.00	7.00– 10.00
☐ Rachmaninoff, Sergel	160.00– 200.00	200.00– 250.00	5.00– 8.00
☐ Ravel, Maurice	300.00– 400.00	190.00– 250.00	5.00– 8.00
☐ Rimsky-Korsakov, Nikolai ...	600.00– 800.00	350.00– 450.00	9.00– 12.00
☐ Rossini, G.	250.00– 300.00	325.00– 425.00	7.00– 10.00
☐ Rubinstein, Anton	150.00– 200.00	225.00– 280.00	4.00– 6.00
☐ Saint-Saens, Camille	120.00– 150.00	125.00– 170.00	4.00– 6.00
☐ Schonberg, Arnold	170.00– 230.00	70.00– 90.00	5.00– 7.00
☐ Schubert, Franz	3750.00– 5500.00		80.00– 120.00

	ALs	Signed Photo	Plain Signature
☐ Schumann, Robert	1200.00– 1700.00		13.00– 18.00
☐ Schumann, William	27.00– 35.00	25.00– 33.00	3.00– 4.00
☐ Scriabin, Alex	320.00– 420.00	325.00– 425.00	7.00– 10.00
☐ Shostakovich, Dmitri	400.00– 500.00	230.00– 280.00	7.00– 10.00
☐ Sibelius, Jean	180.00– 250.00	210.00– 260.00	7.00– 10.00
☐ Smetana, Bedrich	575.00– 700.00	600.00– 800.00	8.00– 12.00
☐ Stockhausen, K.	26.00– 33.00	25.00– 30.00	3.00– 4.00
☐ Strauss, Richard	200.00– 250.00	150.00– 200.00	7.00– 10.00
☐ Stravinsky, Igor	150.00– 200.00	120.00– 170.00	4.00– 6.00
☐ Tchaikovsky, Peter	900.00– 1200.00	675.00– 900.00	15.00– 20.00
☐ Thomas, Ambroise	150.00– 175.00	175.00– 225.00	5.00– 7.00
☐ Thomson, Virgil	35.00– 50.00	25.00– 35.00	3.00– 4.00
☐ Wagner, Richard	550.00– 750.00	675.00– 950.00	25.00– 30.00

INSTRUMENTAL RECORDINGS

The following recordings are all in 78rpm and issued mostly in the years between 1900 and 1925.

By and large the public of this era (1900–1925), while a fair segment of it understood and appreciated classical music, bought instrumental recordings for the composition—not for the artist, as is usually the situation with serious fans of classical music today. In fact, the name of the pianist, cellist, orchestra conductor, etc., was frequently not even noticed. Fortunately, the record companies made the necessary identifications on record labels, otherwise the collecting of these records would now be very confusing.

While the sound quality of full orchestral recordings made before about 1912 is somewhat short of pleasing, selections of concert or chamber work by instrumentalists are more satisfactory. The piano's sound was well captured on early recordings, the violin's perhaps even better, the cello's tolerably well. They failed to meld in orchestral recordings because of the archaic practice of trying to capture all the sound in a studio or hall through a single microphone or horn, a practice which has been replaced with more sophisticated recording techniques.

	Price Range	
□ **ELMAN, MISCHA (violinist), VIctor Red Seal**		
□ "Moment Musical/Perpetual Mobile"	5.00	7.00
□ "Fantasie" (Faust)	5.00	7.00
□ "Swing Song"	5.00	7.00
□ "Gavotte"	5.00	7.00
□ "Serenade"	5.00	7.00
□ "Minuet in G #2"	5.00	7.00
□ "Les Farfadets"	5.00	7.00
□ "Minuet in F"	5.00	7.00
□ "Gavotte in G" (Idomeneo)	5.00	7.00
□ "Traumerei"	5.00	7.00
□ "Capricietto"	5.00	7.00
□ "Waltz in E Flat"	5.00	7.00
□ "Rondo Capriccioso"	9.00	12.00
□ "Souvenir de Moscow"	9.00	12.00
□ "Nocturne in E Flat Opus 9, #2"	9.00	12.00
□ "Melodie Opus 42, #3"	9.00	12.00
□ "Humoresque"	9.00	12.00
□ "Caprice Basque"	9.00	12.00
□ "Sicilienne and Rigaudon"	9.00	12.00
□ "Cavatina Op. 85 #3"	9.00	12.00
□ "Ave Maria"	9.00	12.00
□ "Chanson Louis XIII"	9.00	12.00
□ "Meditation" (Thais)	9.00	12.00
□ "Vogel als Prophet Op. 82 #7"	5.00	7.00
□ "Hungarian Dance #7"	5.00	7.00
□ "In a Gondola"	5.00	7.00
□ "Country Dance"	5.00	7.00
□ "Minuet in D"	5.00	7.00
□ "Rondino on a Theme by Beethoven"	5.00	7.00
□ "Pastorale"	5.00	7.00
□ "Orientale"	5.00	7.00
□ "Capriccio"	5.00	7.00

Price Range

☐ "Valse Caprice Op. 16"	5.00	7.00
☐ "Souvenir"	5.00	7.00
☐ "Tango"	5.00	7.00
☐ "Canto Amoroso"	12.00	17.00
☐ "Dans les Bois"	12.00	17.00
☐ **HEIFETZ, JASCHA (violinist), Victor Red Seal**		
☐ "Valse Bluette"	5.00	7.00
☐ "Ruins of Athens"	5.00	7.00
☐ "Capricieuse Op. 17"	5.00	7.00
☐ "Meditation Op. 32"	5.00	7.00
☐ "Guitarre Op. 45 #2"	5.00	7.00
☐ "Caprice #20"	5.00	7.00
☐ "Minuet"	5.00	7.00
☐ "Sicilienne and Rigaudon"	5.00	7.00
☐ "Serenade Op. 4"	5.00	7.00
☐ "Caprice #13"	5.00	7.00
☐ "Zapateado Op. 23 #6"	5.00	7.00
☐ "Spanish Dance"	5.00	7.00
☐ "Hungarian Dance #1 in G Minor"	5.00	7.00
☐ "Slavonic Dance #1 in G Minor"	5.00	7.00
☐ "Hebrew Lullaby"	5.00	7.00
☐ "Minuet in D"	5.00	7.00
☐ "Widmung"	5.00	7.00
☐ "Scherzo Tarantelle Op. 16"	9.00	12.00
☐ "Ave Marie"	9.00	12.00
☐ "Hebrew Melody"	9.00	12.00
☐ "Spanish Dance Op. 21 #1"	9.00	12.00
☐ "Ronde des Lutins"	9.00	12.00
☐ "Moto Perpetuo"	17.00	23.00
☐ "On Wings of Song"	9.00	12.00
☐ "Concert Op. 22"	9.00	12.00
☐ "Nocturne in E Flat Op. 9 #2"	9.00	12.00
☐ "Introduction and Tarantelle Op. 43"	9.00	12.00
☐ "Serenade Op. 48—Valse"	9.00	12.00
☐ "Symphonie Espagnole—Andante"	9.00	12.00
☐ "Violin Concerto—Canzonetta"	9.00	12.00
☐ "Zigeunerweisen #1"	9.00	12.00
☐ "Zigeunerweisen #2"	9.00	12.00
☐ "Serenade Melancolique Op. 26"	9.00	12.00
☐ "Concerto in E Minor—Finale"	9.00	12.00

	Price Range	
☐ "Rondo in G"	9.00	12.00
☐ "Concerto in A Minor Op. 28—Andante" ...	9.00	12.00
☐ "Nocturne Op. 27 #2"	9.00	12.00
☐ "Slavonic Dance #2 in E Minor"	9.00	12.00
☐ "Slavonic Dance #3 in G"	9.00	12.00
☐ **KREISLER, FRITZ (violinist), Victor Red Seal**		
☐ "Old Refrain"	5.00	7.00
☐ "Song Without Words #25"	5.00	7.00
☐ "Spanish Dance"	5.00	7.00
☐ "Songs My Mother Taught Me"	5.00	7.00
☐ "Berceuse Romantique"	5.00	7.00
☐ "Rondino on a Theme by Beethoven"	5.00	7.00
☐ "Arlesienne Suite: Adagietto"	5.00	7.00
☐ "Minuet"	5.00	7.00
☐ "Bohemian Fantasie"	9.00	12.00
☐ "Humoresque"	9.00	12.00
☐ "Meditation" (Thais)	9.00	12.00
☐ "Liebesfreud"	9.00	12.00
☐ "Caprice Viennois"	9.00	12.00
☐ "Moment Musical"	9.00	12.00
☐ "Tambourin Chinois"	9.00	12.00
☐ "Scherzo"	9.00	12.00
☐ "Chanson"	9.00	12.00
☐ "Praeludium"	9.00	12.00
☐ "Liebeslied"	9.00	12.00
☐ "Indian Lament"	9.00	12.00
☐ "Slavonic Dance #2 in E Minor"	9.00	12.00
☐ "Wienerisch"	9.00	12.00
☐ "Concerto for Two Violins Part I"	20.00	25.00
☐ "Concerto for Two Violins Part II"	20.00	25.00
☐ "Concerto for Two Violins Part III"	20.00	25.00
☐ "Poor Butterfly"	5.00	7.00
☐ "Underneath the Stars"	5.00	7.00
☐ "Rosamunde Ballet"	5.00	7.00
☐ "Paraphrase on Minuet"	5.00	7.00
☐ "Dream of Youth"	5.00	7.00
☐ "Polichinelle Serenade"	5.00	7.00
☐ "Beautiful Ohio"	5.00	7.00
☐ "Nobody Knows the Trouble I See"	5.00	7.00
☐ "Gypsy Serenade"	5.00	7.00

Price Range

☐ "Forsaken"	5.00	7.00
☐ "Who Can Tell"	5.00	7.00
☐ "Love Nest"	5.00	7.00
☐ "On Miami Shore"	5.00	7.00
☐ "Melody in A"	5.00	7.00
☐ "Souvenir"	5.00	7.00
☐ "To Spring Op. 43 #6"	5.00	7.00
☐ "La Gitana"	5.00	7.00
☐ "Paradise"	5.00	7.00
☐ "Waltz Op. 39 #15"	5.00	7.00
☐ "Aucassin and Nicolette"	5.00	7.00
☐ "Pale Moon"	5.00	7.00
☐ "Toy Soldier's March"	5.00	7.00
☐ "Midnight Bells"	5.00	7.00
☐ "Mazurka Op. 33 #2"	5.00	7.00
☐ "Melodie Op. 16 #2"	5.00	7.00
☐ "Cherry Ripe"	5.00	7.00
☐ "Entr'acte"	5.00	7.00
☐ "Love Sends a Little Gift of Roses"	5.00	7.00
☐ "The World Is Waiting for the Sunrise"	5.00	7.00
☐ "Old French Gavotte"	5.00	7.00
☐ "From the Land of the Sky Blue Water"	5.00	7.00
☐ "Farewell to Cucullain"	5.00	7.00
☐ "Serenade"	5.00	7.00
☐ "Miniature"	5.00	7.00
☐ "Syncopation"	5.00	7.00

☐ **PADEREWSKI, JAN (pianist), Victor Red Seal**

☐ "Minuet in G"	20.00	25.00
☐ "Valse Brilliante Op. 34 #1"	20.00	25.00
☐ "Hark Hark the Lark"	20.00	25.00
☐ "La Campanella"	20.00	25.00
☐ "Etude in F Minor"	20.00	25.00
☐ "Maiden's Wish Op. 74 #1"	20.00	25.00
☐ "Chant d'Amour"	20.00	25.00
☐ "Berceuse"	20.00	25.00
☐ "Aufschwung"	20.00	25.00
☐ "La Bandoline"	20.00	25.00
☐ "Carrillon de Cythere"	20.00	25.00
☐ "Warum"	20.00	25.00
☐ "Etude in G Flat Op. 25 #9"	12.00	16.00
☐ "Spinning Song"	12.00	16.00

	Price Range	
☐ "Chant du Voyageur"	12.00	16.00
☐ "Nocturne in F Sharp Op. 15 #2"	12.00	16.00
☐ "Polonaise Militaire Op. 40 #1"	12.00	16.00
☐ "Minuet in G"	12.00	16.00
☐ "Cracovienne Fantastique"	12.00	16.00
☐ "Waltz in C Sharp Minor Op. 64 #2"	12.00	16.00
☐ "Nocturne in F Op. 15 #1"	12.00	16.00
☐ "Valse Brilliante Op. 34 #1"	12.00	16.00
☐ "Hark Hark the Lark"	12.00	16.00
☐ "La Bandoline"	12.00	16.00
☐ "Warum"	12.00	16.00
☐ "La Campanella"	12.00	16.00
☐ "Nocturne in B Flat"	12.00	16.00
☐ "Maiden's Wish Op. 74 #1"	12.00	16.00
☐ "Hungarian Rhapsody #10"	12.00	16.00
☐ "Valse in A Flat Op. 42"	12.00	16.00
☐ "Hungarian Rhapsody #2 Part I"	12.00	16.00
☐ "Hungarian Rhapsody #2 Part II"	12.00	16.00
☐ **POWELL, MAUD (violinist), Victor Red Seal**		
☐ "Sault d'amour"	7.00	10.00
☐ "Gavotte" (Mignon)	7.00	10.00
☐ "Barcarolle" (Tales of Hoffmann)	7.00	10.00
☐ "Chanson a Bercer"	7.00	10.00
☐ "Silver Threads Among the Gold"	7.00	10.00
☐ "Tambourin"	7.00	10.00
☐ "Gondoliers"	7.00	10.00
☐ "Molly on the Shore"	7.00	10.00
☐ "Love's Delight"	7.00	10.00
☐ "Petite Valse"	7.00	10.00
☐ "Sonata in E, Second Movement"	7.00	10.00
☐ "Sonata in E, Fourth Movement"	7.00	10.00
☐ "Minuet in G"	7.00	10.00
☐ "Kol Nidre"	7.00	10.00
☐ "Guitarrero"	7.00	10.00
☐ "Little Firefly"	7.00	10.00
☐ "Poupee Valsante"	7.00	10.00
☐ "Valse Triste"	7.00	10.00
☐ "Largo" (Serse)	7.00	10.00
☐ "Concerto in G, Allegro Maestoso"	7.00	10.00
☐ "Concerto in G, Andante Tranquillo"	7.00	10.00
☐ "Concerto in G, Allegro Moderato"	7.00	10.00

	Price Range	
☐ "Humoresque"	7.00	10.00
☐ "Fifth Nocturne"	7.00	10.00
☐ "Four American Folk Songs"	7.00	10.00
☐ **RACHMANINOFF, SERGEI (pianist), Victor Red Seal**		
☐ "Lilacs"	23.00	30.00
☐ "Le Coucou"	12.00	16.00
☐ "Spinning Song"	12.00	16.00
☐ "De Gradus ad Parnassum"	12.00	16.00
☐ "Prelude in G Sharp Minor Op. 23 #12" ...	12.00	16.00
☐ "Waltz in D Flat Op. 64 #1"	12.00	16.00
☐ "Golliwog's Cake-walk"	12.00	16.00
☐ "Waltz in G Flat Major"	12.00	16.00
☐ "Prelude in C Sharp Minor Op. 3 #2"	12.00	16.00
☐ "Etude in F Minor"	12.00	16.00
☐ "Waltz and Elfin Dance"	12.00	16.00
☐ "Serenade Op. 3 #5"	12.00	16.00
☐ "La Jongleuse"	23.00	30.00
☐ "Waltz in A Flat Op. 40 #8"	23.00	30.00
☐ "Waltz in B Minor Op. 69 #2"	23.00	30.00
☐ "Mazurka in C Sharp Minor Op. 63 #3" ...	23.00	30.00
☐ "If I Were a Bird"	23.00	30.00
☐ "Prelude in G Minor Op. 23 #5"	12.00	16.00
☐ "Troika en traineaux"	12.00	16.00
☐ "Prelude in G Major Op. 32 #5"	12.00	16.00
☐ "Liebeslied"	12.00	16.00
☐ "Polka de W.R."	12.00	16.00
☐ "Polichinelle"	12.00	16.00
☐ "Nocturne in F Sharp Minor Op. 15 #2" ...	23.00	30.00
☐ **ZIMBALIST, EFREM (violinist), Victor Red Seal**		
☐ "Humoresque."	5.00	7.00
☐ "Orientale"	5.00	7.00
☐ "Long Ago"	5.00	7.00
☐ "Larghetto"	5.00	7.00
☐ "Hebraisches Lied und Tanz"	5.00	7.00
☐ "Sonata Op. 42 #2, Andantino"	5.00	7.00
☐ "Polish Dance"	5.00	7.00
☐ "Serenata"	5.00	7.00
☐ "Chant d'Automne"	5.00	7.00
☐ "Massa's in de Cold, Cold Ground"	5.00	7.00

	Price Range	
☐ "Old Black Joe"	5.00	7.00
☐ "Chant Negre"	5.00	7.00
☐ "Chant de la Veslomoy"	5.00	7.00
☐ "Russian Dance"	5.00	7.00
☐ "Spring Song"	5.00	7.00
☐ "Salut d'amour"	5.00	7.00
☐ "Song Without Words"	5.00	7.00
☐ "Madrigale"	9.00	12.00
☐ "Petite Serenade"	7.00	10.00
☐ "Improvisation"	7.00	10.00
☐ "Entr'acte"	7.00	10.00
☐ "Gypsy Love Song" (Fortune Teller)	7.00	10.00
☐ "Hungarian Dances #20 and 21"	7.00	10.00
☐ "Legende"	7.00	10.00
☐ "Alabama"	7.00	10.00
☐ "Broken Melody"	7.00	10.00
☐ "Millions d'Arlequin"	7.00	10.00
☐ "The Lark"	7.00	10.00

COUNTRY AND WESTERN

MEMORABILIA

For reasons not entirely explainable, fans of country and western music have traditionally been more avid collectors of star-related memorabilia than fans of most other kinds of music. From at least as early as the 1930's, devotees of country and western have sought out and devotedly preserved photographs, clothing, instruments, and virtually anything connected with their favorite artists. For a long while, however, this sort of collecting activity was confined to the so-called country and western belt—Tennessee, Kentucky, West Virginia, and other states where this music originated. This is hardly surprising, as it was not until the mid-1950's that country and western recordings began to receive disc-jockey play nationwide. Until then, many of the biggest country and western stars were virtually unknown outside the south and southwest. Today, collecting interest in country and western memorabilia is not only national but international, with strongest buying activity for items pertaining to the early pioneers and big old-time stars, those who recorded in the 1920–39 period. Material relating to modern and current country and western performers is, of course, collected also, but prices on the whole tend to be much lower.

Collectors of country and western memorabilia can purchase from dealers, but a much more exciting—and usually less expensive—way of obtaining this material is "at the source"; from attics and garages of southern music fans, as well as southern secondhand shops. Troves of it certainly exist that have not yet reached the hands of collectors but are waiting to be discovered. In the case of early country and western artists who are still alive, a letter to them (when the address can be learned) almost always brings a signed photo or other reply.

Beware of printed signatures on photos of semi-modern and modern stars, especially Gene Autry, Roy Rogers, Roy Acuff, Ernest Tubb, Eddy Arnold, and Johnny Cash. Photos of these performers with stenciled or facsimile signatures were distributed in large numbers.

	Price Range	
☐ **ACUFF, ROY,** c. 1948, map of Nashville, Tenn., signed by him and several other country and western stars	100.00	125.00
☐ **ACUFF, ROY,** small colored photo on card, unsigned, early	11.00	16.00
☐ **ACUFF, ROY,** c. 1955. 8x10 color photo, signed and inscribed, laminated	60.00	80.00
☐ **ACUFF, ROY,** c. 1940, fiddle used by him	1100.00	1500.00
☐ **ACUFF, ROY,** necktie reputedly worn by him at Grand Old Opry performance	110.00	135.00
☐ **ACUFF, ROY,** sheet music to "Wabash Cannonball," signed and inscribed, stained	95.00	120.00
☐ **ACUFF, ROY,** c. 1938–72, collection of c. 200 press cuttings on his career	110.00	140.00
☐ **ACUFF, ROY,** three large scrapbooks (14x17) with c. 2,500 items pertaining to him, 23 autographed photos, about 200 snapshots and candid photos, some unsigned publicity photos, c. 1,000 press cuttings, etc., mostly in well-preserved condition	3700.00	4500.00
☐ **ACUFF, ROY,** c. 1958, typed letter, signed	32.00	40.00
☐ **ALLEN, REX,** 8x10 photo, signed	11.00	16.00
☐ **ALLEN, REX,** c. 1950's, copy of *Rex Allen Comics,* published by Dell	4.60	6.00
☐ **ALLEN, REX,** autographed copy of *Rex Allen Comics*	15.00	20.00
☐ **ALLEN, REX,** button with his name and picture	5.00	7.00

Price Range

☐ **ARNOLD, EDDY,** 7x9 color photo mounted on stiff paper, signed twice, in original mailing envelope 35.00   45.00

☐ **ARNOLD, EDDY,** 8x10 photo, signed 15.00   20.00

☐ **ARNOLD, EDDY,** 16″ 78rpm transcription of a radio show 120.00   150.00

☐ **ARNOLD, EDDY,** pair of tan leather boots reputedly worn by him 110.00   140.00

☐ **ATKINS, CHET,** c. 1956, 6x7 photo with guitar, signed and dated 20.00   25.00

☐ **ATKINS, CHET,** LP record album cover, signed, no record 33.00   42.00

☐ **ATKINS, CHET,** two small colored photos, unsigned 7.00   10.00

☐ **ATKINS, CHET,** c. 1963, typewritten letter, signed 9.00   12.00

☐ **ATKINS, CHET,** Grand Old Opry poster with his name 16.00   22.00

☐ **ATKINS, CHET,** 8x10 photo with Little Jimmie Dickens, signed by both, inscribed 35.00   45.00

☐ **ATKINS, CHET,** postcard photo with facsimile signature 4.00   6.00

☐ **ATKINS, CHET,** two pieces of sheet music with notes in his hand 35.00   45.00

☐ **ATKINS, CHET,** collection of 67 news cuttings 55.00   70.00

☐ **AUTRY, GENE,** c. 1948, "Autry's Aces," fan club newsletter 30.00   40.00

☐ **AUTRY, GENE,** Gene Autry Flying A Ranch decal, 5x8 . . . . 20.00   25.00

☐ **AUTRY, GENE,** c. 1940's, 5x7 photo, printed inscription "From your pal, Gene Autry" . . . 13.00   17.00

☐ **AUTRY, GENE,** c. 1950, 8x10 photo, signed and inscribed 40.00   50.00

☐ **AUTRY, GENE,** c. 1950, button with his name and picture 15.00   20.00

☐ **AUTRY, GENE,** signature on rodeo souvenir booklet, Madison Square Garden, N.Y 35.00   50.00

☐ **AUTRY, GENE,** cowboy hat reputedly worn by him in film 100.00   115.00

☐ **AUTRY, GENE,** membership card in Gene Autry Fan Club 15.00   20.00

Eddy Arnold

	Price Range	
☐ **AUTRY, GENE,** 4x6 photo on horse, signed	**17.00**	**22.00**
☐ **BRITT, ELTON,** c. 1946, 8x10 photo, signed and inscribed	**16.00**	**21.00**
☐ **BRITT, ELTON,** c. 1932, ALs, two pp.	**23.00**	**33.00**
☐ **BRITT, ELTON,** 78rpm record, signed on the label	**50.00**	**65.00**
☐ **BRITT, ELTON,** two small snapshot photos, one signed	**15.00**	**20.00**
☐ **BRITT, ELTON,** page with photo and biography cut from book, signed, framed	**20.00**	**25.00**
☐ **BRITT, ELTON,** photo with Cowboy Copas, signed by Britt	**16.00**	**22.00**
☐ **BRITT, ELTON,** c. 1951, 78rpm record sleeve, signed, dated	**13.00**	**18.00**
☐ **CARLISLE, CLIFF,** 8x10 studio photo, signed	**15.00**	**20.00**
☐ **CARLISLE, CLIFF,** photo in front of radio mike, signed	**15.00**	**20.00**

Price Range

☐ **CARLISLE, CLIFF,** photo with Dellmore Bros., signed by Carlisle only 16.00   22.00

☐ **CARLISLE, CLIFF,** postcard photo, unsigned   4.00   5.00

☐ **CARLISLE, CLIFF,** signature on advertising poster 10.00   13.00

☐ **CARLISLE, CLIFF,** collection of 32 photos, none signed, mostly cut from magazines and mounted on cards 9.00   12.00

☐ **CARTER, WILF ("MONTANA SLIM"),** c. 1948, 8x10 photo, signed 20.00   25.00

☐ **CARTER, WILF,** c. 1934, ALs, two pp., with envelope 15.00   20.00

☐ **CARTER, WILF,** c. 1941 and 1947, two postcards in his hand 11.00   16.00

☐ **CARTER, WILF,** c. 1932, 4x5 photo, signed, creased 13.00   18.00

☐ **CARTER, WILF,** c. 1975, typewritten letter, signed 7.00   10.00

☐ **CARTER, WILF,** record company ad circular, signed 6.00   8.00

☐ **CARTER, WILF,** 8x10 photo signed "Montana Slim" 15.00   20.00

☐ **COPAS, COWBOY,** sheet music, "Filipino Baby," signed 25.00   35.00

☐ **COPAS, COWBOY,** c. 1957, ALs, one page   24.00   33.00

☐ **COPAS, COWBOY,** c. 1955, 8x10 photo, signed and inscribed 33.00   40.00

☐ **COPAS, COWBOY,** brief memo in his hand, undated, early 15.00   20.00

☐ **DALHART, VERNON,** c. 1925, 8x10 photo, signed 50.00   65.00

☐ **DALHART, VERNON,** c. 1920's, sheet music, "John T. Scopes Trial," signed, in a metal frame 125.00   160.00

☐ **DALHART, VERNON,** 5x7 photo wearing suit and tie, signed 30.00   40.00

☐ **DALHART, VERNON,** photo with Riley Puckett, signed by Dalhart only, browned 70.00   90.00

☐ **DAVIS, JIMMIE,** 8x10 close-up, signed 13.00   16.00

☐ **DAVIS, JIMMIE,** typewritten letter as Governor of Louisiana, 1½ pp., relating to a farm bill, signed 30.00   40.00

Price Range

☐ **DAVIS, JIMMIE,** typewritten letter as Governor of Louisiana, about speculation on his seeking a second term, signed 45.00 60.00

☐ **DAVIS, JIMMIE,** signature on a calling card 5.00 7.00

☐ **DAVIS, JIMMIE,** 78rpm record, signed on the label 50.00 70.00

☐ **DAVIS, JIMMIE,** bumper sticker "Davis for Governor" 15.00 20.00
This is the value as a country and western collectible; collectors of political items would probably pay much less.

☐ **DAVIS, JIMMIE,** celluloid pin, "Davis for Gov." 9.00 12.00

☐ **DAVIS, JIMMIE,** photo behind desk in governor's mansion, signed 42.00 52.00

☐ **DAVIS, JIMMIE,** three Louisiana newspapers with headlines "Davis elected" or other headlines to that effect 9.00 12.00

☐ **DEXTER, AL,** 8x10 photo, signed 11.00 15.00

☐ **DEXTER, AL,** 78rpm record, signed on the label 30.00 37.00

☐ **DEXTER, AL,** sheet music, "Pistol Packin' Mama," signed 17.00 24.00

☐ **DEXTER, AL,** c. 1941, ALs, with envelope 15.00 20.00

☐ **GAYLE, CRYSTAL,** 8x10 publicity photo, framed, signed 9.00 14.00

☐ **GAYLE, CRYSTAL,** four articles and one album review, mounted and signed 14.00 19.00

☐ **JONES, GRANDPA,** 8x10 signed photo 8.00 11.00

☐ **JONES, GRANDPA,** c. 1972, signed photo with "Hee Haw" cast 7.00 10.00

☐ **JONES, GRANDPA,** c. 1933, 5x7 photo at early age, seated with banjo at radio mike, signed 20.00 25.00

☐ **JONES, GRANDPA,** TV Guide issue with feature on "Hee Haw," signed 7.00 10.00

☐ **JONES, GRANDPA,** LP record album cover, signed, record missing 33.00 42.00

☐ **JONES, GRANDPA,** c. 1940's, banjo reputedly used by him 500.00 700.00

☐ **JONES, GRANDPA,** photo with Buck Owens, signed by Jones 7.00 10.00

Price Range

☐ **JONES, GRANDPA,** photo of Dave Macon inscribed to Grandpa Jones 125.00 155.00

☐ **KINCAID, BRADLEY,** c. 1940's, 8x10 close-up photo, signed 15.00 20.00

☐ **KINCAID, BRADLEY,** photo wearing cowboy outfit, signed 16.00 21.00

☐ **KINCAID, BRADLEY,** c. 1930's, record company brochure, signed 9.00 12.00

☐ **KINCAID, BRADLEY,** c. 1930's, photo on stage, signed 15.00 20.00

☐ **KINCAID, BRADLEY,** two snapshot photos, unsigned 6.00 8.00

☐ **KINCAID, BRADLEY,** c. 1930, ALs, with envelope 22.00 27.00

☐ **KINCAID, BRADLEY,** poster advertising an appearance 16.00 22.00

☐ **KINCAID, BRADLEY,** postcard photo, facsimile signature 5.00 7.00

☐ **KINCAID, BRADLEY,** photo on street in Nashville, signed 13.00 17.00

☐ **KRISTOFFERSON, KRIS,** 8x10 publicity photo, signed 15.00 21.00

☐ **KRISTOFFERSON, KRIS,** movie still, signed 20.00 26.00

☐ **KRISTOFFERSON, KRIS,** handwritten note to fan, c. 1975 .... 25.00 32.00

☐ **KRISTOFFERSON, KRIS,** snapshot taken with a fan, signed...................... 19.00 27.00

☐ **LYNN, LORETTA,** 8x10 publicity photo, signed 8.00 13.00

☐ **LYNN, LORETTA,** sheet music, signed 10.00 15.00

☐ **LYNN, LORETTA,** greeting card, signed and inscribed 10.00 15.00

☐ **MACON, "UNCLE" DAVE,** c. 1920, banjo reputedly used by him, with several vintage photographs and other items, in a box 1350.00 1700.00

☐ **MACON, "UNCLE" DAVE,** c. 1950, 30-minute reel-to-reel tape of an amateur interview with him, discussing his career 95.00 120.00

☐ **MACON, "UNCLE" DAVE,** c. 1937, 4x5 photo, signed 32.00 40.00

Price Range

☐ **MACON, "UNCLE" DAVE,** c. 1949, ALs, four pages, reminiscences on his career, written in crayon 250.00   330.00

☐ **MAINER, J. E.,** 8x10 photo with his group, signed by him and one other 90.00   115.00

☐ **MAINER, J. E.,** c. 1930, 4x5 photo, signed and inscribed 45.00   65.00

☐ **MAINER, J. E.,** theater bill with his name .. 55.00   75.00

☐ **McMICHEN, CLAYTON,** 8x10 photo, signed, worn, creased 55.00   77.00

☐ **McMICHEN, CLAYTON,** 78rpm record, signed on the label 70.00   95.00

☐ **MONROE, BILL,** c. 1942, ALs, two pages .. 10.00   13.00

☐ **MONROE, BILL,** postcard photo, facsimile signature 4.00   6.00

☐ **MONROE, BILL,** c. 1953, photo of him on stage, signed, dated 7.00   10.00

☐ **MONROE, BILL,** printed photo, "Blue Grass Boys," signed 10.00   14.00

☐ **MONROE, BILL,** 8x10 photo, signed and inscribed 9.00   12.00

☐ **MONROE, BILL,** necktie reputedly worn by him 22.00   30.00

☐ **MONROE, BILL,** scrapbook with 300-odd clippings, photos 120.00   150.00

☐ **MONROE, BILL,** LP record album cover, signed, no record 35.00   45.00

☐ **MONROE, BILL,** photo with Ernest Tubb, signed by Monroe 11.00   15.00

☐ **MULLICAN, MOON,** c. 1953, photo of him at piano, signed 10.00   13.00

☐ **MULLICAN, MOON,** 8x10 studio portrait, signed 11.00   16.00

☐ **MULLICAN, MOON,** printed discography of his recordings, signed 8.00   11.00

☐ **MULLICAN, MOON,** large poster with his name and picture 30.00   40.00

☐ **NELSON, WILLIE,** 8x10 publicity photo, signed 16.00   24.00

☐ **NELSON, WILLIE,** concert ticket stub, c. 1977 .... 14.00   19.00

Price Range

☐ **NELSON, WILLIE,** bandanna supposedly worn by him in concert, c. 1980 . . . .   30.00   45.00

☐ **PARTON, DOLLY,** 8x10 publicity photo, signed 21.00   28.00

☐ **PARTON, DOLLY,** snapshot taken with fan, signed and inscribed 15.00   21.00

☐ **POOLE, CHARLIE,** 5x7 photo of him, signed, framed 27.00   37.00

☐ **POOLE, CHARLIE,** c. 1928, printed picture, "North Carolina Ramblers," signed 40.00   55.00

☐ **PRIDE, CHARLIE,** 8x10 publicity photo, signed 10.00   16.00

☐ **PRIDE, CHARLEY,** 6x7 photo of him in concert, signed and inscribed 14.00   19.00

☐ **PRIDE, CHARLEY,** photo with Johnny Cash, signed only by Pride 12.00   17.00

☐ **PRIDE, CHARLEY,** album cover, signed, missing record 9.00   14.00

☐ **RITTER, TEX,** c. 1958, check endorsed by him 33.00   44.00

☐ **RITTER, TEX,** motion picture still, signed . .   17.00   22.00

☐ **RITTER, TEX,** printed postcard photo, facsimile signature 7.00   10.00

☐ **RITTER, TEX,** western-style belt worn by him   70.00   95.00

☐ **RITTER, TEX,** sheet music, "Old Chisum Trail," signed 35.00   45.00

☐ **RITTER, TEX,** c. 1946, cover of a 78rpm record album set, signed, two records present (incomplete) 125.00   150.00

☐ **RITTER, TEX,** 37 motion picture stills, unsigned 90.00   120.00

☐ **RITTER, TEX,** motion picture lobby card, 27x41 . . . .   90.00   120.00

☐ **RITTER, TEX,** 8x10 photo, signed and inscribed 22.00   33.00

☐ **RITTER, TEX,** c. 1968–74, six snapshot photos 17.00   22.00

☐ **RITTER, TEX,** membership card "Tex Ritter Fan Club" 13.00   16.00

☐ **RITTER, TEX,** c. 1936, ALs, one page, torn   33.00   44.00

☐ **RITTER, TEX,** photo with Gary Cooper, signed by both 350.00   450.00

Price Range

☐ **ROBERTSON, TEXAS JIM,** c. 1940's, 5x7 photo, signed 10.00   14.00

☐ **ROBERTSON, TEXAS JIM,** full-color photo, 3x4, signed on back 11.00   15.00

☐ **ROBERTSON, TEXAS JIM,** 78rpm record, signed on label 40.00   55.00

☐ **ROBERTSON, TEXAS JIM,** 8x10 photo, signed and inscribed 15.00   20.00

☐ **ROBERTSON, TEXAS JIM,** signature on a record company brochure 6.00   8.00

☐ **ROBISON, CARSON,** c. 1945, small snapshot, inscribed "With best wishes, Carson Robison," ink somewhat faded, mounted on stiff gray cardboard with traces of glue on the back 22.00   30.00

☐ **ROBISON, CARSON,** postcard dated 1938, three lines in his handwriting with signature "Carson," sent to a friend 20.00   25.00

☐ **ROBISON, CARSON,** scrap album containing c. 65 press cuttings and other material relating to him, mostly 1940's, a few unsigned and one small signed photograph, the album damaged, contents mostly in good condition 120.00   150.00

☐ **ROBISON, CARSON,** c. early 1940's, photo with Roy Acuff, signed by both, probably taken at Nashville, framed 80.00   105.00

☐ **RODGERS, JIMMIE,** c. 1932, 8x10 photo with banjo, signed 275.00   350.00

☐ **RODGERS, JIMMIE,** 4x5 postcard photo, facsimile signature 33.00   40.00

☐ **RODGERS, JIMMIE,** photo with Will Rogers, signed by both, shortly before J. R.'s death 575.00   770.00

☐ **RODGERS, JIMMIE,** sheet music, "Waiting for a Train," signed 450.00   570.00

☐ **RODGERS, JIMMIE,** c. 1933, obituary notice from N.Y. Times 9.00   12.00

☐ **RODGERS, JIMMIE,** letter to him from record company executive 27.00   35.00

☐ **ROGERS, ROY,** c. probably 1950, white china plate with colored illustration of Roy and Trigger, lettered "Roy Rogers and Trigger—Many Happy Trails," 9" in diameter .. 60.00   80.00

Price Range

☐ **ROGERS, ROY,** Child's clothes rack, wood, 4 feet tall, die-cut figure of Roy and Trigger, decorated with cattle brands 125.00   160.00

☐ **ROGERS, ROY,** child's cloth bathrobe, gray background with cowboy motifs and Roy's name, belt missing 85.00   110.00

☐ **ROGERS, ROY,** pair of child's gloves, black cloth and plastic, illustration of Roy and Trigger on each glove 22.00   33.00

☐ **ROGERS, ROY,** c. 1955, "Roy Rogers and the Man from Dodge City," booklet advertising Dodge autos, 16 pp., 5x8 ....   15.00   20.00

☐ **ROGERS, ROY,** c. probably 1950's, "Roy Rogers Fix-It Stagecoach." Plastic toy stagecoach with two horses, strongbox, rifle, driver, etc., in original box 125.00   160.00

☐ **ROGERS, ROY,** "Roy Rogers Hauler and Van Trailer with Nellybelle Jeep," with plastic figures of Roy, Dale Evans, etc. The horse hauler is all metal in red, blue and yellow with illustration of Roy and Trigger on both sides. The tailgate drops and inside is a red plastic jeep and additional pieces, 15″ long 80.00   110.00

☐ **ROGERS, ROY,** c. early 1950's, Nellybelle jeep with Pat Brady, Dale Evans, Bullet. Jeep is all metal, painted gray, 12x5, movable hood, windshield and steering wheel, plastic motor 80.00   110.00

☐ **ROGERS, ROY,** "Roy Rogers Bank," white metal bank in the shape of a book, 6″ tall   42.00   52.00

☐ **ROGERS, ROY,** "Roy Rogers Darts," 2′x2′ masonite board with full color target and picture of Roy 55.00   70.00

☐ **ROGERS, ROY,** "Roy Rogers and Trigger 620 Snap Shot Camera," black plastic and metal camera with flash attachment 50.00   70.00

☐ **ROGERS, ROY,** "Roy Rogers and Trigger plastic binoculars," brown plastic 27.00   37.00

☐ **ROGERS, ROY,** c. 1952, "Roy Rogers, King of the Cowboys drinking mug," plastic 22.00   30.00

☐ **SNOW, HANK,** c. 1960, 8x10 photo, signed and inscribed 10.00   13.00

Price Range

☐ **SNOW, HANK,** c. 1950's, guitar used by him, with his name elaborately fashioned on it .. 1000.00   1500.00

☐ **SNOW, HANK,** 5x6½ photo, signed 8.00   11.00

☐ **SNOW, HANK,** 78rpm record, signed on the label 22.00   27.00

☐ **SNOW, HANK,** LP record album cover, signed, record missing 33.00   45.00

☐ **SNOW, HANK,** c. 1930's, three snapshot photos, unsigned 7.00   10.00

☐ **SNOW, HANK,** signature on a card 4.00   5.00

☐ **SNOW, HANK,** c. 1931, ALs, about his future plans 25.00   30.00

☐ **SNOW, HANK,** photo with Ernest Tubb, signed by Snow 13.00   17.00

☐ **SNOW, HANK,** c. 1974, photo standing outside Country Music Hall of Fame, signed .. 11.00   16.00

☐ **SNOW, HANK,** c. early, membership card, "Hank Snow Fan Club" 7.00   10.00

☐ **STONEMAN, E. V.,** 8x10 photo, signed, mounted 37.00   50.00

☐ **TANNER, GID,** photo playing fiddle, signed 55.00   70.00

☐ **TANNER, GID,** photo with Riley Puckett, signed by Tanner 50.00   65.00

☐ **TANNER, GID,** c. 1930, poster advertising "Gid Tanner and His Skillet Lickers," 22x30 100.00   120.00

☐ **TUBB, ERNEST,** 8x10 close-up photo, signed 8.00   11.00

☐ **TUBB, ERNEST,** c. 1972, Catalogue issued by his record shop, Nashville, Tenn. 2.00   3.00

☐ **TUBB, ERNEST,** photo of Mrs. Ernest Tubb and Mrs. Hank Snow, signed by Mrs. Ernest Tubb 6.00   8.00

☐ **TUBB, ERNEST,** sheet music, "Walking the Floor Over You," signed 22.00   27.00

☐ **TUBB, ERNEST,** 4x5 photo, signed 6.00   8.00

☐ **TUBB, ERNEST,** 78rpm record, signed on the label 35.00   45.00

☐ **TUBB, ERNEST,** c. 1975, photo in front of his record shop, Nashville, signed 8.00   11.00

☐ **TUBB, ERNEST,** signature on a 45rpm record sleeve 4.00   5.00

	Price Range	
☐ **TUBB, ERNEST,** necktie with his name and likeness on it	13.00	16.00
☐ **TUBB, ERNEST,** wallet with his name and words "Music City U.S.A."	22.00	27.00
☐ **TYLER, T. TEXAS,** 8x10 portrait photo, signed	13.00	17.00
☐ **TYLER, T. TEXAS,** sheet music, "Deck of Cards" signed	25.00	33.00
☐ **WILLIAMS, HANK,** c. 1945, ALs, with envelope	95.00	120.00
☐ **WILLIAMS, HANK,** c. 1952, cover of a 78rpm record album, signed, records missing, issued by MGM	160.00	220.00
☐ **WILLIAMS, HANK,** 8x10 portrait photo, signed, inscribed	85.00	110.00
☐ **WILLIAMS, HANK,** c. 1950, color photo, unsigned	15.00	20.00
☐ **WILLIAMS, HANK,** signature on a card	17.00	22.00
☐ **WILLS, BOB,** 8x10 photo with "The Texas Playboys," signed by Wills and one other member of group	55.00	70.00

78's

In this section are included all types of recordings that could be classified under the catch-all heading of country and western, including bluegrass, hillbilly, mountain music, cowboy, etc.

The market for 78rpm country records, or "country classics," has grown enormously in recent years. Tens of thousands of such recordings exist, many of them (perhaps most) by artists of whom little or nothing is known today. They span the period from 1924—when Vernon Dalhart recorded the first country and western million-seller and alerted music producers to the salability of country records—to about 1954, when most record companies ceased producing records in 78rpm. In those 30 years, country and western music was a bigger moneymaker than pop or jazz or any other form of commercial recording. Every major record label had its country and western subsidiary company with a stable of artists, and throughout the country (not just in the South) there were innumerable small labels specializing in country and western. Many of the latter were of a "fly by night" nature, working out of barns or wagons, recording nonprofessional local talent without contracts and—usually—without pay. Most of the records they produced were naturally of mediocre quality, but quite a few are rare, and, amid the slush, one will discover occasional gems of talent that deserved to be discovered. All these records are "collectible," though it is not easy to find two collectors who agree on their merits or values. One collector's trash is another's treasure. But it is fairly safe to say that, at least as examples of American folk artistry, they do have some claim to attention.

The most valuable and sought-after country and western 78's are, mainly, early releases by artists who subsequently became stars, such as Gene Autry, Ernest Tubb, Jimmie Davis, Hank Snow, etc. There are important exceptions, however. In the case of Jimmie Rodgers—"The Singing Brakeman"—every single one of his recordings (more than 50 of them) is valuable, worth at minimum $50 in VF condition. This includes records released after he achieved mass popularity, some of which must have been pressed in quantities approaching 500,000. There is no easy explanation for this, except the very strong collector interest in Jimmie Rodgers records. They are certainly obtainable, but the demand outpaces the supply. The fact that many of his recordings have been repressed into LP albums has not only failed to diminish interest in the originals, it has seemed to create an even greater market for them. Their values have more than doubled in the past four to five years.

The collector of country and western 78's should keep in mind that many artists recorded under different names early in their careers, or even later; the classic example is Wilf Carter/"Montana Slim," who made numerous recordings under both names. Gene Autry recorded under about half a dozen names. The country and western connoisseur will recognize the voice even if the name is unfamiliar.

Also: be sure you do not confuse the value of a recording with that of a song. Many tunes were re-recorded by the same artists several times, for different labels or the same label, and the values of each recording can vary considerably. Usually, a version of a song done by an artist for a small label, before he signed with a major recording company, is more valuable than the same song subsequently recorded by the big label. In some cases these are actually not remakes but merely repressings.

	Price Range	
☐ **ACUFF, ROY, Columbia,** "Waiting for My Call to Glory/Tell Me Now or Tell Me Never"	5.00	7.00
☐ "It's Too Late Now to Worry Anymore/Wait for the Light to Shine"	5.00	7.00
☐ "Blues in My Mind/I Heard a Silver Trumpet"	6.00	9.00

Price Range

☐ "Write Me Sweetheart/I'll Forgive You but I Can't Forget" 5.00   7.00

☐ "The Prodigal Son/Not a Word From Home" 5.00   7.00

☐ "I'll Reap My Harvest in Heaven/Don't Make Me Go to Bed" 6.50   9.00

☐ "Night Train to Memphis/Low and Lonely" 5.00   7.00

☐ "Fireball Mail/Wreck on the Highway" 5.00   7.00

☐ "Be Honest With Me/Worried Mind" 5.00   7.00

☐ "Come Back Little Pal/The Precious Jewel" 5.00   7.00

☐ "Beneath That Lonely Mound of Clay/Blue Eyed Darling" 5.00   7.00

☐ "We Live in Two Different Worlds/Pins and Needles" 5.00   7.00

☐ "No One Will Ever Know/I Think I'll Go Home and Cry" 5.00   7.00

☐ "All the World is Lonely Now/That Glory Bound Train" 5.00   7.00

☐ "Great Speckled Bird/My Mountain Home Sweet Home" 5.50   8.00

☐ "Great Speckled Bird #2/Tell Mother I'll Be There" 4.50   7.00

☐ "Steel Guitar Chimes/Steel Guitar Blues" .. 8.00   12.00

☐ "Wabash Cannonball/Freight Train Blues" 7.00   10.00

☐ "Streamlined Cannonball/Mule Skinner Blues" 7.00   10.00

☐ "Let Me Be the First to Say I'm Sorry/Gone, Gone, Gone" 5.00   7.00

☐ "Jole Blon/Tennessee Central" 5.00   7.00

☐ "There's a Big Rock in the Road/Po' Folks" 5.00   7.00

☐ "It Won't Be Long/Just Inside the Pearly Gates" 5.00   7.00

☐ "Things That Might Have Been/No Letter in the Mail" 5.00   7.00

☐ "Brother Take Warning/The Great Judgment Morning" 5.00   7.00

☐ "You're My Darling/Branded Wherever I Go" 5.00   7.00

☐ "Are You Thinking of Me Darling?/I Called and Nobody Answered" 5.00   7.00

☐ "I Talk to Myself About You/Short changed in Love" 5.00   7.00

☐ "New Greenback Dollar/Steamboat Whistle Blues" 5.00   7.00

Price Range

- ☐ "Smoky Mountain Rag/Smoky Mountain Moon" 5.00 7.00
- ☐ "Blue Eyes Crying in the Rain/The Devil's Train" 8.00 12.00
- ☐ "They Can Only Fill One Grave/Do You Wonder Why?" 5.00 7.00
- ☐ "Easy Rockin' Chair/Golden Treasure" 5.00 7.00
- ☐ "The Songbirds are Singing in Heaven/The Waltz of the Wind" 6.00 9.00
- ☐ "I Saw the Light/Thank God" 5.00 7.00
- ☐ "Unloved and Unclaimed/I Had a Dream" 5.00 7.00
- ☐ "Blues in My Mind/I Heard a Silver Trumpet" 6.00 9.00
- ☐ "That Beautiful Picture/Do You Wonder Why" 5.00 7.00
- ☐ "Blue Ridge Sweetheart/Just to Ease My Worried Mind" 5.00 7.00
- ☐ "What Would You Do With Gabriel's Trumpet?/Farther Along" 5.00 7.00
- ☐ "Heartaches and Flowers/When They Take That Last Look at Me" 5.00 7.00
- ☐ "Lonesome Old River Blues/It's Just About Time" 9.00 12.00
- ☐ "You'll Reap These Tears/I'll Always Care" 5.00 7.00
- ☐ **Conqueror.** "Great Speckled Bird/My Mountain Home Sweet Home" 22.00 30.00
- ☐ "You're the Only Star/She No Longer Belongs to Me" 22.00 30.00
- ☐ "Gonna Have a Big Time Tonight/Yes Sir, That's My Baby" 22.00 30.00
- ☐ "Great Speckled Bird #2/Tell Mother I'll Be There" 24.00 33.00
- ☐ "Steel Guitar Chimes/Steel Guitar Blues" .. 22.00 30.00
- ☐ "Singing My Way to Glory/Lonesome Valley" 28.00 39.00
- ☐ "Wabash Cannonball/Freight Train Blues" 22.00 30.00
- ☐ "New Greenback Dollar/Steamboat Whistle Blues" 22.00 30.00
- ☐ "When Lulu's Gone/Doin' it the Old Fashioned Way" 22.00 30.00
- ☐ "An Old Three Room Shack/Bonnie Blue Eyes" 22.00 30.00
- ☐ "One Old Shirt/Tonky Tonk Mamas" 22.00 30.00
- ☐ "Old Fashioned Love/Mule Skinner Blues" 25.00 35.00

Price Range

- ☐ "Answer to Sparkling Blue Eyes/Mother's Prayers Guide Me" 22.00   30.00
- ☐ "Ida Red/Just to Ease My Worried Mind" .. 22.00   30.00
- ☐ "Haven of Dreams/Old Age Pension Check" 22.00   30.00
- ☐ **ALLEN BROTHERS, Vocalion,** "Long Gone from Bowling Green/Red Pajama Sal" 8.00   12.00
- ☐ "Salty Dog Blues/Hey Hey Hey Hey" 15.00   21.00
- ☐ "Misbehavin' Mama/Midnight Mama" 9.00   12.00
- ☐ "Baby When You Come Back Home/Daddy Park Your Car" 9.00   12.00
- ☐ "The Prisoner's Dream/Mercy Mercy Blues" 9.00   12.00
- ☐ "Can I Get You Now/New Deal Blues" 9.00   12.00
- ☐ "Tipple Blues/Mary's Breakdown" 9.00   12.00
- ☐ **ALLEN, ROSALIE, Bluebird,** "Guitar Polka/I Want to Be a Cowboy's Sweetheart" 15.00   21.00
- ☐ "Me Go Where You Go/A Rose of the Alamo" 12.00   18.00
- ☐ "Hitler Lives/I Can't Tell that Lie to My Heart" 9.00   12.00
- ☐ "Never Trust a Man/Take it Back and Change it for a Boy" 9.00   12.00
- ☐ **ARNOLD, EDDY, Bluebird,** "Mommy, Please Stay Home With Me/Mother's Prayer" 40.00   55.00
- ☐ "Cattle Call/Each Year Seems a Million Years" 35.00   45.00
- ☐ "Did You See My Daddy Over There/I Walk Alone" 35.00   45.00
- ☐ "You Must Walk the Line/Many Years Ago" 30.00   40.00
- ☐ "I Talk to Myself About You/Live and Learn" 25.00   35.00
- ☐ "Can't Win, Can't Place, Can't Show/All Alone in This World Without You" 25.00   35.00
- ☐ "Mommy, Please Stay Home With Me/Many Tears Ago" 25.00   35.00
- ☐ "That's How Much I Love You/Chained to a Memory" 25.00   35.00
- ☐ "I'll Hold You in My Heart/Don't Bother to Cry" 14.00   19.00
- ☐ "Easy Rocking Chair/To My Sorrow" 14.00   19.00
- ☐ **AUTRY, GENE, Champion,** "Cowboy Yodel/Hobo Yodel" 70.00   90.00

Price Range

☐ "Dust Pan Blues/Texas Blues" 70.00   90.00

☐ "In the Jailhouse Now #2/Anniversary Blue
Yodel #7" . . . . , ... 70.00   90.00

☐ "Blue Yodel #8/Mean Mama Blues" 80.00   110.00

☐ "Pistol Packin' Papa/Any Old Time" 80.00   90.00

☐ "Blue Days/Money Ain't No Use Anyhow" 70.00   90.00

☐ "T.B. Blues/I've Got the Jailhouse Blues" . . 80.00   110.00

☐ **Clarion,** "Hobo Yodel/That's Why I Left the
Mountains" 60.00   80.00

☐ "No One to Call Me Darling/Frankie and
Johnny" 60.00   80.00

☐ "I'll Be Thinking of You, Little Girl/Why Don't
You Come Back to Me" 60.00   80.00

☐ "My Alabama Home/Cowboy Yodel" 60.00   80.00

☐ "Lullaby Yodel/Red River Valley" (with Car-
son Robison) 55.00   75.00

☐ "Pictures of My Mother/True Blue Bill" 60.00   80.00

☐ "A Gangster's Warning/That's How I Got My
Start" 60.00   80.00

☐ **Columbia,** "Don't Hang Around Me Any-
more/Address Unknown" 11.00   15.00

☐ "I Want to be Sure/Don't Live a Lie" 11.00   15.00

☐ "Over and Over Again/Wave to Me, Lady" 9.00   14.00

☐ "Nobody's Darlin' But Mine/Don't Waste
Your Tears on Me" 9.00   14.00

☐ "There's a Gold Mine in the Sky/Sail Along
Silv'ry Moon" 9.00   14.00

☐ "End of My Round-Up Days/I Want a Pardon
for Daddy" 22.00   30.00

☐ "Back in the Saddle Again/Little Old Band of
Gold" 9.00   12.00

☐ "When I'm Gone You'll Soon For-
get/Goodbye, Little Darlin', Goodbye" 9.00   14.00

☐ "You Waited Too Long/That Little Kid Sister
of Mine" 8.00   14.00

☐ "You Are My Sunshine/It Makes No Differ-
ence Now" 9.00   14.00

☐ "Take Me Back into Your Heart/Tweedle-o-
Twill" 9.00   14.00

☐ "Rainbow on the Rio Colorado/Private Buck-
aroo" 9.00   14.00

Price Range

☐ "Yesterday's Roses/Call For Me and I'll Be
There" 9.00 14.00

☐ "If You Only Believed in Me/Purple Sage in
the Twilight" 9.00 14.00

☐ "I'll Be Back/At Mail Call Today" 9.00 14.00

☐ "Have I Told You Lately That I Love
You/Someday You'll Want Me to Want You" 9.00 14.00

☐ "Tumbling Tumbleweeds/Back in the Saddle
Again" 9.00 14.00

☐ "Home on the Range/Red River Valley" ... 9.00 14.00

☐ "Mexicali Rose/South of the Border" 9.00 14.00

☐ "Ridin' Down the Canyon/Twilight on the
Trail" 9.00 14.00

☐ "Ages and Ages Ago/You Laughed and I
Cried" 9.00 14.00

☐ "When the Snowbirds Cross the Rock-
ies/The Angel Song" 12.00 20.00

☐ "Jingle Jangle Jingle/I'm A Cowpoke Pokin'
Along" 9.00 14.00

☐ "Keep Rollin' Lazy Longhorns/Deep in the
Heart of Texas" 9.00 14.00

☐ "I Hang My Head and Cry/You'll be Sorry" 9.00 14.00

☐ **BATES, DR. HUMPHREY, "And his Possum
Hunters," Brunswick,** "Going Up-Town/
How Many Biscuits Can You Eat" 70.00 95.00

☐ "Billy in the Low Ground/8th of January" .. 70.00 95.00

☐ **BLUE SKY BOYS, Bluebird,** "Sunny Side of
Life/Where the Soul Never Dies" 35.00 52.00

☐ "Down on the Banks of the Ohio/Midnight on
the Stormy Sea" 35.00 52.00

☐ "There'll Come a Time/I'm Troubled, I'm
Troubled" 35.00 52.00

☐ **BOYD, BILL** (NOTE: This was not the Bill
Boyd who portrayed "Hopalong Cassidy."),
Bluebird, "Train Song/Under the Double
Eagle" 9.00 13.00

☐ "Boyd's Blues/David Blues" 9.00 13.00

☐ "The Sweetest Girl/Rio Grande Waltz" 9.00 13.00

☐ "Mama Don't Like No Music/Wind Swept De-
sert" 9.00 13.00

☐ "Floatin' Down/Beale Street Blues" 15.00 20.00

☐ "Hobo's Paradise/Ramshackle Shack" 15.00 20.00

Price Range

☐ "Put Me in Your Pocket/Way Out There" ..	**9.00**	**13.00**
☐ "Ain't She Coming Out Tonight?/You Shall Be Free Monah"	**9.00**	**13.00**
☐ "Draggin' it Around/Right or Wrong"	**9.00**	**13.00**
☐ "Jennie Lee/You're Tired of Me"	**9.00**	**13.00**
☐ **BRITT, ELTON, Bluebird,** "Goodbye, Little Darlin', Goodbye/I'll Never Smile Again" ..	**9.00**	**14.00**
☐ "She Taught Me to Yodel/Where Are You Now?"	**9.00**	**14.00**
☐ "There's a Star Spangled Banner Waving Somewhere/When the Roses Bloom Again"	**9.00**	**14.00**
☐ "Buddy Boy/I Hung My Head and Cried" ..	**9.00**	**14.00**
☐ "I'm a Convict with Old Glory in My Heart/The Best of Travel"	**9.00**	**14.00**
☐ "Someday/Weep No More My Darlin' "	**9.00**	**14.00**
☐ **RCA Victor,** "Wave to Me, My Lady/Blueberry Lane"	**6.00**	**9.00**
☐ "Make Room in Your Heart For a Friend/Detour"	**6.00**	**9.00**
☐ "Thanks for the Heartaches/Blue Texas Moonlight"	**6.00**	**9.00**
☐ "Rogue River Valley/Too Tired to Care" ...	**6.00**	**9.00**
☐ "There's a Star Spangled Banner Waving Somewhere/I Hung My Head and Cried" ..	**8.00**	**11.00**
☐ "Blue Eyes Crying in the Rain/I'd Trade All of My Tomorrows"	**8.00**	**11.00**
☐ "Candlelight and Roses/I Wish You the Best of Everything"	**6.00**	**9.00**
☐ **CARLISLE, CLIFF, Bluebird,** "Look Out, I'm Shifting Gears/Get Her by the Tail"	**37.00**	**55.00**
☐ "A Wildcat Woman and a Tomcat Man/Rambling Yodler"	**37.00**	**55.00**
☐ "My Lovin' Kathleen/A Stretch of 28 Years"	**30.00**	**40.00**
☐ "In a Box Car Around the World/Cowboy Johnny's Last Ride"	**30.00**	**40.00**
☐ "You'll Miss Me When I'm Gone/When the Evening's Sun Goes Down"	**30.00**	**40.00**
☐ "Shufflin' Gal/Wigglin' Mama"	**30.00**	**40.00**
☐ "That Good Old Utah Trail/My Old Saddle Horse is Missing"	**22.00**	**30.00**
☐ "Still There's a Spark of Love/Cowgirl Jean"	**22.00**	**30.00**
☐ "That Nasty Swing/It Ain't No Fault of Mine"	**22.00**	**30.00**

Price Range

☐ "My Rocking Mama/When I'm Dead and Gone"	22.00	30.00
☐ "A Little White Rose/Handsome Blues"	22.00	30.00
☐ **CARSON, FIDDLIN' JOHN, Bluebird,** "Georgia's $3 Tag/The New 'Comin' Round the Mountain' "	75.00	100.00
☐ "When the Saints Go Marching In/Bear Me Away on Your Snowy White Wings"	75.00	100.00
☐ "The Honest Farmer/Taxes on the Farmer Feeds Them All"	75.00	100.00
☐ **CARTER, WILF ("MONTANA SLIM"), Bluebird,** "I Long For Old Wyoming/My Little Swiss and Me"	30.00	40.00
☐ "Keep Smiling, Old Pal/Rescue From Moses River Goldmine"	30.00	40.00
☐ "The Fate of Old Strawberry Roan/Yodeling Hillbilly"	30.00	40.00
☐ "Broken-Down Cowboy/Old Barn Dance"	30.00	40.00
☐ "Dreamy Prairie Moon/Sweetheart of My Childhood Days"	30.00	40.00
☐ "The Fate of Sunset Trail/Midnight the Unconquered Outlaw"	30.00	40.00
☐ "Memories of My Grey-Haired Mother/Roll Along Moonlight Yodel"	30.00	40.00
☐ "Goodbye, Little Pal of My Dreams/The Hobo's Yodel"	30.00	40.00
☐ "Rose of My Heart/Under the Light of the Texas Moon"	30.00	40.00
☐ "Round-up Time in Heaven/Put My Little Shoes Away"	30.00	40.00
☐ "There's a Love-Knot in My Lariat/My Little Yoho Lady"	30.00	40.00
☐ "Where is My Boy Tonight?/Answer to Swiss Moonlight Lullaby"	30.00	40.00
☐ "When the Sun Says Goodnight to the Prairie/The Hindenburg Disaster"	30.00	40.00
☐ "How My Yodeling Days Began/Covered Wagon Headin' West"	30.00	40.00
☐ "Pete Knight's Last Ride/The Last Ride Down Lariat Trail"	30.00	40.00
☐ "Old Alberta Plains/Won't You Be the Same Old Pal"	30.00	40.00

Price Range

- ☐ "I Loved Her Till She Done Me Wrong/My Faithful Pinto Pal" 30.00 40.00
- ☐ "The Preacher and the Cowboy/Roll on Texas Dreamy Moon" 30.00 40.00
- ☐ "Dusty Trails/Everybody's Been Some Mother's Darlin' " 30.00 40.00
- ☐ "You'll Always Be Mine in My Dreams/I Wish I Had Never Seen Sunshine" 30.00 40.00
- ☐ "The Cowboy Wedding in May/I'm Still Waiting For You" 30.00 40.00
- ☐ "Round-Up Time in Sunny Old Alberta/When the Bright Prairie Moon is Rollin' " 30.00 40.00
- ☐ "By the Grave of Nobody's Darling/There'll Be No Blues Up Yonder" 30.00 40.00
- ☐ "Longing For my Mississippi Home/Don't Let Me Down, Old Pal" 30.00 40.00
- ☐ "The Cowboy's Heavenly Dream/Ridin' a Maverick" 30.00 40.00
- ☐ "That Tumbledown Shack By the Trail/My Old Montana Home" 30.00 40.00
- ☐ "What a Friend We Have in Mother/Down the Yodeling Trail at Twilight" 30.00 40.00
- ☐ "It Makes No Difference Now/We'll Meet Again in Peaceful Valley" 30.00 40.00
- ☐ "I'm Only a Dude in Cowboy Clothes/My Honeymoon Bridge Broke Down" 30.00 40.00
- ☐ **DALHART, VERNON, Brunswick,** "Jim Blake/The Death of Laura Parsons" 25.00 35.00
- ☐ "The Miner's Doom/Return of Mary Vickery" 15.00 20.00
- ☐ "The Dying Cowboy/A Home on the Range" 15.00 20.00
- ☐ "Barbara Allen/Wreck of the C & O #5" .. 28.00 39.00
- ☐ "The House at the End of the Lane/My Blue Ridge Mountain Home" (with Carson Robison) 15.00 20.00
- ☐ "Wreck of the Royal Palm/Wreck of the #9" 25.00 35.00
- ☐ "Down on the Farm/My Mother's Old Red Shawl" 15.00 20.00
- ☐ "The Gypsy's Warning/Molling Darling" 15.00 20.00
- ☐ "Billy Richardson's Last Ride/My Little Home in Tennessee" 25.00 35.00
- ☐ "A Cowboy's Herding Song/Cowboy's Evening Song" 15.00 20.00

Price Range

☐ "The Jealous Lover of Lone Green/Nellie Dare and Charlie Brooks"	15.00	20.00
☐ "The Engineer's Dream/The Mississippi Floor"	15.00	20.00
☐ "Billy the Kid/The Three Drowned Sisters"	17.00	25.00
☐ **Clarion,** "When the Work's All Done Next Fall/The Cowboy's Lament" (with Mack Allen)	25.00	35.00
☐ "The Pony Express/Don't Marry a Widow"	17.00	25.00
☐ **Columbia,** "Prisoner's Song/Ain't Ya Coming Out Tonight"	25.00	35.00
☐ "Mother and Home/Chain Gang Song"	27.00	37.00
☐ "Oh Bury Me Not on the Lone Prairie/Get Away Old Man"	15.00	20.00
☐ "Lindbergh/Lucky Lindy"	35.00	45.00
☐ "Boy's Best Friend is His Mother/In the Baggage Coach Ahead"	27.00	37.00
☐ "Crepe on the Little Cabin Door/We Will Meet at the End of the Trail"	26.00	36.00
☐ "Dying Girl's Message/Fatal Wedding"	33.00	42.00
☐ "Putting on the Style/Goin' to Have a Big Time Tonight"	15.00	20.00
☐ "When the Moon Shines Down Upon the Mountain/Golden Slippers" (with Carson Robison, billed as Charlie Wells on this recording)	27.00	37.00
☐ "John T Scopes Trial/Santa Barbara Earthquake"	27.00	37.00
☐ "Wreck of the Shenandoah/Stone Mountain Memorial"	35.00	45.00
☐ **RCA Victor,** "Prisoner's Song/Wreck of Old 97"	35.00	45.00
☐ "Death of Floyd Collins/Dream of a Miner's Child"	35.00	45.00
☐ "Letter Edged in Black/Lightning Express"	35.00	45.00
☐ "Little Rosewood Casket/Convict and Rose"	35.00	46.00
☐ **DAVIS, JIMMIE, Bluebird,** "Bear Cat Mama from Horners Corners/She's a Hum Dinger"	65.00	95.00
☐ "When It's Roundup Time in Heaven/I Wonder if She's Blue"	50.00	70.00
☐ "Beautiful Texas/The Tramp's Mother"	50.00	70.00
☐ "The Shotgun Wedding/Arabelle Blues" ...	50.00	70.00

Price Range

☐ "I'll Be Happy Today/My Arkansas Sweetheart" 35.00 50.00

☐ "Midnight Blues/The Davis Limited" 35.00 50.00

☐ "Yo Yo Mama/Hold 'er, Newt" 35.00 50.00

☐ **Decca,** "Nobody's Darlin' But Mine/Have
You Ever Been in Heaven" 35.00 50.00

☐ "Greatest Mistake of My Life/One, Two,
Three, Four" 35.00 50.00

☐ "It's Been Years/Beautiful Mary" 35.00 50.00

☐ "Good Time Papa Blues/Shirt Tail Blues" .. 45.00 70.00

☐ "Jellyroll Blues/Graveyard Blues" 45.00 70.00

☐ **DELMORE BROTHERS, Bluebird,** "Gonna
Lay Down My Old Guitar/Lonesome Yodel
Blues" 45.00 70.00

☐ "The Frozen Girl/Bury Me Out on the Prairie" 60.00 85.00

☐ "I'm Leaving You/I'm Goin' Back to Alabama" 50.00 75.00

☐ "I Ain't Gonna Stay Here Long/I'm Mississippi Bound" 45.00 70.00

☐ "Smoky Mountain Bill and His Song/The Girls
Don't Worry My Mind" 45.00 70.00

☐ "A New Salt Dog/Brown's Ferry Blues" 45.00 70.00

☐ "I've Got the Big River Blues/Blue Railroad
Train" 45.00 70.00

☐ "I Ain't Got Nowhere to Travel/Ramblin'
Minded Blues" 45.00 70.00

☐ "Lonesome Jailhouse Blues/By the Banks of
the Rio Grande" 45.00 70.00

☐ "Blow Yo' Whistle, Freight Train/Lorena the
Slave" 35.00 50.00

☐ "I Believe it For My Mother Told Me So/Hey!
Hey! I'm Memphis Bound" 35.00 50.00

☐ "I'm Going Away/Brown's Ferry Blues (Part
2)" 35.00 50.00

☐ "Down South/Alabama Lullaby" 35.00 50.00

☐ "The Fugitive's Lament/Keep the Campfires
Burning" 35.00 50.00

☐ "I Guess I've Got to Be Goin'/Kansas City
Blues" 35.00 50.00

☐ "I Long to See My Mother/When it's Summer
Time in a Southern Clime" 35.00 50.00

	Price Range	
☐ "Lonesome Yodel Blues #2/Happy Hickey the Hobo"	35.00	50.00
☐ "I'm Worried Now/I'm Gonna Change My Way"	35.00	50.00
☐ "I Know I'll Be Happy in Heaven/Don't Let Me Be in the Way"	35.00	50.00
☐ "Nashville Blues/It's Takin' Me Down"	35.00	50.00
☐ "No Drunkard Can Enter There/Blind Child"	35.00	50.00
☐ "Southern Moon/I Don't Know Why I Love Her"	35.00	50.00
☐ "Don't You See That Train/The Lover's Warning"	35.00	50.00
☐ "Put Me on the Train to Carolina/Carry Me Back to Alabama"	35.00	50.00
☐ "False Hearted Girl/Memories of My Carolina Girl"	35.00	50.00
☐ "Take Away This Lonesome Day/No One"	35.00	50.00
☐ "Till the Roses Bloom Again/The Budded Rose"	35.00	50.00
☐ **Columbia,** "Alabama Lullaby/Got the Kansas City Blues"	75.00	115.00
☐ **DIXON BROTHERS, Bluebird,** "Sales Tax on the Women/Intoxicated Rat"	32.00	42.00
☐ "Two Little Rosebuds/Weave Room Blues"	32.00	42.00
☐ **FOLEY, RED, Decca,** "Chiquita/Will You Wait for Me"	9.00	13.00
☐ "I'm Looking for a Sweetheart/Is It True?"	9.00	13.00
☐ "Pals of the Saddle/Someday Somewhere Sweetheart"	9.00	13.00
☐ "Smoke on the Water/There's a Blue Star Shining Bright"	9.00	13.00
☐ **FOX, CURLY, King,** "It's Your Time to be Blue/Soldier's Return"	25.00	39.00
☐ "Black Mountain Rag/Come Here Son" ...	25.00	39.00
☐ **GUTHRIE, JACK, Capitol,** "Oklahoma Hills/I'm Branding My Darling With My Heart"	20.00	31.00
☐ "When the Cactus is in Bloom/I Loved You Once"	9.00	13.00
☐ "Chained to a Memory/I'm Telling You" ...	9.00	13.00
☐ "Oakie Boogie/The Clouds Rained Trouble Down"	9.00	13.00

Price Range

☐ "You Laughed and I Cried/It's Too Late to Change Your Mind" 9.00 13.00

☐ **HAWKINS, HAWKSHAW, King,** "After All/The Way I Love You" 14.00 23.00

☐ "I'll Never Cry Over You/I Ain't Goin' Honky Tonkin' Anymore" 12.00 20.00

☐ "There's a Little Bit of Everything in Texas/Soldier's Last Letter" 9.00 12.00

☐ "Blue-Eyed Elaine/Try Me One More Time" 9.00 12.00

☐ "You Nearly Lost Your Mind/Are You Waiting Just for Me?" 9.00 12.00

☐ "Walking the Floor Over You/I'll Get Along Somehow" 9.00 12.00

☐ "That's When It's Coming Home to You/I'm Wondering How" 5.00 8.00

☐ **JONES, GRANDPA, King,** "It's Raining Here This Morning/I'll Be Around If You Need Me" 13.00 21.00

☐ "I'll Never Lose That Loneliness For You/That's a Grave in the Wave of the Ocean" 13.00 21.00

☐ "Steppin' Out Kind/You'll Be Lonesome Too" 13.00 21.00

☐ "Don't Sweet Talk Me/Maybe You'll Miss Me When I'm Gone" 13.00 21.00

☐ **KINCAID, BRADLEY, Decca,** "Ain't We Crazy/The Little Shirt That Mother Made For Me" 7.00 11.00

☐ "Old Wooden Rocker/My Mother's Beautiful Hands" 7.00 11.00

☐ "Red River Valley/Cowboy's Dream" 7.00 11.00

☐ **MACON, "UNCLE" DAVE, Bluebird,** "We Won the Heart of Sarah Jane/She's Got the Money Too" 75.00 100.00

☐ "When the Harvest Days are Over/One More River to Cross" 75.00 100.00

☐ "I'll Tickle Nancy/I'll Keep My Skillet Good and Greasy" 80.00 130.00

☐ "Over the Mountain/Just One Way to the Pearly Gates" 75.00 100.00

☐ "Honest Confession/From Jerusalem to Jericho" 75.00 100.00

Price Range

☐ "Two in One Chewing Gum/Travelin' Down the Road"	75.00	100.00
☐ "Allin, Down and Out Blues/The Bum Hotel"	75.00	100.00
☐ "Johnny Grey/The Gayest Old Dude That's Out"	75.00	100.00
☐ "Give Me Back My Five Dollars/Railroadin' and Gamblin' "	75.00	100.00
☐ "Cumberland Mountain Deer Race/Country Ham and Red Gravy"	75.00	100.00
☐ "Things I Don't Like to See/Working for My Lord"	75.00	100.00
☐ **Brunswick,** "Gal That Got Stuck on Everything She Said/Worthy of Estimation" (with Sam McGee)	110.00	165.00
☐ "Hold on to the Sleigh/Cross-Eyed Butcher"	110.00	165.00
☐ "Never Make Love No More/Diamond in the Rough"	110.00	165.00
☐ "Comin' Round the Mountain/Gov. Al Smith" (with Sam McGee)	110.00	165.00
☐ "Tennessee Jubilee/Uncle Dave's Travels"	110.00	165.00
☐ "New Coon in Town/Uncle Dave's Travels, Part 1"	110.00	165.00
☐ "Over the Road I'm Bound to Go/From Earth to Heaven" (with Sam McGee)	110.00	165.00
☐ "Since Baby's Learned to Talk/Uncle Dave's Travels, Part 4"	110.00	165.00
☐ "Rock About, My Sara Jane/Death of John Henry" (billed as "Uncle" Dave Macon and the Fruit Jar Drinkers)	110.00	165.00
☐ **MAINER, J. E., Bluebird,** "Greenback Dollar/Broken-Hearted Blues"	42.00	70.00
☐ "Maple on the Hill/Take Me in the Lifeboat"	42.00	70.00
☐ "Ship Sailing Now/This World's Not My Home"	42.00	70.00
☐ "New Curly Headed Baby/Let Her Go, God Bless Her"	42.00	70.00
☐ "The Longest Train I Ever Saw/Ride On"	36.00	70.00
☐ "Lights in the Valley/City on the Hill"	42.00	70.00
☐ "Searching For a Pair of Blue Eyes/Write a Letter to Mother"	42.00	70.00
☐ "Fatal Wreck of the Bus/One to Love Me"	35.00	51.00

Price Range

☐ "A Leaf From the Sea/Brown Eyes" (with Wade Mainer) **35.00** **51.00**

☐ "My Little Red Ford/My Wife Went Away and Left Me" (with John Love) **35.00** **51.00**

☐ "Satisfied/Don't Cause Mother's Hair to Turn Grey" **35.00** **51.00**

☐ "Maple on the Hill, Part 2/Where the Red, Red Roses Grow" **35.00** **51.00**

☐ **O'DAY, MOLLY, Columbia,** "The Tramp on the Street/Put My Rubber Doll Away" **20.00** **30.00**

☐ "The Drunken Driver/Six More Miles" **20.00** **30.00**

☐ "When God Comes to Gather His Jewels/The Tear Stained Letter" **20.00** **30.00**

☐ **RENO, DON, and RED SMILEY, King,** "Hear Jerusalem Mourn/I'm Using My Bible for a Roadmap" **5.00** **8.00**

☐ "Lord's Last Supper/Highway to Heaven" .. **5.00** **8.00**

☐ "Choking the Strings/I'm the Talk of the Town" **5.00** **8.00**

☐ "He's Coming Back to Earth Again/My Mother's Bible" **5.00** **8.00**

☐ "Tennessee Breakdown/My Mother's Bible" **5.00** **8.00**

☐ "I Can Hear the Angels Singing/Mountain Church" **5.00** **8.00**

☐ "Tree of Life/Someone Will Love Me in Heaven" **5.00** **8.00**

☐ **ROBERTSON, TEXAS JIM, RCA Victor,** "Filipino Baby/Rainbow at Midnight" **8.00** **11.00**

☐ "Don't Look Now/It Takes a Long, Long Train" **8.00** **11.00**

☐ "Land, Sky and Water/Seven Women to One" **8.00** **11.00**

☐ "Miz O'Reilly's Daughter/Too Blue to Cry" **8.00** **11.00**

☐ **RODGERS, JIMMIE, Bluebird,** "Years Ago/Jimmie Rodger's Last Blue Yodel" ... **100.00** **140.00**

☐ "The Carter Family and Jimmie Rodgers in Texas/Where is My Sailor Boy" (second side by Monroe Bros.) **100.00** **140.00**

☐ "Why There's a Tear in My Eye/We Miss Him When the Evening Shadows Fall" (second side by Mrs. Jimmie Rodgers) **150.00** **200.00**

Price Range

☐ "The One Rose/Yodeling My Way Back Home"	100.00 140.00
☐ "Take Me Back Again/Dreaming with Tears in My Eyes"	100.00 140.00
☐ "I've Only Loved Three Women/The Wonderful City"	100.00 140.00
☐ "My Good Gal's Gone Blues/Blue Yodel #11"	100.00 140.00
☐ "I've Ranged, Roamed, I've Traveled/Why Did You Give Me Your Love"	100.00 140.00
☐ **RCA Victor,** "Sleep, Baby, Sleep/Soldier's Sweetheart"	150.00 200.00
☐ "Whippin' That Old T.B./No Hard Times"	350.00 450.00
☐ "In the Hills of Tennessee/Miss the Mississippi and You"	300.00 400.00
☐ "Hobo's Meditation/Down That Old Road to Home"	120.00 200.00
☐ "Waiting For a Train/Blue Yodel #4"	120.00 175.00
☐ "Rock All Our Babies to Sleep/Mother the Queen of My Heart"	150.00 200.00
☐ "My Blue Eyed Jane/Jimmie the Kid"	100.00 140.00
☐ "Hobo Bill's Last Ride/That's Why I'm Blue"	100.00 140.00
☐ "Train Whistle Blues/Jimmie's Texas Blues"	100.00 140.00
☐ "Blue Yodel #3/Never No More Blues"	70.00 100.00
☐ "Treasures Untold/Mother Was a Lady"	70.00 100.00
☐ "Ben Dew Berry's Final Run/In the Jailhouse Now #1"	70.00 100.00
☐ "Blue Yodel #1/Away Out on the Mountain"	70.00 100.00
☐ "Blue Yodel #2/Brakeman's Blues"	70.00 100.00
☐ "Blue Yodel #10/Mississippi Moon"	150.00 200.00
☐ "Home Call/She Was Happy Till She Met You"	150.00 200.00
☐ "99 Year Blues/My Time Ain't Long"	185.00 230.00
☐ "Roll Along Kentucky Moon/For the Sake of Days Gone By"	150.00 200.00
☐ "Gambling Polka Dot Blues/When the Cactus is in Bloom"	150.00 200.00
☐ "Let Me Be Your Sidetrack/Rodgers' Puzzle Record"	150.00 200.00
☐ "What's It/Why Should I Be Lonely"	150.00 200.00
☐ "Blue Yodel #9/Looking For a New Mama"	150.00 200.00

Price Range

- ☐ "Moonlight and Skies/Jimmie Rodgers Visits the Carter Family" 150.00 200.00
- ☐ "Traveling Blues/I'm Lonesome Too" 100.00 140.00
- ☐ "T.B. Blues/Mississippi River Blues" 125.00 185.00
- ☐ "Nobody Knows But Me/The Mystery of Number Five" 100.00 140.00
- ☐ "Blue Yodel #8/Jimmie's Mean Mama Blues" 100.00 140.00
- ☐ "Those Gambler's Blues/Pistol Packin' Papa" 100.00 140.00
- ☐ "High Powered Mama/In the Jailhouse Now #2" 100.00 140.00
- ☐ "A Drunkard's Child/Whisper Your Mother's Name" 100.00 140.00
- ☐ "Blue Yodel #6/Yodeling Cowbow" 100.00 140.00
- ☐ "My Rough and Rowdy Ways/Tuck Away My Lonesome Blues" 100.00 150.00
- ☐ "The Sailor's Plea/I'm Lonely and Blue" ... 100.00 150.00
- ☐ "My Little Lady/You and My Old Guitar" ... 100.00 150.00
- ☐ "My Carolina Sunshine Girl/Desert Blues" 100.00 150.00
- ☐ "Blue Yodel #5/I'm Sorry We Met" 100.00 150.00
- ☐ "Frankie and Johnnie/Everybody Does it in Hawaii" 100.00 150.00
- ☐ "Long Tall Mama Blues/Gambling Barroom Blues" 250.00 350.00
- ☐ "Southern Cannonball/Land of My Boyhood Dreams" 250.00 350.00
- ☐ "Old Love Letters/Somewhere Below the Dixon Line" 300.00 425.00
- ☐ "Blue Yodel #12/Cowhand's Last Ride" .. 300.00 425.00
- ☐ "Old Pal of My Heart/Mississippi Delta Blues" 250.00 350.00
- ☐ "Blue Yodel #12/Cowhand's Last Ride" (picture record with large portrait of Jimmie Rodgers on the record itself)" .... 2000.00 3000.00 (This is the most valuable of all country and western 78rpm records.)
- ☐ **ROGERS, ROY, Decca,** "Nobody's Fault But My Own/You Waited Too Long" 5.00 8.00
- ☐ "O Come All Ye Faithful/Silent Night, Holy Night" 5.00 8.00

Price Range

☐ "Chapel in the Valley/No Matter What Happens"	5.00	8.00
☐ "New Worried Mind/Melody of the Plains"	5.00	8.00
☐ "Yesterday/Time Changes Everything"	4.00	6.00
☐ "Life Won't Be the Same/Wondering Why"	5.00	8.00
☐ "Don't Be Blue, Little Pal/I'm Trusting in You"	5.00	6.00
☐ "Down By the Old Alamo/A Gay Ranchero"	5.00	8.00
☐ **STANLEY BROTHERS, King,** "Train 45/She's More to Be Pitied"	8.00	12.00
☐ "Midnight Ramble/Love Me Darling Just Tonight"	8.00	12.00
☐ "How Can We Thank Him?/That Home Far Away"	8.00	12.00
☐ "Suwanee River Hoedown/The Memory of Your Smile"	8.00	12.00
☐ "Mother's Footsteps Guide Me On/White Dove"	8.00	12.00
☐ "I'm a Man of Constant Sorrow/How Mountain Girls Can Love"	8.00	12.00
☐ **STONEMAN, ERNEST V. (& HIS DIXIE MOUNTAINEERS), RCA Victor,** "Little Old Log/Sourwood Mountain"	50.00	85.00
☐ "I Love to Walk/Hallelujah Side"	45.00	70.00
☐ "Old Joe Clark/Ida Red"	45.00	70.00
☐ "Going Up Cripple Creek/Sugar in Gourd"	50.00	85.00
☐ "All Go Hungry/West Virginia"	45.00	70.00
☐ **TANNER, GID (& HIS SKILLET LICKERS), Bluebird,** "Tanner's Rag/Tanner's Hornpipe"	40.00	55.00
☐ "Cotton Patch/Whoa, Mule, Whoa"	40.00	55.00
☐ "Georgia Wagner/Mississippi Lawyer"	40.00	55.00
☐ "Skillet Licker Breakdown/Hawkin's Rag"	40.00	55.00
☐ "Ida Red/Git Along"	40.00	55.00
☐ "Down Yonder/Back Up and Push"	40.00	55.00
☐ "Soldier's Joy/Flop Eared Mule"	40.00	55.00
☐ "Keep Your Gal at Home/I Ain't No Better Now"	40.00	55.00
☐ **Columbia,** "Rocky Pallet/Hell's Broke Loose in Georgia"	60.00	85.00
☐ "Leather Breeches/New Arkansas Traveler"	60.00	85.00
☐ "Georgia Wagner/Sugar in the Gourd"	60.00	85.00
☐ "Soldier's Joy/Rock That Cradle Lucy"	65.00	90.00

Price Range

☐ "Cripple Creek/Bonaparte's Retreat" 65.00 90.00
☐ "Flatwoods/Never Seen the Like" 65.00 90.00
☐ "Mississippi Sawyer/Goin' on Down Town" 60.00 85.00
☐ "Fox Chase/Arkansas Traveler" (with Riley Puckett) 70.00 100.00
☐ "Georgia Railroad/John Henry" (with Riley Puckett) 70.00 100.00
☐ "Just Gimme the Leavings/Old Time Tunes" 60.00 85.00
☐ "Darktown Strutter's Ball/Drink 'er Down" 60.00 85.00
☐ **WILLIAMS, HANK, Sterling,** "Calling You/Never Again" 500.00 800.00
☐ "Wealth Won't Save Your Soul/When God Comes and Gathers His Jewels" 400.00 600.00
☐ "My Love For You/I Don't Care" 320.00 450.00
☐ "Honky Tonkin'/Pan American" 250.00 375.00
☐ **MGM,** "Kaw-liga/Your Cheatin' Heart" 14.00 20.00
☐ "I'll Never Get Out of This World Alive/I Could Never Be Ashamed of You" 14.00 20.00
☐ "Jambalaya/Window Shopping" 14.00 20.00
☐ "Settin' the Woods on Fire/You Win Again" 14.00 20.00
☐ "Half as Much/Let's Turn Back the Years" 14.00 20.00
☐ "Honky Tonk Blues/I'm Sorry For You, My Friend" 14.00 20.00
☐ "May You Never Be Alone/I Just Don't Like This Kind of Livin' " 17.00 23.00
☐ "Lovesick Blues/Never Again" 14.00 20.00
☐ "Wedding Bells/I've Just Told Mama Good-bye" 14.00 20.00
☐ "Dear Brother/Lost on the River" 14.00 20.00
☐ "My Son Calls Another Man Daddy/Long Ago Lonesome Blues" 14.00 20.00
☐ "I Can't Help It/Howlin' at the Moon" 14.00 20.00
☐ "Cold Cold Heart/Dear John" 14.00 20.00
☐ "Moanin' the Blues/Nobody's Lonesome For Me" 14.00 20.00
☐ "My Bucket's Got a Hole in It/I'm So Lone-some I Could Cry" 14.00 20.00
☐ "I Saw the Light/Six More Miles" 14.00 20.00
☐ "I'm a Long Gone Daddy/The Blues Come Around" 14.00 20.00
☐ "Mansion on the Hill/I Can't Get You Off My Mind" 14.00 20.00

	Price Range	
☐ "Pan American/I Don't Care"	14.00	20.00
☐ **WILLS, BOB (& HIS TEXAS PLAYBOYS),** **Bluebird,** "Nancy Jane/Sunbonnet Sue" ..	375.00	550.00
☐ **Columbia,** "I Knew the Moment I Lost You/Oh! You Pretty Woman"	17.00	24.00
☐ "Trouble in Mind/New San Antonio Rose"	12.00	19.00
☐ "It's All Your Fault/Dusty Skies"	15.00	21.00
☐ "New Texas Playboy Rag/Texarkana Baby"	15.00	21.00
☐ "Empty Chairs at the Christmas Table/White Cross on Okinawa"	15.00	21.00
☐ "Roly Poly/New Spanish Two-Step"	15.00	21.00
☐ "New Worried Mind/Take Me Back to Tulsa"	12.00	19.00
☐ **Okeh,** "Lil Liza Jane/Bob Wills' Stomp" ...	15.00	19.00
☐ "I Don't Love a Nobody/Lone Star Rag" ...	15.00	21.00
☐ "San Antonio Rose/Convict and the Rose"	15.00	21.00
☐ "You're From Texas/We Might as Well Forget It"	15.00	21.00
☐ **Vocalion,** "Alexander's Ragtime Band/ Gambling Polka Dot Blues"	185.00	300.00
☐ "Little Girl, Go Ask Your Mama/Whoa Babe"	100.00	140.00
☐ "Oozlin' Daddy Blues/New St. Louis Blues"	100.00	140.00

CYLINDER RECORDINGS

The earliest phonograph recordings were of the cylinder type: a hollow tube with the sound grooves cut on the outside. In principle it worked just like a modern disc record but looked very different. When placed on a rotating arm, the cylinder turned, and the phonograph needle engaged the sound grooves. Wax cylinders began to be manufactured in the late 1870's. They continued to be made up to the early 1900's, but sales sharply declined in the 1890's. By then, disc records were available, and just about everybody preferred them over cylinders. The first disc records were introduced in 1887—originally in zinc, then around 1898 in the standard wax type that remained in production up to the early 1950's. Cylinder records are, of course, highly collectible and have many fans among devotees of music history. They are not really difficult to find. Even though they were in production for only a little more than 30 years—and in peak production about 20 years—literally millions of specimens were turned out, to serve the owners of pioneer "talking machines." Finding them in *good condition* is another matter. For every 50 or 60 you'll run across, only about one can really be classified as "mint." And even an absolutely mint cylinder recording, just the way it came from the factory back in the 1880's or 1890's, sounds extremely poor compared to a recording of a later era. If poor sound quality bothers you, you aren't going to be pleased with cylinder recordings. Most of those who collect cylinders are totally undisturbed by this: they approach them as historical objects, relics of the dawning days of recorded sound, and as such they really have no equals. Another thing to keep in mind is that many things are captured on cylinder recordings that would not be preserved in any other way, such as the voices of early presidents and eyewitness accounts of Queen Victoria's funeral procession.

At first, the makers of cylinder recordings did not pay any great attention to what they offered. During the early days of the cylinders, just about anything was slapped on them. When you bought a phonograph in 1880 or 1885, a few cylinder recordings came with it. These showed that the phonograph worked, and of course it was a big novelty to hear sound coming out of a machine—any kind of sound—in those days. If you wanted more, the phonograph dealer had them. Or you could send away to Mr. Edison in New Jersey, who regularly published long lists of his available cylinders. The phonograph companies made the cylinders and had a complete monopoly on the market. But it's very apparent that they were more concerned about selling phonographs than selling cylinders. That's where the money was, at that time, as phonographs by the thousands went into the homes of persons who had never before owned one. And at $15 or $20 for a machine, compared to 50¢ for a cylinder, you can hardly criticize that line of reasoning. Some folks were so thrilled at the novelty of it all that they just kept replaying the complimentary cylinders, and bought others only when the groove wore clear off the complimentaries. The phonograph, you have to remember, was the thing. People would say to their neighbors, "Come over and hear my phonograph," not "Come over and hear my new records." Hardly anybody really cared about the records—at first. It was the era of *"Be the first on your block to own . . .,"* and if you owned one of Edison's magical contraptions, that put you among the elite.

Many of the pioneer cylinders featured talking rather than music. The reasons were obvious. A talking record was much cheaper and simpler to cut than hiring a band, and the bad sound quality was less noticeable on such records. Another thing is that volume was hard to get out of the old machines. The more you cranked up the volume (if there was a volume control at all, which there often wasn't), the more scratchiness and paint-peeling screeches you heard. This is why the early ads show members of a family gathered *around* the phonograph, leaning their ears as close as possible. The best way to listen was to keep the volume soft and move in close. Since voices did not need to project as much as music, they were better suited for that kind of equipment. What were the voices saying? Mostly they were reciting patriotic speeches or poems, or reading something out of *Hamlet.* This was great to kick off the phonograph on its path to commercial stardom, but of course the public got tired of that kind of thing. Gradually the cylinder makers had to provide more alluring material. Little by little, music, vocals, minstrels, funny stories, and all sorts of things worked their way on cylinders. The big push at variety came in the late 1880's and early 1890's when Thomas Edison tried his best (for a while) to make his cylinder records competitive with the disc records of Emile Berliner. When you come across a really good cylinder recording, the odds are good that it dates somewhere between 1887 and about 1892. Needless to say, the best ones are invariably found in the worst condition, since a dance-hall cylinder got played far more often than someone reciting poetry. When these are in reasonable shape, they're certainly worth buying at the right price (see listings for rough guidelines).

In the next five or six years—between the time that cylinder manufacturers woke up and put as much emphasis on the cylinder as on the phonograph, and the cylinder's death at the hands of disc records—some really worthy material got pressed. Most of the "progressive" cylinder recordings fell into one of the following categories (and remember that the world of entertainment was, in the Victorian era, quite a different scene than it later became—our ancestors were totally captivated by many types of performances that we would not enjoy).

Marches. This was the era of John Philip Sousa, the "March King." Sousa composed—and played—stirring patriotic marches with lots of loud brassy punch. Our grandparents thought Sousa's marches were spine-tingling; every amateur band played them, and no parade was complete without several—at least. The patriotic spirit engendered by Sousa's marches was said to have been responsible for many enlistments for the Spanish-American War. You might not be quite so moved by them, hearing them on 90-year-old cylinder recordings. Their effect depended a lot on the ear-crunching volume of their sound, and that just doesn't come across on cylinders. Anyway, plenty of them were pressed, and they're interesting as curiosities even if nothing else. Compared to cylinder recordings on the whole, their values are not prohibitive.

Banjo solos. Our ancestors were very fond of banjo solos. The "modern" era of vaudeville was just coming in, and every vaudeville troupe had a banjo soloist. In the intervening years, from then to now, the banjo has slipped a little in prestige as a solo instrument. The 1880's and 1890's were definitely its "salad days." Why? Chiefly because there were several dozen musicians who could play a banjo for every one who had a trace of talent on the piano or violin. Nearly all of them got started out in minstrel shows, which employed gangs of banjo-players. They were mostly self-taught, and if you listened closely, that fact was painfully evident. But it was not an overly critical age. A good rollicking banjo solo, thumped out by somebody with heart, found plenty of sympathetic ears. They were a natural for early records because they (unlike band music) presented no problems in microphone placement. You just stood the mike in front of the banjo.

Instrumentals. Mostly these were called "orchestra records" in their day, because the word *orchestra* implied class and culture. Classical selections were not presented, however. The fare among instrumentals was largely a mixed bag taken from the music halls and minstrel show stages, heavy on strings and light on brass. Some of it comprised the "Top 40" of the day (though of course there were no popularity charts at the time), blended in with traditional tunes. These records were cut by the hundreds, possibly by the thousands, and surface wherever cylinders are found. If you want to make a collection, you can get most of them pretty reasonably—under $25. For an instrumental-on-cylinder to go as high as $35 or $40, it has to either be in fantastic condition or rank as something genuinely unusual. Premiums are usually attached to minstrel-type numbers with racist titles, having "coon" or "darkie" in the title. Most such tunes were not pressed as instrumental recordings, however, but as "minstrels" (see below). The difference was that in an orchestral recording there was more back-up. A number cut as a "minstrel tune" would usually be played with banjos only. One of the more valuable and worth-looking-for instrumental cylinders is Columbia 515063, "Night Alarm," which features the clanging bell of a fire engine. This was first-rate creativity for the time.

Minstrel tunes. On the whole these are the most valuable cylinder records. They capture a form of entertainment that totally vanished from the American scene not long thereafter—replaced by vaudeville, movies, radio, etc. Therefore, minstrel records are considered more historical than the bulk of cylinder records. The magnitude of the minstrel industry is hard to conceive today. From 1850 to the 1890's, it was the most popular U.S. entertainment. There were more minstrel groups active than any other kind of group. A typical minstrel show consisted of banjo music, vocals, and comedy. The performers were mostly white but painted their faces black, in the belief that this type of entertainment originated among slaves on the southern plantations. Actually, minstrel music as presented on stages bore little resemblance to any native "folk" music, but nobody really cared one way or the other. Some minstrel troupes were all-black, but these were very much in the minority. They were always advertised as "genuine" minstrels. It is highly questionable whether any of the all-black troupes were recorded on cylinder records. If such records exist and could be identified, they would be worth large premium prices. However, the practice in retailing cylinders was to indicate the selection's title and omit the performer's name or names. So it's not too likely that we're ever going to know. As things stand today, the most valuable minstrel cylinders are those of tunes that were recorded infrequently, especially those with racist titles.

Male quartets. Male quartets featured on cylinder records bear no resemblance to modern-day groups. This was the age of so-called "barbershop singing." How that phrase got started is open to question, but every male quartet in the later 1800's was invariably referred to as a "barbershop quartet." Most barbershop quartets were amateur. They entertained at local civic functions and other events, just for the joy of letting loose in song. When you hear the cylinder recordings you will not hesitate in concluding that they, too, were amateurs. That may or may not have been the case. Usually, barbershop quartets sang without accompaniment, and this is how you'll hear them on most cylinder recordings. Their repertoire included everything from Stephen Foster to lullabies. They also sang—and are best remembered for—the popular tunes of their era, which of course seem as antique as parchment scrolls today. But if you like "In the Good Old Summertime" and "In the Shade of the Old Apple Tree," you will enjoy male-quartet cylinders. One thing you have to say for them: they're authentic. Most of these records are not too expensive.

Baritone solos, tenor solos. Whenever a male vocalist sang solo, the cylinder record companies never put the performer's name on the label. They identified such records as "Baritone Solo" or "Tenor Solo," relegating the poor artist to a lifetime of anonymity. This was largely because there were very few recognized names in the world of vocal music at that time. Just about the only "stars" who existed were on the operatic stage, and cylinder companies had no intention of paying them the kind of money they'd demand for recording a popular tune. Why print a name on a label, when not a single buyer would know the name anyway? The philosophy was that everybody was interested in the tune, not in the performer, and this was probably 99% correct—though it did not remain so for very long. Disc records ushered in the era of star recordings, when the name meant much more than the tune. Male solos on cylinder recordings are usually performed to the accompaniment of a piano, which can be heard faintly in the background. The talent is fair—but while you're blaming the artist, don't forget to blame the archaic recording and acoustical gear of the time, too. The tunes are nearly all in the "pop" category or what passed for it, pretty much the same as with male quartets. In fact some of the singers may have been the same, too.

Soprano solos. Some fabulous operatic sopranos were active in the era of cylinder recordings. Unfortunately, they were not the ones who cut Soprano Solo records. Just who these artists were, is difficult to say. One thing you have to realize: the word *soprano* now denotes a classical artist, but in the 1800's any female who sang and whose voice was more or less in the soprano range, was billed as a soprano—even if she sang exclusively dance-hall or minstrel tunes. That's just what cylinder soprano solos are—popular and not-so-popular songs, rather than anything with even a hint of classicism. They included dance-hall numbers that were considered highly risque in their time, with naughty titles like "I Just Can't Make My Eyes Behave" and "Everyone Is in Slumberland But You and Me." The bad thing about soprano-solo cylinders is too much treble and too little bass, resulting in many words (especially those sung on very high notes) being completely unintelligible.

Vaudeville numbers. These comprise a large percentage of cylinder recordings, especially of those pressed in the period from 1887 until the cylinder record demise some years thereafter. Vaudeville was making its splash, pushing out the old traditional minstrel shows, and of course the cylinder manufacturers wanted to bring this new novelty into America's parlors. The term *vaudeville* was already in use when a man named B. F. Keith—a vaudeville manager—inaugurated continuous performances that ran all through the day. It soared like no entertainment medium before had ever done. Vaudeville theaters grew up all across the land, most of which later turned into movie houses. Scores of great stars got their start—or spent the bulk of their careers—on the vaudeville stage. It was a tough proving ground, since five or six shows a day was enough to kill the show business ambition of just about anybody. But if you're looking for star recordings among cylinder records, save your time. Recordings labeled "Vaudeville Numbers" feature tunes made popular in that medium but performed by house artists whose names did not become household words. In fact their names are not even on the records. Nevertheless, this is a nostalgic group of cylinders, in which the long-ago echoes of Old Broadway can be heard.

Comic monologues. This is probably the single most intriguing of all the groups of cylinder recordings—not because the monologues are funny or the performances are good (which is rare), but because of their uniqueness. They show what America was laughing at 90 and 100 years ago and in that sense are social documents of the highest order. The cylinder record was ideal for comic (or any other type of) monologues. They could be edited down or rewritten to fit recording time requirements much better than a song could. Also, they simply sounded better when you played them, as they still do today: the lack of tonal balancing did not hurt the spoken word as much as music, or even as much as the singing voice. Cylinder manufacturers liked to advertise that their comic monologues were taken straight off the vaudeville stage. Some of them no doubt were, but with vaudeville reusing the same routines over and over endlessly, there weren't nearly enough comic monologues to go around. So they made up their own, and some very weird things found their way onto the cylinders, with titles like "Krausmeyer and His Dog" and "Reuben Haskins' Ride on a Cyclone Auto." A large portion of comic monologues were of an ethnic or racial nature, which was par for the course at that time in show biz: foreigners who spoke with accents were heavily lampooned by comics. In fact, Americans who spoke with accents came in for their share of ribbing, too. There are many comic monologue records in which the joke is turned on New England Yankees. Comic monologue selections tend to be snapped up very fast wherever cylinders appear. Even those who don't really collect them have a curiosity interest in them, much more so than in most other types of cylinder recordings.

Having said all of the above, we need to point out one more thing: that to play cylinder recordings, you need a cylinder phonograph. This is a fair-sized investment, but for anybody who has intentions of being a serious collector it will be more than repaid in listening pleasure. Just make sure, before putting down any cash, that the machine is in proper operating condition. See the section on mechanical instruments for further information.

COLUMBIA WAX CYLINDER RECORDINGS

Recordings on the Columbia label (yes, the firm is still in business today) were slightly more expensive, originally, than those of Oxford. Musically and technically they were of about equal quality, but Columbia had the bigger reputation and—especially in the classical field—the bigger artists.

	Price Range	
BAND, MARCHES		
☐ 51544, Admiral's Favorite March	16.00	22.00
☐ 51514, America	16.00	22.00
☐ 532311, Anona	20.00	26.00
☐ 532362, Any Rags	16.00	22.00
☐ 531867, Arkansas Husking Bee	16.00	22.00
☐ 532389, Bedella	20.00	25.00
BANJO SOLOS		
☐ 53861, Bunch of Rags	34.00	51.00
☐ 531412, Coon Band Contest	45.00	60.00
☐ 53816, Darky's Dream	45.00	60.00

Price Range

☐ **53825,** El Capitan March	23.00	38.00
☐ **53856,** Eli Green's Cakewalk	29.00	49.00
☐ **53860,** Old Folks at Home	29.00	49.00
☐ **53830,** Rag Time Medley ("All Coons Look Alike to Me")	37.00	58.00
☐ **53859,** Whistling Rufus	25.00	41.00

INSTRUMENTALS (originally called Orchestra Records)

☐ **515132,** Angel's Serenade	15.00	20.00
☐ **515162,** Blue Danube Waltz	15.00	20.00
☐ **515206,** Bugler's Dream	16.00	23.00
☐ **531688,** Creole Belle	20.00	30.00
☐ **515010,** Dancing in the Kitchen	20.00	30.00
☐ **515145,** Darky's Dream	20.00	30.00
☐ **515159,** Darky's Tickle	21.00	35.00
☐ **532191,** Dixieland March	18.00	30.00
☐ **515064,** Down on the Suwanee River	27.00	42.00
☐ **515114,** Flora Waltz	15.00	21.00
☐ **515202,** Georgia Camp Meeting	15.00	21.00
☐ **515007,** Happy Days in Dixie	20.00	32.00
☐ **515142,** Husking Bee	20.00	32.00
☐ **532283,** Laughing Water	15.00	20.00
☐ **515121,** Let Her Rip	15.00	20.00
☐ **515063,** Night Alarm (with fire-engine sound effects)	34.00	52.00
☐ **515044,** Rose from the South Waltz	15.00	20.00
☐ **515059,** Virginia Skedaddle	20.00	31.00
☐ **515203,** Whistling Rufus	15.00	21.00

MINSTREL TUNES

☐ **31609,** Coon, Coon, Coon	50.00	71.00
☐ **13000,** Dese Bones Shall Rise Again	65.00	95.00
☐ **32986,** Dixie Dear	35.00	55.00
☐ **32952,** Goodbye, Mr. Greenback	35.00	55.00
☐ **13001,** High Old Time	65.00	100.00
☐ **31691,** I'd Leave My Happy Home for You	45.00	75.00
☐ **13004,** Laughing Song	72.00	105.00
☐ **33031,** Moses Andrew Jackson	72.00	105.00
☐ **13002,** Old Log Cabin	35.00	51.00
☐ **33104,** San Antonio	35.00	51.00

QUARTETS, MALE

☐ **33048,** Ain't You Coming Back to New Hampshire, Molly?	16.00	22.00

		Price Range	
☐	**33049,** Alice, Where Art Thou Going?	16.00	22.00
☐	**33201,** Black Jim	30.00	44.00
☐	**32931,** Call to Arms	30.00	44.00
☐	**33033,** Christmas Morning at Flanagan's . .	25.00	39.00
☐	**32836,** Darling Nellie Gray	16.00	22.00
☐	**32907,** Down in Chinkapin Lan	27.00	45.00
☐	**9037,** Farmyard Medley	23.00	38.00
☐	**32690,** Goodbye Sis	23.00	38.00
☐	**32237,** Hoosier Hollow Quilting Party	23.00	38.00
☐	**32764,** In the Shade of the Old Apple Tree	16.00	24.00
☐	**32722,** In the Sweet Bye and Bye	16.00	24.00
☐	**9045,** My Old New Hampshire Home	16.00	24.00
☐	**9042,** Nationality Medley	20.00	35.00
☐	**32704,** Nelle Was a Lady	25.00	41.00
☐	**9030,** The Old Folks at Home	25.00	41.00
☐	**9029,** Way Down Yonder in the Cornfield	27.00	45.00
☐	**33070,** When Daddy Sings the Little Ones to Sleep	16.00	24.00
☐	**32989,** While the Old Mill Wheel Is Turning	14.00	23.00

OXFORD LABEL WAX CYLINDER RECORDINGS

The following cylinders are all Oxford label and date from circa 1905.

BAND MUSIC

☐	**31529,** American Students' Waltz	19.00	15.00
☐	**32413,** By the Sycamore Tree Medley	9.00	14.00
☐	**32982,** Dixie Queen March	10.00	15.00
☐	**514,** El Capitan March	16.00	22.00
☐	**501,** High School Cadets' March	15.00	21.00
☐	**32735,** Hobo Band	15.00	21.00
☐	**500,** Liberty Bell March	16.00	22.00
☐	**32816,** Me and My Banjo	20.00	32.00
☐	**1537,** O Promise Me	25.00	40.00
☐	**32749,** Roosevelt's Inaugural Parade	25.00	40.00
☐	**32815,** Whistler and His Dog	23.00	32.00

BARITONE SOLOS

☐	**32615,** Abraham (minstrel song)	50.00	75.00
☐	**32820,** And the World Goes On	30.00	51.00
☐	**32589,** Come Take a Trip in My Airship . . .	50.00	75.00
☐	**32811,** Girl Who Cares for Me	30.00	50.00
☐	**32854,** Home Sweet Home	23.00	38.00

Price Range

☐ **33058,** I Love the Last One Best of All	30.00	50.00
☐ **32805,** In Dear Old Georgia	37.00	51.00
☐ **33123,** My Irish Rosie	37.00	51.00
☐ **32960,** The Poor Old Man	30.00	50.00
☐ **32882,** Wait Till the Sun Shines Nelly	25.00	38.00
☐ **33057,** We'll Be Sweethearts to the End ..	30.00	51.00
☐ **32889,** When the Mocking Birds are Singing	30.00	51.00
☐ **32939,** You Look Awfully Good to Father	35.00	58.00
☐ **32605,** You Must Think I'm Santa Claus ..	30.00	51.00
☐ **32976,** You're Just the Girl I'm Looking For	35.00	58.00

COMIC MONOLOGUES, ETC.

☐ **11102,** Backyard Conversation Between Two Jealous Irish Washerwomen	50.00	81.00
☐ **330243,** An Evening at Mrs. Clancy's Boarding House	40.00	60.00
☐ **32949,** Flanagan's Night Off	40.00	60.00
☐ **32623,** Hand of Fate	35.00	55.00
☐ **32655,** Krausmeyer and His Dog	50.00	75.00
☐ **32603,** Night Before Christmas	27.00	40.00
☐ **33001,** Punch and Judy	27.00	40.00
☐ **32249,** Reuben Haskins' Ride on a Cyclone Auto	40.00	60.00
☐ **32569,** Rheumatism Cure in Jayville Center	50.00	75.00

SOPRANO SOLOS

☐ **33082,** Everyone is in Slumberland But You and Me	16.00	22.00
☐ **33063,** Fancy Little Nancy	20.00	31.00
☐ **33083,** If the Man in the Moon Were a Coon	28.00	42.00
☐ **33097,** I Just Can't Make My Eyes Believe	20.00	30.00
☐ **33004,** It's All Right in the Summer Time ..	28.00	42.00
☐ **32911,** So Long, Mary	22.00	35.00
☐ **32746,** You Ain't the Man I Thought You Was	20.00	32.00
☐ **32972,** Waiting at the Church	20.00	32.00

TENOR SOLOS

☐ **32533,** A Bit o'Blarney	20.00	32.00
☐ **33179,** Always Leave Them Laughing When You Say Goodbye	16.00	22.00
☐ **32945,** Anxious	21.00	36.00
☐ **33140,** Ask Me Not	16.00	25.00
☐ **32641,** Bunker Hill	16.00	25.00
☐ **32476,** By the Old Oak Tree	15.00	25.00

Price Range

☐ **32946,** Can't You See I'm Lonely	16.00	25.00
☐ **33127,** Captain Baby Bunting	20.00	32.00
☐ **33023,** Cheer Up, Mary	16.00	23.00
☐ **32887,** Will You Love Me in December? ...	11.00	15.00
☐ **33178,** Dreaming	20.00	31.00
☐ **32732,** Farewell, Soldier Boy (Spanish-American War)	20.00	32.00
☐ **32844,** Girl of the U.S.A	22.00	38.00
☐ **32812,** Goodbye, Sweet Old Manhattan Isle	30.00	45.00
☐ **32875,** Goodnight, Little Girl	21.00	33.00
☐ **32997,** Good Old U.S.A	16.00	22.00
☐ **32806,** I'll Be Waiting in the Gloaming	30.00	45.00
☐ **32582,** I'm Longing For You, Sweetheart ..	16.00	22.00
☐ **32664,** In the Shade of the Old Apple Tree	10.00	14.00
☐ **32943,** Is There Any Room in Heaven? ...	30.00	45.00
☐ **32658,** It Makes Me Think of Home	20.00	33.00
☐ **32726,** Just Across the Bridge of Gold	16.00	23.00
☐ **32860,** Just a Little Rocking Chair and You	20.00	31.00
☐ **32798,** Keep a Little Cozy Corner in Your Heart.....................................	23.00	37.00
☐ **32942,** Keep on the Sunny Side	20.00	32.00
☐ **33080,** Lemon in the Garden of Love	27.00	40.00
☐ **32908,** Let Me Write What I Never Dared to Tell	22.00	37.00
☐ **32566,** Little Boy Called Taps	27.00	40.00
☐ **33168,** Little Suit of Blue	25.00	37.00
☐ **32718,** Longing for You	25.00	37.00
☐ **32619,** Mamma's Boy	15.00	23.00
☐ **32909,** Mayor of Tokio, I Like You	30.00	45.00
☐ **32465,** My Cosy Corner Girl	25.00	36.00
☐ **32778,** My Irish Molly O	25.00	36.00
☐ **33015,** Not Because Your Hair is Curly ...	20.00	33.00
☐ **32919,** Nothing Like That in Our Family ...	22.00	37.00
☐ **32773,** On a Summer Night	22.00	37.00
☐ **32877,** Only 45 Minutes from Broadway ...	30.00	45.00
☐ **32774,** Picnic for Two	25.00	37.00
☐ **32859,** Robinson Crusoe's Isle	25.00	37.00
☐ **32427,** Runaway Motor Car	27.00	42.00
☐ **33128,** School Days	13.00	30.00
☐ **32852,** Somebody's Sweetheart	22.00	38.00
☐ **33062,** Street of New York	22.00	38.00
☐ **32513,** Sweetest Girl in Dixie	20.00	33.00

Price Range

☐ **32828,** Sweethearts in Every Town	25.00	36.00
☐ **33196,** Take Me Back to New York Town	25.00	36.00
☐ **32560,** Teasing	20.00	35.00
☐ **33205,** Two Blue Eyes	20.00	35.00
☐ **32941,** We Parted as the Sun Went Down	20.00	35.00
☐ **32881,** What Has the Night Time to Do with the Girl?	22.00	36.00
☐ **33060,** When the Flowers Bloom in the Springtime	16.00	23.00
☐ **32458,** When the Sunset Turns the Ocean's Blue to Gold	20.00	33.00
☐ **32470,** When the Trees are White with Blossoms I'll Return	16.00 ·	22.00
☐ **32814,** Where the Morning Glories Twine	16.00	22.00
☐ **32619,** Why Don't They Play with Me?	22.00	37.00
☐ **32887,** Will You Love Me in December? . . .	11.00	15.00
☐ **32970,** With the Robins I'll Return	23.00	32.00
☐ **32625,** Yankee Doodle Boy	16.00	22.00
☐ **32853,** You Don't Seem Like the Girl I Used to Know	22.00	35.00
☐ **33157,** You'll Have to Get Off and Walk . .	20.00	33.00

VAUDEVILLE NUMBERS

☐ **32795,** Anthony and Cleopatra (satire on Shakespeare)	35.00	52.00
☐ **33182,** At the Village Post Office	40.00	59.00
☐ **33000,** Barnyard Serenade	30.00	43.00
☐ **11024,** Blazing Ray	30.00	43.00
☐ **33206,** Bronco Bob	40.00	53.00
☐ **32981,** Coming Home from Coney Island . .	40.00	53.00
☐ **32980,** Darktown Courtship	50.00	70.00
☐ **32628,** Down the Pike at the St. Louis Exposition	40.00	52.00
☐ **32730,** Ev'ry Little Bit Helps	30.00	42.00
☐ **33170,** Flanagan at the Barber's	37.00	55.00
☐ **33198,** Flanagan at the Doctor's	37.00	55.00
☐ **33183,** Flanagan at the Vocal Teacher's . .	37.00	55.00
☐ **33129,** Flanagan on a Broadway Car	37.00	55.00
☐ **33144,** Flanagan on a Farm	35.00	55.00
☐ **32868,** Fritz and Louisa	32.00	50.00
☐ **32738,** Heinie	37.00	55.00
☐ **33169,** Herman and Minnie	32.00	50.00
☐ **33064,** Jealous	37.00	55.00

		Price Range	
☐	32947, Maggie Clancy's New Piano	32.00	50.00
☐	33143, Meet Me Down at the Corner	32.00	50.00
☐	32998, Monkey on a String	22.00	35.00
☐	32766, Mr. and Mrs. 'Awkins	27.00	39.00
☐	32780, Mr. and Mrs. Murphy	27.00	39.00
☐	33014, Mrs. Hiram Offen Discharges Bridget Sullivan	35.00	50.00
☐	32948, Mrs. Hiram Offen Engaging Bridget Sullivan	35.00	50.00
☐	33002, Mrs. Reilly's Troubles With the Dumb Waiter	35.00	50.00
☐	32700, Musical Congress of Nations	27.00	40.00
☐	32901, Original Cohens	60.00	90.00

VOCAL DUETS, MALE

☐	33150, And a Little Bit More	16.00	22.00
☐	33050, Arrah Wanna	16.00	22.00
☐	33105, Bake Dat Chicken Pie	20.00	31.00
☐	32894, Central, Give Me Back My Dime ...	20.00	31.00
☐	32621, Coax Me	22.00	37.00
☐	32777, Come Along, Little Girl	20.00	31.00
☐	33009, Come, Take a Skate with Me	20.00	31.00
☐	32485, Dixie	20.00	31.00

FOLK

MEMORABILIA

Only in the past 10 to 15 years has folk music memorabilia been actively collected. Undoubtedly, this material is, as a whole, still undervalued and is likely to increase in price in the future.

		Price Range	
☐	**BAEZ, JOAN,** photo cut from "Life" Magazine, signed and inscribed	7.00	10.00
☐	**BAEZ, JOAN,** 10x12 color photo, signed on the back, glue marks on back	8.00	11.00
☐	**BAEZ, JOAN,** 8x10 studio portrait with guitar, signed, dated 1964	6.00	9.00
☐	**BAEZ, JOAN,** 8x10 photo blown up from candid shot, shows her seated on grass in park, signed, inscribed, c. 1967	15.00	20.00

Price Range

☐ **BAEZ, JOAN,** 45rpm recording, "The Night They Drove Old Dixie Down," signed on the label 15.00   20.00

☐ **BAEZ, JOAN,** six snapshot photos, mostly 3½x4, two of them signed, mounted on a stiff cardboard sheet 17.00   22.00

☐ **BRAND, OSCAR,** book, "The Ballad Mongers," signed and inscribed on front endleaf 7.00   10.00

☐ **BRAND, OSCAR,** typewritten letter, signed, radio station letterhead, 1968 .... 3.00   4.00

☐ **BRAND, OSCAR,** postcard in his hand, three lines, 1958 .... 2.00   3.00

☐ **BRAND, OSCAR,** signature on a card 1.00   2.00

☐ **BRAND, OSCAR,** 8x10 studio portrait, signed and inscribed, dated 1962 .... 4.00   5.00

☐ **BRAND, OSCAR,** 3½x4 snapshot with fan, signed on the back 2.00   3.00

☐ **BRAND, OSCAR,** T-shirt with his name and likeness 7.00   10.00

☐ **BRAND, OSCAR,** concert program, signed 2.00   3.00

☐ **BRAND, OSCAR,** magazine article, signed 2.00   3.00

☐ **BRAND, OSCAR,** two checks endorsed by him, 1971 and 1977 .... 7.00   10.00

☐ **BRAND, OSCAR,** scrapbook with 41 photos of him, some with other folk music celebrities, a few signed 70.00   90.00

☐ **CLANCY BROTHERS,** 8x10 group photo, signed by all, 1961 .... 13.00   20.00

☐ **COLLINS, JUDY,** 8x10 studio photo, signed and inscribed, dated 1968 .... 4.00   6.00

☐ **COLLINS, JUDY,** photo cut from LP album cover, signed 7.00   10.00

☐ **COLLINS, JUDY,** ALs, two pages, with envelope, 1961 .... 4.00   6.00

☐ **COLLINS, JUDY,** signature on a card 2.00   3.00

☐ **COLLINS, JUDY,** signature on a record company press release 3.00   5.00

☐ **COLLINS, JUDY,** 5x7 color photo, signed on the back 4.00   6.00

☐ **COLLINS, JUDY,** book, "Poems of the Scottish Highlands," signed by her inside front cover 6.00   9.00

Joan Baez

Price Range

- ☐ **COLLINS, JUDY,** news cutting (record review), signed, laminated .... 2.00 · 3.00
- ☐ **COLLINS, JUDY,** LP phono record, signed on the label .... 20.00 · 30.00
- ☐ **COLLINS, JUDY,** concert program, signed 3.00 · 5.00
- ☐ **COLLINS, JUDY,** record company contract, signed twice .... 20.00 · 25.00
- ☐ **HOUSTON, CISCO,** EP album sleeve, signed, record missing .... 22.00 · 33.00
- ☐ **HOUSTON, CISCO,** ALs, two pages, 1951 17.00 · 25.00
- ☐ **HOUSTON, CISCO,** concert program, signed 8.00 · 11.00
- ☐ **HOUSTON, CISCO,** book, "Songs of the American West," signed on front flyleaf ... 15.00 · 20.00
- ☐ **HOUSTON, CISCO,** 8x10 studio portrait, signed, c. 1955 .... 18.00 · 27.00
- ☐ **HOUSTON, CISCO,** 78rpm phono record, signed on the label .... 60.00 · 80.00

	Price Range	
☐ **HOUSTON, CISCO,** signature on a card ...	3.00	5.00
☐ **HOUSTON, CISCO,** check endorsed by him, 1947	35.00	50.00
☐ **HOUSTON, CISCO,** concert appearance contract, signed	30.00	40.00
☐ **IVES, BURL,** 8x10 portrait photo, signed, dated 1950	4.00	6.00
☐ **IVES, BURL,** sailor's cap reputedly worn by him in concert	15.00	20.00
☐ **IVES, BURL,** motion picture still, "Cat on a Hot Tin Roof," signed	7.00	10.00
☐ **IVES, BURL,** theatrical poster, signed, framed, 18x28	40.00	55.00
☐ **IVES, BURL,** check endorsed by him, 1961	15.00	22.00
☐ **IVES, BURL,** ALs, three pages, New York, 1941	20.00	28.00
☐ **IVES, BURL,** postcard sent by him in 1949, six lines, stained	4.00	5.00
☐ **IVES, BURL,** photo with John Daly, signed by Ives only	5.00	6.00
☐ **IVES, BURL,** article from "TV-Radio Life," signed	6.00	7.00
☐ **IVES, BURL,** 78rpm phono record, signed on the label	18.00	24.00
☐ **IVES, BURL,** record company contract, signed	20.00	26.00
☐ **IVES, BURL,** T-shirt with his name and likeness	8.00	11.00
☐ **NILES, JOHN JACOB,** ALs, two pages, 1935	22.00	33.00
☐ **NILES, JOHN JACOB,** ALs, 1½ pages, to Carl Sandburg	80.00	110.00
☐ **NILES, JOHN JACOB,** Copy of book, Carl Sandburg's "American Songbag," inscribed by Sandburg to Niles, with notes by Niles ..	130.00	175.00
☐ **NILES, JOHN JACOB,** 78rpm record, signed on the label	40.00	55.00
☐ **NILES, JOHN JACOB,** 5x6½ photo, signed and inscribed, c. 1930	18.00	24.00
☐ **NILES, JOHN JACOB,** signature on a card	5.00	7.00
☐ **OCHS, PHIL,** 8x10 studio portrait, signed and inscribed, dated 1966	25.00	33.00

	Price Range	
☐ **OCHS, PHIL,** concert program, signed	20.00	28.00
☐ **OCHS, PHIL,** LP record album cover, signed, record missing	80.00	105.00
☐ **OCHS, PHIL,** signature on a card	8.00	11.00
☐ **OCHS, PHIL,** ALs, one page, 1960	37.00	53.00
☐ **ODETTA,** 8x10 studio photo, signed and inscribed	5.00	7.00
☐ **ODETTA,** sheet music, "The Golden Vanity," signed	4.00	5.00
☐ **ODETTA,** copy of magazine "Thirteen," signed	4.00	5.00
☐ **ODETTA,** snapshot photo on stage, signed on the back	4.00	5.00
☐ **ODETTA,** ALs, two pages, 1969	5.00	6.00
☐ **ODETTA,** ALs, 1½ pages, with autographed photo enclosed, 1973	7.00	10.00
☐ **ODETTA,** guitar reputedly used by her in TV appearance	550.00	800.00
☐ **ODETTA,** book, "Songs of the Southern Highlands," signed on front flyleaf	8.00	11.00
☐ **ODETTA,** scrapbook on her career, containing six 8x10 photos, three of them signed, 56 news cuttings and other items	70.00	90.00
☐ **PAXTON, TOM,** 8x10 studio photo, signed and inscribed	5.00	7.00
☐ **PAXTON, TOM,** concert contract, signed ..	11.00	16.00
☐ **PAXTON, TOM,** ALs, ½ page, 1968	5.00	6.00
☐ **PAXTON, TOM,** LP record album cover, signed, record missing	13.00	19.00
☐ **PAXTON, TOM,** signature on a card	2.00	3.00
☐ **PAXTON, TOM,** photo with Phil Ochs, signed by both	70.00	90.00
☐ **PAXTON, TOM,** T-shirt with his name and likeness	7.00	10.00
☐ **PAXTON, TOM,** postcard sent by him in 1961	4.00	5.00
☐ **PAXTON, TOM,** two 5x6 snapshot photos, signed on the backs	7.00	10.00
☐ **PAXTON, TOM,** check endorsed by him, 1970	11.00	15.00
☐ **PAXTON, TOM,** LP phono record, signed on the label	20.00	25.00

Price Range

☐ **SEEGER, PETE,** 8x10 studio portrait, signed, dated 1958	6.00	8.00
☐ **SEEGER, PETE,** three small snapshot photos, two signed, 1970–75	8.00	11.00
☐ **SEEGER, PETE,** ALs, two pages, 1961	6.00	8.00
☐ **SEEGER, PETE,** concert poster (Carnegie Hall, New York), framed under glass, not signed	13.00	19.00
☐ **SEEGER, PETE,** signature on a card	1.50	2.00
☐ **SEEGER, PETE,** copy of "Rolling Stone" magazine, signed	5.00	7.00
☐ **SEEGER, PETE,** 6x7½ photo standing on shipboard, signed	5.00	7.00
☐ **SEEGER, PETE,** concert program, signed ..	4.00	5.00
☐ **SEEGER, PETE,** check endorsed by him, 1974	11.00	16.00
☐ **SEEGER, PETE,** 647 news cuttings relating to his career, housed in a set of four 14x17 leatherette albums	55.00	75.00
☐ **SEEGER, PETE,** LP record album cover, signed, record missing	15.00	20.00
☐ **WHITE, JOSH,** ALs, two pages, 1937	40.00	55.00
☐ **WHITE, JOSH,** 8x10 photo, signed and inscribed	16.00	22.00
☐ **WHITE, JOSH,** cover of 78rpm album set, signed	16.00	22.00

78's

The traditional definition of folk music is music not originally created to be recorded or performed professionally. Mountain ballads of Kentucky are a perfect and indisputable example of folk music; so are sea chanties and the earlier Polish polkas. But today the term *folk music,* as commonly interpreted, also encompasses a great deal else. Almost any recording made by a recognized folk music artist is labeled folk music, and there is no doubt that buyers are just as interested—if not more so—in the artist as in his music. Therefore, it is difficult to set guidelines for the collector.

Whether the recordings made by current folk artists will be highly regarded by future generations is questionable. In any case, the fact that modern LP albums are pressed in very large quantities, and, being made of vinyl, preserve far better than recordings of the pre-1950 era, it is not likely they will become "collectors' items" to quite the same degree as the old 78's.

Folk music was recorded from the turn of the century onward; it is found even on wax cylinders predating disc records. Nearly all early recordings, however, up to World War I, had the songs performed by popular or operatic artists, which rendered them far from authentic-sounding. John McCormack doing an Irish folk ballad made sense, even though the original singers of these songs probably did not have opera-trained voices; but very often such songs, of whatever origin or nationality, were done in far too dignified and artistic a manner for folk music. It was only later, around 1920, that record companies began to press folk music performed by artists who gave it a suitable rendering.

There is much difference of opinion as to what may or may not be included in a collection of "authentic" folk music. Nor can any strict guidelines be laid. Many of the records listed in our section on Country and Western 78rpms could easily be termed "folk," especially those of such artists as Dave Macon, Gid Tanner, J. E. Mainer, and Ernest Stoneman. They were mountain or bluegrass ballads, performed by natives of the land. "Overlapping" is common in folk music: a tune can fall into several categories.

	Price Range	
☐ **BATES, DR. HUMPHREY and HIS POSSUM HUNTERS, Brunswick 239,** "Eighth of January"	36.00	57.00
☐ **Brunswick 275,** "Run, Nigger, Run"	45.00	65.00
☐ **BAUMAN, MORDY, Musicraft M-75** (album; 4 10-inch records), "Songs of American Sailormen"	50.00	75.00
☐ **BEIRNE and DONOVAN, Decca 12244,** "Green Mossy Banks of the Lee/What Will You Do, Love?"	8.00	12.00
☐ **DYER-BENNETT, RICHARD, Packard D-6,** "Come All Ye/Leprechaun"	15.00	21.00
☐ **Asch 461** (album; 3 12-inch records), "Ballads"	85.00	130.00
☐ **Vox 633** (album; 4 10-inch records), "Singing Minstrel Songs of Germany" (performed in English)	75.00	115.00
☐ **Keynote K-108** (album; 3 10-inch records), "Ballads and Folksongs"	150.00	200.00

	Price Range	

Note: Apparently there was a switch in record-company policy sometime during the marketing of this album, as some copies contain different records than others.

☐ **GUTHRIE, WOODY, Disc 610** (album), "Dust Bowl Ballads"	**250.00**	**350.00**
☐ **Stinson-Asch 347** (album), "Woody Guthrie, Vol. 1"	**175.00**	**250.00**
☐ **Stinson-Asch 360** (album), "American Documentary"	**175.00**	**250.00**
☐ **Stinson-Asch 347, Part II,** "Songs by Woody Guthrie" (with Cisco Houston and Blind Sonny Terry)	**175.00**	**250.00**
☐ **HADDOCK, G. MARSTON, Musicraft 55** (album; 4 10-inch records), "English Folk Songs and Ballads"	**75.00**	**115.00**
☐ **HARLAN MINERS FIDDLERS, Montgomery Ward 3025,** "Skip to My Lou/The Roving Gambler"	**12.00**	**19.00**
☐ **SANDBURG, CARL, Musicraft M-11** (album; four 10-inch records), "American Songbag"	**110.00**	**150.00**
☐ **Decca A-356** (album; four 10-inch records), "Cowboy Songs and Negro Spirituals"	**95.00**	**130.00**
☐ **SCOTT, TOM, Signature S-5** (album; four 10-inch records), "Sing of America"	**110.00**	**145.00**
☐ **SEEGER, PETE, Commodore CR-11,** "Sea Chanteys and Whaling Ballads" (with Woody Guthrie, Peter Hawes and Millard Lampell)	**80.00**	**115.00**
☐ **Disc 604** (album), "School Days" (with Cisco Houston, Charity Bailey and "Leadbelly") ..	**60.00**	**95.00**
☐ **Charter C-500,** "Cumberland Mt. Bear Chase/Keep My Skillet Good and Greasy"	**10.00**	**15.00**
☐ **Charter album** (three 10-inch records), "Bawdy Ballads and Real Sad Songs" (with Betty Sanders)	**70.00**	**110.00**

LP's

AXTON, HOYT

☐ **A and M SP-4376** (stereo), Less Than a Song	**12.00**	**20.00**
☐ **SP-4422** (stereo), Life Machine	**12.00**	**20.00**
☐ **SP-4510** (stereo), Southbound	**12.00**	**20.00**

	Price Range	
☐ **SP-4571** (stereo), Fearless	**12.00**	**20.00**
☐ **SP-4669** (stereo), Road Songs	**12.00**	**20.00**
☐ **Horizon WP-1601** (stereo), The Balladeer	**14.00**	**24.00**

BROONZY, BIG BILL & PETE SEEGER
| ☐ **Folkways FVS-9008** (stereo), Bill Bill Broonzy & Pete Seeger .... | **19.00** | **28.00** |

COLLINS, JUDY
☐ **Elektra EKS-7222** (stereo), Golden Apples of the Sun	**14.00**	**24.00**
☐ **EKS7-243** (stereo), Judy Collins #3	**14.00**	**24.00**
☐ **EKS7-300** (stereo), Judy Collins' Fifth Album	**14.00**	**24.00**
☐ **EKS7-320** (stereo), In My Life	**14.00**	**24.00**
☐ **EKS7-4012** (stereo), Wildflowers	**12.00**	**20.00**
☐ **EKS7-4033** (stereo), Who Knows Where The Time Goes?	**12.00**	**20.00**
☐ **EKS7-4055** (stereo), Recollections	**12.00**	**20.00**

FOGELBERG, DAN
| ☐ **Columbia KC-31751** (stereo), Home Free .. | **10.00** | **16.00** |
| ☐ **Epic PE-33499** (stereo), Captured Angel ... | **10.00** | **16.00** |

GUTHRIE, ARLO
☐ **Reprise MS-2183** (stereo), Arlo Guthrie	**8.00**	**18.00**
☐ **RS-6267** (stereo), Alice's Restaurant	**8.00**	**18.00**
☐ **RS-6299** (stereo), Arlo	**8.00**	**18.00**
☐ **RS-6346** (stereo), Running Down The Road	**8.00**	**18.00**

HENSKE, JUDY
| ☐ **Mercury SR-61010** (stereo), Little Bit of Sunshine .... | **19.00** | **28.00** |

HESTER, CAROLYN
| ☐ **Columbia CL-8596** (mono), Carolyn Hester | **23.00** | **34.00** |

HURT, MISSISSIPPI JOHN
| ☐ **Piedmont PLP-13157** (mono), Folksongs and Blues, Volume I .... | **20.00** | **30.00** |

Though billed as Volume I, no further volumes were issued.

	Price Range	

IVES, BURL
☐ **Decca DL7-8886** (stereo), Cheers	10.00	20.00
☐ **MCA 318** (stereo), Paying My Dues Again ..	8.00	15.00
☐ **2-4089** (stereo), The Best of Burl Ives ...	8.00	15.00
☐ **Columbia CL-1459** (mono), Return of the Wayfaring Stranger	15.00	20.00
☐ **United Artists UAS-6060** (stereo), Ballads	9.00	15.00

LIGHTFOOT, GORDON
☐ **Reprise 2206** (stereo), Cold on the Shoulder	9.00	15.00
☐ **United Artists UAS-6649** (stereo), Did She Mention My Name	9.00	15.00

LOMAX, ALAN
☐ **United Artists 4027** (stereo), Blues in the Mississippi Night	7.00	16.00

MITCHELL, CHAD (Trio)
☐ **Colpix SCP-411** (stereo), The Chad Mitchell Trio Arrives	20.00	28.00
☐ **Kapp KS-3262** (stereo), A Mighty Day on Campus	14.00	23.00
☐ **KS-3313** (stereo), Blowin' in the Wind ...	14.00	23.00
☐ **KS-3324** (stereo), Best of the Chad Mitchell Trio	14.00	23.00
☐ **Mercury SR-60838** (stereo), Singin' Our Mind	14.00	23.00
☐ **SR-60891** (stereo), Reflecting	14.00	23.00
☐ **SR-61067** (stereo), Violets of Dan	14.00	23.00

MITCHELL, JONI
☐ **Reprise RS-6293** (stereo), Joni Mitchell ...	10.00	18.00
☐ **RS-6376** (stereo), Ladies of the Canyon	10.00	18.00
☐ **Asylum 202** (stereo), Miles of Aisles	10.00	18.00

NEW CHRISTY MINSTRELS
☐ **Columbia CS-8672** (stereo), Presenting the New Christy Minstrels	8.00	12.00
☐ **CS-8817** (stereo), Tall Tales	6.00	10.00
☐ **CS-8896** (stereo), Merry Christmas	6.00	10.00
☐ **CS-9103** (stereo), Cowboys & Indians ...	6.00	10.00

The New Christy Minstrels took their name from an old-time blackface band called The Christy Minstrels.

	Price Range	

OCHS, PHIL

☐ **Elektra EKS-7269** (stereo), All the News That's Fit to Sing	12.00	16.00
☐ **EKS-7287** (stereo), I Ain't Marching Anymore	12.00	16.00
☐ **EKS-7310** (stereo), Phil Ochs in Concert	12.00	16.00
☐ **A & M SP-4133** (stereo), Pleasures of the Harbor	10.00	15.00
☐ **SP-4148** (stereo), Tape from California ..	10.00	15.00
☐ **SP-4181** (stereo), Rehearsals for Retirement	10.00	15.00

ODETTA

☐ **Vanguard VSD-2046** (stereo), My Eyes Have Seen	18.00	25.00
☐ **VSD-2057** (stereo), Ballad for Americans	18.00	25.00
☐ **VSD-2072** (stereo), Odetta at Carnegie Hall	18.00	25.00
☐ **Riverside RLP-9417** (stereo), Odetta & The Blues	18.00	25.00

PAXTON, TOM

☐ **Anchor 2012** (stereo), The Paxton Brothers	10.00	18.00
☐ **Reprise 2096** (stereo), Peace Will Come ...	9.00	17.00
☐ **2144** (stereo), New Songs from Old Friends	9.00	17.00
☐ **Elektra 74043** (stereo), Things I Notice Now	9.00	17.00
☐ **74066** (stereo), Tom Paxton 6	9.00	17.00

PETER, PAUL & MARY

☐ **Warner Brothers WS-1449** (stereo), Peter, Paul & Mary	15.00	23.00
☐ **WS-1473** (stereo), Moving	15.00	23.00
☐ **WS-1507** (stereo), In the Wind	15.00	23.00
☐ **WS-1555** (stereo), In Concert	15.00	23.00
☐ **WS-1589** (stereo), A Song Will Rise	12.00	17.00
☐ **WS-1648** (stereo), The Peter, Paul & Mary Album	12.00	17.00

SEEGER, PETE

☐ **Aravel AB-1006** (mono), Live Hootenanny	20.00	30.00
☐ **Folkways FH-5210** (mono), Champlain Valley Song Bag	10.00	15.00

	Price Range	
☐ **31040** (stereo), Banks of Marble	**10.00**	**15.00**
☐ **Tradition 2107** (stereo), Pete Seeger Sings Folk Music of the World	**10.00**	**15.00**
☐ **Columbia CS-8448** (stereo), Pete Seeger Story Songs	**12.00**	**18.00**
☐ **CS-8901** (mono), We Shall Overcome . . .	**12.00**	**18.00**

SHANKAR, RAVI

☐ **Columbia WL-119** (mono), The Sounds of India	**25.00**	**35.00**

HUMOROUS 77–81s

This section consists of 77–81 rpm recordings released prior to 1920. The word *humorous* may be misleading, as this suggests to most modern readers monologues of comedians, etc. However, in the terminology of the early recording industry (1900–1925), humorous records were primarily songs and song-poems that did not fall into the classification of opera, standard, or celebrity recordings. They were, in a sense, the pop records of their day, including show tunes, vaudeville routines, popular ditties and novelty items. Some would still be considered humorous in the true sense of the word—for example, Ethel Levey's "Where Did Robinson Crusoe Go with Friday on Saturday Night?"—but many a ballad or near-ballad went into the humorous section of record catalogues, too, including all of Harry Lauder's recordings.

It should be remembered that the pre-1920 era was without disc jockeys or "Top 40" lists, so there is no tangible evidence, in most instances, of the popularity attained by these recordings in their time. There is no question, though, about some becoming hits. In nearly all instances, the artists were public figures before making recordings, having attained reputations in music halls or vaudeville. Very rarely were recording contracts granted to unknowns, no matter how promising, in the theory that sales were made on the artist's reputation. Persons, for example, who saw Harry Lauder in the music halls and enjoyed his songs might buy his records. The public was not likely to gamble its $1 (or whatever the price) on a performer it had not seen and heard. In the absence of radio, it would be very unlikely that anyone would have heard any of these songs except in a public performance.

Though early record companies prided themselves on their more serious releases—it seems almost criminal that, in the case of Lauder, RCA Victor did not place his recordings on its "celebrity" label—humorous records sold just as well and were produced in nearly equal numbers. A full listing of all such records pressed before 1920 would run to hundreds of pages.

Because humorous recordings did not require the full orchestration of classical, they did not place such challenges on early techniques and equipment. Therefore, the performances were captured somewhat more successfully and can be heard today, even on very old records; truer to the originals than one could expect of grand opera. You get the feeling of being in the vaudeville house or music hall much more readily with a humorous record than you do of being at La Scala when listening to a 78rpm of Caruso.

It would be normal to assume that the values of these discs should depend on artist popularity—that the records made by more celebrated artists, those whose names are still remembered today, ought to outsell those of vaguely recalled performers. Such is not always the situation. The more popular the artist, the better his or her records would sell, and the greater quantities would be manufactured. Thus, they tend to be less scarce and often not worth as much money as one might expect. On the other hand, the records of lesser-known artists might be pressed in fewer numbers, have a limited sale, and be much harder to get today. Anyone who collects rock records of the 1950's knows that the million-sellers are seldom valued above $3 or $4, while obscure recordings by long-forgotten groups or artists can be more valuable.

The following are all 10-inch recordings on the Columbia label, dating from c. 1920–1922.

	Price Range	
☐ **CASEY, MICHAEL**, "Casey at the Dentist's/Casey as a Doctor"	7.00	10.00
☐ "Casey at Home/Marriage Difficulties" (second side by Golden & Marlow)	6.00	9.00
☐ **DUPREZ, FRED**, "Happy Tho' Married/Cohen on the Telephone" (second side by Joe Hayman)	9.00	12.00
☐ **GOLDEN** and **HUGHES**, "Whistling Pete/Turkey in the Straw" (second side by Billy Golden)	6.00	9.00
☐ **PORTER, STEVE**, "Flanagan on a Farm/Down on the Farm" (second side by Columbia Male Quartette)	6.00	9.00
☐ **ROSE, JULIAN**, "Levinsky at the Wedding I/Levinsky at the Wedding II"	12.00	20.00
☐ Levinsky at the Wedding III/Levinsky at the Wedding IV"	12.00	20.00

Price Range

- ☐ **STEWART, CAL,** "Wedding of Uncle Josh and Aunt Nancy/Uncle Josh at Delmonico's" 10.00 15.00
- ☐ "War Talk at Pumpkin Center/Moving Pictures at Pumpkin Center" 12.00 19.00
- ☐ "Uncle Josh and the Insurance Company/Uncle Josh on an Automobile" 10.00 15.00
- ☐ "Uncle Josh at the Dentist's/Uncle Josh and Aunt Nancy Put Up Kitchen Stove" (first side Stewart and Browne, second side Stewart and Jones) 12.00 20.00
- ☐ "Uncle Josh at the Opera/Uncle Josh and Aunt Nancy Visit New York" 12.00 20.00
- ☐ "Uncle Josh at Roller Rink/Uncle Josh Has His Photo Taken" 10.00 15.00
- ☐ "Uncle Josh in a Cafeteria/Uncle Josh and the Sailor" 10.00 15.00
- ☐ "Uncle Josh Invites City Folks/Two Rubies in Eating House" (second side by Stanley and Harlan) 12.00 20.00
- ☐ "Christmas at Punkin' Center/Evening at Punkin' Center" (both with Jones Quartette) 12.00 20.00
- ☐ **WILLIAMS, BERT,** "Ten Little Bottles/Unlucky Blues" 20.00 30.00
- ☐ "Eve Cost Adam Just One Bone/You'll Never Need a Doctor" 15.00 21.00
- ☐ "The Moon Shines on Moonshine/Somebody" 18.00 29.00
- ☐ "Save a Little Dram for Me/Lonesome Alimony Blues" 15.00 21.00
- ☐ "Never Me/Purpostus" 15.00 21.00
- ☐ "I Wish It Was Sunday Night/All the Silver from Silvery Moon" 15.00 21.00
- ☐ "I'm Sorry I Ain't Got It Blues/Checkers" .. 18.00 29.00
- ☐ **WILLIAMS, BILLY,** "Where Does Daddy Go?/When Father Papered the Parlor" 18.00 29.00
- ☐ **WILLS, NAT,** "No News, or What Killed the Dog/Head Waiter, Colored Social Club" ... 24.00 37.00

JAZZ

MEMORABILIA

The collecting of jazz memorabilia had its beginnings in the night clubs and bistros of New Orleans, New York, and elsewhere, where, from as early as the 1920's, the walls were often lined with inscribed photographs of the stars who performed there. Around 1950, "jazz collecting" began to take on interest as a hobby with private collectors. Many of the old-time jazz greats were still alive at that time, and ambitious collectors succeeded in obtaining from them a variety of personal mementos. Though no cash value was then attached to much of this material, the growth of jazz memorabilia collecting has rendered it quite valuable.

	Price Range	
☐ **ADDERLEY, JULIAN,** article from "Downbeat" magazine, signed and inscribed	11.00	15.00
☐ **ADDERLEY, JULIAN,** mimeographed flyer advertising a concert appearance	6.00	8.00
☐ **ADDERLEY, JULIAN,** polaroid color snapshot, backstage at a theater, mounted on a card, signed on the card	17.50	22.00
☐ **ADDERLEY, JULIAN,** collection of obituaries from various newspapers, including NY Times, Washington Post, LA Times, etc . . .	12.00	16.00
☐ **ALLEN, "RED,"** 8x10 photo, signed, thumbtack holes	9.00	12.00
☐ **ALLEN, "RED,"** two small photos, one signed	5.00	7.00
☐ **AMMONS, ALBERT,** piano score, with notations in his hand	32.00	40.00
☐ **AMMONS, ALBERT,** poster advertising an appearance in a New Orleans cafe, folded, worn at the folds	47.00	59.00
☐ **ARMSTRONG, LOUIS,** cover of "Life" magazine picturing him, signed in red crayon, matted in green plush and framed	175.00	250.00
☐ **ARMSTRONG, LOUIS,** c. 1932, trumpet reputedly used by him early in career, in a worn leather box	2375.00	3200.00
☐ **ARMSTRONG, LOUIS,** c. 1975, plastic figurine in his likeness	25.00	33.00

Price Range

☐ **ARMSTRONG, LOUIS,** c. 1970, pen and wash drawing of him playing trumpet, 11x14, matted to 14x17, framed 65.00   85.00

☐ **ARMSTRONG, LOUIS,** photograph of him at age c. 18, somewhat worn 40.00   55.00

☐ **ARMSTRONG, LOUIS,** c. 1962, 8x10 photo with Carol Channing, signed by both 80.00   100.00

☐ **ARMSTRONG, LOUIS,** c. 1955, 8x10 portrait photo, signed 60.00   80.00

☐ **ARMSTRONG, LOUIS,** c. 1942, 8x10 sepia photo, signed 100.00   130.00

☐ **ARMSTRONG, LOUIS,** c. 1955, LP album cover, "Louis Armstrong Plays W. C. Handy," signed, record lacking 85.00   110.00

☐ **ARMSTRONG, LOUIS,** Pair of cuff links reputedly worn by him 60.00   80.00

☐ **ARMSTRONG, LOUIS,** oil portrait on canvas, 33x48, probably copied from a photograph and dating from c. 1975 .... 120.00   160.00

☐ **ARMSTRONG, LOUIS,** signature on a theater program 30.00   40.00

☐ **BAILEY, MILDRED,** c. 1940's, 5x8 photo, signed, ink faded 39.00   50.00

☐ **BAILEY, MILDRED,** postcard sent by her, brief message 35.00   45.00

☐ **BASIE, "COUNT,"** 8x10 photo seated at piano, signed 15.00   20.00

☐ **BASIE, "COUNT,"** pair of white gloves reputedly worn by him, sold with two small unsigned photos and a letter from a previous owner 60.00   80.00

☐ **BASIE, "COUNT,"** 5x7 photo, signed, framed with a 78rpm recording 70.00   90.00

☐ **BASIE, "COUNT,"** signature on a calling card 8.00   11.00

☐ **BEIDERBECKE, BIX,** 8x10 photo standing outside club, signed in white ink, also signed by two others, corners clipped 50.00   70.00

☐ **BEIDERBECKE, BIX,** c. 1930, typed letter, signed, with original envelope (stained) 60.00   80.00

☐ **BEIDERBECKE, BIX,** one page of music notations, unsigned 100.00   130.00

	Price Range	

☐ **BEIDERBECKE, BIX,** c. 1927 and 1929, two postcards addressed to him **30.00** **38.00**

☐ **BERIGAN, BUNNY,** c. 1935, photo with orchestra, signed by him and several other musicians **50.00** **65.00**

☐ **BERIGAN, BUNNY,** c. 1928, 3x4 snapshot photo **6.00** **8.00**

☐ **BERIGAN, BUNNY,** signature on cafe cocktail list **7.50** **10.00**

☐ **BLAKEY, ART,** 8x10 photo playing drums, signed **6.00** **8.00**

☐ **BLAKEY, ART,** pair of drumsticks used by him **15.00** **20.00**

☐ **BLANTON, JIMMY,** 6x7 photo, signed and inscribed across almost the entire photo **30.00** **40.00**

☐ **BOLDEN, CHARLES,** signature on a memo sheet **6.00** **8.00**

☐ **BOLDEN, CHARLES,** contract bearing his signature **23.00** **29.00**

☐ **BOLDEN, CHARLES,** c. 1890's. Poster advertising his band **100.00** **130.00**

☐ **BOLDEN, CHARLES,** 8x10 sepia photo, damaged, unsigned **6.00** **8.00**

☐ **BROONZY, BILL,** 7x9 color photo, boldly signed **20.00** **27.00**

☐ **BROONZY, BILL,** collection of articles and news cuttings, mostly from "Billboard" and "DownBeat" magazines **16.00** **21.00**

☐ **BROONZY, BILL,** Signature on an insurance company circular **7.00** **10.00**

☐ **BRUBECK, DAVE,** c. 1958, charcoal drawing of him at piano, 12x12, matted and framed **75.00** **100.00**

☐ **BRUBECK, DAVE,** typed letter, signed, to a theatrical agent **8.00** **11.00**

☐ **BRUBECK, DAVE,** two LP record album covers, signed, records missing **40.00** **55.00**

☐ **BRUBECK, DAVE,** 8x10 photo, signed in brown ink **7.00** **10.00**

☐ **CARNEY, HARRY,** three small candid photos, one signed on the back **5.50** **7.50**

☐ **CARTER, BENNY,** 8x10 photo, signed, small corner crease **5.00** **7.00**

Price Range

☐ **CARTER, BENNY,** signature on an otherwise blank card 2.50   3.50

☐ **CATLETT, SIDNEY,** 4x5 photo, inscribed, signed with initials 15.00   20.00

☐ **CHRISTIAN, CHARLIE,** c. 1940, envelope addressed by him, letter missing 15.00   20.00

☐ **CHRISTIAN, CHARLIE,** 5x4 photo, signed, margins cut 25.00   33.00

☐ **CHRISTIAN, CHARLIE,** small photo with guitar, signed 30.00   40.00

☐ **CLAYTON, BUCK,** 8x10 photo with two other musicians, signed by all three 9.00   12.00

☐ **CLAYTON, BUCK,** trumpet carrying case once owned by him 23.00   30.00

☐ **CLAYTON, BUCK,** two magazine articles about him, one signed 8.00   11.00

☐ **CLAYTON, BUCK,** ½-page note in his hand, signed 7.00   10.00

☐ **COHN, AL,** two 8x10 photos, one signed .. 9.00   12.00

☐ **COHN, AL,** c. 1967, Typed letter, signed, with envelope 8.00   11.00

☐ **COHN, AL,** postcard in his handwriting 6.00   8.00

☐ **COLTRANE, JOHN,** 8x10 photo, signed in red ink, matted and inscribed on the mat, signed again, framed 30.00   40.00

☐ **COLTRANE, JOHN,** signature on a theatrical agent's card 5.00   7.00

☐ **COLTRANE, JOHN,** signature on an advertising circular 5.00   7.00

☐ **CONDON, EDDIE,** 11x14 color photo, signed in the margin 35.00   45.00

☐ **CONDON, EDDIE,** scrapbook with c. 220 items pertaining to him, mostly news cuttings, two signed photos, etc 75.00   95.00

☐ **CONDON, EDDIE,** Xerox copy of a photo of him, signed on the Xerox 7.00   10.00

☐ **DAVIS, MILES,** LP album cover inscribed and signed on the back, record missing 40.00   55.00

☐ **DAVIS, MILES,** small photo cut from magazine, signed, mounted on heavy card 12.00   17.00

☐ **DAVIS, MILES,** three 8x10 portrait photos, unsigned 7.00   10.00

Price Range

☐ **DeFRANCO, BUDDY,** 8x10 photo, signed and inscribed on the back, tape marks at corners 6.00   8.00

☐ **DESMOND, PAUL,** 16 photos, mostly snapshots, one 8x10 signed studio photo, in a cloth folding case 50.00   65.00

☐ **DESMOND, PAUL,** c. 1971, three-page handwritten letter 52.00   70.00

☐ **DODDS, WARREN,** circular advertising a cafe appearance 7.00   10.00

☐ **DODDS, WARREN,** 5x6 photo, signed 8.00   11.00

☐ **DODDS, WARREN,** notebook used by him, various memos 40.00   50.00

☐ **DORSEY, JIMMY,** c. 1943, poster, 27x41, advertising a concert appearance, New York 110.00   140.00

☐ **DORSEY, JIMMY,** collection of 14 motion picture stills, unsigned 30.00   37.00

☐ **DORSEY, JIMMY,** 8x10 studio photo, signed and inscribed 30.00   40.00

☐ **DORSEY, JIMMY,** c. 1949, 8x10 photo, signed and inscribed to Toots Shore 50.00   65.00

☐ **DORSEY, JIMMY,** record company circular, signed 30.00   37.00

☐ **DORSEY, JIMMY,** c. 1947, 8x10 photo with Tommy Dorsey, signed by both 90.00   115.00

☐ **DORSEY, JIMMY,** c. 1952, one-page typewritten letter, signed 20.00   25.00

☐ **DORSEY, JIMMY,** c. 1944–46, six snapshot photos 16.00   21.00

☐ **DORSEY, TOMMY,** 8x10 studio photo, with trombone, signed 28.00   36.00

☐ **DORSEY, TOMMY,** Five motion picture stills, one creased 11.00   15.00

☐ **DORSEY, TOMMY,** two scrapbooks relating to his career, containing c. 43 photos, mostly cut from magazines, 500 news cuttings, several letters and miscellaneous items 300.00   400.00

☐ **DORSEY, TOMMY,** 8x10 photo with Bing Crosby, signed by both 75.00   100.00

☐ **ELDRIDGE, ROY,** 5x4 photo, signed 6.00   8.00

☐ **ELDRIDGE, ROY,** signature on restaurant menu (faded) 5.00   7.00

Price Range

☐ **ELLINGTON, DUKE,** oil on canvas, 23x29, seated at piano, signed "Clark Tillman," date unknown, possibly copied from a photograph, unframed 100.00   140.00

☐ **ELLINGTON, DUKE,** two piano scores with notes in his hand 110.00   150.00

☐ **ELLINGTON, DUKE,** c. 1927. Early photo of him at piano 25.00   35.00

☐ **ELLINGTON, DUKE,** seven pages from scrap album with various photos, including of him as a youth, two of them signed 175.00   250.00

☐ **ELLINGTON, DUKE,** magazine cover portrait of him, colored, signed, framed 75.00   100.00

☐ **ELLINGTON, DUKE,** caricature in ink, 7x9, artist unknown 50.00   70.00

☐ **ELLINGTON, DUKE,** piano stool reputedly used by him 85.00   110.00

☐ **ELLINGTON, DUKE,** program of a concert appearance 7.00   10.00

☐ **ELLINGTON, DUKE,** photo with Count Basie, signed by both 100.00   150.00

☐ **ELLINGTON, DUKE,** signature on cover of sheet music 25.00   35.00

☐ **ELLINGTON, DUKE,** envelope of obituary notices from various newspapers, some foreign 40.00   55.00

☐ **EVANS, BILL,** 8x10 photo, signed 7.00   10.00

☐ **EVANS, BILL,** c. 1940's, 4x5 photo as a youth, unsigned 5.00   7.00

☐ **FITZGERALD, ELLA,** LP album cover, signed in violet magic marker, record lacking, with two news cuttings 50.00   65.00

☐ **FITZGERALD, ELLA,** sheet music to "A Tisket, A Tasket," signed with large crayon signature 40.00   55.00

☐ **FITZGERALD, ELLA,** 8x10 studio portrait, signed 12.00   16.00

☐ **FITZGERALD, ELLA,** scrapbook with c. 75 news cuttings, etc 60.00   80.00

☐ **FITZGERALD, ELLA,** 45rpm phono record, signed on label 15.00   20.00

Price Range

☐ **FITZGERALD, ELLA,** magazine article, signed, two pages 9.00   12.00

☐ **FITZGERALD, ELLA,** three unsigned 8x10 photos, one dated from the 1940's, mounted on cards 8.00   11.00

☐ **FITZGERALD, ELLA,** photo with Count Basie, signed by Fitzgerald only 15.00   20.00

☐ **FITZGERALD, ELLA,** photo with Duke Ellington, signed by both 45.00   60.00

☐ **FITZGERALD, ELLA,** interview in "DownBeat" magazine, signed 7.00   10.00

☐ **FITZGERALD, ELLA,** two small snapshot photos, one signed 9.00   12.00

☐ **GARNER, ERROLL,** c. 1960, 8x10 photo at piano, signed 10.00   15.00

☐ **GARNER, ERROLL,** two items of sheet music, signed 35.00   45.00

☐ **GARNER, ERROLL,** record album cover, signed, no record 30.00   40.00

☐ **GARNER, ERROLL,** cuff links reputedly worn by him 32.00   41.00

☐ **GARNER, ERROLL,** photo with Art Tatum, signed by Garner 22.00   33.00

☐ **GARNER, ERROLL,** collection of news cuttings and magazine articles, one signed photo, in a cloth folder 75.00   100.00

☐ **GARNER, ERROLL,** signature on a business card 3.00   4.00

☐ **GARNER, ERROLL,** c. 1974, color photo, 5x6½, signed 17.00   23.00

☐ **GETZ, STAN,** photo playing sax, signed, inscribed 5.00   6.00

☐ **GETZ, STAN,** 8x10 studio photo, signed, matted 6.00   8.00

☐ **GETZ, STAN,** magazine photo, signed, mounted on card 4.00   5.00

☐ **GETZ, STAN,** c. 1965, letter to him from record company official 3.00   4.00

☐ **GETZ, STAN,** two snapshots, one signed, New Orleans 4.00   5.00

☐ **GETZ, STAN,** magazine photo with Zutty Singleton, signed by Getz only 5.00   6.00

Price Range

☐ **GETZ, STAN,** book, "Pictorial History of Jazz," signed by him and Gene Krupa 25.00 32.00

☐ **GETZ, STAN,** two items of sheet music, with notes in his hand, not signed 15.00 20.00

☐ **GIBBS, TERRY,** 8x10 studio photo, signed 4.00 5.00

☐ **GIBBS, TERRY,** c. 1970, poster advertising an appearance 12.00 15.00

☐ **GIBBS, TERRY,** c. 1950, ALs, one page, with envelope 4.00 5.00

☐ **GIBBS, TERRY,** novelty $1 bill with his picture in center 2.00 3.00

☐ **GIBBS, TERRY,** 6x7 photo at vibes, signed and inscribed 4.00 5.00

☐ **GILLESPIE, DIZZY,** trumpet reputedly used by him early in career, in carrying case 500.00 650.00

☐ **GILLESPIE, DIZZY,** LP record album cover, signed, record missing 35.00 45.00

☐ **GILLESPIE, DIZZY,** two 8x10 photos, signed, one inscribed 23.00 29.00

☐ **GILLESPIE, DIZZY,** signature on a postcard 3.75 5.00

☐ **GILLESPIE, DIZZY,** c. 1958, magazine article, signed 4.50 6.00

☐ **GILLESPIE, DIZZY,** photo with Billy Taylor, unsigned 2.50 3.50

☐ **GILLESPIE, DIZZY,** Associated Press photo, unsigned 2.50 3.50

☐ **GILLESPIE, DIZZY,** sheet music with notes in his hand.............................. 45.00 60.00

☐ **GILLESPIE, DIZZY,** photo with John Lewis, signed by both 25.00 32.00

☐ **GILLESPIE, DIZZY,** c. 1947–52, five small snapshots 7.00 10.00

☐ **GILLESPIE, DIZZY,** T-shirt with his likeness 9.00 12.00

☐ **GILLESPIE, DIZZY,** close-up cover photo playing horn, signed, matted, framed, signed again on the mat 35.00 45.00

☐ **GOODMAN, BENNY,** c. 1942, 8x10 studio portrait wearing white jacket, holding clarinet, signed.................................. 20.00 25.00

☐ **GOODMAN, BENNY,** three motion picture stills, signed 45.00 58.00

Price Range

☐ **GOODMAN, BENNY,** c. 1938. Photo with Glenn Miller, unsigned 6.00   9.00

☐ **GOODMAN, BENNY,** 78rpm record, signed on the label 35.00   45.00

☐ **GOODMAN, BENNY,** concert program, signed 7.00   10.00

☐ **GOODMAN, BENNY,** signature on cafe menu   5.00   7.00

☐ **GOODMAN, BENNY,** c. 1946, 8x10 photo with band, signed 23.00   30.00

☐ **GOODMAN, BENNY,** 8x10 photo with Paul Whiteman, signed by Goodman only 25.00   32.00

☐ **GOODMAN, BENNY,** c. 1958, magazine article, signed 7.00   10.00

☐ **GOODMAN, BENNY,** c. 1974, typewritten letter, signed 9.00   12.00

☐ **GOODMAN, BENNY,** c. 1951, memo in his hand 7.00   10.00

☐ **GOODMAN, BENNY,** photo with Jimmy Dorsey, signed by both 60.00   80.00

☐ **HACKETT, BOBBY,** 5x7 photo playing trumpet, signed 8.00   11.00

☐ **HACKETT, BOBBY,** c. 1961, ALs, one page, with envelope 11.00   15.00

☐ **HACKETT, BOBBY,** signature on a card . . .   2.50   3.75

☐ **HACKETT, BOBBY,** magazine photo, signed and inscribed 5.00   7.00

☐ **HACKETT, BOBBY,** two 8x10 unsigned photos 4.00   6.00

☐ **HACKETT, BOBBY,** musical score with notes in his hand 23.00   30.00

☐ **HACKETT, BOBBY,** c. 1966, tiny snapshot photo, signed on back 3.00   4.00

☐ **HACKETT, BOBBY,** c. 1972, typewritten letter, signed 4.00   6.00

☐ **HAMPTON, LIONEL,** set of drumsticks used by him, autographed by him, in a velvet case   110.00   135.00

☐ **HAMPTON, LIONEL,** biography of him from jazz book, signed 7.00   10.00

☐ **HAMPTON, LIONEL,** LP record album cover, signed, no record 32.00   40.00

☐ **HAMPTON, LIONEL,** c. 1948, 8x10 studio portrait, signed 20.00   25.00

Price Range

☐ **HAMPTON, LIONEL,** photo with John Kirby, signed by Hampton only	20.00	25.00
☐ **HAMPTON, LIONEL,** c. 1942, ALs, with envelope	20.00	25.00
☐ **HAMPTON, LIONEL,** photo with Perry Como, signed by Hampton only	15.00	20.00
☐ **HAMPTON, LIONEL,** signature on a record company circular	2.50	3.50
☐ **HAMPTON, LIONEL,** scrapbook of c. 320 news cuttings, etc	100.00	130.00
☐ **HAMPTON, LIONEL,** c. 1950's, two short notes in his hand	7.00	10.00
☐ **HAMPTON, LIONEL,** c. 1930's, three early snapshot photos	8.00	11.00
☐ **HARRIS, BILL,** 8x10 studio photo, signed	4.00	5.00
☐ **HARRIS, BILL,** article from "Variety," signed	3.00	4.00
☐ **HARRIS, BILL,** musical score with notes in his hand	12.00	17.00
☐ **HARRIS, BILL,** photo with trombone, signed, framed	12.00	17.00
☐ **HAWKINS, COLEMAN,** sheet music, "Body and Soul", with notes in his hand	170.00	240.00
☐ **HAWKINS, COLEMAN,** 8x10 photo with orchestra, signed	30.00	40.00
☐ **HAWKINS, COLEMAN,** 78rpm record album signed on the front cover, records missing	90.00	120.00
☐ **HAWKINS, COLEMAN,** signature on back of a letter	10.00	15.00
☐ **HAWKINS, COLEMAN,** letter to him from an agent	5.00	7.00
☐ **HAWKINS, COLEMAN,** c. 1964, check endorsed by him	42.00	60.00
☐ **HAWKINS, COLEMAN,** photo playing sax, signed	32.00	43.00
☐ **HAWKINS, COLEMAN,** c. 1950's, two 8x10 unsigned photos	7.00	10.00
☐ **HAWKINS, COLEMAN,** c. 1950, photo with Charlie Parker, signed by both, framed	120.00	150.00
☐ **HENDERSON, FLETCHER,** 8x10 photo, signed, creased	7.00	10.00
☐ **HENDERSON, FLETCHER,** photo from magazine, signed	6.00	8.00

	Price Range	

☐ **HENDERSON, FLETCHER,** one page of music score, signed 15.00 20.00

☐ **HENDERSON, FLETCHER,** 78rpm record, signed on the label 25.00 32.00

☐ **HENDERSON, FLETCHER,** record company advertising poster, signed 32.00 41.00

☐ **HENDERSON, FLETCHER,** photo in Times Square, NY, signed 6.00 8.00

☐ **HENDERSON, FLETCHER,** c. 1930's, two snapshots, one signed 7.00 10.00

☐ **HERMAN, WOODY,** photo with clarinet, signed, inscribed 8.00 11.00

☐ **HERMAN, WOODY,** c. 1940's, photo with Benny Goodman, each holding clarinet, signed by Herman only 17.00 23.00

☐ **HERMAN, WOODY,** caricature in ink, 8x10, unsigned 22.00 30.00

☐ **HERMAN, WOODY,** 4x5 photo as a youth, signed, stained 11.00 15.00

☐ **HERMAN, WOODY,** signature on cover of sheet music..................... 13.00 20.00

☐ **HERMAN, WOODY,** signature on a concert program 6.00 9.00

☐ **HERMAN, WOODY,** c. 1956, 8x10 studio portrait, signed 7.00 10.00

☐ **HERMAN, WOODY,** three letters to him from record company executives 9.00 12.00

☐ **HERMAN, WOODY,** magazine article, signed 4.00 6.00

☐ **HIGGINBOTHAM, JAY C,** 8x10 portrait photo, signed 12.00 17.00

☐ **HILL, BERTHA,** 5x6 portrait photo, signed 35.00 45.00

☐ **HINES, EARL,** photo at piano, signed, matted and framed 11.00 15.00

☐ **HINES, EARL,** c. 1950's, musical score, signed 25.00 35.00

☐ **HINES, EARL,** photo with George Shearing, signed by Hines 12.00 17.00

☐ **HINES, EARL,** c. 1930's, two 5x6 photos, unsigned 5.00 7.00

☐ **HINES, EARL,** 8x10 portrait photo at piano, large signature 12.00 17.00

Price Range

☐ **HINES, EARL,** 11x14 photo, signed in the margin 16.00   22.00

☐ **HINES, EARL,** signature on a card 3.00   4.00

☐ **HINES, EARL,** scrapbook with reviews, photos, etc. 65.00   85.00

☐ **HODGES, JOHNNY,** signature on a card, also signed by Max Roach 3.00   4.00

☐ **HODGES, JOHNNY,** 8x10 studio photo, signed 4.00   5.00

☐ **HODGES, JOHNNY,** notes on back of record company catalogue 4.00   5.00

☐ **HODGES, JOHNNY,** photo outside Philadelphia night club, signed 3.00   4.00

☐ **KRUPA, GENE,** LP record album cover, signed, no record 40.00   55.00

☐ **KRUPA, GENE,** c. 1958, brochure issued by his drum school 4.00   6.00

☐ **KRUPA, GENE,** c. 1936, 8x10 photo at drums, early, signed 20.00   27.00

☐ **KRUPA, GENE,** c. 1962, typewritten letter, signed 5.00   7.00

☐ **KRUPA, GENE,** c. 1941, ALs, half page, with envelope 14.00   20.00

☐ **KRUPA, GENE,** signature on a business card 3.00   4.00

☐ **KRUPA, GENE,** 8x10 color portrait photo, signed on back 13.00   18.00

☐ **KRUPA, GENE,** c. 1937, 4x5 snapshot photo, signed 8.00   11.00

☐ **KRUPA, GENE,** c. 1956, magazine article, signed 4.00   5.00

☐ **KRUPA, GENE,** photo with Miles Davis, signed by both 25.00   32.00

☐ **LADNIER, TOMMY,** photo cut from newspaper, signed 12.00   17.00

☐ **LADNIER, TOMMY,** 8x10 photo, signed, inscribed 22.00   30.00

☐ **LADNIER, TOMMY,** c. 1930, poster advertising an appearance 40.00   55.00

☐ **LADNIER, TOMMY,** signature on a music company catalogue 7.00   10.00

☐ **LADNIER, TOMMY,** c. 1920's, snapshot photo, signed 20.00   25.00

Price Range

☐ **LANG, EDDIE,** photo with guitar, signed, faded 40.00   55.00

☐ **LANG, EDDIE,** c. 1925, two small snapshots, one signed 28.00   36.00

☐ **LANG, EDDIE,** c. 1928, ALs, Atlanta 45.00   60.00

☐ **LEDBETTER, HUDDIE ("LEADBELLY"),** c. 1940's, 5x7 photo, signed, laminated and mounted on a card 60.00   80.00

☐ **LEWIS, JOHN,** four lines of music composition in his hand 30.00   40.00

☐ **LEWIS, JOHN,** 8x10 studio portrait, signed 6.00   9.00

☐ **LEWIS, JOHN,** signature on a card 2.50   3.50

☐ **LEWIS, JOHN,** c. 1971, typewritten letter, signed 4.50   6.00

☐ **LEWIS, JOHN,** c. 1960's, photo with combo, signed 6.00   9.00

☐ **LEWIS, JOHN,** article in "Variety," signed .. 3.50   5.00

☐ **LUNCEFORD, JIMMIE,** c. 1942, 8x10 studio portrait, signed, dated 22.00   30.00

☐ **LUNCEFORD, JIMMIE,** c. 1930's, two snapshots, signed 20.00   27.00

☐ **MANNE, SHELLY,** 8x10 photo at drums, signed 4.50   6.00

☐ **MANNE, SHELLY,** c. 1978, postcard in his hand, 4 lines 3.50   5.00

☐ **MANNE, SHELLY,** c. 1954, ALs, half page 5.50   7.00

☐ **MANNE, SHELLY,** c. 1967, photo with Gene Krupa, signed by both 16.00   22.00

☐ **MANNE, SHELLY,** photo with Billy Taylor, signed by Manne 6.00   8.00

☐ **MANNE, SHELLY,** ½-hour amateur tape of "jam session" with him at drums 17.00   23.00

☐ **MANNE, SHELLY,** signature on a card 2.00   3.00

☐ **MANNE, SHELLY,** photo in front of New York night club, signed 3.50   5.00

☐ **MANNE, SHELLY,** article from "DownBeat" magazine, signed 3.50   5.00

☐ **McPARTLAND, JIMMY,** sheet music autographed 18.00   25.00

☐ **McPARTLAND, JIMMY,** two 6x8 photos, signed 12.00   17.00

Price Range

☐ **McPARTLAND, JIMMY,** 8x10 studio photo
with horn, signed 9.00 12.00

☐ **McPARTLAND, JIMMY,** colored photo cut
from magazine or book, signed, inscribed,
matted and framed 22.00 30.00

☐ **McPARTLAND, JIMMY,** signature on restaurant check 2.50 3.50

☐ **McPARTLAND, JIMMY,** typewritten letter to
him from booking agent 2.50 3.50

☐ **McPARTLAND, JIMMY,** c. 1947, ALs, two
pp. 11.00 15.00

☐ **McPARTLAND, JIMMY,** photo with L. Armstrong, signed by both 60.00 75.00

☐ **McPARTLAND, JIMMY,** straw hat reputedly
worn by him 10.00 20.00

☐ **McPARTLAND, JIMMY,** two small snapshot
photos, unsigned 2.00 3.00

☐ **MILLER, GLENN,** 78rpm phono record,
signed on the label 90.00 110.00

☐ **MILLER, GLENN,** 8x10 studio portrait,
signed, inscribed 60.00 80.00

☐ **MILLER, GLENN,** c. 1938, check endorsed
by him 75.00 95.00

☐ **MILLER, GLENN,** collection of 36 motion picture stills, unsigned, housed in a cloth folder 75.00 100.00

☐ **MILLER, GLENN,** c. 1943, typewritten letter
to a fan, signed 75.00 100.00

☐ **MILLER, GLENN,** 8x10 photo with trombone,
signed, inscribed, framed along with a 78rpm
recording, overall size 26x19 .... 230.00 300.00

☐ **MILLER, GLENN,** brief memo in his hand, two
lines 25.00 32.00

☐ **MILLER, GLENN,** signature on a dance program 12.00 12.00

☐ **MILLER, GLENN,** c. 1940, signature with
brief note on a restaurant menu 26.00 35.00

☐ **MILLER, GLENN,** c. 1942, 8x10 photo with
Benny Goodman, signed by both 150.00 200.00

☐ **MILLER, GLENN,** 78rpm record sleeve,
signed 20.00 25.00

☐ **MILLER, GLENN,** sheet music, "In the
Mood," signed 120.00 140.00

Price Range

☐ **MILLER, GLENN,** sheet music, "Pennsylvania 6-5000," signed .... 120.00 · 150.00

☐ **MILLER, GLENN,** printed postcard photo, facsimile signature 20.00 25.00

☐ **MILLER, GLENN,** c. 1937, large poster advertising his band (size not stated), color illustration 230.00 300.00

☐ **MILLER, GLENN,** c. 1932, envelope addressed by him, postmarked 1932 .... 35.00 45.00

☐ **MINGUS, CHARLIE,** 8x10 studio portrait, signed 6.00 9.00

☐ **MINGUS, CHARLIE,** two pages of notes in his hand 9.00 12.00

☐ **MINGUS, CHARLIE,** LP album cover, signed, no record 20.00 25.00

☐ **MINGUS, CHARLIE,** cover of "DownBeat" magazine, signed 3.50 5.00

☐ **MINGUS, CHARLIE,** signature on a card ... 2.50 3.50

☐ **MINGUS, CHARLIE,** photo with band, signed by him and several others, framed 9.00 12.00

☐ **MINGUS, CHARLIE,** three snapshot photos, one signed 8.00 11.00

☐ **MINGUS, CHARLIE,** two 8x10 photos, unsigned 3.50 5.00

☐ **MONK, THELONIUS,** sheet music, signed 22.00 29.00

☐ **MONK, THELONIUS,** c. 1961, two typewritten letters to publisher, with envelopes 20.00 25.00

☐ **MONK, THELONIUS,** one page of musical composition in his hand, creased 23.00 30.00

☐ **MONK, THELONIUS,** 8x10 photo with Charlie Parker, signed by Monk only 20.00 25.00

☐ **MONK, THELONIUS,** magazine interview, signed 3.50 4.50

☐ **MONK, THELONIUS,** 8x10 studio portrait, signed 6.00 8.00

☐ **MONTGOMERY, WES,** large color photo with guitar, signed 9.00 12.00

☐ **MONTGOMERY, WES,** signature on passport application 7.00 10.00

☐ **MONTGOMERY, WES,** 8x10 studio portrait, signed 4.00 6.00

Price Range

☐ **MONTGOMERY, WES,** 3x4½ snapshot photo, signed 2.00   3.00

☐ **MONTGOMERY, WES,** guitar instructional book, signed on the flyleaf 7.00   10.00

☐ **MONTGOMERY, WES,** c. 1959, photo with boxer Ezzard Charles, signed by Montgomery only 6.00   8.50

☐ **MONTGOMERY, WES,** signature on a bus schedule folder 2.00   3.00

☐ **MONTGOMERY, WES,** collection of 326 news cuttings, articles, pictures relating to his career, in an album 85.00   110.00

☐ **MORTON, JELLY ROLL,** 8x10 photo at piano in club, signed, framed. Photo somewhat faded 140.00   180.00

☐ **MORTON, JELLY ROLL,** 78rpm record, signed on the label 110.00   140.00

☐ **MORTON, JELLY ROLL,** 8x10 photo with W. C. Handy, unsigned, notation on back (perhaps by a third party) 30.00   37.00

☐ **MORTON, JELLY ROLL,** piano score with notes in his hand, soiled, front cover torn, in a cello bag 220.00   265.00

☐ **MORTON, JELLY ROLL,** c. 1920, early photo at piano, unsigned 20.00   25.00

☐ **MORTON, JELLY ROLL,** c. 1930, New Orleans cafe bill advertising him 100.00   120.00

☐ **MORTON, JELLY ROLL,** signature on a card 20.00   25.00

☐ **MOTEN, BENNIE,** 8x10 sepia photo, signed 25.00   32.00

☐ **MOTEN, BENNIE,** c. 1916, ALs, three pages 75.00   100.00

☐ **MOTEN, BENNIE,** canceled check, signed by him 45.00   60.00

☐ **MULLIGAN, GERRY,** 8x10 studio portrait, signed 4.50   6.00

☐ **MULLIGAN, GERRY,** 11x14 montage of small photos clipped from magazines and books, signed, inscribed, framed 17.00   25.00

☐ **MULLIGAN, GERRY,** cover of "DownBeat" magazine, signed 2.50   3.50

☐ **MULLIGAN, GERRY,** LP album cover, signed, record missing 17.00   25.00

Price Range

☐ **MULLIGAN, GERRY,** 8x10 photo with sax, signed and inscribed 4.50 6.00

☐ **MULLIGAN, GERRY,** c. 1954, two brief memos in his hand 5.50 7.50

☐ **MULLIGAN, GERRY,** LP record, signed on the label 22.00 30.00

☐ **MULLIGAN, GERRY,** saxophone reputedly owned by him 900.00 1200.00

☐ **MURPHY, TURK,** c. 1926, photo as a youth, unsigned 1.75 2.50

☐ **MURPHY, TURK,** c. 1975, typewritten letter, signed, ½-page 2.50 3.50

☐ **MURPHY, TURK,** c. 1961, 8x10 studio portrait, signed 3.50 5.00

☐ **MURPHY, TURK,** photo with several other musicians, signed 2.50 3.50

☐ **MURPHY, TURK,** magazine interview, signed 2.50 3.50

☐ **NAVARRO, FATS,** c. 1947. 4x5 photo, signed 11.00 16.00

☐ **NAVARRO, FATS,** three 8x10 photos, one signed 25.00 34.00

☐ **NAVARRO, FATS,** letter to a recording company, typewritten, signed 15.00 20.00

☐ **NICHOLS, RED,** c. 1942, theater poster advertising "Red Nichols & his Five Pennies," 27x41 .... 70.00 90.00

☐ **NICHOLS, RED,** 78rpm record, signed on the label 23.00 29.00

☐ **NICHOLS, RED,** 8x10 photo with Sammy Kaye, signed by both 15.00 20.00

☐ **NICHOLS, RED,** 8x10 photo with Jack Benny, signed by Nichols only 7.00 10.00

☐ **NICHOLS, RED,** 8x10 studio photo, signed 4.50 6.00

☐ **NICHOLS, RED,** printed postcard photo, facsimile signature 1.75 2.50

☐ **NICHOLS, RED,** c. 1953. Check endorsed by him 23.00 29.00

☐ **NICHOLS, RED,** scrapbook containing 6 signed photos, 35 unsigned studio photos and snapshots, 217 news cuttings and various miscellaneous 230.00 300.00

Price Range

☐ **NICHOLS, RED,** c. 1964, typewritten letter,
signed 6.00   9.00
☐ **NICHOLS, RED,** c. 1948, music instrument
catalog, signed 3.50   5.00
☐ **NOONE, JIMMIE,** 8x10 studio portrait, signed   22.00   30.00
☐ **NOONE, JIMMIE,** two small snapshot photos   3.50   5.00
☐ **NORVO, RED,** photo with Lionel Hampton,
signed by both 20.00   27.00
☐ **NORVO, RED,** printed poster, "King of the
Vibes" 4.50   6.00
☐ **NORVO, RED,** c. 1972, 8x10 photo, signed   3.50   5.00
☐ **NORVO, RED,** signature on a restaurant
menu 1.75   2.75
☐ **NORVO, RED,** three pages of notations in his
hand 7.00   10.00
☐ **OLIVER, KING,** 8x10 sepia photo with band,
King Oliver stands holding cornet, faded,
signed 200.00   250.00
☐ **OLIVER, KING,** music hall bill advertising his
band 115.00   140.00
☐ **ORY, KID,** 8x10 portrait photo, signed in pur-
ple ink 5.00   7.50
☐ **ORY, KID,** c. 1971, 4x5 Polaroid photo,
mounted on signed card 6.00   8.50
☐ **ORY, KID,** c. 1932, ALs, two pages, with en-
velope 12.00   17.00
☐ **ORY, KID,** sheet music, "Muskrat Ramble",
signed 65.00   80.00
☐ **ORY, KID,** three bars from "Muskrat Ramble"
in his hand, signed, framed along with a
photo (unsigned) 75.00   95.00
☐ **ORY, KID,** c. 1943, 8x10 photo with trom-
bone, signed 6.00   9.00
☐ **ORY, KID,** two small photos dating from c.
1930, unsigned 2.50   3.50
☐ **PARKER, CHARLIE,** 8x10 portrait photo,
signed 60.00   80.00
☐ **PARKER, CHARLIE,** sheet of musical com-
position 135.00   180.00
☐ **PARKER, CHARLIE,** two photos cut from
"DownBeat" magazine, signed 60.00   80.00

Price Range

☐ **PETERSON, OSCAR,** c. 1977, check endorsed by him 11.00   15.00
☐ **PETERSON, OSCAR,** signature on a card . . 1.75   2.75
☐ **PETERSON, OSCAR,** 8x10 studio portrait, signed 4.50   6.00
☐ **PETERSON, OSCAR,** photo with Joe Turner, signed by both 8.00   11.00
☐ **PETERSON, OSCAR,** three small snapshot photos, unsigned 3.50   5.00
☐ **PETERSON, OSCAR,** 8x10 photo at piano, matted, signed on the mat 7.00   10.00
☐ **PETERSON, OSCAR,** signature on a store receipt 2.00   3.00
☐ **PETERSON, OSCAR,** envelope with about 250 news cuttings relating to him, reviews, etc. 7.00   10.00
☐ **PETTIFORD, OSCAR,** 8x10 studio photo, signed 20.00   25.00
☐ **PETTIFORD, OSCAR,** c. 1958, typewritten letter, signed 11.00   15.00
☐ **PETTIFORD, OSCAR,** bowstring reputedly used by him 45.00   60.00
☐ **PETTIFORD, OSCAR,** biography of him from book, signed 15.00   20.00
☐ **PETTIFORD, OSCAR,** signature on a union card 27.00   34.00
☐ **PETTIFORD, OSCAR,** his Social Security card, signed 35.00   45.00
☐ **PETTIFORD, OSCAR,** 6x8 photo in group outside hotel, signed 15.00   20.00
☐ **PETTIFORD, OSCAR,** LP record album cover, signed, no record 65.00   85.00
☐ **POWELL, BUD,** 8x10 publicity photo, signed and inscribed 9.00   12.00
☐ **POWELL, BUD,** 9x12 color photo at piano, signed 15.00   20.00
☐ **POWELL, BUD,** c. 1947, ALs, ½-page 20.00   25.00
☐ **POWELL, BUD,** c. 1945, two postcards in his hand, signed 11.00   15.00
☐ **POWELL, BUD,** signature on a card 4.50   6.00
☐ **POWELL, BUD,** c. 1930's, two 4x5 snapshot photos, unsigned 4.50   6.00

Price Range

☐ **RAINEY, GERTRUDE,** c. 1908, photo standing on lawn, cut down to 6x8½ (margins trimmed away and photo cut into), signed   115.00   150.00

☐ **REDMAN, DON,** two pages of musical composition in his hand 32.00   40.00

☐ **REDMAN, DON,** photo with Jimmy Dorsey, signed by Redman 15.00   20.00

☐ **REDMAN, DON,** c. 1938, 8x10 studio portrait, signed 10.00   14.00

☐ **REDMAN, DON,** c. 1939, Check endorsed by him 22.00   30.00

☐ **REDMAN, DON,** c. 1941, ALs, one and ½-page 20.00   25.00

☐ **REDMAN, DON,** scrapbook with 16 photos (3 signed), news cuttings, articles, other memorabilia, album damaged 100.00   140.00

☐ **RICH, BUDDY,** 8x10 photo with drums, signed and inscribed 7.00   10.00

☐ **RICH, BUDDY,** photo with Gene Krupa, signed by both 22.00   28.00

☐ **RICH, BUDDY,** signature on a card 2.50   3.50

☐ **RICH, BUDDY,** set of drumsticks autographed by him........................   75.00   100.00

☐ **RICH, BUDDY,** c. 1956, 6x7 photo in night club, signed 4.50   6.00

☐ **RICH, BUDDY,** 8x10 studio portrait, signed   6.00   8.00

☐ **RICH, BUDDY,** 8x10 studio portrait, signed and inscribed, matted and framed 20.00   25.00

☐ **RICH, BUDDY,** advertising poster, signed ..   4.50   6.00

☐ **RICH, BUDDY,** three small snapshots, one signed 6.00   8.00

☐ **ROACH, MAX,** 8x10 photo with Gene Krupa, signed by Roach 9.00   12.00

☐ **ROACH, MAX,** theater pass, signed 3.00   4.00

☐ **ROACH, MAX,** c. 1962, ALs, with envelope   4.00   6.00

☐ **ROACH, MAX,** signature on a card 1.50   2.50

☐ **ROACH, MAX,** 8x10 studio portrait, signed   3.00   4.00

☐ **ROACH, MAX,** two snapshots, signed on the backs 4.00   6.00

☐ **ROACH, MAX,** LP album cover, signed, record missing 13.00   18.00

Price Range

☐ **ROGERS, SHORTY,** two pages of music composition in his hand 25.00   32.00

☐ **ROGERS, SHORTY,** c. 1960, 8x10 studio portrait, signed 4.00   5.00

☐ **ROGERS, SHORTY,** signature on a card ... 2.00   3.00

☐ **ROGERS, SHORTY,** c. 1968, postcard in his hand, 17 words 4.00   5.50

☐ **ROGERS, SHORTY,** $1 bill, signed by him 4.00   5.50

☐ **ROGERS, SHORTY,** LP record, signed on the label 30.00   40.00

☐ **ROGERS, SHORTY,** c. 1959, ALs, one page 7.00   10.00

☐ **ROLLINS, SONNY,** c. 1975, 8x10 photo with sax, signed 3.00   4.00

☐ **ROLLINS, SONNY,** magazine article, signed 2.00   3.00

☐ **ROLLINS, SONNY,** snapshot with a fan, signed and inscribed 2.50   3.50

☐ **ROLLINS, SONNY,** printed sheet music, signed................................. 5.00   8.00

☐ **ROLLINS, SONNY,** two typewritten letters, signed................................. 4.00   6.00

☐ **RUGOLO, PETE,** musical score, signed, in a folder 17.00   22.00

☐ **RUGOLO, PETE,** photo with Johnny Hodges, signed by Rugolo 11.00   15.00

☐ **RUGOLO, PETE,** photo with Red Norvo, signed by both 25.00   30.00

☐ **RUGOLO, PETE,** notebook used by him, c. 62 pp. with musical jottings, addresses, etc. .. 30.00   37.00

☐ **RUGOLO, PETE,** LP album cover, signed, record missing 22.00   27.00

☐ **RUGOLO, PETE,** c. 1968, ½-hour tape interview 7.00   10.00

☐ **RUGOLO, PETE,** 8x10 studio portrait in color, unsigned 2.00   3.00

☐ **RUGOLO, PETE,** article from "Encyclopedia of Jazz," signed 3.50   5.00

☐ **RUGOLO, PETE,** signature on a card 2.00   3.00

☐ **RUGOLO, PETE,** collection of c. 200 news cuttings and magazine articles 13.00   17.00

☐ **RUSSELL, PEE WEE,** c. 1938, photo with clarinet, signed and dated, framed 23.00   30.00

Price Range

☐ **RUSSELL, PEE WEE,** 8x10 studio photo, signed **13.00** **17.00**

☐ **RUSSELL, PEE WEE,** c. 1930's, three early snapshots, signed **17.00** **23.00**

☐ **RUSSELL, PEE WEE,** 78rpm recording, signed on the label **30.00** **40.00**

☐ **RUSSELL, PEE WEE,** photo with Dave Tough, signed by Russell **15.00** **20.00**

☐ **RUSSELL, PEE WEE,** photo with Red Nichols, signed by both **30.00** **40.00**

☐ **RUSSELL, PEE WEE,** magazine article, signed **8.00** **11.00**

☐ **SHAW, ARTIE,** c. 1950, photo with band, signed by him and several others, dated ... **17.00** **23.00**

☐ **SHAW, ARTIE,** c. 1948, poster, signed **30.00** **38.00**

☐ **SHAW, ARTIE,** magazine cover, signed ... **6.00** **9.00**

☐ **SHAW, ARTIE,** c. 1952, snapshot with fan, signed on back **7.00** **10.00**

☐ **SHAW, ARTIE,** musical score, signed **23.00** **30.00**

☐ **SHAW, ARTIE,** collection of 132 news cuttings and photos **45.00** **60.00**

☐ **SHAW, ARTIE,** scrapbook with 12 signed photos, news cuttings, miscellaneous items **115.00** **150.00**

☐ **SHAW, ARTIE,** c. 1955, 8x10 studio photo, signed **6.00** **9.00**

☐ **SHAW, ARTIE,** three early magazine articles, one signed **9.00** **12.00**

☐ **SHAW, ARTIE,** c. 1938–67, 27 snapshot photos, 12 signed, mounted on large cards, laminated **95.00** **120.00**

☐ **SHAW, ARTIE,** 78rpm recording "Begin the Beguine," signed on the label **75.00** **100.00**

☐ **SHAW, ARTIE,** sheet music, "Begin the Beguine", signed **45.00** **65.00**

☐ **SILVER, HORACE,** 8x10 studio portrait, color, signed **6.00** **9.00**

☐ **SILVER, HORACE,** c. 1970, check endorsed by him **11.00** **16.00**

☐ **SILVER, HORACE,** c. 1965, ALs, two pages, with envelope **6.00** **9.00**

☐ **SILVER, HORACE,** poster picture (from a photo), 16x23, signed **13.00** **17.00**

Price Range

☐ **SILVER, HORACE,** T-shirt with his likeness
and name 8.00   11.00

☐ **SILVER, HORACE,** signature on a card 1.50   2.50

☐ **SIMS, ZOOT,** c. 1954, 8x10 photo with several unidentified persons, signed, inscribed,
dated 4.50   6.00

☐ **SIMS, ZOOT,** signature on a cafe menu 2.00   3.00

☐ **SIMS, ZOOT,** two small snapshot photos, unsigned 2.50   3.50

☐ **SIMS, ZOOT,** three 8x10 photos, one signed 7.00   10.00

☐ **SIMS, ZOOT,** c. 1963. Check endorsed by
him 20.00   25.00

☐ **SIMS, ZOOT,** album cover, signed, record
missing 40.00   50.00

☐ **SIMS, ZOOT,** galley proofs of a magazine article, signed 4.50   6.00

☐ **SIMS, ZOOT,** printed poster, signed, creased, stained 9.00   12.00

☐ **SIMS, ZOOT,** record company catalogue, signed on front cover 11.00   16.00

☐ **SINGLETON, ZUTTY,** pair of drumsticks used by him, framed along with a signed 8x10 photo in a gold-colored frame 150.00   185.00

☐ **SINGLETON, ZUTTY,** c. 1961, 8x10 studio
photo, signed 6.00   8.50

☐ **SINGLETON, ZUTTY,** signature on a card 2.50   3.75

☐ **SINGLETON, ZUTTY,** c. 1936, ALs, ½-page,
stained 4.50   6.00

☐ **SINGLETON, ZUTTY,** three small snapshot
photos, signed 13.00   17.00

☐ **SINGLETON, ZUTTY,** magazine photo, signed and inscribed 3.50   5.00

☐ **SINGLETON, ZUTTY,** c. 1949, check endorsed by him 22.00   30.00

☐ **SINGLETON, ZUTTY,** photo with Don Redman, signed by both 20.00   25.00

☐ **SINGLETON, ZUTTY,** photo with Nat Hentoff, signed by both 15.00   20.00

☐ **SINGLETON, ZUTTY,** c. 1944, postcard in
his hand, four lines 4.50   6.00

☐ **SINGLETON, ZUTTY,** 78rpm record, signed
on the label 30.00   42.00

Price Range

☐ **SINGLETON, ZUTTY,** collection of c. 450 news cuttings, etc.	85.00	110.00
☐ **SINGLETON, ZUTTY,** two 8x10 sepia photos, unsigned, early	6.00	8.50
☐ **SMITH, BESSIE,** 8x10 photo, signed and inscribed	200.00	275.00
☐ **SMITH, BESSIE,** c. 1934, poster advertising her appearance at a cafe, framed	185.00	240.00
☐ **SMITH, CLARENCE,** c. 1926, ALs, four lines	75.00	100.00
☐ **SMITH, JOE,** 8x10 photo, signed and inscribed, creased	22.00	30.00
☐ **SMITH, JOE,** c. 1922, 4x5 photo, unsigned	7.00	10.00
☐ **SMITH, WILLIE,** 8x10 studio photo, signed and inscribed	5.00	8.00
☐ **SMITH, WILLIE,** signature on a union card	35.00	45.00
☐ **SMITH, WILLIE,** c. 1950's, four snapshot photos, one signed	20.00	25.00
☐ **SMITH, WILLIE,** 78rpm recording, signed on the label	55.00	75.00
☐ **SMITH, WILLIE,** c. 1962, check endorsed by him	40.00	55.00
☐ **SMITH, WILLIE,** c. 1941, 8x10 photo at piano, signed	12.00	17.00
☐ **SPANIER, MUGGSY,** 8x10 publicity photo, signed, trimmed	5.00	7.50
☐ **SPANIER, MUGGSY,** LP record album cover, signed, no record	55.00	75.00
☐ **SPANIER, MUGGSY,** signature on a card	2.00	3.00
☐ **STITT, SONNY,** 8x10 studio photo, signed and inscribed	3.50	5.00
☐ **STITT, SONNY,** three small snapshots, one signed	4.00	6.00
☐ **STITT, SONNY,** LP album cover, signed, record missing	17.00	23.00
☐ **STITT, SONNY,** two lines of musical notation, unsigned	6.00	9.00
☐ **TATUM, ART,** c. 1948, 8x10 photo, signed and inscribed	30.00	40.00
☐ **TATUM, ART,** c. 1930's, poster advertising a cafe appearance	110.00	150.00
☐ **TATUM, ART,** 78rpm recording, signed on the label	75.00	100.00

Price Range

☐ **TATUM, ART,** 5x6 photo at piano, signed in the margin	35.00	45.00
☐ **TATUM, ART,** printed score with notes in his hand	60.00	80.00
☐ **TATUM, ART,** c. 1950, check endorsed by him	35.00	45.00
☐ **TATUM, ART,** c. 1925, snapshot photo, signed	45.00	60.00
☐ **TATUM, ART,** scrapbook of 56 photos, 6 signed, other items	500.00	650.00
☐ **TAYLOR, BILLY,** 8x10 photo at piano, signed	3.50	5.00
☐ **TAYLOR, BILLY,** signature on a card	2.00	3.00
☐ **TEAGARDEN, JACK,** 78rpm recording, signed on the label	75.00	95.00
☐ **TEAGARDEN, JACK,** signature on a card	3.50	5.00
☐ **TEAGARDEN, JACK,** c. 1932, 8x10 studio photo, signed	30.00	40.00
☐ **WALLER, FATS,** c. 1939, 8x10 photo, signed and inscribed	95.00	120.00
☐ **WALLER, FATS,** three snap photos, various sizes, unsigned	15.00	20.00
☐ **WALLER, FATS,** 78rpm recording, signed on the label	110.00	140.00
☐ **WEATHERFORD, TEDDY,** c. 1936, ALs, one page	15.00	20.00
☐ **WEBB, CHICK,** 8x10 studio photo, signed	17.00	23.00
☐ **WHITEMAN, PAUL,** c. 1922, check endorsed by him	60.00	80.00
☐ **WHITEMAN, PAUL,** c. 1930, photo holding baton, signed	22.00	30.00
☐ **WHITEMAN, PAUL,** snapshot photo at age 21, unsigned	7.00	10.00
☐ **WILLIAMS, COOTIE,** 8x10 studio photo, signed	3.50	5.00
☐ **WINDING, KAI,** "DownBeat" magazine article, signed	4.50	6.50
☐ **WINDING, KAI,** LP album cover, signed, record missing	22.00	30.00
☐ **YANCEY, JIMMY,** 8x10 photo, signed, framed	33.00	45.00
☐ **YANCEY, JIMMY,** signature on a card	2.50	3.50
☐ **YOUNG, LESTER,** 8x10 photo, signed	20.00	25.00

78's

ALABAMA WASHBOARD STOMPERS

☐ Vocalion 1546, I Want a Little Girl		24.00	39.00
☐ 1587, Who Stole the Lock?		24.00	39.00
☐ 1626, I Surrender, Dear		24.00	39.00
☐ 1635, I Need Lovin'		21.00	33.00

ALEXANDER, TEXAS

☐ Okeh 8511, Corn-Bread Blues		17.00	28.00
☐ 8526, Farm Hand Blues		17.00	28.00
☐ 8542, Sabine River Blues		17.00	28.00
☐ 8563, Bell Cow Blues		17.00	28.00
☐ 8578, Death Bed Blues		15.00	23.00
☐ 8591, Deep Blues Sea Blues		15.00	23.00
☐ 8603, West Texas Blues		15.00	23.00
☐ 8624, Sittin' on a Log		15.00	23.00
☐ 8640, Blue Devil Blues		16.00	24.00
☐ 8658, 'Frisco Train Blues		40.00	70.00
☐ 8688, St. Louis Fair Blues		18.00	27.00
☐ 8705, Gold Tooth Blues		15.00	25.00
☐ 8731, Awful Moaning Blues		15.00	25.00
☐ 8751, Peaceful Blues		15.00	25.00
☐ 8764, Broken Yo Yo		15.00	25.00
☐ 8771, Texas Special		15.00	25.00
☐ 8785, Thirty Day Blues		15.00	25.00
☐ 8813, She's So Far		28.00	47.00
☐ 8823, Last Stage Blues		30.00	55.00
☐ 8835, Days Is Lonesome		28.00	47.00
☐ 8890, Seen Better Days		28.00	47.00
☐ Vocalion 02743, Blues in My Mind		13.00	20.00
☐ 02764, Prairie Dog Hole Blues		13.00	20.00
☐ 02772, Worried Blues		13.00	20.00
☐ 02856, Justice Blues		13.00	20.00
☐ 02876, Lonesome Valley Blues		13.00	20.00
☐ 02912, Deceitful Blues		13.00	20.00

ANDERSON, JELLY ROLL

☐ Gennett 6135, Free Women Blues		55.00	90.00
☐ 6181, Good Time Blues		45.00	80.00
☐ Herwin 92014, Salt Tear Blues		75.00	120.00
☐ 92020, Free Women Blues		85.00	135.00

ANTRIM, ROOSEVELT

☐ Bluebird 7149, Complaint to Make		13.00	20.00
☐ 7475, Station Boy Blues		13.00	20.00

Price Range

ARMSTRONG, LOUIS

☐ **Columbia 2574-D,** Star Dust		10.00	17.00
☐ **2606-D,** All of Me		11.00	18.00
☐ **2631-D,** The New Tiger Rag		10.00	17.00
☐ **2688-D,** Rockin' Chair		10.00	17.00
☐ **2709-D,** Body and Soul		11.00	18.00
☐ **2727-D,** After You've Gone		11.00	18.00
☐ **Okeh 8299,** Oriental Strut		45.00	80.00
☐ **8300,** Heebie Jeebies		50.00	90.00
☐ **8318,** Georgia Grind		50.00	90.00
☐ **8320,** Cornet Chop Suey		52.00	95.00
☐ **8343,** I'm Gonna Gitcha		45.00	80.00
☐ **8379,** Sweet Little Papa		50.00	90.00
☐ **8396,** The King of the Zulus		52.00	95.00
☐ **8423,** Big Butter and Egg Man		50.00	90.00
☐ **8436,** Jazz Lips		50.00	90.00
☐ **8447,** Irish Black Bottom		45.00	80.00
☐ **8474,** Wild Man Blues		50.00	90.00
☐ **8482,** Willie the Weeper		40.00	75.00
☐ **8496,** Keyhole Blues		45.00	80.00
☐ **8503,** Potato Head Blues		45.00	80.00
☐ **8535,** Savoy Blues		50.00	90.00
☐ **8551,** Got No Blues		45.00	80.00
☐ **8566,** Struttin' with Some Barbeque		45.00	80.00
☐ **8597,** West End Blues		32.00	57.00
☐ **8609,** Sugar Foot Strut		35.00	60.00
☐ **8631,** Knee Drops		30.00	53.00
☐ **8641,** Squeeze Me		30.00	53.00
☐ **8657,** Save It, Pretty Mama		27.00	50.00
☐ **8669,** No-One Else But You		27.00	50.00
☐ **8690,** Basin Street Blues		27.00	50.00
☐ **8703,** Knockin' a Jug		26.00	47.00
☐ **8714,** Ain't Misbehavin'		23.00	39.00
☐ **8717,** That Rhythm Man		23.00	39.00
☐ **8729,** Some of These Days		23.00	39.00
☐ **8756,** Rockin' Chair		23.00	39.00
☐ **8774,** Bessie Couldn't Help It		23.00	39.00
☐ **41078,** Fireworks		21.00	37.00
☐ **41157,** Knee Drops		12.00	18.00
☐ **41180,** Save It, Pretty Mama		12.00	18.00

Price Range

☐	**41241,** Basin Street Blues	17.00	24.00
☐	**41276,** Black and Blue	17.00	24.00
☐	**41281,** Sweet Savannah Sue	22.00	36.00
☐	**41298,** Some of These Days	22.00	36.00
☐	**41350,** After You've Gone	22.00	36.00
☐	**41415,** My Sweet	22.00	36.00
☐	**41423,** Exactly Like You	20.00	33.00
☐	**41442,** I'm a Ding Dong Daddy	20.00	33.00
☐	**41448,** Confessin'	20.00	33.00
☐	**41454,** Weather Bird	26.00	47.00
☐	**41468,** Body and Soul	17.00	30.00
☐	**41478,** You're Drivin' Me Crazy	16.00	27.00
☐	**41486,** Shine	16.00	27.00
☐	**41497,** Walkin' My Baby Back Home	17.00	30.00
☐	**41501,** Them There Eyes	16.00	27.00
☐	**41504,** When It's Sleepy Time Down South	15.00	26.00
☐	**41530,** Star Dust	15.00	26.00
☐	**41534,** Chinatown, My Chinatown	14.00	25.00
☐	**41538,** The Lonesome Road	14.00	25.00
☐	**41550,** Kickin' the Gong Around	14.00	25.00
☐	**41552,** All of Me	13.00	24.00
☐	**41557,** The New Tiger Rag	13.00	24.00
☐	**41560,** Keepin' Out of Mischief Now	13.00	24.00

AUSTIN, LOVIE

☐	**Paramount 12255,** Steppin' On the Blues	50.00	76.00
☐	**12278,** Charleston Mad	45.00	70.00
☐	**12283,** Heebie Jeebies	44.00	67.00
☐	**12300,** Rampart Street Blues	35.00	56.00
☐	**12313,** Too Sweet For Words	33.00	53.00
☐	**12361,** Frog Tongue Stomp	125.00	180.00
☐	**12380,** Chicago Mess Around	130.00	185.00
☐	**12391,** In the Alley Blues	130.00	185.00

BAILEY, DE FORD

☐	**Bluebird 5147,** Ice Water Blues	10.00	15.00
☐	**Brunswick 146,** Pan-American Blues	22.00	35.00
☐	**147,** Muscle Shoals Blues	22.00	35.00
☐	**148,** Alcoholic Blues	22.00	35.00
☐	**434,** Up Country Blues	17.00	25.00
☐	**Victor 23336,** John Henry	45.00	70.00
☐	**23831,** John Henry	40.00	62.00
☐	**38014,** Ice Water Blues	17.00	25.00

Price Range

BAKER, KATHERINE

☐ **Gennett 6125,** I Helped You, Sick Man	65.00	100.00
☐ **6157,** Chicago Fire Blues	65.00	110.00
☐ **6228,** Money Women Blues	65.00	100.00
☐ **6321,** Mistreated Blues	65.00	100.00
☐ **Herwin 92017,** My Man Left Me Blues	75.00	120.00
☐ **92037,** Daddy Sunshine Blues	70.00	115.00
☐ **92038,** Wild Women Blues	70.00	115.00
☐ **92039,** Mistreated Blues . . . . : .	70.00	115.00

BARBECUE BOB

☐ **Columbia 14222-D,** Mississippi Heavy Water Blues	12.00	19.00
☐ **15246-D,** Honey You Don't Know My Mind	12.00	19.00
☐ **14257-D,** Brown-Skin Gal	12.00	19.00
☐ **14268-D,** It Won't Be Long Now	12.00	19.00
☐ **14280-D,** Crooked Woman Blues	12.00	19.00
☐ **14299-D,** Thinkin' Funny Blues	12.00	19.00
☐ **14331-D,** Waycross Georgia Blues	15.00	25.00
☐ **14350-D,** My Mistake Blues	15.00	25.00
☐ **14372-D,** Blind Pig Blues	15.00	25.00
☐ **14383-D,** Cold Wave Blues	15.00	25.00
☐ **14412-D,** Dollar Down Blues	15.00	25.00
☐ **14436-D,** It's a Funny Little Thing	15.00	25.00
☐ **14461-D,** Bad Time Blues	15.00	25.00
☐ **14507-D,** Me and My Whiskey	24.00	38.00
☐ **14523-D,** Yo Yo Blues No. 2	24.00	38.00
☐ **14546-D,** Telling It To You	24.00	38.00
☐ **14558-D,** The Spider and the Fly	24.00	38.00
☐ **14573-D,** California Blues	24.00	38.00
☐ **14581-D,** Jambooger Blues	24.00	38.00
☐ **14591-D,** Atlanta Moon . . . . . . :	24.00	38.00

BLAKE, EUBIE

☐ **Crown 3086,** When Your Lover Has Gone	23.00	35.00
☐ **3090,** I'm No Account Any More	20.00	32.00
☐ **3105,** It Looks Like Love	20.00	32.00
☐ **3130,** Nobody's Sweetheart	23.00	35.00
☐ **3193,** River Stay 'Way From My Door	20.00	32.00
☐ **3197,** Sweet Georgia Brown	25.00	40.00
☐ **Victor 22735,** My Blue Days Blew Over	25.00	40.00
☐ **22737,** Thumpin and Bumpin'	27.00	42.00

Price Range

BLIND BLAKE

☐ **Paramount 12413**, Skeedle Loo Doo Blues	37.00	56.00
☐ **12431**, Too Tight	35.00	53.00
☐ **12442**, Tampa Bound	34.00	52.00
☐ **12464**, Buck-Town Blues	34.00	52.00
☐ **12479**, One Time Blues	33.00	50.00
☐ **12565**, Southern Rag	32.00	50.00
☐ **12583**, Hard Road Blues	33.00	50.00
☐ **12597**, Wabash Rag	32.00	49.00
☐ **12606**, Brownskin Mama Blues	34.00	52.00
☐ **12643**, Tootie Blues	39.00	60.00
☐ **12657**, Detroit Bound Blues	38.00	57.00
☐ **12673**, Hot Potatoes	50.00	75.00
☐ **12695**, Low Down Loving Gal	38.00	57.00
☐ **12710**, Back Door Slam Blues	37.00	55.00
☐ **12723**, No Dough Blues	37.00	55.00
☐ **12737**, Search Warrant Blues	36.00	53.00
☐ **12754**, Notoriety Woman Blues	36.00	53.00
☐ **12767**, Ramblin' Mama Blues	37.00	55.00
☐ **12810**, Poker Woman Blues	37.00	55.00
☐ **12824**, Georgia Bound	36.00	53.00
☐ **12863**, Fightin' the Jug	65.00	100.00
☐ **12888**, Police Dog Blues	47.00	72.00
☐ **12904**, Ice Man Blues	45.00	69.00

BLIND WILLIE

☐ **Regal 3260**, How About You	20.00	30.00
☐ **Vocalion 02568**, Weary Hearted Blues	16.00	26.00
☐ **02577**, Death Cell Blues	15.00	25.00
☐ **02595**, Warm It Up to Me	15.00	25.00
☐ **02623**, Lord Have Mercy If You Please	14.00	23.00
☐ **02668**, My Baby's Gone	14.00	23.00

BLYTHE'S BLUE BOYS

☐ **Champion 15344**, There'll Come a Day	125.00	190.00
☐ **15528**, My Baby	115.00	165.00
☐ **15551**, Pleasure Mad	110.00	160.00
☐ **15570**, Tell Me, Cutie	110.00	160.00
☐ **15676**, Oriental Man	110.00	160.00
☐ **40023**, Oriental Man	15.00	25.00
☐ **40062**, Tack It Down	14.00	23.00
☐ **40115**, Tell Me, Cutie	14.00	23.00

Price Range

BOGAN, LUCILLE
- ☐ **Brunswick 7083,** Coffee Grindin' Blues 29.00 43.00
- ☐ **7145,** My Georgia Blues 24.00 37.00
- ☐ **7186,** Black Angel Blues 20.00 31.00
- ☐ **7193,** Crawlin' Lizard Blues 23.00 36.00
- ☐ **Paramount 12459,** Sweet Petunia 34.00 60.00
- ☐ **12504,** Kind Stella Blues 32.00 55.00
- ☐ **12514,** Doggone Wicked Blues 31.00 53.00
- ☐ **12560,** War Time Man Blues 31.00 53.00

BOOKER, JOHN LEE
- ☐ **Chance 1108,** Miss Lorraine 10.00 18.00
- ☐ **1110,** Graveyard Blues 10.00 18.00
- ☐ **1122,** 609 Boogie 10.00 18.00
- ☐ **De Luxe 6032,** Stuttering Blues 6.00 11.00
- ☐ **6046,** Real Real Gone 6.00 11.00
- ☐ **Rockin' 525,** Pouring Down Rain 7.00 12.00

BROWN, BESSIE
- ☐ **Banner 1833,** What's the Matter Now? 11.00 18.00
- ☐ **Brunswick 4346,** The Blues Singer from Alabama 20.00 35.00
- ☐ **4409,** He Just Don't Appeal to Me 20.00 35.00
- ☐ **Regal 8143,** What's the Matter Now? 11.00 18.00
- ☐ **Vocalion 1182,** Arkansas Blues 13.00 22.00
- ☐ **15688,** The Man I Love 10.00 17.00

BROWN, HENRY
- ☐ **Paramount 12825,** Twenty-First Street Stomp 75.00 115.00
- ☐ **12934,** Blues Stomp 70.00 110.00
- ☐ **12988,** Eastern Chimes Blues 65.00 105.00

BRYANT, GLADYS
- ☐ **Harmograph 818,** Beale Street Mama 35.00 52.00
- ☐ **2539,** Triflin' Blues 20.00 32.00
- ☐ **2540,** Laughin' Cryin' Blues 20.00 32.00
- ☐ **Paramount 12026,** Laughin' Cryin' Blues .. 20.00 32.00
- ☐ **12031,** Beale Street Mama 30.00 45.00

BUMBLE BEE SLIM
- ☐ **Decca 7021,** Cruel Hearted Woman Blues 13.00 23.00
- ☐ **7045,** The Longest Day You Live 12.00 21.00
- ☐ **7053,** Bleeding Heart Blues 12.00 21.00

Price Range

☐ 7054, Let's Pitch a Boogie Woogie	12.00	21.00
☐ 7071, My Black Gal Blues	17.00	25.00
☐ 7079, Mean Bloody Murder Blues	12.00	21.00
☐ 7089, Good Evening Blues	12.00	21.00
☐ 7101, Sail On Sail On Blues	12.00	21.00
☐ 7121, I'll Take You Back	12.00	21.00
☐ 7126, Smoky Mountain Blues	12.00	21.00
☐ 7138, Happy Life Blues	12.00	21.00
☐ 7145, Some Old Rainy Day	12.00	20.00
☐ 7162, Deep Bass Blues	12.00	20.00
☐ 7170, No Good Woman	13.00	21.00
☐ **Fidelity 3004,** Ida Red	11.00	18.00
☐ **Paramount 13102,** Yo Yo String Blues	65.00	105.00
☐ 13109, Chain Gang Bound	70.00	115.00
☐ 13132, Honey Bee Blues	65.00	105.00
☐ **Vocalion 1691,** Piney Woods Working Man	34.00	57.00
☐ 1719, Greasy Greens	34.00	62.00
☐ 02728, Baby So Long	12.00	19.00
☐ 02742, East St. Louis Blues	10.00	16.00
☐ 02773, Wrecked Life Blues	12.00	19.00
☐ 02809, Helping Hand Blues	10.00	16.00
☐ 02829, Rough Road Blues	9.00	15.00
☐ 02865, Cold-Blooded Murder	12.00	19.00
☐ 02885, Burned Down Mill	10.00	16.00
☐ 02903, Running Bad Luck Blues	10.00	16.00
☐ 02930, Blues Before Daylight	9.00	15.00
☐ 02970, Way Down in Georgia	9.00	15.00
☐ 03005, Lemon Squeezing Blues	10.00	16.00
☐ 03037, I Keep on Drinking	12.00	19.00
☐ 03054, When the Sun Goes Down	10.00	16.00
☐ 03090, Big 80 Blues	9.00	15.00
☐ 03165, Cold-Blooded Murder No. 2	12.00	19.00
☐ 03197, When Somebody Loses	9.00	15.00
☐ 03209, Can't You Trust Me No More? ...	10.00	16.00
☐ 03221, Dumb Tricks Blues	10.00	16.00
☐ 03242, Back in Jail Again	10.00	16.00
☐ 03267, Wet Clothes Blues	12.00	19.00
☐ 03298, Any Time at Night	10.00	16.00
☐ 03328, Hard Rocks in My Bed	12.00	19.00
☐ 03384, Meet Me at the Landing	9.00	15.00
☐ 03446, Fast Life Blues	10.00	16.00
☐ 03473, 12 O'Clock Midnight	9.00	15.00

Price Range

☐ 03506, She Never	10.00	16.00
☐ 03550, Big Six	9.00	15.00
☐ 03582, Woman for Every Man	10.00	16.00
☐ 03611, Good Bye	9.00	15.00
☐ 03637, Rough Treatment	12.00	19.00
☐ 03698, Just Yesterday	10.00	16.00
☐ 03767, This Old Life I'm Living	9.00	15.00
☐ 03870, When Your Deal Goes Down	9.00	15.00
☐ 03929, Rock Hearted Woman	9.00	15.00
☐ 04661, Where Was You Last Night?	9.00	15.00

BUNCH, FRANK

☐ Gennett 6278, Fuzzy Wuzzy	80.00	130.00
☐ 6293, Fourth Avenue Stomp	70.00	110.00
☐ Herwin 92044, Congo Stomp	100.00	160.00

BURSTON, CLARA

☐ Champion 16125, Try That Man O'Mine	45.00	75.00
☐ 16216, Pay with Money	42.00	70.00
☐ 16756, Good and Hot	42.00	70.00
☐ Paramount 12881, Georgia Man Blues	35.00	60.00
☐ 13003, C. P. Blues	33.00	56.00
☐ 13045, Finger Snappin'	35.00	60.00

CAMPBELL, GENE

☐ Brunswick 7139, Bended Knee Blues	36.00	60.00
☐ 7154, Western Plain Blues	33.00	52.00
☐ 7161, Freight Train Yodeling Blues	32.00	50.00
☐ 7170, Wandering Blues	32.00	50.00
☐ 7177, Wash and Iron Woman Blues	31.00	50.00
☐ 7197, Wedding Day Blues	31.00	50.00
☐ 7206, Face to Face Blues	30.00	50.00
☐ 7214, Doggone Mean Blues	31.00	50.00
☐ 7225, Crooked Woman Blues	32.00	53.00
☐ 7226, Turned Out Blues	30.00	50.00
☐ 7227, Married Life Blues	30.00	50.00

CARR, LEROY

☐ Bluebird 5915, Big Four Blues	11.00	18.00
☐ 5946, Just a Rag	11.00	18.00
☐ 5963, Going Back Home	11.00	18.00
☐ Vocalion 1191, My Own Lonesome Blues	15.00	25.00
☐ 1200, Tennessee Blues	18.00	33.00
☐ 1214, Low Down Dirty Blues	19.00	35.00

Price Range

☐	**1232,** Truthful Blues	18.00	33.00
☐	**1241,** Prison Bound Blues	26.00	41.00
☐	**1259,** How About Me?	25.00	40.00
☐	**1261,** Tired of Your Low Down Ways	25.00	40.00
☐	**1290,** Straight Alky Blues	26.00	41.00
☐	**1400,** Naptown Blues	25.00	40.00
☐	**1405,** Wrong Man Blues	25.00	40.00
☐	**1423,** Gettin' All Wet	26.00	41.00
☐	**1432,** Prison Cell Blues	25.00	38.00
☐	**1435,** Love Hides All Faults	25.00	38.00
☐	**1454,** The Dirty Dozen	25.00	38.00
☐	**1473,** Rainy Day Blues	23.00	36.00
☐	**1483,** That's Tellin' 'em	23.00	36.00
☐	**1499,** Blue with the Blues	22.00	35.00
☐	**1519,** I Know That I'll Be Blue	22.00	35.00
☐	**1527,** Memphis Town	22.00	35.00
☐	**1541,** Sloppy Drunk Blues	25.00	37.00
☐	**1549,** Four Day Rider	25.00	37.00
☐	**1574,** Jail Cell Blues	24.00	36.00
☐	**1585,** Big House Blues	24.00	36.00
☐	**1593,** Papa's on the House Top	23.00	35.00
☐	**1605,** Low Down Dog Blues	23.00	35.00
☐	**1624,** Let's Disagree	23.00	35.00
☐	**1636,** Papa's Got Your Water On	24.00	36.00
☐	**1651,** What More Can I Do?	23.00	35.00
☐	**1693,** The Depression Blues	25.00	37.00
☐	**1703,** Midnight Hour Blues	22.00	34.00
☐	**1709,** I Keep the Blues	22.00	34.00
☐	**1716,** Quittin' Papa	22.00	34.00
☐	**02875,** Longing For My Sister	14.00	22.00
☐	**02893,** Cruel Woman Blues	14.00	22.00
☐	**02922,** Stormy Weather Blues	14.00	24.00
☐	**02950,** My Woman's Gone Wrong	14.00	24.00
☐	**02969,** Bo Bo Stomp	14.00	24.00
☐	**02986,** George Street Blues	14.00	24.00
☐	**03034,** Tight Time Blues	14.00	24.00
☐	**03067,** Black Wagon Blues	12.00	21.00
☐	**03107,** Muddy Water	13.00	22.00
☐	**03157,** My Good for Nothin' Gal	12.00	21.00
☐	**03233,** Blue Night Blues	13.00	22.00
☐	**03296,** Good Woman Blues	13.00	22.00
☐	**03349,** Big Four Blues	13.00	22.00

Price Range

CARTER, BO (and Walter Jacobs)

☐ **Bluebird 5489,** Bo Carter Special	14.00	23.00
☐ 5536, Howlin' Tom Cat Blues	14.00	22.00
☐ 5594, Pin in Your Cushion	14.00	22.00
☐ 5629, Beans	12.00	21.00
☐ 5704, Nobody's Business	12.00	21.00
☐ 5825, Backache Blues	14.00	22.00
☐ 5861, Old Shoe Blues	12.00	20.00
☐ 5912, Mashing That Thing	14.00	22.00
☐ 5997, Skin Ball Blues	14.00	22.00
☐ 6024, Blue Runner Blues	12.00	21.00
☐ 6058, Please Warm My Weiner	17.00	28.00
☐ 6295, Cigarette Blues	17.00	28.00
☐ 6315, Ride My Mule	12.00	21.00
☐ 6363, Rolling Blues	12.00	21.00
☐ 6407, It's Too Wet	14.00	22.00
☐ 6444, Fat Mouth Blues	14.00	22.00
☐ 6529, T Baby Blues	14.00	23.00
☐ 6589, I Get the Blues	12.00	20.00
☐ 6659, Doubled Up in a Knot	12.00	20.00
☐ 6735, Worried G Blues	12.00	20.00
☐ 7073, Got to Work Somewhere	12.00	19.00
☐ 7213, The Ins and Outs of My Girl	14.00	23.00
☐ 7927, Shake 'em on Down	12.00	19.00
☐ 7952, Lucille, Lucille	12.00	19.00
☐ 7968, Shoo That Chicken	12.00	19.00
☐ 8045, Let's Get Drunk Again	12.00	19.00
☐ 8093, Old Devil	10.00	17.00
☐ 8122, Whiskey Blues	11.00	19.00
☐ 8147, Santa Claus	10.00	17.00
☐ 8159, Trouble in Blues	10.00	17.00
☐ 8397, The County Farm Blues	10.00	17.00
☐ 8423, Lock the Lock	11.00	19.00
☐ 8459, Baby Ruth	14.00	23.00
☐ 8495, Policy Blues	10.00	17.00
☐ 8514, My Little Mind	10.00	16.00
☐ 8555, Honey	10.00	16.00
☐ **Okeh 8852,** I'm an Old Bumble Bee	30.00	50.00
☐ 8858, Times is Tight Like That	28.00	48.00
☐ 8870, Mean Feeling Blues	27.00	45.00
☐ 8887, Pin in Your Cushion	27.00	45.00
☐ 8888, Loveless Love	26.00	44.00

Price Range

☐	**8889,** Howling Tom Cat Blues	25.00	43.00
☐	**8897,** Ants in My Pants	25.00	43.00
☐	**8923,** What Kind of Scent Is This?	27.00	46.00
☐	**8930,** Last Go Round	25.00	42.00
☐	**8935,** I Want You to Know	25.00	42.00
☐	**8952,** Baby, How Can It Be?	25.00	42.00

CELESTIN'S TUXEDO JAZZ ORCHESTRA

☐	**Columbia 636-D,** Station Calls	17.00	28.00
☐	**14200-D,** I'm Satisfied You Love Me	16.00	26.00
☐	**14220-D,** Papa's Got the Jim-Jams	16.00	26.00
☐	**14259-D,** As You Like It	15.00	25.00
☐	**14396-D,** The Sweetheart of T.K.O	14.00	25.00

COLLINS, SAM

☐	**Gennett 6167,** The Jail House Blues	50.00	70.00
☐	**6181,** Devil in the Lion's Den	43.00	68.00
☐	**6260,** Dark Cloudy Blues	42.00	66.00
☐	**6291,** Lead Me All the Way	41.00	65.00
☐	**6307,** Midnight Special Blues	42.00	66.00
☐	**6379,** Hesitation Blues	42.00	66.00

COX, IDA

☐	**Paramount 12022,** Come Right In	12.00	20.00
☐	**12044,** Weary Way Blues	24.00	37.00
☐	**12045,** Bama Bound Blues	15.00	25.00
☐	**12053,** Blue Monday Blues	15.00	25.00
☐	**12056,** Chicago Bound Blues	15.00	25.00
☐	**12063,** I've Got the Blues for Rampart Street	27.00	44.00
☐	**12064,** Moanin' Groanin' Blues	26.00	43.00
☐	**12085,** Worried Mama Blues	26.00	43.00
☐	**12086,** Confidential Blues	25.00	41.00
☐	**12087,** Mail Man Blues	25.00	41.00
☐	**12094,** Down the Road Bound Blues	16.00	24.00
☐	**12097,** Mean Paper Turn Your Key	26.00	43.00
☐	**12202,** Chicago Monkey Man Blues	15.00	23.00
☐	**12220,** Kentucky Man Blues	14.00	22.00
☐	**12228,** Cherry Picking Blues	13.00	20.00
☐	**12251,** Mississippi River Blues	27.00	44.00
☐	**12258,** Misery Blues	26.00	42.00
☐	**12263,** Georgia Hound Blues	25.00	41.00
☐	**12275,** Mister Man	16.00	24.00
☐	**12282,** Someday Blues	15.00	23.00

			Price Range	
☐	**12291,** Black Crepe Blues		14.00	22.00
☐	**12298,** Southern Woman's Blues		14.00	22.00
☐	**12298,** Lonesome Blues		14.00	22.00
☐	**12318,** Coffin Blues		75.00	120.00
☐	**12325,** One Time Woman Blues		27.00	44.00
☐	**12344,** Trouble Trouble Blues		26.00	43.00
☐	**12353,** Night and Day Blues		26.00	43.00
☐	**12381,** Don't Blame Me		26.00	43.00
☐	**12502,** Mercy Blues		20.00	33.00
☐	**12513,** Pleading Blues		18.00	30.00
☐	**12540,** Mojo Hand Blues		20.00	33.00
☐	**12556,** Seven Day Blues		18.00	30.00
☐	**12582,** Midnight Hour Blues		17.00	28.00
☐	**12664,** Bone Orchard Blues		25.00	38.00
☐	**12667,** Broadcasting Blues		26.00	40.00
☐	**12690,** Fogyism		25.00	37.00
☐	**12704,** You Stole My Man		25.00	37.00
☐	**12727,** Separated Blues		23.00	36.00
☐	**12965,** Jailhouse Blues		55.00	90.00

DAVIS, WALTER

☐	**Bluebird 5031,** M. & O. Blues		10.00	16.00
☐	**5038,** Blue Sea Blues		9.00	15.00
☐	**5077,** Howling Wind Blues		9.00	15.00
☐	**5094,** Hijack Blues		9.00	15.00
☐	**5129,** Worried Man Blues		8.00	14.00
☐	**5143,** Red Cross Blues		8.00	14.00
☐	**5192,** Moonlight Blues		8.00	14.00
☐	**5228,** Evil Woman		9.00	15.00
☐	**5305,** Red Cross Blues—No. 2		9.00	15.00
☐	**5324,** You Don't Smell Right		11.00	17.00
☐	**5361,** What's the Use of Worryin'?		10.00	16.00
☐	**5879,** Sloppy Drunk Again		12.00	20.00
☐	**5931,** Sweet Sixteen		7.00	13.00
☐	**5965,** Minute Man Blues		7.00	13.00
☐	**5982,** Sad and Lonesome Blues		6.00	11.00
☐	**6040,** Dentist Blues		9.00	16.00
☐	**6059,** I Can Tell By the Way You Smell . .		12.00	20.00
☐	**6074,** Pearly May		7.00	13.00
☐	**6125,** Santa Claus		6.00	12.00
☐	**6167,** Moonlight Is My Spread		6.00	12.00
☐	**6201,** Katy Blues		6.00	12.00

Price Range

☐	6228, Blues at Midnight	6.00	12.00
☐	6354, Carpenter Man	7.00	13.00
☐	6410, Fallin' Rain	6.00	11.00
☐	6468, Jacksonville	7.00	13.00
☐	6996, Good Gal	7.00	13.00
☐	7021, Fifth Avenue Blues	10.00	18.00
☐	7064, Angel Child	7.00	12.00
☐	7292, Guiding Rod	7.00	12.00
☐	7329, Holiday Blues	7.00	12.00
☐	7375, Black Jack Engine Blues	7.00	12.00
☐	7512, Walking the Avenue	7.00	12.00
☐	7551, Easy Goin' Mama	7.00	12.00
☐	7589, Million-Dollar Baby	7.00	12.00
☐	7643, Candy Man	7.00	12.00
☐	7663, Friendless Blues	7.00	12.00
☐	7745, Call Me Anytime	7.00	12.00
☐	7792, Love Will Kill You	8.00	15.00
☐	7978, Cuttin' Off My Days	7.00	12.00
☐	8002, Early This Mornin'	7.00	12.00
☐	8026, Smoky Mountain	8.00	15.00
☐	8058, Mercy Blues	8.00	15.00
☐	8107, Troubled and Weary	8.00	15.00
☐	8261, Big Four Blues	8.00	15.00
☐	8282, Green and Lucky	7.00	12.00
☐	8312, Bachelor Blues	7.00	13.00
☐	8343, Froggy Bottom	7.00	13.00
☐	8367, Doctor Blues	6.00	11.00
☐	8393, Sundown Blues	7.00	13.00
☐	8434, Jungle Blues	7.00	13.00
☐	8470, Western Land	6.00	11.00
☐	8510, Come Back Baby	6.00	11.00

DEE, MERCY

☐	**Bayou 003,** Please Understand	14.00	25.00
☐	013, Happy Bachelor	13.00	23.00
☐	**Colony 102,** Straight and Narrow	12.00	21.00
☐	111, Birdbrain Baby	11.00	18.00
☐	**Imperial 5104,** Empty Life	12.00	20.00
☐	5110, Big Foot Country	12.00	20.00
☐	5118, Bought Love	11.00	18.00
☐	5127, Pay Off	11.00	18.00
☐	**Spire 11-001,** Lonesome Cabin Blues	14.00	25.00
☐	11-002, Travelin' Alone Blues	13.00	22.00

Price Range

DIXIE JAZZ BAND

☐ **Challenge 958,** Icky Blues	16.00	25.00
☐ 999, Makin' Friends	11.00	19.00
☐ **Jewel 5547,** Icky Blues	13.00	22.00
☐ 5569, Makin' Friends	11.00	18.00
☐ 5575, Sweet Liza	11.00	18.00
☐ 5648, Twelfth Street Rag	11.00	18.00
☐ 5685, It's So Good	16.00	25.00
☐ 5729, The Way He Loves Is Just Too Bad	15.00	27.00
☐ 5730, Broadway Rhythm	19.00	30.00
☐ **Oriole 565,** Wait Till See You My Baby Do the Charleston	13.00	21.00
☐ 717, Old Folks' Shuffle	13.00	21.00
☐ 880, I'm in Love Again	10.00	17.00
☐ 883, Rosy Cheeks	9.00	16.00
☐ 952, Memphis Blues	9.00	16.00
☐ 984, Tiger Rag	11.00	18.00
☐ 1100, Sorry	9.00	16.00
☐ 1515, Icky Blues	11.00	18.00
☐ 1540, Sweet Liza	9.00	16.00
☐ 1624, Twelfth Street Rag	11.00	18.00
☐ 1668, It's So Good	12.00	20.00
☐ 1726, The Way He Loves Is Just Too Bad	13.00	21.00
☐ 1728, Broadway Rhythm	14.00	23.00
☐ 1730, Doin' the Voom Voom	15.00	25.00
☐ **Regal 8874,** Flaming Youth	22.00	35.00

ELLINGTON, DUKE

☐ **Brunswick 3480,** Birmingham Breakdown . .	13.00	21.00
☐ 3987, Tishomingo Blues	12.00	20.00
☐ 4110, Louisiana	12.00	20.00
☐ 4122, The Mooche	13.00	21.00
☐ 4705, Jolly Wog	12.00	20.00
☐ 6093, Creole Rhapsody	13.00	21.00
☐ **Buddy 8010,** If You Can't Hold the Man You Love	70.00	110.00
☐ 8063, Animal Crackers	70.00	110.00
☐ **Columbia 953-D,** Hop Head	18.00	32.00
☐ **1076-D,** Down in Our Alley Blues	16.00	26.00
☐ **Gennett 3291,** Wanna Go Back Again Blues	45.00	70.00
☐ 3342, Animal Crackers	50.00	75.00
☐ **Okeh 8521,** Black and Tan Fantasy	20.00	30.00

Price Range

☐ **8602,** Diga Diga Doo	20.00	32.00
☐ **8636,** Black Beauty	18.00	28.00
☐ **8662,** Misty Mornin'	18.00	28.00
☐ **40955,** Black and Tan Fantasy	18.00	28.00
☐ **41013,** Jubilee Stomp	18.00	28.00
☐ **Pathe-Actuelle 7504,** Georgia Grind	70.00	100.00
☐ **Perfect 104,** Georgia Grind	50.00	70.00
☐ **14514,** Trombone Blues	40.00	65.00
☐ **Victor 21137,** Creole Love Call	13.00	21.00
☐ **21284,** Washington Wobble	12.00	20.00
☐ **21490,** The Blues I Love to Sing	13.00	21.00
☐ **21580,** Black Beauty	12.00	20.00
☐ **21703,** Got Everything But You	12.00	20.00
☐ **22528,** Three Little Words	8.00	12.00
☐ **22586,** What Good Am I Without You? ...	12.00	20.00
☐ **22587,** Mood Indigo	9.00	14.00
☐ **22603,** Blue Again	9.00	14.00
☐ **22614,** Keep a Song in Your Soul	13.00	22.00
☐ **22743,** Limehouse Blues	10.00	16.00
☐ **22791,** It's Glory	13.00	22.00
☐ **22800,** The Mystery Song	11.00	17.00
☐ **22938,** Bugle Call Rag	12.00	20.00
☐ **23017,** You're Lucky to Me	25.00	34.00
☐ **23022,** Jungle Nights in Harlem	30.00	47.00
☐ **23036,** Sam and Delilah	16.00	27.00
☐ **23041,** Shout 'em, Aunt Tillie	23.00	31.00
☐ **24431,** Rude Interlude	13.00	21.00
☐ **24501,** Daybreak Express	8.00	12.00
☐ **24622,** Ebony Rhapsody	10.00	17.00
☐ **24651,** My Old Flame	9.00	16.00
☐ **24755,** Delta Serenade	9.00	16.00
☐ **38007,** Bandanna Babies	11.00	17.00
☐ **38008,** Diga Diga Doo	11.00	17.00
☐ **38034,** The Mooche	35.00	50.00
☐ **38035,** Flaming Youth	20.00	34.00
☐ **38036,** Saturday Night Function	20.00	34.00
☐ **38053,** Stevedore Stomp	19.00	32.00
☐ **38058,** Saratoga Swing	19.00	32.00
☐ **38065,** Hot Feet	20.00	35.00
☐ **38079,** Cotton Club Stomp	20.00	35.00

ELKINS, W. C.

☐ **QRS 7045,** Climbing Up the Mountain	23.00	37.00

		Price Range	
☐	7046, Oh, Mother, Don't You Weep	21.00	35.00
☐	7047, Roll, Roll, Chariot	20.00	36.00
☐	7063, Eloi	20.00	36.00
☐	7068, A Wheel in a Wheel	20.00	36.00

ESTES, JOHN

☐	**Bluebird 8871,** Little Laura Blues	12.00	20.00
☐	8950, Working Man Blues	11.00	19.00
☐	**Champion 50001,** Stop That Thing	17.00	29.00
☐	50048, Drop Down Mama	16.00	28.00
☐	50068, Someday Baby Blues	15.00	26.00
☐	**Decca 7279,** Someday Baby Blues	11.00	18.00
☐	7289, Married Woman Blues	10.00	17.00
☐	7325, Down South Blues	11.00	18.00
☐	7342, Vernita Blues	11.00	18.00
☐	7354, Hobo Jungle Blues	10.00	17.00
☐	7365, Need More Blues	9.00	16.00
☐	7414, Government Money	9.00	16.00
☐	7442, Floating Bridge	10.00	17.00
☐	7473, Brownsville Blues	9.00	16.00
☐	7491, Liquor Store Blues	8.00	14.00
☐	7516, Easin' Back to Tennessee	8.00	14.00
☐	7571, Everybody Oughta Make a Change	9.00	16.00
☐	7766, Drop Down	8.00	14.00
☐	7814, Jailhouse Blues	8.00	14.00
☐	**Victor 23318,** Expressman Blues	8.00	14.00
☐	23397, Stack O'Dollars	70.00	115.00
☐	38549, Diving Duck Blues	65.00	105.00
☐	38582, Black Mattie Blues	70.00	115.00
☐	38595, T-Bone Steak Blues	60.00	100.00
☐	38628, Poor John Blues	60.00	100.00

EZELL, WILL

☐	**Paramount 12688,** Mixed Up Rag	55.00	85.00
☐	12729, Crawlin' Spider Blues	52.00	80.00
☐	12753, Barrel House Woman	50.00	78.00
☐	12773, Bucket of Blood	55.00	80.00
☐	12914, Freakish Mistreater Blues	55.00	80.00

FOSTER, JIM

☐	**Champion 15301,** Riverside Blues	45.00	70.00
☐	15320, The Jail House Blues	42.00	67.00
☐	15397, Dark Cloudy Blues	40.00	63.00

		Price Range	
☐	**15453,** It Won't Be Long	**38.00**	**62.00**
☐	**15472,** Hesitation Blues	**38.00**	**62.00**

GEORGIA MELODIANS
☐	**Edison 51336,** Wop Blues	**15.00**	**24.00**
☐	**51338,** Wait'll You See My Gal	**10.00**	**17.00**
☐	**51346,** Savannah	**11.00**	**18.00**
☐	**51347,** Tea Pot Dome Blues	**10.00**	**17.00**
☐	**51359,** How You Gonna Keep Kool?	**9.00**	**16.00**
☐	**51378,** Why Did You Do It?	**9.00**	**16.00**
☐	**51412,** San	**9.00**	**16.00**
☐	**51419,** Everybody Loves My Baby	**9.00**	**16.00**
☐	**51420,** Do Wacka Doo	**8.00**	**14.00**
☐	**51425,** I'm Satisfied Beside That Sweetie O'Mine	**9.00**	**16.00**
☐	**51437,** I'm Bound for Tennessee	**9.00**	**16.00**
☐	**51588,** Give Us the Charleston	**12.00**	**20.00**
☐	**51598,** She's Drivin' Me Wild	**12.00**	**20.00**
☐	**51678,** Charleston Ball	**12.00**	**20.00**
☐	**51730,** Rhythm of the Day	**12.00**	**20.00**

GEORGIA TOM
☐	**Champion 16237,** Been Mistreated Blues ..	**55.00**	**80.00**
☐	**16360,** Don't Leave Me Blues	**45.00**	**72.00**
☐	**Decca 7362,** Levee Bound Blues	**6.00**	**9.00**
☐	**Gennett 6919,** My Texas Blues	**42.00**	**75.00**
☐	**6933,** Suicide Blues	**40.00**	**70.00**
☐	**7008,** Pig Meat Blues	**42.00**	**75.00**
☐	**7041,** Rollin' Mill Stomp	**43.00**	**75.00**
☐	**7130,** Six Shooter Blues	**41.00**	**70.00**
☐	**Supertone 9506,** My Texas Blues	**41.00**	**70.00**
☐	**9507,** Pig Meat Blues	**44.00**	**75.00**
☐	**9508,** Eagle Ridin' Papa	**41.00**	**70.00**
☐	**9512,** Rollin' Mill Stomp	**41.00**	**70.00**
☐	**Vocalion 1216,** Grievin' Me Blues	**20.00**	**31.00**
☐	**1246,** Lonesome Man Blues	**18.00**	**30.00**
☐	**1282,** If You Want Me to Love You	**18.00**	**30.00**
☐	**1685,** Don't Leave Me Here	**13.00**	**22.00**

GIBSON, CLIFFORD
☐	**Paramount 12866,** Tired of Being Mistreated	**55.00**	**80.00**
☐	**12923,** Stop Your Rambling	**50.00**	**76.00**
☐	**QRS 7079,** Tired of Being Mistreated	**100.00**	**150.00**

Price Range

☐ **7082**, No No Blues	110.00	170.00
☐ **7083**, Stop Your Rambling	90.00	140.00
☐ **7087**, Whiskey Moan Blues	100.00	150.00
☐ **7090**, Morgan Street Blues	100.00	150.00
☐ **Victor 23255**, Old Time Rider	45.00	75.00
☐ **38562**, Ice and Snow Blues	41.00	70.00
☐ **38572**, Don't Put That Thing On Me	40.00	65.00
☐ **38577**, Levee Camp Moan	34.00	62.00
☐ **38290**, Bad Luck Dice	40.00	65.00
☐ **38612**, Society Blues	40.00	65.00

GLINN, LILLIAN

☐ **Columbia 14275-D**, Doggin' Me Blues	10.00	17.00
☐ **14300-D**, Come Home Daddy	9.00	16.00
☐ **14315-D**, Shake It Down	9.00	16.00
☐ **14360-D**, Lost Letter Blues	9.00	16.00
☐ **14421-D**, Atlanta Blues	15.00	27.00
☐ **14433-D**, Black Man Blues	14.00	25.00
☐ **14493-D**, Don't Leave Me Daddy	14.00	25.00
☐ **14559-D**, I Love That Thing	13.00	23.00
☐ **14617-D**, Cannon Ball Blues	14.00	25.00

GORDON, ROSCOE

☐ **Duke 109**, Too Many Women	6.00	9.00
☐ **Flip 227**, Weeping Blues	12.00	20.00
☐ **RPM 322**, Roscoe's Boogie	6.00	9.00
☐ **336**, Dime a Dozen	6.00	9.00
☐ **350**, No More Doggin'	6.00	9.00
☐ **365**, Two Kinds of Women	6.00	9.00
☐ **Sun 227**, Weeping Blues	15.00	22.00

GRIFFIN, TOMMY

☐ **Bluebird 6696**, I'm Gonna Try That Meat	10.00	17.00
☐ **6734**, Young Heifer Blues	9.00	15.00
☐ **6756**, Dream Book Blues	9.00	15.00
☐ **6793**, On My Way Blues	9.00	15.00
☐ **6834**, Dying Sinner Blues—Part 2	10.00	17.00
☐ **Vocalion 1479**, Bell Tolling Blues	23.00	37.00
☐ **1507**, Mistreatment Blues	21.00	34.00

GROSS, HELEN

☐ **Ajaz 17042**, I Wanna Jazz Some More	36.00	52.00
☐ **17046**, Rockin' Chair Blues	34.00	50.00
☐ **17049**, What'll I Do?	33.00	50.00

Price Range

☐	**17051,** My Man Ain't Yo' Man	32.00	49.00
☐	**17060,** Ticket Agent, Ease Your Window Down	31.00	47.00
☐	**17062,** Chicago Monkey Man Blues	32.00	48.00
☐	**17071,** Neglected Blues	33.00	49.00
☐	**17077,** If You Can't Ride Slow and Easy	32.00	48.00
☐	**17082,** Conjure Man Blues	33.00	49.00
☐	**17086,** Bitter Feelin' Blues	31.00	47.00
☐	**17090,** Last Journey Blues	30.00	46.00
☐	**17133,** Workin' Woman's Blues	33.00	49.00

HANDY, W. C.

☐	**Banner 1036,** St. Louis Blues	17.00	27.00
☐	**1053,** She's a Mean Job	16.00	25.00
☐	**Black Swan 2053,** Yellow Dog Blues	25.00	40.00
☐	**2054,** Muscle Shoals Blues	27.00	42.00
☐	**Lyratone 4211,** Beale Street Blues	21.00	34.00
☐	**4212,** Yellow Dog Blues	20.00	32.00
☐	**Paramount 20098,** St. Louis Blues	15.00	22.00
☐	**20012,** She's a Mean Job	14.00	21.00

HARLEM FOOTWARMERS

☐	**Columbia 14670-D,** Sweet Chariot	29.00	45.00
☐	**Okeh 8720,** Jungle Jamboree	28.00	43.00
☐	**8746,** Syncopated Shuffle	24.00	40.00
☐	**8760,** Lazy Duke	28.00	43.00
☐	**8836,** Big House Blues	29.00	45.00
☐	**8869,** Old Man Blues	27.00	42.00

HARRIS, WILLIAM

☐	**Gennett 6306,** I'm Leavin' Town	36.00	55.00
☐	**6661,** Bull Frog Blues	35.00	53.00
☐	**6677,** Kitchen Range Blues	34.00	50.00
☐	**6693,** Leavin' Here Blues	36.00	52.00
☐	**6707,** Kansas City Blues	36.00	52.00
☐	**6737,** I'm a Roamin' Gambler	33.00	51.00
☐	**6752,** Electric Chair Blues	35.00	52.00
☐	**6904,** Nothin' Right Blues	32.00	50.00

HAYES, CLIFFORD

☐	**Victor 20955,** Blue Guitar Stomp	12.00	20.00
☐	**21489,** Bare-Foot Stomp	26.00	41.00
☐	**21583,** Blue Harmony	13.00	21.00

		Price Range	
☐	**23346,** Tenor Guitar Fiend	37.00	52.00
☐	**23407,** Automobile Blues	55.00	90.00
☐	**38011,** Clef Club Stomp	26.00	41.00
☐	**38022,** Ool Chord's Stomp	25.00	39.00
☐	**38514,** Frog Hop	33.00	53.00
☐	**38557,** Hey! Am I Blue	40.00	60.00

HENDERSON, FLETCHER

☐	**Ajax 17016,** Bull Blues	24.00	37.00
☐	**17017,** Chattanooga	23.00	35.00
☐	**17022,** Mistreatin' Daddy	22.00	34.00
☐	**17023,** House Rent Ball	23.00	35.00
☐	**17029,** Just Blues	22.00	34.00
☐	**17030,** I'm Crazy Over You	23.00	35.00
☐	**17109,** Everybody Loves My Baby	50.00	70.00
☐	**17113,** Alabama Bound	27.00	45.00
☐	**17114,** I'll See You in My Dreams	27.00	44.00
☐	**17123,** Why Couldn't It Be Poor Little Me?	25.00	41.00
☐	**Apex 8300,** Everybody Loves My Baby	43.00	63.00
☐	**8309,** Alabama Bound	12.00	22.00
☐	**8311,** I'll See You in My Dreams	12.00	22.00
☐	**8316,** Why Couldn't It Be Poor Little Me?	12.00	22.00
☐	**8419,** Sleepy Time Gal	12.00	22.00
☐	**Black Swan 2022,** My Oriental Rose	13.00	21.00
☐	**2026,** The Unknown Blues	22.00	34.00
☐	**2076,** Love Days	14.00	25.00
☐	**2079,** Blue	14.00	25.00
☐	**10072,** Love Days	14.00	25.00
☐	**10075,** Blue	13.00	21.00
☐	**10083,** Dumbell	12.00	19.00
☐	**Bluebird 5682,** Hocus Pocus	9.00	16.00
☐	**Brunswick 2592,** War Horse Mama	6.00	9.00
☐	**3460,** Stockholm Stomp	11.00	19.00
☐	**3521,** Sensation	11.00	19.00
☐	**4119,** Hop Off	11.00	19.00
☐	**Cameo 9033,** Old Black Joe's Blues	12.00	20.00
☐	**9174,** Freeze and Melt	11.00	17.00
☐	**9175,** Raisin' the Roof	10.00	16.00
☐	**Columbia 1543-D,** King Porter Stomp	8.00	13.00
☐	**1913-D,** Blazin'	7.00	12.00
☐	**126-D,** Somebody Stole My Gal	9.00	16.00
☐	**164-D,** Muscle Shoals Blues	8.00	15.00

Price Range

☐	**202-D,** That's Georgia	8.00	15.00
☐	**209-D,** He's the Hottest Man in Town	7.00	13.00
☐	**228-D,** Manda	13.00	21.00
☐	**249-D,** The Meanest Kind of Blues	12.00	20.00
☐	**292-D,** Play Me Slow	11.00	18.00
☐	**383-D,** Money Blues	14.00	23.00
☐	**395-D,** Sugar Foot Stomp	13.00	23.00
☐	**509-D,** Carolina Stomp	13.00	23.00
☐	**532-D,** Pensacola	14.00	25.00
☐	**654-D,** The Stampede	13.00	23.00
☐	**817-D,** The Chant	14.00	25.00
☐	**854-D,** Sweet Thing	12.00	21.00
☐	**970-D,** Rocky Mountain Blues	14.00	25.00
☐	**1059-D,** Whiteman Stomp	15.00	26.00
☐	**1543-D,** King Porter Stomp	11.00	18.00
☐	**1913-D,** Blazin'	13.00	22.00
☐	**2329-D,** Somebody Loves Me	13.00	22.00
☐	**2353-D,** Keep a Song In Your Soul	14.00	23.00
☐	**2414-D,** Sweet and Hot	13.00	22.00
☐	**2513-D,** Clarinet Marmalade	13.00	22.00
☐	**2559-D,** Sugar	14.00	23.00
☐	**2565-D,** Singin' the Blues	14.00	23.00
☐	**2586-D,** My Gal Sal	13.00	22.00
☐	**2615-D,** Business in F	14.00	23.00
☐	**2732-D,** Honeysuckle Rose	14.00	23.00
☐	**2825-D,** Nagasaki	15.00	25.00
☐	**A-3995,** Dicty Blues	9.00	16.00
☐	**14392-D,** Easy Money	21.00	32.00
☐	**2329-D,** Somebody Loves Me	14.00	23.00
☐	**2352-D,** Keep a Song In Your Soul	13.00	22.00
☐	**2414-D,** Sweet and Hot	14.00	25.00
☐	**2513-D,** Clarinet Marmalade	13.00	22.00
☐	**2559-D,** Sugar	14.00	25.00
☐	**2586-D,** My Gal Sal	14.00	25.00
☐	**2615-D,** Business in F	13.00	21.00
☐	**2732-D,** Honeysuckle Rose	14.00	25.00
☐	**2825-D,** Nagasaki	17.00	30.00
☐	**14392-D,** Easy Money	14.00	23.00
☐	**Crown 3093,** After You've Gone	18.00	28.00
☐	**3107,** Tiger Rag	17.00	27.00
☐	**Edison 51276,** Shake Your Feet	10.00	12.00
☐	**51277,** Linger Awhile	10.00	12.00

	Price Range	
☐ **Emerson 10714,** Steppin' Out	12.00	20.00
☐ **10744,** Ghost of the Blues	13.00	22.00
☐ **Gennett 3285,** When Spring Comes Peeping Through	19.00	29.00
☐ **3286,** Honeybunch	17.00	28.00
☐ **Lincoln 3062,** Old Black Joe's Blues	12.00	17.00
☐ **3201,** Freeze and Melt	15.00	23.00
☐ **3202,** Raisin' the Roof	14.00	22.00
☐ **Paramount 12143,** Chime Blues	20.00	30.00
☐ **12486,** Off to Buffalo	28.00	40.00
☐ **20367,** Prince of Wails	37.00	60.00
☐ **Romeo 837,** Old Black Joe's Blues	12.00	21.00
☐ **976,** Freeze and Melt	13.00	22.00
☐ **977,** Raisin' the Roof	12.00	21.00
☐ **Victor 22775,** Malinda's Wedding Day	9.00	16.00
☐ **22786,** Oh, It Looks Like Rain	9.00	16.00
☐ **22955,** Strangers	9.00	16.00
☐ **24008,** Poor Old Joe	9.00	16.00
☐ **24699,** Harlem Madness	9.00	16.00
☐ **Vocalion 14636,** Gulf Coast Blues	10.00	16.00
☐ **14654,** Dicty Blues	11.00	18.00
☐ **14691,** Just Hot	10.00	16.00
☐ **14726,** Charleston Crazy	10.00	16.00
☐ **14740,** Potomac River Blues	9.00	13.00
☐ **14759,** Lots O'Mama	10.00	16.00
☐ **14788,** Chicago Blues	11.00	17.00
☐ **14828,** Strutter's Drag	11.00	17.00
☐ **14838,** Do That Thing	11.00	17.00
☐ **14880,** A New Kind of Man	11.00	17.00
☐ **14892,** Forsaken Blues	9.00	15.00
☐ **14926,** Copenhagen	16.00	27.00
☐ **14935,** Shanghai Shuffle	16.00	27.00
☐ **15030,** Memphis Bound	36.00	60.00

HOKUM BOYS

☐ **Broadway 5060,** It's All Worn Out	33.00	50.00
☐ **5078,** Cut That Out	33.00	50.00
☐ **Champion 16081,** Pig Meat Strut	70.00	110.00
☐ **16237,** Hip Shakin' Strut	60.00	95.00
☐ **16360,** Hokum Stomp	60.00	95.00
☐ **Okeh 8747,** Gin Mill Blues	27.00	45.00
☐ **8788,** That's My Business	26.00	43.00

Price Range

☐ **Paramount 12714,** Selling That Stuff	25.00	42.00
☐ **12746,** Pat-A-Foot Blues	24.00	41.00
☐ **12777,** Better Cut That Out	30.00	47.00
☐ **12778,** Selling That Stuff	28.00	46.00
☐ **12811,** Hokum Blues	30.00	47.00
☐ **12821,** Ain't Goin' That Way	26.00	43.00
☐ **12858,** Went To His Head	26.00	43.00
☐ **12882,** I Was Afraid of That	27.00	45.00
☐ **12897,** Let Me Have It	26.00	43.00
☐ **12919,** Gambler's Blues—No. 2	26.00	43.00
☐ **12935,** The Folks Down Stairs	27.00	45.00

HOWELL, PEG LEG

☐ **Columbia 14194-D,** Coal Man Blues	18.00	30.00
☐ **14210-D,** New Jelly Roll Blues	17.00	27.00
☐ **14238-D,** Sadie Lee Blues	16.00	26.00
☐ **14270-D,** Hobo Blues	17.00	27.00
☐ **14298-D,** Peg Leg Stomp	16.00	26.00
☐ **14320-D,** Rock and Gravel Blues	15.00	25.00
☐ **14356-D,** Fairy Blues	16.00	27.00
☐ **14426-D,** Monkey Man Blues	16.00	27.00
☐ **14438-D,** Rolling Mill Blues	15.00	25.00
☐ **14456-D,** Turtle Dove Blues	15.00	25.00
☐ **14473-D,** Skin Game Blues	18.00	30.00

HUNTER, ALBERTA

☐ **Black Swan 2008,** Bring Back the Joys	37.00	60.00
☐ **2019,** Someday Sweetheart	30.00	50.00
☐ **Columbia 14450-D,** My Particular Man	17.00	27.00
☐ **Okeh 8268,** Your Jelly Roll Is Good	19.00	30.00
☐ **8278,** Everybody Does It Now	14.00	23.00
☐ **8294,** I'm Hard to Satisfy	14.00	23.00
☐ **8315,** Empty Cellar Blues	14.00	23.00
☐ **8365,** You For Me, Me For You	12.00	18.00
☐ **8383,** Everybody Mess Around	16.00	23.00
☐ **8393,** Wasn't It Nice?	14.00	24.00
☐ **8409,** Don't Forget to Mess Around	12.00	18.00
☐ **Paramount 12001,** Daddy Blues	14.00	22.00
☐ **12005,** Down Hearted Blues	15.00	25.00
☐ **12006,** Jazzin' Baby Blues	15.00	25.00
☐ **12008,** You Can't Have It All	14.00	24.00
☐ **12010,** After All These Years	14.00	24.00
☐ **12012,** Someday Sweetheart	12.00	18.00

		Price Range	
☐	**12014,** Bring Back the Joys	**14.00**	**24.00**
☐	**12016,** 'Tain't Nobody's Bizness	**13.00**	**19.00**
☐	**12017,** Chirping the Blues	**14.00**	**24.00**
☐	**12018,** Bring It With You When You Come	**19.00**	**30.00**
☐	**12019,** Loveless Love	**18.00**	**28.00**
☐	**12021,** Bleeding Hearted Blues	**20.00**	**30.00**
☐	**12036,** Michigan Water Blues	**20.00**	**32.00**
☐	**12043,** Mistreated Blues	**20.00**	**30.00**
☐	**12049,** Stingaree Blues	**20.00**	**30.00**
☐	**12065,** Experience Blues	**27.00**	**40.00**
☐	**12093,** Old-Fashioned Love	**13.00**	**22.00**
☐	**Victor 20497,** I'll Forgive You 'Cause I Love You	**12.00**	**21.00**
☐	**20771,** Sugar	**14.00**	**25.00**
☐	**21539,** I'm Going to See My Ma	**27.00**	**40.00**

JACKSON, CHARLIE

☐	**Okeh 8954,** Skoodle-Um-Skoo	**15.00**	**23.00**
☐	**8957,** If I Got What You Want	**16.00**	**25.00**
☐	**Paramount 12219,** Papa's Lawdy Lawdy Blues	**12.00**	**20.00**
☐	**12236,** Salty Dog Blues	**13.00**	**21.00**
☐	**12259,** The Cat's Got the Measles	**12.00**	**20.00**
☐	**12264,** Coffee Pot Blues	**12.00**	**20.00**
☐	**12281,** Shake That Thing	**12.00**	**20.00**
☐	**12289,** Drop That Sack	**12.00**	**20.00**
☐	**12305,** Mama, Don't You Think I Know?	**12.00**	**20.00**
☐	**12320,** Maxwell Street Blues	**12.00**	**20.00**
☐	**12335,** Texas Blues	**10.00**	**16.00**
☐	**12348,** Jackson's Blues	**10.00**	**17.00**
☐	**12358,** Butter and Egg Man Blues	**9.00**	**16.00**
☐	**12366,** The Judge Cliff Davis Blues	**11.00**	**18.00**
☐	**12375,** Up the Way Bound	**11.00**	**18.00**
☐	**12383,** Bad Luck Woman Blues	**10.00**	**17.00**
☐	**12422,** Fat Mouth Blues	**11.00**	**18.00**
☐	**12461,** Coal Man Blues	**13.00**	**22.00**
☐	**12501,** Skoodle-Um-Skoo	**13.00**	**22.00**
☐	**12574,** Bright Eyes	**14.00**	**23.00**
☐	**12602,** Long Gone Lost John	**13.00**	**21.00**
☐	**12660,** Ash Tray Blues	**14.00**	**23.00**
☐	**12700,** Lexington Kentucky Blues	**16.00**	**27.00**

Price Range

☐	**12721,** Corn Liquor Blues	17.00	28.00
☐	**12736,** Don't Break Down On Me	17.00	28.00
☐	**12765,** We Can't Buy It No More	20.00	30.00
☐	**12797,** Tailor Made Lover	17.00	29.00
☐	**12853,** Forgotten Blues	17.00	29.00
☐	**12905,** I'll Be Gone Babe	16.00	25.00
☐	**12911,** Papa Charlie and Blind Blake Talk About It	36.00	55.00
☐	**12956,** Self Experience	24.00	38.00

JACKSON, JIM

☐	**Victor 21268,** Bootlegging Blues	18.00	30.00
☐	**21387,** Old Dog Blue	17.00	27.00
☐	**21671,** I'm Gonna Move to Louisiana	18.00	30.00
☐	**38505,** What a Time	16.00	25.00
☐	**38517,** Traveling Man	17.00	27.00
☐	**38525,** Going 'Round the Mountain	17.00	27.00
☐	**Vocalion 1145,** Mobile Central Blues	18.00	29.00
☐	**1146,** He's in the Jailhouse Now	17.00	26.00
☐	**1164,** I'm a Bad Bad Man	17.00	26.00
☐	**1284,** Hey Mama, It's Nice Like That	18.00	29.00
☐	**1295,** Foot Achin' Blues	17.00	26.00
☐	**1413,** Ain't You Sorry Mama?	16.00	25.00
☐	**1428,** Jim Jackson's Jamboree	16.00	24.00
☐	**1477,** Hesitation Blues	15.00	23.00

JAMES, SKIP

☐	**Paramount 13065,** Cherry Ball Blues	120.00	185.00
☐	**13066,** 22-20 Blues	130.00	210.00
☐	**13072,** Illinois Blues	120.00	185.00
☐	**13085,** How Long 'Buck'	110.00	175.00
☐	**13088,** Devil Got My Woman	120.00	185.00
☐	**13098,** Special Rider Blues	110.00	175.00
☐	**13106,** Hard Luck Child	110.00	175.00
☐	**13108,** Be Ready When He Comes	105.00	170.00
☐	**13111,** Drunken Spree	120.00	185.00

JEFFERSON, BLIND LEMON

☐	**Paramount 12347,** Booster Blues	27.00	42.00
☐	**12354,** Got the Blues	26.00	40.00
☐	**12367,** Black Horse Blues	27.00	41.00
☐	**12373,** Jack O'Diamond Blues	26.00	40.00
☐	**12394,** Beggin' Back	25.00	38.00

		Price Range	
☐	12407, Stockin' Feet Blues	25.00	38.00
☐	12425, Wartime Blues	25.00	38.00
☐	12443, Bad Luck Blues	24.00	37.00
☐	12454, Rabbit Foot Blues	24.00	37.00
☐	12493, Weary Dog Blues	34.00	50.00
☐	12510, Right of Way Blues	33.00	48.00
☐	12541, Rambler Blues	30.00	47.00
☐	12551, Chinch Bug Blues	31.00	48.00
☐	12578, Gone Dead on You Blues	32.00	50.00
☐	12585, He Arose from the Dead	34.00	52.00
☐	12593, Lonesome House Blues	34.00	52.00
☐	12608, 'Lectric Chair Blues	35.00	54.00
☐	12622, Prison Cell Blues	35.00	54.00
☐	12631, Mean Jumper Blues	33.00	52.00
☐	12639, Lemon's Cannon Ball Moan	32.00	50.00
☐	12650, Piney Woods Mama Blues	31.00	49.00
☐	12666, Blind Lemon's Penitentiary Blues	45.00	70.00
☐	12679, Lock Step Blues	31.00	52.00
☐	12685, How Long How Long	31.00	52.00
☐	12712, Maltese Cat Blues	31.00	52.00
☐	12728, Competition Bed Blues	32.00	55.00
☐	12739, Eagle Eyed Mama	31.00	48.00
☐	12756, Tin Cup Blues	32.00	55.00
☐	12771, Oil Well Blues	31.00	48.00
☐	12801, Peach Orchard Mama	31.00	48.00
☐	12852, Long Distance Moan	30.00	47.00
☐	12872, Bed Springs Blues	32.00	55.00
☐	12880, Pneumonia Blues	31.00	48.00
☐	12921, Cat Man Blues	31.00	48.00
☐	12933, The Cheaters Spell	31.00	48.00
☐	12946, Empty House Blues	30.00	47.00

JACKSON, BIG BILL

		Price Range	
☐	Champion 16081, Saturday Night Rub	50.00	75.00
☐	16172, That Won't Do	48.00	72.00
☐	16327, The Baker's Blues	47.00	70.00
☐	16396, Worried in Mind Blues	46.00	70.00
☐	16426, Mr. Conductor Man	47.00	70.00
☐	50060, Big Bill Blues	13.00	22.00
☐	50069, Too Too Train Blues	13.00	22.00

JOHNSON, LONNIE

		Price Range	
☐	Columbia 14667-D, Home Wreckers Blues	27.00	40.00

Price Range

☐	**14674-D,** Unselfish Love	**26.00**	**37.00**
☐	**Okeh 8253,** Mr. Johnson's Blues	**16.00**	**26.00**
☐	**8282,** Love Story Blues	**14.00**	**23.00**
☐	**8291,** Bed of Sand	**13.00**	**23.00**
☐	**8340,** A Good Happy Home	**13.00**	**23.00**
☐	**8358,** Good Old Wagon	**15.00**	**23.00**
☐	**8376,** Baby Please Tell Me	**15.00**	**23.00**
☐	**8391,** Oh! Doctor, The Blues	**13.00**	**23.00**
☐	**8417,** Johnson Trio Stomp	**15.00**	**23.00**
☐	**8435,** Ball and Chain Blues	**13.00**	**23.00**
☐	**8451,** You Drove a Good Man Away	**12.00**	**21.00**
☐	**8466,** South Bound Water	**14.00**	**23.00**
☐	**8484,** Treat 'em Right	**14.00**	**23.00**
☐	**8505,** Fickle Mamma Blues	**14.00**	**23.00**
☐	**8512,** St. Louis Cyclone Blues	**14.00**	**23.00**
☐	**8524,** Tin Can Alley Blues	**14.00**	**23.00**
☐	**8537,** Kansas City Blues	**13.00**	**23.00**
☐	**8557,** Life Saver Blues	**13.00**	**23.00**
☐	**8558,** Playing With the Strings	**13.00**	**23.00**
☐	**8574,** Crowing Rooster Blues	**12.00**	**21.00**
☐	**8575,** Blues in G	**13.00**	**23.00**
☐	**8586,** Bed Bug Blues No. 2	**13.00**	**22.00**
☐	**8601,** Wrong Woman Blues	**14.00**	**23.00**
☐	**8618,** Broken Levee Blues	**13.00**	**22.00**
☐	**8635,** Careless Love	**13.00**	**22.00**
☐	**8664,** It Feels So Good—Parts 1 and 2 ..	**9.00**	**14.00**
☐	**8691,** Death is on Your Track	**13.00**	**22.00**
☐	**8695,** Bull Frog Moan	**12.00**	**20.00**
☐	**8697,** It Feels So Good—Parts 3 and 4 ..	**9.00**	**14.00**
☐	**8709,** Mr. Johnson's Blues—No. 2	**13.00**	**22.00**
☐	**8754,** Sundown Blues	**13.00**	**22.00**
☐	**8762,** Wipe It Off	**20.00**	**34.00**
☐	**8768,** She's Making Whoopee in Hell Tonight	**22.00**	**35.00**
☐	**8775,** The Dirty Dozen	**20.00**	**32.00**
☐	**8786,** Headed for Southland	**18.00**	**31.00**
☐	**8796,** Don't Drive Me From Your Door ...	**16.00**	**27.00**
☐	**8802,** The Bull Frog and the Toad	**17.00**	**30.00**
☐	**8812,** Keep it to Yourself	**15.00**	**26.00**
☐	**8822,** Deep Sea Blues	**15.00**	**26.00**
☐	**8831,** No More Troubles Now	**17.00**	**27.00**
☐	**8846,** Let All Married Women Alone	**17.00**	**27.00**

Price Range

☐ **8875,** Just a Roaming Man	18.00	28.00
☐ **8886,** I Just Can't Stand These Blues	18.00	28.00
☐ **8898,** Beautiful But Dumb	18.00	28.00
☐ **8909,** I Have To Do My Time	16.00	27.00
☐ **8916,** The Best Jockey in Town	16.00	27.00
☐ **8926,** Sleepy Water Blues	18.00	28.00
☐ **8937,** Sam, You're Just a Rat	16.00	27.00
☐ **8946,** Racketeers Blues	17.00	28.00
☐ **40695,** Nile of Genago	9.00	13.00
☐ **Paradise 110,** Tomorrow Night	15.00	26.00
☐ **123,** Lonesome Day Blues	15.00	26.00

JOHNSON, MARGARET

☐ **Okeh 8107,** E Flat Blues	10.00	15.00
☐ **8162,** Absent Minded Blues	10.00	15.00
☐ **8185,** Changeable Daddy of Mine	27.00	41.00
☐ **8193,** Who'll Chop Your Suey When I'm Gone.	15.00	24.00
☐ **8220,** Nobody's Blues But Mine	11.00	18.00
☐ **8230,** I'm a Good-Hearted Mama	17.00	26.00
☐ **8405,** Mama, Papa Don't Wanna Come Back Home	9.00	16.00
☐ **8506,** Stinging Bee Blues	14.00	23.00
☐ **Victor 20178,** My Man's Done Me Dirty	9.00	16.00
☐ **20333,** Graysom Street Blues	18.00	30.00
☐ **20982,** Dead Drunk Blues	17.00	27.00

JOHNSON, STUMP

☐ **Bluebird 5159,** Don't Give My Lard Away . .	13.00	22.00
☐ **5247,** Money Johnson	12.00	20.00
☐ **Paramount 12862,** Kind Babe Blues	45.00	70.00
☐ **12906,** Soaking Wet Blues	43.00	67.00
☐ **12938,** You Buzzard You	41.00	65.00
☐ **Victor 23327,** Barrel of Whiskey Blues	43.00	67.00

BLIND WILLIE JOHNSON

☐ **Columbia 14303-D,** Nobody's Fault But Mine	15.00	22.00
☐ **14343-D,** Mother's Children Have a Hard Time	13.00	21.00
☐ **14391-D,** Jesus Is Coming Soon	15.00	22.00
☐ **14490-D,** Let Your Light Shine On	14.00	21.00
☐ **14520-D,** God Moves on the Water	14.00	21.00
☐ **14530-D,** John the Revelator	42.00	65.00

Price Range

☐	**14537-D,** The Rain Don't Fall on Me	15.00	21.00
☐	**14545-D,** When the War Was On	15.00	23.00
☐	**14556-D,** Can't Nobody Hide From God ..	15.00	23.00
☐	**14582-D,** The Soul of a Man	14.00	21.00
☐	**14597-D,** Go With Me to That Land	14.00	21.00
☐	**14624-D,** Take Your Stand	14.00	21.00

JONES, ALBERTA

☐	**Buddy 8024,** Sud Bustin' Blues	29.00	42.00
☐	**8025,** Home Alone Blues	27.00	40.00
☐	**8033,** It Must Be Hard	58.00	90.00
☐	**8034,** Take Your Fingers Off It	62.00	100.00
☐	**Gennett 3306,** Take Your Fingers Off It ...	12.00	20.00
☐	**3402,** Lucky Number Blues	33.00	50.00
☐	**6424,** Dying Blues	29.00	43.00
☐	**6439,** Shake a Little Bit	27.00	40.00
☐	**6535,** My Slow and Easy Man	25.00	38.00
☐	**6642,** Wild Geese Blues	37.00	59.00
☐	**7252,** On Revival Day	27.00	39.00
☐	**7274,** I Lost My Man	28.00	41.00
☐	**Silvertone 4052,** Home Alone Blues	12.00	20.00
☐	**5025,** Lucky Number Blues	27.00	41.00
☐	**Supertone 9284,** Dying Blues	23.00	34.00

JUNGLE BAND

☐	**Brunswick 3956,** Tiger Rag	9.00	15.00
☐	**4238,** Tiger Rag	12.00	20.00
☐	**4309,** Paducah	11.00	19.00
☐	**4345,** Doin' the Voom Voom	11.00	19.00
☐	**4450,** Dog Bottom	13.00	21.00
☐	**4492,** Jungle Jamboree	11.00	19.00
☐	**4760,** Sweet Mama	12.00	20.00
☐	**4776,** Maori	11.00	19.00
☐	**4783,** Double Check Stomp	11.00	19.00
☐	**4889,** Wall Street Wall	9.00	16.00
☐	**4936,** St. Louis Blues	12.00	20.00
☐	**4952,** Runnin' Wild	12.00	20.00
☐	**6038,** Rockin' in Rhythm	10.00	17.00
☐	**6732,** Rockin' Chair	8.00	13.00

KANSAS JOE

☐	**Bluebird 6260,** Something Gonna Happen to You	10.00	16.00
☐	**Columbia 14439-D,** When the Levee Breaks	18.00	29.00

		Price Range	
☐	**14542-D,** I Want That	17.00	26.00
☐	**Vocalion 1500,** What Fault You Find of Me?	16.00	25.00
☐	**1523,** Can I Do It For You?	17.00	26.00
☐	**1535,** Cherry Ball Blues	16.00	25.00
☐	**1550,** North Memphis Blues	15.00	24.00
☐	**1570,** Botherin' That Thing	15.00	24.00
☐	**1612,** Pile Drivin' Blues	16.00	25.00
☐	**1631,** I Called Up This Morning	16.00	25.00
☐	**1643,** Preachers Blues	15.00	24.00
☐	**1660,** Pickin' the Blues	22.00	38.00
☐	**1668,** My Wash Woman's Gone	15.00	24.00
☐	**1686,** Joliet Bound	14.00	23.00
☐	**1688,** You Stole My Cake	15.00	25.00
☐	**1705,** Dresser Drawer Blues	21.00	36.00

KELLY, WILLIE

☐	**Victor 23259,** Kelly's Special	50.00	85.00
☐	**23263,** Side Door Blues	48.00	80.00
☐	**23270,** Big Time Woman	47.00	75.00
☐	**23299,** Nasty But It's Clean	47.00	75.00
☐	**23320,** Hard Luck Man Blues	45.00	70.00
☐	**23416,** Sad and Lonely Day	45.00	70.00
☐	**38619,** 32-20 Blues	40.00	60.00

KIRK, ANDY

☐	**Brunswick 4694,** Blue Clarinet Stomp	18.00	30.00
☐	**4803,** I Lost My Gal From Memphis	17.00	28.00
☐	**4863,** Once or Twice	18.00	30.00
☐	**4878,** Snag It	19.00	32.00
☐	**4893,** Froggy Bottom	18.00	30.00
☐	**4981,** Honey, Just For You	17.00	28.00

LENOIR, J. B.

☐	**Chess 1449,** My Baby Told Me	11.00	18.00
☐	**1463,** Deep in Debt Blues	10.00	16.00
☐	**J.O.B. 112,** Let's Roll	13.00	21.00
☐	**1008,** The Mountain	7.00	12.00
☐	**1012,** The Mojo	6.00	10.00
☐	**1016,** I'll Die Trying	7.00	12.00
☐	**Parrot 802,** Eisenhower Blues/I'm in Korea	9.00	15.00
☐	**802,** Tax Paying Blues/I'm in Korea	9.00	15.00
☐	**809,** Mama Talk to Your Daughter	6.00	9.00
☐	**814,** What Have I Done	7.00	10.00

Price Range

LOUISIANA RHYTHM KINGS:

☐ **Vocalion 15657,** Nobody's Sweetheart		18.00	27.00
☐ **15710,** I Can't Give You Anything But Love		23.00	33.00
☐ **15716,** Dusky Stevedore		20.00	30.00
☐ **15729,** Skinner's Sock		18.00	27.00
☐ **15779,** Futuristic Rhythm		22.00	32.00
☐ **15784,** That's a Plenty		23.00	34.00
☐ **15810,** I'm Walking Through Clover		33.00	49.00
☐ **15815,** Last Cent		35.00	52.00
☐ **15828,** Ballin' the Jack		35.00	52.00
☐ **15841,** Little by Little		31.00	47.00

LOVIN' SAM

☐ **Bluebird 7514, 7629, 7916**		7.00	12.00
☐ **Brunswick 7073,** She's Givin' It Away		17.00	28.00
☐ **7075,** What You Gonna Do?		16.00	27.00
☐ **7090,** Get Your Mind On It		16.00	27.00
☐ **7098,** You Rascal You		17.00	29.00
☐ **7117,** Huggin' and Kissin' Gwine On		17.00	29.00
☐ **7131,** Get It In Front		18.00	30.00
☐ **7167,** You Rascal! You—No. 2		16.00	27.00
☐ **7198,** Three Sixes		16.00	27.00
☐ **7218,** That New Kinda Stuff		15.00	24.00
☐ **Vocalion 03686,** Spo-Dee-O-Dee		9.00	15.00

McCLENNAN, TOMMY

☐ **Bluebird 8347,** You Can Mistreat Me Here		8.00	12.00
☐ **8373,** Bottle It Up and Go		9.00	15.00
☐ **8408,** Cotton Patch Blues		8.00	12.00
☐ **8444,** Brown Skin Girl		7.00	11.00
☐ **8545,** My Baby's Doggin' Me		9.00	15.00
☐ **8605,** My Little Girl		8.00	12.00
☐ **8669,** My Baby's Gone		8.00	12.00

McCRACKLIN, JIMMY

☐ **Aladdin 3089,** Bad Luck and Trouble		6.00	10.00
☐ **Courtney 123,** You Had Your Chance		9.00	15.00
☐ **Down Town 2023,** Bad Condition Blues ...		10.00	16.00
☐ **2027,** Low Down Mood		11.00	17.00
☐ **Excelsior 182,** You Deceived Me		12.00	20.00
☐ **Globe 102,** Miss Mattie Left Me		6.00	9.00
☐ **104,** Highway 101		7.00	10.00
☐ **109,** Street Loafin' Woman		7.00	10.00
☐ **J & M Fullbright 123,** Special For You		9.00	15.00

		Price Range	
☐	**124,** Rock and Rye	9.00	15.00
☐	**RPM 317,** Your Heart Ain't Right	7.00	10.00
☐	**Trilon 197,** Rock and Rye	8.00	12.00
☐	**231,** Big Foot Mama..................	8.00	12.00

MEMPHIS MINNIE & KANSAS JOE

☐	**Bluebird 6187,** When the Sun Goes Down	10.00	16.00
☐	**6199,** Doctor, Doctor Blues	9.00	15.00
☐	**6202,** Hustlin' Woman Blues	9.00	15.00
☐	**Checker 771,** Me and My Chauffeur	7.00	11.00
☐	**Decca 7019,** Chickasaw Train Blues	10.00	17.00
☐	**7023,** Hole in the Wall	9.00	14.00
☐	**7037,** Keep It To Yourself	9.00	14.00
☐	**7038,** You Got To Move	8.00	13.00
☐	**7048,** You Can't Give It Away	10.00	17.00
☐	**7084,** Sylvester and His Mule Blues	9.00	15.00
☐	**7102,** Down in New Orleans	9.00	15.00
☐	**7125,** Jockey Man Blues	8.00	14.00
☐	**7146,** Squat It	8.00	14.00
☐	**J.O.B. 1101,** Kissing in the Dark	9.00	15.00
☐	**Okeh 8948,** My Butcher Man	13.00	21.00
☐	**Regal 3259,** Kidman Blues	11.00	17.00
☐	**Vocalion 1476,** Bumble Bee	11.00	17.00
☐	**1512,** I'm Gonna Bake My Biscuits	12.00	20.00
☐	**1556,** Bumble Bee—No. 2	12.00	20.00
☐	**1588,** Frankie Jean	11.00	17.00
☐	**1601,** Garage Fire Blues	26.00	45.00
☐	**1603,** Good Girl Blues	14.00	21.00
☐	**1618,** New Dirty Dozen	13.00	20.00
☐	**1631,** Plymouth Rock Blues	13.00	20.00
☐	**1638,** Dirt Dauber Blues	12.00	20.00
☐	**1653,** Tricks Ain't Walkin' No More	11.00	19.00
☐	**1673,** Don't Bother It	11.00	19.00
☐	**1682,** Minnie Minnie Bumble Bee	13.00	20.00
☐	**1688,** Socket Blues	11.00	19.00
☐	**1698,** Outdoor Blues	11.00	19.00
☐	**1711,** Fishin' Blues	9.00	15.00
☐	**1718,** Jailhouse Trouble Blues	17.00	28.00
☐	**02711,** Stinging Snake Blues	14.00	21.00

MILES, JOSIE

☐	**Ajax 17057,** Lovin' Henry Blues	32.00	53.00

Price Range

☐	**17066,** Believe Me, Hot Mama	31.00	50.00
☐	**17070,** South Bound Blues	30.00	49.00
☐	**17076,** Sweet Man Joe	31.00	50.00
☐	**17080,** A to Z Blues	32.00	53.00
☐	**17083,** Picnic Time	19.00	29.00
☐	**17087,** Cross Word Papa	17.00	26.00
☐	**17092,** It Ain't Gonna Rain No Mo'	13.00	21.00
☐	**17127,** At the Cake Walk Steppers Ball ..	31.00	48.00
☐	**17134,** Give Me Just a Little Bit of Love ..	30.00	47.00
☐	**Banner 1498,** Bitter Feelin' Blues	10.00	16.00
☐	**1499,** Let's Agree to Disagree	13.00	19.00
☐	**1516,** Ghost Walkin' Blues	14.00	21.00
☐	**1534,** Low Down Daddy Blues	10.00	16.00
☐	**Black Swan 14133,** When I Dream of Old Tennessee Blues	19.00	31.00
☐	**14136,** Four O'Clock Blues	18.00	23.00
☐	**14139,** Low Down 'Bama Blues	16.00	28.00
☐	**Domino 3468,** Bitter Feelin' Blues	10.00	16.00
☐	**3469,** Let's Agree to Disagree	13.00	19.00
☐	**3485,** Ghost Walkin' Blues	13.00	21.00
☐	**3504,** Low Down Daddy Blues	10.00	16.00
☐	**Edison 51476,** Sweet Man Joe	50.00	80.00
☐	**51477,** Temper'mental Papa	55.00	85.00
☐	**Gennett 5359,** War Horse Mama	13.00	21.00
☐	**Paramount 12157,** If You Want to Keep Your Daddy Home	20.00	30.00
☐	**12158,** When I Dream of Old Tennessee Blues	13.00	22.00
☐	**12159,** Four O'Clock Blues	13.00	22.00
☐	**12160,** Low Down 'Bama Blues	14.00	22.00
☐	**Regal 9796,** Let's Agree to Disagree	11.00	17.00
☐	**9797,** Bitter Feelin' Blues	10.00	15.00
☐	**9831,** Low Down Daddy Blues	9.00	14.00

LUCKY MILLINDER

☐	**Brunswick 6156,** Moanin'	20.00	35.00
☐	**6199,** Snake Hips	11.00	20.00
☐	**6229,** Savage Rhythm	12.00	20.00
☐	**Columbia 2963-D,** Let's Have a Jubilee ...	11.00	20.00
☐	**2994-D,** Keep the Rhythm Going	10.00	17.00
☐	**3020-D,** Back Beats	9.00	15.00
☐	**3038-D,** African Lullaby	12.00	20.00

		Price Range	
☐ **3071-D,** Harlem Heat		12.00	20.00
☐ **3078-D,** Truckin'		10.00	17.00
☐ **3087-D,** Congo Caravan		9.00	15.00
☐ **3111-D,** Yes! Yes!		10.00	17.00
☐ **3134-D,** Everything Is Still Okay		9.00	16.00
☐ **3147-D,** Merry-Go-Round		9.00	16.00
☐ **3148-D,** In a Sentimental Mood		9.00	16.00
☐ **3156-D,** Balloonacy		8.00	14.00
☐ **3157-D,** Showboat Shuffle		9.00	16.00
☐ **3158-D,** Algiers Stomp		9.00	16.00
☐ **3162-D,** Big John's Special		8.00	14.00
☐ **Variety 503,** Jungle Madness		7.00	13.00
☐ **546,** Rhythm Jam		7.00	13.00
☐ **604,** The Lucky Swing		8.00	15.00
☐ **624,** Camp Meeting Jamboree		7.00	14.00
☐ **634,** Jammin' For the Jack-Pot		7.00	14.00
☐ **Victor 22763,** Heebie Jeebies		8.00	15.00
☐ **22800,** Moanin'		8.00	15.00
☐ **24442,** Harlem After Midnight		15.00	27.00
☐ **24482,** Break It Down		12.00	23.00
☐ **Vocalion 3808,** Blue Rhythm Fantasy		7.00	13.00

OLIVER, JOE ("King Oliver")

☐ **Autograph 617,** King Porter		500.00	900.00
☐ **Brunswick 3398,** Showboat Shuffle		15.00	23.00
☐ **3741,** Farewell Blues		15.00	27.00
☐ **4028,** Four or Five Times		23.00	40.00
☐ **4469,** I'm Watching the Clock		24.00	43.00
☐ **6053,** Papa De Da Da		24.00	43.00
☐ **6065,** I'm Crazy 'Bout My Baby		23.00	40.00
☐ **Claxtonola 40292,** Riverside Blues		110.00	170.00
☐ **Columbia 13003-D,** Chattanooga Stomp . . .		37.00	51.00
☐ **14003-D,** Camp Meeting Clues		34.00	46.00
☐ **Gennett 5132,** Weather Bird Rag		165.00	280.00
☐ **5133,** Cana Street Blues		175.00	300.00
☐ **5134,** Mandy Lee Blues		165.00	280.00
☐ **5135,** Froggie Moore		160.00	265.00
☐ **5184,** Snake Rag		165.00	280.00
☐ **5274,** Krooked Blues		220.00	350.00
☐ **5275,** Zulus Blues		900.00	1300.00
☐ **Okeh 4906,** Sobbin' Blues		90.00	135.00
☐ **4918,** Dipper Mouth Blues		95.00	145.00

Price Range

☐ 4933, Snake Rag	95.00	145.00
☐ 4975, Jazzin' Babies' Blues	110.00	165.00
☐ 8148, Room Rent Blues	90.00	135.00
☐ 8235, Mabel's Dream	85.00	125.00
☐ 40000, Buddy's Habits	85.00	125.00
☐ 40034, Riverside Blues	95.00	135.00
☐ **Paramount 20292,** Mabel's Dream	80.00	125.00
☐ **Puritan 11292,** Mabel's Dream	85.00	130.00
☐ **Victor 22298,** When You're Smiling	10.00	15.00
☐ 22681, Olga	20.00	30.00
☐ 23001, Struggle Buggy	32.00	47.00
☐ 23009, Shake It and Break It	33.00	50.00
☐ 23011, You Were Only Passing Time With Me	33.00	50.00
☐ 23029, I Can't Stop Loving You	32.00	49.00
☐ 23388, New Orleans Shout	65.00	100.00
☐ 38034, West End Blues	22.00	35.00
☐ 38039, Call of the Freaks	36.00	50.00
☐ 38090, Too Late	35.00	47.00
☐ 38101, Sweet Like This	34.00	47.00
☐ 38109, Frankie and Johnny	34.00	47.00
☐ 38134, Boogie Woogie	34.00	47.00
☐ 38137, Edna	33.00	45.00
☐ 38521, Freakish Light Blues	32.00	44.00
☐ **Vocalion 1007,** Too Bad	42.00	63.00
☐ 1014, Jackass Blues	43.00	65.00
☐ 1033, Sugar Foot Stomp	43.00	65.00
☐ 1049, Tack Annie	65.00	95.00
☐ 1059, Dead Man Blues	26.00	39.00
☐ 1112, Willie the Weeper	67.00	100.00
☐ 1114, Showboat Shuffle	65.00	90.00
☐ 1152, Farewell Blues	45.00	70.00
☐ 1189, West End Blues	65.00	95.00
☐ 1190, Sweet Emmeline	61.00	90.00
☐ 1225, Speakeasy Blues	61.00	90.00
☐ 15394, Deep Henderson	31.00	50.00
☐ 15493, Dead Man's Blues	32.00	55.00
☐ 15503, Snag It	32.00	55.00

ORIGINAL WOLVERINES

☐ **Brunswick 3707,** Shim-Me-Sha-Wabble ...	13.00	21.00
☐ **Vocalion 15635,** Royal Garden Blues	18.00	30.00
☐ 15708, Limehouse Blues	20.00	32.00

		Price Range	
☐ **15732,** There's a Rainbow Round My Shoulder		12.00	18.00
☐ **15751,** Sweethearts on Parade		12.00	18.00
☐ **15768,** I'll Never Ask for More		12.00	20.00
☐ **15784,** He, She and Me		24.00	35.00
☐ **15795,** Some Sweet Day		12.00	20.00

PATTON, CHARLEY

☐ **Paramount 12792,** Banty Rooster Blues		75.00	120.00
☐ **12854,** It Won't Be Long		72.00	115.00
☐ **12869,** A Spoonful Blues		70.00	110.00
☐ **12877,** Pea Vine Blues		68.00	105.00
☐ **12883,** Lord I'm Discouraged		65.00	100.00
☐ **12909,** High Water Everywhere		75.00	120.00
☐ **12924,** Rattlesnake Blues		65.00	95.00
☐ **12943,** Magnolia Blues		80.00	130.00
☐ **12972,** Green River Blues		85.00	135.00
☐ **12986,** I Shall Not Be Moved		85.00	135.00
☐ **12998,** Hammer Blues		95.00	140.00
☐ **13014,** Moon Going Down		85.00	135.00
☐ **13031,** Some Happy Day		90.00	140.00
☐ **13040,** Devil Sent the Train		100.00	150.00
☐ **13070,** Dry Well Blues		90.00	140.00
☐ **13110,** Frankie and Albert		95.00	150.00
☐ **13133,** Joe Kirby		100.00	165.00
☐ **Vocalion 02651,** Poor Me		22.00	37.00
☐ **02680,** High Sheriff Blues		21.00	35.00
☐ **02782,** Love My Stuff		21.00	35.00
☐ **02931,** Revenue Man Blues		20.00	34.00

PARHAM, TINY

☐ **Victor 21553,** Cuckoo Blues		33.00	48.00
☐ **21659,** Snake Eyes		30.00	45.00
☐ **22778,** Sud Buster's Dream		31.00	46.00
☐ **22842,** Rock Bottom		26.00	41.00
☐ **23027,** Blue Moon Blues		34.00	49.00
☐ **23386,** Nervous Tension		75.00	110.00
☐ **23410,** Steel String Blues		80.00	120.00
☐ **23426,** Golden Lily		75.00	110.00
☐ **38009,** Jogo Rhythm		27.00	41.00
☐ **38041,** Subway Sobs		26.00	39.00
☐ **38047,** Blue Melody Blues		25.00	38.00

		Price Range	
☐	**38060,** Stompin' on Down	32.00	49.00
☐	**38076,** Echo Blues	33.00	51.00

RAINEY, MA

☐	**Paramount 12080,** Last Minute Blues	22.00	38.00
☐	**12081,** Bad Luck Blues	21.00	36.00
☐	**12082,** Walking Blues	22.00	38.00
☐	**12083,** Southern Blues	23.00	40.00
☐	**12098,** Dream Blues	15.00	25.00
☐	**12200,** Ma Rainey's Mystery Record	26.00	42.00
☐	**12215,** Lucky Rock Blues	25.00	42.00
☐	**12222,** Farewell Daddy Blues	18.00	30.00
☐	**12227,** South Bound Blues	33.00	47.00
☐	**12238,** Jelly Bean Blues	95.00	135.00
☐	**12242,** Toad Frog Blues	30.00	47.00
☐	**12252,** See See Rider Blues	100.00	145.00
☐	**12257,** Cell Bound Blues	32.00	50.00
☐	**12284,** Explaining the Blues	31.00	48.00
☐	**12290,** Louisiana Hoo Doo Blues	30.00	46.00
☐	**12295,** Stormy Sea Blues	31.00	48.00
☐	**12303,** Night Time Blues	30.00	46.00
☐	**12311,** Rough and Tumble Blues	30.00	45.00
☐	**12332,** Slave to the Blues	30.00	45.00
☐	**12338,** Chain Gang Blues	28.00	42.00
☐	**12357,** Stack O'Lee Blues	28.00	42.00
☐	**12364,** Broken Hearted Blues	27.00	41.00
☐	**12374,** Titanic Man Blues	27.00	41.00
☐	**12384,** Sissy Blues	28.00	43.00
☐	**12395,** Down in the Basement	28.00	43.00
☐	**12419,** Grievin' Hearted Blues	24.00	37.00
☐	**12438,** Don't Fish in My Sea	23.00	36.00
☐	**12508,** Misery Blues	70.00	110.00
☐	**12526,** Gone Daddy Blues	60.00	95.00
☐	**12548,** Big Boy Blues	60.00	95.00
☐	**12566,** Oh Papa Blues	70.00	110.00
☐	**12590,** Georgia Cake Walk	50.00	95.00
☐	**12603,** Moonshine Blues	52.00	100.00
☐	**12612,** Ice Bag Papa	52.00	100.00
☐	**12668,** Prove It On Me Blues	53.00	105.00
☐	**12687,** Victim of the Blues	51.00	100.00
☐	**12706,** Traveling Blues	51.00	100.00
☐	**12718,** Big Feeling Blues	30.00	50.00
☐	**12735,** Tough Luck Blues	28.00	48.00

		Price	Range
☐	12760, Sleep Talking Blues	28.00	48.00
☐	12804, Log Camp Blues	50.00	90.00
☐	12902, Runaway Blues	33.00	55.00
☐	12926, Sweet Rough Man	32.00	53.00

REDMAN, DON

☐	Brunswick 6211, Chant of the Weed	14.00	24.00
☐	6233, I Heard	13.00	21.00
☐	6273, How'm I Doin'?	10.00	19.00
☐	6344, It's a Great World After All	10.00	19.00
☐	6354, Tea for Two	9.00	16.00
☐	6368, Hot and Anxious	9.00	16.00
☐	6401, Ain't I The Lucky One?	9.00	15.00
☐	6412, Two-Time Man	9.00	15.00
☐	6429, Nagasaki	9.00	15.00
☐	6517, Doin' the New Low-Down	9.00	15.00
☐	6523, How Ya Feelin'?	9.00	15.00
☐	6560, Sophisticated Lady	7.00	12.00
☐	6585, I Won't Tell	8.00	14.00
☐	6622, Lazy Bones	9.00	16.00
☐	6684, I Found a New Way to Go	9.00	15.00
☐	6745, Got the Jitters	9.00	15.00
☐	6935, Lonely Cabin	9.00	15.00

ROBINSON, ELZADIE

☐	Paramount 12417, Barrel House Man	50.00	95.00
☐	12420, Houston Bound	48.00	90.00
☐	12469, Baltimore Blues	47.00	87.00
☐	12509, Whiskey Blues	45.00	85.00
☐	12544, Tick Tock Blues	42.00	80.00
☐	12573, St. Louis Cyclone Blues	38.00	62.00
☐	12627, Love Crazy Blues	36.00	59.00
☐	12635, Elzadie's Policy Blues	42.00	80.00
☐	12676, Mad Blues	39.00	70.00
☐	12689, Wicked Daddy	39.00	70.00
☐	12701, Arkansas Mill Blues	40.00	75.00
☐	12745, Unsatisfied Blues	39.00	70.00
☐	12768, Cheatin' Daddy	39.00	70.00
☐	12900, Driving Me South	38.00	65.00

RUSSELL, LUIS

☐	Okeh 8424, Plantation Joys	22.00	36.00
☐	8454, Sweet Mumtaz	21.00	34.00
☐	8656, The Call of the Freaks	21.00	34.00

Price Range

☐	8734, Jersey Lightnin'	20.00	33.00
☐	8760, Savoy Shout	20.00	33.00
☐	8780, Saratoga Shout	19.00	32.00
☐	8811, Louisiana Swing	21.00	35.00
☐	8830, Muggin' Lightly	21.00	35.00
☐	8849, High Tension	19.00	32.00
☐	Victor 22789, Goin' to Town	22.00	36.00
☐	22793, You Rascal, You	21.00	35.00
☐	22815, Freakish Blues	21.00	35.00

SCRUGGS, IRENE

☐	Champion 16102, Borrowed Love	26.00	41.00
☐	16148, My Back to the Wall ..../..	25.00	40.00
☐	16756, The Voice of the Blues	25.00	39.00
☐	Gennett 7296, You've Got What I Want ...	25.00	39.00
☐	Paramount 13023, Good Meat Grinder	37.00	58.00
☐	13046, Back to the Wall	36.00	56.00
☐	Vocalion 1017, Home Town Blues	62.00	90.00

SMITH, BESSIE

☐	Columbia 14042-D, Weeping Willow Blues	14.00	23.00
☐	14056-D, Sobbin' Hearted Blues	17.00	30.00
☐	14064-D, Cold in Hand Blues	16.00	27.00
☐	14075-D, Soft Pedal Blues	11.00	20.00
☐	14079-D, You've Been a Good Old Wagon	19.00	29.00
☐	14083-D, Careless Love	19.00	29.00
☐	14090-D, Nashville Woman's Blues	19.00	29.00
☐	14095-D, J. C. Holmes Blues	11.00	19.00
☐	14115-D, Red Mountain Blues	12.00	21.00
☐	14179-D, Young Woman's Blues	11.00	19.00
☐	14197-D, After You've Gone	12.00	21.00
☐	14209-D, Them's Graveyard Words	11.00	19.00
☐	14219-D, Alexander's Ragtime Band	10.00	18.00
☐	14232-D, Trombone Cholly	10.00	18.00
☐	14260-D, Sweet Mistreater	11.00	19.00
☐	14273-D, Dyin' By the Hour	12.00	23.00
☐	14435-D, I've Got What It Takes	11.00	19.00
☐	14451-D, Take It Right Back	11.00	19.00
☐	14464-D, He's Got Me Goin'	12.00	23.00
☐	14476-D, Wasted Life Blues	13.00	24.00
☐	14487-D, You Don't Understand	13.00	24.00
☐	14527-D, Blue Spirit Blues	13.00	24.00
☐	14538-D, Moan, You Moaners	13.00	24.00

Price Range

☐	**14554-D,** Hustlin' Dan	15.00	27.00
☐	**14569-D,** Hot Springs Blues	15.00	27.00
☐	**14611-D,** In the House Blues	20.00	36.00
☐	**14634-D,** Safety Mama	18.00	34.00
☐	**14663-D,** Shipwreck Blues	18.00	34.00

SMITH, CLARA

☐	**Black Patti 8034,** Sand Raisin' Blues	70.00	110.00
☐	**Columbia 14062-D,** Broken Busted Blues ..	15.00	25.00
☐	**14073-D,** Courthouse Blues	15.00	24.00
☐	**14077-D,** My John Blues	15.00	24.00
☐	**14419-D,** Got My Mind On That Thing ...	15.00	24.00
☐	**14462-D,** Papa I Don't Need You Now ...	15.00	24.00
☐	**14536-D,** Where Is My Man?	12.00	20.00
☐	**14553-D,** Don't Fool Around on Me	9.00	15.00
☐	**14568-D,** You're Getting Old on Your Job	10.00	16.00
☐	**14580-D,** Woman to Woman	9.00	15.00
☐	**14592-D,** Good Times	9.00	15.00
☐	**14619-D,** Ol' Sam Tages	9.00	15.00
☐	**14633-D,** You Dirty Dog	12.00	20.00
☐	**14653-D,** So Long Jim	12.00	20.00

SMITH, SUSIE

☐	**Ajax 17064,** House Rent Blues	23.00	40.00
☐	**17073,** Salt Water Blues	22.00	39.00
☐	**17079,** The Bye Bye Blues	21.00	36.00
☐	**17081,** Meat Man Pete	23.00	40.00
☐	**17089,** Sore Bunion Blues	23.00	40.00
☐	**17093,** Scandal Blues	22.00	39.00
☐	**17095,** How Can I Miss You	21.00	36.00
☐	**17127,** Texas Special Blues	21.00	36.00
☐	**17132,** Undertaker's Blues	21.00	36.00
☐	**17134,** Crepe Hanger Blues	21.00	36.00

SMITH, TRIXIE

☐	**Black Swan 2039,** Trixie's Blues	19.00	28.00
☐	**2044,** Long Lost Weary Blues	20.00	30.00
☐	**14114,** Pensacola Blues	19.00	28.00
☐	**14127,** My Man Rocks Me	18.00	27.00
☐	**14132,** I'm Through With You	19.00	28.00
☐	**14138,** I'm Gonna Get You	16.00	27.00
☐	**14142,** Log Cabin Blues	16.00	27.00
☐	**14149,** Triflin' Blues	17.00	27.00
☐	**Paramount 12161,** Trixie's Blues	14.00	23.00

Price Range

☐	**12162,** Long Lost Weary Blues	**14.00**	**23.00**
☐	**12163,** Pensacola Blues	**14.00**	**23.00**
☐	**12164,** My Man Rocks Me	**14.00**	**23.00**
☐	**12165,** I'm Through With You	**14.00**	**23.00**
☐	**12167,** Log Cabin Blues	**12.00**	**20.00**
☐	**12168,** Triflin' Blues	**12.00**	**20.00**
☐	**12208,** Sorrowful Blues	**23.00**	**36.00**
☐	**12211,** Freight Train Blues	**22.00**	**34.00**
☐	**12232,** Praying Blues	**23.00**	**36.00**
☐	**12262,** Railroad Blues	**65.00**	**110.00**
☐	**12330,** Love Me Like You Used To Do	**32.00**	**50.00**
☐	**12336,** Black Bottom Hop	**32.00**	**50.00**

TENNESSEE MUSIC MEN

☐	**Clarion 5389-C,** Georgia On My Mind	**15.00**	**25.00**
☐	**5446-C,** Loveless Love	**12.00**	**20.00**
☐	**5461-C,** Bugle Call Rag	**13.00**	**22.00**
☐	**5467-C,** Choo Choo	**15.00**	**25.00**
☐	**5469-C,** Baby Won't You Please Come Home	**13.00**	**22.00**
☐	**5474-C,** Shim-Me-Sha-Wabble	**12.00**	**20.00**
☐	**Harmony 1378-H,** You Rascal You	**15.00**	**25.00**
☐	**1406-H,** Loveless Love	**13.00**	**22.00**
☐	**1415-H,** Bugle Call Rag	**11.00**	**19.00**
☐	**1420-H,** Choo Choo	**12.00**	**20.00**
☐	**1422-H,** Baby, Won't You Please Come Home	**12.00**	**20.00**
☐	**1427-H,** Shim-Me-Sha-Wabble	**13.00**	**22.00**
☐	**Velvet Tone 2453-V,** Georgia On My Mind	**12.00**	**20.00**
☐	**2456-V,** You Rascal You	**13.00**	**22.00**
☐	**2506-V,** Loveless Love	**12.00**	**20.00**
☐	**2521-V,** Bugle Call Rag	**11.00**	**19.00**
☐	**2527-V,** Choo Choo	**11.00**	**19.00**
☐	**2529-V,** Baby, Won't You Please Come Home	**12.00**	**20.00**
☐	**2534-V,** Shim-Me-Sha-Wabble	**12.00**	**20.00**

THOMAS, HENRY

☐	**Bluebird 5343,** My Sweet Candy	**11.00**	**18.00**
☐	**5411,** Sick with the Blues	**12.00**	**20.00**
☐	**Vocalion 1094,** John Henry	**21.00**	**36.00**
☐	**1137,** Red River Blues	**23.00**	**37.00**
☐	**1138,** The Little Red Caboose	**23.00**	**37.00**

		Price Range	
☐	**1139,** Woodhouse Blues	**21.00**	**36.00**
☐	**1141,** Run, Mollie, Run	**23.00**	**37.00**
☐	**1197,** Texas Easy Street Blues	**24.00**	**41.00**
☐	**1230,** Bull Doze Blues	**23.00**	**39.00**
☐	**1249,** Texas Worried Blues	**24.00**	**41.00**
☐	**1443,** Don't Leave Me Here	**23.00**	**39.00**
☐	**1468,** Lovin' Babe	**24.00**	**41.00**

THOMAS, RAMBLIN'

☐	**Paramount 12616,** Sawmill Moan	**55.00**	**80.00**
☐	**12637,** Lock and Key Blues	**52.00**	**75.00**
☐	**12670,** No Baby Blues	**60.00**	**85.00**
☐	**12708,** Jig Head Blues	**55.00**	**80.00**
☐	**12722,** Ramblin' Man	**53.00**	**75.00**
☐	**12752,** Good Time Blues	**53.00**	**75.00**

THREE JOLLY MINERS

☐	**Vocalion 1003,** Pig Alley Stomp	**13.00**	**21.00**
☐	**1004,** Chicago Back Step	**12.00**	**20.00**
☐	**15009,** Freakish Blues	**12.00**	**20.00**
☐	**15051,** Black Cat Blues	**13.00**	**21.00**
☐	**15087,** Lake George Blues	**11.00**	**18.00**
☐	**15141,** Texas Shuffle	**12.00**	**19.00**
☐	**15164,** House Party Stomp	**13.00**	**21.00**
☐	**15269,** Pig Alley Stomp	**11.00**	**18.00**

TUCKER, BESSIE

☐	**Victor 21692,** Black Name Moan	**16.00**	**27.00**
☐	**21708,** The Dummy	**16.00**	**27.00**
☐	**23385,** Bogey Man Blues	**27.00**	**41.00**
☐	**23392,** T. B. Moan	**26.00**	**40.00**
☐	**38018,** Fryin' Pan Skillet Blues	**17.00**	**29.00**
☐	**38538,** Old Black Mary	**17.00**	**29.00**
☐	**38542,** Katy Blues	**17.00**	**29.00**

VENUTI, JOE

☐	**Columbia 2535-D,** There's No Other Girl . . .	**11.00**	**18.00**
☐	**2589-D,** The Wolf Wobble	**11.00**	**18.00**
☐	**2765-D,** Raggin' the Scale	**11.00**	**18.00**
☐	**2782-D,** Vibraphonia	**11.00**	**18.00**
☐	**2783-D,** Isn't It Heavenly?	**11.00**	**18.00**
☐	**2834-D,** Doin' the Uptown Lowdown	**12.00**	**20.00**
☐	**3103-D,** Eeny Meeny Miney Mo	**11.00**	**18.00**

	Price Range	
☐ **3104-D,** Stop, Look and Listen	10.00	16.00
☐ **3105-D,** Red Velvet	10.00	16.00
☐ **Melotone 12277,** Farewell Blues	29.00	44.00
☐ **12294,** Beale Street Blues	25.00	39.00
☐ **Okeh 40762,** Wild Cat	10.00	16.00
☐ **40825,** Doin' Things	9.00	15.00
☐ **40853,** Kickin' the Cat	11.00	19.00
☐ **40897,** A Mug of Ale	10.00	18.00
☐ **40947,** Penn Beach Blues	11.00	18.00
☐ **41025,** The Wild Dog	12.00	20.00
☐ **41051,** 'Tain't So, Honey, 'Tain't So	11.00	18.00
☐ **41076,** The Man From the South	11.00	18.00
☐ **41087,** Pickin' Cotton	10.00	17.00
☐ **41133,** I Must Have That Man	10.00	17.00
☐ **41144,** The Blue Room	11.00	18.00
☐ **41251,** My Honey's Lovin' Arms	11.00	18.00
☐ **41263,** I'm In Seventh Heaven	9.00	15.00
☐ **41320,** Chant of the Jungle	11.00	18.00
☐ **41361,** Apple Blossoms	10.00	17.00
☐ **41432,** Raggin' the Scale	12.00	20.00
☐ **41451,** Out of Breath	12.00	20.00
☐ **41469,** I've Found a New Baby	12.00	20.00
☐ **41506,** Pardon Me, Pretty Baby	12.00	20.00
☐ **41586,** Fiddlesticks	12.00	20.00
☐ **Victor 21561,** Doin' Things	16.00	27.00
☐ **23015,** My Man from Caroline	17.00	28.00
☐ **23018,** Wasting My Love On You	16.00	27.00
☐ **23039,** Gettin' Hot	21.00	37.00
☐ **Vocalion 15858,** Farewell Blues	27.00	45.00
☐ **15864,** Beale Street Blues	31.00	50.00

WALLER, FATS

☐ **Columbia 14593-D,** I'm Crazy 'Bout My Baby	35.00	55.00
☐ **Okeh 4757,** Birmingham Blues	29.00	46.00
☐ **Victor 20357,** St. Louis Blues	12.00	20.00
☐ **20470,** Soothin' Syrup Stomp	19.00	32.00
☐ **20492,** Rusty Pail	18.00	30.00
☐ **20655,** Stompin' the Bug	19.00	32.00
☐ **20890,** Beale Street Blues	21.00	35.00
☐ **21127,** I Ain't Got Nobody	19.00	32.00
☐ **21202,** He's Gone Away	18.00	30.00
☐ **21525,** Hog Maw Stomp	18.00	30.00
☐ **22092,** Ain't Misbehavin'	12.00	20.00

		Price Range	
☐	22108, Sweet Savannah Sue	14.00	25.00
☐	22371, St. Louis Blues	9.00	15.00
☐	23260, That's All	33.00	51.00
☐	23331, Sugar	21.00	34.00
☐ Victor 38050, Harlem Fuss		34.00	51.00
☐	38086, Lookin' Good But Feelin' Bad	31.00	46.00
☐	38110, When I'm Alone	32.00	47.00
☐	38119, Ridin' But Walkin'	32.00	47.00
☐	38508, Numb Fumblin'	18.00	30.00
☐	38554, Valentine Stomp	27.00	41.00
☐	38568, Turn on the Heat	18.00	30.00
☐	38613, Smashing Thirds	23.00	35.00

WASHBOARD RHYTHM BOYS

☐ Bluebird 6157, Arlena		11.00	19.00
☐	6186, Street Walkin' Blues	12.00	20.00
☐	6278, Hot Nuts	11.00	19.00
☐ Victor 22719, A Porter's Love Song to a Chambermaid		19.00	30.00
☐	22814, Shoot 'em	18.00	27.00
☐	22958, Pepper Steak	35.00	51.00
☐	23301, Georgia on My Mind	29.00	46.00
☐	23323, If You Don't Love Me	28.00	45.00
☐	23337, All This World Is Made of Glass ..	29.00	46.00
☐	23348, My Silent Love	25.00	43.00
☐	23357, Depression Stomp	28.00	46.00
☐	23364, Say It Isn't So	25.00	43.00
☐	23368, The Boy in the Boat	26.00	46.00
☐	23373, How Deep Is the Ocean?	27.00	43.00
☐	23375, A Nickel for a Pickle	23.00	41.00
☐	23380, Sloppy Drunk Blues	24.00	40.00
☐	23403, Nobody's Sweetheart	24.00	40.00
☐	23405, Sophisticated Lady	24.00	40.00
☐	23408, Bug-A-Boo	24.00	40.00
☐	23415, Hard Corn	27.00	43.00
☐ Vocalion 1725, The Scat Song		19.00	32.00
☐	1729, Syncopate Your Sins Away	18.00	31.00
☐	1730, Oh! You Sweet Thing	18.00	31.00
☐	1731, Angeline	17.00	30.00
☐	1732, Blue Drag	18.00	31.00
☐	1733, Old Yazoo	17.00	30.00
☐	1734, Spider Crawl	16.00	28.00

Price Range

WATERS, ETHEL

☐	**Black Swan 2010,** Down Home Blues	22.00	37.00
☐	**2021,** There'll Be Some Changes Made ..	21.00	36.00
☐	**2035,** Royal Garden Blues	21.00	35.00
☐	**2037,** Bugle Blues	20.00	33.00
☐	**2038,** Dyin' with the Blues	21.00	36.00
☐	**2074,** Struggle	20.00	33.00
☐	**2077,** Tiger Rag	21.00	36.00
☐	**10077,** Struggle	20.00	31.00
☐	**14117,** Jazzin' Babies Blues	20.00	31.00
☐	**14120,** Georgia Blues	22.00	36.00
☐	**14128,** At the New Jump Steady Ball	22.00	35.00
☐	**14145,** Brown Baby	24.00	39.00
☐	**14146,** Memphis Man	20.00	31.00
☐	**14148,** Long-Lost Mama	20.00	31.00
☐	**14151,** Lost Out Blues	19.00	29.00
☐	**14155,** All The Time	19.00	29.00
☐	**Cardinal 2036,** The New York Guide	24.00	37.00
☐	**Columbia 2222-D,** My Kind of Man	10.00	17.00
☐	**2346-D,** I Got Rhythm	12.00	20.00
☐	**2409-D,** When Your Lover Has Gone	14.00	23.00
☐	**2481-D,** Without That Gal	13.00	21.00
☐	**2511-D,** River, Stay 'Way From My Door	14.00	23.00
☐	**2826-D,** Harlem On My Mind	15.00	26.00
☐	**2853-D,** A Hundred Years from Today ...	13.00	21.00
☐	**14353-D,** My Handy Man	9.00	16.00
☐	**14380-D,** Do What You Did Last Night ...	9.00	16.00
☐	**14411-D,** Lonesome Swallow	11.00	17.00
☐	**14458-D,** Long Lean Lanky Mama	9.00	15.00
☐	**14565-D,** Georgia Blues	9.00	15.00
☐	**Paramount 12169,** Down Home Blues	13.00	21.00
☐	**12170,** There'll Be Some Changes Made	14.00	23.00
☐	**12171,** Royal Garden Blues	13.00	21.00
☐	**12173,** Bugle Blues	15.00	24.00
☐	**12174,** Dyin' with the Blues	15.00	24.00
☐	**12175,** Jazzin' Babies' Blues	15.00	24.00
☐	**12176,** At the New Jump Steady Ball	15.00	24.00
☐	**12178,** Brown Baby	13.00	21.00
☐	**12179,** Memphis Man	14.00	23.00
☐	**12180,** Long-Lost Mama	13.00	21.00
☐	**12181,** Lost Our Blues	13.00	21.00
☐	**12182,** Ethel Sings 'em	14.00	25.00

		Price Range	
☐	**12189,** All the Time	13.00	21.00
☐	**12214,** Tell 'em 'Bout Me	12.00	20.00
☐	**12230,** Black Splatch Blues	27.00	41.00
☐	**12313,** Craving Blues	29.00	43.00

WASHINGTON, LIZZIE

☐	**Black Patti 8054,** Mexico Blues	100.00	150.00
☐	**Champion 15282,** Skeleton Key Blues	90.00	135.00
☐	**15303,** East Coast Blues	37.00	56.00
☐	**15319,** Sport Model Mamma Blues	40.00	62.00
☐	**Gennett 6126,** Working Man Blues	37.00	56.00
☐	**6134,** Skeleton Key Blues	35.00	52.00
☐	**6321,** Brick Flat Blues	36.00	54.00
☐	**Herwin 92013,** East Coast Blues	41.00	67.00
☐	**92021,** My Low Down Brown	43.00	69.00
☐	**92039,** Lord Have Mercy Blues	41.00	67.00
☐	**92040,** Mexico Blues	44.00	70.00
☐	**92041,** Brick Flat Blues	41.00	67.00
☐	**Vocalion 1459,** Whiskey Head Blues	20.00	33.00

WHEATSTRAW, PEETIE

☐	**Bluebird 5451,** Devil's Son-in-Law	12.00	20.00
☐	**5626,** Ice and Snow Blues	12.00	20.00
☐	**Conqueror 8858, 8858, 8925, 9027, 9028**	10.00	16.00
☐	**Decca 7007,** Doin' the Best I Can	11.00	18.00
☐	**7018,** Throw Me in the Alley	12.00	20.00
☐	**7061,** Good Home Blues	12.00	20.00
☐	**7082,** Numbers Blues	12.00	20.00
☐	**Vocalion 1552,** Tennessee Peaches Blues	29.00	49.00
☐	**1569,** School Days	26.00	43.00
☐	**1597,** Strange Man Blues	27.00	46.00
☐	**1620,** Mama's Advice	26.00	43.00
☐	**1649,** Ain't It a Pity and a Shame	27.00	46.00
☐	**1672,** C and A Blues	25.00	40.00
☐	**1722,** Police Station Blues	25.00	40.00
☐	**1727,** Can't See Blues	25.00	40.00
☐	**02783,** Back Door Blues	15.00	25.00
☐	**02810,** C and A Train Blues	15.00	25.00
☐	**02843,** Keyhole Blues	15.00	25.00
☐	**03066,** King of Spades	11.00	16.00
☐	**03119,** Sorrow Hearted Blues	10.00	15.00
☐	**03155,** Johnnie Blues	10.00	15.00

Price Range

WHOOPEE MAKERS

☐ **Banner 6548,** Saturday Night Function	15.00	24.00
☐ **Cameo 9036,** Hottentot	13.00	21.00
☐ 9037, Misty Mornin'	14.00	24.00
☐ 9306, Saturday Night Function	12.00	20.00
☐ **Conqueror 7428,** Flaming Youth	12.00	20.00
☐ **Lincoln 3065,** Hottentot	12.00	20.00
☐ 3066, Misty Mornin'	11.00	18.00
☐ 3330, Saturday Night Function	11.00	18.00
☐ **Pathe-Actuelle 36781,** Jubilee Stomp	15.00	26.00
☐ 36787, Take It Easy	14.00	23.00
☐ 36899, The Mooche	14.00	21.00
☐ 36915, Hot and Bothered	15.00	21.00
☐ 36923, Misty Mornin'	14.00	23.00
☐ 36945, Bugle Call Rag	13.00	21.00
☐ 37013, Tiger Rag	11.00	17.00
☐ 37042, Dirty Dog	10.00	16.00
☐ 37059, Doin' the Voom Voom	16.00	26.00
☐ **Perfect 14962,** East St. Louis Toodle-oo ...	17.00	29.00
☐ 14968, Take It Easy	17.00	26.00
☐ 15080, Move Over	17.00	29.00
☐ 15096, Hot and Bothered	18.00	32.00
☐ 15104, Misty Mornin'	18.00	32.00
☐ 15194, Tiger Rag	11.00	18.00
☐ 15217, Twelfth Street Rag	10.00	17.00
☐ 15223, The Sorority Stomp	10.00	17.00
☐ 15376, Happy Feet	9.00	15.00
☐ 15418, Them There Eyes	11.00	18.00
☐ **Romeo 840,** Misty Mornin'	11.00	18.00

WILLIAMS, CLARENCE

☐ **Oriole 2141,** Papa De-Da-Da	11.00	18.00
☐ 2164, Hot Lovin'	10.00	17.00
☐ **Paramount 12435,** Shut Your Mouth	47.00	65.00
☐ 12517, Bottomland	32.00	53.00
☐ 12839, Midnight Stomp	90.00	140.00
☐ 12870, Pane in the Glass	110.00	155.00
☐ 12884, Speakeasy	95.00	145.00
☐ 12885, Squeeze Me	90.00	140.00
☐ **Perfect 15403,** Hot Lovin'	11.00	20.00
☐ **QRS 7004,** Speakeasy	110.00	175.00
☐ 7005, Squeeze Me	100.00	160.00

		Price Range	
☐	**7039,** Midnight Stomp	110.00	175.00
☐	**7034,** Bozo	110.00	175.00
☐	**7044,** Sister Kate	105.00	160.00
☐	**Romeo 1529,** Hot Lovin'	12.00	20.00
☐	**Victor 38063,** Lazy Mama	21.00	33.00
☐	**38524,** Too Low	23.00	36.00
☐	**38630,** I'm Not Worryin'	31.00	50.00
☐	**Vocalion 2541,** Breeze	7.00	11.00
☐	**2563,** The Right Key But the Wrong Keyhole	12.00	20.00
☐	**2584,** Chocolate Avenue	11.00	19.00
☐	**2602,** Harlem Rhythm Dance	10.00	17.00
☐	**2616,** Swaller-Tail Coat	11.00	18.00
☐	**2629,** Jimmy Had a Nickel	9.00	16.00
☐	**2630,** How Can I Get It?	11.00	18.00
☐	**2654,** New Orleans Hop Scop Blues	11.00	18.00
☐	**2674,** As Long As I Live	10.00	18.00
☐	**2676,** St. Louis Blues	11.00	19.00
☐	**2689,** I Can't Dance, I Got Ants In My Pants	11.00	19.00
☐	**2718,** Pretty Baby, Is It Yes or No?	10.00	17.00
☐	**2736,** After Tonight	9.00	15.00
☐	**2759,** Let's Have a Showdown	10.00	17.00
☐	**2778,** Bimbo	9.00	15.00
☐	**2788,** Trouble	10.00	17.00
☐	**2838,** Big Fat Mama	10.00	17.00
☐	**2854,** Chizzlin' Sam	9.00	15.00
☐	**2871,** Organ Grinder Blues	10.00	17.00
☐	**2889,** Tell the Truth	11.00	18.00
☐	**2899,** I Saw Stars	10.00	17.00
☐	**2909,** Jungle Crawl	9.00	15.00
☐	**2938,** Black Gal	10.00	17.00
☐	**2958,** I Can See You All Over the Place ..	10.00	17.00

WILLIAMSON, SONNY BOY

☐	**Bluebird 7012,** Skinny Woman	12.00	18.00
☐	**7059,** Sugar Mama Blues	12.00	18.00
☐	**7098,** Blue Bird Blues	12.00	18.00
☐	**7302,** Early in the Morning	12.00	18.00
☐	**7352,** Suzanne Blues	12.00	18.00
☐	**7404,** Frigidaire Blues	12.00	18.00
☐	**7428,** Collector Man Blues	12.00	18.00
☐	**7500,** Sunny Land	10.00	16.00
☐	**7536,** You Can Lead Me	12.00	18.00

		Price Range	
☐	7576, Miss Louisa Blues	10.00	16.00
☐	7665, Decoration Blues	10.00	16.00
☐	7707, Honey Bee Blues	9.00	15.00
☐	7756, You Give an Account	10.00	16.00
☐	7805, Deep Down in the Ground	10.00	16.00
☐	7847, Shannon Street Blues	9.00	15.00
☐	**Bluebird 8034, 8094**	9.00	15.00
☐	8237, Good for Nothing Blues	10.00	16.00
☐	8265, Bad Luck Blues	10.00	16.00
☐	8307, Doggin' My Love Around	12.00	18.00
☐	8333, T. B. Blues	12.00	18.00
☐	8357, Good Gal Blues	10.00	16.00
☐	8383, New Jail House Blues	12.00	18.00
☐	8403, Joe Louis and John Henry Blues ..	12.00	18.00
☐	8439, Miss Ida Lee	10.00	16.00
☐	8474, Honey Bee Blues	12.00	18.00
☐	**Trumpet 139,** Do It If You Wanna	9.00	15.00
☐	140, Stop Crying	9.00	15.00
☐	144, West Memphis Blues	3.00	13.00
☐	145, Pontiac Blues	8.00	13.00

OPERA

MEMORABILIA

		Price Range	
☐	**ADLER, KURT,** 8x10 photograph, signed and inscribed	15.00	22.00
☐	**ADLER, KURT,** c. mid-1950's, printed score of "The Magic Flute," signed and inscribed	10.00	15.00
☐	**ALBANESE, LICIA,** 5x7 photo in "Butterfly" costume, signed in light blue ink, mounted on stiff paper, laminated, signature somewhat faded	17.00	22.00
☐	**ALBANESE, LICIA,** c. 1947, typewritten letter, signed, half page	15.00	20.00
☐	**ALBANESE, LICIA,** four photos of her, ranging in size from 4x3 to 8x10, two in costume, one signed, one damaged	33.00	45.00
☐	**ALCOCK, MERLE,** c. 1920's, photo in costume from "Amico Fritz," 8x10, signed in the margin	30.00	40.00

Price Range

☐ **ALDA, FRANCES,** c. 1920, sepia photo, 12x14½, with lengthy inscription and large bold signature **52.00** **75.00**

☐ **ALDA, FRANCES,** Metropolitan Opera program, signed (also signed by several others) **26.00** **40.00**

☐ **ALTGLASS, MAX,** 7x9 photo in costume from "Boris," signed in green ink, framed under glass **43.00** **55.00**

☐ **ALVARY, LORENZO,** 8x10 studio photo, signed **10.00** **13.00**

☐ **ALVARY, LORENZO,** six photos, various sizes, in costume, four of them signed, in a cloth folding case **77.00** **100.00**

☐ **ALVARY, LORENZO,** hotel menu signed, stained **8.00** **13.00**

☐ **AMARA, LUCINE,** article from "Opera News" magazine, signed and with handwritten comments **12.00** **17.00**

☐ **AMARA, LUCINE,** pair of 8x10 photos, signed, one in costume, one framed against green velvet in a simple wood frame **53.00** **70.00**

☐ **AMARA, LUCINE,** pair of long black gloves worn by her in an operatic role **30.00** **40.00**

☐ **AMARA, LUCINE,** plain signature on an otherwise blank sheet **5.00** **6.00**

☐ **ANTHONY, CHARLES,** 8x10 photo, signed **9.00** **12.00**

☐ **BACCALONI, SALVATORE,** 8x10 photo in "Leporello" costume, signed and inscribed **20.00** **30.00**

☐ **BACCALONI, SALVATORE,** 8x10 photo, signed, framed **25.00** **35.00**

☐ **BACCALONI, SALVATORE,** c. 1940's, poster advertising a concert appearance .. **12.00** **17.00**

☐ **BACCALONI, SALVATORE,** 14x17 photo in costume, signed and inscribed, mounted on bristol board **65.00** **85.00**

☐ **BADA, ANGELO,** 4x3 photo, signed, wrinkled **10.00** **14.00**

☐ **BADA, ANGELO,** c. 1932, postcard with handwritten message and signature **12.00** **17.00**

☐ **BAMPTON, ROSE,** handwritten note to a student **30.00** **40.00**

☐ **BAMPTON, ROSE,** c. 1938, typed letter, signed, NY **32.00** **42.00**

Price Range

☐ **BAUM, KURT,** 8x10 photo in costume, signed twice 20.00   25.00

☐ **BERGONZI, CARLO,** newspaper review of an opera, signed in pencil 10.00   15.00

☐ **BJOERLING, JUSSI,** 8x10 photo in "Cavaradossi" costume, signed and inscribed 22.00   28.00

☐ **BJOERLING, JUSSI,** 8x10 photo in "Boheme" costume, signed 25.00   33.00

☐ **BJOERLING, JUSSI,** scrapbook on his career, with c. 200 news cuttings, several 8x10 and other photos, a few signed items 110.00   150.00

☐ **BORI, LUCREZIA,** 8x10 sepia photo, signed and inscribed 35.00   44.00

☐ **BORI, LUCREZIA,** c. 1917, handwritten letter, signed, with the original envelope. Sold with two small unsigned photos 90.00   115.00

☐ **BRANZELL, KARIN,** seven photos, 3x4 to 8x10, two duplicates, one signed. Enclosed in a leatherette envelope 35.00   44.00

☐ **BROWNLEE, JOHN,** 8x10 photo in "Don Giovanni" costume, signed and inscribed to a friend 17.00   25.00

☐ **BROWNLEE, JOHN,** c. 1940, 8x10 photo in "Rigoletto" costume, signed 21.00   30.00

☐ **BROWNLEE, JOHN,** 5x7½ color photo from magazine, signed and inscribed. Mounted on stiff paper 17.00   23.00

☐ **BROWNLEE, JOHN,** artist's caricature of him in role, 5x7, pen and wash, matted 45.00   60.00

☐ **CABALLE, MONTSERRAT,** 8x10 photo in costume, signed 10.00   14.00

☐ **CABALLE, MONTSERRAT,** seven different 8x10 photos, three of them signed, along with several news cuttings 50.00   63.00

☐ **CABALLE, MONTSERRAT,** LP album cover, signed and inscribed (lacking record) 44.00   55.00

☐ **CARUSO, ENRICO,** c. 1911, handwritten letter, signed 175.00   220.00

☐ **CARUSO, ENRICO,** c. 1915, two-page letter, typed, signed 150.00   190.00

Price Range

☐ **CARUSO, ENRICO,** handwritten letter with caricature of old man and dog, signed, framed in a metal frame 250.00   320.00

☐ **CARUSO, ENRICO,** caricature of bearded man holding umbrella, on 6x7½ sheet of greenish paper, a few handwritten notes, signed 185.00   240.00

☐ **CARUSO, ENRICO,** c. 1915, restaurant menu with small caricature, signed, stained and worn 170.00   210.00

☐ **CARUSO, ENRICO,** c. 1908, restaurant menu, signed 115.00   150.00

☐ **CARUSO, ENRICO,** signature on calling card   65.00   85.00

☐ **CARUSO, ENRICO,** c. 1902, check endorsed by him 100.00   130.00

☐ **CARUSO, ENRICO,** handwritten note on stationery of the Ansonia Hotel, New York ... 175.00   225.00

☐ **CARUSO, ENRICO,** 8x10 photo in "I Pagliacci" costume, signed and inscribed, matted and framed 220.00   300.00

☐ **CARUSO, ENRICO,** 5x7 photo in "Rigoletto" costume, signed, ink faded, lightly watermarked 150.00   200.00

☐ **CARUSO, ENRICO,** 8x10 photo in "Girl of the Golden West" costume, matted, unsigned   65.00   85.00

☐ **CARUSO, ENRICO,** half-page handwritten note, framed along with a signed 5x7 portrait and a 78rpm recording in a 17x22 wood frame 385.00   450.00

☐ **CARUSO, ENRICO,** c. 1906, 8x10 portrait photo in street dress, signed and inscribed 170.00   220.00

☐ **CARUSO, ENRICO,** two 3x4 photos, one on shipboard 45.00   60.00

☐ **CARUSO, ENRICO,** opera review from the New York Times, signed. Enclosed in a cloth folding case, along with an unsigned photo 110.00   130.00

☐ **CARUSO, ENRICO,** scrapbook with 27 photos, 17 of them signed, and c. 300 other items, news cuttings, tickets, etc 1800.00   2300.00

☐ **CARUSO, ENRICO,** poster advertising his appearance in a Metropolitan Opera production 250.00   330.00

Price Range

☐ **CHALIAPIN, FYODOR,** 8x10 sepia photo, signed as "Boris"	230.00	330.00
☐ **CHALIAPIN, FYODOR,** handwritten letter, signed, in Russian	475.00	650.00
☐ **CHALIAPIN, FYODOR,** five 8x10 movie stills, unsigned	33.00	45.00
☐ **CHALIAPIN, FYODOR,** c. 1925, 5x7 portrait photo, signed	210.00	275.00
☐ **CHALIAPIN, FYODOR,** 22x31 poster as "Boris," apparently a recent enlargement by a collector from a small early Metropolitan Opera photo	45.00	66.00
☐ **CHALIAPIN, FYODOR,** signature on an otherwise blank sheet	60.00	80.00
☐ **CHOOKASIAN, LILI,** 8x10 portrait photo (unsigned)	3.00	4.00
☐ **CLAUSSEN, JULIA,** c. 1920's, series of five letters to her, mostly on musical matters ..	45.00	65.00
☐ **CLEVA, FAUSTO,** 8x10 photo with baton, signed	45.00	67.00
☐ **CONNER, NADINE,** 6x7½ color photo, trimmed into margins, inscribed and signed	22.00	30.00
☐ **CONTINI, LUDOVICO,** 5x7 photo in "Faust" costume, signed	62.00	80.00
☐ **CORELLI, FRANCO,** two 8x10 photos, signed	25.00	35.00
☐ **CORELLI, FRANCO,** concert program, signed	11.00	15.00
☐ **CRESPIN, REGINE,** 8x10 color photo, signed and inscribed, mounted on stiff paper, laminated and framed	28.00	37.00
☐ **CRESPIN, REGINE,** LP album cover signed, record missing	12.00	16.00
☐ **CRESPIN, REGINE,** copy of "Metropolitan Opera Annual," signed	10.00	14.00
☐ **DELLA CASA, LISA,** collection of 7 photos, c. 35 press cuttings and various miscellaneous items, three signatures, in a manila envelope	55.00	75.00
☐ **DeLOS ANGELES, VICTORIA,** 8x10 photo in "Faust" costume, with lengthy inscription and signature, thumbtack holes at corners	45.00	60.00

	Price Range	
☐ **DeLOS ANGELES, VICTORIA,** signature on page torn from a magazine	9.00	13.00
☐ **DELUCA, GIUSEPPE,** small sepia photo in "Barber" costume, signed in pencil	25.00	35.00
☐ **DELUCA, GIUSEPPE,** opera contract signed by him, stained	75.00	100.00
☐ **DESTINN, EMMY,** 8x10 photo, signed in violet ink, framed	100.00	125.00
☐ **DESTINN, EMMY,** three unsigned early photos, one in costume	23.00	31.00
☐ **DESTINN, EMMY,** c. 1909, handwritten letter, ¾ers page	80.00	105.00
☐ **DIAZ, JUSTINO,** copy of "Opera News" magazine, with photo of him on front cover, signed on the cover	25.00	35.00
☐ **DIAZ, JUSTINO,** 8x10 photo, signed	10.00	14.00
☐ **DIAZ, JUSTINO,** small color photo of him and Beverly Sills in rehearsal, signed and inscribed by him	12.00	16.00
☐ **DIAZ, JUSTINO,** sword used by him in Metropolitan Opera	50.00	70.00
☐ **DIAZ, JUSTINO,** helmet worn by him in Metropolitan Opera production, gold colored ..	55.00	75.00
☐ **DUNN, MIGNON,** 8x10 photo, signed and inscribed	12.00	16.00
☐ **DUNN, MIGNON,** two 5x7 photos, one cut from a magazine. Not signed, mounted on a card	7.00	10.00
☐ **ELIAS, ROSALIND,** 8x10 photo in costume, signed	10.00	14.00
☐ **ELIAS, ROSALIND,** small color photo from "Walkure," signed	11.00	15.00
☐ **FARRAR, GERALDINE,** 8x10 photo in "Butterfly" costume, inscribed and signed, framed	100.00	125.00
☐ **FARRAR, GERALDINE,** c. 1921–1942, six letters written by her, all but one in holograph	200.00	250.00
☐ **FARRAR, GERALDINE,** 8x10 photo as "Juliet," signed, somewhat damaged	85.00	115.00
☐ **FARRAR, GERALDINE,** c. 1933, postcard, handwritten	40.00	55.00

	Price Range	
☐ **FARRELL, EILEEN,** 8x10 photo, signed ...	9.00	12.00
☐ **FITZPATRICK, LESLIE,** 8x10 photo, signed	7.00	10.00
☐ **FLAGSTAD, KIRSTEN,** opera libretto, signed and inscribed	50.00	75.00
☐ **FLAGSTAD, KIRSTEN,** six 8x10 photos, signed, four in costume, two with inscriptions, all collected into one frame along with a short handwritten note	325.00	400.00
☐ **FLAGSTAD, KIRSTEN,** c. 1930's, 8x10 photo in costume, signed	40.00	55.00
☐ **FLAGSTAD, KIRSTEN,** inscribed Metropolitan Opera program	39.00	50.00
☐ **FLAGSTAD, KIRSTEN,** U.S. $1 bill, signed	50.00	66.00
☐ **GALLI-CURCI, AMELITA,** 5x4 photo in "Traviata" costume, signed in the margin ..	40.00	55.00
☐ **GALLI-CURCI, AMELITA,** 8x10 photo, matted to 11x13½. Not signed	26.00	36.00
☐ **GALLI-CURCI, AMELITA,** scrapbook with c. 85 new cuttings relating to her career, also a few items on other artists	90.00	115.00
☐ **GEDDA, NICOLAI,** opera poster, signed in crayon	23.00	28.00
☐ **GEDDA, NICOLAI,** photo in costume, signed, size not given	10.00	13.00
☐ **GOBBI, TITO,** album cover, signed	34.00	43.00
☐ **GOBBI, TITO,** c. 1959, 8x10 photo, signed and dated	30.00	38.00
☐ **GOBBI, TITO,** 26 photographs, some cut from publications, two of them signed	80.00	100.00
☐ **GOBBI, TITO,** Western Union telegram addressed to him	10.00	14.00
☐ **GRAMM, DONALD,** c. 1975, 8x10 portrait photo, signed	12.00	17.00
☐ **GRAMM, DONALD,** photo of him playing the organ, signed	20.00	25.00
☐ **GRAMM, DONALD,** 8x10 photo in costume, signed in margin, matted	20.00	25.00
☐ **JERITZA, MARIA,** photo in "Tote Stadt" costume, signed on the back, traces of glue staining	55.00	70.00
☐ **JERITZA, MARIA,** c. 1923, two-page letter in her hand, signed, with original envelope ...	90.00	115.00

Price Range

☐ **KEITH, GEORGE,** libretto to "Tosca," signed in pencil 7.00   10.00

☐ **KIRSTEN, DOROTHY,** framed montage consisting of two small signed photos of her, a 78rpm record and three press cuttings 120.00   150.00

☐ **KIRSTEN, DOROTHY,** 8x10 studio photo, hand-colored, signed 55.00   75.00

☐ **KIRSTEN, DOROTHY,** huge poster photo, 27x41, unsigned, mounted on thin wooden board, some defects 60.00   80.00

☐ **LOVE, SHIRLEY,** 8x10 photo in costume, signed 10.00   14.00

☐ **MARTINELLI, GIUSEPPE,** 10x12 sepia portrait photo, signed 70.00   90.00

☐ **McCORMACK, JOHN,** sheet music "When Irish Eyes Are Smiling," signed and inscribed 90.00   110.00

☐ **McCORMACK, JOHN,** c. 1928, typed letter, signed 33.00   45.00

☐ **McCORMACK, JOHN,** c. 1915, 8x10 photo in "Traviata" costume, signed 55.00   70.00

☐ **McCORMACK, JOHN,** card signed, "Best Wishes, John McCormack" 23.00   35.00

☐ **McCORMACK, JOHN,** small snapshot photo. Corner creased 12.00   16.00

☐ **McCRACKEN, JAMES,** 8x10 photo in costume, signed 10.00   14.00

☐ **McCRACKEN, JAMES,** color photo from cover of "Opera News" magazine, signed in Magic Marker 12.00   16.00

☐ **McCRACKEN, JAMES,** three LP album covers signed, with records 70.00   90.00

☐ **MELBA, NELLIE,** c. 1901, one-page holograph letter on her stationery, framed against pink velvet along with a photograph 90.00   115.00

☐ **MELBA, NELLIE,** 7x9 photo signed, brief inscription 120.00   150.00

☐ **MELCHIOR, LAURITZ,** 8x10 photo in Wagnerian costume, with lengthy inscription and signature 80.00   100.00

☐ **MELCHIOR, LAURITZ,** c. 1925–1945, collection of 17 posters advertising his appearances in operas and concerts 225.00   300.00

Price Range

☐ **MELCHIOR, LAURITZ,** photo of him and Jimmy Durante, signed by both 65.00   85.00

☐ **MELCHIOR, LAURITZ,** snapshot photo of him in Central Park, New York, signed on the back 40.00   53.00

☐ **MELCHIOR, LAURITZ,** five unsigned photos, various sizes 45.00   60.00

☐ **MELCHIOR, LAURITZ,** letter to him from James J. Rorimer, president of the Metropolitan Museum, New York, regarding artworks given to the museum by Melchior 40.00   55.00

☐ **MELTON, JAMES,** 8x10 photo in costume, signed 22.00   34.00

☐ **MELTON, JAMES,** collection of c. 150 press cuttings relating to his career, contained in a vinyl-covered album 60.00   80.00

☐ **MERRILL, ROBERT,** photo of him with Danny Kaye, signed by both 35.00   45.00

☐ **MERRILL, ROBERT,** copy of his autobiography, inscribed on the flyleaf 20.00   25.00

☐ **MERRILL, ROBERT,** c. 1952, 8x10 portrait photo, signed 19.00   24.00

☐ **MERRILL, ROBERT,** record company contract, signed by him 43.00   57.00

☐ **MERRILL, ROBERT,** 6x8 color photo in costume, signed 25.00   32.00

☐ **MERRILL, ROBERT and JAN PEERCE,** 8x10 photo of both in costume, signed by both 80.00   110.00

☐ **MILANOV, ZINKA,** magazine article signed in blue pencil 20.00   26.00

☐ **MILANOV, ZINKA,** pair of earrings worn by her 60.00   80.00

☐ **MILANOV, ZINKA,** 8x10 photo in costume, signed 22.00   33.00

☐ **MILANOV, ZINKA,** LP record album cover, signed (no record) 45.00   63.00

☐ **MILNES, SHERRILL,** small photo cut from magazine, mounted on card, signed on the card, inscribed on back of card 20.00   26.00

☐ **MILNES, SHERRILL,** album cover, signed and inscribed 17.00   25.00

Price Range

☐ **MILNES, SHERRILL,** handkerchief used by him in "Otello" .... | 35.00 | 45.00

☐ **MILNES, SHERRILL,** three 8x10 photos, one in costume, all signed .... | 38.00 | 48.00

☐ **MILNES, SHERRILL,** c. 1969, photo of him with Leontyne Price, signed by him .... | 20.00 | 25.00

☐ **MOFFO, ANNA,** article on her from "Life" magazine, signed .... | 30.00 | 37.00

☐ **MOFFO, ANNA,** card signed "Best Wishes, Anna Moffo" .... | 9.00 | 13.00

☐ **MOFFO, ANNA,** Christmas card sent by her, signed .... | 21.00 | 27.00

☐ **MOFFO, ANNA,** LP album cover, signed, record missing .... | 33.00 | 45.00

☐ **MOORE, GRACE,** photo with Bob Hope, signed by both .... | 27.00 | 37.00

☐ **MOORE, GRACE,** six motion picture stills, unsigned .... | 13.00 | 17.00

☐ **MOORE, GRACE,** photo as Mimi in "Boheme," signed .... | 35.00 | 45.00

☐ **MOORE, GRACE,** fan used by her in opera production .... | 30.00 | 40.00

☐ **MOORE, GRACE,** five small snapshot photos, one signed .... | 25.00 | 33.00

☐ **MORELL, BARRY,** LP record album cover, signed, record missing .... | 12.00 | 16.00

☐ **MORELL, BARRY,** photo with James Levine, signed by both .... | 25.00 | 33.00

☐ **MUNSEL, PATRICE,** pair of long silver gloves worn by her in opera production, with letter of authentication .... | 42.00 | 55.00

☐ **MUNSEL, PATRICE,** 8x10 photo, signed and inscribed .... | 12.00 | 16.00

☐ **MUNSEL, PATRICE,** c. 1940's, two 8x10 studio portraits, one of them signed .... | 15.00 | 22.00

☐ **MUNSEL, PATRICE,** signature on an opera company contract .... | 31.00 | 40.00

☐ **MUNSEL, PATRICE,** photo with Helen Traubel, signed by Munsel only, framed, glass cracked .... | 20.00 | 26.00

☐ **MUNSEL, PATRICE,** two small snapshot photos, signed .... | 12.00 | 16.00

	Price Range	

☐ **MUNSEL, PATRICE,** libretto to "Boheme,"
signed 21.00 28.00

☐ **MUNSEL, PATRICE,** photo in "Mignon" costume, signed 27.00 35.00

☐ **MUNSEL, PATRICE,** 6x8 color photo, laminated, signed 21.00 28.00

☐ **NAGY, ROBERT,** 8x10 photo, signed 7.00 10.00

☐ **NILSSON, BIRGIT,** photo in "Tristan" costume, signed 20.00 28.00

☐ **NILSSON, BIRGIT,** LP album cover signed, records missing 27.00 35.00

☐ **NILSSON, BIRGIT,** cover of "Opera News" magazine, signed 15.00 22.00

☐ **NILSSON, BIRGIT,** helmet reputedly worn by her on stage 80.00 105.00

☐ **NILSSON, BIRGIT,** scrapbook containing c. 800 items pertaining to her, press cuttings, photos, several signed, etc. Bound in ½ green leather, 19½x24½ inches. In a buckram slipcase 800.00 1000.00

☐ **NILSSON, BIRGIT,** signature on an opera circular 6.00 8.00

☐ **ORDASSY, CARLOTTA,** 8x10 studio photo, signed and inscribed 9.00 12.00

☐ **PATTI, ADELINA,** c. 1893, ALs, with envelope 55.00 70.00

☐ **PATTI, ADELINA,** c. 1897, ALs, 2½ pp. regarding her role in an opera 110.00 140.00

☐ **PATTI, ADELINA,** 7x9½ photo in costume, framed, soiled, not signed 20.00 26.00

☐ **PATTI, ADELINA,** oil on canvas portrait, 25x38, seated in chair with flowers, framed 1000.00 1250.00

☐ **PATTI, ADELINA,** 8x10 photo, signed and inscribed, framed 160.00 200.00

☐ **PATTI, ADELINA,** two small unsigned photos 12.00 16.00

☐ **PATTI, ADELINA,** signature cut from a letter, glue stained 8.00 11.00

☐ **PAVAROTTI, LUCIANO,** 8x10 photo in "Pagliacci" costume, signed 12.00 18.00

☐ **PAVAROTTI, LUCIANO,** 8x10 photo in "Elisir" costume, mounted, signed, and inscribed 17.00 25.00

	Price Range	
☐ **PAVAROTTI, LUCIANO,** pallet used by him in "Boheme"	30.00	45.00
☐ **PEERCE, JAN,** photo with Leonard Warren, signed by both	70.00	85.00
☐ **PEERCE, JAN,** 8x10 photo with Richard Tucker, signed by Peerce only, both in costume	75.00	110.00
☐ **PEERCE, JAN,** photo in costume, signed and inscribed	23.00	30.00
☐ **PEERCE, JAN,** c. 1971, typed letter, signed	23.00	30.00
☐ **PEERCE, JAN,** c. 1970, brief handwritten note, undated	20.00	26.00
☐ **PEERCE, JAN,** photo with Robert Merrill, signed by Peerce only, matted and framed	70.00	90.00
☐ **PEERCE, JAN,** signature on opera program	12.00	16.00
☐ **PEERCE, JAN,** 8x10 photo in costume, signed	20.00	27.00
☐ **PEERCE, JAN,** magazine article on opera, signed by him and several others	33.00	42.00
☐ **PETERS, ROBERTA,** c. 1965, LP record album cover, signed, record missing	65.00	80.00
☐ **PETERS, ROBERTA,** 8x10 photo standing next to piano, long gown, signed and inscribed	35.00	45.00
☐ **PETERS, ROBERTA,** concert program, signed	9.00	12.00
☐ **PETERS, ROBERTA,** c. 1968, Christmas card, signed	20.00	26.00
☐ **PETERS, ROBERTA,** photo in "Don Giovanni" costume, signed	15.00	20.00
☐ **PETERS, ROBERTA,** c. 1972, colored magazine photo, signed	12.00	16.00
☐ **PETERS, ROBERTA,** c. 1965, ALs, half page	15.00	20.00
☐ **PINZA, EZIO,** 8x10 photo in "Carmen" costume, signed	40.00	53.00
☐ **PINZA, EZIO,** c. 1923, ALs, two pp. with envelope	60.00	80.00
☐ **PINZA, EZIO,** c. 1932, ALs, mentions Lawrence Tibbett	66.00	85.00
☐ **PINZA, EZIO,** 4x5 portrait, signed, framed along with a 78rpm phono record	75.00	95.00

Price Range

☐ **PINZA, EZIO,** c. 1948, 8x10 portrait photo, inscribed 33.00 50.00

☐ **PINZA, EZIO,** printed score, "Fanny," signed 32.00 45.00

☐ **PINZA, EZIO,** sheet music, "Some Enchanted Evening," signed 39.00 50.00

☐ **PINZA, EZIO,** 8x10 photo with Lauritz Melchior, signed by both 95.00 120.00

☐ **PINZA, EZIO,** signature on a news cutting 10.00 14.00

☐ **PINZA, EZIO,** c. 1928–1940, six Metropolitan Opera posters advertising his appearances in various operas, unsigned 180.00 235.00

☐ **PONS, LILY,** c. 1930's, 8x10 photo with drum from "Daughter of the Regiment," signed and inscribed 45.00 60.00

☐ **PONS, LILY,** c. 1937, 8x10 studio photo, signed 35.00 47.00

☐ **PONS, LILY,** c. 1935, ALs, one page, about an opera role 50.00 65.00

☐ **PONS, LILY,** c. 1946, ALs, one page, declining an invitation 35.00 45.00

☐ **PONS, LILY,** 8x10 photo with Robert Merrill, signed by Pons only 30.00 40.00

☐ **PONS, LILY,** 8x10 signed photo, framed with a 78rpm phonograph record and two news cuttings 60.00 80.00

☐ **PONS, LILY,** scrapbook with c. 200 items pertaining to her career, mostly magazine and news cuttings, a few snapshot photos, etc. 200.00 250.00

☐ **PONSELLE, ROSA,** 11x14 sepia photo in costume, signed in blue ink with lengthy inscription, matted and framed (frame damaged) 190.00 240.00

☐ **PONSELLE, ROSA,** c. 1917, ALs, ½ page, with envelope 70.00 100.00

☐ **PONSELLE, ROSA,** c. 1976, typewritten letter, signed, lengthy, 5 pp., discussing her life in opera, etc. 235.00 300.00

☐ **PONSELLE, ROSA,** signature on an opera libretto 35.00 43.00

☐ **PONSELLE, ROSA,** c. 1937, 8x10 studio portrait, signed 44.00 59.00

	Price Range	
☐ **PONSELLE, ROSA,** four small photos, unsigned, mounted	12.00	16.00
☐ **PONSELLE, ROSA,** 78rpm record signed on the label	30.00	38.00
☐ **PONSELLE, ROSA,** c. 1920's, hand-colored photo in costume	12.00	16.00
☐ **PRICE, LEONTYNE,** 8x10 portrait photo, signed and inscribed	15.00	20.00
☐ **PRICE, LEONTYNE,** T-shirt with her likeness	8.00	11.00
☐ **PRICE, LEONTYNE,** c. 1972, typewritten letter, signed	23.00	28.00
☐ **PRICE, LEONTYNE,** 8x10 color photo in costume, signed	33.00	40.00
☐ **PRICE, LEONTYNE,** two LP record album covers, signed, one with records present ..	125.00	165.00
☐ **PRICE, LEONTYNE,** six 8x10 photos in costume, unsigned	10.00	14.00
☐ **PRICE, LEONTYNE,** gold-colored bracelet worn by her in opera production, sold at benefit auction	60.00	80.00
☐ **PRICE, LEONTYNE,** 27x41 poster portrait	75.00	95.00
☐ **RAMEY, SAMUEL,** 8x10 photo in "Mefistofele" costume, signed	11.00	18.00
☐ **RASKIN, JUDITH,** 8x10 studio portrait, signed	11.00	16.00
☐ **RESNIK, REGINA,** c. 1948, opera libretto, signed	12.00	16.00
☐ **RESNIK, REGINA,** 8x10 photo in costume, signed	12.00	16.00
☐ **RESNIK, REGINA,** magazine article with colored photos, signed	15.00	20.00
☐ **RESNIK, REGINA,** c. 1952, signature on an opera company brochure	7.00	10.00
☐ **RESNIK, REGINA,** two 8x10 photos in costume, one signed	20.00	28.00
☐ **RESNIK, REGINA,** photo with Mario Lanza, signed by both	45.00	60.00
☐ **RESNIK, REGINA,** c. 1945–1965, collection of 325 news cuttings	105.00	130.00
☐ **SAYAO, BIDU,** c. 1930's, 8x10 photo in costume, matted, signed on the mount. Sold with several news cuttings	70.00	90.00

Price Range

☐ **SAYAO, BIDU,** c. 1940, 78rpm phono record, signed on the label 25.00 33.00

☐ **SAYAO, BIDU,** opera libretto, signed and inscribed (in Spanish) 32.00 40.00

☐ **SAYAO, BIDU,** c. 1932, handwritten note (in Spanish) 33.00 42.00

☐ **SAYAO, BIDU,** book, "Folk Songs of South America," signed 31.00 39.00

☐ **SCHWARZKOPF, ELIZABETH,** color cover of "Opera News" magazine, signed and inscribed, framed 20.00 25.00

☐ **SCHWARZKOPF, ELIZABETH,** c. 1955, 8x10 photo in costume, signed 26.00 33.00

☐ **SCHWARZKOPF, ELIZABETH,** three unsigned 8x10 studio portraits 10.00 15.00

☐ **SCHWARZKOPF, ELIZABETH,** c. 1960's, signed concert program 9.00 13.00

☐ **SCHWARZKOPF, ELIZABETH,** LP record album cover, signed, record missing 33.00 41.00

☐ **SCHWARZKOPF, ELIZABETH,** three snapshots, signed on backs 21.00 28.00

☐ **SCHWARZKOPF, ELIZABETH,** c. 1959, ALs, 2½ pp., N.Y. hotel stationery 30.00 40.00

☐ **SCHWARZKOPF, ELIZABETH,** c. 1962, ALs, one page 21.00 27.00

☐ **SCHWARZKOPF, ELIZABETH,** signature on a greeting card 21.00 27.00

☐ **SCHWARZKOPF, ELIZABETH,** photo cut from album cover, signed 12.00 17.00

☐ **SIEPI, CESARE,** 8x10 photo in costume, signed 8.00 11.00

☐ **SIEPI, CESARE,** 6x8 photo with Richard Tucker, signed by Siepi only 11.00 15.00

☐ **SIEPI, CESARE,** c. 1978, typewritten letter, signed 7.00 10.00

☐ **SIEPI, CESARE,** 8x10 portrait photo, signed and inscribed 10.00 14.00

☐ **SIEPI, CESARE,** c. 1969, check endorsed by him 21.00 28.00

☐ **SIEPI, CESARE,** three small unsigned photos (candid) 9.00 12.00

Price Range

☐ **SILLS, BEVERLY,** ALs from Pittsburgh hotel, mentioning bad weather **21.00** **30.00**

☐ **SILLS, BEVERLY,** 8x10 photo in "Daughter of the Regiment" costume, signed **25.00** **35.00**

☐ **SILLS, BEVERLY,** huge portrait of her mounted on heart-shaped heavy cardboard, c. three feet, in color, inscribed **125.00** **175.00**

☐ **SILLS, BEVERLY,** copy of her autobiography, "Bubbles," signed **31.00** **40.00**

☐ **SILLS, BEVERLY,** 8x10 portrait photo, signed **20.00** **27.00**

☐ **SILLS, BEVERLY,** c. 1975, large poster of the New York City Opera, picturing her in roles from the "Three Queens," signed by her in Magic Marker **13.00** **20.00**
(The low price of this item—which under normal conditions would be worth at least $50—results from the fact that she signed hundreds of these posters so they could be sold at the New York City Opera's gift shop.)

☐ **SUTHERLAND, JOAN,** 8x10 photo in "Traviata" costume, signed **14.00** **20.00**

☐ **SUTHERLAND, JOAN,** two unsigned 8x10 photos in costume **7.00** **10.00**

☐ **SUTHERLAND, JOAN,** LP record album set, signed on box, records present **125.00** **150.00**

☐ **SUTHERLAND, JOAN,** review of a concert from the "London Times," signed **8.00** **11.00**

☐ **SUTHERLAND, JOAN,** c. 1948, ALs, one page **35.00** **45.00**

☐ **SUTHERLAND, JOAN,** colored magazine cover, signed **25.00** **31.00**

☐ **SUTHERLAND, JOAN,** 8x10 photo with Richard Bonynge, signed by both **55.00** **71.00**

☐ **SUTHERLAND, JOAN,** Christmas card, signed by her and Richard Bonynge **45.00** **60.00**

☐ **SUTHERLAND, JOAN,** c. 1968, 8x10 studio portrait, signed **15.00** **21.00**

☐ **SUTHERLAND, JOAN,** 22x30 color blow-up of a photo of her in costume, signed with large signature, framed **90.00** **115.00**

Price Range

☐ **SUTHERLAND, JOAN,** six scrapbooks with c. 1,500 items on her career, including 56 signed photos, mostly cut from magazines, etc. 1500.00   1900.00

☐ **SUTHERLAND, JOAN,** signature on a restaurant menu 7.00   10.00

☐ **SUTHERLAND, JOAN,** snapshot photo at age about 18, unsigned, mounted 5.00   7.00

☐ **SUTHERLAND, JOAN,** c. 1975, typewritten letter, signed, Brooklyn 20.00   27.00

☐ **SUTHERLAND, JOAN,** five photos mounted on heavy paper, signed on the paper, inscribed, dated 1976 . . . .   90.00   115.00

☐ **SWARTHOUT, GLADYS,** 8x10 potrait photo, signed 15.00   21.00

☐ **SWARTHOUT, GLADYS,** c. 1932, ALs, 1½ pp., with envelope 36.00   45.00

☐ **SWARTHOUT, GLADYS,** 78rpm record, signed on the label 25.00   33.00

☐ **SWARTHOUT, GLADYS,** signature on opera libretto 10.00   15.00

☐ **THOMAS, JOHN CHARLES,** copy of book, "Songs of Stephen Foster," signed on flyleaf   25.00   35.00

☐ **THOMAS, JOHN CHARLES,** 5x6 photo in dressing room, signed 17.00   23.00

☐ **THOMAS, JOHN CHARLES,** c. 1945, 8x10 studio portrait, signed and inscribed 20.00   28.00

☐ **THOMAS, JOHN CHARLES,** 8x10 photo, signed, framed along with a 78rpm record   55.00   75.00

☐ **THOMAS, JOHN CHARLES,** typewritten letter, signed, undated 15.00   22.00

☐ **THOMAS, JOHN CHARLES,** early photo at age c. 15, signed 31.00   43.00

☐ **THOMAS, JOHN CHARLES,** two small snapshots, unsigned 6.00   9.00

☐ **THOMAS, JOHN CHARLES,** c. 1948, 78rpm record album set, signed on the front cover, records present 70.00   90.00

☐ **THOMAS, JOHN CHARLES,** signature on a card 5.00   7.00

Price Range

- ☐ **TIBBETT, LAWRENCE,** 8x10 photo from "Emperor Jones," matted, signed on the mat, framed .... **120.00** | **150.00**
- ☐ **TIBBETT, LAWRENCE,** printed score, "Emperor Jones," signed .... **70.00** | **90.00**
- ☐ **TIBBETT, LAWRENCE,** 8x10 photo in costume, signed .... **44.00** | **60.00**
- ☐ **TIBBETT, LAWRENCE,** c. 1926, ALs, 1½ pp. **77.00** | **100.00**
- ☐ **TIBBETT, LAWRENCE,** 8x10 photo with Amelita Galli-Curci, signed by both, framed **120.00** | **150.00**
- ☐ **TIBBETT, LAWRENCE,** Metropolitan Opera poster for "Emperor Jones," signed .... **250.00** | **350.00**
- ☐ **TRAUBEL, HELEN,** c. 1952, 8x10 photo with Jimmy Durante, signed by both, matted and framed .... **60.00** | **80.00**
- ☐ **TRAUBEL, HELEN,** 5x7 photo with Lauritz Melchior in scene from opera, signed by Traubel only .... **42.00** | **55.00**
- ☐ **TRAUBEL, HELEN,** signature on opera libretto .... **12.00** | **17.00**
- ☐ **TRAUBEL, HELEN,** 4x5 snapshot photo on street, unsigned .... **6.00** | **7.00**
- ☐ **TRAUBEL, HELEN,** c. 1961, typewritten letter, signed .... **12.00** | **17.00**
- ☐ **TRAUBEL, HELEN,** 8x10 studio portrait, signed, thumbtack holes in corners .... **15.00** | **20.00**
- ☐ **TUCKER, RICHARD,** c. 1948, 8x10 studio portrait, signed .... **12.00** | **17.00**
- ☐ **TUCKER, RICHARD,** two photos in costume, one signed .... **20.00** | **30.00**
- ☐ **TUCKER, RICHARD,** c. 1974, typewritten letter, signed .... **12.00** | **17.00**
- ☐ **TUCKER, RICHARD,** colored photo from magazine, signed .... **15.00** | **20.00**
- ☐ **TUCKER, RICHARD,** signature on opera program .... **7.00** | **10.00**
- ☐ **TUCKER, RICHARD,** LP album cover signed, no record .... **42.00** | **55.00**
- ☐ **TUCKER, RICHARD,** c. 1962, magazine cover photo, signed .... **20.00** | **27.00**
- ☐ **WARREN, LEONARD,** opera program to "Tosca," signed and inscribed .... **30.00** | **40.00**

	Price Range	
☐ **WARREN, LEONARD,** 8x10 photo in costume, signed	36.00	46.00

POSTERS

A thorough listing of opera posters from the 19th century to today would be exhaustive, insofar as virtually every opera company in the world—even small companies that perform out of auditoriums rather than actual opera theaters—uses posters of one kind or another to promote its productions. All of these are collectible to varying degrees. Of course, the most desirable and usually most expensive posters are (a) the oldest, (b) those of acclaimed opera companies, (c) posters with names of celebrated artists, (d) highly pictorial posters, especially those with graphic work by noted artists. The price range of opera posters goes from about $5 to at least $500—not counting special copies that carry signatures of artists or are in some other way specially desirable (some of which will be found listed in the preceding section with star memorabilia).

Certainly, posters dating from before 1900 are very highly collectible and seem to be the overall favorite of collectors. Standards of condition are rather high, as it is possible in most cases to find specimens of these posters in nearly mint condition.

	Price Range	
☐ **Foreign Opera Houses,** posters 1850–99	50.00	220.00
☐ **Foreign Opera Houses,** posters pre-1900, with names of artists who later became celebrated in U.S	100.00	285.00
☐ **Foreign Opera Houses,** pre-1800 (generally rather small and printed on thinner paper than later posters; these were designed to be pasted on walls)	250.00	500.00
☐ **Foreign Opera Posters,** pre-1700. Very rare	500.00	2000.00
☐ **Metropolitan Opera House,** unillustrated posters dating before 1900	75.00	100.00
☐ **Metropolitan Opera House,** unillustrated posters, 1900–10	50.00	75.00
☐ **Metropolitan Opera House,** unillustrated posters, 1911–20	45.00	60.00
☐ **Metropolitan Opera House,** posters 1900–10 with illustration of a member or members of the cast	90.00	150.00

Price Range

☐ **Metropolitan Opera House,** most illustrated posters, 1911–20	**75.00**	**125.00**
☐ **Metropolitan Opera House,** most illustrated posters, 1920's	**65.00**	**125.00**
☐ **Metropolitan Opera House,** most illustrated posters, 1965–75	**15.00**	**25.00**
☐ **New York City Opera,** most posters prior to 1970	**15.00**	**30.00**
☐ **U.S. Opera Houses outside New York,** most posters before 1900	**70.00**	**110.00**

(The values of posters are increased by framing. The proportion of increase depends on the type of framing and, of course, the value of the frame itself. Generally, a poster in a frame of average design is worth $20 to $40 more than unframed, but this is only a rough guideline.)

SCRAPBOOKS

Since about 1890, the keeping of scrapbooks has been a favorite pastime among opera fans. Scrapbooks are found pertaining to individual artists as well as to opera in general, and range in scope from collections of news cuttings to autographed photographs and sometimes letters by the artists to the scrapbook keeper. It is not a simple matter to place value guidelines on these collections, as each differs from the other. As a general rule, the older scrapbooks are of greater interest and value than those more recent, as they are likely to contain out-of-print photographs and other memorabilia that is no longer easily obtainable. News cuttings, however, even those of an early vintage, have very little cash value; nor do snippings from magazines, unless autographed, as the magazines from which they were obtained can usually be supplied by "back-date" dealers at a nominal cost.

The values of scrapbooks can roughly be figured as follows:

In scrapbooks in which the majority of material dates before 1920, figure $4 to $8 for original photographs (not cut from magazines or books) of major artists, 50¢–$1 for significant news cuttings, and add to this the values of any autographed items that might be included, referring to the list of artists' memorabilia as a guide.

Condition is a factor only with the items in the album. The condition of the album itself is not important. The use of paste or glue to affix an item will lower its value 10 to 20 percent.

RECORDINGS

CARUSO, ENRICO

Listed below are exclusively 78 (or, as was occasionally the case, 79) rpm recordings, the great majority of them issued while Caruso was alive (he died in 1921). Some posthumous releases are included but none dating later than the 1920's.

Caruso was called upon to make a great number of recordings. His name on a record, after he achieved fame at the Metropolitan and other opera houses, guaranteed a good sale. Many people bought Caruso records who never bought other classical music. He was, in fact, the only operatic performer of the time (1903–21) who could be called popular with the average record-buying public. Though most of his records were of operatic arias or selections, he also recorded a number of non-operatic light-classical songs and even an occasional folk song (such as "O Sole Mio.")

The sound quality on his earlier recordings is understandably quite bad. They date to as early as 1903, when recording techniques and equipment were in a primitive state. Recording technology improved with the years, however, and his later recordings are much better.

These recordings, old though some may be, are by no means impossible to find, and the building of a complete collection of original "Carusos" is certainly attainable with time, patience, and some care. If you choose to collect Caruso 78rpms, do not settle for worn-out copies of the earlier discs, in the belief that their age makes it unlikely to find better ones. Well-preserved specimens of all the Caruso recordings are available and can be found; they cost somewhat more than worn copies but are well worth the investment.

A word of caution: don't play these albums very often. Most are available on LP repressings, if you wish to listen to them—though listening to records is often a secondary consideration to a serious collector. If you have Caruso 78's that are not to be found in LP repressing and want to listen to them, you should record the album and play the recording instead. In any event, you are apt to be far more pleased with the tonal quality of LP repressings than with the original records. A record made in 1905 or 1910 was not designed for play on modern equipment. Tone arms of present-day phonographs are too light; they do not dig deeply enough into the grooves to bring out the full sound. And if you use an old phono with a heavy tone arm, the record will be that much more rapidly worn out. Record companies usually achieve very satisfactory results on their repressings.

The prices given are for specimens in VG and VF condition, but of course one must realize that these standards, for records 60–70 years old, are not quite the same as for more recent recordings. Surface noise is inevitable even in well-preserved specimens but is more noticeable on worn copies.

	Price Range	
☐ **VICTOR RED SEAL (IMPORTED)**, 1903, "Celeste Aida" (Aida)	45.00	70.00
☐ "Cielo e mar" (Gioconda)	45.00	70.00
☐ "E lucevan le stelle" (Tosca)	45.00	70.00
☐ "La Mia Canzone"	45.00	70.00
☐ "Siciliana" (Cavalleria Rusticana)	45.00	70.00
☐ "Non t'amo piu"	72.00	110.00
☐ "Vesti la giubba" (Pagliacci)	42.00	62.00
☐ **VICTOR RED SEAL**, 1904–1905, "Questa o quella" (Rigoletto)	17.00	25.00
☐ "La donna e mobile" (Rigoletto)	17.00	25.00
☐ "Una furtiva lagrima," Part One (Elisir d'Amore)	20.00	30.00
☐ "E lucevan le stelle" (Tosca)	17.00	25.00
☐ "Recondita armonia" (Tosca)	22.00	35.00
☐ "Siciliana" (Cavalleria Rusticana)	17.00	25.00
☐ "Il sogno" (Manon)	22.00	35.00
☐ "Vesti la giubba" (Pagliacci)	18.00	27.00
(The first phonograph recording to sell 1 million copies.)		
☐ "Brindisi" (Cavalleria Rusticana)	17.00	25.00
☐ "Una furtiva lagrima," Part Two (Elisir d'Amore)	37.00	55.00
☐ "Celeste Aida" (Aida)	23.00	32.00
☐ "Com'e gentil" (Don Pasquale)	26.00	35.00
☐ "Canzone del fior" (Carmen)	37.00	54.00
☐ "Cielo e mar" (Gioconda)	31.00	43.00
☐ "Bianca al par" (Huguenots)	37.00	55.00
☐ **VICTOR RED SEAL**, 1906–1908, "Di quella pira" (Trovatore)	19.00	27.00
☐ "La donna e mobile" (Rigoletto)	12.00	19.00
☐ "Questa o quella" (Rigoletto)	12.00	19.00
☐ "M'appari" (Martha)	12.00	19.00
☐ "Che gelida manina" (Boheme)	23.00	34.00
☐ "Salut demeure" (Faust)	23.00	34.00
☐ "Spirto gentil" (La Favorita)	23.00	34.00

Price Range

☐ "Triste Ritorno"	23.00	34.00
☐ "Ideale"	20.00	30.00
☐ "O Paradiso" (Africana)	20.00	30.00
☐ "Improvviso" (Andrea Chenier)	20.00	32.00
☐ "Vesti la giubba" (Pagliacci)	17.00	25.00
☐ "In terra sola" (Don Sebastiano)	21.00	33.00
☐ "Adorables tourments"	21.00	33.00
☐ "Lolita"	17.00	25.00
☐ "Ah se ben mio" (Trovatore)	21.00	32.00
☐ "Celeste Aida" (Aida)	12.00	17.00
☐ "Solenne" (Forza del Destino), with Scotti	14.00	22.00
☐ "Ah Mimi" (Boheme), with Scotti	14.00	22.00
☐ "Del Tempio" Pearl Fishers	22.00	32.00
☐ "O quanti occhi" (Butterfly), with Geraldine Farrar	32.00	47.00

(This was the first duet recording made by Caruso and Geraldine Farrar and is considered a prize collector's item. They later teamed up again for selections from Faust and other recordings.)

☐ "Ai nostri monti" (Trovatore)	20.00	30.00
☐ "O soave fanciulla" (Boheme), with Nellie Melba	32.00	45.00
☐ "Quartet" (Rigoletto), record #96000	21.00	31.00
☐ "Quartet" (Rigoletto), record #96001	20.00	30.00
☐ "Addio dolce" (Boheme)	22.00	31.00
☐ "Sextet" (Lucia)	20.00	30.00
☐ **VICTOR RED SEAL,** 1909–1911, "Magiche note" (Queen of Sheba)	31.00	43.00
☐ "Pour un baiser"	21.00	31.00
☐ "Recondita armonia" (Tosca)	12.00	18.00
☐ "E lucevan le stelle" (Tosca)	17.00	18.00
☐ "Studenti, udite" (Germania)	31.00	46.00
☐ "Non chiuder" (Germania)	30.00	44.00
☐ "For You Alone"	10.00	15.00
☐ "Ora e per sempre addio" (Otello)	30.00	44.00
☐ "Siciliana" (Cavalleria Rusticana)	10.00	15.00
☐ "Mamma Mia"	12.00	19.00
☐ "O tu che in seno" (Forza del Destino)	12.00	19.00
☐ "Air de la fleur" (Carmen)	25.00	36.00
☐ "Canzone del fior" (Carmen)	21.00	32.00

	Price Range	
☐ "Bianca al par" (Huguenots)	25.00	36.00
☐ "Cielo e mar" (La Gioconda)	20.00	29.00
☐ "No, Pagliaccio non son" (Pagliacci)	15.00	23.00
☐ "Addio"	10.00	15.00
☐ "La fatal pietra" (Aida)	21.00	34.00
☐ "O terra addio" (Aida)	21.00	34.00
☐ "Miserere" (Trovatore)	10.00	15.00
☐ "Eternelle" (Faust)	20.00	30.00
☐ "Laisse-moi" (Faust)	20.00	30.00
☐ "Mon coeur" (Faust)	23.00	34.00
☐ "Voici la rue" (Faust)	23.00	34.00
☐ "Solo, profugo" (Martha)	23.00	34.00
☐ "O Merveille" (Faust)	12.00	18.00
☐ "Amore o grillo" (Butterfly)	23.00	34.00
☐ "Ve lo dissi" (Butterfly)	23.00	34.00
☐ "Mal reggendo" (Trovatore)	19.00	29.00
☐ "Gia i sacerdoti" (Aida)	23.00	34.00
☐ "Aida a me togliesti" (Aida)	23.00	34.00
☐ "Alerte" (Faust)	19.00	29.00
☐ "Seigneur Dieu" (Faust)	23.00	32.00
☐ "Eh quoi" (Faust)	27.00	40.00
☐ "Que voulez-vouz" (Faust)	23.00	34.00
☐ **VICTOR RED SEAL,** 1912–1915, "Barcarola" (Masked Ball)	10.00	15.00
☐ "Canta pe' me"	14.00	21.00
☐ "Love Is Mine"	10.00	15.00
☐ "Because"	15.00	23.00
☐ "Pimpinella"	15.00	23.00
☐ "Donna non vidi mai" (Manon Lescaut)	20.00	30.00
☐ "Your Eyes Have Told"	14.00	21.00
☐ "Lasciati amar"	20.00	29.00
☐ "Guardann'a luna"	21.00	32.00
☐ "Serenade Espagnole"	21.00	32.00
☐ "Amor Mio"	20.00	29.00
☐ "Parted"	15.00	23.00
☐ "Trusting Eyes"	15.00	23.00
☐ "Hantise d'amour"	25.00	40.00
☐ "La Mia Canzone"	14.00	21.00
☐ "Cielo Turchino"	20.00	29.00
☐ "Brindisi" (Traviata)	20.00	29.00
☐ "Celeste Aida" (Aida)	10.00	15.00
☐ "Testa adorata" (Boheme)	20.00	30.00

	Price Range	
☐ "Eternamente"	20.00	30.00
☐ "Core 'ngrato"	20.00	30.00
☐ "Io non ho" (Boheme)	20.00	30.00
☐ "Una furtiva lagrima" (Elisir d'Amore)	10.00	15.00
☐ "Quando Nascesti Tu" (Lo Schiavo)	24.00	38.00
☐ "Ma se m'e forza" (Masked Ball)	24.00	35.00
☐ "Tarantella Sincera"	16.00	24.00
☐ "Ah fuyez" (Manon)	25.00	37.00
☐ "Danza"	16.00	24.00
☐ "Dreams of Long Ago"	12.00	19.00
☐ "Lost Chord"	12.00	19.00
☐ "Hosanna"	16.00	27.00
☐ "Agnus dei"	16.00	27.00
☐ "Parmi veder le lagrime" (Rigoletto)	15.00	27.00
☐ "Fenesta che lucive"	15.00	27.00
☐ "Addio alla madre" (Cavalleria Rusticana) ..	22.00	30.00
☐ "Les Rameaux"	16.00	27.00
☐ "Cuius Animam" (Stabat Mater)	16.00	27.00
☐ "Manella Mia"	22.00	30.00
☐ "Tiempo antico"	22.00	30.00
☐ "Ingemisco" (Requiem)	22.00	30.00
☐ "Angelo casto" (The Duke of Alba)	27.00	42.00
☐ "Pecche"	21.00	30.00
☐ "Invano, Alvaro" (Forza del Destino)	25.00	39.00
☐ "Le minaccie" (Forza del Destino)	25.00	39.00
☐ "Crucifix"	21.00	29.00
☐ "On l'appelle" (Manon)	26.00	39.00
☐ "Ai nostri monti" (Trovatore)	16.00	25.00
☐ "Dio che nell'alma" (Don Carlos)	24.00	37.00
☐ "Elegie"	12.00	17.00
☐ "Si per ceil (Othello)	21.00	30.00
☐ "E scherzo" (Masked Ball)	28.00	40.00
☐ "La rivedro" (Masked Ball)	28.00	40.00
☐ "Sento un forza" (Guaranty)	31.00	48.00
☐ "Si vous l'avez compris"	15.00	27.00
☐ "Deux Serenades"	15.00	27.00
☐ "Siam giunti" (Martha)	22.00	29.00
☐ "Che vuol dir" (Martha)	22.00	29.00
☐ "Presto, Presto" (Martha)	22.00	29.00
☐ "Quartetto Notturno" (Martha)	16.00	25.00
☐ "Qual volutta" (Lombardi)	25.00	36.00
☐ "Sextet" (Lucia)	25.00	36.00

	Price Range	
☐ **VICTOR RED SEAL,** 1916–20 and some later, "Luna d'estate"	18.00	26.00
☐ "O Sole Mio"	12.00	19.00
☐ "Come un bel di" (Andrea Chernier)	21.00	30.00
☐ "De mon amie" (Pearl Fishers)	21.00	30.00
☐ "Pourquoi"	18.00	26.00
☐ "L'Alba separa"	18.00	26.00
☐ "Over There"	21.00	30.00
☐ "Inno de Garibaldi"	21.00	30.00
☐ "A Vucchella"	18.00	26.00
☐ "Vieni sul mar"	12.00	19.00
☐ "Addio a Napoli"	12.00	19.00
☐ "A Dream"	8.00	11.00
☐ "Messe Solennelle"	21.00	29.00
☐ "Nina"	18.00	26.00
☐ "M'appari" (Martha)	12.00	19.00
☐ "Inspirez-moi" (Queen of Sheba)	25.00	38.00
☐ "O Souverain" (El Cid)	25.00	38.00
☐ "Mia sposa"	25.00	38.00
☐ "La Procession"	23.00	32.00
☐ "Ah la paterna mano" (Macbeth)	27.00	40.00
☐ "Sancta Maria"	23.00	32.00
☐ "Santa Lucia"	17.00	25.00
☐ "Noel"	17.00	25.00
☐ "Chanson de Juin"	23.00	32.00
☐ "Je crois entendre" (Pearl Fishers)	12.00	19.00
☐ "Vois, ma misere" (Samson)	23.00	32.00
☐ "Echo lointain" (Eugene Onegin)	27.00	39.00
☐ "Musica Proibita"	23.00	32.00
☐ "Uocchie Celeste"	23.00	32.00
☐ "Ah mon sort" (Nero)	27.00	39.00
☐ "Pieta Signore"	23.00	32.00
☐ "Regiment de Sambre et Meuse"	21.00	30.00
☐ "Campana de San Giusto"	17.00	25.00
☐ "Campane a Sera"	17.00	25.00
☐ "Love Me or Not"	21.00	33.00
☐ "Largo" (Serse)	16.00	25.00
☐ "A Granada"	16.00	25.00
☐ "Rachel quand du Seigneur" (La Juive)	12.00	18.00
☐ "Mia piccirella" (Salvator Rosa)	21.00	30.00
☐ "A la luz de la Luna"	17.00	25.00
☐ "Il segreto fu dunque" (Forza del Destino)	23.00	34.00

	Price Range	
☐ "Je viens celebrer" (Samson)	23.00	34.00
☐ "Venti scudi" (Elisir d'Amore)	23.00	34.00
☐ "Quartet" (Rigoletto)	12.00	19.00
☐ "Sextet" (Lucia)	12.00	19.00

HOMER, LOUISE

☐ **VICTOR RED SEAL,** 1903–1905, "Le parlate d'amor" (Faust)	23.00	32.00
☐ "Annie Laurie"	21.00	29.00
☐ "May Day"	30.00	42.00
☐ "Sing Me a Song"	23.00	32.00
☐ "Stella del mariner" (La Gioconda)	37.00	51.00
☐ "Old Folks at Home"	23.00	32.00
☐ "Habanera" (Carmen)	37.00	51.00
☐ "Filles de Cadiz"	37.00	51.00
☐ "Scene de la prison" (La Phophete)	57.00	82.00
☐ "Nobil Signori" (Huguenots)	41.00	58.00
☐ "He Shall Feed His Flock (Messiah)	35.00	46.00
☐ "Mon coeur" (Samson)	38.00	50.00
☐ "Away with Crying" (Orfeo)	48.00	61.00
☐ "O don fatale" (Don Carlos)	46.00	60.00
☐ "Turn Ye to Me"	38.00	50.00
☐ "O Rest in the Lord" (Elijah)	31.00	43.00
☐ "Ah mon fils" (La Prophete)	38.00	55.00
☐ **VICTOR RED SEAL,** 1906–1911, "Stride la vamps" (Trovatore)	23.00	33.00
☐ "Voce di donna" (La Gioconda)	25.00	38.00
☐ "Esser mesto" (Martha)	40.00	59.00
☐ "Quanto a te lieta" (Faust)	31.00	45.00
☐ "Le parlate d'amor" (Faust)	29.00	40.00
☐ "Acerbe volunta" (Adriana Lecouvreur)	39.00	51.00
☐ "At Parting"	17.00	25.00
☐ "Banjo Song"	8.00	14.00
☐ "Vengeance at Last" (Samson)	29.00	40.00
☐ "Lost Chord"	12.00	19.00
☐ "Old Black Joe"	12.00	19.00
☐ "Fac ut portem" (Stabat Mater)	16.00	23.00
☐ "Quanto a te lieta" (Faust)	25.00	40.00
☐ "Amour, viens aider" (Samson)	16.00	23.00
☐ "Die Lorelei"	16.00	23.00

	Price Range	
☐ "Die Allmacht"	35.00	51.00
☐ "Che faro senza Euridice" (Orfeo)	16.00	22.00
☐ "Fatal Divinita" (Alceste)	35.00	51.00
☐ "There Is a Green Tree"	12.00	19.00
☐ "Mesta ognor" (Martha)	44.00	65.00
☐ "Dome epais" (Lakme)	44.00	65.00
☐ "Du Aermste" (Lohengrin)	44.00	65.00
☐ **VICTOR RED SEAL,** 1912–1918, "I Cannot Sing the Old Songs"	8.00	14.00
☐ "Boats Sail/Sing to Me"	12.00	17.00
☐ "Annie Laurie"	8.00	14.00
☐ "Oh Promise Me" (Robin Hood)	8.00	14.00
☐ "Last Night"	8.00	14.00
☐ "Janet's Choice"	12.00	19.00
☐ "Don't Cease"	12.00	19.00
☐ "Where Is My Boy Tonight?"	8.00	14.00
☐ "Nur wer die Sehnsucht kennt"	8.00	14.00
☐ "Star Spangled Banner"	12.00	19.00
☐ "Come Unto Me"	25.00	40.00
☐ "Dearest" (Requiem)	25.00	40.00
☐ "Babylon"	25.00	40.00
☐ "He Was Despised" (Messiah)	16.00	23.00
☐ "My Heart Ever Faithful"	16.00	23.00
☐ "Largo" (Serse)	16.00	23.00
☐ "Love's Old Sweet Song"	12.00	17.00
☐ **VICTOR RED SEAL,** 1919–1925, "I Love to Tell the Story"	8.00	14.00
☐ "Hard Times"	8.00	14.00
☐ "Oh, Boys, Carry Me 'Long"	8.00	14.00
☐ "When the Roses Bloom"	8.00	14.00
☐ "Just for Today"	8.00	14.00
☐ "My Ain Folk"	8.00	14.00
☐ "My Ain Countrie"	8.00	14.00
☐ "Christ the Lord"	8.00	14.00
☐ "Lane to Ballybree"	8.00	14.00
☐ "Ring Out Wild Bells"	17.00	25.00
☐ "Sheep and Lambs"	17.00	25.00
☐ "Auld Scotch Sangs"	17.00	25.00
☐ "Barnyard Song"	17.00	25.00
☐ "Little Orphan Annie"	27.00	40.00

McCORMACK, JOHN

John McCormack was the all-around singer supreme, at home with folk songs, popular tunes and operatic arias. Although best remembered today as the classic balladeer of Irish traditional melodies, he also enjoyed a long career on the opera stage, notably at the Metropolitan, and made a number of operatic recordings. Most of his records are, however, in the nature of ballads or comic tunes sung to the accompaniment of a piano only. They have been repressed very often, but collectors, being collectors, will always try to locate the originals.

The discs listed here date from the period 1910 to 1925 and are, of course, one-sided. On the whole, the sound quality of McCormack's recordings was not too bad, though one can only wonder how he might have sounded with modern recording techniques. He was under exclusive contract with the Eldridge Johnson Victor Co., and all of his records were released on the Victor Red Seal label, that label being assigned to classical music, and were then called "celebrity recordings."

	Price Range	
☐ **VICTOR RED SEAL,** 1910–1912, "The Minstrel Boy"	8.00	14.00
☐ "I Hear You Calling Me"	8.00	14.00
☐ "When Shadows Gather"	14.00	20.00
☐ "Annie Laurie"	8.00	14.00
☐ "Dear Little Shamrock"	8.00	14.00
☐ "My Lagen Love"	16.00	23.00
☐ "I'm Falling in Love" (Naughty Marietta)	12.00	19.00
☐ "Believe Me if All Those Endearing Young Charms"	8.00	14.00
☐ "Mother Machree"	8.00	14.00
☐ "Take, Oh Take Those Lips Away"	8.00	14.00
☐ "A Child's Song"	15.00	22.00
☐ "A Farewell"	15.00	22.00
☐ "I Know of Two Bright Eyes"	15.00	22.00
☐ "Eileen Aroon"	15.00	22.00
☐ "The Rosary"	8.00	14.00
☐ "The Wearing of the Green"	8.00	14.00
☐ "The Harp That Once Thro' Tara's Halls"	8.00	14.00
☐ "Silver Threads Among the Gold"	8.00	14.00
☐ "Killarney"	12.00	19.00
☐ "Come Back to Erin"	12.00	19.00
☐ "Snowy Breasted Pearl"	12.00	19.00
☐ "Molly Bawn"	12.00	19.00

	Price Range	
☑ "Has Sorrow Thy Young Days Shaded"	12.00	19.00
☐ "Drink To Me Only With Thine Eyes"	12.00	19.00
☐ "Ah, Moon of My Delight"	14.00	20.00
☐ "Kathleen Mavoureen"	12.00	19.00
☐ "Irish Emigrant"	12.00	19.00
☐ "She is Far From the Land"	12.00	19.00
☐ "An Evening Song"	12.00	19.00
☐ "Paul's Address" (Natoma)	27.00	39.00
☐ "Like Stars Above"	21.00	30.00
☐ "Marie, My Girl"	21.00	30.00
☐ "Asthore"	14.00	20.00
☐ "Vieni al contento" (Lakme)	21.00	30.00
☐ "Li Mariani"	29.00	45.00
☐ "Del Tempio" (Pearl Fishers)	29.00	45.00
☐ "Fra poco a me" (Lucia)	29.00	45.00
☐ "Canzone del fior" (Carmen)	29.00	45.00
☐ "Una furtiva lagrima" (Elisir d'Amore)	29.00	45.00
☐ "Che gelida manina" (Boheme)	29.00	45.00
☐ "Salve dimora" (Faust)	29.00	45.00
☐ "Per viver vicino (Daughter of the Regiment)	29.00	45.00
☐ "Tu che a Dio" (Lucia)	29.00	45.00
☐ "Ah Mimi" (Boheme)	35.00	50.00
☐ **VICTOR RED SEAL,** 1913–1915, "At Dawning"	8.00	12.00
☐ "Dai campi" (Mefistofele)	17.00	25.00
☐ "Giunto sul passo" (Mefistofele)	17.00	25.00
☐ "Mi par d'udire (Pearl Fishers)	17.00	25.00
☐ "There Is a Flower" (Maritana)	14.00	20.00
☐ "Sweet Genevieve"	8.00	12.00
☐ "My Dreams"	8.00	12.00
☐ "Where the River Shannon Flows"	8.00	12.00
☐ "Il sogno" (Manon)	21.00	33.00
☐ "Molly Brannigan"	12.00	19.00
☐ "Within the Garden of My Heart"	8.00	14.00
☐ "Dear Love, Remember Me"	8.00	14.00
☐ "Foggy Dew"	8.00	14.00
☐ "Say Au Revoir"	8.00	14.00
☐ "Low Back'd Car"	8.00	14.00
☐ "Down in the Forest"	14.00	25.00
☐ "Mother o' Mine"	8.00	14.00
☐ "Sospiri Miei"	21.00	30.00
☐ "I Hear a Thrush at Eve"	8.00	14.00

	Price Range	
☐ "Eileen Allanna"	12.00	17.00
☐ "Good Bye, Sweetheart"	8.00	14.00
☐ "A Little Love"	8.00	14.00
☐ "Questa o quella" (Rigoletto)	15.00	25.00
☐ "Nearer, My God, to Thee"	8.00	14.00
☐ "Le Portrait"	26.00	40.00
☐ "I'll Sing Thee Songs of Araby"	8.00	14.00
☐ "Somewhere a Voice is Calling"	8.00	14.00
☐ "Mavis"	8.00	14.00
☐ "Come Where My Love Lies"	8.00	14.00
☐ "Who Knows"	8.00	14.00
☐ "Little Grey Home"	8.00	14.00
☐ "My Wild Irish Rose"	8.00	14.00
☐ "Bonnie Wee Thing"	8.00	14.00
☐ "Beautiful Isle of Somewhere"	15.00	23.00
☐ "Golden Love"	8.00	14.00
☐ "Because"	15.00	23.00
☐ "Mavoureen"	8.00	14.00
☐ "Mary of Argyle"	8.00	14.00
☐ "Ben Bolt"	8.00	14.00
☐ "A Dream"	8.00	14.00
☐ "Funiculi Funicula"	15.00	22.00
☐ "Lily of Killarney"	13.00	19.00
☐ "It's a Long, Long Way to Tipperray"	8.00	14.00
☐ "Until"	8.00	14.00
☐ "Evening Song"	8.00	14.00
☐ "When the Dew Is Falling"	8.00	14.00
☐ "Morning"	15.00	22.00
☐ "Vacant Chair"	8.00	14.00
☐ "De' miei bollenti spiriti" (Traviata)	35.00	50.00
☐ "Nirvana"	21.00	30.00
☐ "Parle-moi de ma mere" (Carmen)	25.00	37.00
☐ "Good Bye"	11.00	19.00
☐ "O terra addio" (Aida)	20.00	30.00
☐ "When My Ships Come Sailing Home"	13.00	19.00
☐ "The Trumpeter"	13.00	19.00
☐ "Come Into the Garden"	13.00	19.00
☐ "Turn Ye to Me"	22.00	35.00
☐ "Adeste Fideles"	13.00	19.00
☐ "Serenade"	13.00	19.00
☐ "Ave Marie" (record #87192)	13.00	19.00
☐ "Serenata"	13.00	19.00

Price Range

☐ "Carme"	16.00	25.00
☐ "Flirtation"	11.00	17.00
☐ "Calm as the Night"	11.00	17.00
☐ "O soave fanciulla" (Boheme)	15.00	23.00
☐ "Parigi o cara" (Traviata)	20.00	30.00
☐ "Angel's Serenade"	15.00	23.00
☐ "Ave Maria" (record #88481)	15.00	23.00
☐ "Le Nil"	15.00	23.00
☐ "Berceuse" (Jocelyn)	15.00	23.00
☐ "Ave Maria" (record #88484)	15.00	23.00
☐ "Quartet" (Rigoletto)	20.00	30.00
☐ **VICTOR RED SEAL,** 1916–1919, "Sing, Sing Birds on the Wing"	8.00	14.00
☐ "A Little Bit of Heaven"	7.00	13.00
☐ "Forgotten"	7.00	13.00
☐ "Venetian Song"	7.00	13.00
☐ "Old Refrain"	7.00	13.00
☐ "Parted"	7.00	13.00
☐ "Then You'll Remember Me" (Bohemian Girl)	11.00	19.00
☐ "Dreams"	8.00	14.00
☐ "Your Eyes"	8.00	14.00
☐ "Little Boy Blue"	8.00	14.00
☐ "Cradle Song 1915"	8.00	14.00
☐ "Sunshine of Your Smile"	8.00	14.00
☐ "Love, Here Is My Heart"	8.00	14.00
☐ "Tommy Lad"	8.00	14.00
☐ "When Irish Eyes Are Smiling"	8.00	14.00
☐ "Star Spangled Banner"	12.00	19.00
☐ "Ireland My Sireland" (Eileen)	12.00	19.00
☐ "Eileen Alanna Asthore" (Eileen)	12.00	19.00
☐ "There's a Long, Long Trail"	8.00	14.00
☐ "Keep the Home Fires Burning"	8.00	14.00
☐ "Any Place Is Heaven"	8.00	14.00
☐ "Crucifix"	8.00	14.00
☐ "Lord Is My Light"	8.00	14.00
☐ "Rainbow of Love"	8.00	14.00
☐ "Trumpet Call"	12.00	19.00
☐ "Send Me Away With a Smile"	12.00	19.00
☐ "God Be With Our Boys"	12.00	19.00
☐ "Little Mother of Mine"	8.00	14.00
☐ "Dear Old Pal of Mine"	8.00	14.00

	Price Range	
☐ "Love's Garden of Roses"	8.00	14.00
☐ "When You Come Back"	12.00	19.00
☐ "My Irish Song of Songs"	8.00	14.00
☐ "Calling Me Home to You"	8.00	14.00
☐ "When You Look in the Heart of a Rose" ..	8.00	14.00
☐ "First Rose of Summer"	8.00	14.00
☐ "Roses of Picardy"	8.00	14.00
☐ "Prize Song" (Meistersinger)	12.00	20.00
☐ "Il mio tesoro" (Don Giovanni)	14.00	21.00
☐ "Kerry Dance"	10.00	15.00
☐ "Non e ver"	18.00	27.00
☐ "Champs paternels" (Joseph)	21.00	32.00
☐ "Barcarolle" (Tales of Hoffman)	10.00	15.00
☐ **VICTOR RED SEAL,** 1920–1925, "The Tumble-Down Shack"	6.50	11.00
☐ "Only You"	6.50	11.00
☐ "Your Eyes"	6.50	11.00
☐ "Barefoot Trail"	6.50	11.00
☐ "Thank God for a Garden"	6.50	11.00
☐ "Honour & Love" (Monsieur Beaucaire)	10.00	15.00
☐ "When You & I Were Young"	6.50	11.00
☐ " 'Tis an Irish Girl"	6.50	11.00
☐ "Next Market Day"	10.00	15.00
☐ "Beneath the Moon of Lombardy"	6.50	11.00
☐ "Somewhere"	6.50	11.00
☐ "Learn to Smile"	6.50	12.00
☐ "Little Town in Ould County Down"	6.50	11.00
☐ "Rose of My Heart"	6.50	11.00
☐ "The Road That Brought You"	6.50	11.00
☐ "Sweet Peggy O'Neil"	6.50	11.00
☐ "Wonderful World of Romance"	6.50	11.00
☐ "O Sleep" (Semele)	6.50	11.00
☐ "Three O'Clock in the Morning"	12.00	19.00
☐ "Mother in Ireland"	6.50	11.00
☐ "Jesus, My Lord"	6.50	11.00
☐ "Kingdom Within Your Eyes"	6.50	11.00
☐ "Remember the Rose"	6.50	11.00
☐ "Sometime You'll Remember"	6.50	11.00
☐ "Love Sends a Little Gift of Roses"	6.50	11.00
☐ "Wonderful One"	6.50	11.00
☐ "Somewhere in the World"	6.50	11.00

	Price Range	
☐ "Where the Rainbow Ends"	6.50	11.00
☐ "Bard of Armagh"	11.00	17.00
☐ "Would God I Were the Tender Apple Blossom"	6.50	11.00
☐ "Take a Look Molly"	6.50	11.00
☐ "Marcheta"	11.00	17.00
☐ "Indiana Moon"	11.00	17.00
☐ "Lost Chord"	6.50	11.00
☐ "When Night Descends"	11.00	17.00
☐ "Since You Went Away"	11.00	17.00
☐ "O Cease Thy Singing"	11.00	17.00
☐ "The Last Hour"	6.50	11.00

MELBA, NELLIE

Nellie Melba's recordings are collectors' items in the truest sense of the term. Having reached the peak of her stardom not long after the introduction of 78rpm records, her voice was among the most frequently recorded of early-20th-century opera artists. A star she was in every respect, the only female opera singer before 1910 whose public notoriety could be said to equal Caruso's. Modern opinion of her talents does not perhaps equal those of her contemporaries; nevertheless, her recordings are still very much in demand.

☐ **IMPORTED VICTOR MAUVE LABEL,** 1904–1905, "Les Anges Pleurent"	30.00	44.00
☐ "Chant Venetien"	30.00	44.00
☐ "Come Back to Erin"	22.00	30.00
☐ "Auld Lang Syne"	22.00	30.00
☐ "Old Folks at Home"	22.00	30.00
☐ "Good Night"	22.00	35.00
☐ "Away on the Hill"	22.00	35.00
☐ "Goodbye"	27.00	37.00
☐ "Mad scene" (Lucia)	38.00	53.00
☐ "Ah forse lui" (Traviata)	38.00	53.00
☐ "Sempre libera" (Traviata)	38.00	53.00
☐ "Sweet Bird" (Penseroso)	38.00	53.00
☐ "Three Green Bonnets"	38.00	53.00
☐ "Caro nome" (Rigoletto)	38.00	53.00
☐ "Se Saran Rose"	38.00	53.00
☐ "A vos jeux" (Hamlet)	38.00	53.00
☐ "Pale et blonde" (Hamlet)	38.00	53.00

Price Range

☐ "Martinata" (Tosti)	38.00	53.00
☐ "Nymphes et Sylvainus"	38.00	53.00
☐ "Si Mes Vers"	38.00	53.00
☐ "Porgi amor" (Marriage of Figaro)	38.00	53.00
☐ "Home Sweet Home"	27.00	40.00
☐ "Lo, Hear the Gentle Lark"	27.00	40.00
☐ "Sur le Lac"	36.00	51.00

NIELSEN, ALICE

The rich soprano voice of Alice Nielsen, who long enticed opera audiences with her renditions of roles from Tosca, Butterfly, Marriage of Figaro, and others, was well represented on recordings, of which the following is only a mere selection. On the whole, her recordings are somewhat more valuable than those of most other opera singers.

☐ **COLUMBIA,** 1911–1915. "Deh Vieni" (Marriage of Figaro)	30.00	43.00
☐ "Le roi de Thule" (Faust)	30.00	43.00
☐ "Annie Laurie"	15.00	22.00
☐ "Kathleen Mavoureen"	15.00	22.00
☐ "From the Land of the Sky-Blue Water"	30.00	45.00
☐ "Chonita's Prayer" (Sacrifice)	30.00	45.00
☐ "Home Sweet Home"	20.00	30.00
☐ "Il Bacio"	20.00	30.00
☐ "Ancora un passo" (Butterfly)	30.00	45.00
☐ "Piccolo Iddio" (Butterfly)	30.00	45.00
☐ "Un bel di" (Butterfly)	30.00	45.00
☐ "Addio" (Boheme)	20.00	30.00
☐ "L'altra notte" (Mefistofele)	30.00	45.00
☐ "Vissi d'arte" (Tosca)	30.00	45.00
☐ "Je dis que rien" (Carmen)	30.00	45.00
☐ "Ieri son salito" (Butterfly)	30.00	45.00
☐ "Fardi si fa" (Faust)	36.00	51.00
☐ "Sweet Genevieve"	16.00	25.00
☐ "In the Gloaming"	16.00	25.00
☐ "Oh I'm Not Myself"	16.00	25.00
☐ "Believe Me if All Those Endearing Young Charms"	16.00	25.00
☐ "Love's Old Sweet Song"	16.00	25.00
☐ "Bendemeer's Stream"	16.00	25.00
☐ "Day Is Done"	16.00	25.00
☐ "Spirit Flower"	16.00	25.00

	Price Range	
☐ "Low Back'd Car"	16.00	25.00
☐ "Killarney"	16.00	25.00
☐ "Barney O'Hea"	16.00	25.00
☐ "By the Water of Minnetonka"	12.00	19.00
☐ "From the Land of the Sky-Blue Water" ...	12.00	19.00

ROSA, PONSELLE

The voice of Rosa Ponselle, a long-time favorite at the Metropolitan and other opera houses, is still regarded by those who heard it live as one of the finest in operatic history. On these recordings she tackled a wide range of selections, usually with memorable results.

☐ **COLUMBIA RECORDS,** 1919–1923, "O Patria mia" (Aida)	17.00	25.00
☐ "La vergine" (Forza del Destino)	17.00	25.00
☐ "D'amor sull'ali" (Trovatore)	17.00	25.00
☐ "Good Bye"	17.00	25.00
☐ "Vissi d'arte" (Tosca)	17.00	25.00
☐ "Un bel di" (Butterfly)	17.00	25.00
☐ "Keep the Home Fires Burning"	17.00	25.00
☐ "Bolero" (Vespri Siciliani)	21.00	32.00
☐ "Casta diva" (Norma)	17.00	25.00
☐ "O terra addio" (Aida)	17.00	25.00
☐ "Suicidio" (La Gioconda)	17.00	25.00
☐ "Pace, pace" (Forza del Destino)	17.00	25.00
☐ "Kiss Me Again" (Mme. Modiste)	17.00	25.00
☐ "Maria Mari"	17.00	25.00
☐ "Song of India" (Sadko)	17.00	25.00
☐ "Mira d'acerbe" (Trovatore)	19.00	25.00
☐ "Rachem"	17.00	25.00
☐ "Old Folks at Home"	12.00	17.00
☐ "Home Sweet Home"	12.00	17.00
☐ "Scenes That Are Brightest" (Maritana)	17.00	24.00
☐ "O Sole Mio"	18.00	25.00

RUFFO, TITTA

Unfortunately, the early recordings of this noted baritone were made at a time when equipment and techniques did not permit the full range of his voice to be captured at its best. Still, his records are of historical interest and popular with collectors.

Price Range

☐ **IMPORTED VICTOR RED SEAL,** 1907–		
1909, "Veglia o donna" (Rigoletto)	20.00	32.00
☐ "Si vendetta" (Rigoletto)	20.00	32.00
☐ "Brindis" (Hamlet)	20.00	32.00
☐ "Per me giunto" (Don Carlos)	20.00	32.00
☐ "Largo al factotum" (Barber of Seville)	15.00	23.00
☐ "Prologo" (Pagliacci)	15.00	23.00
☐ "Pari siamo" (Rigoletto)	22.00	34.00
☐ "Monologo—Essere o non essere" (Hamlet)	22.00	34.00
☐ "Dio possente" (Faust)	22.00	34.00
☐ "Come il romito Fior" (Hamlet)	22.00	34.00
☐ "Canzon del toreador" (Carmen)	22.00	34.00
☐ "Cortigiani" (Rigoletto)	22.00	34.00
☐ "Nega se puoi la luce" (Hamlet)	25.00	38.00
☐ "Dunque io son" (Barber of Seville)	22.00	34.00
☐ "Piangi Fanciulla" (Rigoletto)	22.00	34.00
☐ "Dite alla giovine" (Traviata)	22.00	34.00
☐ "Le minaccie" (Forza del Destino)	25.00	42.00
☐ "La ci darem" (Don Giovanni)	21.00	30.00
☐ "Lassu in cielo" (Rigoletto)	25.00	42.00

SCOTTI, ANTONIO

The 78rpm discography of Antonio Scotti includes a number of rare and costly recordings. He was one of the comparatively few artists to switch labels, beginning with Columbia and going over to the then-more-prestigious Victor.

☐ **COLUMBIA RECORDS,** 1903, "Canzone del		
Toreador" (Carmen)	215.00	325.00
☐ "Prologo" (Pagliacci)	215.00	325.00
☐ "Serenata" (Don Giovanni)	215.00	325.00
☐ "Canzone del Toreador" (Carmen) (reissue)	140.00	215.00
☐ **VICTOR RED SEAL,** 1903–1905, "Dio pos-		
sente" (Faust)	65.00	110.00
☐ "Prologo" (Pagliacci)	28.00	45.00
☐ "Dio possente" (Faust)	28.00	45.00
☐ "Suo padre" (Aida)	28.00	45.00
☐ "Bella siccome un angelo" (Don Pasquale)	28.00	45.00
☐ "Brindis" (Othello)	28.00	45.00
☐ "Mandolinata"	23.00	34.00
☐ "O casto fior" (Rio de Lahore)	27.00	43.00
☐ "Alla vita" (Masked Ball)	27.00	43.00

	Price Range	
☐ "Deh non parlare" (Rigoletto)	55.00	80.00
☐ "Fin ch'han del vino" (Don Giovanni)	55.00	80.00
☐ "Eri tu" (Masked Ball)	55.00	80.00
☐ "Credo" (Othello)	55.00	80.00
☐ "Per me giunto" (Don Carlos)	55.00	80.00
☐ "Come pande vezzoso" (Elisir d'Amore) ...	55.00	80.00
☐ "Triste Aprile"	40.00	57.00

STRACCIARA, RICCARDO

A baritone popular in his day, Stracciara is now much better known to record collectors than to the public.

☐ **COLUMBIA RECORDS,** 1907–1912, "Prologo" (Pagliacci)	17.00	25.00
☐ "Largo al Factotum" (Barber of Seville)	17.00	25.00
☐ "Dio Possente" (Faust)	17.00	25.00
☐ "Di Provenza" (Traviata)	17.00	25.00
☐ "Il balen" (Trovatore)	17.00	25.00
☐ "Eri tu" (Masked Ball)	17.00	25.00
☐ "Elegie"	17.00	25.00
☐ "There's a Long, Long Trail"	17.00	25.00
☐ "The Sunshine of Your Smile"	13.00	19.00
☐ "Solenne" (Forza del Destino)	17.00	25.00
☐ " 'Cause of You"	17.00	25.00
☐ "La Paloma"	13.00	19.00
☐ "Mira d'acerbe" (Trovatore)	21.00	30.00
☐ "Canzone del Toreador" (Carmen)	17.00	25.00
☐ "Ideale"	17.00	25.00
☐ "Pari siamo" (Rigoletto)	17.00	25.00
☐ "Elegie"	13.00	19.00
☐ "O Sole Mio"	13.00	19.00
☐ "Until"	13.00	19.00
☐ "Santa Lucia"	13.00	19.00
☐ "Canta pe' me"	13.00	19.00
☐ "When the Evening Bells Are Ringing"	13.00	19.00

WILSON, MARGARET WOODROW

Margaret Woodrow Wilson, daughter of the president, aspired to be an opera singer and, in the opinion of some, thanks only to the celebrity of her father she succeeded in obtaining a recording contract with Columbia Records. Her records were mostly in the folk song category.

Price Range

☐ **COLUMBIA RECORDS,** 1914–1918, "Low
Back'd Car" 8.00 13.00
☐ "Will Ye Not Come Back" 8.00 13.00
☐ "My Laddie" 7.00 11.00
☐ "My Lovely Celia" 7.00 11.00
☐ "Leezie Lindsay" 7.00 11.00
☐ "Star Spangled Banner" 7.00 11.00
☐ "My Old Kentucky Home" 7.00 11.00

ORCHESTRA LEADERS AND MUSICIANS MEMORABILIA

Price Range

☐ **ALPERT, HERB,** 8x10 photo with combo,
signed, dated 1966 .... 7.00 10.00
☐ **ALPERT, HERB,** restaurant menu, signed,
with small sketch of man playing horn 8.00 11.00
☐ **ALPERT, HERB,** LP record album cover,
signed, record missing 20.00 30.00
☐ **ALPERT, HERB,** record company contract,
signed, three pages 15.00 20.00
☐ **ALPERT, HERB,** postcard in his hand, three
lines, 1961 .... 5.00 7.00
☐ **ALPERT, HERB,** two typed letters, signed,
1972 and 1973 .... 7.00 10.00
☐ **ALPERT, HERB,** poster, advertising "Tijuana
Brass," matted, framed, 27x41, c. 1968 ... 27.00 35.00
☐ **ALPERT, HERB,** three Polaroid snapshots
taken by fans, not signed 3.00 4.00
☐ **ARNAZ, DESI,** 8x10 studio photo, inscribed
and signed, 1945 .... 15.00 20.00
☐ **ARNAZ, DESI,** 8x10 portrait with Lucille Ball,
signed by both, matted and framed, c. 1953 45.00 60.00
☐ **ARNAZ, DESI,** magazine cover, signed, cor-
ner torn 6.00 8.00
☐ **ARNAZ, DESI,** article from "TV Guide,"
signed, c. 1951 .... 8.00 11.00
☐ **ARNAZ, DESI,** motion picture company publicity photo on card, facsimile signature,
5x6½, c. 1949 .... 3.00 4.00
☐ **ARNAZ, DESI,** Mexican-style hat reputedly
worn by him in revue, c. 1946 .... 60.00 80.00

	Price Range	
☐ **ARNAZ, DESI,** signature on a card	3.00	4.00
☐ **ARNAZ, DESI,** postcard from him to film producer, 1950	7.00	10.00
☐ **ARNAZ, DESI,** typewritten letter, signed, Desilu letterhead, 1955	7.00	10.00
☐ **ARNAZ, DESI,** Desilu Productions contract, signed by him and several others, 1956 . . .	11.00	15.00
☐ **ARRAU, CLAUDIO,** concert program, signed, 1955	13.00	18.00
☐ **ARRAU, CLAUDIO,** 8x10 studio portrait, signed, 1968	15.00	20.00
☐ **ARRAU, CLAUDIO,** scrapbook containing mementos of his career, with 34 photos, mostly candid, 7 signed, three postcards written by him, two letters, one contract, 61 news cuttings, and other items	235.00	330.00
☐ **ARRAU, CLAUDIO,** 5x7 photo, signed and inscribed	12.00	16.00
☐ **ARRAU, CLAUDIO,** copy of "Opera News," signed on interior page	7.00	10.00
☐ **ARRAU, CLAUDIO,** signature on a 3x5 sheet of paper	4.00	5.00
☐ **ARRAU, CLAUDIO,** signature on label of a 12" LP record	45.00	60.00
☐ **ARRAU, CLAUDIO,** candid snapshot outside Alice Tully Hall, N.Y., signed on the back . .	10.00	15.00
☐ **ARRAU, CLAUDIO,** ALs, three pages, with envelope, 1946	30.00	40.00
☐ **BERNSTEIN, LEONARD,** ALs, one page, NY, 1951	25.00	35.00
☐ **BERNSTEIN, LEONARD,** 6x8 color photo, signed and inscribed	16.00	23.00
☐ **BERNSTEIN, LEONARD,** musical score, "The Mass," signed	13.00	18.00
☐ **BERNSTEIN, LEONARD,** four sheets of original manuscript composition for "The Mass," in plastic folder	115.00	150.00
☐ **BERNSTEIN, LEONARD,** concert program, signed	13.00	20.00
☐ **BERNSTEIN, LEONARD,** membership card, "ASCAP," signed	35.00	45.00

Price Range

☐ **BERNSTEIN, LEONARD,** performance contract, signed three times, 1961	70.00	100.00
☐ **BERNSTEIN, LEONARD,** LP record album cover, signed, record missing	55.00	75.00
☐ **BERNSTEIN, LEONARD,** signature on a card	5.00	7.00
☐ **BLOCH, RAY,** 8x10 photo, signed, 1955 ...	4.00	6.00
☐ **BLOCH, RAY,** ALs, two pages, 1967	5.00	7.00
☐ **BLOCH, RAY,** photo with Milton DeLugg, signed by both, 1967	10.00	14.00
☐ **BLOCH, RAY,** photo with Rosemary Clooney, signed by Bloch only	6.00	8.00
☐ **BLOCH, RAY,** magazine article, signed, c. 1957	3.00	4.00
☐ **BLOCH, RAY,** TV contract, signed, seven pages	12.00	16.00
☐ **BLOCH, RAY,** photo with orchestra, signed by him and 7 members of orchestra, c. 1954	9.00	13.00
☐ **CASALS, PABLO,** instructional booklet on cello playing, signed and inscribed, dated 1928	60.00	80.00
☐ **CASALS, PABLO,** 8x10 photo with cello, signed, c. 1968	50.00	65.00
☐ **CASALS, PABLO,** handwritten postcard from Mrs. Jacqueline K. Onassis to Pablo Casals, four lines, large signature, 1966	220.00	300.00
☐ **CASALS, PABLO,** 5x7 photo at age about 50, signed on back, pinholes in corners, traces of glue on back	60.00	80.00
☐ **CASALS, PABLO,** ALs, four pages, in Spanish, concerns musical engagements, 1919	150.00	200.00
☐ **CASALS, PABLO,** ALs, one page, 1927 ...	80.00	105.00
☐ **CASALS, PABLO,** ALs, half page, declining a speaking invitation, 1951	65.00	80.00
☐ **CASALS, PABLO,** ALs, two pages, concerning cello lessons for a student, 1958	120.00	160.00
☐ **CASALS, PABLO,** envelope addressed by him, 1957	45.00	60.00
☐ **CASALS, PABLO,** concert program, signed	75.00	100.00
☐ **CASALS, PABLO,** poster advertising an appearance at Carnegie Hall, New York, unsigned	26.00	34.00

	Price Range	
☐ **CAVALLARO, CARMEN,** 8x10 photo with band, signed	7.00	10.00
☐ **CAVALLARO, CARMEN,** handbill advertising his appearance at a Chicago cafe, signed	5.00	7.00
☐ **CAVALLARO, CARMEN,** ALs, two pages, 1960	7.00	10.00
☐ **CAVALLARO, CARMEN,** two-page article from newspaper, signed and inscribed, laminated	8.00	11.00
☐ **CAVALLARO, CARMEN,** book, "The Big Bands," inscribed on front endleaf	7.00	10.00
☐ **CAVALLARO, CARMEN,** two 4x5½ snapshot photos, one signed on the back, the other unsigned	4.00	5.00
☐ **CAVALLARO, CARMEN,** signature on a card	2.00	2.75
☐ **CAVALLARO, CARMEN,** postcard written by him to newspaper columnist, 1952	4.00	5.00
☐ **CAVALLARO, CARMEN,** photo with Sammy Kaye, signed by Cavallaro only	4.00	5.00
☐ **CLIBURN, VAN,** 8x10 photo, signed, at piano, 1958	20.00	25.00
☐ **CLIBURN, VAN,** photo of him in Red Square, Moscow, signed	14.00	18.00
☐ **CLIBURN, VAN,** printed musical score, signed, inscribed	25.00	32.00
☐ **CLIBURN, VAN,** collection of 327 news cuttings relating to his career, mostly from Philadelphia Inquirer and Life magazine. Mounted in three loose-leaf albums	70.00	90.00
☐ **CLIBURN, VAN,** ALs, half page, with envelope, 1959	25.00	31.00
☐ **CLIBURN, VAN,** contract for a concert appearance, signed twice	40.00	50.00
☐ **CLIBURN, VAN,** signature on a concert program	13.00	18.00
☐ **CLIBURN, VAN,** LP record album cover, signed, record missing	45.00	60.00
☐ **CLIBURN, VAN,** two 4x5 fan snapshots, unsigned, c. 1958	4.00	5.00
☐ **CLIBURN, VAN,** signature on a small concert poster	25.00	35.00
☐ **CONNIFF, RAY,** 8x10 studio portrait, signed	4.00	5.50

Price Range

☐ **CONNIFF, RAY,** 12″ LP recording, signed on label **25.00** **35.00**

☐ **CONNIFF, RAY,** 8x10 color photo with Perry Como, signed by Conniff only **7.00** **10.00**

☐ **CONNIFF, RAY,** scrapbook containing c. 200 items on him, including 16 photos, most of them autographed, news cuttings, etc., also some material on other music personalities. Album worn, cover detached **150.00** **200.00**

☐ **CONNIFF, RAY,** 22x30 blow-up poster of him, full color, homemade, not signed, c. 1970 . . . . **4.00** **5.00**

☐ **CONNIFF, RAY,** 45rpm record sleeve, signed (no record) **2.00** **2.50**

☐ **CONNIFF, RAY,** signature on a card **1.00** **2.00**

☐ **CONNIFF, RAY,** magazine article, signed . . **3.00** **4.00**

☐ **CUGAT, XAVIER,** 8x10 studio photo, signed on back **7.00** **10.00**

☐ **CUGAT, XAVIER,** ALs, 1½ pages, in Spanish, regarding Spanish Civil War, with envelope, 1938 . . . . **45.00** **65.00**

☐ **CUGAT, XAVIER,** ALs, one page, about an engagement in Los Angeles, 1948 . . . . **9.00** **12.00**

☐ **CUGAT, XAVIER,** pencil sketch of him, 9x12, matted and framed, signed "S.W.L., 1967" **15.00** **21.00**

☐ **CUGAT, XAVIER,** 5x7 photo of living room in his Manhattan apartment, lengthy inscription on reverse, not signed **8.00** **11.00**

☐ **CUGAT, XAVIER,** 8x10 photo with Abby Lane, signed by both **25.00** **32.00**

☐ **CUGAT, XAVIER,** magazine cover boldly signed in pink ink **7.00** **10.00**

☐ **CUGAT, XAVIER,** three photos of him in early 1920's, unsigned, in a wallet-like folder, worn **7.00** **10.00**

☐ **CUGAT, XAVIER,** signature on a card **2.00** **3.00**

☐ **DUCHIN, PETER,** LP record album cover, signed, record missing **13.00** **20.00**

☐ **DUCHIN, PETER,** 8x10 studio photo, signed and inscribed **4.00** **5.00**

Price Range

☐ **DUCHIN, PETER,** motion picture company contract, signed in three places, in a cloth folder 20.00   25.00

☐ **DUCHIN, PETER,** ALs, one page, 1971 .... 6.00   8.00

☐ **DUCHIN, PETER,** photo with Peggy Lee, signed by Duchin only 7.00   10.00

☐ **DUCHIN, PETER,** check endorsed by him, 1975 .... 13.00   20.00

☐ **DUCHIN, PETER,** magazine article, signed 3.00   4.00

☐ **DUCHIN, PETER,** three Polaroid snapshots made by fans, mounted on heavy paper, one signed 5.00   7.00

☐ **DUCHIN, PETER,** 45rpm phonograph record, signed on the label 7.00   10.00

☐ **DUCHIN, PETER,** collection of 227 news cuttings and photos, no autographs, covering the period 1962–1977, in a manila portfolio 55.00   70.00

☐ **ELGART, LES,** 8x10 studio photo, signed, dated 1944 .... 4.00   6.00

☐ **ELGART, LES,** 8x10 portrait, Associated Press stamp on back, signed in margin 4.00   6.00

☐ **ELGART, LES,** postcard in his hand, seven lines, New Orleans, 1961 .... 4.00   6.00

☐ **ELGART, LES,** 8x10 color photo with Larry Elgart, signed by both, dated 1969 .... 13.00   20.00

☐ **ELGART, LES,** two-page printed musical score, signed 5.00   7.00

☐ **ELGART, LES,** ALs, two pages, with envelope, 1949 .... 7.00   10.00

☐ **ELGART, LES,** record company contract, signed, three pages 13.00   20.00

☐ **ELGART, LES,** signature on a restaurant menu 3.00   4.00

☐ **ELGART, LES,** signature on a card 2.00   2.75

☐ **ELGART, LES,** page of notes kept by him, addresses, etc 3.00   4.00

☐ **FIEDLER, ARTHUR,** LP record album cover, signed, record missing 45.00   60.00

☐ **FIEDLER, ARTHUR,** copy of "Thirteen" magazine, signed on the cover 8.00   11.00

☐ **FIEDLER, ARTHUR,** 8x10 studio portrait, signed, c. 1940 .... 13.00   20.00

Price Range

☐ **FIEDLER, ARTHUR,** 8x10 photo with baton, signed, c. 1947 .... **15.00** **21.00**

☐ **FIEDLER, ARTHUR,** magazine article, signed **10.00** **15.00**

☐ **FIEDLER, ARTHUR,** ALs, three pages, with envelope, 1933 .... **35.00** **45.00**

☐ **FIEDLER, ARTHUR,** ALs, one page, to Columbia Records, 1945 .... **20.00** **25.00**

☐ **FIEDLER, ARTHUR,** 328 news cuttings relating to his career, mounted in three leatherette albums, 1936–1978 .... **100.00** **130.00**

☐ **FIEDLER, ARTHUR,** check endorsed by him, 1951 .... **33.00** **44.00**

☐ **FIEDLER, ARTHUR,** 5x7 color glossy photo on podium, signed **21.00** **28.00**

☐ **FIEDLER, ARTHUR,** printed musical score, signed **25.00** **35.00**

☐ **GRECO, BUDDY,** 8x10 photo, signed and inscribed, dated 1955 .... **7.00** **10.00**

☐ **GRECO, BUDDY,** three 5½x7 photos, two signed, various dates **10.00** **15.00**

☐ **GRECO, BUDDY,** collection of 18 pieces of sheet music, signed by him **85.00** **110.00**

☐ **GRECO, BUDDY,** signature on cafe menu, dated 1960 .... **4.00** **6.00**

☐ **GRECO, BUDDY,** check endorsed by him, 1966 .... **13.00** **20.00**

☐ **GRECO, BUDDY,** postcard sent by him, large signature **5.00** **7.00**

☐ **GRECO, BUDDY,** photo with Guy Lombardo, signed by Greco only **7.00** **10.00**

☐ **GRECO, BUDDY,** typewritten letter, signed, 1969 .... **4.00** **6.00**

☐ **GRECO, BUDDY,** two small pocket photos, signed and inscribed for fans **5.00** **7.00**

☐ **HEIFETZ, JASCHA,** ALs, two pages (written at age 17), 1918 .... **60.00** **80.00**

☐ **HEIFETZ, JASCHA,** ALs, one page, regarding an engagement, 1931 .... **35.00** **47.00**

☐ **HEIFETZ, JASCHA,** ALs, ½ page, regarding state of the arts in America as a result of the war and financial depression, 1941 .... **43.00** **60.00**

Price Range

☐ **HEIFETZ, JASCHA,** ALs, ½ page, declining an invitation, 1962	25.00	35.00
☐ **HEIFETZ, JASCHA,** check endorsed by him, 1950	50.00	65.00
☐ **HEIFETZ, JASCHA,** photo of him as a youth, not signed, dated 1916	11.00	15.00
☐ **HEIFETZ, JASCHA,** 8x10 studio portrait at an early age, signed and inscribed, photo touched with hand-coloring, matted and framed, c. 1930	45.00	60.00
☐ **HEIFETZ, JASCHA,** magazine photo, signed, c. 1960	9.00	12.00
☐ **HEIFETZ, JASCHA,** studio portrait, signed, inscribed, dated 1968	25.00	32.00
☐ **HEIFETZ, JASCHA,** signature on a concert program	15.00	21.00
☐ **HEIFETZ, JASCHA,** signature on a card ...	5.00	7.00
☐ **HEIFETZ, JASCHA,** booklet on violin instruction, signed	25.00	32.00
☐ **HEIFETZ, JASCHA,** copy of "Hi-Fi-Stereo Review," signed	8.00	11.00
☐ **HENDERSON, SKITCH,** 8x10 studio photo, signed, dated 1958	4.00	6.00
☐ **HENDERSON, SKITCH,** photo with Sammy Kaye, signed by Henderson only	5.00	7.00
☐ **HENDERSON, SKITCH,** photo with Steve Allen, signed by both	8.00	11.00
☐ **HENDERSON, SKITCH,** check endorsed by him, 1966	12.00	17.00
☐ **HENDERSON, SKITCH,** taped radio interview, 30 minutes, c. 1964	7.00	10.00
☐ **HENDERSON, SKITCH,** T-shirt with his likeness and name	8.00	11.00
☐ **HENDERSON, SKITCH,** signature on a restaurant napkin	3.00	4.00
☐ **HENDERSON, SKITCH,** record company contract, signed (three signatures)	13.00	20.00
☐ **HENDERSON, SKITCH,** copy of "Billboard" magazine, signed on front page	4.00	6.00
☐ **HENDERSON, SKITCH,** two 5x7 photos, signed	6.00	8.00

Price Range

☐ **HENDERSON, SKITCH,** copy of "TV Guide,"
signed on interior page, also signed by several other musicians 12.00   16.00

☐ **HENDERSON, SKITCH,** signature on a card   2.00   2.50

☐ **HIRT, AL,** poster advertising his appearance
at a New Orleans club, signed, c. 1972 .... 20.00   30.00

☐ **HIRT, AL,** 8x10 studio photo with trumpet,
signed, dated 1975 .... 6.00   8.00

☐ **HIRT, AL,** celluloid button with his likeness
and name, 2″ diameter, c. 1970 .... 4.00   6.00

☐ **HIRT, AL,** ALs, two pages, with envelope,
1953 .... 8.00   11.00

☐ **HIRT, AL,** 8x10 publicity photo, in street parade, signed on back, with lengthy inscription 10.00   15.00

☐ **HIRT, AL,** T-shirt with his name and likeness 8.00   11.00

☐ **HIRT, AL,** 8x10 studio photo, close-up,
signed, dated 1966 .... 5.00   7.00

☐ **HIRT, AL,** 4x5½ snapshot photo with Benny
Goodman, signed by Hirt only 5.00   7.00

☐ **HIRT, AL,** magazine article, signed 3.00   4.00

☐ **HIRT, AL,** signature on a card 2.25   3.00

☐ **HIRT, AL,** 12″ LP record, signed on the label 26.00   36.00

☐ **HOROWITZ, VLADIMIR,** ALs, four pages,
one page stained, in a cloth folder with morocco spine, 1923 .... 95.00   115.00

☐ **HOROWITZ, VLADIMIR,** ALs, 1½ pages,
1941 .... 60.00   80.00

☐ **HOROWITZ, VLADIMIR,** ALs, two pages, on
music theory, 1947 .... 85.00   110.00

☐ **HOROWITZ, VLADIMIR,** concert program,
signed, 1971 .... 15.00   21.00

☐ **HOROWITZ, VLADIMIR,** 5x7 color photo
mounted on stiff card, signed on the card 20.00   30.00

☐ **HOROWITZ, VLADIMIR,** 8x10 studio photo,
sepia, signed and inscribed, c. 1935 ...... 55.00   70.00

☐ **HOROWITZ, VLADIMIR,** 8x10 photo, signed,
dated 1969 .... 26.00   38.00

☐ **HOROWITZ, VLADIMIR,** signature on a receipt 15.00   22.00

☐ **HOROWITZ, VLADIMIR,** signature on LP
record album box, records missing 50.00   70.00

Price Range

☐ **HOROWITZ, VLADIMIR,** concert contract, signed three times 85.00 110.00

☐ **HOROWITZ, VLADIMIR,** signature on a card 5.00 7.00

☐ **HOROWITZ, VLADIMIR,** musical score (printed), signed 50.00 65.00

☐ **HOROWITZ, VLADIMIR,** poster advertising an appearance at Carnegie Hall, N.Y., not signed 7.00 10.00

☐ **ITURBI, JOSE,** 8x10 studio portrait, signed on front and back 20.00 30.00

☐ **ITURBI, JOSE,** cartoon sketch of him in charcoal by "Franz S.," bristol board, unframed, 11x14, c. 1960 .... 35.00 45.00

☐ **ITURBI, JOSE,** ALs, in Spanish, with envelope, 1917 .... 31.00 40.00

☐ **ITURBI, JOSE,** ALs, two pages, 1933 ..... 34.00 45.00

☐ **ITURBI, JOSE,** concert poster, signed in Magic Marker, matted and framed 65.00 90.00

☐ **ITURBI, JOSE,** LP record album cover, signed, record missing 35.00 45.00

☐ **ITURBI, JOSE,** cancelled check, endorsed by him 30.00 42.00

☐ **ITURBI, JOSE,** five postcards in his hand, three sent from London, total of 25 lines of writing, mounted on album sheets 60.00 80.00

☐ **ITURBI, JOSE,** photo with James Levine, signed by Iturbi only 14.00 20.00

☐ **ITURBI, JOSE,** Christmas card sent by him in 1973, inscribed 26.00 33.00

☐ **ITURBI, JOSE,** signature on a card 3.00 4.00

☐ **KAYE, SAMMY,** newspaper article, signed and inscribed, 1948 .... 6.00 8.00

☐ **KAYE, SAMMY,** baton autographed by him 13.00 19.00

☐ **KAYE, SAMMY,** TV Guide article, signed, framed along with an unsigned portrait 14.00 20.00

☐ **KAYE, SAMMY,** 8x10 studio photo, signed, dated 1950 .... 4.00 5.00

☐ **KAYE, SAMMY,** 78rpm phonograph record, signed on the label 18.00 27.00

☐ **KAYE, SAMMY,** photo with Hoagy Carmichael, signed by both 13.00 17.00

Price Range

☐ **KAYE, SAMMY,** collection of 22 candid snapshots, mostly on street, not signed, mostly from the 1940's 7.00 10,00

☐ **KAYE, SAMMY,** check endorsed by him, 1969 .... 14.00 20.00

☐ **KAYE, SAMMY,** LP record album cover, signed, record missing 18.00 27.00

☐ **KAYE, SAMMY,** pair of kidskin gloves reputedly owned by him 13.00 17.00

☐ **KLEMPERER, WERNER,** 8x10 studio portrait, signed 14.00 20.00

☐ **KLEMPERER, WERNER,** ALs, in German, two pages, 1944 .... 33.00 45.00

☐ **KLEMPERER, WERNER,** signature on a card 5.00 7.00

☐ **KLEMPERER, WERNER,** record company contract, signed 40.00 50.00

☐ **KLEMPERER, WERNER,** two 8x10 blow-ups of candid photos, one signed 22.00 30.00

☐ **KLEMPERER, WERNER,** LP record album cover, signed, record missing 40.00 55.00

☐ **KLEMPERER, WERNER,** concert poster, signed in margin 30.00 40.00

☐ **KLEMPERER, WERNER,** check endorsed by him, 1977 .... 21.00 27.00

☐ **KLEMPERER, WERNER,** signature on a restaurant menu 6.00 8.00

☐ **KOSTELANETZ, ANDRE,** ALs, two pages, with envelope, 1926 .... 10.00 15.00

☐ **KOSTELANETZ, ANDRE,** ALs, ½ page, about appearing on a TV show, 1971 ..... 6.00 8.00

☐ **KOSTELANETZ, ANDRE,** 8x10 studio portrait, signed, c. 1955 .... 8.00 11.00

☐ **KOSTELANETZ, ANDRE,** 8x10 color portrait photo, inscribed on back, dated 1958 ..... 13.00 20.00

☐ **KOSTELANETZ, ANDRE,** letter to him from NBC program department 3.00 4.00

☐ **KOSTELANETZ, ANDRE,** LP record, signed on the label 24.00 35.00

☐ **KOSTELANETZ, ANDRE,** two postcards sent by him in 1966 .... 10.00 15.00

☐ **KOSTELANETZ, ANDRE,** record company contract, signed in two places 26.00 33.00

	Price Range	

☐ **KOSTELANETZ, ANDRE,** two 5x7 color photos cut from periodicals, signed and inscribed, mounted on stiff cards **13.00**   **20.00**

☐ **KOSTELANETZ, ANDRE,** signature on a card **3.00**   **4.00**

☐ **KYSER, KAY,** photo with Bing Crosby, signed by both, dated 1942 . . . .   **75.00**   **100.00**

☐ **KYSER, KAY,** printed postcard photo, facsimile signature **7.00**   **10.00**

☐ **LEINSDORF, ERICH,** ALs, two pages, in German, 1930 . . . .   **30.00**   **40.00**

☐ **LEINSDORF, ERICH,** concert poster, signed, 22x28 . . . .   **60.00**   **80.00**

☐ **LEINSDORF, ERICH,** 8x10 studio portrait, signed on back **15.00**   **21.00**

☐ **LEINSDORF, ERICH,** photo with Martina Arroyo, signed by Leinsdorf only **20.00**   **26.00**

☐ **LEINSDORF, ERICH,** check endorsed by him, 1977 . . . .   **35.00**   **45.00**

☐ **LEINSDORF, ERICH,** copy of "Opera News," signed on front cover **11.00**   **15.00**

☐ **LEINSDORF, ERICH,** photo debarking from plane, signed **9.00**   **14.00**

☐ **LEINSDORF, ERICH,** printed musical score, signed **26.00**   **32.00**

☐ **LEINSDORF, ERICH,** book, "Complete Opera Book," signed on front endleaf **13.00**   **18.00**

☐ **LEINSDORF, ERICH,** LP record album cover, signed, record missing **35.00**   **45.00**

☐ **LEINSDORF, ERICH,** two postcards sent by him from Paris **20.00**   **27.00**

☐ **LEINSDORF, ERICH,** three 5x6½ snapshot photos, signed **20.00**   **27.00**

☐ **LEINSDORF, ERICH,** signature on an opera libretto **8.00**   **11.00**

☐ **LEINSDORF, ERICH,** signature on a card . .   **3.00**   **4.00**

☐ **LIBERACE,** copy of "TV Guide," signed on cover **20.00**   **27.00**

☐ **LIBERACE,** 8x10 photo in costume at piano, signed, 1952 . . . .   **15.00**   **20.00**

☐ **LIBERACE,** 8x10 photo in front of swimming pool, signed, undated **11.00**   **16.00**

Price Range

☐ **LIBERACE,** 8x10 studio portrait, signed, c. 1953	11.00	16.00
☐ **LIBERACE,** postcard photo (printed), facsimile signature	4.00	5.00
☐ **LIBERACE,** magazine article, signed (fan magazine), c. 1951	10.00	15.00
☐ **LIBERACE,** scrapbook containing 33 photos, 11 of them signed, four ALs's, several typed letters and other items related to him	350.00	425.00
☐ **LIBERACE,** jacket said to have been worn by him, pink silk with sequins	205.00	240.00
☐ **LIBERACE,** check endorsed by him, 1954	40.00	50.00
☐ **LIBERACE,** printed musical score (Chopin), signed	30.00	39.00
☐ **LIBERACE,** signature on a card	3.00	4.00
☐ **LIBERACE,** TV contract, signed (three signatures)	70.00	90.00
☐ **LIBERACE,** 78rpm record, signed on the label	35.00	45.00
☐ **LOMBARDO, GUY,** check endorsed by him, 1940	41.00	55.00
☐ **LOMBARDO, GUY,** 8x10 photo with Ted Weems, signed by both	40.00	55.00
☐ **LOPEZ, TRINI,** 8x10 studio portrait, signed, dated 1969	5.00	7.00
☐ **LOPEZ, TRINI,** 45rpm record, signed on the label	9.00	13.00
☐ **LOPEZ, TRINI,** record company contract, signed	33.00	41.00
☐ **LOPEZ, TRINI,** copy of "Billboard" magazine, signed	7.00	10.00
☐ **LOPEZ, TRINI,** collection of 41 news cuttings relating to his career, reviews of his records, etc., 1968–1975	12.00	16.00
☐ **LOPEZ, TRINI,** 8x10 color photo with band, signed by him and several band members	13.00	18.00
☐ **LOPEZ, TRINI,** ALs, one page, on hotel stationery, 1970	6.00	8.00
☐ **LOPEZ, TRINI,** poster in full colors, 17x24, signed	10.00	13.00
☐ **LOPEZ, TRINI,** two small snapshot photos, one signed on the back	4.00	6.00

	Price Range	
☐ **LOPEZ, TRINI,** check endorsed by him, 1977	13.00	18.00
☐ **LOPEZ, TRINI,** photo with Mac Davidson, signed by Lopez only	5.00	7.00
☐ **MAAZEL, LORIN,** ALs, two pages, in French, 1950	10.00	13.00
☐ **MAAZEL, LORIN,** ALs, 1½ pages, with envelope, 1956	8.00	11.00
☐ **MAAZEL, LORIN,** 8x10 studio portrait, signed and inscribed	10.00	13.00
☐ **MAAZEL, LORIN,** concert program, signed, 1971	7.00	10.00
☐ **MAAZEL, LORIN,** two postcards sent by him, lengthy messages, 1976 and 1977	7.00	10.00
☐ **MAAZEL, LORIN,** 11x14 color portrait photo with baton, signed and inscribed, matted and framed along with an LP phonograph record	50.00	65.00
☐ **MAAZEL, LORIN,** LP record album cover, signed, record missing	25.00	33.00
☐ **MAAZEL, LORIN,** check endorsed by him, stained, 1971	10.00	13.00
☐ **MAAZEL, LORIN,** typewritten letter, signed, large signature	5.00	7.00
☐ **MAAZEL, LORIN,** copy of "Hi-Fi-Stereo Review," signed	5.00	7.00
☐ **MAAZEL, LORIN,** signature on a card	2.00	3.00
☐ **MAAZEL, LORIN,** collection of 31 unsigned snapshot photos, mostly dating 1957–1975	20.00	28.00
☐ **MANTOVANI, ANNUZIO,** check endorsed by him, 1955	15.00	20.00
☐ **MANTOVANI, ANNUZIO,** 8x10 portrait photo, signed and inscribed	8.00	11.00
☐ **MANTOVANI, ANNUZIO,** ALs, two pages, 1955	14.00	20.00
☐ **MANTOVANI, ANNUZIO,** postcard sent by him in 1961	6.00	8.00
☐ **MANTOVANI, ANNUZIO,** sheet music, signed	14.00	20.00
☐ **MANTOVANI, ANNUZIO,** two 4x5 snapshots, one signed on the back	8.00	11.00
☐ **MANTOVANI, ANNUZIO,** LP record album cover, signed, record missing	18.00	26.00

Price Range

☐ **MANTOVANI, ANNUZIO,** concert poster, signed, 1961 .... **12.00**   **16.00**

☐ **MANTOVANI, ANNUZIO,** 45rpm phonograph record, signed on the label **15.00**   **20.00**

☐ **MANTOVANI, ANNUZIO,** magazine article, signed twice, preserved in a cloth folder along with an unsigned snapshot photo ... **10.00**   **13.00**

☐ **MENUHIN, YEHUDI,** 8x10 portrait photo in concert, signed on the back **40.00**   **52.00**

☐ **MENUHIN, YEHUDI,** 8x10 color photo, close-up, signed and inscribed, dated 1974 ..... **52.00**   **70.00**

☐ **MENUHIN, YEHUDI,** musical score (printed), signed **30.00**   **38.00**

☐ **MENUHIN, YEHUDI,** ALs, New York, two pages, 1938 .... **35.00**   **45.00**

☐ **MENUHIN, YEHUDI,** concert program, signed, 1970 .... **13.00**   **20.00**

☐ **MENUHIN, YEHUDI,** two postcards sent by him from London, total of 11 lines of writing **20.00**   **28.00**

☐ **MENUHIN, YEHUDI,** envelope addressed by him, postmarked 1950 .... **7.00**   **10.00**

☐ **MENUHIN, YEHUDI,** 4x5 photo, signed and inscribed **15.00**   **21.00**

☐ **MENUHIN, YEHUDI,** LP record album cover, signed, record missing **40.00**   **50.00**

☐ **MENUHIN, YEHUDI,** three snapshot photos, various sizes, one signed and dated 1968, others unsigned, mounted on a 14x16 card **20.00**   **26.00**

☐ **MENUHIN, YEHUDI,** cancelled check, endorsed by him, 1975 .... **35.00**   **45.00**

☐ **MENUHIN, YEHUDI,** typewritten letter, signed, ½ page, 1976 .... **11.00**   **15.00**

☐ **SCHIPPERS, THOMAS,** 8x10 photo, signed, dated 1978 .... **9.00**   **12.00**

☐ **SCHIPPERS, THOMAS,** opera libretto, signed **7.00**   **10.00**

☐ **SCHIPPERS, THOMAS,** check endorsed by him, 1971 .... **22.00**   **26.00**

☐ **SCHIPPERS, THOMAS,** baton used by him in leading orchestra, signed **50.00**   **65.00**

☐ **SCHIPPERS, THOMAS,** photo cut from "Opera News," signed, framed **13.00**   **18.00**

	Price Range	
☐ **SCHIPPERS, THOMAS,** concert program, signed	6.00	9.00
☐ **SCHIPPERS, THOMAS,** two 4x5 snapshot photos outside Metropolitan Opera House, signed on the backs	9.00	12.00
☐ **SERKIN, RUDOLF,** ALs, three pages, in German, 1929	30.00	38.00
☐ **SERKIN, RUDOLF,** 8x10 portrait photo, signed and inscribed, 1976	15.00	20.00
☐ **SERKIN, RUDOLF,** 8x10 color photo, matted and framed, signed in pencil on the mat	20.00	25.00
☐ **SERKIN, RUDOLF,** postcard sent by him in 1973, three lines	8.00	11.00
☐ **SERKIN, RUDOLF,** concert program, signed	9.00	12.00
☐ **SERKIN, RUDOLF,** pen-and-ink caricature, 8x10, matted and framed, artist unknown	20.00	28.00
☐ **SERKIN, RUDOLF,** set of three scrapbooks containing 15 photos, nine of them signed, plus numerous memorabilia relating to his career	200.00	245.00
☐ **SERKIN, RUDOLF,** snapshot photo, signed on the back	6.00	9.00
☐ **SOLTI, GEORGE,** 8x10 portrait photo, signed and inscribed	10.00	14.00
☐ **SOLTI, GEORGE,** news cutting, signed (review of an LP recording)	6.00	9.00
☐ **SOLTI, GEORGE,** ALs, one page, New York, 1961	11.00	15.00
☐ **SOLTI, GEORGE,** ALs, 3½ pages, Los Angeles, with envelope, 1974	16.00	22.00
☐ **SOLTI, GEORGE,** check endorsed by him, 1971	20.00	29.00
☐ **SOLTI, GEORGE,** concert program, signed	8.00	11.00
☐ **SOLTI, GEORGE,** LP record album cover, signed, record missing	30.00	38.00
☐ **SOLTI, GEORGE,** 5x7 color photo, signed on the back	11.00	15.00
☐ **SOLTI, GEORGE,** six postcards sent by him, 1971–1976	35.00	45.00
☐ **SOLTI, GEORGE,** collection of 147 news cuttings relating to his career, enclosed in a vinyl folder	40.00	50.00

Price Range

☐ **STERN, ISAAC,** ALs, two pages, New York, 1967 .... 30.00   37.00

☐ **STERN, ISAAC,** photo with Beverly Sills, signed by Stern only 27.00   35.00

☐ **STERN, ISAAC,** Carnegie Hall recital poster, signed in crayon, matted and framed 85.00   110.00

☐ **STERN, ISAAC,** New York Philharmonic program, signed 15.00   20.00

☐ **STERN, ISAAC,** two 4x5½ snapshot photos with fans, one signed 15.00   20.00

☐ **STERN, ISAAC,** typewritten letter, signed, one page, 1977 .... 16.00   22.00

☐ **STERN, ISAAC,** 8x10 portrait photo, signed and inscribed, with violin 20.00   25.00

☐ **STERN, ISAAC,** check endorsed by him, 1966 .... 45.00   65.00

☐ **STERN, ISAAC,** LP record, signed on the label 70.00   95.00

☐ **STERN, ISAAC,** concert program, signed twice, mounted and framed along with an unsigned snapshot photo 35.00   45.00

☐ **STOKOWSKI, LEOPOLD,** poster for "Fantasia," signed by Walt Disney and Stokowski, matted and framed 675.00   800.00

☐ **STOKOWSKI, LEOPOLD,** ALs, two pages, London, 1906 .... 45.00   60.00

☐ **STOKOWSKI, LEOPOLD,** concert program, signed 17.00   25.00

☐ **STOKOWSKI, LEOPOLD,** check endorsed by him, 1931 .... 55.00   75.00

☐ **STOKOWSKI, LEOPOLD,** LP record album cover, signed, record missing, matted and framed 75.00   100.00

☐ **STOKOWSKI, LEOPOLD,** 8x10 portrait photo, sepia, signed, dated 1929 .... 30.00   37.00

☐ **STOKOWSKI, LEOPOLD,** 8x10 studio photo, signed and inscribed, c. 1955 .... 23.00   32.00

☐ **STOKOWSKI, LEOPOLD,** Photo with Fritz Chrysler, signed by both 65.00   80.00

☐ **STOKOWSKI, LEOPOLD,** signature on a card 6.00   9.00

	Price Range	
☐ **ZIMBALIST, EFREM, Sr.,** 8x10 portrait photo, signed	**15.00**	**20.00**

POPULAR MUSIC

ARTISTS' MEMORABILIA

Though "pop" (short for popular, as opposed to classical) music has been around since the 1800's and available on commercial recordings since the 1890's, the collecting of pop memorabilia did not become a major hobby until the 1950's. Elvis Presley's impact on his fans is thought by some to have started it all; others feel that the Beatles made collectors out of pop music fans. In any event, the collecting of pop memorabilia was not taken seriously until pretty recently. Most collectors were the very young, who obtained autographs in person at concerts, etc., and who adoringly preserved shirts, neckties, or other personal items that once belonged to their favorites, while adults scoffed at the possibility of this material ever having more than emotional value. Gradually, as a market developed (in the 1960's), dealers began to print catalogues and auction lists of this memorabilia, with prices that were at first very modest. Today, pop music memorabilia is big business all across the country. It is sold by specialist dealers as well as by dealers in comic books, movie memorabilia, and nostalgia, and some of it fetches healthy sums indeed. Many souvenirs obtained free at stage doors by admiring fans are now worth $10, $20, or even more, depending on the star and the item's nature.

Nostalgia buffs, many of them born too late to remember stars of the 1940's or earlier, are buying the early, pre-Presley items. Because of space limitations, the following listings exclude material relating to stars whose careers were completed before 1940. This should not be taken to mean that such memorabilia is not of value; it surely is, and in many instances of greater value than more modern items.

	Price Range	
☐ **ALDA, ROBERT,** c. 1952, 8x10 studio photo, signed	**5.00**	**7.00**
☐ **ALDA, ROBERT,** printed copy, "Guys and Dolls," signed	**8.00**	**11.00**
☐ **ALDA, ROBERT,** c. 1958, typed letter, signed, one page	**7.00**	**10.00**
☐ **ALDA, ROBERT,** collection of 26 motion picture stills, none of them signed	**55.00**	**70.00**

Price Range

☐ **ALDA, ROBERT,** 8x10 color photo in "Guys and Dolls" costume, signed 12.00 16.00

☐ **ALPERT, HERB,** c. 1969, fan magazine article, signed 11.00 15.00

☐ **ALPERT, HERB,** 8x10 studio portrait, signed 11.00 15.00

☐ **ALPERT, HERB,** photo with band, signed twice 12.00 17.00

☐ **ALPERT, HERB,** two LP album covers, signed, records missing 50.00 65.00

☐ **AMES, ED,** c. 1956, 8x10 photo of group "The Ames Bros.," signed by all 35.00 45.00

☐ **AMES, ED,** snapshot photo taken by fan, signed on back 5.00 7.00

☐ **AMES, ED,** magazine photo, signed, pasted on card 4.00 6.00

☐ **AMES, ED,** 45rpm phono record signed on label (indistinct) 10.00 14.00

☐ **AMES, ED,** 8x10 color photo, signed and inscribed 12.00 16.00

☐ **ANDERSON, LYNN,** sheet music, "Rose Garden," signed, framed along with a colored magazine photo (unsigned) 36.00 45.00

☐ **ANDERSON, LYNN,** 8x10 studio portrait, signed 8.00 11.00

☐ **ANDERSON, LYNN,** two small outdoor snapshots, Polaroid 5.00 7.00

☐ **ANDREWS, JULIE,** lobby card, "Sound of Music," signed 27.00 35.00

☐ **ANDREWS, JULIE,** sheet music, "A Spoonful of Sugar," signed 20.00 27.00
(Note: "Spoonful of Sugar," in the motion picture "Mary Poppins," was mouthed by Julie Andrews but sung on the soundtrack by Marni Nixon.)

☐ **ANDREWS, JULIE,** press review, "Sound of Music," signed 8.00 11.00

☐ **ANDREWS, JULIE,** fan magazine photo, signed and inscribed 9.00 12.00

☐ **ANDREWS, JULIE,** collection of 76 motion picture stills, unsigned 180.00 210.00

Price Range

☐ **ANDREWS, JULIE,** gown worn by her at Academy Awards presentation, with letter of authentication 325.00 420.00

☐ **ANDREWS, JULIE,** 5x7 photo signed, with balloon 8.00 11.00

☐ **ANDREWS, JULIE,** strip of 32mm film (41 frames), scene from "Mary Poppins." Framed along with a signed photo 120.00 165.00

☐ **ANDREWS, PATTY,** c. 1947, typed letter, signed 10.00 14.00

☐ **ANDREWS, PATTY,** signature on a card ... 4.00 5.00

☐ **ANDREWS, PATTY,** 8x10 photo, signed and inscribed 10.00 14.00

☐ **ANDREWS, PATTY,** 8x10 photo with Bing Crosby, signed by Andrews only 20.00 28.00

☐ **ANN-MARGRET (OLSON),** color photo from "Playboy" magazine, signed 25.00 33.00

☐ **ANN-MARGRET,** motion picture still with Elvis Presley, signed by Ann-Margret only 50.00 65.00

☐ **ANN-MARGRET,** 8x10 photo (pin-up), signed 26.00 36.00

☐ **ANN-MARGRET,** six stills from the motion picture "Tommy," three of them signed, in a folder 38.00 49.00

☐ **ANN-MARGRET,** photo with Anthony Hopkins, signed by her only 15.00 23.00

☐ **ANN-MARGRET,** small photo of her, topless, from a movie scene, cut from a magazine or book, matted, signed on the mat 36.00 45.00

☐ **BELAFONTE, HARRY,** 8x10 motion picture still with Sidney Poitier, signed by both 80.00 100.00

☐ **BELAFONTE, HARRY,** sheet music, "Banana Boat Song," signed 20.00 26.00

☐ **BELAFONTE, HARRY,** LP record album cover signed, no record 33.00 43.00

☐ **BELAFONTE, HARRY,** colored photo from "Life" magazine, signed 20.00 25.00

☐ **BELAFONTE, HARRY,** two 8x10 studio portraits, one signed 20.00 25.00

☐ **BELAFONTE, HARRY,** signature on a concert program, NY 8.00 11.00

☐ **BELAFONTE, HARRY,** five miscellaneous items signed by him..................... 22.00 33.00

Price Range

- ☐ **BELAFONTE, HARRY,** c. 1955, 8x10 photo in calypso outfit, signed 26.00 35.00
- ☐ **BENNETT, TONY,** sheet music, "I Left My Heart in San Francisco," signed, inscribed. Framed along with a portrait and a 45rpm record 110.00 140.00
- ☐ **BENNETT, TONY,** sheet music (as above), signed 30.00 38.00
- ☐ **BENNETT, TONY,** 8x10 studio portrait, signed and inscribed 10.00 14.00
- ☐ **BENNETT, TONY,** snapshot on stage, signed in crayon 8.00 11.00
- ☐ **BENNETT, TONY,** c. 1971, cancelled check endorsed by him 20.00 25.00
- ☐ **BENNETT, TONY,** lock of hair reputedly his, framed with an unsigned photo 32.00 40.00
  (We list items of this nature only out of curiosity interest; collectors should be wary of them, as they frequently are not authentic.)
- ☐ **BENNETT, TONY,** early LP record album cover signed, record missing 36.00 45.00
- ☐ **BENNETT, TONY,** signature on concert program 12.00 16.00
- ☐ **BENNETT, TONY,** c. 1966, typed letter to a fan, signed 12.00 16.00
- ☐ **BERGEN, POLLY,** c. 1956, 8x10 photo signed 8.00 11.00
- ☐ **BERGEN, POLLY,** ad for skin cream, signed 10.00 14.00
- ☐ **BERGEN, POLLY,** signature on the back of an envelope 4.00 5.00
- ☐ **BERGEN, POLLY,** c. 1968, typed letter, signed 6.00 9.00
- ☐ **BERGEN, POLLY,** 8x10 color portrait photo, unsigned 5.00 7.00
- ☐ **BOONE, PAT,** 8x10 publicity photo, signed 10.00 16.00
- ☐ **BOONE, PAT,** signed album cover 13.00 17.00
- ☐ **BOONE, PAT,** typed letter, signed 8.00 13.00
- ☐ **BOONE, PAT,** concert program, signed 13.00 18.00
- ☐ **BREWER, TERESA,** c. 1957, 8x10 photo in stage costume (probably from a TV show), signed 8.00 12.00

Price Range

☐ **BREWER, TERESA,** 45rpm phono record, "Ricochet Romance," signed on the label, framed 20.00   26.00

☐ **BREWER, TERESA,** 5x7 photo as a young girl 5.00   7.00

☐ **BREWER, TERESA,** 8x10 studio portrait, signed and inscribed 9.00   12.00

☐ **BREWER, TERESA,** signature on leaf from autograph book 3.00   4.00

☐ **CANTRELL, LANA,** 5x6 photo from magazine, full color, signed in red magic marker 5.00   7.00

☐ **CANTRELL, LANA,** c. 1977, 8x10 studio photo, signed 6.00   8.00

☐ **CANTRELL, LANA,** LP record album cover, signed, no record 14.00   18.00

☐ **CANTRELL, LANA,** c. 1975, signature on a fan club card 5.00   7.00

☐ **CARPENTER, KAREN,** sheet music to four of her song hits, signed, in a large plastic frame 75.00   90.00

☐ **CARPENTER, KAREN,** c. 1976, small photo taken by fan, mounted on a card, signed on the card 9.00   12.00

☐ **CARPENTER, KAREN,** c. 1975, 8x10 studio photo with Richard Carpenter, signed by both 20.00   30.00

☐ **CARPENTER, KAREN,** signature on a concert brochure 8.00   11.00

☐ **CARR, VICKI,** c. 1963, typed letter, signed 6.00   9.00

☐ **CARR, VICKI,** brief memo on pink stationery, undated 5.00   7.00

☐ **CARR, VICKI,** T-shirt with her photo 8.00   11.00

☐ **CARR, VICKI,** Christmas card signed by her 8.00   11.00

☐ **CARR, VICKI,** magazine ad signed 4.00   5.00

☐ **CARR, VICKI,** photo clipped from magazine, signed, mounted 5.00   7.00

☐ **CARROLL, DIAHANN,** two motion picture stills, signed 12.00   16.00

☐ **CARROLL, DIAHANN,** 8x10 photo with Alan Alda, signed by Carroll only 9.00   13.00

☐ **CARROLL, DIAHANN,** 8x10 photo inscribed to David Frost 30.00   40.00

☐ **CARROLL, DIAHANN,** studio portrait, inscribed and signed 9.00   13.00

Price Range

☐ **CARROLL, DIAHANN,** LP record album cover signed, no record 15.00 20.00

☐ **CARROLL, DIAHANN,** c. 1971, typed letter, signed 8.00 11.00

☐ **CHANNING, CAROL,** Printed score, "Hello Dolly," signed and inscribed. Framed along with an unsigned photo 90.00 115.00

☐ **CHANNING, CAROL,** review of show "Gentlemen Prefer Blondes," clipped from N.Y. Times, signed, framed 41.00 55.00

☐ **CHANNING, CAROL,** 8x10 photo in "Dolly" costume, signed 36.00 46.00

☐ **CHANNING, CAROL,** 8x10 color photo with Barbra Streisand, both dressed as "Dolly," signed by both 100.00 120.00

☐ **CHANNING, CAROL,** 8x10 color photo with Louis Armstrong, signed by Channing only 90.00 115.00

☐ **CHANNING, CAROL,** hat worn by her in "Hello Dolly," sold at benefit auction 125.00 140.00

☐ **CHANNING, CAROL,** book "The Matchmaker," signed on flyleaf, signed again on interior page, soft covered 60.00 80.00

☐ **CHANNING, CAROL,** signature on a theater program 9.00 12.00

☐ **CHARLES, RAY,** LP album cover, signed .. 22.00 27.00

☐ **CHARLES, RAY,** 8x10 publicity photo, signed 14.00 20.00

☐ **CHARLES, RAY,** three pieces of sheet music, all signed, one inscribed 35.00 50.00

☐ **CLARK, PETULA,** sheet music, "Downtown," signed 15.00 20.00

☐ **CLARK, PETULA,** article from British fan magazine, signed 8.00 11.00

☐ **CLARK, PETULA,** 8x10 photo performing on stage 3.00 4.00

☐ **CLARK, PETULA,** postcard photo with facsimile signature 4.00 5.00

☐ **CLARK, PETULA,** poster advertising a concert, 24x37 .... 70.00 90.00

☐ **CLARK, PETULA,** signature on a shop circular 5.00 7.00

☐ **CLOONEY, ROSEMARY,** c. 1957, 8x10 studio portrait, signed 10.00 13.00

	Price Range	
☐ **CLOONEY, ROSEMARY,** color photo from fan magazine, cover signed	7.00	10.00
☐ **CLOONEY, ROSEMARY,** sheet music, "This Old House," signed	20.00	26.00
☐ **CLOONEY, ROSEMARY,** snapshot with Perry Como, signed by Clooney only	13.00	17.00
☐ **CLOONEY, ROSEMARY,** c. 1964, LP record album cover signed on the back with lengthy message, record present	70.00	90.00
☐ **COMO, PERRY,** c. 1930, handwritten letter, 1½ pp	56.00	70.00
☐ **COMO, PERRY,** c. 1925, exercise book used by him in grade school	80.00	100.00
☐ **COMO, PERRY,** 8x10 photo with Dinah Shore, signed by both	34.00	44.00
☐ **COMO, PERRY,** c. 1953, 8x10 photo on stage, possibly TV	5.00	7.00
☐ **COMO, PERRY,** three signed and inscribed 8 x10 photos	33.00	42.00

Perry Como

Price Range

☐ **COMO, PERRY,** c. 1960, Christmas card, signed 25.00 33.00

☐ **COMO, PERRY,** c. 1964, LP album cover, signed, no record 36.00 44.00

☐ **COMO, PERRY,** typed letter, signed, regarding his TV show 22.00 30.00

☐ **COMO, PERRY,** signature on a record sleeve 6.00 8.00

☐ **COMO, PERRY,** book "Pictorial History of Television," signed by him 25.00 34.00

☐ **CONNIFF, RAY,** c. 1967, photo with orchestra, signed 8.00 11.00

☐ **CONNIFF, RAY,** c. 1971, typed letter, signed 6.00 9.00

☐ **CONNIFF, RAY,** photo with Mike Douglas, signed by Conniff 11.00 16.00

☐ **CONNIFF, RAY,** signature on an advertising circular 3.00 4.00

☐ **CONNIFF, RAY,** LP record album cover signed, record inside also signed (on the label) 35.00 45.00

☐ **CROSBY, BING,** c. 1932, 8x10 photo, signed and inscribed 70.00 90.00

☐ **CROSBY, BING,** collection of 236 motion picture stills, six of them signed, housed in looseleaf albums 600.00 750.00

☐ **CROSBY, BING,** pipe smoked by him, sold at auction in War Bonds drive 85.00 100.00

☐ **CROSBY, BING,** 78rpm record album cover, signed and inscribed, all four records missing, somewhat worn 110.00 140.00
(The value would not be so high, if it were not possible to replace the records.)

☐ **CROSBY, BING,** 8x10 photo with Barry Fitz-Gerald, signed by both 130.00 175.00

☐ **CROSBY, BING,** c. 1948, 6x8 photo cut from magazine, signed and inscribed 25.00 33.00

☐ **CROSBY, BING,** 5x6 color photo with Danny Kaye, signed by both 45.00 60.00

☐ **CROSBY, BING,** motion picture poster "Country Girl," signed at the top, stained .. 350.00 450.00

☐ **CROSBY, BING,** golf ball signed by him ... 90.00 130.00

☐ **CROSBY, BING,** baseball autographed by him and Mel Allen 120.00 160.00

	Price Range	
☐ **CROSBY, BING,** c. 1970, typed letter, signed	20.00	25.00
☐ **CROSBY, BING,** signature on a hotel desk receipt	8.00	11.00
☐ **CROSBY, BING,** 8x10 photo with Harry James, unsigned	5.00	7.00
☐ **DAMONE, VIC,** c. 1955, 8x10 studio portrait, signed	10.00	13.00
☐ **DAMONE, VIC,** c. 1958, cabaret handbill advertising him, with small photo	4.00	5.00
☐ **DAMONE, VIC,** color cover of a fan magazine, signed	10.00	13.00
☐ **DAMONE, VIC,** "Top 60" chart from "Cashbox" magazine, signed and inscribed, framed	25.00	33.00
☐ **DAMONE, VIC,** 4x5 snapshot photo on street, signed on back	5.00	7.00
☐ **DAMONE, VIC,** two 8x10 studio photos, unsigned, early	6.00	8.00
☐ **DAMONE, VIC,** c. 1961, typed letter, signed	5.00	7.00
☐ **DAMONE, VIC,** large cardboard figure of him, almost lifesize, apparently from a theater display	55.00	70.00
☐ **DAVIS, SAMMY, Jr.,** c. 1960, 8x10 photo with Frank Sinatra and Dean Martin, signed by all	120.00	150.00
☐ **DAVIS, SAMMY, Jr.,** LP record album cover signed, no record	45.00	65.00
☐ **DAVIS, SAMMY, Jr.,** signature on a milk carton (indistinct)	10.00	13.00
☐ **DAVIS, SAMMY, Jr.,** early 1950's. Bill advertising Will Maston Trio	6.00	8.00
☐ **DAVIS, SAMMY, Jr.,** c. 1953, ALs, nearly one full page	30.00	38.00
☐ **DAVIS, SAMMY, Jr.,** photo with Peter Lawford, signed by Davis only	31.00	40.00
☐ **DAVIS, SAMMY, Jr.,** 8x10 studio portrait, signed and inscribed	12.00	16.00
☐ **DAVIS, SAMMY, Jr.,** three snapshots on stage, unsigned	9.00	12.00
☐ **DAVIS, SAMMY, Jr.,** c. 1968, check endorsed by him	30.00	40.00

Price Range

☐ **DAVIS, SAMMY, Jr.,** c. 1957–1974, collection of 64 magazine articles on him, unbound, in a folder 110.00   140.00

☐ **DAY, DORIS,** large photo from "Life" magazine, signed 12.00   16.00

☐ **DAY, DORIS,** sheet music, "Secret Love," signed and inscribed 42.00   60.00

☐ **DAY, DORIS,** c. 1948, 8x10 publicity photo   4.00   6.00

☐ **DAY, DORIS,** collection of 91 motion picture stills from about 15 films, none signed 220.00   275.00

☐ **DAY, DORIS,** "Doris Day Coloring Book," mint 15.00   20.00

☐ **DAY, DORIS,** sheet music, "Ten Cents a Dance," signed 25.00   35.00

☐ **DAY, DORIS,** matted, signed photo of Ruth Etting, signed on the mat by Doris Day (who portrayed her in motion picture) 130.00   155.00

☐ **DAY, DORIS,** 11x14 color photo, signed ... 24.00   34.00

☐ **DAY, DORIS,** LP record album cover, signed, no record 36.00   46.00

☐ **DAY, DORIS,** 8x10 photo with James Cagney, signed by both 70.00   90.00

☐ **DeHAVEN, GLORIA,** 8x10 motion picture still, signed 10.00   14.00

☐ **DESMOND, JOHNNY,** c. 1957, concert program, signed 5.00   7.00

☐ **DESMOND, JOHNNY,** membership card "Johnny Desmond Fan Club" 8.00   11.00

☐ **DESMOND, JOHNNY,** 8x10 portrait photo, signed 9.00   13.00

☐ **DESMOND, JOHNNY,** two fan magazine covers from the 1950's with his portrait in color, unsigned 4.00   5.00

☐ **DESMOND, JOHNNY,** c. 1963, typed letter, signed, with envelope 6.00   8.00

☐ **DESMOND, JOHNNY,** c. 1956, signature on cafe check 6.00   8.00

☐ **DESMOND, JOHNNY,** photo with Vic Damone, signed by both 25.00   35.00

☐ **DESMOND, JOHNNY,** 45rpm record, "That Old Gang of Mine," signed on the label ... 15.00   20.00

Price Range

☐ **EDDY, NELSON,** c. 1938, 8x10 studio portrait, signed and inscribed 21.00 27.00

☐ **EDDY, NELSON,** 8x10 motion picture still with Jeanette MacDonald, signed by both 85.00 110.00

☐ **EDDY, NELSON,** collection of 57 motion picture stills 130.00 160.00

☐ **EDDY, NELSON,** series of 8 scrapbooks 11x14 inches, containing items on his life and career, 23 signed photos, c. 250 unsigned photos (including motion picture stills), magazine articles, news cuttings 1500.00 2000.00

☐ **EDDY, NELSON,** sheet music, "Shortnin' Bread," signed 130.00 160.00

☐ **EDDY, NELSON,** c. 1945, pen and wash caricature by Al Capp 300.00 350.00

☐ **EDDY, NELSON,** bulletin of the "Nelson Eddy Fan Club" 25.00 33.00

☐ **EDDY, NELSON,** c. 1939, postcard photo with facsimile signature 12.00 16.00

☐ **FISHER, EDDIE,** c. 1953, 8x10 studio portrait, signed 21.00 26.00

☐ **FISHER, EDDIE,** magazine cover photo with Elizabeth Taylor 4.00 6.00

☐ **FISHER, EDDIE,** c. 1953, "Enjoy Coke Time with Eddie Fisher," 11x14 ad, signed 26.00 32.00

☐ **FISHER, EDDIE,** signature on a "TV Guide" cover 6.00 9.00

☐ **FISHER, EDDIE,** 45rpm record, "O My Papa," signed on the label. Framed along with a small unsigned portrait 80.00 100.00

☐ **FISHER, EDDIE,** c. 1968, 5x7 photo, signed 8.00 11.00

☐ **FISHER, EDDIE,** c. 1978, 6x8 photo with Carrie Fisher, signed by both 12.00 16.00

☐ **FISHER, EDDIE,** 8x10 photo with Debbie Reynolds 5.00 7.00

☐ **FRANCIS, CONNIE,** 8x10 publicity photo, signed 5.00 9.00

☐ **FRANCIS, CONNIE,** handwritten note, signed 6.50 11.50

☐ **FRANCIS, CONNIE,** magazine article, signed, good condition 7.00 11.00

Price Range

☐ **FRANCIS, CONNIE,** card, inscribed and signed 9.00 14.00

☐ **FRANCIS, CONNIE,** signature on a notebook page 6.00 9.00

☐ **FROMAN, JANE,** c. 1952, 8x10 studio portrait, signed 7.00 10.00

☐ **GARLAND, JUDY,** c. 1969, N.Y. Times newspaper with story on her death 9.00 13.00

☐ **GARLAND, JUDY,** c. 1946, 8x10 photo, signed and inscribed 180.00 240.00

☐ **GARLAND, JUDY,** sheet music, "Over the Rainbow," signed, framed along with a signed, inscribed early photo 500.00 650.00

☐ **GARLAND, JUDY,** concert program, Palace Theater, N.Y., unsigned 22.00 28.00

☐ **GARLAND, JUDY,** three stills from "The Wizard of Oz," all signed by her, two also signed by Jack Haley, one by Jack Haley and Bert Lahr. In a brown leatherette folder 550.00 700.00

☐ **GARLAND, JUDY,** c. 1962, Typed letter, signed 100.00 120.00

☐ **GARLAND, JUDY,** c. 1937, ALs, two pp., Hollywood 400.00 500.00

☐ **GARLAND, JUDY,** LP record album cover, signed, no record 310.00 390.00

☐ **GARLAND, JUDY,** Newspaper clipping, signed 85.00 110.00

☐ **GORME, EYDIE,** 8x10 photo with Steve Lawrence, signed by both 21.00 26.00

☐ **GORME, EYDIE,** record company ad, signed by her 8.00 11.00

☐ **GORME, EYDIE,** 5x7 photo on stage, signed on the back 9.00 12.00

☐ **GORME, EYDIE,** signature on a card 4.00 5.00

☐ **GORME, EYDIE,** scrapbook with c. 250 news cuttings, photos, a few signed, other items pertaining to her and Steve Lawrence 95.00 115.00

☐ **GORME, EYDIE,** c. 1966, typed letter, signed 6.00 8.00

☐ **HORNE, LENA,** 8x10 publicity photo, signed 20.00 25.00

☐ **HORNE, LENA,** concert program, inscribed and signed 13.00 19.00

☐ **HORNE, LENA,** snapshot taken with a fan 14.00 20.00

Price Range

☐ **HUMPERDINCK, ENGELBERT,** LP record album, cover signed and inscribed to a fan, record present 50.00   70.00

☐ **HUMPERDINCK, ENGELBERT,** 8x10 studio portrait, signed 25.00   33.00

☐ **HUMPERDINCK, ENGELBERT,** collection of color photos from fan magazine covers, mounted on stiff paper sheets, unsigned .. 15.00   20.00

☐ **HUMPERDINCK, ENGELBERT,** T-shirt with his likeness 10.00   13.00

☐ **HUMPERDINCK, ENGELBERT,** bumper sticker 8.00   11.00

☐ **HUMPERDINCK, ENGELBERT,** four 8x10 color photos, one signed 90.00   115.00

☐ **HUMPERDINCK, ENGELBERT,** membership card in his fan club 5.00   7.00

☐ **HUMPERDINCK, ENGELBERT,** c. 1970. "Win a Date with Engelbert," rules for promotional contest, one page 4.00   5.00

☐ **HUMPERDINCK, ENGELBERT,** signature on a card 6.00   8.00

☐ **HUNTER, TAB,** c. 1958, 8x10 photo, signed 5.00   7.00

☐ **JOLSON, AL,** c. 1920's, 8x10 sepia photo, signed and inscribed 110.00   135.00

☐ **JOLSON, AL,** sheet music, "Mammy," signed, framed 150.00   210.00

☐ **JOLSON, AL,** c. 1908, ALs, 1½ pp., with envelope 100.00   125.00

☐ **JOLSON, AL,** cardboard cut-out portrait of Jolson in black-face, possibly from a motion picture poster, signed 240.00   310.00

☐ **JOLSON, AL,** c. 1944, typewritten letter, two pages, concerning the war and his observations on its effect on show biz, signed 225.00   300.00

☐ **JOLSON, AL,** c. 1940, 8x10 photo with Eddie Cantor, signed by Jolson only, framed 110.00   125.00

☐ **JOLSON, AL,** c. 1936, signature on the back of a press pass 16.00   21.00

☐ **JOLSON, AL,** c. 1912, vaudeville bill advertising him as one of the attractions 60.00   80.00

☐ **JOLSON, AL,** 8x10 photo with George Jessel, unsigned 12.00   17.00

Price Range

☐ **JOLSON, AL,** 8x10 motion picture still, boldly signed 100.00   115.00

☐ **JOLSON, AL,** c. 1925, handwritten memo, three lines 50.00   70.00

☐ **JOLSON, AL,** 17 unsigned publicity photos, various sizes 120.00   150.00

☐ **KAZAN, LAINIE,** c. 1971, 8x10 photo, signed   9.00   13.00

☐ **KAZAN, LAINIE,** LP record album cover, signed, no record 21.00   26.00

☐ **KAZAN, LAINIE,** signature on a food company brochure 4.00   6.00

☐ **KYSER, KAY,** postcard photo with facsimile signature 8.00   11.00

☐ **KYSER, KAY,** c. 1944, 8x10 photo with band, signed 12.00   16.00

☐ **KYSER, KAY,** diploma in "Kollege of Musical Knowledge," facsimile signature 10.00   13.00

☐ **KYSER, KAY,** c. 1941, snapshot photo signed on back 6.00   8.00

☐ **KYSER, KAY,** photo with "Ish Kabibble," signed by both 17.00   25.00

☐ **KYSER, KAY,** photo with Bob Crosby, signed by both 15.00   20.00

☐ **LAINE, FRANKIE,** sheet music, "Mule Train," signed 55.00   70.00

☐ **LAINE, FRANKIE,** c. 1954, magazine article, signed 5.00   7.00

☐ **LAINE, FRANKIE,** c. 1960, typewritten letter, signed 8.00   11.00

☐ **LAINE, FRANKIE,** LP album cover, signed, record inside also signed (on the label) 60.00   80.00

☐ **LAINE, FRANKIE,** c. 1952, sheet music, "High Noon," signed 50.00   70.00

☐ **LAINE, FRANKIE,** photo with Tex Ritter, signed by both, framed along with sheet music of "High Noon" and 78rpm records of the song done by both 120.00   160.00

☐ **LAINE, FRANKIE,** signature on a cash voucher 4.00   5.00

☐ **LAINE, FRANKIE,** c. 1958, 8x10 photo, signed 10.00   13.00

Price Range

☐ **LANSON, SNOOKY,** 8x10 photo with Dorothy Collins, signed by Lanson only	6.00	8.00
☐ **LaROSA, JULIUS,** c. 1956, 6x8 color photo from magazine, signed	6.00	8.00
☐ **LaROSA, JULIUS,** c. early 1950's, advertisement for Arthur Godfrey radio program with his picture and others	3.00	4.00
☐ **LaROSA, JULIUS,** c. 1951, handwritten letter, with envelope	8.00	11.00
☐ **LaROSA, JULIUS,** c. 1953, 8x10 studio portrait	3.00	4.00
☐ **LaROSA, JULIUS,** collection of c. 85 news clippings on LaRosa/Godfrey affair	22.00	28.00
☐ **LaROSA, JULIUS,** two candid photos, one signed on back	9.00	12.00
☐ **LaROSA, JULIUS,** signature on cover of LP album, no record	21.00	28.00
☐ **LEE, PEGGY,** 8x10 studio portrait, signed and inscribed, framed along with a 45rpm recording	50.00	65.00
☐ **LEE, PEGGY,** sheet music, "Fever," signed	33.00	41.00
☐ **LEE, PEGGY,** typewritten letter to a music agent, signed	12.00	16.00
☐ **LEE, PEGGY,** 8x10 publicity photo, close-up, signed	15.00	20.00
☐ **LEE, PEGGY,** two 8x10 photos, one holding a gold record	12.00	16.00
☐ **LEE, PEGGY,** snapshot photo with Duke Ellington, signed by Lee only	17.00	25.00
☐ **LEE, PEGGY,** c. 1955, photo in long gown, photo service stamp on back	4.00	5.00
☐ **LEE, PEGGY,** sheet music, "Is That All There Is?" signed	30.00	38.00
☐ **LEE, PEGGY,** LP record album cover, signed, record missing	33.00	45.00
☐ **LEE, PEGGY,** poster advertising an album, signed	60.00	75.00
☐ **MacRAE, GORDON,** 8x10 studio portrait, signed	5.00	7.00
☐ **MacRAE, GORDON,** c. 1958, three small fan snapshots	6.00	8.00

Price Range

☐ **MacRAE, GORDON,** c. 1963, 8x10 photo with Sheila MacRae, signed by both 25.00   33.00

☐ **MacRAE, GORDON,** photo with Vic Damone, signed by MacRae only 12.00   16.00

☐ **MacRAE, GORDON,** typewritten letter to a fan, signed 6.00   8.00

☐ **MacRAE, GORDON,** magazine article, signed 5.00   7.00

☐ **MacRAE, GORDON,** c. 1960, photo with Dean Martin, unsigned 4.00   5.00

☐ **MARTIN, DEAN,** c. 1951, 8x10 photo with Jerry Lewis, signed by both, CBS stamp on back 70.00   90.00

☐ **MARTIN, DEAN,** photo-spread from "Life" magazine, signed 30.00   40.00

☐ **MARTIN, DEAN,** 8x10 portrait photo holding gold record, signed 13.00   18.00

☐ **MARTIN, DEAN,** c. 1970, signature on restaurant menu........................... 5.00   7.00

☐ **MARTIN, DEAN,** LP record album cover, signed and inscribed on the back, record missing 38.00   48.00

☐ **MARTIN, DEAN,** 45rpm record, "That's Amore," signed on the label 30.00   40.00

☐ **MARTIN, DEAN,** c. 1954, postcard photo with Jerry Lewis, facsimile signatures 6.00   8.00

☐ **MARTIN, DEAN,** 8x10 photo with Sammy Davis, Jr. and Frank Sinatra, signed by Martin only 30.00   40.00

☐ **MARTIN, DEAN,** 43 motion picture stills, two in color 115.00   145.00

☐ **MARTIN, DEAN,** c. 1975, typewritten letter, signed.................................... 9.00   13.00

☐ **MARTIN, DEAN,** sheet music, "That's Amore," signed......................... 45.00   57.00

☐ **MATHIS, JOHNNY,** 8x10 publicity photo, signed.................................... 8.00   13.00

☐ **MATHIS, JOHNNY,** magazine article, signed 6.00   10.00

☐ **MATHIS, JOHNNY,** typewritten note to a fan, signed.................................... 5.00   8.00

☐ **MATHIS, JOHNNY,** signature on a restaurant check 5.00   8.00

Price Range

☐ **MATHIS, JOHNNY,** sheet music to "Misty," signed 8.00   15.00

☐ **MATHIS, JOHNNY,** concert program, signed   7.00   11.00

☐ **MERMAN, ETHEL,** 8x10 photo with Mary Martin, signed by both, matted and framed   110.00   145.00

☐ **MERMAN, ETHEL,** printed score, "Annie Get Your Gun," signed 50.00   65.00

☐ **MERMAN, ETHEL,** c. 1944, 8x10 studio portrait, signed 42.00   50.00

☐ **MERMAN, ETHEL,** c. 1948, 8x10 studio portrait, signed 36.00   45.00

☐ **MERMAN, ETHEL,** 8x10 photo in "Annie" costume, signed 50.00   70.00

☐ **MERMAN, ETHEL,** c. 1970, 6x8 color photo, inscribed 26.00   33.00

☐ **MERMAN, ETHEL,** two pages from a notebook in her hand 31.00   40.00

☐ **MERMAN, ETHEL,** three small snapshots taken by fans 6.00   8.00

☐ **MERMAN, ETHEL,** poster advertising "Annie Get Your Gun," 27x41, color, soiled 160.00   210.00

☐ **MILLER, MITCH,** printed record company circular, signed 5.00   7.00

☐ **MILLER, MITCH,** typewritten letter on Columbia Record Co. stationery, signed 9.00   12.00

☐ **MILLER, MITCH,** sheet music, "Yellow Rose of Texas," signed 31.00   36.00

☐ **MILLER, MITCH,** c. 1958, 8x10 studio photo, signed 8.00   11.00

☐ **MILLER, MITCH,** c. 1966, 7x8½ magazine photo with Skitch Henderson, signed by both   21.00   26.00

☐ **MILLER, MITCH,** 8x10 photo with Al Hirt, signed by Miller only 12.00   16.00

☐ **MILLER, MITCH,** c. 1958 & 1960. Two checks endorsed by him 36.00   43.00

☐ **MILLER, MITCH,** LP record album cover, signed, record missing 31.00   40.00

☐ **MILLER, MITCH,** signature on a notebook page 4.00   5.00

☐ **MITCHELL, GUY,** c. 1957, 45rpm record, "Singing the Blues," autographed on the label, framed with an unsigned photo 31.00   40.00

Price Range

☐ **MITCHELL, GUY,** "Billboard" magazine Top 100 chart, showing "Singing the Blues" #1, signed 24.00   32.00

☐ **MITCHELL, GUY,** 8x10 photo on stage, signed, inscribed 10.00   13.00

☐ **MITCHELL, GUY,** sheet music to three songs recorded by him, signed 55.00   70.00

☐ **MITCHELL, GUY,** 4x5 snapshot photo in car, signed 7.00   9.00

☐ **MITCHELL, GUY,** 5x7 photo with Perry Como, signed by Mitchell only 9.00   12.00

☐ **MONROE, VAUGHN,** sheet music, "Ghost Riders in the Sky," signed, framed along with a photo and a 78rpm recording 80.00   100.00

☐ **MONROE, VAUGHN,** 8x10 studio portrait, signed 12.00   16.00

☐ **MONROE, VAUGHN,** c. 1941, typewritten letter, signed 14.00   19.00

☐ **MONROE, VAUGHN,** c. 1949, signature on a card 7.00   10.00

☐ **MONROE, VAUGHN,** 8x10 photo at party, signed 12.00   16.00

☐ **MONROE, VAUGHN,** scrapbook with 34 photos, 17 of them signed, c. 135 news cuttings and magazine articles relating to him 300.00   350.00

☐ **MONROE, VAUGHN,** c. 1958, Christmas card, signed 12.00   16.00

☐ **MONROE, VAUGHN,** two small photos taken with fans, signed 15.00   20.00

☐ **MONROE, VAUGHN,** 8x10 photo, unsigned, Associated Press stamp on back 5.00   7.00

☐ **NEWLEY, ANTHONY,** printed score, "Stop the World," signed 14.00   18.00

☐ **NEWLEY, ANTHONY,** LP record album cover, signed, no record 30.00   37.00

☐ **NEWLEY, ANTHONY,** LP album cover, "Stop the World," original Broadway cast, signed on front, inscribed on back, no record 45.00   60.00

☐ **NEWLEY, ANTHONY,** 8x10 photo in costume, signed 12.00   16.00

☐ **NEWLEY, ANTHONY,** 4x5 photo, signed, mounted 8.00   11.00

Price Range

☐ **NEWLEY, ANTHONY,** signature on a small slip of paper 3.00 4.00

☐ **O'CONNELL, HELEN,** c. 1944, 8x10 photo in group, signed 9.00 12.00

☐ **O'CONNELL, HELEN,** color photo from magazine or book, signed 8.00 11.00

☐ **O'CONNELL, HELEN,** c. 1953, typewritten letter, signed 8.00 11.00

☐ **O'CONNELL, HELEN,** record company reply to a fan of O'Connell's, detailing plans for releases of forthcoming records, etc 4.00 5.00

☐ **O'CONNELL, HELEN,** c. 1936, early photo of her, signed 9.00 12.00

☐ **O'CONNELL, HELEN,** 8x10 photo with Bob Hope, signed by O'Connell only 10.00 14.00

☐ **O'CONNELL, HELEN,** scrapbook with c. 350 news cuttings, etc. 80.00 110.00

☐ **PAGE, PATTI,** sheet music, "How Much is That Doggie in the Window?" signed, framed 45.00 60.00

☐ **PAGE, PATTI,** c. 1964, 8x10 studio photo, signed 8.00 11.00

☐ **PAGE, PATTI,** photo with two gold disc records, signed 10.00 13.00

☐ **PAGE, PATTI,** two news clippings, signed .. 5.00 7.00

☐ **PAGE, PATTI,** cover of a fan magazine with colored photo, signed 8.00 11.00

☐ **PAGE, PATTI,** signature on a 45rpm record sleeve 3.00 4.00

☐ **PAGE, PATTI,** c. 1950's, three 8x10 studio photos, unsigned 8.00 11.00

☐ **PAGE, PATTI,** photo with Perry Como, signed by both 25.00 33.00

☐ **RAY, JOHNNY,** c. 1952, sheet music, "Little White Cloud That Cried," signed 31.00 42.00

☐ **RAY, JOHNNY,** 8x10 photo with Liberace, signed by both 50.00 65.00

☐ **RAY, JOHNNY,** two small magazine photos mounted on card, signed on the card 10.00 13.00

☐ **RAY, JOHNNY,** c. 1951, typewritten letter, signed 12.00 16.00

Price Range

☐ **REYNOLDS, DEBBIE,** 45rpm phono record, "Tammy," signed on the label, framed with a signed 8x10 photo 70.00   90.00

☐ **REYNOLDS, DEBBIE,** Collection of 147 unsigned motion picture stills, 23 of them in color 370.00   450.00

☐ **REYNOLDS, DEBBIE,** c. 1948, 8x10 photo, signed 10.00   13.00

☐ **REYNOLDS, DEBBIE,** c. 1942, photo as a youth, signed 15.00   20.00

☐ **REYNOLDS, DEBBIE,** five lobby cards of motion pictures 175.00   210.00

☐ **REYNOLDS, DEBBIE,** c. 1959, 8x10 photo with Doris Day, signed by Reynolds only . . . 12.00   16.00

☐ **REYNOLDS, DEBBIE,** typewritten letter to Warner Bros. studios, signed, with envelope 15.00   20.00

☐ **REYNOLDS, DEBBIE,** sheet music, "Abba Dabba Honeymoon," signed and inscribed 40.00   50.00

☐ **REYNOLDS, DEBBIE,** c. 1961, magazine article, signed 7.00   11.00

☐ **REYNOLDS, DEBBIE,** 8x10 color photo portrait, signed 15.00   21.00

☐ **SHORE, DINAH,** c. 1973, 8x10 photo on golf course, signed 8.00   11.00

☐ **SHORE, DINAH,** signature on a department store receipt 4.00   5.00

☐ **SHORE, DINAH,** c. 1951, photo on stage (TV show), signed 8.00   11.00

☐ **SHORE, DINAH,** c. 1949, ALs, one page, with envelope 9.00   12.00

☐ **SHORE, DINAH,** list of recordings made by her, signed 5.00   7.00

☐ **SHORE, DINAH,** photo with Perry Como, signed by Shore only 12.00   16.00

☐ **SHORE, DINAH,** photo with Montgomery Clift, signed by both 33.00   44.00

☐ **SHORE, DINAH,** Christmas card, signed, undated 12.00   16.00

☐ **SHORE, DINAH,** photo in record studio, signed, mounted 12.00   16.00

☐ **SHORE, DINAH,** large portrait photo, 16x23, signed 26.00   31.00

Price Range

☐ **SHORE, DINAH,** three items of sheet music, signed 44.00 52.00

☐ **SHORE, DINAH,** photo with Dean Martin, signed by Shore only 12.00 16.00

☐ **SINATRA, FRANK,** c. 1941, Paramount theater poster advertising an appearance by him, unsigned 150.00 200.00

☐ **SINATRA, FRANK,** c. 1957, 8x10 portrait photo, signed 30.00 40.00

☐ **SINATRA, FRANK,** LP record album cover signed, no record 90.00 120.00

☐ **SINATRA, FRANK,** c. 1960, memo in his hand 15.00 20.00

☐ **SINATRA, FRANK,** 8x10 photo on stage, Madison Square Garden, N.Y., autographed, matted, framed 70.00 100.00

☐ **SINATRA, FRANK,** c. 1962, pen-and-ink caricature of him, 10x12, matted and framed . . 100.00 125.00

☐ **SINATRA, FRANK,** photo with Frank, Jr., signed by both 70.00 100.00

☐ **SINATRA, FRANK,** photo with Dean Martin, signed by Sinatra only 35.00 45.00

☐ **SINATRA, FRANK,** 43 motion picture stills, black and white, one of them signed, several signed by other performers 120.00 150.00

☐ **SINATRA, FRANK,** c. 1958, photo holding a gold record, signed 30.00 40.00

☐ **SINATRA, FRANK,** sheet music, "My Way," signed, also signed by Paul Anka 150.00 200.00

☐ **SINATRA, FRANK,** c. 1972, photo with Paul Anka, signed by both 100.00 150.00

☐ **SINATRA, FRANK,** 45rpm record, "All the Way," signed on the label 75.00 100.00

☐ **SINATRA, FRANK,** T-shirt with his likeness 10.00 13.00

☐ **SINATRA, FRANK,** c. 1944, membership card in fan club 15.00 20.00

☐ **SINATRA, FRANK,** photo at age 17, signed "Frank" 60.00 80.00

☐ **SINATRA, FRANK,** c. 1975, photo with Nancy Sinatra, signed by both 70.00 100.00

☐ **SINATRA, FRANK,** c. 1940's, photo with Tommy Dorsey, signed by Sinatra only 65.00 90.00

Price Range

☐ **SINATRA, FRANK,** Motion picture still, "Man with the Golden Arm," signed, also signed by Kim Novak and Robert Strauss **100.00** **160.00**

☐ **SMITH, KATE,** c. 1950, sheet music, "When the Moon Comes Over the Mountain," signed and inscribed **44.00** **60.00**

☐ **SMITH, KATE,** c. 1951, photo from TV show, signed **9.00** **12.00**

☐ **SMITH, KATE,** c. 1939, 8x10 portrait photo, signed **14.00** **19.00**

☐ **SMITH, KATE,** 8x10 photo on stage, signed **12.00** **16.00**

☐ **SMITH, KATE,** c. 1955, signature on theater program **4.00** **5.00**

☐ **SMITH, KATE,** c. 1974, photo at hockey game, Canada, signed **8.00** **11.00**

☐ **SMITH, KATE,** two colored photos from magazine, signed **11.00** **15.00**

☐ **SMITH, KATE,** c. 1957, Christmas card, signed **12.00** **16.00**

☐ **SMITH, KATE,** 78rpm recording signed on the label **26.00** **33.00**

☐ **SMITH, KATE,** snapshot photo with fan, signed **5.00** **6.00**

☐ **STAFFORD, JO,** c. 1952. 8x10 studio portrait, signed **9.00** **12.00**

☐ **STAFFORD, JO,** c. 1953. Colored photo from magazine, signed **8.00** **11.00**

☐ **STAFFORD, JO,** 8x10 photo with Frankie Laine, signed by both **16.00** **22.00**

☐ **STAFFORD, JO,** signature on a card **3.00** **4.00**

☐ **STAFFORD, JO,** c. 1969, typewritten letter, signed **6.00** **8.00**

☐ **STAFFORD, JO,** c. 1961, brief memo in her hand **5.00** **7.00**

☐ **STARR, KAY,** sheet music, "Side by Side," signed **16.00** **22.00**

☐ **STARR, KAY,** c. 1953. 8x10 studio portrait, signed **8.00** **11.00**

☐ **STARR, KAY,** 78rpm recording signed on the label **20.00** **27.00**

☐ **STARR, KAY,** c. 1958, postcard with five lines in her hand **5.00** **7.00**

Price Range

☐ **STARR, KAY,** 8x10 photo on stage (possibly TV), signed 9.00 13.00

☐ **STARR, KAY,** snapshot photo at about age 16, signed 9.00 13.00

☐ **STARR, KAY,** record company contract signed 20.00 27.00

☐ **STARR, KAY,** c. 1954, magazine article, signed 5.00 7.00

☐ **STARR, KAY,** record company advertisement, signed 4.00 5.00

☐ **STARR, KAY,** c. mostly 1952–56, scrapbook with c. 90 news cuttings, several signed photos, etc. 50.00 65.00

☐ **STREISAND, BARBRA,** 8x10 photo with Garry Moore, signed by Streisand only, age 19 .... 30.00 40.00

☐ **STREISAND, BARBRA,** printed score, "Funny Girl," signed 40.00 55.00

☐ **STREISAND, BARBRA,** gown worn by her in film, sold at benefit auction 400.00 550.00

☐ **STREISAND, BARBRA,** c. 1962, 8x10 studio portrait, signed 25.00 33.00

☐ **STREISAND, BARBRA,** c. 1975, 8x10 studio portrait, signed 20.00 27.00

☐ **STREISAND, BARBRA,** c. 1972, typewritten letter, signed 20.00 27.00

☐ **STREISAND, BARBRA,** c. 1968, ALs, one-page, with envelope 40.00 60.00

☐ **STREISAND, BARBRA,** collection of 166 motion picture stills, all black and white, none signed, in a cloth box 370.00 445.00

☐ **STREISAND, BARBRA,** 8x10 photo with Elliot Gould, signed by Streisand only 50.00 70.00

☐ **STREISAND, BARBRA,** 8x10 photo with Woody Allen, signed by both, framed 100.00 150.00

☐ **STREISAND, BARBRA,** LP record album cover, signed, record missing 175.00 250.00

☐ **STREISAND, BARBRA,** two pages of notes in her hand 100.00 135.00

☐ **STREISAND, BARBRA,** sheet music, "Memories," signed 75.00 100.00

Price Range

☐ **STREISAND, BARBRA,** T-shirt with her likeness	10.00	13.00
☐ **STREISAND, BARBRA,** pen sketch of her, 8x10, framed	23.00	30.00
☐ **STREISAND, BARBRA,** portrait of her done in stained glass, 22x25, framed	130.00	180.00
☐ **STREISAND, BARBRA,** photo of her with Oscar award, signed	80.00	110.00
☐ **TORME, MEL,** c. 1954, 8x10 studio portrait, signed	8.00	11.00
☐ **TORME, MEL,** c. 1949, ALs, half page	6.00	8.00
☐ **TORME, MEL,** c. 1953, hand puppet, "Velvet Frog" (after his nickname "Velvet Frog"), plush	12.00	16.00
☐ **TORME, MEL,** 8x10 photo on stage, signed	7.00	10.00
☐ **TORME, MEL,** 5x7 photo on street, signed, creased	4.00	5.00
☐ **TORME, MEL,** magazine photo in turtleneck sweater, signed	5.00	7.00
☐ **VALE, JERRY,** c. 1960, 8x10 studio portrait, signed	8.00	11.00
☐ **VALE, JERRY,** c. 1964, restaurant ad, signed	6.00	8.00
☐ **VALE, JERRY,** three unsigned photos, various sizes	5.00	7.00
☐ **VALE, JERRY,** c. 1972, handwritten note . .	5.00	7.00
☐ **VALE, JERRY,** LP album cover, signed, record present	14.00	20.00
☐ **VALE, JERRY,** signature on restaurant napkin	3.00	4.00
☐ **VALLEE, RUDY,** c. 1930, 8x10 photo, signed and inscribed	25.00	33.00
☐ **VALLEE, RUDY,** score, "How to Succeed," signed	22.00	29.00
☐ **VALLEE, RUDY,** c. 1934, Yale football pennant, signed	70.00	95.00
☐ **VALLEE, RUDY,** photo at about age 14, signed	50.00	65.00
☐ **VALLEE, RUDY,** photo with Robert Morse, signed by both	41.00	55.00
☐ **VALLEE, RUDY,** 78rpm recording, signed on the label	25.00	33.00

	Price Range	
☐ **VALLEE, RUDY,** c. 1959, 8x10 photo with microphone, signed	**20.00**	**27.00**
☐ **WILLIAMS, ANDY,** 4x5 snapshot, signed, mounted	**5.00**	**7.00**
☐ **WILLIAMS, ANDY,** c. 1970, LP record album cover, signed	**25.00**	**33.00**
☐ **WILLIAMS, ANDY,** 8x10 color photo on golf course, signed	**12.00**	**16.00**
☐ **WILLIAMS, ANDY,** c. 1969, Photo with gold records and other awards, signed	**10.00**	**14.00**

ROCK AND ROLL

Rock music's beginnings can be traced back to roots in country, bluegrass, and jazz; its closest ancestor was Negro rhythm and blues. A number of the earlier rock stars came out of that musical style. To name the first pure rock record or rock performer would be impossible. Some would say Bill Haley & the Comets. This group had the first million-selling pure rock record, "Rock Around the Clock," in 1955. Without doubt, Bill Haley and his band were more of an influence on early rock performers than any other pioneers in the field. The success of "Rock Around the Clock" also encouraged record companies previously skeptical of rock's sales appeal to bring out rock records. By the end of 1955, it was the biggest selling type of popular music.

The so-called "golden age" of rock was the 1950's, or more specifically the years from 1955 to 1959. All rock records of that era are collectible, though many carry just minimal value depending on the artist, label, recording, and scarcity. Many post-1960 records are also sought by rockaphiles. There is no line of demarcation on age. Undoubtedly, today's rock records will be collector's items in time, perhaps a very short time.

As far as collectibility goes, in terms of artist, the most desirable rock recordings are early (pre-popularity) releases by artists who later became stars. It is very rare in the rock field—or in any form of pop music, for that matter—for an unknown artist's first recording to become a big hit. Usually, unknowns who score Top Ten hits have made previous recordings; the big hit is believed by the public to be their first record because few persons are aware earlier records were released. Everyone, including many disc jockeys, thought the Everly Brothers' "Bye Bye Love," a 1956 million-seller, was their first recording. It was their first on the Cadence label but had been preceded by a Columbia disc. That

Columbia recording, "Keep A-Loving Me/The Sun Keeps Shining," is now a prime collector's item, worth $20 to $30 depending on condition. "Bye Bye Love" brings $3 at most.

Generally speaking, records that made the hit charts are of minimal value, because of the vast quantities manufactured. As many as 4 million copies can exist of a super hit. In fact, there have been many million sellers—"gold records"—that never made Number One. On the other hand, a recording that fails badly will probably only get about ten to twenty thousand pressings (possibly less), and will be quite scarce and collectible. For more complete information on the field of rock music collecting, see *The Official Guide to Collectible Rock Records* by Randal C. Hill, published by The House of Collectibles.

Rock music collecting. The logical and most popular approach is to concentrate on the recordings of a single artist, or several artists. Some collectors try to assemble a complete "Billboard" or "Cashbox" hit list—the fifty or sixty recordings that appeared on the list in a given week, but this will invariably include non-rock titles. Others make a specialty of recordings by artists who never became famous. These records, usually very popular among '50's cultists (more so today than originally), tend to be quite scarce and costly. Some had very limited pressings. They were issued by small companies with low budgets, which could not afford to take gambles. No complete list of all rock recordings has ever been compiled, so it is possible that some obscure releases of the 1950's or later exist that are not even known to collectors. Advanced collectors are also interested in demo records, many of which were never publicly released or, if released, were not identical to the demo.

The best source for rock records are the dealers who make a specialty of buying and selling them. Occasional "finds" may be made in junkshops, flea markets, etc., but in general the condition of records found in this fashion is undesirable. Specialist dealers stock only specimens in fine or better condition and can supply hard-to-get titles that would probably not be obtainable anywhere else. Another possibility is to trade with fellow collectors, using this guide or dealer price lists to establish values.

	8x10 Signed Photo	Plain Signature	Other
AUTOGRAPHS			
☐ **ACE, JOHNNY**	3.25	2.50	
☐ **ADAMS, LINK**	3.25	2.50	

	8x10 Signed Photo	Plain Signature	Other
☐ **ADDEO, NICKY**	5.25	2.50	
☐ **ALAIMO, STEVE**	3.25	1.75	
☐ **ALEXANDER, ARTHUR**	3.25	1.75	
☐ **ALLEN, DAVIE**	4.25	2.50	
☐ Typed letter with signature			3.00
☐ **ALLEN, LEE**	3.00	1.75	
☐ **ALPERT, HERB**	4.00	2.00	
☐ **ANDREWS, LEE**	4.00	2.00	
☐ **ANKA, PAUL**	3.50	1.50	
☐ Typed letter			3.00
☐ Signed cover of record album			15.00
☐ **AVALON, FRANKIE**	4.00	2.00	
☐ Signed album cover			14.00
☐ **BAKER, KENNY**	5.00	2.00	
☐ **BAKER, LAVERN**	5.00	2.50	
☐ **BALIN, MARTY**	6.50	3.50	
☐ **BALLARD, HANK**	3.00	1.50	
☐ **BARRI, STEVE**	3.00	1.50	
☐ **BARRY, JEFF**	9.00	3.00	
Most memorabilia is scarce.			
☐ **BEAUMONT, JIMMY**	3.00	1.50	
☐ **BELLUS, TONY**	5.00	2.00	
☐ **BENNETT, BOYD**	4.00	2.00	
☐ **BERRY, CHUCK**	4.75	2.50	
☐ Signed album cover			20.00
☐ **BERRY, JAN**	4.00	2.00	
☐ **BEST, PETER**	25.00	5.00	
☐ **BIG BOPPER (J. P. Richardson)**	105.00	25.00	
☐ **BLACK, JACK**	3.00	1.50	
☐ **BLAND, BILLY**	3.00	1.50	
☐ **BLANE, MARCIE**	3.00	1.50	
☐ **BONDS, GARY**	5.50	2.00	
☐ **BONO, SONNY**	5.00	2.00	
☐ **BOWEN, JIMMY**	10.00	3.00	
☐ **BOWIE, DAVID**	25.00	8.00	
☐ **BOYCE, TOMMY**	3.50	1.50	
☐ **BRADLEY, JAN**	3.00	1.50	
☐ **BROOKS, DONNIE**	3.00	1.50	

	8x10 Signed Photo	Plain Signature	Other
☐ BURNETTE, DORSEY	4.00	1.50	
☐ BURNETTE, JOHNNY	22.00	6.00	
Most memorabilia is scarce.			
☐ BUTLER, JERRY	3.00	1.50	
☐ BYRNES, ED	6.00	2.00	
☐ CAMPBELL, GLEN	6.25	1.75	
☐ Signed album cover			12.00
☐ CAMPBELL, JO-ANN	3.00	1.50	
☐ CANNON, FREDDY	3.00	1.50	
☐ CAPEHART, JERRY	6.00	3.00	
☐ CARR, VICKI	4.00	1.50	
☐ CASEY, AL	6.00	3.00	
☐ CASTRO, VINCE	6.00	3.00	
☐ CHECKER, CHUBBY	7.50	3.75	
☐ CHRISTIE, LOU	6.00	3.00	
☐ CLANTON, JIMMY	4.00	1.50	
☐ CLARK, SANFORD	3.00	1.50	
☐ CLIFFORD, BUZZ	4.00	1.50	
☐ COCHRAN, EDDIE	6.00	3.00	
☐ COCKER, JOE	7.00	3.50	
☐ CONNORS, CAROL	6.00	3.00	
☐ COOKE, SAM	25.00	5.00	
☐ Signed album cover			75.00
☐ CORTEZ, DAVE	4.00	1.50	
☐ CRAWFORD, JOHNNY	4.00	1.50	
☐ CYMBAL, JOHNNY	4.00	1.50	
☐ DALE, DICK	5.00	2.00	
☐ DALTREY, ROGER	10.00	5.00	
☐ DARIN, BOBBY	40.00	7.00	
☐ Signed album cover			150.00
☐ DARREN, JAMES	4.00	1.50	
☐ DAVIES, DAVE	3.00	1.50	
☐ DEANE, JANET	6.00	3.00	
☐ DEE, JOHNNY	7.00	3.00	
☐ DEE, TOMMY	5.00	2.00	
☐ DENSON, LEE	6.00	2.00	
☐ DeSHANNON, JACKIE	6.00	2.00	
☐ DIDDLEY, BO	15.00	5.50	
☐ DIMEOLA, AL	4.00	1.50	
☐ DION	6.00	2.00	

	8x10 Signed Photo	Plain Signature	Other
☐ **DOBKINS, CARL**	4.00	1.50	
☐ **DOLENZ, MICKEY**	7.50	2.50	
☐ Signed album cover			12.00
☐ **DOMINO, FATS**	12.00	3.00	
☐ **DONNER, RAL**	20.00	5.00	
☐ **DORMAN, HAROLD**	2.00	1.00	
☐ **DYLAN, BOB**	30.00	5.00	
Very strong collector interest in all memorabilia.			
☐ **EDDY, DUANE**	5.00	2.00	
☐ **ENGLISH, SCOTT**	5.00	2.00	
☐ **FABIAN**	3.50	1.50	
☐ Signed album cover			12.00
☐ **FAITH, ADAM**	3.00	1.00	
☐ **FORD, FRANKIE**	3.00	1.00	
☐ **FOWLEY, KIM**	5.00	2.00	
☐ **FRAMPTON, PETER**	25.00	5.00	
☐ **FREEMAN, BOBBY**	6.00	2.00	
☐ **FRENCH, DON**	4.00	1.00	
☐ **FULLER, JERRY**	5.00	1.50	
☐ **FURY, BILLY**	4.00	1.00	
☐ **GALLANT, BILLY**	4.00	1.00	
☐ **GARCIA, JERRY**	6.50	2.00	
☐ **GARFUNKEL, ART**	10.00	2.25	
☐ **GATES, DAVID**	5.00	1.50	
☐ **GAYE, MARVIN**	25.00	5.00	
☐ **GIBBS, GEORGIA**	5.00	1.50	
☐ Signed contract with record company			22.00
☐ **GORE, LESLEY**	4.00	2.00	
☐ **GRACIE, CHARLIE**	4.00	1.50	
☐ **GRANAHAN, JERRY**	4.00	1.50	
☐ **HALEY, BILL**	35.00	4.00	
☐ **HALL, LARRY**	5.00	1.50	
☐ **HAMILTON, GEORGE**	5.00	1.50	
☐ **HARRISON, WILBERT**	8.00	2.00	
☐ **HARRY, DEBORAH**	6.75	2.25	
☐ **HART, BOBBY**	3.00	1.00	
☐ **HAWKINS, DALE**	5.00	1.50	

	8x10 Signed Photo	Plain Signature	Other
☐ HAWKINS, RONNIE	5.00	1.50	
☐ HAWKS, MICKEY	6.00	1.50	
☐ HEAD, ROY	3.00	1.00	
☐ HELMS, BOBBY	2.50	1.00	
☐ HENDRIX, JIMI	40.00	8.00	
☐ HICKEY, ERSEL	5.00	1.50	
☐ HILL, JOEL	6.00	1.50	
☐ HOLLY, BUDDY	120.00	20.00	
☐ HUNTER, IVORY JOE	10.00	2.00	
☐ HYLAND, BRIAN	6.00	1.50	
☐ JACKSON, JOE	7.00	3.00	
☐ JACKSON, MICHAEL	125.00	35.00	
☐ IAN, JANIS	4.00	1.50	
☐ JOHNSON, MARV	4.00	1.00	
☐ JONES, DAVY	7.50	2.00	
☐ JONES, JIMMY	3.00	1.00	
☐ JOPLIN, JANIS	17.00	6.00	
☐ JUSTIS, BILL	7.50	2.00	
☐ KENDRICKS, EDDIE	4.50	1.50	
☐ KENNER, CHRIS	3.00	1.00	
☐ KNIGHT, SONNY	7.50	2.00	
☐ KNOX, BUDDY	15.00	3.00	
☐ Signed album cover			50.00
☐ LEE, CURTIS	5.00	1.50	
☐ 4x5 photo signed from magazine			4.00
☐ LEWIS, BOBBY	4.50	1.50	
☐ LINDEN, KATHY	4.00	1.50	
☐ LITTLE ANTHONY	8.00	3.00	
☐ LITTLE EVA	6.00	2.00	
☐ LITTLE RICHARD	10.00	3.00	
☐ LUKE, ROBIN	5.00	2.00	
☐ LYMON, FRANKIE	80.00	11.00	
☐ MACK, LONNIE	4.00	2.00	
☐ MANN, CARL	6.00	2.00	
☐ MANUEL, RICHIE	5.00	2.50	
☐ MARENO, LEE	11.00	3.00	
☐ MARTIN, GEORGE	4.00	2.00	
☐ MARTIN, JANIS	6.00	2.50	
☐ MASON, DAVE	5.00	1.50	

	8x10 Signed Photo	Plain Signature	Other
☐ MAYER, NATHANIEL	4.00	1.50	
☐ McDANIELS, GENE	4.00	1.50	
☐ McKUEN, ROD	11.00	4.00	
☐ McPHATTER, CLYDE	10.00	3.00	
☐ MILES, GARRY	4.00	1.50	
☐ MILLS, HAYLEY	4.00	1.50	
☐ MINEO, SAL	25.00	5.00	
☐ Signed movie stills			30.00
☐ MONEY, EDDIE	5.50	1.75	
☐ MONTEZ, CHRIS	5.00	1.50	
☐ MORRISON, VAN	6.50	2.75	
☐ NEAL, JERRY	6.00	2.00	
☐ NELSON, RICKY	10.00	3.50	
☐ Signed album cover			17.00
☐ Article from a fan magazine, signed			13.00
☐ 8x10 publicity photo, signed ...			15.00
☐ NELSON, SANDY	6.00	2.00	
☐ NESMITH, MIKE	8.00	3.00	
☐ NEWMAN, TED	3.00	1.50	
☐ NICKS, STEVIE	6.50	2.50	
☐ NORVUS, NERVOUS	11.00	4.00	
☐ ORBISON, ROY	4.00	1.50	
☐ ORLANDO, TONY	6.00	1.50	
☐ 8x10 photo with "Dawn," signed by all			12.00
☐ PAGE, JIMMY	7.00	3.00	
☐ PARSONS, BILL	5.00	1.50	
☐ PAXTON, GARY	4.00	1.50	
☐ PETERSON, PAUL	4.50	1.50	
☐ PETTY, TOM	5.00	2.00	
☐ PHILLIPS, PHIL	6.00	2.00	
☐ PITNEY, GENE	4.00	1.50	
☐ POWERS, JOEY	3.00	1.50	
☐ PRESTON, JOHNNY	6.00	2.00	
☐ PRICE, LLOYD	9.00	3.00	
☐ PROBY, P. J	4.00	1.50	
☐ RELF, KEITH	6.00	2.00	
☐ RENAY, DIANE	4.00	1.50	
☐ RESTIVO, JOHNNY	4.00	1.50	

	8x10 Signed Photo	Plain Signature	Other
☐ RICHARD, CLIFF	5.00	1.50	
☐ RITCHIE, LIONEL	65.00	18.00	
☐ RIVERS, JOHNNY	3.00	1.50	
☐ ROBERTSON, ROBBIE	5.50	2.00	
☐ ROBINSON, FLOYD	3.50	1.50	
☐ ROE, TOMMY	3.00	1.50	
☐ ROGERS, TIMMIE	4.00	1.50	
☐ RONSTADT, LINDA	7.00	2.00	
☐ RUSSELL, LEON	6.00	2.00	
☐ RYDELL, BOBBY	6.00	1.50	
☐ SANDS, TOMMY	4.50	1.50	
☐ SCOTT, JACK	4.00	1.50	
☐ SCOTT, LINDA	3.50	1.50	
☐ SEDAKA, NEIL	3.00	1.50	
☐ SELF, RONNIE	6.00	2.00	
☐ SHANNON, DEL	3.50	1.50	
☐ SHARP, DEE DEE	3.00	1.50	
☐ SHARPE, RAY	3.00	1.50	
☐ SHERMAN, BOBBY	7.00	2.00	
☐ "Bobby Sherman Coloring Book," 1971			6.00
☐ SHONDELL, TROY	5.00	1.50	
☐ SIMON, PAUL	10.00	2.00	
☐ Photo with Art Garfunkel, signed by both			35.00
☐ SMITH, HUEY	8.00	3.00	
☐ SMITH, RAY	4.00	1.50	
☐ SOUL, JIMMY	5.00	1.50	
☐ SPRINGSTEEN, BRUCE	100.00	30.00	
☐ STAFFORD, TERRY	3.00	1.50	
☐ STANLEY, PAT	6.00	2.00	
☐ STEVENS, CONNIE	5.00	1.50	
☐ STITES, GARY	3.00	1.50	
☐ STORM, GALE	3.00	1.50	
☐ STRONG, BARRETT	4.00	1.50	
☐ SUMMERS, GENE	7.00	2.00	
☐ TAYLOR, AUSTIN	4.00	1.50	
☐ THOMAS, GENE	3.50	1.50	
☐ THOMPSON, SUE	3.00	1.50	

	8x10 Signed Photo	Plain Signature	Other
☐ TOROK, MITCHELL	8.00	3.00	
☐ TOWNSHEND, PETE	10.00	5.00	
☐ TURNER, JOE	11.00	4.00	
☐ TWITTY, CONWAY	4.00	1.50	
☐ USHER, GARY	8.00	3.00	
☐ VALENS, RITCHIE	75.00	10.00	
☐ VEE, BOBBY	5.00	1.50	
☐ VINCENT, GENE	50.00	8.00	
☐ Signed album cover			150.00
☐ VINTON, BOBBY	6.00	2.00	
☐ WALLACE, JERRY	4.00	1.50	
☐ WARD, DALE	4.00	1.50	
☐ WAYNE, THOMAS	5.00	1.50	
☐ WEIR, BOB	4.00	1.50	
☐ WONDER, STEVIE	50.00	15.00	
☐ WILLIAMS, LARRY	5.00	1.50	
☐ WILLIS, CHUCK	8.00	2.50	
☐ WILSON, JACKIE	8.00	2.50	
☐ WRAY, LINK	6.00	1.50	
☐ YOUNG, KATHY	4.00	1.50	

ROCK MEMORABILIA

	Price Range	

ABBA

☐ **Magazine,** issue of *Record World,* October 1979, with cover photo and article on them — 4.00 / 5.00

☐ **Picture Sleeve** from 45rpm (no record), *Knowing Me* .... .50 / .75

☐ **Poster,** group picture, commercial, 21x30″ — 4.50 / 6.00

AC/DC

☐ **Poster,** *AC/DC in Concert* with white snake, German promotional, 24x33″ .... 6.00 / 8.00

☐ **Poster,** *Back in Black,* U.S. promotional, 24x24″ .... 3.50 / 4.50

☐ **Poster,** *Flick of the Switch,* promotional, 24x24″ .... 6.00 / 8.00

☐ **Poster,** *For Those About to Rock,* gold color, promotional, 18x27″ .... 3.50 / 4.50

Price Range

☐ **Poster,** *Let There Be Rock,* concert picture, U.S. promotional, 24x24″ 4.50   6.00

AEROSMITH
☐ **Poster,** *Coming Soon to Madison Square Garden,* tour, 20x30″ 7.00   10.00
☐ **Poster,** *Toys in the Attic,* blue/red/green, tour, 26x45″ 9.00   12.00
☐ **Tour Book,** 1979 .... 4.00   5.00

ALLMAN, GREG
☐ **Poster,** picture playing guitar, black and white, commercial, 28x38″ 4.50   6.00

BEE GEES
☐ **Poster,** *Sgt. Pepper's Lonely Hearts Club Band,* 24x36″ 4.00   5.00

BENATAR, PAT
☐ **Poster,** *Get Nervous,* promotional, 24x24″ 9.00   12.00
☐ **Poster,** *Live from Earth,* promotional, 24x24″ 9.00   12.00

BLACK SABBATH
☐ **Poster,** *Born Again,* red and blue, promotional, 23x23″ 5.00   7.00
☐ **Poster,** *Live Evil,* promotional, 23x23″ 5.00   7.00
☐ **Poster,** *Mob Rules,* promotional, 23x24″ ... 6.00   8.00
☐ **Ticket Stub,** *Tempe,* Arizona, 1980 .... 2.50   3.50
☐ **Tour Book,** *Mob Rules,* 1982 .... 3.00   4.00

BLONDIE
☐ **Tour Book,** 1979, color photos 8.00   11.00
☐ **Bumper Sticker,** *Eat to the Beat* 2.00   3.00
☐ **Button,** *Best of Blondie* 2.00   3.00
☐ **Button,** square *Autoamerican,* 2″ 3.00   4.00
☐ **Calendar,** *Autoamerican,* 1981 .... 3.00   4.00
☐ **Poster,** Deborah Harry topless wearing white shorts 6.00   8.00
☐ **Poster,** *Koo Koo,* promotional, 36x36″ 7.00   10.00
☐ **Press Kit,** *Autoamerican,* custom folder, one photo plus three-page biography 10.00   15.00
☐ **Tour Program,** *Parallel Lines,* 1979 .... 6.00   8.00

BOWIE, DAVID
☐ **Book,** *David Bowie* by Vivian Claire, 80 pages, 1977 .... 20.00   25.00

Price Range

☐ **Book,** *David Bowie: A Chronology* by Kevin Cann, paperback, 240 pages 8.00 11.00

☐ **Book,** *David Bowie Black Book* by Miles (author who uses no last name), paperback .. 12.00 15.00

☐ **Booklet,** Rotterdam 1983, 26 pages with vinyl flexi record inserted 9.00 12.00

☐ **Poster,** *China Girl,* promotional color poster, 36x36" 5.00 7.00

☐ **Poster,** *Gigolo,* Italian, 55x40" 18.00 23.00

CHER

☐ **Book,** *Cher* by Vicki Pellagrino, paperback, 1975 .... 3.00 4.00

☐ **Poster,** *Prisoner,* 23x35" 7.00 10.00

CLAPTON, ERIC

☐ **Book,** *Eric Clapton Deluxe,* paperback, 156 pages 10.00 14.00

☐ **Poster,** *Money and Cigarettes,* promotional, 24x24" 4.50 6.00

CLASH

☐ **Poster,** *Bond's International Casino,* black and white, promotional, 23x36" 7.00 10.00

☐ **Poster,** *Combat Rock,* 48x32" 9.00 12.00

☐ **Poster,** *Sandinista,* red and black, tour, French, 15x22" 7.00 10.00

COSTELLO, ELVIS

☐ **Handbill,** *Grand Ole Opry Concert,* 1982 ... 1.00 1.50

☐ **Postcard,** *Imperial Bedroom,* issued in Great Britain 4.50 6.00

☐ **Poster,** *Almost Blue,* 23x23" 11.00 14.00

☐ **Poster,** *Bottom Line,* concert, December 13 and 14, year unspecified, 24x34" 11.00 15.00

☐ **T-Shirt,** *My Aim Is True* from tour, said to be only 500 made, called "official tour t-shirt" 15.00 20.00

CROSBY, STILLS, NASH AND YOUNG

☐ **Book,** *The Authorized Biography* by Dave Zimmer and Henry Diltz, paperback, 256 pages 11.00 15.00

☐ **Poster,** 1982 tour, 18x31" 5.00 7.00

Price Range

DOORS, THE
- [ ] **Book,** *Jim Morrison and the Doors* by Mike Jahn, an unauthorized biography, 95 pages, 1969 .... 10.00   15.00
- [ ] **Book,** *The Doors* by John Tobler and Andrew Doe, paperback, 127 pages 10.00   13.00
- [ ] **Poster,** *Alive She Cried,* promotional, 24x24″   5.00   7.00
- [ ] **Ticket Stub,** *Whisky-a-Go-Go,* Los Angeles, 1967 .... 45.00   57.00

DURAN DURAN
- [ ] **Book,** *Duran Duran Scrapbook* Volume Three, paperback 6.00   8.00
- [ ] **Book,** *Inside Duran Duran* by Robyn Flans, paperback, 64 pages 4.50   6.00
- [ ] **Book,** *Rio,* paperback, 32 pages 5.00   7.00
- [ ] **Poster,** promotional, from *Rolling Stone* magazine, 19x23″ 5.00   7.00

FRAMPTON, PETER
- [ ] **Poster,** *Art of Control,* promotional, 24x36″   3.50   4.50
- [ ] **Press Kit,** *I'm in You,* two pictures plus biography 6.00   8.00

GARCIA, JERRY
- [ ] **Poster,** *Cats Under the Stars,* promotional, 24x36″ 5.00   7.00

GENESIS
- [ ] **Poster,** *Mountain Dew,* U.S. promotional, 17x22″ 2.50   3.50

GRATEFUL DEAD
- [ ] **Ticket Stub,** Fillmore Auditorium, San Francisco, 1966 .... 37.00   46.00

HALL and OATS
- [ ] **Poster,** Lexington tour, February 20 but year not specified, 14x23″ 5.00   7.00

HOLLY, BUDDY
- [ ] **Book,** *The Buddy Holly Collector's Guide* by Bill Griggs and Jim Black, paperback 6.00   8.00
- [ ] **Ticket Stub,** Clear Lake, Iowa, 1959 ...... 100.00   125.00

Price Range

JACKSON, MICHAEL
☐ **Book,** *Body and Soul* by Geoff Brown, paperback, 128 pages 9.00 12.00
☐ **Book,** *Soul of the Jackson Five* by James Gregory, paperback, 1973 .... 4.00 5.00
☐ **Poster,** *The Making of Thriller,* 36x24" 4.50 6.00

JAGGER, MICK
☐ **Book,** *Mick Jagger* by J. Marks, paperback, 1973 .... 4.00 6.00

ELTON JOHN
☐ **Book,** *Elton John* by Cathi Stern, paperback, 1975 .... 4.00 5.00
☐ **Book,** *Elton John Anthology,* paperback, 208 pages 11.00 14.00
☐ **Program,** 1972 concert tour 11.00 14.00

MONKEES
☐ **Book,** *The Monkees* by Gene Fawcett and Howard Liss, paperback, 1966 .... 9.00 12.00

MOODY BLUES
☐ **Program** for 1978 tour, color 9.00 12.00
☐ **Poster,** *Past Present and Future,* 32x22" .. 11.00 14.00
☐ **Tour Book,** Octave, 1978 .... 5.00 7.00

MOTHERS OF INVENTION
☐ **Poster,** *The Mothers of Invention This Week,* apparently for concert but does not further specify, 24x36" 35.00 45.00

PETTY, TOM
☐ **Tour Book,** *Damn the Torpedos,* 1980 .... 3.00 4.00

PINK FLOYD
☐ **Poster,** *The Wall,* 40x27" 9.00 12.00
☐ **Ticket Stub,** Marquee Club, London, 1968 32.00 40.00

PLANT, ROBERT
☐ **Poster,** *Pictures at Eleven,* 36x36" 4.00 5.00
☐ **Tour Book,** *Principle of Moments* 6.00 8.00

POLICE
☐ **Book,** *The Police Chronicles* by Philip Kamin and Peter Goddard, 127 pages 9.00 12.00

Price Range

☐ **Poster,** *Synchronicity,* 24x36"	4.50	6.00
☐ **Poster,** *Synchronicity II,* 24x24"	4.50	6.00

ROLLING STONES

☐ **Book,** *Rolling Stones: An Unauthorized Biography* by David Dalton, paperback, 128 pages	6.00	8.00
☐ **Book,** *Rolling Stones from A to Z* by Sue Weiner and Lisa Howard, paperback, 149 pages	10.00	13.00
☐ **Poster,** *Gimme Shelter,* promotional for motion picture, 18x26"	6.00	8.00

SPRINGFIELD, RICK

☐ **Figure,** cardboard stand-up promoting *Hard to Hold,* 24" tall	6.00	8.00
☐ **Napkins,** set of paper napkins promoting *Hard to Hold*	2.00	2.50
☐ **Poster,** *Hard to Hold,* for video cassette, 35x23"	4.50	6.00

TALKING HEADS

☐ **Press Kit,** *More Songs,* one picture and three pages of biographies	10.00	15.00

TOWNSHEND, PETER

☐ **Book,** *Through the Eyes of Peter Townshend,* paperback, 113 pages with illustrations, 1974	9.00	12.00

THE WHO

☐ **Poster,** *Face Dancing,* orange and black, promotional, 24x30"	5.00	7.00
☐ **Poster,** *It's Hard,* issued in Great Britain, 60x40"	4.50	6.00
☐ **Ticket Stub,** Metropolitan Opera, New York, year unspecified	38.00	48.00

45's AND LP's

LEE ANDREWS AND THE HEARTS

☐ **RAINBOW, 252,** Maybe You'll Be There/ Baby Come Back	90.00	175.00
☐ **256,** White Cliffs of Dover/Much Too Much	90.00	175.00

	Price Range	
☐ **259,** The Bells of St. Mary's/Fairest	90.00	175.00
☐ **GOTHAM, 318,** Bluebird of Happiness/Show Me the Merengue	30.00	55.00
☐ **320,** Lonely Room/Leona	30.00	55.00
☐ **321,** Just Suppose/It's Me	30.00	55.00
☐ **GRAND, 156,** Teardrops/The Girl Around the Corner	30.00	55.00
☐ **157,** Long Lonely Nights/The Clock	30.00	55.00
☐ **MAINLINE, 102,** Long Lonely Nights/The Clock	25.00	45.00
☐ **CHESS, 1665,** Long Lonely Nights/The Clock	4.00	7.00
☐ **1675,** Tear Drops/The Girl Around the Corner	3.50	5.50
☐ **ARGO, 1000,** Tear Drops/The Girl Around the Corner	6.00	11.00
☐ **CASINO, 110,** I Wonder/Baby Come Back	11.00	18.00
☐ **452,** Try the Impossible/Nobody's Home . . .	11.00	18.00
☐ **UNITED ARTISTS, 123,** Try the Impossible/Nobody's Home	3.50	5.50
☐ **136,** Who Do I/Glad to Be Here	4.00	6.50
☐ **151,** All I Ask Is Love/Maybe You'll Be There	4.00	6.50
☐ **162,** Just Suppose/Boom	4.00	6.50

PAUL ANKA, 45's

☐ **RPM 472,** I Confess/Blau-Wile Deveest Fontaine (with the Jacks)	19.00	35.00
☐ **ABC-Paramount 9831,** Diana/Don't Gamble With Love	2.50	5.00
☐ **9855,** I Love You Baby/Tell Me That You Love Me	2.25	4.00
☐ **9880,** You Are My Destiny/When I Stop Loving You	2.25	4.00
☐ **9907,** Crazy Love/Let the Bells Keep Ringing	2.25	4.00
☐ **9937,** Midnight/Verboten	2.25	4.00
☐ **9956,** Just Young/So It's Goodbye	2.25	4.00
☐ **9987,** My Heart Sings/That's Love	2.25	4.00
☐ **10011,** I Miss You So/Late Last Night	2.25	4.00
☐ **10022,** Lonely Boy/Your Way	2.25	4.00
☐ **10040,** Put Your Head on My Shoulder/Don't Ever Leave Me	2.25	4.00
☐ **10064,** It's Time to Cry/Something Has Changed Me	2.25	4.00

Price Range

☐ **10082,** Puppy Love/Adam and Eve	2.25	4.00
☐ **10106,** My Home Town/Something Happened	2.25	4.00
☐ **10132,** Hello Young Lovers/I Love You in the Same Old Way	2.25	4.00
☐ **10147,** Summer's Gone/I'd Have to Share	2.25	4.00
☐ **10163,** I Saw Mommy Kissing Santa Claus/Rudolph the Red-Nosed Reindeer ..	3.00	5.00
☐ **10168,** The Story of My Love/Don't Say You're Sorry	2.00	3.50
☐ **10169,** Li's Christmas Everywhere/Rudolph the Red-Nosed-Reindeer	3.00	5.00
☐ **10194,** Tonight My Love Tonight/I'm Just Your Fool Anyway	2.00	3.50
☐ **10220,** Dance on Little Girl/I Talk to You ...	2.00	3.50
☐ **10239,** Cinderella/Kissin' on the Phone	2.00	3.50
☐ **10279,** Loveland/The Bells at My Wedding	2.00	3.50
☐ **10282,** The Fool's Hall of Fame/Far From the Lights of Town	2.00	3.50
☐ **10311,** I'd Never Find Another You/Uh Huh	2.00	3.50
☐ **10338,** I'm Coming Home/Cry	2.00	3.50
☐ **RCA 7977,** Love Me Warm and Tender/I'd Like to Know	1.75	3.00
☐ **8030,** A Steel Guitar and a Glass of Wine/I Never Knew Your Name	1.75	3.00
☐ **8068,** Every Night/There You Go	1.75	3.00
☐ **8097,** Eso Beso/Give Me Back My Heart ..	1.75	3.00
☐ **8115,** Love/Crying in the Wind	1.75	3.00
☐ **8170,** Remember Diana/At Night	1.75	3.00
☐ **8195,** Hello Jim/You've Got the Nerve to Call This Love	1.75	3.00
☐ **8237,** Wondrous Are the Ways of Love/Hurry Up and Tell Me........................	1.75	3.00
☐ **8272,** Did You Have a Happy Birthday?/For No Good Reason at All	1.75	3.00
☐ **8311,** From Rocking Horse to Rocking Chair/Cheer Up	1.75	3.00
☐ **8349,** Baby's Coming Home/No, No	1.75	3.00
☐ **8396,** It's Easy to Say/In My Imagination ...	1.75	3.00

PAUL ANKA, ALBUMS

☐ **ABC-Paramount 240 (M),** Paul Anka	29.00	38.00

	Price Range	
□ 240 (S), Paul Anka	35.00	45.00
□ 296 (M), My Heart Sings	15.00	25.00
□ 296 (S), My Heart Sings	30.00	40.00
□ 323 (M), Paul Anka Sings His Big 15	20.00	30.00
□ 323 (S), Paul Anka Sings His Big 15	35.00	45.00
□ 347 (M), Swings for Young Lovers	15.00	22.00
□ 347 (S), Swings for Young Lovers	25.00	35.00
□ 353 (M), Anka at the Copa	15.00	25.00
□ 353 (S), Anka at the Copa	20.00	30.00
□ 360 (M), It's Christmas Everywhere	20.00	28.00
□ 360 (S), It's Christmas Everywhere	23.00	27.00
□ 371 (M), Strictly Instrumental	14.00	20.00
□ 371 (S), Strictly Instrumental	20.00	30.00
□ 390 (M), Paul Anka Sings His Big 15, Vol. II	17.00	27.00
□ 390 (S), Paul Anka Sings His Big 15, Vol. II	25.00	35.00
□ 409 (M), Paul Anka Sings His Big 15, Vol. III	17.00	28.00
□ 409 (S), Paul Anka Sings His Big 15, Vol. III	23.00	33.00
□ 420 (M), Diana	14.00	20.00
□ 420 (S), Diana	15.00	25.00
□ RCA 2502 (M), Young, Alive and in Love . . .	14.00	24.00
□ 2502 (S), Young, Alive and in Love	17.00	27.00
□ 2575 (M), Let's Sit This One Out	14.00	24.00
□ 2575 (S), Let's Sit This One Out	17.00	27.00
□ 2614 (M), Our Man Around the World	12.00	18.00
□ 2614 (S), Our Man Around the World	14.00	24.00
□ 2691 (M), 21 Golden Hits (redone)	10.00	20.00
□ 2691 (S), 21 Golden Hits (redone)	12.00	16.00
□ 2744 (M), Songs I Wish I'd Written	12.00	16.00
□ 2744 (S), Songs I Wish I'd Written	14.00	24.00
□ 2966 (M), Excitement on Park Avenue	12.00	18.00
□ 2966 (S), Excitement on Park Avenue	10.00	18.00
□ 3580 (M), Strictly Nashville	8.00	15.00

CHUCK BERRY, 45's

□ Chess 1604, Maybellene/Wee Wee Hours	4.00	7.00
□ 1610, Thirty Days/Together	5.00	9.00
□ 1615, No Money Down/The Downbound Train	5.00	9.00
□ 1626, Roll Over Beethoven/Drifting Heart . .	4.00	7.00
□ 1635, Too Much Monkey Business/Brown Eyed Handsome Man	5.00	9.00
□ 1645, You Can't Catch Me/Havana Moon . .	4.00	7.00
□ 1653, School Day/Deep Feeling	3.00	5.00

	Price Range	
☐ **1664,** Oh Baby Doll/Lajunda	**3.00**	**5.00**
Above issues featured the silver-and-blue chess-top labels.		
☐ **1671,** Rock and Roll Music/Blue Feeling ...	**3.00**	**5.00**
☐ **1683,** Sweet Little Sixteen/Reelin' and Rockin'	**3.00**	**5.00**
☐ **1691,** Johnny B. Goode/Around and Around	**3.00**	**5.00**
☐ **1697,** Beautiful Delilah/Vacation Time	**2.50**	**4.00**
☐ **1700,** Carol/Hey Pedro	**2.50**	**4.00**
☐ **1709,** Sweet Little Rock and Roll/Joe Joe Gun	**2.50**	**4.00**
☐ **1714,** Merry Christmas Baby/Run Rudolph Run	**2.50**	**4.00**
☐ **1716,** Anthony Boy/That's My Desire	**2.50**	**4.00**
☐ **1722,** Little Queenie/Almost Grown	**2.00**	**3.50**
☐ **1729,** Back in the U.S.A./Memphis, Tennessee	**2.00**	**3.50**
☐ **1736,** Childhood Sweetheart/Broken Arrow	**2.00**	**3.50**
☐ **1747,** Too Pooped to Pop/Let It Rock	**2.00**	**3.50**
☐ **1754,** Bye Bye Johnny/Worried Life Blues	**2.00**	**3.50**
☐ **1763,** Mad Lad/I Got to Find My Baby	**2.00**	**3.50**
☐ **1767,** Jaguar and the Thunderbird/Our Little Rendezvous	**1.75**	**3.00**
☐ **1779,** Little Star/I'm Talking About You	**1.75**	**3.00**
☐ **1799,** Go Go Go/Come On	**1.75**	**3.00**
☐ **1853,** I'm Talking About You/Diploma for Two	**1.75**	**3.00**
☐ **1866,** Sweet Little Sixteen/Memphis (reissue)	**1.75**	**3.00**
☐ **1883,** Nadine/Orangutang	**1.75**	**3.00**
☐ **1898,** No Particular Place to Go/You Two ..	**1.75**	**3.00**
☐ **1906,** You Never Can Tell/Brenda Lee	**1.75**	**3.00**
☐ **1912,** Little Marie/Go Bobby Soxer	**1.75**	**3.00**
☐ **1916,** Promised Land/Things I Used to Do	**1.75**	**3.00**
☐ **1926,** Dear Dad/Lonely School Days	**1.75**	**3.00**
☐ **1943,** It Wasn't Me/Welcome Back Pretty Baby	**1.75**	**3.00**
☐ **1963,** Lonely School Days/Ramona, Say Yes	**1.75**	**3.00**
☐ **2090,** Tulane/Have Mercy Judge	**1.75**	**3.00**
☐ **2131,** My Ding-A-Ling/Johnny B. Goode ...	**1.75**	**3.00**
☐ **2136,** Reelin' and Rockin'/Let's Boogie	**1.75**	**3.00**
☐ **2140,** Bio/Roll 'em Pete	**1.75**	**3.00**

Price Range

☐ **2169,** Shake, Rattle and Roll/Baby What You
Want Me to Do 1.75   3.00

CHUCK BERRY, ALBUMS

☐ **Chess 1426 (M),** After School Session	25.00	35.00
☐ **1432 (M),** One Dozen Berrys	17.00	27.00
☐ **1435 (M),** Chuck Berry Is on Top	14.00	24.00
☐ **1448 (M),** Rockin' at the Hops	14.00	24.00
☐ **1456 (M),** More Juke Box Hits	14.00	24.00
☐ **1465 (M),** More Chuck Berry	14.00	24.00
☐ **1485 (M),** Chuck Berry's Greatest Hits	14.00	24.00
☐ **1488 (M),** St. Louis to Liverpool	14.00	24.00
☐ **1495 (M),** Chuck Berry in London	14.00	24.00
☐ **1498 (M),** Fresh Berry's	12.00	22.00
☐ **1514 (S),** Chuck Berry's Golden Decade . . .	8.00	18.00
☐ **1550 (S),** Back Home	8.00	18.00
☐ **Mercury 21103 (M),** Golden Hits	8.00	18.00
☐ **61103 (S),** Golden Hits	8.00	18.00
☐ **21123 (M),** In Memphis	8.00	18.00
☐ **61123 (S),** In Memphis	8.00	18.00
☐ **21138 (M),** Live at Fillmore Auditorium	8.00	18.00
☐ **61138 (S),** Live at Fillmore Auditorium	8.00	18.00
☐ **61176 (S),** From St. Louis to Frisco	8.00	18.00
☐ **61223 (S),** Concerto in B. Goode	8.00	18.00

BREAD, Featured: David Gates

☐ **ELECTRA 45365,** Change of Heart/Lost
Without Your Love 2.25   4.50
☐ **45666,** Any Way You Want Me/Dismal Day   3.50   6.50
☐ **45668,** Could/I Can't Measure the Cost 3.50   6.50
☐ **45686,** (I Wanna) Make It With You/Why Do
You Keep Me Waiting 2.00   5.00
☐ **45701,** It Don't Matter to Me/Call on Me . . . 2.00   5.00
☐ **45711,** Too Much Love/Let Your Love Go   2.50   5.00
☐ **45720,** If/Take Comfort 2.50   5.00
☐ **45740,** Live in Your Love/Mother Freedom   2.50   5.00
☐ **45751,** Baby I'm-A Want You/Truckin' 2.50   5.00
☐ **45784,** (I Found Her) Diary/Down on My
Knees 2.50   5.00

BIG BOPPER

☐ **D 1008,** Chantilly Lace/Purple People Eater
Meets the Witch Doctor 45.00   95.00

Price Range

☐ **MERCURY 71343,** Chantilly Lace/Purple People Eater Meets the Witch Doctor	3.25	5.50
☐ **71375,** Big Bopper's Wedding/Little Red Riding Hood	3.25	5.50
☐ **71416,** Walking Through My Dreams/ Someone Watching Over You	6.00	11.00
☐ **71451,** It's the Truth, Ruth/That's What I'm Talking About	6.00	11.00
☐ **71482,** Pink Petticoats/The Clock	6.00	11.00

BIG BOPPER, ALBUM

☐ **MERCURY 20402 (M),** Chantilly Lace	65.00	125.00

JAMES BROWN

☐ **FEDERAL 12258,** Please Please Please/ Why Do You Do Me	5.50	9.00
☐ **12277,** Hold My Baby's Hand/No, No, No, No	8.50	14.00
☐ **12289,** Just Won't Do Right/Let's Make It . .	8.50	14.00
☐ **12290,** I Won't Plead No More/Chonnie On Chon	8.50	14.00
☐ **12292,** Gonna Try/Can't Be the Same	8.50	14.00
☐ **12295,** Messing With the Blues/Gonna Try	8.50	14.00
☐ **12300,** I Walked Alone/You're Mine, You're Mine	8.50	14.00
☐ **12311,** That Dood It/Baby Cries Over the Ocean	8.50	14.00
☐ **12316,** Begging, Begging/That's When I Lost My Heart	8.50	14.00
☐ **12337,** Try Me/Tell Me What I Did Wrong . .	5.00	9.00
☐ **12348,** I Want You So Bad/There Must Be a Reason	5.00	9.00
☐ **12352,** I've Got to Change/It Hurts to Tell You	5.00	9.00
☐ **12361,** Good Good Lovin'/Don't Let It Happen to Me	5.00	9.00
☐ **12364,** It Was You/Got to Cry	5.00	9.00
☐ **12369,** I'll Go Crazy/I Know It's True	5.00	9.00

Price Range

☐ **12370,** Think/You've Got the Power	5.00	9.00
☐ **12378,** This Old Heart/Wonder When You're Coming Home	5.00	9.00
☐ **KING 5423,** The Bells/And I Do What I Want	5.00	9.00
☐ **5438,** Hold It/The Scratch	5.00	9.00
☐ **5442,** Bewildered/If You Want Me	5.00	9.00
☐ **5466,** I Don't Mind/Love Don't Love Nobody	5.00	9.00
☐ **5485,** Sticky Suds (Pt. 1/Pt. 2)	5.00	9.00
☐ **5524,** Baby You're Right/I'll Never Let You Go	5.00	9.00
☐ **5547,** I Love You, Yes I Do/Just You and Me, Darling	5.00	9.00
☐ **5573,** Lost Someone/Cross Firing	5.00	9.00
☐ **5614,** Night Train/Why Does Everything Happen to Me?	5.00	9.00
☐ **5657,** Shout and Shimmy/Come Over Here	5.00	9.00
☐ **5672,** Mashed Potatoes U.S.A./You Don't Have to Go	· 5.00	9.00
☐ **5701,** Three Hearts in a Tangle/I've Lost Money	5.00	9.00
☐ **5710,** Every Beat of My Heart/Like a Baby	5.00	9.00
☐ **5739,** Prisoner of Love/Choo-Choo	5.00	9.00
☐ **5767,** These Foolish Things/Feel It (Pt. 1)	5.00	9.00
☐ **5803,** Signed, Sealed and Delivered/Waiting in Vain	5.00	9.00
☐ **5829,** I've Got to Change/The Bells	5.00	9.00
☐ **5842,** Oh Baby Don't You Weep (Pt. 1)/(Pt. 2)	5.00	9.00
☐ **5853,** Please Please Please/In the Wee Wee Hours	5.00	9.00
☐ **5876,** How Long Darling/Again	4.50	6.00
☐ **5899,** So Long/Dancin' Little Thing	4.50	7.00
☐ **5956,** Fine Old Foxy Self/Medley	4.50	7.00
☐ **5968,** Have Mercy Baby/Just Won't Do Right	4.50	7.00
☐ **5999,** Papa's Got a Brand New Bag/ (Pt. 2)	3.00	5.00
☐ **6015,** I Got You (I Feel Good)/I Can't Help It	3.00	5.00
☐ **6020,** I'll Go Crazy/Lost Someone	3.00	5.00
☐ **6025,** Ain't That a Groove/(Pt. 2)	3.00	5.00
☐ **6032,** Come Over Here/Tell Me What You're Gonna Do	3.00	5.00
☐ **6035,** It's a Man's Man's Man's Man's World/Is It Yes or Is It You?	3.00	5.00

Later King singles worth up to $3.00 mint

Price Range

JAMES BROWN, EPs

☐ **KING 430,** Please, Please, Please	5.50	10.00
☐ **826,** Live at the Apollo	4.50	9.00

JAMES BROWN, ALBUMS

☐ **KING 610 (M),** Please, Please, Please	17.00	38.00
☐ **635 (M),** Try Me	14.50	34.00
☐ **683 (M),** Think	14.50	34.00
☐ **743 (M),** The Always Amazing James Brown and the Famous Flames	12.00	28.00
☐ **771 (M),** Jump Around	12.00	28.00
☐ **780 (M),** The Exciting James Brown	10.00	25.00
☐ **804 (M),** Tour the U.S.A.	10.00	25.00
☐ **826 (M),** The James Brown Show	10.00	25.00
☐ **851 (M),** Prisoner of Love	10.00	25.00
☐ **883 (M),** Pure Dynamite	8.50	20.00
☐ **909 (M),** Please, Please, Please	8.50	20.00
☐ **919 (M),** The Unbeatable 16 Hits	8.50	20.00
☐ **938 (M),** Papa's Got a Brand New Bag	7.50	17.00
☐ **946 (M),** I Got You (I Feel Good)	7.50	17.00
☐ **985 (M),** Soul Brother #1	6.50	15.00

COASTERS

☐ **Date Records 2-1607,** She Can/Everybody's Woman (Radio Station copy)	12.00	19.00
☐ **Atco 6064,** Down in Mexico/Turtle Dovin' (maroon label)	10.00	17.00
☐ **6073,** One Kiss Led to Another/Brazil (maroon label)	8.50	14.00
☐ **6087,** Searchin'/Young Blood (maroon label)	5.00	7.50
☐ **6087,** Searchin'/Young Blood (yellow-and-white label)	3.50	5.50
☐ **6098,** Idol with the Golden Head/My Baby Comes to Me	3.50	5.50
☐ **6104,** Sweet Georgia Brown/What's the Secret of Your Success	3.50	5.50
☐ **6111,** Gee Golly/Dance	8.50	14.00
☐ **6116,** Yakety Yak/Zing! Went the Strings of My Heart	3.50	5.50
☐ **6126,** The Shadow Knows/Sorry But I'm Gonna Have to Pass	4.50	7.50

	Price Range	
☐ **6132,** Charlie Brown/Three Cool Cats	**3.50**	**5.50**
☐ **6141,** Along Came Jones/That Is Rock 'N' Roll	**3.50**	**5.50**
☐ **6146,** Poison Ivy/I'm a Hog for You	**3.50**	**5.50**
☐ **6153,** Run Red Run/What About Us	**3.25**	**5.25**
☐ **6163,** Besame Mucho (Pt. 1)/(Pt.2)	**3.25**	**5.25**
☐ **6168,** Wake Me, Shake Me/Stewball	**3.25**	**5.25**
☐ **6178,** Shoppin' for Clothes/Snake and the Bookworm	**3.25**	**5.25**
☐ **6186,** Wait a Minute/Thumbin' a Ride	**3.25**	**5.25**
☐ **6192,** Little Egypt/Keep on Rolling	**3.25**	**5.25**
☐ **6204,** Girls, Girls, Girls (Pt. 1)/(Pt. 2)	**3.25**	**5.25**
☐ **6210,** Just Like Me/Bad Blood	**3.25**	**5.25**
☐ **6219,** Ridin' Hood/Teach Me How to Shimmy	**3.25**	**5.25**
☐ **6234,** The Climb/The Climb (instrumental)	**3.25**	**5.25**
☐ **6251,** The PTA/Bull Tick Waltz	**3.25**	**5.25**
☐ **6287,** 'T'Ain't Nothing to Me/Speedoo's Back in Town	**3.25**	**5.25**
☐ **6300,** Bad Detective/Lovey Dovey	**3.25**	**5.25**
☐ **6321,** Wild One/I Must Be Dreaming	**3.25**	**5.25**
☐ **6341,** Hongry/Lady Like	**3.25**	**5.25**
☐ **6356,** Let's Go Get Stoned/Money Honey ..	**3.25**	**5.25**
☐ **6379,** Bell Bottom Slacks/Crazy Baby	**3.25**	**5.25**
☐ **6407,** She's a Yum Yum/Saturday Night Fish Fry	**3.25**	**5.25**

COASTERS, EPs
☐ **Atco 4501,** Rock And Roll with the Coasters	**15.50**	**30.00**
☐ **4502,** Keep Rockin' with the Coasters	**15.50**	**30.00**
☐ **4506,** The Coasters	**15.50**	**30.00**
☐ **4507,** Top Hits	**15.50**	**30.00**

COASTERS, ALBUMS
☐ **Atco 101 (M),** The Coasters	**17.00**	**39.00**
☐ **111 (M),** The Coasters' Greatest Hits	**15.00**	**34.00**
☐ **123 (M),** One by One	**12.00**	**29.00**
☐ **123 (S),** One by One	**17.00**	**39.00**
☐ **135 (M),** Coast Along with the Coasters	**12.00**	**29.00**
☐ **135 (S),** Coast Along with the Coasters	**17.00**	**39.00**
☐ **371,** The Coasters: The Early Years—Their Greatest Recordings	**7.50**	**10.00**

Price Range

FIVE SATINS

☐ **Standard 5105,** All Mine/Rosemarie	25.00	50.00
☐ **105,** All Mine/Rosemarie	60.00	120.00
☐ **106,** In the Still of the Night/The Jones Girl	45.00	80.00
☐ **Ember 1005,** I'll Remember (In the Still of the Nite)/The Jones Girl	12.00	21.00
☐ **1005,** In the Still of the Night/The Jones Girl	9.00	17.00
☐ **1008,** Wonderful Girl	9.00	17.00
☐ **1014,** Oh Happy Day/Our Love Is Forever	9.00	17.00
☐ **1019,** To the Aisle/Wish I Had My Baby ...	6.00	12.00
☐ **1025,** Our Anniversary/Pretty Girl	6.00	12.00
☐ **1038,** A Night to Remember/Senorita Lolita	6.00	12.00
☐ **1056,** Shadows/Toni My Love	6.00	12.00
☐ **1061,** I'll Be Seeing You/A Night Like This	6.00	12.00
☐ **1066,** Candlelight/The Time	6.00	12.00
☐ **1070,** Wishing Ring/Tell Me Dear	6.00	12.00
☐ **Musictone 1108,** Just to Be Near You/To the Aisle	6.00	12.00
☐ **Kirshner 4251,** You are Love/Very Precious Oldies	6.00	12.00
☐ **Cub 9071,** Your Memory/I Didn't Know	6.00	12.00
☐ **Chancellor 1110,** The Masquerade Is Over/Raining in My Heart	6.00	12.00
☐ **Nighttrain 901,** All Mine/The Voice	6.00	12.00

FIVE SATINS—EPs

☐ **Ember 100,** The Five Satins Sing	18.00	29.00
☐ **101,** To the Aisle	9.50	17.00
☐ **102,** Our Anniversary	9.50	17.00

FIVE SATINS, ALBUMS

☐ **Ember 100 (M),** The Five Satins Sing	40.00	98.00
☐ **401 (M),** Five Satins: Encore	29.00	64.00
☐ **Mt. Vernon 108 (M),** The Five Satins Sing	14.00	34.00

ERSEL HICKEY

☐ **Epic 9263,** Bluebirds Over the Mountain/Hangin' Around	3.25	6.00
☐ **9278,** Goin' Down the Road/Lover's Land	5.50	11.00
☐ **9298,** You Never Can Tell/Wedding Day ...	3.25	6.00
☐ **9309,** Don't Be Afraid of Love/You Threw a Dart	3.00	5.00
☐ **9357,** What Do You Want?/Love in Bloom	3.00	5.00
☐ **Toot 602,** Tryin' to Get to You/Blue Skies	3.00	5.00

	Price Range	

☐ **Laurie 3165,** Some Enchanted Evening/Put Your Mind at Ease .... | 3.00 | 5.00
☐ **Janus 151,** Bluebirds Over the Mountain/Self Made Man .... | 2.75 | 4.50

MONKEES
☐ **Colgems 1001,** Last Train to Clarksville/Take a Giant Step .... | 3.00 | 5.00
☐ **1002,** I'm a Believer (I'm Not Your) Stepping Stone .... | 3.00 | 5.00
☐ **1004,** A Little Bit Me, A Little Bit You/The Girl I Knew Somewhere .... | 3.00 | 5.00
☐ **1007,** Pleasant Valley Sunday/Words ...... | 3.00 | 5.00
☐ **1012,** Daydream Believer/Goin' Down ..... | 3.00 | 5.00
☐ **1019,** Valleri/Tapioca Tundra .... | 3.00 | 5.00
☐ **1023,** D. W. Washburn/It's Nice to Be with You .... | 3.00 | 5.00
☐ **1031,** Porpoise Song/As We Go Along .... | 3.00 | 5.00
☐ **5000,** Tear Drop City/A Man Without a Dream | 3.00 | 5.00
☐ **5004,** Listen to the Band/Someday Man ... | 3.00 | 5.00
☐ **5005,** Good Clean Fun/Mommy Daddy .... | 3.00 | 5.00
☐ **5011,** Oh My My/I Love You Better .... | 3.00 | 5.00
MONKEES, ALBUMS
☐ **Colgems 101 (M),** Meet the Monkees ..... | 6.00 | 15.00
☐ **101 (S),** Meet the Monkees .... | 8.00 | 21.00
☐ **102 (M),** More of the Monkees .... | 6.00 | 15.00
☐ **102 (S),** More of the Monkees .... | 8.00 | 21.00
☐ **103 (M),** Headquarters .... | 6.00 | 15.00
☐ **103 (S),** Headquarters .... | 8.00 | 21.00
☐ **104 (M),** Pisces, Aquarius, Capricorn and Jones, LTD .... | 6.00 | 15.00
☐ **104 (S),** Pisces, Aquarius, Capricorn and Jones, LTD .... | 8.00 | 17.00
☐ **109 (M),** The Birds, the Bees, and the Monkees .... | 6.00 | 15.00
☐ **109 (S),** The Birds, the Bees, And the Monkees .... | 8.00 | 17.00
☐ **113 (S),** Instant Replay .... | 12.00 | 24.00
☐ **115 (S),** Greatest Hits .... | 10.00 | 20.00
☐ **117 (S),** The Monkees Present .... | 9.00 | 25.00
☐ **5008 (S),** Head (soundtrack) .... | 30.00 | 50.00
☐ **1001 (S),** A Barrel Full of Monkees .... | 25.00 | 45.00

Price Range

SIMON AND GARFUNKEL, 45's

☐ **Columbia 43396,** Sounds of Silence/We've Got a Groovy Thing Goin'	1.75	3.00
☐ **43511,** Homeward Bound/Leaves That Are Green	1.75	3.00
☐ **43617,** I Am a Rock/Flowers Never Bend with the Rainfall	1.75	3.00
☐ **43728,** Dangling Conversation/Big Bright Green Pleasure Machine	1.75	3.00
☐ **43873,** A Hazy Shade of Winter/For Emily, Wherever I May Find Her	1.75	3.00
☐ **44046,** At the Zoo/59th Street Bridge Song (Feelin' Groovy)	1.75	3.00
☐ **44232,** Fakin' It/You Don't Know Where Your Interest Lies	1.75	3.00
☐ **44465,** Scarborough Fair/April Come She Will	1.75	3.00
☐ **44465,** Scarborough Fair/Canticle	1.75	3.00
☐ **44511,** Mrs. Robinson/Old Friends-Bookends	1.75	3.00
☐ **44785,** The Boxer/Baby Driver	1.75	3.00
☐ **45079,** Bridge Over Troubled Water/Keep the Customer Satisfied	1.75	3.00
☐ **45133,** Cecelia/The Only Living Boy in New York City	1.75	3.00
☐ **45237,** El Condor Pasa/Why Don't You Write Me?	1.75	3.00
☐ **45663,** For Emily, Wherever I May Find Her/America	1.75	3.00
☐ **10230,** My Little Town/Rag Doll-You're Kind	1.50	2.50

SIMON AND GARFUNKEL, ALBUMS

☐ **Pickwick 3059 (S),** Hit Sounds of Simon and Garfunkel (pre-Columbia material)	30.00	40.00
☐ **Columbia 2249 (M),** Wednesday Morning, 3 A.M	10.00	20.00
☐ **9049 (S),** Wednesday Morning, 3 A.M	14.00	24.00
☐ **2469 (M),** Sounds of Silence	10.00	20.00
☐ **9269 (S),** Sounds of Silence	12.00	22.00
☐ **2563 (M),** Parsley, Sage, Rosemary & Thyme	10.00	20.00
☐ **9363 (S),** Parsley, Sage, Rosemary & Thyme	12.00	22.00
☐ **9529 (S),** Bookends	9.00	19.00
☐ **9914 (S),** Bridge Over Troubled Water	9.00	19.00
☐ **31350 (S),** Greatest Hits	9.00	19.00

Price Range

BRUCE SPRINGSTEEN
☐ **Columbia 45805,** Blinded by the Light/The
  Angel 26.00   46.00
☐ **45864,** For You/Spirit in the Night 22.00   40.00
☐ **10209,** Born to Run/Meeting Across the
  River 3.00   5.00
☐ **10274,** Tenth Avenue Freeze-Out/She's the
  One 3.25   4.00
☐ **10763,** Prove It All Night/Factory 2.75   4.50
☐ **10801,** Badlands/Streets of Fire 2.75   4.50

ZAGER AND EVANS
☐ **Truth 8082,** In the Year 2525/Little Kids ... 8.25   17.00

THE BEATLES

Along with Elvis Presley, the Beatles rank as the most heavily collected of all recording personalities in history—in terms of both records and memorabilia. While hobbyists may regret having to pay more and more, the price increases have served to fully vindicate their enthusiasm for Beatles material. Back in 1964 when the group first burst upon the American scene, autograph hunters were accused of wasting their time by seeking signatures of the Fab Four. Today these signatures, often scrawled on wrinkled bits of paper, are fetching higher sums than those of many presidents and other historical celebrities. Furthermore the significance—social and financial—of Beatles memorabilia has been acknowledged by its appearance in the most prestigious auction sales, alongside genuine antiques. It has not only "arrived;" it has far surpassed, in collecting interest and status, the wildest dreams of its most devoted collectors. Unbelievable though it may seem, Beatles items now rank on a level with souvenirs of Abraham Lincoln, when they appear for sale. And this may be only the beginning. Never in the history of collecting has any celebrity material soared so high in price within less than two decades.

The tragic death of John Lennon in December 1980 understandably resulted in higher prices for his autographs and other items than for those of the other Beatles. At the same time it has generated higher prices for all material bearing autographs of all four Beatles. Hobbyists and investors will now stretch further for these items because of the Lennon autograph. But there is much more than just autographs for the Lennon collector. He left behind numerous drawings and other material, much of which has not yet reached the market. It may be another ten years, or longer, before we know the full extent of Lennon memorabilia that exists.

The extraordinary collecting activity on Beatles items has spilled over into those associated with them—a phenomenon that seldom occurs even in the case of great historical celebrities. Prices now being paid for autographs and other ephemera of Yoko Ono are virtually on a par with those of the Beatles themselves. There is likewise an active market for all memorabilia of Brian Epstein (the Beatles' first manager) and for Peter Best (the drummer who was replaced by Ringo Starr). It seems almost as though whatever the Beatles touched turned to gold.

A selection is included here, but is—for reasons of space—far from complete. The interested buyer will discover an enormous variety offered by specialist dealers and, as mentioned, in the auction galleries. Of course, a certain amount of discrimination needs to be exercised in collecting. Any autograph can be faked, and some fakes are quite skillful. As far as printed items, toys, dolls, and the like are concerned, each piece must be judged on its merits for age and significance. The mere fact that something pictures the Beatles is no excuse for a price of $500 or $800. All of it may be worthy to collect, but it is certainly not equally rare or equally significant. Today anyone can stamp out a Beatles statuette and advertise it as a "collector's item." Anyone can print the names of John, Paul, George, and Ringo on a pencil or watchband. If an item is of recent origin and obviously not rare or exclusive, the fact that it relates to the Beatles is not, in itself, magic. Serious collectors want early material, as far as group items are concerned. Any souvenirs or toys picturing the Beatles but manufactured after their break-up is not considered as collectible as pre-1970 material.

In attempting to date items, which can be difficult at best, do not be misled by dates which may appear on the piece or by the physical appearance of the portraits. Manufacturers who want their items to be taken for collector's pieces are careful to show the group as very youthful, to give the impression of mid-1960s origin. The best proof of an item's origin is to compare it against a listing in the price list of an established dealer. The dealers have done extensive research on most kinds of Beatles memorabilia—not as a social service but to protect themselves from getting taken by items of little or no value. The whole job is far from done yet, however. Newly discovered items turn up regularly.

Similar effort has been directed toward Beatles records and has borne even more fruit, simply because that task is not quite as challenging. Variations exists of covers, labels, etc., and fakes are inevitable from time to time; but the range of records is not nearly as extensive as that of memorabilia, and the pitfalls are fewer. An amateur could, by using the information in this book and supplementing this knowledge through dealers' catalogues, collect even the most expensive Beatles recordings without danger. With memorabilia he will need to use more care.

The following listings are broken down as follows:
1. Memorabilia.
2. Beatles singles, arranged alphabetically.
3. Beatles LP's, also arranged alphabetically.

Prices are as accurate as possible at the time of going to press. The reader is reminded, though, that this is an extremely volatile market in which values can change within a matter of weeks.

Supplementary collecting and/or historical information has been supplied whenever possible.

Japanese releases. Many of the Beatles' records were released in Japan, bearing labels with Japanese imprints. These are sought by collectors and have in recent years been entering the American market in increasing quantity. At this point the values on most Japanese pressings are fluctuating too sharply to establish fair market prices.

Price Range

MEMORABILIA

☐ **Album, Help!,** LP record album (Parlophone/EMI, 1965), autographed on the sleeve by each of the four Beatles	900.00	1300.00
☐ **"Bag One."** "Bag One" was a set of 14 lithographs from drawings made by John Lennon in 1969, published in 1970 by the Cinnamon Press of New York. The drawings relate to Lennon's marriage and honeymoon. Each lithograph was limited to 300 numbered copies, and enclosed in a white leather portfolio. They measure 20″ x 30″. Of the 300 issued, it is believed that very few full sets are still in existence, as most owners broke them up for framing. The current market value for a full set is:	37,000.00	47,000.00
The individual prints from this set have been selling in the range of $2000.00–$3000.00.		
☐ **Belt Buckle,** with "BEATLES" in swirled script-type lettering, and portrait illustrations	60.00	90.00
☐ **Bobbing Head Auto Mascots,** set of 4, dating to the mid-1960's	700.00	1000.00

Price Range

When sold individually, the value is around $150.00–$200.00, but the John Lennon specimen is worth a premium.

☐ **Book,** *A Cellarful of Noise* by Brian Epstein, published by Souvenir Press, 1964. This is the British first edition, with dust jacket. Issued when Epstein was still alive **140.00**   **200.00**
For a copy autographed by him (and such do exist), the price would be at least double this amount.

☐ **Book,** *A Cellarful of Noise* by Brian Epstein, clothbound reprint of the now-scarce 1964 first edition **13.00**   **20.00**

☐ **Book,** *A Day in the Life* by Tom Schultheiss, paperback, 334 pages **8.00**   **12.00**

☐ **Book,** *A Hard Day's Night* by John Burke, published by Dell, paperback **15.00**   **22.00**

☐ **Book,** *A Spaniard in the Works* by John Lennon, cloth-bound first edition **20.00**   **30.00**
This price represents the average range, but published offers differ considerably. When autographed by Lennon it is, of course, worth substantially more.

☐ **Book,** *A Spaniard in the Works* by John Lennon, paperback, 94 pages **4.00**   **8.00**

☐ **Book,** *A Tribute to John Lennon* by various authors, clothbound **7.00**   **10.00**

☐ **Book,** *A Twist of Lennon* by Cynthia Lennon, paperback, 190 pages **2.00**   **3.00**
Cynthia was John's first wife.

☐ **Book,** *Abbey Road* by Brian Southall, clothbound, printed in Great Britain, 210 pages   **12.00**   **17.00**

☐ **Book,** *All You Need Is Ears* by George Martin, paperback, 285 pages **7.00**   **10.00**
George Martin was a record producer who worked with the Beatles as well as with many other rock artists.

☐ **Book,** *Apple to the Core* by Peter McCabe and Robert D. Schonfeld, paperback, 209 pages **4.00**   **6.00**

☐ **Book,** *As I Write This Letter* by Marc Catone, clothbound, 254 pages **15.00**   **21.00**

Price Range

A collection of fan letters written to the Beatles.

☐ **Book,** *As Time Goes By* by Derek Taylor, clothbound, 231 pages, 1983 reprint 13.00 18.00
Derek Taylor was Brian Epstein's press agent.

☐ **Book,** *The Ballad of John and Yoko* by the editors of *Rolling Stone* magazine, paperback, 306 pages 10.00 15.00

☐ **Book,** *The Beatles* by Geoffrey Stokes, clothbound, 245 pages 14.00 20.00

☐ **Book,** *The Beatles* by Helen Spence, clothbound, 96 pages 7.00 11.00

☐ **Book,** *Beatles Diary,* published in Scotland, miniature 3″ x 4″ size, 1965 .... 50.00 70.00

☐ **Book,** *The Beatles after the Beatles* by John Blake, paperback, 286 pages 6.00 10.00
The rather confusing title refers to the fact that this work deals with the Beatles after their break-up.

☐ **Book,** *The Beatles: An Illustrated Diary* by H. V. Fulpen, paperback, 176 pages 10.00 15.00

☐ **Book,** *The Beatles: An Illustrated Record* by Roy Carr and Tony Tyler, paperback 8.00 12.00

☐ **Book,** *The Beatles Again* by Harry Castleman and Walter Podrazik, clothbound, 302 pages 14.00 18.00

☐ **Book,** *The Beatles Apart* by Bob Woffinden, paperback, unpaginated 8.00 12.00

☐ **Book,** *The Beatles at the Beeb* by Kevin Howlett, clothbound, unpaginated 11.00 15.00
"Beeb" is British slang for BBC, the British Broadcasting Company. This is the story of the various performances given by the Beatles for the BBC.

☐ **Book,** *The Beatles: The Biography* by Hunter Davis, clothbound, 380 pages 13.00 18.00

☐ **Book,** *The Beatles Down Under* by Glenn Baker, paperback, 128 pages 13.00 18.00
Story of the group's Australian tour.

☐ **Book,** *The Beatles for the Record,* authorship uncredited, 96 pages, measures 12″ square 8.00 12.00

Vee Jay 581, 45 rpm.

Vee Jay 587, 45 rpm.

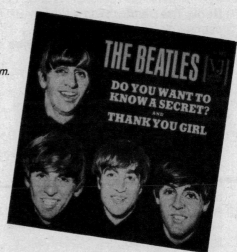

Price Range

☐ **Book,** *The Beatles Forever* by Nicholas Schaffner, clothbound, 218 pages 13.00   17.00
An identical edition in paperback is selling at $6–8.

☐ **Book,** *The Beatles in Their Own Words* by Miles (author who uses no last name), paperback 5.00   8.00

☐ **Book,** *John Lennon in His Own Words* by Miles, paperback 5.00   8.00

☐ **Book,** *The Beatles on Record* by J. P. Russell, paperback, 682 pages 6.00   8.00

☐ **Book,** *The Beatles' Record in Australia* by Bruce Hamlin, paperback, published in Australia 8.00   12.00

☐ **Book,** *The Beatles Reader* by Charles P. Neises, clothbound 13.00   17.00

☐ **Book,** *The Beatles Submarine,* Yellow Submarine pop-out book, features 20 different characters from the movie, paperbound, King Features Books pub., copyright 1968, 15″ x 9½″ 15.00   20.00

☐ **Book,** *The Beatles Who's Who* by Bill Harry, paperback, 190 pages 8.00   11.00
Biographies of everyone who played a role in the Beatles' lives.

☐ **Book,** *The Book of Lennon* by Bill Harry, paperback, 223 pages 9.00   13.00

☐ **Book,** *Come Together* by Jon Wiener, paperback, 379 pages 10.00   13.00

☐ **Book,** *The Complete Beatles Quiz Book* by Edwin Goodgold and Dan Carlinsky, clothbound, 128 pages 3.00   3.50

☐ **Book,** *Dakota Days* by John Green, clothbound, 260 pages 11.00   14.00

☐ **Book,** *George Harrison Yesterday and Today* by Ross Michaels, paperback, 96 pages, published in Great Britain 6.00   8.00

☐ **Book,** *Growing Up with the Beatles* by Ron Schaumburg, paperback, 160 pages 7.00   10.00

☐ **Book,** *In His Own Write* by John Lennon, clothbound first edition 25.00   30.00

Price Range

Multiply that by about 10 if it's personally autographed.

☐ **Book,** *In the Footsteps of the Beatles,* by Ron Jones, paperback, illustrated, Merseyside City Council pub., 72 pages, copyright 1981 — 6.00 — 8.00

☐ **Book,** *Lennon and Me* by Pete Shotton, paperback, 399 pages .... — 3.50 — 4.50

☐ **Book,** *Lennon and McCartney* by Malcolm Doney, clothbound, 126 pages .... — 8.00 — 11.00

☐ **Book,** *John Lennon: A Family Album* by Nishi F. Saimaru, paperback, 128 pages .... — 32.00 — 40.00

☐ **Book,** *John Lennon in His Own Write* by John Lennon, paperback, 79 pages .... — 4.50 — 6.50
Lennon not only wrote and illustrated this book but wrote reviews of it.

☐ **Book,** *John Lennon In My Life* by Pete Shotton and Nicholas Schaffner, paperback, 208 pages .... — 13.00 — 18.00
Shotten was a childhood chum of Lennon in Liverpool.

☐ **Book,** *John Lennon: One Day at a Time* by Anthony Fawcett, paperback, 190 pages .. — 8.00 — 12.00

☐ **Book,** *Lennon: The Solo Years,* author uncredited, paperback, 164 pages .... — 10.00 — 15.00

☐ **Book,** *The Literary Lennon* by James Sauceda, clothbound, 232 pages .... — 13.00 — 18.00
Counting his books, letters, and various miscellania, John Lennon did almost as much writing as a professional author.

☐ **Book,** *The Long and Winding Road* by John Tobler and Neville Stannard, paperback ... — 7.00 — 10.00

☐ **Book,** *The Longest Cocktail Party* by Richard DiLello, clothbound, 284 pages .... — 16.00 — 20.00
An insight into the day-to-day operations of Apple Records while the Beatles were still together.

☐ **Book,** *The Love You Make* by Peter Brown and Steven Gaines, clothbound, 438 pages — 13.00 — 17.00

☐ **Book,** *The Playbook Interviews with John Lennon and Yoko Ono* by David Sheff, paperback, 236 pages .... — 3.00 — 5.00

Price Range

☐ **Book,** *Pocket Beatles for Guitar* by Milton Okun, paperback, 256 pages **4.00** **7.00**

☐ **Book,** *Shout* by Philip Norman, paperback, 398 pages **7.00** **10.00**

☐ **Book,** *Wings Tour USA,* paperback **7.00** **10.00**

☐ **Book,** *With the Beatles* by Dezo Hoffman, paperback, 130 pages **10.00** **14.00**

☐ **Book,** *Working Class Heroes* by Neville Stannard, 240 pages **11.00** **15.00**

☐ **Book,** *Yesterday: The Beatles from 1963 to 1965* by Robert Freeman, clothbound **10.00** **13.00**

☐ **Book,** *You Can't Do That* by Charles Reinhart, clothbound, 410 pages **15.00** **20.00**
Deals with bootleg versions of the Beatles' records.

☐ **Button,** commemorates the 1964 Australian tour, "Be a Beatle Booster" is printed on front with pictures of the group surrounding it, 2¼" diameter **3.00** **5.00**

☐ **Calendar,** *Make a Date with the Beatles,* mid-1960's. Mint condition **40.00** **60.00**

☐ **Cardboard Figures,** set of 4 advertising promotion figures on very heavy cardboard, almost life-size, issued for display in record shops in the mid-1960's. Full color, self-standing **800.00** **1200.00**

☐ **Coasters,** set of six plastic coasters (different colors), each bearing the same illustration and wording, probably 1960's **30.00** **40.00**

☐ **Coloring Book.** *Beatles Coloring Book* by the Saalfield Publishing Co., 1964. Softcover .. **50.00** **65.00**
Value stated is for a copy in which no coloring has been attempted; otherwise, the price is lower.

☐ **Commemorative Coin,** issued in 1964 to mark the group's tour, one side shows American flag, the other has a group portrait of the boys in relief, brass, 1¼" diameter **10.00** **15.00**

☐ **Concert Tickets,** tickets to Beatles' concerts are scarce collector's items **35.00** **50.00**

	Price Range	

☐ **Drum Stick,** autographed by Ringo Starr ...   800.00   1000.00

☐ **EPSTEIN, BRIAN,** candid snapshot photograph, signed. Undated 100.00   150.00
Brian Epstein managed the Beatles in their early years. He met a tragic death at an early age. All autograph material of his is scarce.

☐ **Fan Club membership card,** measuring 4½″ x 5½″, picturing all four Beatles in characteristic pose, signed by each, 1963 .....   900.00   1200.00

☐ **Flasher Pins,** four different buttons, each shows a different Beatle, when viewed from another angle, the image changes to a group portrait of the group 4.00   6.50

☐ **Frisbee,** Beatles logo surrounded by imprints of the group, dark blue, white imprinting, 9¼″ diameter 3.00   6.00

☐ **Gum Cards,** set of 64 cards issued by Topps, 1964. Orange backs. Question and answer series, in color 50.00   65.00
Individual cards from this set normally sell for .65¢–85¢.

☐ **Gum Cards,** set of 50 Yellow Submarine cards issued by Primrose Confectionary (Britain), 1968. Cards measure $1^5/_{16}$″ by 2½″. They were originally distributed in packets of candy cigarettes 95.00   135.00
Individual cards from this set normally sell for $1.25–$1.75.

☐ **Hairbrush,** plastic hairbrush carrying cartoon likenesses of the Beatles, apparently marketed in the 1960's 60.00   80.00

☐ **HARRISON, GEORGE,** restaurant check signed (for wine), 1964 ....   200.00   275.00
Even as early as 1964, the Beatles were signing their restaurant bills.

☐ **HARRISON, GEORGE,** lock of hair (about 1″) said to be that of George Harrison, enclosed in a plastic brooch-type mounting set with a chain. Accompanied by a written statement by the former owner, telling how it was obtained 100.00   135.00

Price Range

Readers are cautioned that many items of this sort are not authentic and that making a positive authentication is just about impossible. Hence their value—regardless of how much they may fetch at sales—is very questionable.

☐ **Jigsaw Puzzle,** "Illustrated Lyrics Puzzle in a Puzzle," bearing a copyright date of 1970, in the original box 40.00   55.00

☐ **LENNON, JOHN,** paperback book containing two writings by him, *John Lennon in His Own Write* and *A Spaniard in the Works,* published by Penguin Books. Signed by Lennon on the front flyleaf 400.00   600.00
Obviously it's the signature that makes the price. Plain copies of this book are still on the market.

☐ **LENNON, JOHN,** "Two Virgins" LP record album (Apple Records, 1968), autographed on the sleeve. Accompanying the autograph is a small sketch 450.00   579.00
Though this record was released in 1968, the autograph and sketch date to 1979.

☐ **LENNON, JOHN,** ink sketch on paper, a profile drawing of an unidentified male subject, signed on the back by Lennon and Ringo Starr, 5½" x 3". Undated 600.00   800.00

☐ **LENNON, JOHN,** "Whatever Gets You Through the Night," master disc used in the pressing of this 45 rpm record, signed by Lennon (first name only). Apple Records, 1974 450.00   550.00

☐ **Lunchbox,** laminated tin, with colored portraits (drawings) of the Beatles, no contents 200.00   250.00

☐ **Magazine,** *The Beatles Book,* published in England, a complete run of 77 issues beginning August, 1963 and concluding December, 1969. This fan magazine terminated when the Beatles went their separate ways. It was a popular item, but full sets are hard to find 350.00   450.00

Price Range

☐ **McCARTNEY, PAUL,** small b/w snapshot showing him standing on a street, signed on the back in violet ink, with a pencil notation (in another hand) that the photo was snapped in Paris. Undated, probably c. 1970 .... 290.00 360.00

☐ **McCARTNEY, PAUL,** pencil sketch by him of a young girl, signed, 8″ x 5″, 1965 .... 525.00 650.00
Sketching has been merely a pastime for Paul McCartney, but his skills with a pencil are clearly above average.

☐ **McCARTNEY, PAUL,** small candid photograph of John Lennon, signed by Paul McCartney, 3½″ x 5″, 1968. Snapped at a press function 325.00 400.00
It wasn't too unusual for the Beatles to do zany things like autographing each other's pictures.

☐ **McCARTNEY, PAUL,** picture postal card with 16 words in his handwriting plus partial signature ("Paul"), and some doodles. Apparently not sent through the mails. Creased at one corner 450.00 575.00

☐ **Pen Holder,** cube 2½″ square, one side is a group portrait, another side shows the Beatles logo, two other sides show autographs, ballpoint pen is included, in box ... 10.00 14.00

☐ **Pennant,** a felt pennant (size not specified) with the name BEATLES printed in block letters and with likenesses of the group's members. Believed to date from 1964 .... 50.00 65.00

☐ **Pin,** in the shape of a guitar, with group portrait on body of guitar, black with gold highlights 5.00 8.00

☐ **Platinum Record,** awarded to John Lennon for sales of his album "Rock 'n' Roll," 1975, signed by Lennon, enclosed in a simple frame. Overall size 20″ x 16″ 9000.00 12000.00

☐ **Playing Cards,** group portrait on each card 4.00 6.00

☐ **Pocketbook or Carrybag,** canvas, imprinted "BEATLES" with illustrations 45.00 60.00

☐ **Pocket Mirror,** glass mirror with group portrait of the group playing, 2″ x 3″ 5.00 7.00

Price Range

☐ **Poster** for the motion picture *A Hard Day's Night,* approximately 22″ x 30″, colored illustration, stained in the margins from having been amateurishly mounted on a stiff backing | 300.00 | 400.00

☐ **Poster.** Italian poster for the motion picture *Yellow Submarine,* 1969, approximately 18½″ x 26½″ .... | 175.00 | 275.00

☐ **Poster,** fan club souvenir poster dated 1968, measuring approximately 20″ x 30″, full color. With traces of old folds, mostly smoothed out .... | 200.00 | 250.00

☐ **Press Kit** for Paul McCartney and Wings, 1973 .... | 80.00 | 110.00

☐ **Press Photographs,** when these are unsigned (printed signatures do not count, of course), the value is quite low, because of large quantities distributed—in most instances no more than $5 unless very early.

☐ **Promotion Card,** issued by Parlophone Records for the Beatles in 1963, picturing all (looking very young) and signed by all, 5″ x 7½″ .... | 900.00 | 1150.00

☐ Above, without signatures .... | 40.00 | 55.00

☐ **Record Shop Poster,** 4-color poster advertising *A Hard Day's Night,* mint condition .. | 180.00 | 230.00

☐ **Song Sheet,** "Scrambled Egg," composed by John Lennon and Paul McCartney, signed and inscribed by John Lennon, dated 1978 | 800.00 | 1000.00

☐ **Strap** for carrying schoolbooks, imprinted "BEATLES" with musical notes .... | 17.00 | 23.00

☐ **Starbucks,** uncirculated United States Federal Reserve Notes with images of each of the Beatles on them. These are legal tender! | 3.00 | 6.00

☐ **Wristwatch,** Beatles wristwatch, the dial consisting of a printed photograph of the Beatles in close-up. Above the portraits appear the words THE BEATLES, and the date "1964" beneath. With a corrugated leather band .. | 275.00 | 350.00
The watch has no numerals but simply stars where each numeral should appear. The price stated is for a specimen without the original box. In the original box it would have

Price Range

some slight premium. Collectors are cautioned that reproductions of an item such as this are very apt to turn up.

☐ **Writing Tablet,** a blank writing tablet (note size) with cover photo of the Beatles in color, dating to the mid or later 1960's 35.00   50.00
If any of the sheets were used or missing, the value would be somewhat less. For the cover alone, the value would be in the range of 18.00/25.00.

☐ **Yellow Submarine,** animation cell, matted and framed, from the Beatles motion picture *Yellow Submarine* 250.00   325.00
The range of price is rather wide as it depends to some extent on the scene. Cells showing all four Beatles normally fetch the highest sums—those with no members of the group go lowest. As of this date, comparatively few cells have reached the market.

☐ **Yellow Submarine Flasher,** a plastic disc measuring approximately 2½" in diameter, carrying on one side a colored picture printed on a plastic grid (network of impressed lines), when tilted, the picture appears to move, c. 1967 . . . .   85.00   110.00

45's

☐ **Atco 6308.** "Nobody's Child/Ain't She Sweet?" promo 27.00   62.00
☐ As above, commercial, with picture sleeve   45.00   100.00
☐ As above, commercial, without picture sleeve   3.50   7.50
When offered separately, the sleeve of Atco 6308 brings as much as $75 in mint condition. It is rare to be offered separately, however, as the accompanying record is easily obtainable—so most sellers will automatically take their empty sleeve and marry it up with a record.

☐ **Polydor 52-317.** "Ain't She Sweet?/If You Love Me, Baby" with picture sleeve 50.00   120.00

Price Range

This is a German release dating to 1964. The label is red, the picture sleeve blue.

☐ As above, without picture sleeve	25.00	60.00
☐ **Polydor 52-317.** "Ain't She Sweet?/Take Out Some Insurance" with picture sleeve ..	50.00	120.00

As you will note, the serial number of this disc is the same as that of the previous. Polydor used the 52-317 number for "Ain't She Sweet?" but issued two versions of the record, one backed with "If You Love Me, Baby" and the other with "Take Out Some Insurance." This practice is not uncommon in Germany. As with the previous, label is red but the picture sleeve is red rather than blue.

☐ As above, without picture sleeve	25.00	60.00
☐ **Capitol 5964.** "All You Need is Love/Baby, You're a Rich Man" promo	35.00	80.00
☐ As above, commercial, orange label	2.00	4.50
☐ As above, commercial, orange label, picture sleeve	7.00	11.00
☐ As above, commercial, orange and yellow label	3.00	6.00
☐ As above, commercial, orange an yellow label, picture sleeve	10.00	18.00
☐ As above, commercial, red and orange "bullseye" label	6.00	12.00
☐ As above, commercial, red and orange "bullseye" label, picture sleeve	12.00	20.00
☐ **Apple 5235.** "And I Love Her/If I Fell"	2.50	5.50
☐ **Capitol 5235.** "And I Love Her/If I Fell," orange label	2.00	4.50
☐ As above, orange and yellow label	3.00	6.00
☐ As above, orange label, picture sleeve	12.00	25.00
☐ As above, orange and yellow label	3.00	6.00
☐ As above, orange and yellow label, picture sleeve	16.00	31.00
☐ As above, red and orange "bullseye" label	7.00	13.00
☐ As above, red and orange "bullseye" label, picture sleeve	23.00	45.00

No promotional copies have been discovered.

Price Range

☐ **Apple 2531.** "The Ballad of John and Yoko/Old Brown Shoe" .... | 2.50 | 5.50
☐ As above, picture sleeve .... | 10.00 | 21.00
☐ As above, bearing Apple and Capitol markings .... | 7.00 | 17.00
☐ As above, bearing apple and Capitol markings, picture sleeve .... | 13.00 | 28.00
☐ As above, Apple marking only, orange label | 2.00 | 4.00
☐ As above, Apple marking only, orange label, picture sleeve .... | 9.00 | 18.00
☐ **Apple 5150.** Can't Buy Me Love/You Can't Do That" .... | 3.00 | 5.50
☐ **Capitol 5150,** "Can't Buy Me Love/You Can't Do That," orange label .... | 4.00 | 6.00
☐ As above, orange label, picture sleeve ..... | 75.00 | 150.00
☐ As above, orange and yellow label .... | 7.00 | 13.00
☐ As above, orange and yellow label, picture sleeve .... | 85.00 | 185.00
☐ As above, red and orange "bullseye" label | 7.00 | 13.00
☐ As above, red and orange "bullseye" label, picture sleeve .... | 85.00 | 185.00

All existing picture sleeves for this disc bear the Capitol name. Apple did not issue a picture sleeve. However, it is possible to find an Apple pressing in a Capitol picture sleeve. The value would be around $75–$150, almost wholly on the strength of the sleeve.

☐ **Capitol Starline 6064,** "Do You Want to Know a Secret?/Thank You, Girl" .... | 7.00 | 17.00
☐ **VeeJay 587,** "Do You Want to Know a Secret?/Thank You Girl," label name contained in brackets .... | 6.00 | 13.00
☐ As above, picture sleeve .... | 25.00 | 55.00
☐ As above, label name contained in oval .... | 7.00 | 17.00
☐ As above, label name contained in oval, picture sleeve .... | 26.00 | 56.00
☐ As above, promo (no picture sleeve) ...... | 21.00 | 45.00
☐ **Oldies 149,** "Do You Want to Know a Secret?/Thank You Girl" .... | 4.00 | 9.00

The picture sleeve was printed only for use on VeeJay pressings.

Price Range

☐ **Apple 5371,** "8 Days a Week/I Don't Want to Spoil the Party" 2.50   5.50

☐ **Capitol 5371,** "8 Days a Week/I Don't Want to Spoil the Party," orange label 4.00   6.00

☐ As above, orange label, picture sleeve 7.00   13.00

☐ As above, orange and yellow label 3.00   5.50

☐ As above, orange and yellow label, picture sleeve 8.00   17.00

☐ As above, red and orange "bullseye" label 7.00   13.00

☐ As above, red and orange "bullseye" label, picture sleeve 11.00   21.00

The picture sleeve was printed by Capitol only. So far there are no reports of discovery of promotional copies.

☐ **VeeJay 522,** "From Me to You/Thank You, Girl," promo 25.00   60.00

☐ As above, commercial, label name contained in brackets 5.00   11.00

☐ As above, commercial, label name contained in oval 8.00   19.00

No picture sleeves were printed for this disc.

☐ **Apple 2490,** "Get Back/Don't Let Me Down" 3.00   6.50

☐ As above, bearing Apple and Capitol markings 4.00   9.00

☐ **Capitol 2490,** "Get Back/Don't Let Me Down" 2.00   4.00

☐ **Capitol 4506,** Girl/You're Gonna Lose That Girl," promo 35.00   80.00

☐ As above, promo, picture sleeve 40.00   95.00

☐ **Apple 5222,** "Hard Day's Night/I Should Have Known Better" 2.50   5.50

☐ **Capitol 5222,** "Hard Day's Night/I Should Have Known Better," orange label 2.00   4.50

☐ As above, orange label, picture sleeve 11.00   21.00

☐ As above, orange and yellow label 4.00   9.00

☐ As above, orange and yellow label, picture sleeve 13.00   25.00

☐ As above, red and orange "bullseye" label 6.00   13.00

☐ As above, red and orange "bullseye" label, picture sleeve 16.00   33.00

The picture sleeve was printed by Capitol only.

Price Range

☐ **Apple 2056,** "Hello Goodbye/I Am the Walrus" 2.50   5.50
No promotional copies have been found on Apple—nor picture sleeve bearing that label's name.

☐ **Capitol 2056,** "Hello Goodbye/I Am the Walrus," promo 37.00   83.00
☐ As above, commercial, orange label 2.00   4.50
☐ As above, commercial, orange label, picture sleeve 13.00   25.00
☐ As above, commercial, orange and yellow label 3.00   6.00
☐ As above, commercial, orange and yellow label, picture sleeve 15.00   33.00
☐ As above, commercial, red and orange "bullseye" label 5.00   11.00
☐ As above, commercial, red and orange "bullseye" label, picture sleeve 19.00   40.00
☐ **Apple 5476,** "Help/I'm Down" 2.50   5.50
☐ **Capitol 5476,** "Help/I'm Down," orange label 2.00   4.50
☐ As above, orange label, picture sleeve 9.00   20.00
☐ As above, orange and yellow label 3.00   6.00
☐ As above, orange and yellow label, picture sleeve 10.00   23.00
☐ As above, red and orange "bullseye" label 6.00   13.00
☐ As above, red and orange "bullseye" label, picture sleeve 12.00   27.00
No promotion copies have been found.

☐ **Capitol 4274,** "Helter Skelter" (both sides), promo 7.00   16.00
☐ **Capitol 4274,** "Helter Skelter/Got to Get You into My Life," promo 7.00   16.00
☐ As above, commercial 2.00   4.50
Note that the serial numbers are the same on both promo pressings of "Helter Skelter," even though the reverse sides aren't.

☐ **Apple 2276,** "Hey Jude/Revolution" 3.00   6.50
☐ As above, bearing Apple and Capitol markings 4.00   9.00
☐ **Capitol 2276,** "Hey Jude/Revolution" 2.00   4.50
☐ **Apple 5327,** "I Feel Fine/She's a Woman" 2.50   5.50

Price Range

☐ **Capitol 5327,** "I Feel Fine/She's a Woman,"
orange label 2.00 4.50
☐ As above, orange label, picture sleeve 9.00 20.00
☐ As above, orange and yellow label 3.00 6.00
☐ As above, orange and yellow label, picture
sleeve 10.00 23.00
☐ As above, red and orange "bullseye" label 6.00 13.00
☐ As above, red and orange "bullseye" label,
picture sleeve 12.00 27.00
No promotional copies seem to have been
pressed.
☐ **Apple 5112,** "I Want to Hold Your Hand/I
Saw Her Standing There" 2.50 5.50
☐ **Capitol 5112,** "I Want to Hold Your Hand/I
Saw Her Standing There," orange label . . . 4.00 7.50
☐ As above, orange label, Capitol picture sleeve 16.00 35.00
☐ As above, orange label, WMCA picture sleeve 400.00 900.00
The WMCA picture sleeve was printed by
radio station WMCA in New York. It had the
Capitol picture on the front with pictures of
the WMCA "Good Guys" (the station's disc
jockeys) on the back. It was used as part of
a giveaway promotion, and the number of
copies printed, compared to those of the reg-
ular Capitol sleeve, was apparently very
small.
☐ As above, orange and yellow label 6.00 13.00
☐ As above, orange and yellow label, Capitol
picture sleeve 18.00 38.00
☐ As above, orange and yellow label, WMCA
picture sleeve 450.00 975.00
☐ As Above, red and orange "bullseye" label 6.00 13.00
☐ As above, red and orange "bullseye" label,
Capitol picture sleeve 21.00 45.00
☐ As above, red and orange "bullseye" label,
WMCA picture sleeve 450.00 975.00
No promotional copies have been found.
☐ **Apple 5235,** "If I Fell/And I Love Her" 2.50 5.50
☐ **Capitol 5235,** "If I Fell/And I Love Her," or-
ange label 2.00 4.50
☐ As above, orange label, picture sleeve 11.00 23.00
☐ As above, orange and yellow label 3.00 6.00

Price Range

☐ As above, orange and yellow label, picture sleeve	**13.00**	**26.00**
☐ As above, red and orange "bullseye" label	**6.00**	**13.00**
☐ As above, red and orange, "bullseye" label, picture sleeve	**15.00**	**33.00**

No promotional copies have been traced.

☐ **Apple 5234,** "I'll Cry Instead/I'm Happy Just to Dance with You"	**2.50**	**5.50**
☐ **Capitol 5234,** "I'll Cry Instead/I'm Happy Just to Dance with You," orange label	**2.00**	**4.50**
☐ As above, orange label, picture sleeve	**11.00**	**24.00**
☐ As above, orange and yellow label	**3.00**	**6.00**
☐ As above, orange and yellow label, picture sleeve	**13.00**	**28.00**
☐ As above, red and orange "bullseye" label	**6.00**	**13.00**
☐ As above, red and orange "bullseye" label, picture sleeve	**14.00**	**31.00**

No promotional copies have been discovered.

☐ **Swan 4152-1,** "I'll Get You" (uniface)	**75.00**	**180.00**

This one-sided disc was pressed as a promo in 1964. It was not turned into a commercial release.

☐ **Capitol Starline 6066,** "Kansas City/Boys," red and orange "bullseye" label	**7.00**	**15.00**
☐ As above, green label	**8.00**	**20.00**
☐ **Apple 2138,** "Lady Madonna/The Inner Light"	**2.50**	**5.50**
☐ **Capitol 2138,** "Lady Madonna/The Inner Light," promo	**35.00**	**87.00**
☐ As above, commercial, orange label	**2.00**	**4.50**
☐ As above, commercial, orange label, picture sleeve	**10.00**	**23.00**
☐ As above, commercial, orange label, picture sleeve, accompanied by flyer on Beatles fan club	**15.00**	**33.00**

The Beatles fan club flyer was included only with discs in the picture sleeve. It frequently became separated, however, and copies (on any of the label variations) with both picture sleeve and fan club flyer are worth more than with the picture sleeve alone.

Price Range

☐ As above, commercial, orange and yellow label	3.00	6.00
☐ As above, commercial, orange and yellow label, picture sleeve	11.00	23.00
☐ As above, commercial, orange and yellow label, picture sleeve, accompanied by flyer on Beatles fan club	14.00	36.00
☐ As above, commercial, red and orange "bull-seye" label	6.00	13.00
☐ As above, commercial, red and orange "bull-seye" label, picture sleeve	13.00	29.00
☐ As above, commercial, red and orange "bull-seye" label, picture sleeve, accompanied by flyer on Beatles fan club	17.00	39.00
☐ **Apple 2764,** "Let It Be/You Know My Name"	2.50	5.50
☐ As above, picture sleeve	11.00	21.00
☐ As above, bearing Apple and Capitol markings	4.00	9.00
☐ As above, bearing Apple and Capitol markings, picture sleeve	13.00	28.00
☐ **Capitol 2764,** "Let It Be/You Know My Name"	2.00	4.00
☐ **Apple 2832,** "Long and Winding Road/For You Blue"	2.50	4.00
☐ As above, picture sleeve	9.00	19.00
☐ As above, bearing Apple and Capitol markings	6.00	13.00
☐ As above, bearing Apple and Capitol markings, picture sleeve	13.00	27.00
☐ **Capitol 2764,** "Long and Winding Road/For You Blue"	2.00	4.00
☐ **Capitol Starline 9008,** "Love Me Do/P.S. I Love You"	8.00	20.00
☐ **Oldies 151,** "Love Me Do/P.S. I Love You"	4.00	9.00
☐ **Tollie 9008,** "Love Me Do/P.S. I Love You," promo	30.00	70.00
☐ As above, commercial	3.50	7.50
☐ As above, commercial, picture sleeve	14.00	34.00

This might be more of a collector's item with the picture sleeve than meets the eye. It was the only picture sleeve ever printed by Tollie for a Beatles disc. This record was *not*

Price Range

pressed on the regular Capitol label, nor on
Apple. (Apple Records was not in existence
at the time of its release, in 1964.)

□ **Polydor 24 948,** "Madison Kid/Let's Dance" One of the earliest examples of the Beatles on disc, this German release was billed as by Tony Sheridan and the Beat Brothers.	240.00	610.00
□ As above, picture sleeve	710.00	1750.00
□ **Capitol Starline 6065,** "Misery/Roll Over, Beethoven," green label	8.00	20.00
□ As above, red and orange "bullseye" label	7.00	14.00
□ **Polydor 24 673,** "My Bonnie/The Saints"	420.00	950.00
□ As above, picture sleeve	825.00	1950.00

The sleeve does not bill the Beat Brothers—it
notes only that the recording is Tony Sheridan.

□ As above, picture sleeve, with the numbers referred to as "twist" music on the sleeve	865.00	1950.00
□ As above, picture sleeve, with the numbers referred to as "twist" music on the sleeve	865.00	2050.00
□ **Polydor 52 273,** "My Bonnie/The Saints," red label	30.00	70.00

This disc was released two years after Polydor 24 673. It was on "red label Polydor," intended for circulation to Germany and Austria.

□ As above, red label, picture sleeve	80.00	190.00
□ **Polydor NH 66 833,** "My Bonnie/The Saints"	1400.00	3000.00

The most valuable Beatles 45. It dates to
1962 and gives the name of the group as
Tony Sheridan and the Beatles (not Beat
Brothers, as was the case on most Polydor
releases). This disc was intended for circulation in England. Unfortunately—as it compli-
cates the collector's life—a reissue appeared
the following year, with the same serial number. They can be told apart only by the printing on the label, which is thinner and curvier
on the original. Value of the reissue is less
than $1/10$th as much—$55.–$130.

□ **Decca 9-31382,** "My Bonnie/The Saints," promo, pink label	375.00	860.00

Price Range

The above, like all Decca pressings of "My Bonnie," is billed as by Tony Sheridan and the **Beat Brothers.**

☐ As above, commercial	1350.00	2850.00
☐ As above, silver and black label (BNA release)	700.00	1500.00

This was the only appearance of the Beatles on Decca, which allowed a multibillion-dollar property slip away to Capitol.

☐ **MGM K-13213,** "My Bonnie/The Saints," promo	35.00	85.00

Billed as by the Beatles with Tony Sheridan. This was released at about the time the group was making its first American tour.

☐ As above, commercial, with LP number on label	5.00	11.00
☐ As above, commercial, without LP number on label	8.00	17.00
☐ **Apple 5587,** "Nowhere Man/What Goes On"	2.00	4.00
☐ **Capitol 5587,** "Nowhere Man/What Goes On," orange label	2.00	4.50
☐ As above, orange label, picture sleeve	7.00	16.00
☐ As above, orange and yellow label	3.00	6.00
☐ As above, orange and yellow label, picture sleeve	9.00	20.00
☐ As above, red and orange "bullseye" label	5.00	12.00
☐ As above, red and orange "bullseye" label, picture sleeve	11.00	24.00

No promotional copies seems to have been released.

☐ **Capitol 4347,** "Ob-La-Di Ob-La-Da/Julia," promo	6.00	13.00
☐ As above, commercial	2.50	5.50
☐ As above, commercial, picture sleeve	5.00	11.00

This disc was not pressed on the Apple label

☐ **Apple 5651,** "Paperback Writer/Rain"	2.00	4.00
☐ **Capitol 5651,** "Paperback Writer/Rain," orange label	2.00	4.50
☐ As above, orange label, picture sleeve	9.00	20.00
☐ As above, orange and yellow label	3.00	6.00
☐ As above, orange and yellow label, picture sleeve	11.00	23.00

Price Range

☐ As above, red and orange "bullseye" label	6.00	13.00
☐ As above, red and orange "bullseye" label, picture sleeve	13.00	28.00

No promotional copies have been found.

☐ **Apple 5810,** "Penny Lane/Strawberry Fields Forever"	2.00	4.00
☐ **Capitol 5810,** "Penny Lane/Strawberry Fields Forever," orange label	2.00	4.50
☐ As above, orange label, picture sleeve	20.00	40.00
☐ As above, orange and yellow label	3.00	6.00
☐ As above, orange and yellow label, picture sleeve	15.00	33.00
☐ As above, red and orange "bullseye" label	5.00	11.00
☐ As above, red and orange "bullseye" label, picture sleeve	22.00	46.00
☐ **Capitol Starline 6063,** "Please Please Me/From Me to You"	8.00	20.00
☐ **Oldies 150,** "Please Please Me/From Me to You"	4.00	9.00
☐ **VeeJay 498,** "Please Please Me/Ask Me Why," promo	127.00	270.00
☐ As above, commercial, label name contained within brackets	110.00	235.00
☐ As above, commercial, label name contained within oval	130.00	275.00
☐ As above, commercial, group's name shown as BEATTLES (two t's), thin lettering	700.00	1475.00

There are two versions of the misspelled label rarity. The one listed above is the most desirable. They can be told apart only by the lettering style, which is thin in the more valuable variety and thick in the less valuable. But the latter is by no means an item to be lightly regarded, as it sells for $130–$275.

☐ **VeeJay 581,** "Please Please Me/From Me to You," promo	35.00	75.00
☐ As above, commercial, label name contained within brackets	6.00	12.50
☐ As above, commercial, label name contained within brackets, picture sleeve	50.00	110.00
☐ As above, commercial, label name contained within oval	13.00	27.00

Price Range

☐ As above, commercial, label name contained within oval, picture sleeve **55.00**   **120.00**
VeeJay 581 was not simply a re-pressing of that label's #498. A new flip side was added, and this is the way it appeared when pressed by Capitol Starline. It was never issued by the regular Capitol label nor by Apple.

☐ **Polydor 52 025,** "Ruby Baby/What'd I Say?"   **280.00**   **580.00**
Billed as by Tony Sheridan and the Beat Brothers. Issued on "red label Polydor" for circulation in Germany and Austria.

☐ As above, picture sleeve **600.00**   **1300.00**
On this Polydor sleeve, the Beat Brothers were credited along with Tony Sheridan—not always the case with Polydor. This was the first Beatles 45 rpm record, dating a full four years prior to their first American visit.

☐ **Capitol 4612,** "Sergeant Pepper's Lonely Hearts Club Band/A Day in the Life" **2.00**   **4.00**

☐ As above, picture sleeve **4.00**   **9.00**

☐ **Swan 4152,** "She Love You/I'll Get You," early pressing **75.00**   **125.00**
Early pressing specimens are identified by the absence of the words DON'T DROP OUT on the label

☐ As above, later pressing **30.00**   **65.00**
Later pressings are identified by the presence of the words DON'T DROP OUT on the label.

☐ As above, final pressing **3.25**   **5.50**
Final pressing specimens are identified by the black and silver coloring used on the label.

☐ As above, promo **90.00**   **175.00**
This disc was also released (by Swan) with special labels showing the title of "She Loves You" in the German language. There are two variations, one in which the German and English are shown on the same line ($13–$30.00) and another in which the English equivalent is placed on a second line ($6–$12).

Price Range

☐ **Apple 5255,** "Slow Down/Matchbox" 2.00 4.50
☐ **Capitol 5255,** "Slow Down/Matchbox," orange label 2.00 4.50
☐ As above, orange label, picture sleeve 25.00 60.00
☐ As above, orange and yellow label 3.00 6.00
☐ As above, orange and yellow label, picture sleeve 28.00 69.00
☐ As above, red and orange "bullseye" label 6.00 13.00
☐ As above, red and orange "bullseye" label, picture sleeve 32.00 75.00
Promotional copies have not been discovered. The value of an Apple disc in a Capitol picture sleeve would be in the neighborhood of $25–$60.
☐ **Apple 2645,** "Something/Come Together" 2.50 5.50
☐ As above, bearing Apple and Capitol markings 5.00 11.00
There were no picture sleeves or promotional records issued for this disc, so far as can be determined.
☐ **Atco 6302,** "Sweet Georgia Brown/Take Out Some Insurance," promo 35.00 70.00
☐ As above, commercial 8.50 20.00
☐ **Polydor 52 324,** "Sweet Georgia Brown/Skinny Minny" 35.00 72.00
This was a Polydor (German) "red label" release, for circulation in Germany and Austria. It dates from 1964.
☐ As above, picture sleeve 90.00 195.00
☐ **Apple 5407,** "Ticket to Ride/Yes It Is" 2.50 5.50
☐ **Capitol 5407,** "Ticket to Ride/Yes It Is," orange label 4.00 6.00
☐ As above, orange label, picture sleeve 11.00 23.00
☐ As above, orange and yellow label 6.00 11.00
☐ As above, orange and yellow label, picture sleeve 15.00 33.00
☐ As above, red and orange "bullseye" label 8.00 18.00
☐ As above, red and orange "bullseye" label, picture sleeve 20.00 41.00
No promotional copies have been discovered.

Price Range

☐ **Capitol Starline 6061,** "Twist and Shout/There's a Place"	8.00	20.00
☐ **Oldies 152,** "Twist and Shout/There's a Place"	4.00	9.00
☐ **Tollie 9001,** "Twist and Shout/There a Place"	4.50	9.50
☐ **Apple 5555,** "We Can Work It Out/Day Tripper"	2.50	5.50
☐ **Capitol 5555,** "We Can Work It Out/Day Tripper," orange label	2.00	4.50
☐ As above, orange label, picture sleeve	11.00	23.00
☐ As above, orange and yellow label	3.00	6.00
☐ As above, orange and yellow label, picture sleeve	13.00	28.00
☐ As above, red and orange "bullseye" label	6.00	13.00
☐ As above, red and orange "bullseye" label, picture sleeve	18.00	38.00

No promotional copies have been discovered.

☐ **Polydor 0462,** "What'd I Say?/Ya Ya"	420.00	950.00
☐ **MGM K-13227,** "Why/Cry for a Shadow," promo	35.00	80.00

Billed as by the Beatles with Tony Sheridan. This disc dates to 1964, when the group's meteoric rise to stardom prompted companies holding old Beatles tracks to dust them off and give them a fresh try.

☐ As above, commercial	11.00	18.00
☐ **Apple 5715,** "Yellow Submarine/Eleanor Rigby"	2.50	5.50
☐ **Capitol 5715,** "Yellow Submarine/Eleanor Rigby," orange label	2.00	4.50
☐ As above, orange label, picture sleeve	10.00	21.00
☐ As above, orange and yellow label	3.00	6.00
☐ As above, orange and yellow label, picture sleeve	12.00	25.00
☐ As above, red and orange "bullseye" label	6.00	13.00
☐ As above, red and orange "bullseye" label, picture sleeve	15.00	33.00

No promotional copies have been found.

☐ **Apple 5498,** "Yesterday/Act Naturally"	2.50	5.50

Price Range

☐ **Capitol 5498,** "Yesterday/Act Naturally," orange label .... 2.00 | 4.50

☐ As above, orange label, picture sleeve ..... 9.00 | 19.00

☐ As above, orange and yellow label .... 3.00 | 6.00

☐ As above, orange and yellow label, picture sleeve .... 12.00 | 27.00

☐ As above, red and orange "bullseye" label 6.00 | 13.00

☐ As above, red and orange "bullseye" label, picture sleeve .... 16.00 | 35.00
No promotional copies have turned up.

☐ **Polydor 24 849,** "You Are My Sunshine/Swanee" .... 230.00 | 590.00
This was a German "red label Polydor" release. It billed the group as Tony Sheridan and the Beat Brothers.

☐ As above, picture sleeve .... 700.00 | 1700.00

LP's

☐ **Apple SO-383** (stereo), "Abbey Road" .... 8.00 | 20.00

☐ **R.P.N.** (unnumbered), "The Beatles American Tour" (with Ed Ruby), #2 .... 36.00 | 76.00
A collection of interviews, packaged with a booklet (which must still be present to command the values stated).

☐ **R.P.N.** (unnumbered), "The Beatles American Tour" (with Ed Ruby), #3 .... 45.00 | 85.00
Fakes have turned up. The ones reported to date lack printing on the sleeve's spine.

☐ **Apple SWBO-101** (stereo), "The Beatles" 13.00 | 30.00
Double-record album with embossed printing on the front cover. Can still be found at retail in some shops but fast disappearing.

☐ **Apple SBC-100** (stereo), "The Beatles Christmas Album" .... 33.00 | 75.00

☐ **Apple SKBO-3403** (stereo), "The Beatles, 1962–1966" .... 6.00 | 13.00
Still on retail sale at many record shops.

☐ **Apple SKBO-3404** (stereo), "The Beatles, 1967–1970" .... 6.00 | 13.00

Price Range

Still on retail sale at many record shops.
- [ ] **Capitol SXA-2080** (stereo), "The Beatles Second Album" 65.00   148.00
A compact 33 rpm extended play, to be used in jukeboxes. Copies that have been "on the route" (played in jukeboxes) aren't touched by collectors with a long pole.
- [ ] **Capitol ST-2080** (stereo), "The Beatles Second Album", green label 10.00   24.00
- [ ] As above, black label 8.00   18.00
This was the regular commercial version of SXA-2080 (see above).
- [ ] **Apple ST-2080** (stereo), "The Beatles Second Album" 4.00   9.00
Still readily available in the record shops.
- [ ] As above, bearing Capitol and Apple markings on the label 6.00   13.00
You can still find this one in the shops, too, but it may take a bit more looking.
- [ ] **Vee Jay DX 30** (mono), "The Beatles vs. The Four Seasons" 26.00   60.00
- [ ] As above, in stereo 60.00   142.00
- [ ] **MGM LP-4215** (mono), "The Beatles with Tony Sheridan and Guests" 11.00   25.00
- [ ] As above, in stereo 28.00   64.00
- [ ] **Apple ST-2358** (stereo), "Beatles VI" 7.00   16.00
- [ ] As above, bearing Capitol and Apple markings on the label 5.00   11.00
- [ ] **Capitol ST-2358** (stereo), "Beatles VI" 4.00   8.50
As above, with sleeve reading "SEE LABEL FOR CORRECT PLAYING ORDER" 9.00   20.00
- [ ] **Apple ST-2228** (stereo), "Beatles '65" 5.00   11.00
The label has both the Apple and Capitol names.
- [ ] **Capitol LP-2309** (stereo), "The Early Beatles" (green label) 7.00   13.00
- [ ] As above, black label 8.00   17.00
- [ ] **United Artists LP-6366** (mono), "A Hard Day's Night" 12.00   25.00
- [ ] As above, in stereo (tan label) 5.00   11.00
- [ ] As above, in stereo (black label) 7.00   16.00

Price Range

☐ As above, in stereo (salmon label) 6.00   13.00

☐ **VeeJay PRO-202** (mono), "Hear the Beatles Tell All" 25.00   634.00

An early interview album, played to death by radio stations as a substitute for a live Beatles interview.

☐ **Capitol SMAS-2386** (stereo), "Help," green label 6.00   13.00

☐ As above, black label 7.00   16.00

The Capitol pressing also exists in mono but is not the big collector's item in mono that some people mistakenly believe. Actually its value, even in mint, is under $15.

☐ **VeeJay LP-1062** (mono), "Introducing The Beatles" 50.00   120.00

☐ As above, in stereo 100.00   250.00

☐ **VeeJay LP-1062** (mono), "Introducing The Beatles" (with "Love Me Do")" 18.00   38.00

☐ As above, in stereo 27.00   60.00

☐ **VeeJay LP-1962** (Mono) "Introducing The Beatles" (with "Please Please Me") 12.00   25.00

☐ As above, in stereo 27.00   60.00

☐ **Lingasong 2-7001,** "Live at the Star Club" (Hamburg) 7.00   15.00

Cuts on this LP were recorded when the group was performing in Germany, very early in their career (when under contract to Polydor).

☐ **Capitol SKBL-11711** (stereo), "Love Songs"   5.00   11.00

☐ **United Artists SKBL-11711** (stereo), "Love Songs" 5.00   11.00

☐ **Apple SMAL-2835** (stereo), "Magical Mystery Tour" 6.00   13.00

The label has both the Apple and Capitol names.

☐ **Capitol SMAL-2835** (mono), "Magical Mystery Tour" 9.00   20.00

☐ As above, stereo, green label 8.00   20.00

☐ As above, stereo, black label 6.00   13.00

☐ **Capitol ST-2407** (stereo), "Meet the Beatles," green label 7.00   13.00

Price Range

☐ As above, black label 8.00   23.00
This album also exists as a compact 33, for
jukebox use. It is considerably scarcer in that
form and carries a value of $60.–$139.00.
However, copies that were actually used in
jukeboxes (which comprise the majority) are
not considered to be in "collector condition"
and sell for much less. The serial number is
SXA-2047 . . . .   75.00   150.00

☐ **Apple ST-2576** (stereo), "Revolver" 6.00   13.00
The label has both the Apple and Capitol
names.

☐ **Capitol ST-2576** (stereo), "Revolver," green
label 7.00   16.00

☐ As above, black label 7.00   16.00

☐ **Capitol SKBO-11537** (stereo), "Rock and
Roll Music" 4.00   9.00
This album was not pressed on Apple.

☐ **Capitol ST-2442** (stereo), "Rubber Soul,"
green label 6.00   13.00

☐ As above, black label 7.00   16.00

☐ **Savage BM-69** (mono), "Savage Young
Beatles" 12.00   29.00

☐ **Apple SMAS-2652** (stereo), "Sergeant Pep-
per's Lonely Hearts Club Band" 5.00   11.00
The label has both the Apple and Capitol
names.

☐ **Capitol SMAS-2652** (stereo), "Sergeant
Pepper's Lonely Hearts Club Band," green
label 6.00   13.00

☐ As above, black label 7.00   15.00
Not to be confused with the soundtrack
album of the film "Sergeant Pepper," released a number of years later (which feature
the BeeGees, not the Beatles).

☐ **Apple ST-2108** (stereo), "Something New,"   5.00   11.00
The label has both the Apple and Capitol
names.

☐ **Capitol ST-2108** (stereo), "Something New,"
green label 6.00   13.00

Price Range

☐ As above, black label	8.00	19.00
This album also exists as a compact 33, for jukebox use. It is considerably scarcer in that form and carries a value of $77–$195.00. However, copies that were actually used in jukeboxes (which comprises the majority) are not considered to be in "collector condition" and sell for much less. The serial number is SXA-2108	85.00	200.00
☐ **Apple SW-153** (stereo), "Yellow Submarine" (sound track)	4.00	9.00
Still readily available in the record shops.		
☐ **Apple ST-2553** (stereo), "Yesterday and Today"	13.00	20.00
☐ **Capitol T-2553** (mono), "Yesterday and Today," butcher cover	165.00	330.00
☐ As above, in stereo	310.00	625.00
☐ As above, revised cover	100.00	225.00
☐ **Capitol T-2553** "Yesterday and Today," revised cover	100.00	225.00
☐ As above, in stereo	150.00	325.00

ELVIS PRESLEY

When Elvis Presley first burst upon the recording scene, in 1956, critics called his meteoric popularity a fad. Once again, following his death in 1977 and the sharply increased prices paid for his records and memorabilia, the cry of "fad" was heard. All of this buying activity will soon subside, some claimed. Today, almost a decade later, it has not only failed to subside but has grown. Collecting interest—and values—are stronger at the present time than at any time in the past. In fact the *rate* of increase, in market value, has outstripped most other types of music collectibles. There are now estimated to be more than a million Elvis collectors scattered around the world. Of these, many (because of financial circumstances) buy only the re-pressings of his records, rather than the scarce originals, and ignore memorabilia. But there is certainly a considerable number of hobbyists competing for the cream of Elvis collectibles, spending sums of money that are said to reach 60 million dollars annually. Old and young are involved in the Elvis hobby, from fans who followed him since the earliest days of his career to persons far too young to remember "Love Me Tender" or "Hound Dog." During his 20 years in the spotlight, Elvis picked up many new fans along the way, and the same appears to be true of Elvis collecting. More and more individuals are coming into the hobby, some of whom, quite possibly, were not even Elvis fans in his lifetime.

The advanced Elvis specialists have brought their hobby down to a science. They've researched every aspect of Elvis's life and career, his family and friends. They've traced his day-to-day movements and know where he was and what he was doing virtually every day of his life—which is not really difficult in light of the enormous press coverage he received. They know what exists in the way of memorabilia, how scarce it is, and—usually—where to find it, and how much to pay for it. They can sort out the good from the bad, the rare from the common, without any trouble. They know when to say no and when to stretch a few extra dollars—or even a few extra hundred—for a really exceptional item. To the beginner, the world of Elvis collecting may seem a vast jungle of potential pitfalls and entanglements. To a degree it is. The problems arise, of course, because of profiteers, who always stand ready to take advantage of a "good thing." If the public is anxious to buy Elvis Presley memorabilia, these individuals are just as anxious to provide it, even if it means manufacturing fakes, facsimiles, and cheap souvenirs. This has been going on for quite some time and has saturated the market with Elvis "memorabilia" of very questionable nature and value. Thus, the first piece of advice to a beginner is to develop a sense of discrimination. Don't fall into the trap of believing that everything is collectible just because it carries Elvis's name or likeness. Anyone can put Elvis's name and picture on a button, pennant, scarf, etc., and call it a "collectors' item." The Elvis memorabilia now being sold in retail shops and in the souvenir stands around Graceland is of current manufacture. Obviously, there is a market for these things, but the serious collector ought to stay away from them. It is very doubtful if they will increase in value or even gain recognized collector status. The collectible Elvis memorabilia falls basically into two groups: personal items such as signed photographs, and souvenir-type merchandise manufactured during his lifetime. As far as the souvenir-type items are concerned (bowls, clocks, spoons, etc.), the older the better, with the highest level of desirability attached to those from the very earliest days of his popularity. These objects were made for sale to fans, not to entice hobbyists or investors. Although nationally and sometimes internationally sold, they were still manufactured in smaller quantities than most of today's Elvis souvenirs—and most of them were of better quality, too.

When modern items have gotten into private hands and are then offered for resale, it may be difficult to judge their age. Fortunately, it is very easy to recognize many modern Elvis souvenirs as "noncollectibles," or, at the very best, collectibles of secondary interest and value. Any object giving the dates of his birth and death were obviously manufactured after his death; and anything picturing an older Elvis is just as obviously not from the early years of his career. Likewise it can be automatically presumed that objects bearing slogans such as "The King Lives On" were manufactured after his passing. But some pieces exist—which would have to be categorized as fakes—that are of current or very recent manufacture, yet bear a youthful likeness of Elvis. These can easily be mistaken for originals dating from the fifties or early sixties. Sometimes the manufacturer will add to the aura of "age" by using a black-and-white photo, or imprinting one of Elvis' early song titles on the object. Proceed with caution, and do not pay a premium price unless you feel assured of the item's authenticity. Buying from established dealers in Elvis collectibles will eliminate most of the uncertainty. This is one of the advantages of the hobby's vast expansion. It is now profitable for specialist dealers to trade exclusively in Elvis collectibles. These people serve a very valuable purpose. They may charge "top of the market" prices (such as are indicated in our listings), but they succeed in turning up many Elvis collectibles that the hobbyist, operating on his own, would never encounter. Also, and perhaps most vitally, they screen out the fakes and doubtful pieces and offer only worthy material to their customers. The specialist dealers see and handle so much Elvis memorabilia that they can spot the good ones without much trouble.

Obviously, this hobby is never going to be as standardized as, say, coin collecting. We don't know (and aren't likely to, ever) how many Elvis souvenirs were manufactured during his lifetime, or how many specimens of each were placed on the market. There are no "Mint figures," and no hope of getting such info through manufacturer's files. Mistakes are probable. Some items may be scarcer than they're assumed to be; others may be more common than dealers and collectors believe. But the market itself is the final analyst. If something appears for sale very seldom on the market, it is presumed to be scarce or rare, and this presumption must be treated as valid until proven otherwise. On the other hand, if an object is offered repeatedly by dealers and shows up in just about every auction sale of Elvis collectibles, no amount of sales talk can make anyone believe it to be scarce. With just a little experience in the market, you will learn which items and which types of items are the scarcest.

There is no space to get into detail about the various techniques used by sellers to advertise currently made items to give them glamor and appearance. If they can give the suggestion that a current item is 15 or 20 years old, it naturally has a much greater sales potential. They are then in the position of having to "explain it away," because if the item was truly old and scarce, how could they be offering dozens or hundreds of them? Usually this is taken care of by the phrase "warehouse find." It is not restricted to Elvis collectibles but is used throughout the collectibles market, as any reader of the antiques and hobbyist newspapers knows. The seller advertises that a lucky find occurred, in which "forgotten stock" was discovered in a manufacturer's warehouse. This not only satisfies the buyer's doubt about authenticity, but gives a good excuse for the items being in mint condition. This is not to say that every claim of "warehouse find" is a fraud, but many of them are. You have been forewarned!

MEMORABILIA

	Price Range	
☐ **Book,** *The Army Years* by Nick Corvino, 93 pages, clothbound, 5½″ x 8½″ .... Fictionalized story of the years spent by Elvis in the army.	5.00	7.00
☐ **Book,** *The Complete Elvis* by Martin Torgoff, paperback, 256 pages	9.00	12.00
☐ **Book,** *Elvis* by Dave Marsh, clothbound, 246 pages	30.00	40.00
☐ **Book,** *Elvis* by Albert Goldman, clothbound	13.00	17.00
☐ **Book,** *Elvis: The Final Years* by Jerry Hopkins, clothbound, 258 pages	11.00	15.00
☐ **Book,** *Elvis: The Illustrated Discography* by Martin Hawkins and Colin Escott, paperback	5.00	8.00
☐ **Book,** *Elvis: The Illustrated Record* by Roy Carr and Mick Farren, 12″ square format ..	11.00	15.00
☐ **Book,** *Elvis in His Own Words* by Mick Farren and Pearce Marchbank, paperback, 128 pages	5.00	7.00
☐ **Book,** *Elvis: The Legend and the Music* by John Tobler and Richard Wooten, clothbound, 192 pages	10.00	13.00
☐ **Book,** *Elvis Presley: A Complete Reference* by Wendy Sauers, clothbound, 194 pages	15.00	20.00
☐ **Book,** *Elvis Presley Reference Guide and Discography* by John Whisler, clothbound, 250 pages	12.00	18.00
☐ **Book,** *Elvis Presley: A Study in Music* by Robert Matthew-Walker, paperback, 154 pages	5.00	8.00
☐ **Book,** *Elvis Presley News Diary* by Bill Johnson, 230 pages, spiral binding, 9½″ x 12″, 1981	8.00	10.00

Price Range

☐ **Book,** *The Illustrated Elvis* by W. A. Harbinson, 160 pages, softbound, 8″ x 10½″	2.00	3.00
☐ **Book,** *Jailhouse Rock* by Lee Cotten and Howard A. DeWitt, clothbound, 368 pages	16.00	20.00
☐ **Book,** *Private Elvis,* author uncredited, 199 pages, softbound, 8½″ x 11″, 1978	10.00	13.00
☐ **Book,** *Up and Down with Elvis Presley* by Marge Crumbaker and Gabe Tucker, clothbound, 254 pages	11.00	15.00
☐ **Book,** *When Elvis Died* by Neal Gregory and Janice Gregory, clothbound, 290 pages ...	12.00	16.00
☐ Elvis Presley child's guitar, plastic	28.00	38.00
☐ Elvis Presley school bag	35.00	50.00
☐ Elvis Presley lunch box, c. 1965	10.00	18.00
☐ 8 x 10 photo with guitar, signed and inscribed, 1957	350.00	450.00
☐ Printed postcard photo, facsimile signature	5.00	8.00
☐ Life-size cardboard figure of Elvis, c. 1961, used for theater promotion, full color	375.00	475.00
☐ 8 x 10 color photo, signed	400.00	600.00
☐ Signature on label of 45rpm record—add $225–$300 to value of record as listed above.		
☐ Signature on label of 33⅓rpm long-play record—add $275–$375 to value of album as listed above.		
☐ Signature on cover of 33⅓rpm long-play album—add $300–$400 to value of album if record is present. If record is not present, cover alone is worth $300–$400.		
☐ Elvis Presley drinking mug, ceramic, picture on side	25.00	30.00
☐ Handkerchief, colored silk, illustrated	25.00	30.00
☐ Typewritten note by Col. Tom Parker (his manager), signed	9.00	12.00
☐ 8 x 10 photo, unsigned, black and white ...	2.00	4.00
☐ 8x 10 motion picture still, unsigned, black and white	1.50	3.00
☐ 8 x 10 color photo, unsigned (*not* clipped from magazine or book)	5.00	10.00
☐ 8 x 10 motion picture still, unsigned, color ..	5.00	9.00
☐ 8 x 10 motion picture still, black and white, signed	250.00	375.00

RCA Victor, LSP 2426.

RCA Victor, LSP 4776.

Price Range

☐ 8 x 10 motion picture still, color, signed	300.00	450.00
☐ Typewritten letter, signed, ½ page	150.00	225.00
☐ Typewritten letter, signed, 1 page	180.00	250.00
☐ Typewritten letter, signed, 2 pages	275.00	375.00
☐ Handwritten letter, signed, ½ page	275.00	375.00
☐ Handwritten letter, signed, 1 page	450.00	600.00
☐ Handwritten letter, signed, 2 pages	600.00	800.00
☐ Handwritten letter, signed, 3 pages	750.00	1100.00
☐ Note in his handwriting, one line	160.00	210.00
☐ Signature on an otherwise blank sheet of paper or card	80.00	100.00
☐ Typewritten letter to him from record company executive	40.00	50.00
☐ Typewritten letter to him from motion picture executive	35.00	50.00
☐ Typewritten letter to him from TV producer	30.00	45.00
☐ Typewritten letter to him from music agent	30.00	40.00
☐ Typewritten letter to him from U.S. Armed Forces	235.00	310.00
☐ Typewritten letter to him from author seeking an interview	10.00	15.00
☐ Typewritten letter to him from Ed Sullivan ..	140.00	200.00
☐ Draft card issued to him by Selective Service	1750.00	3000.00
☐ Magazine cover with full color photo	.50	1.00
☐ News cuttings (most)	.50	2.00

ELVIS PRESLEY, 45's

☐ **Sun 209,** That's All Right/Blue Moon of Kentucky	195.00	350.00
☐ **210,** Good Rockin' Tonight/ I Don't Care If the Sun Don't Shine	175.00	275.00
☐ **215** Milkcow Blues Boogie/You're a Heartbreaker	250.00	375.00
☐ **217,** Baby Let's Play House/I'm Left, Your Right, She's Gone	140.00	240.00
☐ **223,** Mystery Train/I Forgot to Remember to Forget	130.00	240.00
☐ **RCA6357,** Mystery Train/I Forgot to Remember to Forget	15.00	24.00
☐ **6380,** That's All Right/Blue Moon of Kentucky	15.00	24.00

Price Range

☐ **6381,** Good Rockin' Tonight/I Don't Care If the Sun Don't Shine	15.00	24.00
☐ **6382,** Milkcow Blues Boogie/You're a Heartbreaker	15.00	24.00
☐ **6383,** Baby Let's Play House/I'm Left, You're Right, She's Gone	15.00	24.00
☐ **6420,** Heartbreak Hotel/I Was the One	5.00	9.00
☐ **6540,** I Want You, I Need You, I Love You/My Baby Left Me	5.00	9.00
☐ **6604,** Don't Be Cruel/Hound Dog	5.00	9.00
☐ **6636,** Blue Suede Shoes/Tutti Fruitti	15.00	24.00
☐ **6637,** I Got a Woman/I'm Countin' on You	15.00	24.00
☐ **6638,** I'm Gonna Sit Right Down and Cry Over You/I'll Never Let You Go	15.00	24.00
☐ **6639,** Tryin' to Get to You/I Love You Because	15.00	24.00
☐ **6640,** Blue Moon/Just Because	15.00	24.00
☐ **6641,** Money Honey/One-Sided Love Affair	15.00	24.00
☐ **6642,** Shake, Rattle and Roll/Lawdy Miss Clawdy	15.00	24.00
☐ **6643,** Love Me Tender/Anyway You Want Me	4.50	8.00
☐ **6800,** Too Much Playing For Keeps	4.50	8.00
☐ **6870,** All Shook Up/That's When Your Heartaches Begin	4.50	8.00
☐ **7000,** Teddy Bear/Loving You	4.50	8.00
☐ **7035,** Jailhouse Rock/Treat Me Nice	4.50	8.00
☐ **7150,** Don't/I Beg of You	4.50	8.00
☐ **7240,** Wear My Ring Around Your Neck/Doncha Think It's Time	4.50	8.00
☐ **7280,** Hard Headed Woman/Don't Ask Me Why	4.50	8.00
☐ **7410,** One Night/I Got Stung	4.50	8.00
☐ **7506,** A Fool Such As I/I Need Your Love Tonight	3.75	6.00
☐ **7600,** A Big Hunk O' Love/My Wish Came True	3.75	6.00
☐ **7740,** Stuck on You/Fame and Fortune	3.25	5.50
☐ **7740,** Stuck on You/Fame and Fortune (stereo single)	70.00	125.00
☐ **7777,** It's Now or Never/A Mess of Blues ..	3.25	5.50
☐ **7777,** It's Now or Never/A Mess of Blues (stereo single)	70.00	125.00

Price Range

☐ **7810,** Are You Lonesome Tonight?/I Gotta Know 3.25 5.50

☐ **7810,** Are You Lonesome Tonight?/I Gotta Know (stereo single) 70.00 125.00

☐ **7850,** Surrender/Lonely Man 3.25 5.50

☐ **7850,** Surrender/Lonely Man (stereo single) 95.00 165.00

☐ **7880,** I Feel So Bad/Wild in the Country ... 3.50 6.00

☐ **7880,** I Feel So Bad/Wild in the Country (stereo single) 95.00 165.00

☐ **7908,** His Latest Flame/Little Sister 3.00 5.00

☐ **7968,** Can't Help Falling in Love/Rock-a-Hula-Baby 3.00 5.00

☐ **7992,** Good Luck Charm/Anything That's a Part of You 3.00 5.00

☐ **8041,** She's Not You/Just Tell Her Jim Said Hello 3.00 5.00

☐ **8100,** Return to Sender/Where Do You Come From? 3.00 5.00

☐ **8134,** One Broken Heart for Sale/They Remind Me Too Much of You 3.00 5.00

☐ **8188,** Devil in Disguise/Please Don't Drag That Sting Around 3.00 5.00

☐ **8234,** Kissin' Cousins/It Hurts Me 3.00 5.00

☐ **8360,** What's I Say/Viva Las Vegas 3.00 5.00

☐ **8400,** Such a Night/Never Ending 3.00 5.00

☐ **8440,** Ask Me/Ain't That Loving You Baby 3.00 5.00

☐ **8500,** Do the Clam/You'll Be Gone 3.00 5.00

☐ **8585,** (Such An) Easy Question/It Feels So Right 3.00 5.00

☐ **8657,** I'm Yours/It's a Long, Lonely Highway 3.25 5.50

☐ **8740,** Tell Me Why/Blue Rider 3.00 5.00

☐ **8780,** Frankie and Johnny/Please Don't Stop Loving Me 3.00 5.00

☐ **8870,** Love Letters/Come What May 3.00 5.00

☐ **8941,** If Every Day Was Like Christmas/How Would You Like to Be 4.50 8.00

☐ **8950,** If Everyday Was Like Christmas/How Would You Like to Be? 3.75 5.50

☐ **9056,** Indescribably Blue/Fools Fall in Love 3.00 5.00

☐ **9115,** Long Legged Girl/That's Someone You Never Forget 3.00 5.00

		Price Range
☐ **9287,** There's Always Me/Judy	3.00	5.00
☐ **9341,** Big Boss Man/You Don't Know Me . .	3.00	5.00
☐ **94258,** Guitar Man/High Heeled Sneakers	3.00	5.00
☐ **9465,** U.S. Male/Stay Away Joe	3.00	5.00
☐ **9547,** Let Yourself Go/Your Time Hasn't Come Yet Baby	3.00	5.00
☐ **9600,** You'll Never Walk Alone/We Call on Him	3.00	5.00
☐ **9610,** A Little Less Conversation/Almost in Love	3.00	5.00
☐ **9670,** If I Can Dream/Edge of Reality	2.75	4.50
☐ **9731,** Memories/Charro	2.75	4.50
☐ **9741,** In the Ghetto/Any Day Now	2.75	4.50
☐ **9747,** Clean Up Your Own Back Yard/The Fair Is Moving On	2.75	4.50
☐ **9764,** Suspicious Minds/You'll Think of Me	2.75	4.50
☐ **9768,** Don't Cry Daddy/Rubberneckin'	2.75	4.50
☐ **9791,** Kentucky Rain/My Little Friend	2.75	4.50
☐ **9835,** The Wonder of You/Mama Liked the Roses	2.75	4.50
☐ **9873,** I've Lost You/The Next Step Is Love	2.75	4.50
☐ **9916,** You Don't Have to Say You Love Me/Patch It Up	2.75	4.50
☐ **9960,** I Really Don't Want to Know/There Goes My Everything	2.75	4.50
☐ **9980,** Where Did They Go, Lord?/Rags to Riches	2.75	4.50
☐ **9985,** Life/Only Believe	2.75	4.50
☐ **9998,** I'm Leavin'/Heart of Rome	2.75	4.50
☐ **1017,** It's Only Love/The Sound of Your Cry	2.75	4.50
☐ **0619,** Until It's Time for You to Go/We Can Make the Morning	2.75	4.50
☐ **0672,** An American Trilogy/The First Time I Ever Saw Your Face	2.75	4.50
☐ **0769,** Burning Love/It's a Matter of Time . .	2.75	4.00
☐ **0815,** Separate Ways/Always on My Mind	2.50	4.00
☐ **0910,** Steamroller Blues/Fool	2.50	4.00
☐ **0088,** Raised on Rock/For Ol' Time Sake . .	2.50	4.00
☐ **0196,** I've Got a Thing About You Baby/Take Good Care of Her	2.50	4.00
☐ **0280,** If You Talk in Your Sleep/Help Me . .	2.50	4.00
☐ **10074,** Promised Land/It's Midnight	2.50	4.00

	Price Range	
☐ **10191**, My Boy/Thinking about You	2.50	4.00
☐ **10278**, T-R-O-U-B-L-E/Mr. Songman	2.50	4.00
☐ **10401**, Bringing It Back/Pieces of My Life ..	2.50	4.00
☐ **10601**, Hurt/For the Heart	2.50	4.00
☐ **18057**, Moody Blue/She Thinks I Still Care	2.50	4.00

EXTENDED PLAY (EP)

☐ **RCA 1254**, Elvis Presley (double-pocket) ...	90.00	165.00
☐ **747**, Elvis Presley	12.00	25.00
☐ **821**, Heartbreak Hotel	14.00	27.00
☐ **830**, Elvis Presley	14.00	27.00
☐ **940**, The Real Elvis	14.00	27.00
☐ **965**, Anyway You Want Me	14.00	27.00
☐ **4006**, Love Me Tender	12.00	25.00
☐ **992**, Elvis, Vol. I	12.00	25.00
☐ **993**, Elvis, Vol. II	14.00	27.00
☐ **994**, Strictly Elvis	14.00	27.00
☐ **1-1515**, Loving You, Vol. I	14.00	27.00
☐ **2-1515**, Loving You, Vol. II	14.00	27.00
☐ **4041**, Just for You	14.00	27.00
☐ **4054**, Peace in the Valley	12.00	25.00
☐ **4108**, Elvis Sings Christmas Songs	14.00	27.00
☐ **4114**, Jailhouse Rock	14.00	27.00
☐ **4319**, King Creole, Vol. I	14.00	27.00
☐ **4321**, King Creole, Vol. II	14.00	27.00
☐ **4325**, Elvis Sails	27.00	48.00
☐ **4340**, Christmas with Elvis	14.00	27.00
☐ **4368**, Follow That Dream	8.25	14.00
☐ **4371**, Kid Galahad	8.25	14.00
☐ **4382**, Easy Come, Easy Go	9.50	18.00
☐ **4383**, Tickle Me	9.50	18.00
☐ **5088**, A Touch of Gold, Vol. I (maroon label)	35.00	56.00
☐ **5088**, A Touch of Gold, Vol. I (black label)	12.00	25.00
☐ **5120**, The Real Elvis (reissue) (maroon label)	35.00	54.00
☐ **5120**, The Real Elvis (reissue) (black label)	9.50	15.00
☐ **5121**, Peace in the Valley (reissue) (maroon label)	35.00	54.00
☐ **5151**, Peace in the Valley (reissue) (black label)	9.50	15.00
☐ **5122**, King Creole, Vol. I (reissue) (maroon label)	35.00	54.00

	Price Range	
☐ **5122,** King Creole, Vol. I (reissue) (black label)	9.50	15.00
☐ **5101,** A Touch of Gold, Vol. II (maroon label)	35.00	54.00
☐ **5101,** A Touch of Gold, Vol. II (black label)	12.00	25.00
☐ **5141,** A Touch of Gold, Vol. II (maroon label)	35.00	54.00
☐ **5141,** A Touch of Gold, Vol. III (black label)	12.00	25.00
☐ **5157,** Elvis Sails (reissue) (maroon label) ..	40.00	70.00
☐ **5157,** Elvis Sails (reissue) (maroon label) ..	12.00	25.00

COMPACT 33's

☐ **RCA 37-7850,** Surrender/Lonely Man	48.00	115.00
☐ **37-7880,** I Feel So Bad/Wild in the Country	75.00	175.00
☐ **37–7908,** His Latest Flame/Little Sister	75.00	175.00
☐ **37-7968,** Can't Help Falling in Love/Rock-a-Hula Baby	75.00	175.00
☐ **37-7992,** Good Luck Charm/Anything That's Part of You	75.00	175.00
☐ **37-8041,** She's Not You/Just Tell Her Jim Said Hello	90.00	250.00
☐ **37-8100,** Return to Sender/Where Do You Come From?	90.00	250.00

LP's

The Albums Below Were First Issued Only in Mono

☐ **RCA 1254 (M),** Elvis Presley	25.00	56.00
☐ **1382 (M),** Elvis	25.00	56.00
☐ **1515 (M),** Loving You	17.00	39.00
☐ **1035 (M),** Elvis' Christmas Album (double-pocket)	75.00	190.00
☐ **1707 (M),** Elvis' Golden Records	17.00	39.00
☐ **1884 (M),** King Creole	17.00	39.00
☐ **1951 (M),** Elvis' Christmas Album (reissue) (photo on back)	17.00	39.00
☐ **1990 (M),** For LP Fans Only	24.00	56.00
☐ **2011 (M),** A Date with Elvis (double pocket)	34.00	84.00
☐ **2011 (M),** A Date with Elvis (single pocket)	17.00	39.00
☐ **2075,** Elvis' Golden Records, Vol. II	17.00	39.00

The Albums Below Have Equivalent Value in Mono and Stereo

☐ **2231 (M),** Elvis is Back	17.00	39.00
☐ **2256 (M),** G.I. Blues	17.00	39.00

Price Range

☐ **2328 (M),** His Hand in Mine	12.00	29.00
☐ **2370 (M),** Something for Everybody	17.00	39.00
☐ **2436 (M),** Blue Hawaii	17.00	39.00
☐ **2523 (M),** Pot Luck	17.00	39.00
☐ **2621 (M),** Girls! Girls! Girls!	17.00	39.00
☐ **2697 (M),** It Happened at the World's Fair ..	17.00	39.00
☐ **2697 (M),** Fun in Acapulco	15.00	35.00
☐ **2765 (M),** Elvis' Golden Records, Vol. III ...	15.00	35.00
☐ **2894 (M),** Kissin' Cousins	15.00	35.00
☐ **2999 (M),** Roustabout	15.00	35.00
☐ **3338 (M),** Girl Happy	15.00	35.00
☐ **3450 (M),** Elvis for Everyone	15.00	35.00
☐ **3468 (M),** Harum Scarum (with photo enclosed)	20.00	35.00
☐ **3553 (M),** Frankie and Johnny	17.00	39.00
☐ **3643 (M),** Paradise, Hawaiian Style	15.00	35.00
☐ **3702 (M),** Spinout	17.00	39.00
☐ **3758 (M),** How Great Thou Art	15.00	35.00

INDEX